MEDITERRANEAN
HARVEST

"Martha Rose Shulman's cuisine has always been blessed by the sun, fired by her own personal energy, colored by the rainbow-hued produce of the Mediterranean. Martha's experience, expertise, and professionalism shine through loud and clear in this marvelous book!"

— *Patricia Wells, author of* Vegetable Harvest

"*Mediterranean Harvest* is Martha Rose Shulman's most delectable harvest of recipes yet! This is a treasure trove for all good eaters."

— *Deborah Madison, author of* Vegetarian Cooking for Everyone *and* Local Flavors

"I love Martha Rose Shulman's food. It is always comforting and full of love. She brings us on a culinary journey, sharing wonderful recipes that jump from the pages with tips that seem endless. Pleasure pours from the pages with the perfect juxtaposition of exotic and comfort food. Travel with Martha on an unhurried journey of flavor and adventure. Just as Mediterranean food must be savored, Martha's recipes make you want to create and savor every bite."

— *Sherry Yard, Executive Pastry Chef, Spago*

"There's nobody's table I'd rather eat at than Martha Rose Shulman's. Her food is always delicious and direct to the point, the way home cooking is supposed to be—good cooking not as an ostentatious display, but as a natural and necessary component of good living. *Mediterranean Harvest* captures that spirit perfectly. If you want endlessly complicated dishes you will slave over for a whole weekend, look elsewhere. If you just want to feed your friends and family good food you know they'll enjoy, this is the book for you."

— *Russ Parsons,* Los Angeles Times *food columnist and author of* How to Pick a Peach

"*Mediterranean Harvest* proves that eating vegetables can be the greatest of pleasures. The recipes are fabulous and easy to follow. Even better, they are Mediterranean, which means they could not be more delicious. I can't think of a healthier or happier way of eating."

— *Marion Nestle, professor of nutrition, food studies, and public health at New York University and author of* What to Eat

"What I love about Martha Shulman's newest creation is . . . everything. Her vast experience and knowledge, her voice, the luscious breadth of flavor and textures in the recipes, all of which are calculated to get the cook—whether experienced or novice—into the kitchen. This book is a must in anyone's collection."

— *Susan Herrmann Loomis, author of* Cooking at Home on Rue Tatin

MEDITERRANEAN HARVEST

VEGETARIAN RECIPES FROM THE WORLD'S HEALTHIEST CUISINE

MARTHA ROSE SHULMAN

RODALE

© 2007 by Martha Rose Shulman

Rodale books may be purchased for business or promotional use or for special sales. For information, please write to:
Special Markets Department, Rodale, Inc., 733 Third Avenue, New York, NY 10017

Printed in the United States of America
Rodale Inc. makes every effort to use acid-free ♾, recycled paper ♻.

The recipes for Lentil Salad, Harissa, and Homemade Ricotta Cheese originally appeared
in *Little Foods of the Mediterranean*, by Clifford A. Wright, published by The Harvard Common Press (2003).
They are reprinted with permission of the author and publisher.

Map that appears on next spread © MapResource

Book design by Carol Angstadt

Library of Congress Cataloging-in-Publication Data

Shulman, Martha Rose.
    Mediterranean harvest : vegetarian recipes from the world's healthiest cuisine / Martha Rose Shulman.
        p.   cm.
    Includes bibliographical references and index.
    ISBN-13 978–1–59486–234–2   hardcover
    ISBN-13 978–1–60529–428–5   paperback
    1. Vegetarian cookery.   2. Cookery, Mediterranean.   I. Title.
TX837.S322   2007
641.5'636—dc22   2007031561

Distributed to the book trade by Macmillan

4   6   8   10   9   7   5   3   hardcover
2   4   6   8   10   9   7   5   3   1   paperback

RODALE
LIVE YOUR WHOLE LIFE

We inspire and enable people to improve their lives and the world around them

For more of our products visit **rodalestore.com** or call 800-848-4735

To Liam Max Shulman Grantham,

world traveler, fearless eater,

cool dude, wonderful boy

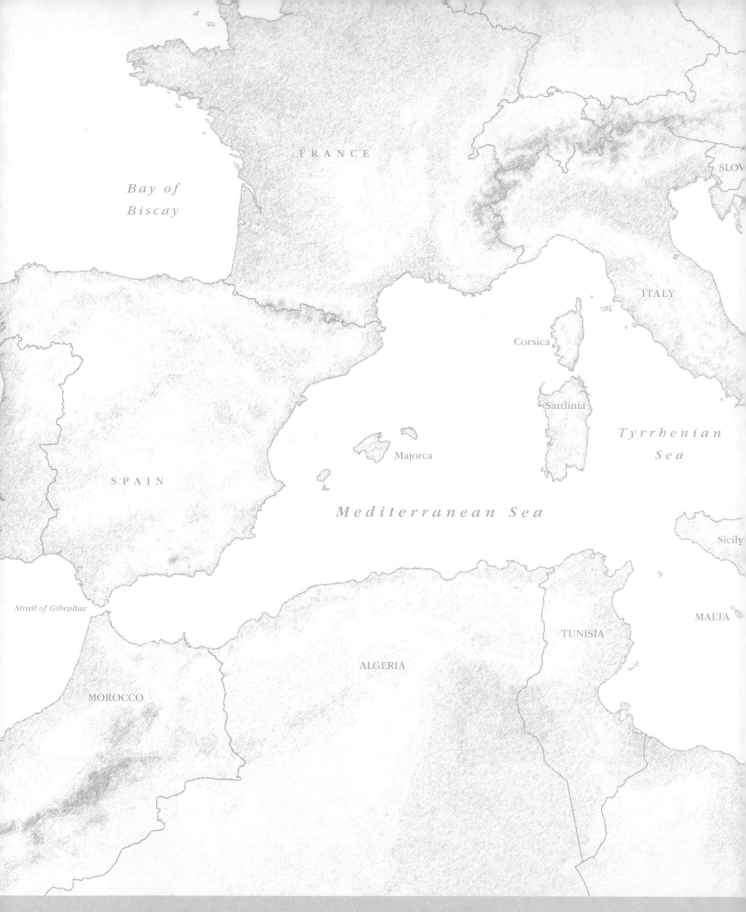

The Countries of the Mediterranean

CONTENTS

1   *Preface*

7   *Introduction*

11   COOKING MEDITERRANEAN FOOD

31   A FEW APERITIFS TO WHET YOUR APPETITE

37   BREADS, PIZZA, AND PANINI

69   SAUCES, DRESSINGS, AND CONDIMENTS

89   LITTLE FOODS: STARTERS, SNACKS, MEZE, AND MORE

143   SOUPS

173   EGGS AND CHEESE

201   PASTA

227   SAVORY PIES AND GRATINS

263   VEGETABLES AND BEANS

313   RICE, COUSCOUS, AND OTHER GRAINS

343   SWEETS AND DESSERTS

369   *Acknowledgments*

370   *Online Sources for Mediterranean Ingredients*

371   *Select Bibliography*

373   *Recipes by Region*

380   *Index*

398   *About the Author*

PREFACE

THE CUISINES OF THE MEDITERRANEAN CAPTURED MY TASTE BUDS long ago, certainly long before I knew I was going to have a career as a cook and cookbook author. I can trace it back to a poetic moment. I was fifteen years old, picnicking on a canal somewhere in the South of France with a bunch of privileged teenagers and a couple of French counselors, on a high school kids' European tour. I held in my hand the largest peach I'd ever seen. I took a big bite. The sensations went on and on: juice, sweetness, perfume, a flavor deeper than any peach flavor I'd ever known. The color was a dark, expressive yellow with tinges of pink. The aroma continued long after I'd swallowed.

I'm not as cavalier about discussing my age as I used to be. So let us just say that more than a few decades have gone by since that moment. Yet the memory doesn't fade. I can recall every bite of the peach, right down to the pit. I have only one other food memory from that trip, which took my brother Peter and me all over Europe, from Switzerland to Germany and Austria, to Paris and Spain, and to Italy. It was a plate of pasta. We'd just arrived in Venice and gone to lunch at a small trattoria. It was spaghetti, or maybe tagliatelle, with a smooth tomato sauce, nothing more. What I remember about that pasta is that there wasn't too much of it (it was a novelty to me that pasta was just the first course of a meal, followed by fish, salad, and cheese); that the sauce was a pure, concentrated expression of ripe tomatoes; and that the pasta wasn't swimming in it. You could see the noodles through the sauce, and when I finished eating them no sauce remained on the plate.

Eight years passed between that moment on the canal and a moment when, at the age of 23, I had an epiphany and decided I would make cooking my work. During those years I finished high school, went to college, dropped out of college and worked with Mexican American migrant farmworkers in south Texas, moved to Austin, Texas, and again enrolled in school. I had learned to cook along the way and loved doing it, but back in those days you didn't go to culinary school just because you loved to cook. You just cooked.

I had also become a vegetarian. Because I loved good food, I sought out recipes that fit into my diet but still tasted good. Cookbooks of the day introduced me to Middle Eastern food like hummus, tabbouleh, and baba gannouj, albeit not very authentic versions. A well-traveled vegetarian cookbook writer named Anna Thomas presented Greek dishes like spanakopita and *tiropites* in her best-selling *The Vegetarian Epicure*. I discovered pesto. These foods became part of my repertoire; they're in my catering brochures from the 1970s.

Mediterranean food appealed to me then, as it does now, because its flavors are so vivid. It tastes good. No matter where you go in the region, cooks know how to make eating a pleasure. They do it simply, with olive oil, garlic, and salt; with herbs and spices, tomatoes and eggplant, peppers and squash, and other seasonal fruits and vegetables; with great bread, cheeses, yogurt, and wine. They know what their food should taste like because they've been eating the same dishes for centuries; recipes have been passed down from mother to daughter, from one generation to the next. Of course, culinary traditions are changing in these faster-paced times, but they have a long way to go before they're lost. Furthermore, because food producers and food lovers know what is at stake, many of the most important ingredients in the Mediterranean repertoire are protected by government decree.

Early on in my cooking career, I became enamored of France, eventually going to Paris for an "open-ended year" that stretched into 12 years. The apartment I rented belonged to Christine Picasso, the painter's daughter-in-law, whom I grew to call my "French mother." Christine, who is my son, Liam's, godmother, lives on a farm in the Lubéron region of Provence, and since 1981 I have spent part of every summer vacation in her massive stone farmhouse. When I lived in France, not a season of the year went by that I didn't visit; I spent the better part of a year there when I was working on my book *Provençal Light*. My summer trips to Christine's didn't stop when I moved to California in the 1990s. Provence is where Liam developed his penchant for olives, tapenade, and *sirop à l'eau*.

Much of what I learned in Provençal kitchens I learned from Lulu Peyraud, proprietress of the famous Bandol winery Domaine Tempier. I spent the month-long harvest there in 1981, and moved quickly from the vineyards into the kitchen to assist Lulu with the daily midday feasts that she made for the workers. I rarely made a trip to Provence without visiting the Peyrauds and eating one of Lulu's amazing meals. The *aïoli monstre* she made to celebrate the end of the harvest—a feast of vegetables, fish, and garlic mayonnaise—made a lasting impression. Each time I went I learned something new about food and something new about wine.

But Provence isn't the only part of the Mediterranean that enthralls me. Greece, Italy, Spain, the Middle East, Turkey, North Africa, the Balkans—all of these places beckoned. Whenever I left Paris I traveled south, beyond the French borders to Italy and Spain, and Greece. The dishes I sampled on these trips would find their way to my table at my Paris "Supper Club Chez Martha," monthly paying dinners I held for two dozen people in my apartment.

Sometimes I traveled in search of authentic dishes, other times I simply sought sunshine and sea after months of gray skies in Paris. But I always acquired new recipes, no matter what my intent. I summered with four friends on a Croatian island called Korčula and lived on the sweetest, biggest tomatoes I'd ever tasted and the freshest, most succulent sardines; they were brought to us daily by the owners of the house we rented. I spent a wintry 10 days in Venice during Carnevale, where I resolved to eat a different risotto each day. I went to southern Spain in search of authentic gazpacho and tapas, ate wonderful Catalan eggplant dishes and paellas in Barcelona, and spent a September in the sun, swimming off rocks and living on *meze* on the Greek island of Simi.

I often visited my friends Marco de Stefani and Lorella Grossi in Bologna, and every time I came they would take me to out-of-the-way places for great food—to a country inn for fresh nettle pasta; to a grandmother's for homemade ravioli. They took me to a porcini festival in Modena, where I ate grilled mushrooms that were as thick and juicy as steaks, and to a huge Communist Party fair called the *Festa dell'Unità,* where I watched Lorella's mother and father, with a team of other cooks, prepare immense cauldrons of polenta that they poured out into wooden frames and served with local catfish. I explored Sicily, and afterwards I got my first taste of southern Italian cuisine in Basilicata, at Marco's uncle's hotel, perched on a hillside above the Mediterranean. The chef grilled zucchini and eggplant with red pepper flakes and topped bruschetta with wild mushrooms; he used delicate spring vegetables in his minestrone and seasoned thin swordfish steaks with capers and lemon.

At a food conference in northern Greece, I savored leek and winter squash pies that I will never forget, made by women from the local villages. One March, when I was working on *Mediterranean Light,* my mother and I took a trip to Egypt, going back in time from Paris to Venice by train and on to Egypt by ferryboat. The flavors of the Middle Eastern food I ate there—the *fattet* and the elaborate salads, the *ful midammes* and the falafel, the garlicky tahini dips and baba gannouj that tasted of wood smoke—still linger on my palate, as intense a memory as the stunning antiquities I saw.

When I moved to California in the 1990s, it was a fairly soft landing, at least culinarily speaking. The produce I found at the farmers' markets, and the breads that were being produced in Bay Area and Los Angeles bakeries, were the fruits, vegetables, and breads I had become used to working with in Europe. So I went on cooking Mediterranean food. My repertoire continued to expand as my travels took me back to the region, to countries I had not had a chance to visit when I lived on that side of the Atlantic.

I toured Tunisia with a like-minded group of colleagues on a trip sponsored by Oldways Preservation Trust and the International Olive Oil Council, and there discovered a world of vegetable tagines spiced with caraway, coriander, cumin, and harissa. I sampled couscous dishes I'd never dreamed of, like *mesfouf*—a mixture of fine couscous, citrus, and dates perfumed with orange flower water and crowned with pomegranate seeds. A year later, with the same group, I traveled to Morocco, and got to taste the sweet-and-savory, elegantly seasoned tagines and salads I had so often read about and eaten when I was living in Paris. A Moroccan restaurateur, Fatima Hal, had once been a guest chef at my supper club in Paris, and had made an unforgettable *bastilla,* the famous Moroccan phyllo pie filled with shredded pigeon and almonds, and seasoned with sweet Moroccan spices. This followed a medley of bright Moroccan salads—beets, carrots, romaine, and oranges. I was thrilled to meet up with Fatima again in her own country, and taste real Moroccan food *sur place.*

After I had my son, Liam, my Mediterranean travels were limited to Provence for a while, but by the time I'd begun work on this book, Liam was old enough to take on the road with me. When he was seven, he and I set out for a six-week journey to Spain, Italy, Greece, and Croatia. Our 19-year-old friend Rachel, Liam's beloved babysitter, traveled with us, and the three of us had quite a time sharing food and adventures. We ate well everywhere.

We began our travels in Andalusia, then drove to Valencia, and from Valencia we flew to Rome. We were only a few days in Rome, but it was enough time for me to be completely smitten with the city. We flew on to Athens for two weeks in

Greece, which in many ways was the highlight of that trip (it certainly was for Liam). I had signed up for a week-long cooking class on the island of Ikaria with cookbook author Diane Kochilas, and it proved to be more than I could have hoped for. I knew that I loved Greek food, that Greek cuisine was incredibly varied, an especially rich source of vegetarian recipes. Were it not for Diane's huge volume of work, we would know little about this diverse and interesting cuisine, and I had the chance to spend a week cooking with her. We cooked at least six dishes at each session (usually more) up at Diane's house in the village of Raches. We visited a farm and learned to make fresh goat's cheese, went out with a honey producer to his hives, toured a winery, and had fabulous meals in different tavernas. We stayed at a hotel overlooking the sea, and every day I would dive off the rocks and take long swims in the sometimes rough, but always warm, Aegean, the bluest sea I have ever laid eyes on. I took long, hot walks in the hills, and joined Liam and Rachel, Diane and her children at the beach every afternoon.

From Greece we took a long, slow voyage by boat, from Patras to Venice, and from Venice we sailed again, across the Adriatic to Pula, on the Istrian peninsula of Croatia. We met Croatian friends there and had another magical week eating great food and exploring the island of Brijuni, a national park where bicycles are the only mode of transportation. The food of Istria is unique, bringing together especially Italian, but also Balkan and Austro-Hungarian, influences.

After a week in Croatia we sailed back across the Adriatic to Rimini, picked up a car and drove up to see Marco and Lorella and their kids in Bologna, then spent a few days driving down the length of the boot. The drive was spectacular, taking us down the Adriatic coast, through tunnels that cut through the mountains of the Abruzzo that drop right into the sea. Puglia, the heel of the boot, was our final destination. I was especially interested in the cuisine of this region of Italy because vegetables play such an important role in it. I knew that I would be eating wonderful dishes like Dried Fava Beans and Greens and Orecchiette with Broccoli Rabe, as well as pastas I'd never seen or tasted before.

We spent our last four days in one of the most beautiful places on earth, an old olive oil farm that is also an *azienda agrituristica,* or farmhouse hotel, called Il Frantoio. To call Il Frantoio simply a farmhouse hotel hardly does it justice. The owners, Rosalba and Armando Ciannamea, have lovingly restored every room in the elegant house. Wherever your eye falls, it falls on something pleasing to look at. Olive groves, some of them more than 500 years old, with beautiful, huge trees, stretch for miles within the whitewashed walls of the property. Armando produces several different olive oils, and the farm also produces wheat, fruit, and vegetables—everything organic.

When you cross the quiet courtyard and enter the dining room for breakfast at Il Frantoio, you will encounter a linen-covered buffet with bowls of fruit from the farm's orchards—plums and peaches, apricots and nectarines in summer, apples and pears in the late fall—and baked goods from the kitchen—cookies and cakes, breads and pastries made with flour ground from Il Frantoio's own heirloom wheat. Rosalba is a passionate cook who has become locally well known for the multicourse feasts that she makes twice a week using ingredients from the farm. Guests sit outside under the stars in warm weather, the oleander blossoms gently dropping, as they work their way through seven to thirteen courses, while Armando goes from table to table to talk about the food and pour a different wine to go with each course.

By the time I returned to Los Angeles I had a list of well over 100 dishes from the trip that I wanted to include in this book. It being August, the same produce I'd been enjoying in Europe was at its peak here. I couldn't wait to start cooking, and did so, feverishly, for there was a lot to test before the summer produce gave way to fall fruits and vegetables.

Now, as I put the finishing touches on this book, a year has passed and we're back to summer vegetables. Through the fall, winter, and spring there has been no shortage of Mediterranean dishes to test. I've used the time to pore over my cookbook library, discovering and comparing, exploring through books those dishes that I haven't gotten to experience through travel. We've eaten a lot of good food in my kitchen, and there's a lot that remains to cook. This well won't run dry for a very long time.

Martha Rose Shulman
Los Angeles, California
July 2007

INTRODUCTION

I LOVE THE COOKING OF THE MEDITERRA-NEAN BECAUSE its heart is produce, with bread and grains as backbone.

Meat is certainly present, particularly in the more festive dishes. It is a great symbol of hospitality; when I went to Morocco, I don't think I was served a meal that didn't include a roasted lamb. Used in small quantities, meat adds flavor to many dishes, particularly sauces, soups, and stews. But the day-to-day diets of the Mediterranean have always been sparing of meat. A typical Middle Eastern or Greek *meze* table will sparkle with vegetable dishes—hummus or puréed yellow split peas; bright green fava purée; glistening grape leaves stuffed with rice and herbs; taboulleh and *fattoush* salads; salads made with purslane and arugula, with feta, tomatoes, and cucumbers; fried potatoes seasoned with oregano; eggplant topped with tomato sauce and feta; crispy hot phyllo triangles filled with cheese or spinach, or both. Walk into a food shop along the Riviera from Nice to Genoa and you'll find a variety of enticing vegetable tortes made with greens, ratatouille, or squash (both winter and summer varieties), with artichokes, leeks, or fennel; there will be tomato pizzas and onion pizzas (*pissaladière*); dumplings made of chick pea flour; bowls of pesto; ravioli filled with local greens and soft, creamy sheep's milk cheese; and vegetables stuffed with savory mixtures of rice and herbs.

I am not a vegetarian today, though I once was. But I tend to eat this way most of the time in my own home. Oh, I like a good rare steak or a shiny piece of fresh tuna as much as the next person, but I don't get excited about meat and fish; I do about produce. Tell me I can have any three ingredients to cook with, and I guarantee you that two of them will be garlic and olive oil, and the third will be a vegetable. So it makes perfect sense that the book of Mediterranean recipes that I wanted to put together for you would be a book of meatless dishes that reflect the way I like to eat. As you can see by the heft of this book, there is no shortage of material.

I hope that you will find this book useful whether or not you're vegetarian. If you do eat meat or fish, you'll use the dishes here to supplement your diet, or to vary the way you eat. If your family and/or your friends include both carnivores and vegetarians, the recipes in these pages will ease the daily dilemmas you face about what to cook so that everyone gets something good to eat. There is plenty here that is substantial enough to satisfy the most dedicated meat eaters while providing enough protein for those who choose not to get theirs from animal sources.

If you have kids and you're concerned about feeding them well, the food of the Mediterranean is a good place to start. It's a lot easier to get a child to like different kinds of foods, vegetables included, when they taste good. And since kids love grains, pasta, couscous, bread, and beans, all Mediterranean staples, this is a diet that allows parents the luxury of not catering separately to their children. The sooner you start, the better. I'm blessed that my own son is a good eater, but

I'm sure that it has something to do with the kind of food I've always given him. He's certainly crazy about junk food, candy, and sodas; but he was also a willing eater for every recipe in this book. He loves to eat but carries no extra weight; he's solid and strong, and hardly ever gets sick.

The Mediterranean Diet and Health

There is no single Mediterranean cuisine; there are many. They include not only the cuisines of the dozen or so countries with shorelines on the Mediterranean Sea, but within those countries, the cooking of specific regions. You will find types of pasta and cheese in the Italian regions of Puglia or Abruzzo, for example, that you won't find in Bologna, and vice versa. Foodways have evolved over the centuries, a result of geography and climate; conquests, expansion, and migrations; religion and custom. Yet despite all of this variation, every cuisine in the Mediterranean reflects a way of eating that we refer to collectively as the *Mediterranean diet,* a diet that is inherently healthy and very long on big flavors.

We know that the Mediterranean diet is a healthy one because it has been the focus of many studies, going back to the late 1950s. In 1958 an epidemiologist named Ancel Keys began a now-famous study to investigate the relationship between diet and coronary artery disease. The study, known as the Seven Countries Study, tracked 12,763 men aged 40 to 59 years in Greece, Italy, Yugoslavia, Japan, Finland, the Netherlands, and the United States. The men were initially examined and interviewed, so that all of their risk factors for coronary heart disease could be identified (including blood pressure, serum cholesterol, tobacco use, physical activity, dietary

habits), and they were followed for 10 years or longer.

Among the findings, it was reported that the Mediterranean groups had lower mortality rates from all causes compared to men from the other groups, and in particular there was a striking difference in mortality and incidence of coronary artery disease. The Keys study confirmed that a diet low in saturated fat can reduce total serum cholesterol and the risk of coronary heart disease. Other studies determined that the mono-unsaturated fat in olive oil plays an important role in reducing serum cholesterol levels.

Subsequent studies have backed up these findings many times over. In 2003 researchers from the Harvard School of Public Health and the University of Athens Medical School published a study of over 22,000 Greeks from all over that country in the *New England Journal of Medicine.* Their findings showed that those who adhered to a Mediterranean diet had improved longevity compared with study participants who did not adhere as closely. In July 2006 Spanish researchers found that people following a Mediterranean diet that included a relatively high amount of fat from olive oil and nuts, and also a certain amount of saturated fat from cheese and whole milk yogurt, had lower cholesterol, blood pressure, and blood sugar than those following a low-fat diet.

The widespread use of olive oil is only one of a number of characteristics that link the Mediterranean diet with longevity. Just as significant is the fact that this is a diet rich in fresh fruits and vegetables. We don't yet fully understand why, but many studies have shown that fresh fruits and vegetables have a protective role against a variety of illnesses, including several types of cancer, atherosclerosis, Alzheimer's, and other chronic diseases. Moderate consumption of red wine, too, has been shown to be associated with a lowered risk of coronary artery disease. The way in which wine is consumed in the Mediterranean is significant; it is taken at meals, thus it has an association with food and with friends and family.

The Mediterranean diet is also high in complex carbohydrates: couscous in North Africa; pasta, polenta, rice, and potatoes in southern Europe; bulgur and rice in the eastern Mediterranean and Middle East; bread, often made with whole grain flours, everywhere. No matter what the complex carbohydrates are, they are always eaten in conjunction with fresh vegetables and legumes, and supplemented with small amounts of dairy products, meat, poultry, and fish.

This may be very confusing to those of you on a low-carb diet. You may have had some success, but I can assure you that study after study has proven the long-lasting positive effects that the Mediterranean diet, with its emphasis on plant rather than animal protein, can have on health. My purpose here is not to pit one diet against another. I can only go by what has worked for me. People always have a difficult time believing I write cookbooks because I'm so small. Since I began my career my weight has not fluctuated. I always explain that it's a combination of regular swimming and my healthy diet. I love food, I eat heartily, I drink wine, bread is an important part of my life; but I never have to "go on a diet." When food is satisfying, it's much easier to know when you've had enough.

A Question of Lifestyle

Scientists can measure HDL and LDL cholesterol in the blood; they can assess the amount of monounsaturated fat and saturated fat in a person's diet; they can count calories and record their source. What is a little more elusive is the manner in which food is consumed, and the effect this may have on one's overall health, both physical and spiritual.

Mediterranean food isn't supposed to be eaten in the car. It is meant to be savored. Its far-reaching flavors have the effect of slowing you down. Enjoying food in the presence of other people, at a table, with or without wine but with the pleasure of company, has got to be good for your health. To be sure, plenty of the recipes in this book are dishes that are popular as street food in Mediterranean countries, but even a person eating falafel or a piece of pizza on a busy city street cannot help but be aware of how wonderful that food tastes, and of the satisfaction it provides.

I believe that America's and the world's growing obesity epidemic has something to do with a loss of awareness about how we eat. The thing that's so wonderful about Mediterranean food is that it can't help but get your attention. Whether you eat in the company of others or savor a meal on your own, when you sit down to eat the food in this book, you will sit up and take notice.

Cooking
Mediterranean Food

Mediterranean food is easy to cook. That's one of the things I like about it: It's straightforward. It's also forgiving. When you follow one of these recipes, you might find yourself short on an ingredient, like garlic, or parsley. If you use two cloves instead of four, or have to forgo that tablespoon of parsley, your dish will still taste good (as long as you make sure to taste it). Forgot to buy peppers for your ratatouille? Make an eggplant and zucchini stew without the peppers; it'll be wonderful.

I myself use much less olive oil than cooks in the Mediterranean are accustomed to using. In that sense, some of the recipes in this book are not quite authentic. When I approach a dish, I always ask myself how much oil is really needed for the dish to taste good and to cook the ingredients sufficiently. To my palate, it's usually less than is called for in the authentic recipe. Not that you won't find a few deep-fried dishes here, like falafel and a deep-fried cauliflower dish from the Middle East that I have always found irresistible. But I have left out others, like beignets and other fritters, which could have had a place in these pages.

Kitchen Equipment

You need little in the way of fancy equipment and kitchen skills for these recipes. All that is required is that you pay attention, as you must do in all cooking. A good knife and the ability to use it to chop produce; a large, heavy frying pan and some wooden spoons and spatulas; a couple of lidded saucepans and a soup pot will easily get you started.

The list of equipment that follows covers the items I used for testing the recipes in *Mediterranean Harvest.*

KNIVES AND CUTTING BOARDS

Chef's knife: The most important tool in your kitchen is your chef's knife. I use a sturdy stainless-steel 8-inch knife. (Some cooks prefer a longer blade.) Keep it sharp by honing it and sharpening it regularly. A dull knife can be more dangerous than a sharp one.

Paring knife: The other essential knife is a good, sturdy paring knife.

Knife steel: For regular honing of your knives; get into the habit of honing before and after each use.

Serrated bread knife: You can also use it for slicing tomatoes.

Large cutting board (or boards): It's important to have a large, heavy cutting board. You'll be amazed by how much space two chopped onions can take up, and it's so convenient to have them all in front of you and not spilling onto the floor. I prefer wood, though I have some small plastic ones for the odd job. I like to use a wooden or plastic cutting board with a lip for tomatoes and other juicy foods like stone fruits, melons, and citrus, so that the juice runs into the canal and not onto my floor.

GADGETS

Mortar and pestle: This is still not a common item in most American kitchens, but a mortar and pestle really is essential in the Mediterranean kitchen. Once you have one around, you'll use it all the time. I have a small marble one for crushing small amounts of spices or garlic, and a larger, olive wood mortar for larger quantities of food.

Kitchen scale: I have a mechanical scale with a large, wide bowl, and a digital one. You don't need both. Just choose a scale with a surface large enough to rest a medium-size bowl on.

Kitchen timer: I am totally dependent on my digital kitchen timers. Especially for long-simmering dishes, you'll need to be reminded to check them as you go about the rest of your day's business. Using a timer can be a great stress-reducer when it comes to cooking; you don't have to be watching your own watch. I like the digital timers because they will ring for a minute, and I can hear mine from two rooms away. And once they stop ringing, they begin to count up, so you will know exactly how long you've continued to cook something if you didn't get to it right away.

Wooden spoons and spatulas: Look for large, long-handled spoons with wide bowls. If you travel, always look for wooden spoons in markets. Some of my best, widest spoons, with really useful long handles, came from markets in Brazil and Mexico. Wooden implements will last much longer if you don't wash them in the dishwasher.

Chinese wire-mesh deep-fry skimmer (or spider): I use this wire-mesh implement all the time, and not for deep-frying. Mostly I use it to transfer blanched greens and other vegetables from boiling water to a bowl of cold water, or pasta to a serving bowl. It's one of my most useful tools.

Cheese grater: I find that the one I use most often is the little rotary Mouli that I've had since I began to cook.

Microplane: One of the great new gadgets to come into our kitchens in the last 20 years is this long, fine grater that looks like a carpenter's plane. I use mine for zesting citrus, for grating small amounts of Parmesan and Romano cheese, and for grating nutmeg.

Strainer: A medium-size strainer, the kind you can find in a supermarket, is an item I could not be without.

Salad spinner: Another essential. I find it as useful for cleaning herbs and greens like Swiss chard as I do for washing lettuce.

Heavy rolling pin: For rolling out crusts.

Stainless-steel bowls: Have as many as you have room for. Large ones are very useful for mixing up ingredients for tarts, gratins, casseroles, and for all sorts of food prep.

Pyrex measuring cups: Have a 2-cup and a 4-cup for liquids.

Nesting measuring cups: Stainless or plastic for dry ingredients.

Measuring spoons: Have two sets, one for dry ingredients and one for wet.

Spray bottle, or mister: I use mine to spray breads when I bake them. The moisture helps the bread to develop a hard, crunchy crust.

Pasta rolling machine: You can buy attachments for some standing mixers, but the most reliable machine for rolling and cutting pasta may be the inexpensive hand-crank models that clamp to a table or work surface.

Heavy Nonstick Cookware

The quality of nonstick cookware has improved tremendously. As restaurants have begun to choose them for their high-volume line-cooking, manufacturers have had to come up with nonstick cookware that can withstand restaurant wear-and-tear and the high heat of commercial stoves. You can now find this heavy-duty cookware in a range of stores, from fancy cookware stores, to hardware stores, to restaurant supply outlets. Make sure to look for the heavy restaurant pans. I have great, moderately priced pans made by WearEver, NordicWare, and my current favorite, Anolon.

CARE OF NONSTICK COOKWARE

Nonstick cookware has come a long way since the days of peeling Teflon. But you still have to take precautions so the pots and pans won't scratch. You should also take care not to expose them to extremely high temperatures.

- Always use wooden spoons or heatproof plastic when stirring food.

- Wash nonstick cookware carefully in warm water, and avoid using rough surfaces to clean. The cookware will last longer if you keep it out of the dishwasher.

- If you have to stack the pans to store them, place paper towels between them, or stack in reverse order of size so that the bottom of one pan doesn't scratch the inside of another.

- Do not heat nonstick cookware when empty. Once food has been removed, remove the pan from the heat. Overheating the cookware could release volatile elements from the nonstick surface into the air.

12-inch skillet: I use this pan more than any other single item in my *batterie de cuisine*.

12-inch straight-sided, lidded pan (5.3-quart/5-liter capacity): This sauté pan is known as a *sauteuse* in traditional French cooking. I use mine quite often for braises and stews. It doubles as a casserole or Dutch oven and is very useful because of its nonstick surface.

10-inch skillet: I use this much less often than my 12-inch, but it's useful for cooking smaller amounts, and for making frittatas.

8-inch omelet pan: I use this pan to make small omelets, of course, but I also use it all the time for toasting nuts and cooking small amounts of garlic.

Casseroles and Dutch Ovens

Heavy 5-quart casserole: For beans, stews, ragouts, and soups. I like a heavy heatproof and ovenproof Dutch oven that can be used both on top of the stove and in the oven. The cookware that I have been using since I began to cook, and that I still swear by, is Le Creuset enameled cast iron. Every recipe in this book that calls for a large, heavy casserole or Dutch oven was made in my 5.3-quart (5-liter) round lidded casserole. These are expensive, but they will last more than a lifetime (I am also using some of my mother's enameled cast iron bought in the 1940s). They hold the heat beautifully and are attractive enough to double as serving dishes.

Earthenware casseroles: These are traditional in Spanish and North African cooking. Placed on a flame tamer, earthenware pots are wonderful for long, slow, gentle simmers. The next best thing is the enameled cast iron I discuss above.

Saucepans and Other Pots

Heavy nonaluminum saucepans: I use my heavy Le Creuset 2½-quart, 2-quart, and 1-quart saucepans the most, for making rice and sauces. I am specifying nonaluminum here, because aluminum reacts with acidic foods like tomatoes and iron-rich foods like spinach, and changes their flavor.

Light saucepans: A set of light enameled, stainless, or nonstick, saucepans, inexpensive ones that you can find in a supermarket, is useful for steaming and blanching vegetables, and for boiling eggs.

8-quart (or larger) pasta pot: A pasta pot with a basket insert can be very useful. I use the pot as often to blanch vegetables as I do for cooking pasta. The pot can double as a stockpot.

Couscoussière: This large double boiler, the traditional piece of equipment for making couscous, has small holes in the upper portion, which allows steam to reach the nuggets of semolina. You substitute with a colander or sieve (see How to Prepare Packaged Couscous, page 337).

Baking Dishes

2-quart and 3-quart gratin or rectangular baking dishes: I have both earthenware and Le Creuset, and use them interchangeably, both for savory baked dishes and desserts.

Lasagna pan: This is optional, but it's just the right size for making lasagnas with no-boil pasta. Mine measures 10 × 12 inches.

Tart pan and pie pan: I use both my 10½-inch fluted white porcelain tart pan and my classic 10-inch metal tart pan with a removable bottom. I recommend that you have two, so that you can keep a frozen crust on hand in the freezer. I also use my 10-inch Pyrex pie pan.

Half-sheet pans (aka baking sheets, sheet trays): That's what standard 12½ × 17½-inch baking sheets with the ½-inch lip are called in the restaurant trade. Have at least two; you will use them all the time.

14-inch pizza pan: For pizzas and galettes. It also doubles as a cover for my 12-inch nonstick skillet.

9-inch or 10-inch springform pan: I use mine as often for savory pies as I do for cakes. There are now a number of excellent nonstick springform pans available.

Baking stone: A ceramic baking stone will radiate the heat in your oven, mimicking a bread stone or pizza oven. If you are a baker, you'll want one for country breads and pizzas. Terra-cotta tiles can be substituted.

ELECTRICS

Electric spice mill: It's worth investing in an extra coffee mill so that you can grind spices in seconds. Put a piece of tape on the top that says SPICES ONLY! And label your coffee mill with COFFEE ONLY! That way your spices won't end up smelling like coffee and vice versa.

Mini processor: This is a miniature food processor that I use all the time when I need more than one minced garlic clove or minced ginger. It's also great for pesto.

Food processor: Worth the investment for purées like hummus and baba gannouj. But don't use it for chopping; it massacres onions and doesn't chop evenly.

Electric mixer: An electric mixer isn't called for too often in this book, except for mixing up breads. If you bake a lot, it's worth your while to have a free-standing mixer like a KitchenAid.

Hand-held blender: This blender on a stick, also known as an immersion blender, is terrific for puréeing soups right in the pot.

Blender: When a silky texture is important, as with gazpacho, a blender works better than a food processor.

Ice cream maker: Even the simplest ice cream makers now seem to be powered by electricity. You will need one to make the sorbets and gelatos in the book.

Panini grill: These hinged, double-sided grills make a wonderful addition to your kitchen. Use them for grilling sandwiches and also for grilling vegetables like sliced eggplant and zucchini, and quartered bell peppers.

The Mediterranean Pantry

Each region of the Mediterranean has its own set of indispensable ingredients, many of them overlapping from one area to another. The story of the Mediterranean is a story of the rise and fall of empires and city-states, of trade between nations. Foods have traveled and taken root as different conquerors have come and gone. Long after the conquering peoples have retreated, foodways have remained.

OLIVES AND OLIVE OIL

The olive is the defining food of the entire Mediterranean basin. If there is one ingredient that runs through all of the cuisines, the olive is it. Foods of all kinds are cooked in and dressed with its oil; olives that are not destined for oil are cured and eaten everywhere, at breakfast (particularly in Turkey and the Middle East), lunch, and dinner.

When freshly picked, olives are incredibly bitter. In order for olives to be edible, the bitter compounds must be leached out through a curing process. There are essentially three different ways to cure olives. The industrial olives produced in large quantities are usually cured in a lye solution, which is very fast but unfortunately also leaches out much of the olives' flavor. Water- and brine-curing is a slower, more natural method for curing olives. The fruit is soaked in vats of fresh water or saltwater brine, or in the case of kalamata olives, a red wine vinegar brine, for several weeks or months, until the bitter compounds leach out. The liquid is changed regularly, and as the olives are cured, they are also seasoned.

Dry-cured olives are rubbed with salt and left to cure in the salt for several weeks or months. The salt draws out the moisture and with it the bitter compounds. Then the salt is removed, and the olives are either coated with olive oil (as in North Africa) or aged in brine (as in Nice and Nyons). Dry-cured olives are intense, and those that are not brined have a wrinkled appearance and the texture of dried fruit. I find that oiled dry-cured olives can sometimes be too salty for my taste. My favorite olives, the ones I find most versatile, are those that have first been salted, then aged in brine.

Buying Olives

Thanks to the growing popularity of imported olives in the United States, it's now possible to find a wide variety here, even in supermarkets. When I lived in Berkeley, California, I used to love to shop at Andronico's Market, where about two dozen different types of olives were sold in bulk. My local French deli in Los Angeles offers 42 varieties. While you may live someplace where the best you can do when it comes to imported olives is the jar of Greek kalamatas at your local supermarket, you can still make a good start.

This being the 21st century, you can purchase many different types of olives and olive oils online. I especially recommend the website www.zingermans.com.

Imported olives to look for are Greek Amphissa olives, which are fleshier and less briny than kalamatas; small, delicate black Niçoise olives; and green picholines from Provence. Niçoise olives have a vivid, nutty, almost sweet flavor. Picholines are mild, crisp-textured salt-brined green olives. Also from the South of France, but rarer in the United States, are the luscious, slightly bitter, fleshy black Nyons olives; and Lucques olives, crescent-shaped, nutty light green olives from Languedoc-Roussillon. Spanish imports include Manzanilla olives, the most familiar of the Spanish olives, often stuffed with pimiento or garlic, or sold cracked and dressed with olive oil and garlic; as well as fat, meaty, rich-tasting green gordal olives. Morocco and Tunisia are the source of intense, salty dry-cured black olives and green olives that are marinated with spices or chiles or preserved lemon. From Italy look for purple-brown, mild-tasting Gaeta Itri olives.

Buying Olive Oil

Buying olive oil is a little bit like buying wine. You have to know what you like, and what you're using it for. If you've never been to an olive oil tasting, I urge you to do so, so that you can see what an incredible range of styles there are. They range from mild and fruity to strong and assertive. In general I've found that the darker and greener the color, the stronger the oil. No matter what the style or intensity, olive oil should never leave a disagreeable aftertaste in your mouth or on the sides of your tongue.

When I call for olive oil in a recipe, that olive oil must be extra virgin olive oil. Extra virgin means that the oil is minimally processed. It is a product of the first pressing of the olives. With the exception of deep-fat cooking, of which I do very little, I use extra virgin olive oil for virtually all of my Mediterranean cooking. If the olive oil is the main feature of a recipe—a salad dressing, say, or a mayonnaise—then I'll use a quality olive oil, which may cost a little more than my daily workhorse oil. That workhorse olive oil, however, is a perfectly serviceable Greek extra virgin oil that I buy at Trader Joe's. It costs me $7.99 a bottle, and I never grow tired of it.

SALT

From ancient times through the Middle Ages, salt was a valuable trading commodity in the Mediterranean. It was gathered from ancient mountain salt mines and salt pans in the Languedoc, Venice, and Trapani. Europeans everywhere needed it. They used it primarily to preserve food and to make cheese. So valuable was it that a Tuscan farmer would have hardly imagined sprinkling it on his boiled egg. In fact, traditional Tuscan bread is made without salt, which can be a bit jarring if you're not used to it.

Now, of course, salt is cheap, and has been for some time. In my opinion, salt is the most important seasoning in cooking. If you think the food you make isn't tasty enough, try adding a little salt. This is especially true when it comes to vegetarian cooking. Close your eyes and taste a piece of a good, ripe tomato. Now sprinkle a piece with a little bit of salt, and take another bite. Taste the sweetness and the contrast of acids and sugars; just a little bit of salt makes these flavors ever so much more vivid. Try this same

experiment with other foods, like cucumbers, and cooked foods, particularly beans, eggplant, and soups.

We now have access to a range of different kinds of salt, and the choices can be daunting. If you are going to use only one type of salt, I strongly recommend fine sea salt. This may come as a surprise to you, but different salts taste different, and sea salt tastes of the sea.

Kosher salt is a great salt to use because its flat crystals dissolve so nicely. You get more flavor with less salt when you use kosher salt.

For seasoning food that isn't cooked, or as a final garnish for some cooked foods, there is nothing like fleur de sel. This coarse hand-raked and hand-harvested sea salt has a sweet, delicate flavor. It shouldn't be used in cooking (it's expensive!) but as a finishing salt for a dish.

GARLIC

This is an essential ingredient in all of the Mediterranean cuisines, though it's used less widely in some areas. In Provence and Catalonia, they like their food sharp with garlic (think aïoli), whereas in other Spanish provinces it isn't as prevalent a flavor. In Turkey, garlic is very pronounced in dishes from Anatolia, but much more subtle in the palace cooking of Istanbul. Ligurians use a lot of it, but the Milanese don't, and in the south of Italy onion is more prevalent as a seasoning. Still, you'll be buying garlic regularly as you cook your way through this book.

In the spring, take advantage of the green garlic that farmers sell at farmers' markets. It's fresh, juicy young garlic that you might confuse with the leeks or green onions that the same farmer is selling. Cut the bulbs from the green stems, remove the moist, flexible outer skin, and use like regular garlic. In fact, you can use more of it because it's milder. As garlic gets older, green shoots grow from the center of each clove. These are bitter, and should be removed. Cut the clove in half and lift out the shoots, then proceed with your recipe.

CHEESES

With the exception of the North African countries, where vast deserts limit the amount of land available for grazing, cheese is an important food throughout the Mediterranean. Shepherds have always been part of the landscape. Cheeses made from goat's milk and from sheep's milk dominate in Greece, Provence, Spain, and certain parts of southern Italy, and indeed, I associate the distinctive flavors of goat's and sheep's milk cheese with these countries and regions. But the most famous Italian cheeses—mozzarella, Parmesan, fontina, provolone—are made from cow's milk, or in the case of the best mozzarella, from buffalo milk.

If I wrote about all of the cheeses produced in the countries of the Mediterranean I would be writing another book—and many excellent books have been written on the subject. So I'll limit myself here to cheeses that come up in my recipes, and cheeses that are relatively easy to find in the United States.

Cheeses from Spain

Spain produces many wonderful cheeses, but only a few of them are widely available in the United States. Manchego is the one exception.

Manchego: Spain's most popular cheese, Manchego is produced in the interior region of Castile–La Mancha. The sheep's milk cheese is available in a variety of degrees of ripeness, each with a different texture. Young Manchego, aged for 2 months, is mild and soft. Semi-aged (for 1 year) Manchego is more piquant and harder, and extra-aged (for 2 years) is harder still and more piquant. I love the simple sheep's milk flavor of Manchego, whether I'm eating it as a table cheese or grating it into soups or vegetable dishes.

Cheeses from France

France is the world's leading producer of great cheeses, with more than 350 types produced. But only a handful are associated with the Mediterranean cuisines of Provence, the Languedoc-Roussillon, and the Pyrenees.

Brousse: This is a fresh curd cheese made from goat's or sheep's milk, the Provençal version of ricotta.

Goat cheese: In Provence, goat cheeses prevail. They are sold in various stages of ripeness, fresh and moist to aged and dry. They come in logs, disks (*crotins*) both thick and thin, and pyramids. Cheesemongers sell selections of thimble-size cheeses that are often dipped in spices like paprika or pepper or curry. One of the most famous cheeses of the region, Banon, comes wrapped in a chestnut leaf or vine leaf that has been dipped in eau de vie and tied with raffia. Goat cheese is now easy to come by in the United States. Some is imported from France, some is domestic; we now have some excellent dairies producing very fine cheeses.

Gruyère: This cheese isn't produced in the South of France, but the firm, nutty cow's milk cheese is a staple ingredient in every Provençal kitchen. It's widely used as a grating cheese, for gratins, soups, and pasta dishes.

Roquefort: As you move into southwestern France, you find yourself in the region where

Roquefort is made. This is a strong, complex blue cheese. It can be eaten with salads, crumbled onto focaccia, or served at the end of the meal with a dessert wine. That, for me, is the best way to enjoy Roquefort.

Cheeses from Italy

There are entire books about Italian cheese. Every region of the country produces cheese, and prides itself on the cheese it makes. The cheeses that I'm listing here are only those that will come up in the recipes in this book. I urge you, though, to familiarize yourself with all that Italy has to offer in the United States.

Asiago: This firm cow's milk cheese, from the northern part of the Veneto region, is a mild, nutty cheese, very good for grating and cooking, and is also good on its own.

Burrata: Americans have caught on to burrata, those luxurious balls of thin fresh mozzarella curd enclosing a buttery cream. Eat them sparingly, with salads and as an antipasto. Burrata must be eaten the day it's made.

Fontina d'Aosta: A rich, semi-firm cow's milk cheese from the Piedmont, and one of the great cheeses of the world. It has a nutty flavor and is an excellent melter. A great choice for panini. Also wonderful on its own, with a robust glass of red wine from the Piedmont, such as Barolo.

Gorgonzola: This is the most famous cheese of Lombardy, the northern Italian region that includes the Lake Country and Milan. A blue-type cheese, Gorgonzola *dolce* is creamy and mild and a bit smelly in the nice way that blue cheeses are smelly; Gorgonzola *naturale* (also called *picante, del monte,* or *stagionato*), which is aged for a longer time, is sharper but has the same creamy blue cheese qualities of Gorgon-

zola *dolce.* The cheese is wonderful on its own or crumbled into salads. It's terrific melted over polenta or focaccia.

Grana Padano: Parmigiano-Reggiano (see below) is a "grana" type cheese, a hard cheese that forms fine grains or flakes when grated. When you eat it as a table cheese, it has a grainy texture. Grana Padano is another such cheese, made from cow's milk throughout Emilia-Romagna, and in Lombardy and the Piedmont. It is aged for only 6 months, unlike Parmigiano-Reggiano, which is aged for 14 months to 2 years or even longer, and because it is not as highly regulated, it isn't nearly as expensive. It has a pleasant nutty flavor and is quite serviceable for pasta and soups, though it won't be as spectacular as Parmigiano-Reggiano.

Mozzarella: There is mozzarella made from cow's milk, and there is *mozzarella di bufalo,* made from buffalo milk. The latter is richer, with more depth of flavor, but fresh mozzarella made from cow's milk can be good too. The important thing is that it be fresh and not industrial; industrial mozzarella, the kind we get on most American pizzas, tends to be rubbery and flavorless. But try making a pizza with fresh mozzarella and you'll see what I'm talking about. The cheese is made in southern Italy and is a spun- or pulled-curd cheese. Bocconcini are small balls of fresh mozzarella (usually cow's milk) that are often marinated in olive oil and served sprinkled with parsley, garlic, and/or hot red pepper flakes. Fresh mozzarella should be eaten up quickly.

Parmigiano-Reggiano: This is probably Italy's most famous and widely used cheese. Parmigiano-Reggiano, which we often simply call Parmesan, is made within the strictly delineated D.O.C. region in Emilia-Romagna and a very small portion of Lombardy on the right bank of the river Po. Parmigiano-Reggiano must be aged for a minimum of 14 months, and most are aged for 2 years. When I call for "Parmesan" in my recipes, I am hoping that you will use Parmigiano-Reggiano, for no other cheese that calls itself Parmesan has the magnificent qualities of this cheese. Always buy Parmigiano-Reggiano in pieces and grate it as you need it.

Pecorino Romano: Also referred to simply as Romano, this hard sheep's cheese is the most famous pecorino in the country. A grating cheese, Romano is sharp and salty, with a pronounced sheep's milk flavor. It is widely used in southern Italian cooking. Pecorino is also produced in Sardinia, Tuscany, Marche, Umbria, Sicily, and Calabria (in Sicily and Calabria it's known as *incanestrato* and *canestrato*).

Provolone: Provolone is a rather simple spun- or pulled-curd cheese made from cow's milk. Sort of like a drier, aged version of mozzarella, it's good on its own and it's a good melter. We're most familiar with the industrial provolone that goes into deli sandwiches. The real Italian product is much more interesting.

Ricotta: True Italian ricotta is made from whey, the liquid by-product of cheese-making, and is more often made from sheep's or water buffalo milk whey than from cow's milk. In the United States it is made from cow's milk. It is a creamy, pillowy curd with a sweet, mild flavor. It's terrific in pasta dishes, drizzled with a little honey for dessert or for breakfast, or eaten on its own like cottage cheese. The difference between fresh ricotta and commercially made ricotta is stark; once you've tasted the fresh product, it will be difficult to return to the other.

Ricotta salata: This cheese originated in Sicily but is produced widely in the southern regions of Italy. It's grated into many Apulian pasta dishes, and because it is available in the United States, I found that I could duplicate many of the dishes I ate there that contained a rarer, pungent Apulian firm sheep's milk cheese called canestrato Pugliese, which is available only in the region. Ricotta salata is made from a lightly salted sheep's milk curd that is pressed and dried, then aged for at least 3 months. It has a wonderful light texture, holds its shape when sliced, and can also be grated. Even better for grating is Sicilian ricotta salata *per lat grattugia,* which is aged for a year and shaped into cylinders. I love using ricotta salata with pasta when I want a sheep's milk flavor that isn't as pungent and as salty as that of pecorino.

Cheeses from Greece, Turkey, the Balkans, and the Middle East

If you have ever gone walking in Greece, chances are you've said hello to some goats or sheep along the way. Goats are everywhere, and they have always struck me as quite sociable. Sheep are as important today for their milk and their wool as they were in ancient times. The cheeses made throughout the country contribute defining flavors to many of the Greek signature dishes, like spanakopita and other vegetable pies.

Feta: This is the cheese we associate with Greece, and the cheese that comes up most often in the Greek recipes in this book. Feta is a brined cheese, which is why it has that distinctive salty flavor. Its name comes from the Greek word for "slice," which describes the way feta is cut into large chunks or slices before being brined. Authentic feta is made with goat's milk or sheep's milk. It is only made with cow's milk in the

United States; American feta tends to be dry and very salty, nothing like imported feta. According to food writer Diane Kochilas, there are five different types of feta: soft, medium, hard, barrel feta, and tinned feta, which is quite mild. Goat's milk feta tends to be harder and more piquant than sheep's milk feta. Feta is also made in Bulgaria, France, Israel (I buy a delicious, creamy sheep's milk feta made in Israel at my local Trader Joe's), Turkey, the countries of the former Yugoslavia, Romania, and Lebanon.

Graviera, kefalograviera: This is a semi-hard Greek cheese that is made from both cow's and sheep's milk. Both versions are made in the way Gruyère is made, and are similar in texture and nutty flavor, though the sheep's milk graviera has a nuttier sheep's milk flavor.

Haloumi: This is a Cypriot cheese that is also popular in Turkey, Greece, and throughout the Arab world. Made from goat's milk or sheep's milk, haloumi is often flavored with mint. It has a semisoft, layered texture not unlike mozzarella, and because it has a high melting point, it is often fried or grilled. It is always part of the Cypriot *meze* table, and is often served with watermelon.

Kashkaval: This sheep's milk cheese is found in Turkey, Bulgaria, and the countries of the former Yugoslavia. I buy mine, which is made in Bulgaria, at a small Bosnian café that sells Balkan foods. It has an earthy but mild sheep's flavor and a firm, supple texture. It can be grated, but I prefer this cheese as a slicing cheese to serve with *meze*.

Kasseri: This is a basic Greek sheep's milk cheese that resembles provolone in consistency. It's fairly easy to find in the United States. It is eaten as a table cheese in Greece, and is grilled or fried for saganaki. I find it less interesting than the other Greek cheeses.

Kefalotyri: This is a very pleasant grating cheese made from sheep's milk. It's similar to Romano, but less salty and softer, so that it can also be eaten as a table cheese. It's made in Greece, Cyprus, and Syria. You can substitute Parmesan or a mixture of Parmesan and Romano for kefalotyri in recipes.

Syrian white cheese (jubna bayda'): This semi-soft sheep's milk cheese is readily available in Middle Eastern markets. It is often cut into squares or rectangles and served with olives and other appetizers as part of a *meze*.

YOGURT

Yogurt plays an important role in the cuisines of Greece, Turkey, and the Middle East. The yogurt you use should be thick and creamy. I have had very good results with low-fat yogurt in all of these dishes, but nonfat yogurt is too watery. Try to find yogurt made in a local dairy, or organic yogurt, because commercial brands tend to have gelatin or other stabilizers that make them unlike anything you would get in the Mediterranean. The Greek yogurt Fage Total is now available in the United States, and it's a good choice.

Drained yogurt is called for in many of the recipes in this book; this is yogurt that has been thickened by draining in a cheesecloth-lined strainer for several hours or overnight (in the Mediterranean it would be hung in a muslin bag). The resulting yogurt is thick and creamy.

WINE

Wine, along with olives and wheat, is part of the triumvirate of foods that are at the heart of the Mediterranean diet. The hot, dry Mediterranean summers and the relatively mild, wet winters are well suited to viticulture. The Mediterranean is where wine-making began; by classical times grapes were grown and wine produced in every country that bordered the Mediterranean Sea. It is still the case, even in countries whose Islamic religion does not sanction the drinking of alcohol.

Wines from Spain, southern France, and Italy are widely available in the United States, and I urge you to explore them. There are many fine books devoted to the subject, particularly the wines of Spain, the Rhône Valley and Provence, and Italy; and Diane Kochilas writes very informatively on Greek wines in *The Food & Wine of Greece*.

Furthermore, wines produced in Mediterranean climates in other parts of the world, like California, Chile, Australia, and South Africa, are also enjoying a renaissance. Some New World wines you may be familiar with that are produced from Mediterranean grapes include Shiraz (Syrah), Semillon, Mourvèdre, and Viognier.

One of the nice things about Mediterranean wines is that it's not difficult to find quite good ones at reasonable prices. There are, of course, top-of-the-line Rhône wines and Barolos, but you will be able to find many wines for under $10 a bottle that go hand in hand with this food. I urge you to become acquainted not only with red and white wines, but also with the many wonderful dry rosés that are produced particularly in southern France, but also in Spain and to a smaller extent in California.

HERBS AND SPICES

Herbs and spices are essential components of the cuisines of the Mediterranean region. Mediterranean cooks know instinctively how to balance these ingredients so that they can make a dish memorable without overpowering it.

Each region has a different flavor palette, a whole new array of tastes and sensations to play with. Spain loves paprika, saffron, and, to a certain extent, cumin. It's not as enamored of fresh herbs as its neighbors to the east and south. Provençal cooks use a lot of basil, as well as thyme, bay laurel, rosemary, and parsley, the herbs that grow locally. The Italian palate varies from one end of the peninsula to the other. Ligurians, like the Provençals, love basil. Farther south, oregano steps in. Sage is much loved in Tuscany. Oregano is popular in Greece, as are dill, fennel, mint, and parsley. In Turkey, dill, parsley, and mint make up a trio of so-called "warming" herbs. During the Ottoman period, palace chefs determined that certain foods were "warm" and others "cool," much in the way the Chinese see foods as yin and yang. The dishes they developed kept these foods in balance. Spices are particularly prevalent in the cuisines of the eastern and southern Mediterranean. The Arabs were great spice traders during the Middle Ages, and their cuisines are infused with many sweet and savory flavors.

I recommend that you keep your spices in the freezer. I use the door of mine to store my spices. They will stay fresh for a much longer time if they're kept cold.

Here are the herbs and spices frequently used in this book:

Allspice (Balkans, Greece, Turkey, Middle East): Ground, crushed allspice berries are used in rice and vegetable dishes throughout these countries. In Turkey, allspice is one of the two main spices (cinnamon being the other) used in a rice stuffing for cold stuffed vegetables (dolmades), and it is sometimes called *dolma spice.*

Aniseed (France, Greece, Turkey, Middle East, North Africa): The flavor component that defines pastis, ouzo, arak, and raki is also used in savory stews and breads in North Africa, and in breads and sweets in France, Spain, and Italy.

Basil (France, Italy, Greece): Equally important in Provence and in Italy, particularly in Liguria (the home of pesto), the sweet/peppery leaves of basil partner especially well with tomatoes. Along the French and Italian Rivieras, basil is equally popular. The leaves are thought to be an antidote to flies, so there are always a few pots by the doors to Provençal farmhouses.

Bay leaf (France, Italy, Greece, Turkey): A savory herb that deepens the flavors of soups, and vegetable and bean dishes. According to Penzeys Spices (www.penzeys.com), Turkish bay leaves are the best in the world, though interestingly, they are not much used in Turkish cuisine.

Caraway (North Africa): In Algeria and Tunisia the ground seeds are an indispensable spice, a key ingredient in the spice mix *tabil* (page 24).

Cardamom (Middle East, North Africa): These fragrant, astringent seeds are used in spice mixes and in some desserts. They are enclosed in papery pods, which are easy to split open. Squeeze on the pods to split, open them up, and pick out the seeds—then grind in a spice mill or crush in a mortar and pestle.

Cayenne (Spain, North Africa, Provence): Also known as hot red pepper, this is a fiery ground chile that will add heat to any dish. It has a deep, rich flavor, and a little goes a long way. Algeria is especially fond of cayenne.

Chervil (France): This sweet/anisy herb looks like a feathery, delicate parsley but has a flavor all its own. I like it best in salads (it should be present in an authentic mesclun mix), and it goes well with carrots.

Chives (France): Chives are probably used elsewhere in the Mediterranean, but the mild oniony herb is particularly popular in France, where it's used as a salad herb and to season eggs, potatoes, and other foods.

Cilantro, fresh coriander (Middle East, North Africa): Cilantro is very popular in North African cuisines, particularly Tunisian and Algerian, and it's also used in the Middle East. The astringent herb is used abundantly in vegetable and bean stews, soups, and salads.

Cinnamon (Greece, Turkey, Middle East, North Africa in savory dishes; Italy, Spain, France in desserts): Cinnamon is particularly prominent in Greek, Turkish, and Middle Eastern cooking. It's a subtle/sweet spice that adds a rich, intriguing dimension to savory foods.

Cloves (Greece, Turkey, North Africa): Cloves are crushed and used in sweets, breads, and pastries, in stews, and with meat and fish. Algerians use cloves in sweet and savory dishes. In France, a clove is sometimes stuck into a simmering onion.

Coriander seeds (France, Turkey, Middle East, North Africa): Crushed coriander seeds have an intriguing, savory/citrusy flavor that adds a wonderful dimension to many vegetable dishes and marinades.

Cumin seeds (Spain, Greece, Turkey, Middle East, North Africa): Cumin seeds, most often ground, are especially popular in

MEDITERRANEAN SPICE BLENDS

Spice mixes are an integral part of the cuisines of the Middle East and North Africa, and they will come up in some of the recipes in this book. All of them have many variations, probably as many as there are Mediterranean cooks. I've taken my cues from Clifford Wright, Mediterranean food expert extraordinaire.

The spice mixes that follow are all-purpose blends that cooks use along with salt to season all kinds of savory dishes—soups and stews, meat and egg dishes, and in some instances, salads. Some, like the Middle Eastern blend *za'tar*, are also used as condiments, sprinkled over flat bread. Whenever you visit food markets, you will see these blends piled high in the spice stands.

I use an electric spice mill for the blends; local cooks would be more likely to use a mortar and pestle. Store in the freezer; they will keep for about 1 year.

Toasting spices before using them in a recipe releases their aromatic oils. Heat a small skillet over medium-high heat and add the spice. Stir constantly until the spice begins to smell fragrant and darkens ever so slightly. Immediately transfer to a bowl and allow to cool.

Tabil

Tunisia • Makes about ⅓ cup

Tabil is Tunisia's all-purpose spice mix, typically used in stews, tagines, and soups. The word comes from the Tunisian Arabic word meaning "seasoning" and is pronounced like "table."

- 2 large garlic cloves, chopped and left out on a piece of paper towel to air-dry for 2 days, or 2 teaspoons garlic powder or granulated garlic
- 4 tablespoons coriander seeds
- 1 tablespoon caraway seeds
- 2 teaspoons cayenne

In a mortar or spice mill, grind the ingredients together until homogeneous. Store in the refrigerator or freezer.

Ras al-Hanut

Morocco • Makes about ¼ cup

This intriguing Moroccan spice mix will vary from spice merchant to spice merchant. It is always complex and can contain up to 27 ingredients. The name means "head of the shop." That's how important it is to the food seller.

- 6 teaspoons ground cinnamon
- 3 teaspoons turmeric
- 1½ teaspoons freshly ground black pepper
- ¾ teaspoon freshly grated nutmeg
- ¾ teaspoon freshly ground cardamom seeds
- ¾ teaspoon freshly ground cloves

Mix together all the ingredients and store in a jar in the refrigerator or freezer.
Traditionally used with lamb and chicken tagine, it can be an aromatic addition to any couscous.

Za'tar

Middle East and Turkey • Makes about ⅔ cup

Za'tar, which means "thyme"—the most important ingredient in this mix—is used in the Middle East and in Turkey as both seasoning and condiment.

- ½ cup dried thyme
- 2 tablespoons sesame seeds
- 1½ teaspoons ground sumac
- ¼ teaspoon salt, or to taste

Mix together all the ingredients and store in a jar, preferably in the freezer.

Turkey, the Middle East, and North Africa, and they also come up in Spanish dishes. In addition to being used with meat and fish, cumin seeds are often an ingredient in salads and vegetable dishes.

Dill (Greece, Turkey, Balkans, Middle East): This feathery herb defines many Greek and Turkish dishes. It's used abundantly in Greek vegetable pies, and is used in conjunction with mint and parsley in many Turkish dishes.

Fennel and fennel seeds (France, Italy, Balkans, Greece, Turkey, North Africa): Wild fennel grows abundantly in these countries. The Greeks use the anisy, feathery herb more than the others, though in France a favorite dish is sea bass cooked with fennel. Throughout the Mediterranean the crushed seeds are used to season breads, soups, fish, and vegetable dishes. They are a favorite seasoning in North Africa.

Ginger, ground (North Africa): Ground ginger is spicy and pungent; it's popular in Algerian cooking.

Marjoram (France, Italy): I love this somewhat astringent, savory herb in salads, and it's good for some pasta dishes and pizzas.

Mint (Spain, Italy, Balkans, Greece, Turkey, Middle East, North Africa): This herb, most often spearmint, is used in both its fresh and dried form. It's an essential ingredient in many Turkish and Greek dishes, and the Romans love it too. The North Africans use it in salads, vegetable dishes, and especially for their sweet, strong mint tea. In Turkey, it is part of the "warming" trinity of parsley, dill, and mint.

Nigella or charnushka (Turkey, Middle East): These little black seeds, sometimes inac-curately called black cumin (they taste nothing like cumin), are often sprinkled on breads in Turkey and the Middle East. I love their distinctive smoky/aromatic flavor. Nigella is listed as "Charnushka (*Nigella sativa*)" in the Penzeys Spices catalogue (www.penzeys.com).

Nutmeg (France, Italy): A sweet, nutty spice, nutmeg is used in desserts but also in some savory dishes, notably in béchamel, with spinach, winter squash, and potatoes. Use just a pinch; a little goes a long way.

Oregano (Spain, France, Italy, Greece, Turkey, Balkans): I don't know who loves oregano more, the Greeks or the Italians. It's a wonderful seasoning for tomatoes and pizza, Greek salads and potatoes, and vegetable stews. It's most often used in its dried form. Make sure to buy the Mediterranean variety and not the Mexican herb, which is in the verbena family and has a different flavor altogether.

Paprika (Spain, Balkans, Greece, Turkey, North Africa): Sweet Hungarian paprika is used widely in Spain, the Balkans, and North Africa, and to a lesser degree in Turkey and Greece. It has a deep, sweet, rich flavor, more the flavor of sweet red pepper than hot chile.

Parsley: Flat-leaf parsley is used everywhere in the Mediterranean, but it's used in the greatest quantities in Turkey, the Middle East, and North Africa. In the Middle East it could almost be considered a vegetable or lettuce, so abundant is it in salads like tabbouleh. Flat-leaf parsley is the parsley you will use for all of the recipes in this book. It's incredibly healthy and has a wonderful fresh flavor.

Pepper, Aleppo (Turkey, Middle East): In

Turkey and Syria, dried red chile peppers are roughly chopped, crushed into flakes and rubbed with oil, then roasted until deep dark red, almost black. If you were to go to a market in Istanbul, you would see many different grades of red pepper laid out in large sacks, their vendors urging shoppers to taste, as there is a range of sweetness, tartness, and heat. Although the Turkish *kirmizi biber* is not easy to find, several spice companies are now importing its first cousin, Aleppo pepper. You can find it at Middle Eastern markets and through the Internet. I buy mine through Penzeys Spices (www.penzeys.com). Aleppo pepper has a sweet, mild to hot, rich flavor.

Pepper, black: Black pepper is used as a seasoning everywhere. The Italians love it with pasta, and it is widely used in Balkan vegetable pies. It lends heat to many North African dishes. I prefer it freshly ground.

Pepper, red (Spain, southern Italy, North Africa): Hot red pepper flakes are particularly popular in southern Italy. When cooking Turkish and Middle Eastern dishes that call for Aleppo pepper (above), you can substitute a combination of hot red pepper flakes and paprika (half and half).

Pepper, red, Turkish; or kirmizi biber: Crushed or ground dried red chiles are essential in Turkish cuisine. The crushed peppers are rubbed with oil. To increase hotness, the flakes are roasted until almost black. I substitute Aleppo pepper, which is similar and easier for me to find, for Turkish pepper in my recipes.

Rose geranium (Greece, Middle East): Rose geranium petals and leaves are sometimes infused in syrups for spoon sweets, perfuming them with their remarkable floral aroma. If you

do this, make sure that you use rose geranium that has not been treated with pesticides.

Rosemary (France, Italy, Greece): This resinous herb grows in huge bushes and makes a great seasoning for grilled and roasted foods. It seasons tapenade, goes into vegetable pies, and is particularly good with roasted potatoes. If fresh isn't available, use dried, crumbling it and using one-third to one-half of the amount of fresh called for.

Saffron (Spain, France, Italy, North Africa): The stigma of the flowering crocus are gathered by hand, a very labor-intensive process that makes this seasoning an expensive one. But it weighs next to nothing, and a little goes a long way. One pinch, crushed briefly between your thumb and finger, will add a huge flavor dimension and the most gorgeous yellow-orange color to a paella, a soup, or a risotto. Do not buy imitation saffron; it doesn't work, and it's not fragrant. Saffron powder is not nearly as fragrant as the threads but can be added to dishes for color. Don't substitute it for the threads.

Sage (France, Italy, Turkey): In Turkey, sage is mainly used as a tea. But in Italy and Provence, it's a wonderful seasoning, used in vegetable dishes and pasta dishes. The flavor is strong, earthy, somewhat astringent; it goes well with mushrooms, potatoes, and winter squash. Italians heat the leaves in butter, then toss cheese or squash ravioli in the sage-infused butter.

Sumac or sumak (Turkey, Middle East): Sumac is a deep red, tangy berry that is ground and sprinkled on salads, vegetables, meats, fish, soups, egg dishes, and rice dishes. It's an essential ingredient in the Middle Eastern bread salad *fattoush*. If you can only find sumac in berry form, grind it in a spice mill with some salt.

Tarragon (France): Tarragon has a marvelous sweet, slightly anisy flavor. It's wonderful in salads, with eggs, fish, or chicken, and sprinkled over crostini.

Thyme (Spain, France, Italy, Greece, Turkey, Middle East): This savory herb grows wild all over the hills of the Mediterranean. It is always present, with parsley and bay leaf, in the bouquet garni that seasons French soups, and with parsley and bay leaf it's used in many a French gratin. Though thyme is less prevalent in the cooking of Greece, the honey that bees make from mountain thyme is famous. In Turkey and the Middle East, thyme is combined with sumac to make a ubiquitous condiment called *za'tar* (page 24).

Vanilla beans (France, Italy, Spain): I use the tiny seeds from vanilla beans in many of my desserts. I always keep the pods, dry them out, and bury them in a jar of sugar, for fragrant vanilla-scented sugar.

NUTS AND SEEDS

Nuts and seeds are integral to the cuisines of the Mediterranean, adding unforgettable flavors and textures to dishes. Keep these on hand if you can, but only if you have room to store them in your freezer once you open them. The oils in nuts are volatile, and they will become rancid quickly if you don't. They keep well, though, in the freezer.

I toast most nuts in a 350°F oven; I put them on a baking sheet and place them on the middle rack for about 10 minutes, until they smell toasty. The exception is pine nuts, which are very oily and can burn quickly if not watched. These I toast in a pan over medium-high heat, shaking the pan until the pine nuts are golden. Once nuts are toasted, transfer immediately to a bowl or

they will continue to toast on the hot surface of the pan or baking sheet. You can store toasted nuts airtight in the freezer for a month.

Almonds: One of the most memorable food tastings I have ever participated in was on a trip to Tunisia organized by the Oldways Preservation Trust. We were taken to a desert oasis and treated to a tasting of almonds and dates. It was astounding to see what a variety of both items there are. Almonds—raw, roasted, salted, unsalted, chopped, ground, and whole—figure somewhere in all of the Mediterranean cuisines. They're served as snacks, they thicken sauces, and they go into pastries and desserts, into confections and sweet couscous dishes. The Arabs took almonds wherever they went, and so they are firmly rooted in the cuisines of Spain and Sicily. During the days of the Ottoman Empire, palace chefs transformed almonds into marzipan and sweet puddings, and cooked them with meat and fish.

Chestnuts (Spain, France, Italy, Turkey): Chestnuts are winter treats, beloved in Europe and Turkey, where they are eaten roasted in their shells and made into soups and confections. In both Spain and Turkey they are used in two very different vegetable stuffings, and in Italy the flour is used.

Hazelnuts: The hazelnut, too, is a noble nut, much loved by the Arabs. They are roasted and ground for savory sauces like *tarator* (the Turkish version of skordalia) and Spanish Romesco sauce; chopped and added to other savory dishes and salads; and used everywhere in desserts.

Hazelnuts have a papery shell that is bitter and must be removed before you use them. To do this, roast them at 350°F until dark and toasty. A handful at a time, enclose the hazelnuts in a kitchen towel and rub the towel between your hands, or between your hands and your work surface. The shells will loosen and come off.

Pine nuts: Pine nuts have a wonderful, delicate flavor, and it's not surprising that those who have them at their disposal have used them in cooking. They appear in the cuisines of all of the countries with pine-covered hills, which means just about everyplace.

Pistachios (Spain, France, Italy, Greece, Turkey, Middle East, North Africa): Used mostly in sweets in the eastern and southern Mediterranean, pistachios are found in both sweet and savory dishes in Spain, France, and Italy. Salted, they are served everywhere as snacks.

Sesame seeds (Italy, Greece, Turkey, Middle East, North Africa): These are used to make the Middle Eastern condiment *za'tar* (page 24), and are sprinkled onto many breads. Ground, they are the essence of tahini.

Walnuts (France, Italy, Greece, Turkey, Middle East): Walnuts are considered the king of nuts in Istanbul cuisine, where they are used in both sweet and savory dishes. The ground nuts add texture and flavor to dishes throughout the region, and are the key ingredients in sauces like Ligurian walnut sauce and skordalia. In the Hautes-Alpes of northern Provence, the olive tree gives way to the walnut tree, and the oil is widely used.

GRAINS, BEANS, AND FLOURS

Keep these on hand in your pantry and you'll be able to make any number of recipes in this book at a moment's notice.

Borlotti or pinto beans

Dried fava beans: Skinned and split if possible.

White beans

Bulgur: Medium and fine grain.

Chick peas: Both dried and canned.

Couscous

Farro (spelt): These whole wheat berries can be used in soups, risotto, and salads.

Semolina flour: Keep on hand if you like to make bread or pasta; also, the Semolina Gnocchi on page 225 are wonderful.

Unbleached all-purpose flour

Whole wheat flour

Lentils

Dried pasta

Black-eyed peas

Yellow split peas

Polenta: By this I mean the cornmeal used for polenta, not the tubes of already cooked polenta you can find in the supermarket.

Rice: Keep a long-grain rice like basmati for pilafs and some stuffed vegetables, and Arborio or Carnaroli rice for risottos and some gratins and stuffed vegetables.

OTHER INGREDIENTS FOR THE PANTRY

You will also want to have the following ingredients on hand:

Artichoke hearts: Either canned or frozen. Add them to pasta dishes, pizza, and savory tortes.

Capers (France, Italy, Greece): These are unopened flower buds that are gathered and pickled in brine, or in salt. They add a pungent dimension to vegetable dishes and are a particularly important ingredient in tapenade.

Dried fruit: Keep especially raisins, currants, and dried apricots.

Harissa (North Africa): You should make your own fiery pepper paste (the recipe is on page 86), but just in case, get a tube of the definitely inferior imported stuff and keep it on hand in the refrigerator for emergencies.

Honey (everywhere, but especially Provence, Greece, Turkey, Middle East): Every region in the Mediterranean has a culture of beekeeping. The sound of bees buzzing is an unmistakable element of the landscape, as reliable as the purple Provençal lavender that blooms in July, spring's yellow broom and citrus flowers, and the scent of pine forests. Honeys range in color from practically clear (acacia is one of these) to golden (lavender, linden blossom) to amber (thyme and orange blossom) to almost black. The dark honeys, made from chestnut pollen, buckwheat, pine, and some mountain flowers, can be almost bitter, they're so strong; but they have their place, drizzled over a mound of white cheese or feta, or on bread. The lighter honeys are the ones to choose for cooking, as their flavors won't dominate.

Pomì (Italy) marinara sauce: There are a lot of bad marinara sauces out there, whose rancid garlic aftertaste is most objectionable. It's easy to make your own (page 78), but there is one brand imported from Italy, called Pomì, that is absolutely delicious. It's packaged in cardboard cartons and I strongly recommend having one in your pantry at all times. If you only use part of a carton, you can freeze the rest. I usually divide it into ¼-cup servings and freeze them in small bags.

Dried mushrooms (France, Italy, Balkans, Greece): For mushroom ragouts, risotto, and sauces. Porcini are the most aromatic.

Orange flower water (France, Balkans, Greece, Turkey, Middle East, North Africa): Sometimes called orange blossom water and added to some desserts and salads, this perfumes a dish more than flavors it, with the wonderful citrus/floral aroma of orange blossoms.

Phyllo dough (Greece, Balkans): Keep a box in your freezer so you can make wonderful savory pies or baklava. Always thaw phyllo dough in the refrigerator overnight, not at room temperature. If you thaw it too quickly, it becomes soggy.

Rose water (Turkey, Greece, Middle East): Like orange flower water, this perfumes a dish in the most wonderful, floral way. I flavor pastry cream with it for some of my fruit tarts.

Tahini (Turkey, Middle East): A thick, rich paste made from ground sesame seeds, tahini is a key ingredient in many Middle Eastern and Turkish dishes, such as hummus and baba gannouj. It's sold in jars, like peanut butter, in Middle Eastern markets and many supermarkets. Try to find tahini that has a runny consistency. It won't separate and is easier to measure and work with. Once opened, store in the refrigerator, and stir before using, because the oil and sesame paste separate out as it sits.

Canned tomatoes: Out of season, the only tomatoes to use are tomatoes you buy in a can. The imported ones and organic Muir Glen tomatoes consistently win taste contests, but I have no qualms about using the best buy from my supermarket. Have 14-ounce and 28-ounce cans on hand, always at least one of each. And to save time in the kitchen, buy diced tomatoes in juice.

Tomato paste: If you have to buy it in a 6-ounce can, once you use what you've needed, spoon it out by the tablespoonful, wrap each tablespoon in plastic, and freeze. If you can find tomato paste in a tube, get it, as you rarely need more than a tablespoon at a time.

Active dry yeast: For making breads or pizza. I keep mine in the freezer.

A Few Aperitifs
to Whet Your Appetite

Every summer since 1981, the year I moved to Paris, I visit Provence to spend time with my dear friend Christine Picasso, who is also my son's godmother. She lives on a spectacular farm called Terres de Cavalier, in the Luberon region of Provence, about 60 miles east of Avignon. We spend our days in and out of surrounding villages and markets, or just lazing around the pool and napping in the hot afternoons. And every evening we cook. But before dinner, before the sun sets—late on summer nights in this part of the world—we always sit in the beautiful light and enjoy an aperitif, a before-dinner cocktail. It may be wine, or champagne, or something more elaborate like a Mauresque (page 34), a kir, or a vermouth.

One summer evening, Christine announced at about 7:30 that it was time for *L'Apero Megalo*, the giant aperitif. We were invited to get into her four-wheel-drive vehicle, and off we went, ascending the hairpin turns of a rocky unpaved country road until we reached a ridge high above the farm. Christine stopped the car, put it in park (rather precariously perched by the edge of the ridge, in my mind), and removed a basket from the back. In it was a chilled bottle of champagne, champagne glasses, olives, and salted almonds.

The landscape provided us with a natural seat from which we could see clear across the valley to the next set of hills where Viens, the village closest to Cavalier, sits. It was "the pink time," when the sun is just about to set and the sky turns many shades of pink, lavender, orange, and turquoise. We sipped our champagne in the soft, warm evening air, awed by the grandeur of the landscape and fully understanding why Christine had come to call this ritual the giant aperitif.

All over the Mediterranean, at that peaceful time of day when night has not yet arrived but the heat of the day is gone and work is done, people congregate in cafés and bars to visit, people-watch, and relax with a drink. I have sat on many a Mediterranean terrace sipping an aperitif before dinner. If I'm in Italy, it's more often than not of a bubbly nature: Prosecco embellished with peach purée or melon liqueur, or a little CampariSoda. In Spain, there is nothing like a glass of ice-cold, fruity sangria on a hot summer day. And in France, Greece, Turkey, and Lebanon, you might whet your appetite or accompany your *meze* with a strong anise-flavored liqueur mixed with ice-cold spring water.

Not all of these drinks will have alcohol. Part of the fun of traveling with kids is discovering new types of treats, and right up there with Italian gelato are the cream sodas made with fruit syrup, milk, and sparkling water that you can get in Italy or make in your kitchen. Simpler—and so much better and prettier than a soda—are the similar spritzers, without the milk, that we love to order in cafés in France.

In midsummer, when I'm trying to work on a hot afternoon, nothing goes down better for me than a good iced coffee. Traveling through Italy, I never had a problem finding this. I remember stopping for gas and asking for *caffè freddo* in the gas station café. The bartender pulled a large water bottle filled with sweetened espresso from the refrigerator, and I was set for the next 100 miles. But nothing matched the special iced coffee the hosts at the bed-and-breakfast Il Frantoio, in Puglia, used to serve me. They guarded their secret, but I think I've figured out something pretty close.

So before we sit down to eat, I'd like to share some of my favorite Mediterranean cocktails and other beverages with you.

PROSECCO AND MIDORI COCKTAIL
(aka Biz Fizz)

This drink was inspired by an aperitif I had at the Escoffier Restaurant, at the Culinary Institute of America in Hyde Park, New York. It was a champagne cocktail with a little bit of the green melon liqueur called Midori. I was taken with it because it reminded me of summer in Italy and Provence. The perfume of the melon liqueur came through the champagne with an elegance that didn't overpower the champagne.

A few weeks after I returned to Los Angeles, I had dinner with close friends who have a law practice called Business Affairs. They wanted to have a cocktail party, and to create a special Business Affairs cocktail for it. I immediately thought of the champagne and Midori cocktail; it would be perfect, because we could call it the Biz Fizz! I began to play around with the drink. It needed something more than just the Midori. Port, I thought. White port, which wouldn't alter the beautiful color of the drink. Port with melon is a classic combination, a favorite first course during the summer months in restaurants all over France. Sure enough, that whisper of white port added the little bit of *je ne sais quoi* that makes everybody love this cocktail.

FOR EACH DRINK

Place about ½ inch of Midori and ½ teaspoon white port in a champagne flute. Fill with Prosecco. Place 2 ripe honeydew balls on a toothpick and place in the glass.

BELLINI
(Sparkling Wine and Peach Cocktail)
Italy

The Bellini was invented in 1948 at Harry's Bar in Venice. It's a wonderful, fruity combination of Prosecco and white peach purée. You can make a Bellini using yellow peach purée or peach syrup, and it will be delicious. But know that Giuseppe Cipriani, the bartender who invented the Bellini,

was looking specifically for something that would show off Italian white peaches. You can find excellent white peach purée in gourmet groceries and specialty stores.

FOR EACH DRINK

1 ounce (2 tablespoons) white peach purée

5 ounces (10 tablespoons) chilled Prosecco

Pour the peach purée into a champagne flute and top with Prosecco.

CAMPARISODA
Italy

I discovered the pleasures of CampariSoda many years ago on my first trip to Italy. The carbonated drink, which comes in a signature cone-shaped single-serving bottle, is the perfect aperitif to sip in the early evening at an outdoor *caffè* as you watch people out for their evening stroll. Campari, the bitter Italian distillate, is made from a mixture of aromatic herbs and was invented in 1860 by Gaspare Campari in Novara. The Campari company began to produce it commercially in 1904, and in the 1930s they were brilliant enough to develop the world's first premixed drink, a single-serve aperitif. The bottle was designed by Fortunato Depero and has not changed since the drink was introduced. It's easier to find CampariSoda in Europe than it is in the United States, but it's certainly easy to mix your own. Which is what I do often in the summer.

FOR EACH DRINK

Put 3 or 4 ice cubes in a highball glass. Fill one-third full with Campari and top off with club soda or sparkling water. Garnish with a round of orange.

CAMPARI ORANGE COCKTAIL
Italy

Sweeter than CampariSoda, this is another drink I love to sip on a summer night in Italy ... or in Southern California.

FOR EACH DRINK

Put 3 or 4 ice cubes in a highball glass. Fill one-third full with Campari and top off with orange juice. Garnish with a round of orange. If you want to make this a spritzer, add a little sparkling water to the mix.

SANGRIA
Spain • **Makes 1 quart**

I must admit I'd never been a big sangria fan. Then I went to Spain in July. The drink can be incredibly refreshing on a hot summer day. The trick is not making it too sweet. Sangria is really about wine and fruit—oranges and lemons, apples and sometimes peaches. It needs time; the fruit should macerate in the wine for a day.

> 1 bottle full-bodied red wine, preferably from Spain
>
> ¼ cup orange juice
>
> 1 tablespoon sugar
>
> 1 tablespoon apricot, orange, or peach liqueur (optional)
>
> 1 orange, sliced
>
> 1 lemon or lime, sliced
>
> 1 apple, cored and cut in wedges
>
> 1 peach, pitted and cut in wedges (optional)
>
> 1 cup sparkling water or club soda
>
> Ice

1. In a large pitcher, mix together the wine, orange juice, sugar, liqueur, and fruit. Cover and refrigerate for several hours, preferably all day or overnight.

2. Just before serving, add the club soda. Serve very cold, over ice.

THE MAURESQUE
France

This is a popular aperitif in Nice, where it is often enjoyed at the start of a leisurely lunch. It's pastis (see box, opposite) that has a little bit of almond syrup (orgeat) added to it. The sweet almond flavor has Moorish overtones, which explains the name. It's a perfect aperitif for a hot summer night.

FOR EACH DRINK

Pour 1 ounce (2 tablespoons) pastis into a bistro glass or highball glass. Add 2 teaspoons almond syrup (orgeat) and fill with water. Add 2 or 3 ice cubes and serve.

SYRUP SPRITZERS (Sirops à l'Eau)
France and Italy

The success of Coca-Cola, Sprite, and other sweet sodas in France and Italy is a testament to the success of marketing. Before these made their inroads, kids (and adults) had bubbly treats that parents and barmen made by pouring a small amount of flavored syrup into a glass and then filling it with sparkling mineral water. They're incredibly tasty, and the colors are beautiful. I am always impressed by the emerald green mint drink (*menthe à l'eau*) that's popular in France. My son favors the grenadine drinks. Torani syrups are widely available in the United States. They're the same syrups that are used in Europe.

FOR EACH DRINK

Pour 1 ounce (2 tablespoons) flavored syrup into a glass and fill with ice and sparkling water.

ITALIAN CREAM SODAS
Italy

The same syrups used for the Syrup Spritzers (above) are used for Italian cream sodas, but milk and sometimes half-and-half is added, for a wonderful creamy flavor.

FOR EACH DRINK

Combine 1 ounce (2 tablespoons) flavored syrup and 1 ounce (2 tablespoons) milk in a glass. Fill with ice and sparkling water. If you wish, top off with a spoonful of half-and-half.

IL FRANTOIO'S "SPECIAL CAFFÈ FREDDO"

Italy • **Makes 1¼ cups, serving 3**

Il Frantoio is a sumptuous *azienda agrituristica,* or bed-and-breakfast, in Puglia, near the village of Ostuni. When you are sitting in the beautiful court-yard on a hot summer midmorning or afternoon, you might ask for an iced coffee, or *caffè freddo.* "Would you like one of our special *caffè freddos?*" you will be asked, and of course you will say yes. What comes is a short glass of sweet, almond-scented coffee with a froth on the top. The staff at Il Frantoio guards the recipe, but I think I've fig-ured it out.

¾ cup strong brewed espresso

1 tablespoon brown sugar

1 tablespoon almond syrup (orgeat)

⅛ teaspoon almond extract

½ cup cold water

Milk (to taste)

Ice cubes (optional)

1. Make the espresso, and while it is still hot, add the sugar, almond syrup, and almond extract. Stir until the sugar has dissolved. Add the cold water. Transfer to a jar, cover, and refrigerate until very cold.

2. Just before serving, add milk to taste. Transfer to a blender (or use a hand-held blender) and blend until frothy. Fill short tumblers with ice cubes if desired (not necessary if the coffee is good and cold). Pour in the coffee and serve.

Note: *In the summer I keep the base in the refrigerator and add it to milk for instant iced coffees.*

THE ANISE-FLAVORED APERITIFS OF THE MEDITERRANEAN

No other drink is as emblematic of the South of France, particularly Marseille and the Côte d'Azur, as pastis. The strong, anise-flavored liqueur evolved in the early part of the 20th century when the French government banned absinthe, which was also flavored with anise but contained wormwood (and wormwood, it was determined, was a danger-ous substance). The absinthe producers Pernod and Ricard (now one company) reformulated an aperitif that did not contain wormwood but tasted a lot like absinthe, with a heavier emphasis on the anise fla-vor. People all over France, but especially in the Midi, have been drinking pastis ever since.

Here is my enduring image of pastis. Two men sit at a café bar or table on a hot summer afternoon in the Midi; the waiter brings bistro glasses, pours about an ounce of pastis from a bottle into the glasses, and sets a yellow ceramic Ricard pitcher full of cool water and a glass of ice cubes on the table.

The men pour water into the glasses, and the liquid immediately changes from dark transparent yellow to milky light yellow. With little tongs, they add an ice cube or two, and linger for as long as they like.

Anise-flavored drinks are popular in other Medi-terranean countries as well. Ouzo is Greece's equiva-lent and, according to food writer Diane Kochilas, their national drink. Raki is what the Turks drink (in Greece, raki also refers to a grape eau de vie, like grappa), and in Lebanon and Syria, those who do consume alcohol drink arak. They are all distillates, clear when poured into a glass, clouding immediately upon contact with water. Whereas pastis becomes pale yellow and opaque when diluted with water, the others become milky white.

I don't associate pastis with food, but in Greece, Turkey, and the Middle East, it's usually enjoyed with *meze* (*mezedes* in Greek), and is particularly refreshing during the hot Mediterranean summer.

Breads, Pizza, and Panini

When I lived in Paris in the 1980s, I used to make sourdough bread every week. When I summered in Provence, I would take my starter with me. This amused my hosts, because it's so easy to find good bread in France. Why make your own? To this I couldn't even answer that my bread was better; it was just that I loved to make bread.

In July of 1985, some friends and I rented a small house on the Croatian island of Korčula. We drove from Paris to Rijeka, then took a ferryboat down the Adriatic coast to the island. I brought my starter along on that trip, too, and made fantastic rustic country breads every other day, with coarse white flour and cornmeal. One afternoon, the family that lived downstairs brought us a huge box of fresh sardines, which we grilled on the hearth in the middle of our kitchen. It was quite a feast: the luscious fish, a large bowl of tomato and cucumber salad, and my bread. I will never forget the relish with which our Croatian friends tore huge hunks off the loaf and dipped them into the juices from the tomatoes. For me, what was special about that meal were the tomatoes and the fresh sardines; for them, it was clearly the freshly baked bread.

Bread is as vital to the Mediterranean diet as rice is to Chinese cuisine. Along with olives and olive oil, it has always been a staple. No matter where you are, a meal without bread is inconceivable. If bread is your passion, and it is certainly one of mine, you can spend a lot of time in Italian and French bakeries. You will discover much, much more than what you'll find in these pages. What I've chosen for this chapter is a small selection of my favorite signature breads from around the Mediterranean basin.

Country breads are big, rustic loaves, made from white flour alone or a combination of white and whole wheat. In Turkey, the country bread has cornmeal in it. Sicilian and Pugliese breads are made with white flour and semolina. They tend to have thick, chewy crusts and porous interiors, whereas the flat breads of the eastern and southern Mediterranean are soft-crusted, with spongy interiors. They are rarely baked at home, though the dough might be assembled there. Villagers and city dwellers alike in North African countries take their shaped loaves to neighborhood bakers at midmorning to be baked in communal ovens, and pick them up before the midday meal. Elsewhere, the local baker does it all.

Many a Mediterranean meal has bread at its core. Pizza is a case in point. In Italy, pizza can be a meal or it can be a snack. All over Italian cities, you'll find pizzerias offering scores of different kinds by the slice. These aren't sit-down establishments, just counters displaying long or large, round pizzas that continually emerge from large, hot ovens.

One summer afternoon in Rome, after a long siesta, we went for a walk, and because we were hungry we stopped in one of these shops to buy a slice. It took a while to choose from the huge selection, written on a chalkboard and set out before our eyes. The vegetarian choices alone included *funghi porcini* with tomatoes and basil, *patate* (sliced potatoes), *patate mozzarella* (sliced potatoes and mozzarella), *quattro formaggi* (four cheeses), *marinara piccante* (spicy marinara), *pepperoni* (peppers), *fiori di Zucca* (zucchini flowers) with cherry tomatoes, *zucchini mozzarelli*, *melanzane* (eggplant), and *bianca* (white). Then there was pizza with sausage, with prosciutto, with salami, with pepperoni. Between the ice cream places and the pizza vendors, we spent a lot of our time in Italy deciding between one enticing form of street food and another!

BIGA

Italy • **Makes 2 cups, enough for 2 big country loaves**

Biga is the Italian word for the starter that is used for many country breads. It isn't sour, like French sourdough starter. It could be, if you let it go for a longer time and fed it regularly. Its function is more that of giving the bread a boost rather than being the sole leavening used in the bread. I always use it in conjunction with yeast. I mix it up the day before I plan on making bread.

¼ teaspoon active dry yeast

1 cup water

2¼ cups unbleached all-purpose flour

1. If mixing by hand or in a standing mixer: Dissolve the yeast in the water. In a large bowl or in the bowl of a standing mixer fitted with the paddle, combine the water-yeast mixture and the flour. Mix until blended to a thick, sticky mixture. Scrape down the sides of the bowl and cover tightly with plastic wrap.

If mixing in a food processor: Dissolve the yeast in the water. Fit the bowl with the steel blade and add the flour. Pour in the water/yeast mixture with the machine running and process until blended into a thick, sticky mixture. Scrape into a bowl and cover tightly with plastic wrap.

2. Leave at room temperature for 24 hours. The biga should look very spongy by this time. Use as directed in country breads.

ADVANCE PREPARATION: This is best the day after it's made, but you could let it go for a couple of days.

WHOLE WHEAT COUNTRY BREAD

Italy • **Makes 1 large loaf**

This is the bread I've been making regularly for my family for years. It's based on an Italian country bread, and has a marvelous, rich, grainy flavor. I like Italian country breads because the biga, or starter, gives them body and moisture, but they aren't sour. I use very little yeast in this bread and let it rise and develop flavor for a long time before punching it down.

1¼ teaspoons active dry yeast

2 cups warm water

1 cup (½ recipe) Biga (at left)

3 cups whole wheat flour

1 to 1½ cups unbleached all-purpose flour

2½ teaspoons salt

1. Dissolve the yeast in the water in the bowl of a standing mixer and let sit until the yeast is creamy, about 5 minutes. Add the biga and mix on low speed until broken up. Add the whole wheat flour, 1 cup of the all-purpose flour, and the salt, and mix together using the paddle until the dough is amalgamated. Change to the dough hook and mix on low speed for 2 minutes. Turn the speed to medium and mix for another 6 to 8 minutes. The dough should be sticky and somewhat wet, but it should come together on the dough hook. Add more all-purpose flour if necessary. Scrape onto a floured work surface and finish kneading the dough by hand for about a minute.

2. Clean, dry, and lightly oil your bowl. Shape the dough into a ball. Place in the bowl, rounded side down first, then turn it so the rounded side is up. Cover with plastic and allow to rise until tripled in size and full of air bubbles, about 3 hours.

3. Moisten your fingers and tap the dough to deflate. Scrape onto a lightly oiled work surface and shape into 1 large loaf, pulling the sides down tightly and pinching together underneath to form a taut ball. If you have a banneton (page 40), flour it generously and allow the loaf to rise in it, rounded side down. Otherwise, place on a cornmeal-dusted or parchment-lined baking peel or on a lightly oiled or parchment-lined baking sheet. Cover with a clean, dry kitchen towel, then with a moistened one, and let rise in a warm place until there are air bubbles under the skin, about 1 hour.

4. Thirty minutes before baking, place a baking stone on the center rack and heat the oven to 450°F. Dimple the top of the loaf and let rest 10 to 15 minutes. If using a banneton or parchment, just before baking, sprinkle the stone with cornmeal.

5. If using a banneton or parchment: Invert the loaf onto the stone and slash the top with a razor or moistened serrated knife. Or, slide the loaf off the peel.

If using a baking sheet: Place the sheet directly on the stone.

6. Bake for 15 minutes. Reduce the heat to 400°F and bake another 30 to 40 minutes, until dark brown and the loaf responds to tapping with a hollow sound. Cool on a rack. I usually make 1 large loaf, which I cut in half or quarters once it has cooled. I wrap half, first in plastic wrap and then in aluminum foil, and freeze it. The other half stays very fresh for about 3 days, as long as I cover the cut side with foil.

THE BANNETON

A traditional French banneton is a muslin-lined wicker basket with slanted sides. Free-form loaves are set, rounded side down, in the baskets to rise. When the bread is ready to be baked, the dough is reversed onto a hot baking stone or the oven floor. Because you flour the muslin, the resulting bread usually has a rustic, floury surface.

You can improvise a banneton by lining any bowl or basket with a linen dish towel. You can also buy a banneton at kitchen and baking stores.

DURUM FLOUR BREAD FROM ALTAMURA

Italy • **Makes 2 medium loaves**

Altamura is a town in the southern Italian region of Puglia, in the heel of the boot. It is famous for its bread, which is made from high-gluten durum wheat flour, the same type of wheat that is used for pasta. I love this bread, as I do the Sicilian semolina bread on page 42.

You can find durum flour in specialty baking stores and some Italian delis. If you can't find it, substitute a mixture of fine semolina and all-purpose flour. This recipe is adapted from Carol Field's recipe in *The Italian Baker*.

If you don't have two baking stones, follow the instructions in the sidebar on the opposite page.

> 1¼ teaspoons active dry yeast
>
> 2 cups warm water
>
> 1½ cups Biga (page 39)
>
> 1 tablespoon salt
>
> 5 to 6 cups durum flour (as needed) or 3⅔ cups fine semolina plus 1½ scant cups unbleached all-purpose flour
>
> Unbleached all-purpose flour for kneading

1. If making the dough in a standing mixer: Combine the yeast and water in the bowl of a standing mixer fitted with the paddle. Let stand until the yeast is creamy, about 5 minutes. Add the biga and stir together with the paddle until it breaks up slightly. Add the flour and salt, and mix together for about 2 minutes, until the ingredients are blended. If the dough seems very dry, gradually add more water, a tablespoon at a time. Change to the dough hook and knead at medium speed for about 5 minutes, until the dough is smooth on the surface but slightly tacky when you knead it. Finish kneading on a lightly floured surface.

If making the dough by hand: Combine the yeast and water in a large bowl. Let stand until the yeast is creamy, about 5 minutes. Add the biga and stir until it breaks up. Add the salt, and the flour 2 cups at a time, then stir with a large wooden spoon until you can scrape the dough out onto your work surface. Flour your hands and the work surface and knead until smooth and elastic, about 10 minutes. To develop the gluten, periodically pick the dough up and slam it down on the work surface.

2. Clean and dry your bowl, and oil it lightly. Shape the dough into a ball and place in the bowl, rounded side down, then turn it so the rounded side is up. Cover the bowl tightly with plastic wrap and set in a warm place to rise until doubled, about 2 hours.

3. Turn the dough out onto a lightly floured work surface and cut in half. Shape each half into a ball, then shape the balls into football-shaped ovals, tapered at the ends. Using a razor or a moistened serrated knife, make a deep slash down the center of each loaf. Flour a board or a baker's peel and set the loaves on it, cut side down. Cover the loaves with a kitchen towel, and cover the first towel with a dampened towel. Let rise for another 45 minutes to 1 hour.

4. Thirty minutes before baking, set 2 baking stones on the center rack and heat the oven to 400°F.

5. Right before baking, turn the dough over and cut the slash again. Sprinkle the baking stones with cornmeal and slide or place the loaves on them, cut side up. Bake for 35 to 40 minutes, until golden brown and hollow-sounding when tapped. Cool on a rack.

PUGLIESE BREAD

Italy • Makes 1 large round or 2 smaller round loaves

The bread of Puglia is porous, with a dark, crunchy, thick crust. It's great for bruschetta, and is meant to accompany Pugliese specialties like Dried Fava Beans and Greens (page 309). I learned to make this bread following Carol Field's recipe in *The Italian Baker*.

BAKING TWO LOAVES WITH ONE STONE

What do you do when a recipe instructs you to form two loaves and you have only one baking stone? What I do is, form the two loaves and put one of them in the refrigerator for the last rise. Let the other loaf rise in a warm spot, and when it's ready to go into the oven, take the other loaf out of the refrigerator. Bake the first loaf, then bake the second loaf. Don't slash the loaf until just before you put it in the oven.

¾ teaspoon active dry yeast

1⅔ cups lukewarm water

½ cup Biga (page 39)

3¾ to 4 cups unbleached all-purpose flour

2 teaspoons salt

1. Place the yeast and warm water in the bowl of a standing mixer fitted with the paddle and stir together. Let stand until the water is cloudy, about 5 minutes. Add the biga and mix until blended. Add 3¾ cups of the flour and the salt, and mix with the paddle until the dough comes together, about 2 minutes. If the dough doesn't come together, add a couple of additional tablespoons of flour. Change to the dough hook and knead at medium speed for 8 minutes. The dough will not come away from the bottom of the bowl. Scrape out onto a floured work surface, flour your hands, and finish kneading for 30 seconds to a minute by hand. The dough should not be sticky.

2. Clean and dry your bowl and oil it lightly. Place the dough in it, then turn the dough over and cover the bowl tightly with plastic wrap. Let rise until tripled, about 3 hours.

3. Flour your work surface generously and place some flour in a pile for dusting. Flour your hands and scrape the dough out onto the work surface. Flour the top of the dough and cut into 2 pieces if making 2 loaves. Flatten each piece of dough and roll up lengthwise. Turn the dough 90 degrees, pat it flat, and roll it up again. Then shape the dough into a ball by rolling it between cupped hands on your work surface. Place on floured parchment paper set on baking sheets or peels, cover with a slightly damp heavy towel or cloth, and let rise until doubled, about 1 hour.

4. Thirty minutes before baking, set a baking stone on the center rack and heat the oven to 450°F.

5. Five to 10 minutes before baking, flour the tops of the loaves and dimple them all over with your fingertips. (The imprints will disappear when the bread bakes.) Let stand for 5 to 10 minutes, until the loaves feel soft and smooth. Sprinkle the baking stone with cornmeal and slide the dough onto it, or place the baking sheet directly on the stone. Bake until golden brown and crusty, 50 to 60 minutes for a large loaf, 30 to 35 minutes for the smaller loaves. The bread is ready when it responds to tapping with a hollow sound. Cool on a rack.

SEMOLINA BREAD WITH SESAME SEEDS

Italy • **Makes 1 medium loaf**

I have always loved this nutty, rich-tasting bread. In Sicily, it's made with a fine semolina flour that is milled especially for the bread. At home, I make it with fine semolina and flour, and I've always had good results.

  2½ teaspoons active dry yeast

  1¼ cups warm water

  1 tablespoon olive oil

  1 teaspoon malt syrup or honey

  2 teaspoons salt

  2 cups plus 3 tablespoons durum flour
    or fine semolina for pasta

  1 cup plus 1 tablespoon unbleached
    all-purpose flour

  ¼ cup sesame seeds

1. Dissolve the yeast in the warm water in a large bowl or in the bowl of your standing mixer. Let stand until the yeast is creamy, about 5 minutes.

2. If making the dough by hand: Add the oil, malt syrup, and salt. Mix in the flours 1 cup at a time, and as soon as you can scrape the mixture out of your bowl in one piece, scrape onto a lightly floured work surface. Knead for 10 minutes, slamming the dough down from time to time to develop the gluten.

If making the dough in a standing mixer: Add the oil, malt syrup, and salt. Mix in the flours with the paddle for 2 minutes, then change to the dough hook. Knead for 5 to 8 minutes on medium speed, until you have a firm, elastic dough. Knead for a minute or so on a lightly floured surface to finish.

3. Clean and dry your bowl and oil it lightly. Shape the dough into a ball and place in the bowl, rounded side down, then turn so the rounded side is up. Cover the bowl with plastic wrap and allow the dough to rise until doubled, 1½ to 2 hours.

4. Punch down the dough and knead it for a couple of minutes. Shape the dough into a ball, pulling the sides down tightly towards the middle and pinching together. Place the sesame seeds on your work surface. Moisten the surface of the dough with wet hands, and roll in the sesame seeds. Set on floured parchment paper, on a peel sprinkled with cornmeal or semolina, or on an oiled baking sheet. Or place upside down in a banneton. Cover with a kitchen towel and place a second, damp towel on top. Allow to rise until doubled, 1 to 1½ hours.

5. Thirty minutes before baking, set a baking stone on the center rack and heat the oven to 425°F.

6. Just before baking, sprinkle the stone with cornmeal. Slide in the loaf and bake for 10 minutes, spraying three times with water. Reduce the heat to 400°F and bake another 25 to 30 minutes, until the bread is golden-brown and responds to tapping with a hollow sound. Cool on a rack.

SEMOLINA BREAD WITH TOMATO AND ZUCCHINI: I had this beautiful bread at a restaurant called Alla Beccaccia, on Istria. You can use the dough in this recipe as a base, and just before the end of kneading, add ½ cup chopped zucchini and ½ cup diced peeled, seeded tomatoes. Knead until evenly distributed. Proceed with the recipe as directed, but omit the sesame seeds.

FOCACCIA

Italy • **Makes one 11 × 17-inch focaccia**

A close relative to pizza, focaccia is a flat bread that is traditionally baked in a wood-burning oven. It has a dimpled top, and can be filled or topped with a number of ingredients. There are hundreds of different types of focaccia in Italy. At its simplest, it is topped with olive oil and coarse salt. I like to make my focaccia with a small amount of whole wheat flour (see the variation that follows).

FOR THE SPONGE

1 teaspoon active dry yeast

½ cup warm water

¾ cup unbleached all-purpose flour

FOR THE DOUGH

1 teaspoon active dry yeast

1 cup warm water

3 tablespoons olive oil

3¼ cups unbleached all-purpose flour

2 teaspoons salt

FOR THE TOPPING

2 tablespoons olive oil

1 teaspoon coarse sea salt

1. *Make the sponge:* Combine the yeast and water in a large bowl or the bowl of a stand mixer and stir to dissolve. Let stand for 5 to 10 minutes, until the yeast is creamy. Whisk in the flour. Cover with plastic wrap and let rise in a warm place until bubbly and doubled in volume, about 45 minutes.

2. *Make the dough:* If making the dough in a standing mixer, whisk together the yeast and water in a small bowl and let stand until the yeast is creamy, 5 to 10 minutes. Add to the sponge in the mixer bowl along with the olive oil. Mix on low speed with the paddle until well blended. Add the flour and salt and mix for 1 to 2 minutes, until the ingredients are amalgamated. Change to the dough hook and knead on medium speed until the dough comes together and is soft, velvety, and slightly tacky. Flour the work surface lightly, scrape out the dough, and finish kneading by hand until you can shape it into a ball.

If making the dough by hand: Combine the yeast and water as directed above and whisk into the sponge along with the olive oil. Whisk in 1 cup of the flour. Add the salt and remaining flour, 1 cup at a time, folding it in with a wooden spoon. When you can, scrape the dough out onto a floured work surface and knead for 8 to 10 minutes, until soft and velvety.

3. Clean, dry, and lightly oil your bowl. Shape the dough into a ball and place in the bowl, rounded side down, then turn so the rounded side is up. Cover the bowl tightly with plastic wrap and let the dough rise until doubled, 1¼ to 1½ hours.

4. Oil an 11 × 17-inch baking sheet with olive oil. Turn the dough onto the baking sheet. Oil or moisten your hands and press the dough out until it just about covers the bottom of the pan. The dough will be sticky. Cover with a towel and allow it to relax for 10 minutes, then continue to press it out until it reaches the edges of the pan. Cover with a damp towel and let rise for 45 minutes to 1 hour, or until the dough is full of air bubbles.

5. Thirty minutes before baking, set a baking stone on the center rack and heat the oven to 425°F.

6. *Top the focaccia:* With lightly oiled fingertips or with your knuckles, dimple the dough, pressing down hard so that you leave indentations. Drizzle on the olive oil and sprinkle with the salt. Place in the oven on the baking stone. Spray the dough three times with water during the first 10 minutes of baking, and bake for 20 to 25 minutes, until the edges are crisp and the top is golden. If you wish, remove the focaccia from the pan and bake directly on the stone during the last 10 minutes of baking. Remove from the oven, remove from the pan at once, and cool on a rack. If you want a softer focaccia, cover with a towel when you remove it from the oven. Serve warm or at room temperature.

ADVANCE PREPARATION: The dough can be made through Step 3 and refrigerated for up to 5 days. Punch it down, oil it lightly, and seal in a plastic bag. Allow it to come to room temperature before proceeding with Step 4. Once baked, focaccia will not keep well, but you will probably eat it up quickly anyway.

VARIATIONS

- **WHOLE WHEAT FOCACCIA:** Substitute ¾ cup of whole wheat flour for ¾ cup of the all-purpose flour in the dough.
- **BELL PEPPER FOCACCIA:** Knead in 2 red bell peppers, roasted, seeded, and chopped, or scatter them over the top.
- **TOMATO FOCACCIA:** Knead in ½ cup drained chopped sun-dried tomatoes.
- **CHEESE FOCACCIA:** Mix together 1 cup crumbled Gorgonzola or ricotta and ¼ cup Parmesan and dollop over the top. Drizzle with olive oil.
- **HERB FOCACCIA:** Knead in 3 tablespoons chopped fresh sage or rosemary or sprinkle over the top.
- **TOMATO AND MOZZARELLA FOCACCIA:** Top with 6 ounces grated or sliced mozzarella and ½ to ¾ pound sliced tomatoes before baking. Sprinkle the tomatoes with coarse salt and thyme and drizzle with olive oil.

PROVENÇAL BREAD WITH OLIVES
(Fougasse aux Olives)
France • Makes 2 flat breads

Fougasse is the Provençal version of focaccia. It's the signature bread of the region, found in different shapes in bakeries and markets in every Provençal village and town. It's usually a yeast bread, although I've also seen brioche-type *fougasses*. I prefer the former. Some bakers shape their *fougasses* into ladders, others into wheat shafts, while others shape theirs into leaves, which is my favorite. In addition to olives, *fougasses* can be filled with cured bacon, walnuts, or anchovies, and you can also substitute whole wheat flour for some of the unbleached all-purpose flour (see the variations that follow).

    2 teaspoons active dry yeast
    1 teaspoon sugar
    1½ cups warm water
    1 tablespoon olive oil
    3½ to 4 cups unbleached all-purpose flour
    2 teaspoons salt
    1 cup imported black olives, halved and pitted

1. In the bowl of a standing mixer or in a large bowl, dissolve the yeast and sugar in the water. Let stand until the yeast is creamy, about 5 minutes, and stir in the olive oil.

2. If making the dough in a standing mixer: Add 3½ cups of the flour and the salt to the yeast mixture and mix together briefly using the paddle. Change to the dough hook and beat for 8 to 10 minutes at medium speed, adding flour as necessary, until the dough forms a ball and is no longer sticky. Remove from the bowl, knead for a minute on a lightly floured surface, and shape into a ball.

If making the dough by hand: Stir the salt and the flour into the yeast mixture, a cup at a time, until the dough can be scraped out onto a floured work surface. Knead, adding flour as necessary, for 10 minutes, until the dough is elastic and smooth. Shape into a ball.

3. Clean and dry your bowl and oil lightly with olive oil. Place the dough in it, rounded side down, then turn so the rounded side is up. Cover tightly with plastic and let rise in a warm spot until doubled, about 1½ hours, or in the refrigerator for 4 to 8 hours.

4. Punch down the dough. A handful at a time, knead the olives into the dough, until they are evenly distributed. Divide into 2 equal pieces. Cover with lightly oiled plastic and let the dough rest for 15 minutes.

5. Place a baking stone on the center rack and heat the oven to 450°F. Line 2 baking sheets with parchment paper and spray the paper with cooking spray. Roll or press each half of the dough into an oval or rectangle measuring about 9 × 12 inches. Using a pastry scraper or a serrated knife, make 3 diagonal slashes out from the center of the bread toward the edge and 1 down from the top, to look like the veins of a leaf. Leave a 2-inch border at the edge of the dough.

6. Transfer the loaves to the baking sheets. Gently pull the bread apart at the slashes. Cover with lightly oiled plastic wrap and a towel, and let rest for 30 minutes.

7. One at a time, bake the breads on the baking stone for 20 to 25 minutes, until golden. Let rest for at least 10 minutes before serving, or let cool completely.

ADVANCE PREPARATION: You can make the dough through Step 3 and refrigerate in a plastic freezer bag. It will keep for up to a week.

VARIATIONS

WHOLE WHEAT FOUGASSE: Substitute 1½ cups whole wheat flour for 1½ cups of the all-purpose flour. You will use less flour overall if you use some whole wheat flour.

WALNUT FOUGASSE: Follow the instructions for Whole Wheat Fougasse. Substitute 1 cup chopped walnuts for the olives and walnut oil for the olive oil.

ITALIAN FLAT BREAD
Italy • **Makes 2 small round loaves**

I call this bread *pizza bread,* because you can make it with the same dough you use for pizza. It's a very versatile formula, open to endless variations. I make up the dough in seconds in the food processor and keep it on hand in the refrigerator, where the flavor only gets better over 2 or 3 days, or even a week.

> **1 batch Pizza Dough (page 56), replacing ¾ to 1 cup of the all-purpose flour with whole wheat flour**

1. Make the dough through Step 3, allowing the dough to rise until doubled, about 1½ hours.

2. Line a baking sheet with parchment and lightly oil the parchment. Divide the dough into 2 equal balls. Roll or press out to a 1-inch thickness. Cover with lightly oiled plastic and a damp kitchen towel and let rise in a warm spot for 30 minutes while you heat the oven.

3. Place a baking stone on the center rack and heat the oven to 450°F. Bake the breads for 20 to 25 minutes, until puffed and light brown. Remove the breads from the baking sheet and wrap in kitchen towels, so the crust will be soft. Cool on a rack.

VARIATIONS

- Substitute ¾ cup semolina for the whole wheat flour.
- Use all unbleached all-purpose flour.

WHY I LOVE FLAT BREADS

There's something about the ratio of crust to crumb that makes flat breads incredibly appealing to me. The centers tend to be very moist and chewy, and the crusts thick and toothsome. To prevent all that crust from becoming too hard, wrap flat breads in a towel after you remove them from the oven, and store in plastic bags.

ROSEMARY AND THYME BREAD

Makes 1 large or 2 small round loaves

Rosemary bread has become a fairly common item in high-end bakeries on this side of the Atlantic. I like to add thyme to the mix, and I use some whole wheat flour in my country loaf. Use fresh rosemary for this; the dried rosemary will be too spiky. However, if you don't feel like picking 2 tablespoons thyme leaves off the stems, you can use dried.

> 2½ teaspoons active dry yeast
>
> 2 cups lukewarm water
>
> 1 teaspoon honey
>
> 2 tablespoons olive oil (optional)
>
> 2 cups whole wheat flour
>
> 2½ teaspoons salt
>
> 2 tablespoons finely chopped fresh rosemary leaves
>
> 2 tablespoons fresh thyme leaves (or 1 tablespoon dried)
>
> 3 to 3½ cups unbleached all-purpose flour

1. Dissolve the yeast in the warm water in a large bowl or in the bowl of a standing mixer. Stir in the honey and let sit for a few minutes, until creamy. Add the olive oil, if using, and the whole wheat flour, and stir or whisk in one direction until thoroughly combined. Cover with plastic and allow to sit in a warm place for 1 hour, by which time the mixture should be bubbly.

2. If making the dough by hand: Add the salt and the herbs to the sponge. Add the all-purpose flour, a cup at a time, and as soon as you can, scrape the dough out onto a lightly floured work surface. Knead, adding flour as necessary, for 10 minutes, until smooth and elastic.

If making the dough in a standing mixer: Add the salt, herbs, and 3 cups of the all-purpose flour to the sponge. Mix together with the paddle, then change to the dough hook. Mix on medium speed for 8 to 10 minutes, adding flour as needed if the dough does not come away from the sides of the bowl. Scrape out of the bowl and finish kneading on a lightly floured surface for about a minute.

3. Clean, dry, and oil your bowl. Shape the dough into a ball and place in the bowl, rounded side down, then turn so the rounded side is up. Cover the bowl tightly with plastic wrap and set in a warm spot to rise until doubled, about 1½ hours.

4. Punch down the dough and shape into 1 or 2 balls. If you have a banneton (see page 40), place the dough rounded side down in it and cover with a piece of oiled plastic and a damp dish towel. If you don't have a banneton, place the dough on a lightly oiled, cornmeal-sprinkled baking sheet and cover with lightly oiled plastic and a damp towel. Let rise until doubled, about 1 hour.

5. Thirty minutes before baking, place a baking stone on the center rack and heat the oven to 400°F. Dust the baking stone with cornmeal if baking the bread directly on the stone.

6. Reverse the loaf or loaves from the banneton onto the stone, or place the baking sheet on top of the stone. Slash the loaf or loaves across the top with a sharp knife or a razor blade. Spray the loaf or loaves with water. Bake for 10 minutes, spraying with water a few times. Reduce the heat to 375°F and continue to bake for another 40 to 45 minutes, until the bread is nicely brown and responds to tapping with a hollow sound. Cool on a rack. The bread will keep for a few days at room temperature, wrapped in foil. It freezes well, wrapped airtight.

VARIATION

Add 1 cup imported black olives, pitted and cut in half, to the dough along with the herbs.

BOSNIAN FLAT BREAD

Bosnia • **Makes four 6-inch loaves**

Amra Slipac, a wonderful Bosnian cook, makes this bread daily at the café she and her husband have in Los Angeles. I love everything she makes at the aptly named Aroma Café, especially her vegetable pies (pages 247 to 249) and this crusty bread. The dough is a very moist one. If you use too much flour, the bread will be too tight. Amra uses a mixer to mix up the large amounts of dough she must make for the café, but she prefers to knead the bread by hand. "That's the only way I can really tell if it's right, by touch." You may not wish to have such sticky hands, however, so I'm giving you a mechanical option.

> 2 teaspoons active dry yeast
>
> 2 cups warm water
>
> 5 cups unbleached all-purpose flour
>
> 2¼ teaspoons salt

1. In the bowl of a standing mixer or a large bowl, dissolve the yeast in the water. Let sit for 2 to 3 minutes, until the yeast is beginning to get creamy. Add 2 cups of the flour and stir 100 times in the same direction to combine. Cover with plastic and set in a warm spot to rise for 1 hour.

2. If making the dough in a standing mixer: Combine the remaining flour and the salt and add to the yeast mixture all at once. Mix together using the paddle, then change to the dough hook. Knead at low speed for 2 minutes, then turn up to medium speed and knead until the dough comes cleanly away from the sides of the bowl, clusters around the dough hook, and slaps against the sides of the bowl, about 8 minutes. Add flour as needed. Hold on to the machine if it bounces around. Turn out onto a clean work surface and knead by hand for 2 to 3 minutes longer. The dough should be sticky.

If making the dough by hand: Stir the salt into the dough. Fold in the flour a cup at a time, using a large wooden spoon. As soon as you can scrape the dough out in one piece, scrape out onto a lightly floured work surface, and knead for 10 min-

utes, adding flour as necessary, until the dough is elastic. It should be sticky.

3. Transfer the dough to a clean, lightly oiled bowl, rounded side down, then turn so the rounded side is up. Cover the bowl tightly with plastic wrap and leave it in a warm spot to rise until doubled, about 1½ hours.

4. Punch down the dough and let rise again until doubled, about 45 minutes.

5. Line 2 baking sheets with parchment and lightly oil the parchment. Divide the dough into 4 equal balls. Roll or press out to a 1-inch thickness, and place 2 on each baking sheet. Cover with lightly oiled plastic and a damp kitchen towel and let rise in a warm spot for 30 minutes while you heat the oven.

6. Place a baking stone on the center rack and heat the oven to 450°F. Bake the breads for 20 to 25 minutes, until puffed and light brown. Cool on a rack.

ADVANCE PREPARATION: Follow the recipe through Step 3. Then punch down the dough, form into a ball, oil the ball lightly with olive oil, and place in a plastic freezer bag. Refrigerate for up to 1 week.

GREEK COUNTRY BREAD

Greece • **Makes 2 oval loaves**

When I was on the island of Ikaria, one morning I walked the 5 kilometers up the mountain road from the seaside village of Armenistís to the village of Raches. I passed the village bakery just as the baker, a strong-armed woman named Demetra Gerali, was shaping her loaves. She weighed out the dough, formed the loaves, and set them to rise in the folds of sheets of heavy white linen set in long wooden boxes. I continued on my way, and by the time I descended the hill and passed the bakery again, 150 oval loaves were standing on their ends cooling, waiting for people to pick them up for the midday meal. I took a warm loaf back with me, and devoured it with feta and tomatoes for lunch. This bread is an approximation of that wonderful loaf.

    2½ teaspoons active dry yeast

    1 teaspoon sugar

    2 cups warm water

    5½ to 6 cups bread flour or unbleached
        all-purpose flour

    4 tablespoons olive oil

    2½ teaspoons salt

1. In the bowl of a standing mixer or in a large bread bowl, dissolve the yeast and sugar in the water. Let sit until the yeast is creamy, about 5 minutes. Stir in 2 cups of the flour and stir until the mixture is smooth. Cover with plastic and leave for 1 hour in a warm spot. The mixture should be bubbly.

2. If making the dough by hand: Stir 3 tablespoons of the olive oil and the salt into the sponge. Add the flour, a cup at a time, until you can scrape the dough out onto a lightly floured work surface. Knead, adding flour as necessary, for 10 minutes, until the dough is smooth and elastic.

If making the dough in a standing mixer: Stir 3 tablespoons of the olive oil and the salt into the sponge. Add 3½ cups of the flour. Mix together on low speed using the paddle until amalgamated. Change to the dough hook and knead on medium speed for 8 to 10 minutes, adding flour as necessary, until the dough comes away from the sides of the bowl. Scrape out onto a lightly floured work surface and finish kneading for about 1 minute by hand.

3. Clean, dry, and lightly oil the bowl with olive oil. Shape the dough into a ball. Place the dough in the bowl, rounded side down, then turn so the rounded side is up. Cover the bowl tightly with plastic and let the dough rise in a warm spot until doubled in size, about 2 hours.

4. Punch down the dough, knead for about a minute, and shape into a ball. Rub the ball of dough with the remaining 1 tablespoon olive oil and return to the bowl. Cover tightly and allow to rise again until doubled, 1½ to 2 hours.

5. Turn the dough out onto your lightly floured work surface and divide into 2 equal pieces. Shape into log-shaped loaves. Take a heavy linen dish towel and place a loaf in the middle. Make a sort of cradle for the dough by folding up the sides of the towel on either side of the dough, and place on a baking sheet. Repeat with the other loaf. Cover the loaves with a lightly oiled piece of plastic wrap and a damp towel, and let rise for 30 minutes while you heat the oven.

6. Set a baking stone on the center rack and heat the oven to 450°F. Lightly oil a baking sheet and sprinkle with cornmeal. Carefully transfer the loaves from the towels to the baking sheet. Brush or spray the surface with water, and run a knife or razor blade down the length of each loaf. Bake for 15 minutes, reduce the heat to 400°F, and bake another 25 minutes, spraying the oven with water every 10 minutes or so, until the bread is golden brown and responds to tapping with a hollow sound. Cool on a rack.

ADVANCE PREPARATION: The bread will be good for about 3 days, and it freezes well, wrapped airtight.

VARIATIONS

● You can use a starter for this dough. Reduce the yeast to 1 teaspoon and add 1 cup Biga (page 39) to the sponge in Step 1. The rising time for the first rise will be 3 hours instead of 2.

● Substitute 1 cup barley or whole wheat flour for 1 cup of the all-purpose flour in the sponge in Step 1. Reduce the amount of all-purpose flour in Step 2 by ½ cup and add more as needed.

RUSKS (Paximathia)

Greece • **Makes 1 dozen rusks**

Stacked in multicolored piles in bakeries all over Greece, these twice-baked breads were traditionally carried to the fields by agricultural workers, who would moisten them with water at midday to enjoy them with olive oil, feta, olives, and tomatoes. You can find *paximathia* in Greek markets; they are usually from Crete, made with barley flour or chick pea flour. But you can also make them yourself.

**1 batch dough for Greek Country Bread
(page 47)**

1. Mix up the dough, let rise, and shape as directed. Once shaped, let rise until doubled. Using kitchen scissors or a pastry scraper, cut 2-inch wedges along one side of each loaf. Place in the oven but bake only halfway, 20 to 25 minutes. The bread will be brown on the outside but will not ring hollow when tapped. Let cool.

2. When the bread is completely cool, break off the wedges and place on a baking sheet. Heat the oven to its lowest setting, about 170°F. If you have a pilot light, that might be enough without turning on the oven. Place in the oven for 6 to 8 hours, until the bread is hard and golden brown.

3. To reconstitute, for salads and to accompany cheese and tomatoes, douse with water or dunk briefly in water.

 TIP USE WHAT YOU HAVE
You can make rusks with any other country bread you have on hand. Cut the bread into thick slices and place on a baking sheet. Follow the directions in Step 2, above.

TURKISH COUNTRY BREAD

Turkey • **Makes 1 large round loaf**

This bread is popular in the villages of central and eastern Anatolia. There are different versions of it throughout Turkey, some made entirely with whole wheat flour and cornmeal (see the variation that follows). Cornmeal has been a traditional ingredient in Turkish breads since it was introduced in Europe in the 16th century, after the discovery of the Americas. It contributes a wonderful texture to the breads.

> 2 teaspoons active dry yeast
>
> ½ teaspoon sugar
>
> 2 cups warm water
>
> 2 cups unbleached all-purpose flour
>
> 1 cup finely ground cornmeal
>
> 2½ teaspoons salt
>
> 2 cups whole wheat flour

1. Combine the yeast, sugar, and water in a large bowl or the bowl of a standing mixer and stir until dissolved. Add the all-purpose flour and stir together until smooth. Cover with plastic wrap and let sit in a warm spot until bubbly, about 30 minutes.

2. *If making the dough by hand:* Stir the cornmeal into the sponge. Add the salt and whole wheat flour, a cup at a time, folding until you can turn your dough out onto a lightly floured work surface. Knead the dough for about 10 minutes, until smooth and elastic. Shape into a ball.

If making the dough in a standing mixer: Stir the cornmeal into the sponge. Add the salt and whole wheat flour all at once and beat at low speed with the paddle until combined. Change to the dough hook and beat at medium speed for 8 to 10 minutes, until the dough is smooth and elastic. Shape into a ball.

3. Clean, dry, and lightly oil the bowl with olive oil. Place the dough in the bowl, rounded side down, then turn so the rounded side is up. Cover with plastic wrap and set in a warm spot to rise until doubled, about 1½ hours. ▶

4. Punch down the dough and shape into a large round. With a razor or moistened serrated knife, slash an "X" across the top. Oil a baking sheet and sprinkle with cornmeal. Place the loaf on the baking sheet and cover with a damp towel. Let rise until doubled in size, about 45 minutes to 1 hour. Meanwhile, heat the oven to 425°F.

5. Place the dough in the oven and bake for 10 minutes. Reduce the heat to 400°F. Bake 40 minutes, or until the loaf responds to tapping with a hollow sound. Cool on a rack. The bread will keep for 3 or 4 days, and it freezes well.

VARIATIONS

● Use 4 cups unbleached all-purpose flour and omit the whole wheat flour.

● Use all whole wheat flour.

SOFT TURKISH POCKET BREAD

Turkey • **Makes 4 large flat breads or 16 small breads**

Real pita bread is nothing like the thin, dry, airy pocket bread we get in supermarkets and many Middle Eastern restaurants all over North America. The bread made in bakeries throughout the Middle East is spongy, moist, and fragrant. If the bread is baked quickly, in the bottom of a very hot oven, it will puff up to produce a slightly crisp outside with a hollow inside that can be filled with any number of foods. This Turkish version, when shaped into large, flat loaves, is reminiscent of Indian and Afghani naans, especially when topped with nigella seeds. It differs from other pita breads from the Mediterranean because it contains yogurt, and is brushed with egg and sprinkled with the nigella just before baking.

> 2 teaspoons active dry yeast
>
> 2 cups lukewarm water
>
> ¼ cup drained yogurt (page 21)
>
> ¼ cup olive oil or melted butter
>
> 5 to 6 cups unbleached all-purpose flour (as needed)

> 1 tablespoon salt
>
> 1 egg, beaten
>
> 1 tablespoon nigella seeds

1. Stir together the yeast and water in a large bowl or the bowl of a standing mixer. Add the yogurt and oil, and stir or beat in 2½ cups of the flour. Cover with plastic and let stand for 30 minutes to 1 hour, until bubbly.

2. If making the dough by hand: Add the salt and the remaining flour, a cup at a time, until you can scrape the dough out onto a lightly floured work surface. Knead, adding flour as necessary, for 10 minutes, until the dough is smooth and elastic.

If making the dough in a standing mixer: Add 2½ cups flour and the salt and beat in with the paddle. Change to the dough hook and knead for 10 minutes, until smooth and elastic.

3. Clean, dry, and lightly oil the bowl with olive oil. Form the dough into a ball and place in the bowl, rounded side down, then turn so the rounded side is up. Cover tightly with plastic wrap and let the dough rise in a warm spot until doubled in size, about 1½ hours.

4. Meanwhile, place a baking stone or a baking sheet on the rack set at the lowest level and heat the oven to 450°F.

5. Divide the dough into 4 equal pieces and shape each piece into a ball. One at a time, roll out or press out the dough balls using the heel of your hand into large, uneven ovals or circles about ¼ inch thick. Cover the rest of the dough with a damp towel. To make smaller pitas, divide the dough into 8 to 16 pieces and roll them out to thin circles, less than ¼ inch thick. Brush with the beaten egg and sprinkle with nigella seeds.

6. One or two at a time, place a bread on the hot baking stone or baking sheet. Place in the oven and check small rounds after 4 minutes, large rounds after 8. Small rounds will puff up completely; this usually takes about 4 minutes. Large breads will blister in places and will take 8 to 10 minutes to cook and puff up completely. Wrap the breads in a large kitchen towel while you continue to bake the remaining breads. These are best eaten on the day they're made, but they freeze well. If you keep them, seal them in plastic bags so they don't dry out.

ADVANCE PREPARATION: You can prepare the dough through Step 3 and store it, sealed in a plastic bag, in the refrigerator for 3 or 4 days. Shape the breads and bring back to room temperature before baking.

VARIATIONS

- Substitute 1 to 3 cups whole wheat flour for the equivalent number of cups of unbleached all-purpose flour.

- Omit the nigella and egg topping.

ARAB BREAD

Middle East • **Makes eight 6- to 7-inch breads**

This round pocket bread is only slightly different from the Turkish flat bread on the opposite page. It's really quite easy to make.

> 2½ teaspoons active dry yeast
>
> 1 teaspoon sugar
>
> 2 cups warm water (or 2¼ cups if using whole wheat flour)
>
> 2 tablespoons extra virgin olive oil
>
> 5 to 6 cups unbleached all-purpose flour, whole wheat flour, or a combination (I like to use half and half)
>
> 2 teaspoons salt

1. Stir together the yeast, sugar, and water in a large bowl or the bowl of a standing mixer. Add the olive oil and stir or beat in 2½ cups of the flour. Cover with plastic and let stand for 30 minutes to 1 hour, until bubbly.

2. If making the dough by hand: Add the salt and the remaining flour, a cup at a time, until you can scrape the dough out onto a lightly floured work surface. Knead, adding flour as necessary, for 10 minutes, until the dough is smooth and elastic.

If making the dough in a standing mixer: Add 2½ cups flour and the salt and beat with the paddle. Change to the dough hook and knead for 10 minutes, until smooth and elastic.

3. Clean, dry, and lightly oil the bowl with olive oil. Form the dough into a ball and place in the bowl, rounded side down, then turn so the rounded side is up. Cover tightly with plastic wrap and let the dough rise in a warm spot until doubled in size, about 1½ hours.

4. Lightly dust a baking sheet with flour or semolina. Place a large kitchen towel or a folded cotton sheet on your work surface and dust with flour. Punch down the dough and divide into 8 equal pieces. Shape the pieces into balls and place on the baking sheet. Cover with lightly oiled plastic.

5. Take 1 ball at a time, flatten it on a lightly floured work surface, and roll it out with a lightly floured rolling pin until it is about ¼ inch thick and 6 inches in diameter. Transfer to the floured towel or sheet and sprinkle lightly with flour. Repeat with the remaining pieces of dough, laying the rolled out pieces on the floured towel. Cover them with another towel and let rest for 30 minutes. Meanwhile, place a baking stone or a baking sheet on the rack set at the lowest level and heat the oven to 500°F.

6. Bake 2 breads at a time on the baking sheet, placing the breads 1 inch apart (you might only be able to fit one at a time on a baking stone). Bake for 5 to 7 minutes, until the breads puff. Transfer to a wire rack and cover with a towel so that the breads remain soft.

ADVANCE PREPARATION: Arab bread dries out quickly and should be kept in plastic bags. You can prepare the dough through Step 3 and store it for up to 5 days, sealed in a plastic bag, in the refrigerator. Bring back to room temperature before baking. Or, you can stack the baked loaves and freeze them in resealable bags. Thaw them in the bags in the refrigerator, or wrapped in a towel in the microwave. You can warm the bread in a 300°F oven for 10 minutes, but be sure to wrap it quickly in a towel to keep it from drying out.

PROVENÇAL ORANGE-SCENTED BRIOCHE (Pompe à l'Huile)

France • Makes 1 very large round loaf or 2 smaller loaves

This is a traditional Christmas bread, one of the famous "Thirteen Desserts" served at the Provençal Christmas Eve feast called *Le Gros Souper*. It's an orange-scented bread enriched with olive oil, and sometimes (as here) with eggs. Some Provençal bakers shape their *pompe à l'huile* into rings; others roll them out into flattened circles or ovals and cut out spaces to make them look like *fougasse* (page 44). The bread is wonderful with tea and it's a great breakfast bread. Use leftovers for out-of-this-world French toast.

> 2½ teaspoons active dry yeast
>
> 1 cup warm water
>
> ⅓ cup sugar
>
> 4½ to 5 cups unbleached all-purpose flour
>
> 2 large eggs, at room temperature
>
> ⅓ cup olive oil, plus additional for brushing the loaf
>
> 1½ teaspoons salt
>
> Grated zest of 2 oranges
>
> 2 teaspoons orange flower water

1. In a large bowl or the bowl of a standing mixer, dissolve the yeast in the water. Add 1 teaspoon of the sugar and let stand until the yeast is creamy, about 5 minutes. Add 1½ cups of the flour and stir together until smooth. Cover with plastic wrap and set in a warm place for 45 minutes, or until the mixture is bubbling.

2. Add the remaining sugar, the eggs, olive oil, salt, orange zest, and orange flower water to the sponge and stir in.

3. If making the dough by hand: Fold in the remaining flour a cup at a time. When the dough holds together, scrape it out onto your work surface and begin to knead, adding flour as necessary. The dough will be quite sticky. Knead for 10 minutes, until the dough is elastic, then form into a ball.

If making the dough in a standing mixer: Add 3 cups of flour all at once and mix briefly using the paddle. Change to the dough hook and knead for 10 minutes at medium speed. Add a little more flour if the dough seems very sticky (it should be somewhat sticky). Scrape onto a lightly floured work surface and knead briefly with your hands to finish. Shape into a ball.

4. Wash and dry your bowl, and coat it lightly with olive oil. Place the dough in it, rounded side down, then turn so the rounded side is up. Cover with plastic wrap and let rise in a warm spot until doubled, 2 to 3 hours.

5. Punch down the dough and scrape out onto a lightly floured work surface. Shape the dough into 1 large or 2 smaller flat rounds, about 1½ inches thick. If you wish, make three 2-inch-long slits on each side of the dough and pull apart gently at the cuts. Place on an oiled baking sheet, cover with lightly oiled plastic and a damp dish towel, and set in a warm spot to rise for 45 minutes. Meanwhile, heat the oven to 400°F.

6. Place the baking sheet in the oven and bake for 20 minutes. Brush the bread with olive oil, return to the oven, reduce the heat to 375°F, and bake for another 20 minutes, until the bread is brown and responds to tapping with a hollow thumping sound. Brush again with olive oil and cool on a rack.

ADVANCE PREPARATION: You can make the dough a day ahead and keep it in the refrigerator. Bring back to room temperature before shaping the breads or baking. The bread freezes well and will keep for a day or two.

NIÇOISE CHICK PEA FLOUR PANCAKE
(Socca)

France • Serves 4 to 6

Socca is my favorite thing to eat in Nice. It's an addictive polenta-like pancake made with chick pea flour (available in Mediterranean markets), water, salt, and olive oil. *Socca* vendors in Nice make it in huge round heavy pans in hot pizza ovens, and scrape it out by the order into grease-proof brown paper packages. It's meant to be eaten with your fingers, which will become irresistibly greasy with olive oil. There is no better accompaniment to *socca* than a glass of dry Provençal rosé wine and a handful of imported black olives.

My friend Cliff Wright and I like to make *socca* on the grill. We use a paella pan and get it nice and hot over the coals, then pour in the batter. When I make it inside, I make two batches in a heavy-gauge 10-inch pie plate.

- 1½ cups chick pea flour
- 1¼ teaspoons salt
- 3 cups water
- 4 tablespoons olive oil

1. Heat the oven to 500°F, preferably with a baking stone set on the center rack, or prepare a hot grill.

2. Whisk together the chick pea flour, salt, and water in a medium bowl until smooth. Whisk in 2 tablespoons of the olive oil. Let sit for 30 minutes to 1 hour, then whisk again and put through a strainer.

3. Place a 10-inch heavy-gauge cake pan, a 15-inch paella pan, or a 3-quart enameled gratin in the oven or over the coals and heat for 5 minutes, until very hot. Add the remaining 2 tablespoons oil to the pan and brush to cover. It should almost smoke.

4. Whisk the batter and carefully pour into the hot pan. Use only half the batter if using a 10-inch pan. It will sizzle immediately. Place in the oven on the baking stone, or over the coals. Cook for 20 to 22 minutes, or until the *socca* is brown on top and beginning to pull away from the pan. Watch carefully to make sure it doesn't burn. Remove from the heat, allow to sit for a couple of minutes, then scrape out onto plates with a spatula.

ADVANCE PREPARATION: The batter keeps well in the refrigerator for about 3 days. That makes *socca* a really quick fix!

LEFTOVERS: The pancake can be warmed in a medium oven, crisped in a little more olive oil in a pan, or even eaten cold. If you can keep it around, it will be good for 5 days.

SESAME BREAD RINGS

Eastern Mediterranean • Makes 4 large rings or 8 to 12 smaller rings

I first discovered these savory sesame-coated breads—known as *simit* in Turkey, *koulouria* in Greece, *ka'kat* in Cairo—on the streets of Athens. I found them again in Cairo, and so it went. There are many variations of this bread, but all over the eastern Mediterranean it's a beloved street food, sold from long poles or loops of rope, or piled high on vendors' carts.

I find the food processor to be the easiest tool to use for mixing up this small amount of dough.

- 1 teaspoon active dry yeast
- 1 teaspoon sugar
- ⅔ cup warm water
- 2 to 2½ cups unbleached all-purpose flour or bread flour
- ¾ teaspoon salt
- 1 egg white mixed with 2 tablespoons water, or 1 egg, beaten
- ¾ cup sesame seeds

1. Mix together the yeast, sugar, and water in a small bowl or measuring cup. Place the flour and salt in a food processor fitted with the steel blade. Pulse once or twice, then, with the machine running, pour in the yeast mixture. Process until the dough forms a ball on the blades. Remove from the processor and knead on a lightly floured surface for a couple of minutes, adding flour as necessary to form a smooth, elastic dough.

2. Transfer the dough to a clean, lightly oiled bowl, rounded side down, then turn so the rounded side is up. Cover the bowl tightly with plastic wrap and let rise in a warm spot for 1½ hours, until nearly doubled.

3. Punch down the dough and divide into 4 pieces. Roll each piece into a long, thin rope 20 to 24 inches long, or into shorter, fatter ropes about 14 inches long.

4. Heat the oven to 400°F. Line 2 baking sheets with parchment. For smaller bread rings, cut each log into halves or thirds. Twist one of the ends a couple of times, then join the two ends and pinch together. Cover with lightly oiled plastic wrap and a dish towel and allow to rest for 30 minutes.

5. Brush the rings with the egg wash, or one by one, dip each into the egg wash, then flip over so that the entire ring is coated. Place the sesame seeds in a wide bowl, dip the breads in, and flip over to coat thoroughly. Place on the parchment-covered baking sheets.

6. Bake the rings for 20 to 25 minutes, until crisp and brown. Cool on racks. These are best when freshly baked, but freeze well. Cool, then wrap airtight and freeze.

VARIATION

Substitute ⅓ cup pomegranate molasses mixed with ⅓ cup water for the beaten egg. Dip the rings into this mixture, or brush them with it, then cover with sesame seeds.

MOROCCAN FLAT BREAD

Morocco • *Makes 2 round loaves about 10 inches in diameter*

There is a lovely black-and-white photo on page 239 of Jeffrey Alford and Naomi Duguid's wonderful book *Flatbreads & Flavors* of a young Moroccan girl in the town of Taroudannt, in southern Morocco, carrying a tray on her head. The tray is filled with bread dough ready to be baked at the local bakery. I probably have some similar photos. Women walking to the bakery late in the morning with trays of dough was one of my favorite sights in that beautiful country. Each household sends their dough on a recognizable tray or covered with a distinctive cloth, and the baker always knows whose is whose. I loved those flat, chewy country breads, perfect for sopping up sauces from delicious Moroccan tagines. The small amount of cornmeal gives this bread a great texture.

> 2 teaspoons active dry yeast
>
> 2½ cups warm water
>
> 3½ to 4 cups unbleached all-purpose flour
>
> 2¼ teaspoons salt
>
> ¼ cup cornmeal, plus additional for the baking sheets
>
> 2½ cups whole wheat flour

1. In the bowl of a standing mixer or in a large bowl, dissolve the yeast in the water and let stand for 5 minutes, until the yeast is creamy. Stir in the all-purpose flour, a cup at a time, and whisk together or stir about 100 times, until the mixture is smooth. Cover and leave for 1 to 2 hours, until bubbly.

2. If making the dough by hand: Stir the salt and cornmeal into the sponge. Add the whole wheat flour, a cup at a time, until the dough is stiff enough to scrape out onto a lightly oiled work surface. Knead, adding flour as necessary, for 8 to 10 minutes, until the dough is smooth and elastic.

If making the dough in a standing mixer: Stir the salt and cornmeal into the sponge. Add the whole wheat flour all at once and stir together with the paddle, until the ingredients are amalgamated. Change to the dough hook and knead the dough on medium speed for 8 to 10 minutes, until it pulls away from the bowl. Scrape out onto a lightly floured work surface and finish kneading by hand for about a minute.

3. Clean and dry your bowl, and oil it lightly. Shape the dough into a ball and place in the bowl, rounded side down, then turn so the rounded side is up. Cover the bowl tightly with plastic wrap and set in a warm spot to rise until doubled, about 1½ hours.

4. Punch down the dough, knead for about a minute, and divide into 2 equal pieces. Roll or press each piece into a flat round about 10 inches in diameter. Oil 2 large baking sheets and sprinkle with cornmeal. Place the shaped loaves on the baking sheets, cover with a damp towel, and let rest for 30 to 40 minutes. Meanwhile, heat the oven to 400°F, with the rack in the upper third of the oven.

5. Prick the bread in several places with a fork and place in the hot oven. Bake for 25 to 30 minutes, until the bread is nicely browned and responds to tapping with a hollow sound.

LEFTOVERS: This is best eaten freshly baked. If you are keeping it for any length of time, wrap in a towel, and when it is completely cool, wrap airtight.

VARIATION

Anise bread is one of the most widely eaten breads in Morocco. To the above recipe add 1 tablespoon anise seeds along with the salt when mixing up the dough.

PROVENÇAL GREEN OLIVE AND CHEESE BREAD

France • **Makes one 8 × 4-inch loaf**

This quick bread would be called a "cake" in France, and it's a relative newcomer to the Provençal repertoire. Traditionally, it contains diced ham or bacon as well as the olives and cheese. I like this simpler vegetarian version better. It's rich and savory, and is wonderful, thinly sliced, as an hors d'oeuvre.

    1 cup unbleached all-purpose flour

    1 teaspoon baking powder

    ½ teaspoon baking soda

    ½ teaspoon salt

    ¼ teaspoon freshly ground pepper

    3 large eggs

    ⅓ cup milk

    3 tablespoons olive oil

    1 cup tightly packed grated Gruyère
      cheese

    1 cup imported green olives, pitted
      and sliced or coarsely chopped

1. Heat the oven to 375°F. Oil an 8 × 4-inch loaf pan.

2. Sift together the flour, baking powder, baking soda, and salt. Stir in the pepper.

3. Beat the eggs in a large bowl and whisk in the milk and olive oil. Stir in the flour mixture, cheese, and olives, and combine well. Scrape into the loaf pan.

4. Bake for 45 minutes to 1 hour, until a tester comes out clean. Cool in the pan for 10 minutes, then reverse onto a rack. Cool completely before slicing.

ADVANCE PREPARATION: This bread freezes well, and if well wrapped, it can be made up to 2 days before you wish to serve it.

QUICK OLIVE AND CHEESE BREAD

Makes one 5 × 9-inch loaf

This is another lovely savory quick bread. When I entertain, I like to serve this with drinks. I slice it very thin and lay it out on platters, with the Provençal Green Olive and Cheese Bread on page 55.

- 1⅔ cups unbleached all-purpose flour
- 1 teaspoon baking powder
- ½ teaspoon baking soda
- ½ teaspoon salt
- ¼ teaspoon freshly ground pepper
- 4 large eggs
- ⅓ cup white wine
- ⅓ cup olive oil
- 1 cup imported black olives, pitted and sliced
- 1¼ cups tightly packed grated Gruyère cheese

1. Heat the oven to 375°F, with the rack in the center. Butter or oil a 9 × 5-inch loaf pan.

2. Sift together the flour, baking powder, baking soda, and salt. Stir in the pepper.

3. In a large bowl, beat the eggs and whisk in the white wine and olive oil. Quickly whisk or stir in the dry ingredients, then the olives and cheese. Scrape into the loaf pan.

4. Bake for 1 hour, until the bread is nicely browned and a tester comes out clean. Cool for 10 minutes in the pan, then reverse onto a rack to cool completely.

ADVANCE PREPARATION: This quick bread keeps for a couple of days, wrapped airtight; it also freezes very well.

PIZZA DOUGH

Italy • Makes enough for two 12- to 14-inch pizzas

This is a very easy, no-hassle dough. You use a food processor, so you can put it together in about 5 minutes. The dough is easy to stretch or roll out and very forgiving. If you have to forget about it for a day or two, just keep it in the refrigerator.

- 2 teaspoons active dry yeast
- 1 teaspoon sugar
- 1 cup warm water
- 1 tablespoon extra virgin olive oil, plus additional for brushing the pizza crusts
- 2¾ to 3 cups unbleached all-purpose flour
- 1¼ teaspoons salt

1. Mix together the yeast, sugar, water, and olive oil in a small bowl or measuring cup. Let sit for 2 or 3 minutes, until the water is cloudy. Place 2¾ cups of the flour and the salt in a food processor fitted with the steel blade. Pulse once or twice, then with the machine running, pour in the yeast mixture. Process until the dough forms a ball on the blades. Remove from the processor and knead on a lightly floured surface for a couple of minutes, adding flour as necessary for a smooth dough.

2. Transfer the dough to a clean, lightly oiled bowl, rounded side down, then turn so the rounded side is up. Cover the bowl tightly with plastic wrap and let rise in a warm spot for 1 hour. When it is ready, the dough will stretch as it is gently pulled.

3. Divide the dough into 2 equal balls. Shape each ball by gently pulling down the sides of the dough and tucking each pull under the bottom of the ball, working round and round the ball four or five times. Then, on a smooth, unfloured surface, roll the ball around under your palm until the ball feels smooth and firm, about 1 minute. Place the balls on a lightly oiled tray or platter, cover with lightly oiled plastic wrap or a damp towel, and let rest for 15 to 20 minutes.

4. Place a baking stone on the center rack and heat the oven to 450°F (or as instructed in the pizza recipe). Lightly oil pizza pans and dust with semolina.

5. Roll or press out the dough one ball at a time: Place a ball of dough on a lightly floured surface. Lightly flour the dough if it is sticky. While turning the dough, press down on its center with the heel of your hand, gradually spreading it out to a circle 12 to 14 inches in diameter; alternatively, use a rolling pin, turning the dough or the pin to get an even circle. Place the dough on the pizza pan. With your fingers, form a slightly thicker raised rim around the edge of the circle. Brush everything but the rim with a little olive oil. Top the pizza with toppings of your choice, or choose from recipes for pizzas on the following pages.

6. Place the pizza pan on the stone. Bake for 12 minutes. Pull out the lower rack of the oven and carefully slide the pizza from the pan onto the lower rack. Return to the oven for 1 minute to get a nice crisp brown bottom on the crust. Slide the pizza back onto the pan, or onto a paddle, and serve.

ADVANCE PREPARATION: You can keep the dough in the refrigerator, before rolling out, for a couple of days. Prepare it through Step 3 and refrigerate in a resealable plastic bag. The rolled-out dough freezes well, for 6 weeks: Roll it out, place it in pizza pans, wrap airtight in plastic, and freeze. Top the frozen dough and bake as directed. It will take a minute or two longer to bake.

VARIATION

WHOLE WHEAT PIZZA DOUGH: Substitute ¾ cup whole wheat flour for ¾ cup of the all-purpose flour.

PIZZA DOUGH FOR A THICKER CRUST
Makes enough for two 12- to 14-inch pizzas

For most of my pizzas I prefer the thin crust that the previous recipe yields. If you prefer a thicker crust, try this formula. This also works well for the Italian Flat Bread on page 45.

- 2 teaspoons active dry or fresh yeast
- 1 teaspoon sugar
- 1½ cups warm water
- 1 tablespoon extra virgin olive oil, plus additional for brushing the pizza crusts
- 3¾ to 4 cups unbleached all-purpose flour
- 1½ teaspoons salt

Follow the instructions for making Pizza Dough, opposite, using 3¾ cups flour plus ¼ cup for kneading. Bake for 15 to 20 minutes rather than 12 minutes.

PIZZA MARINARA WITH TOMATOES AND GARLIC
Italy • **Makes one 12- to 14-inch pizza**

Also known as *Pizza Napoletana* (Naples being the birthplace of pizza), this is the simplest of pizzas, with nothing more than tomato sauce and herbs. You can throw it together quickly, without cooking the tomatoes, or, as I prefer, you can quickly cook the tomatoes and garlic for a more intensely flavored sauce. Whichever method you choose, note that the pizza is spread with only a thin layer of tomato sauce.

- One 12- to 14-inch pizza crust (opposite page), ready for the oven
- 2 tablespoons extra virgin olive oil
- 2 tablespoons freshly grated Parmesan
- 1 to 2 garlic cloves (to taste), minced
- 1 pound ripe tomatoes, peeled, seeded, chopped, and drained in a strainer for 30 minutes; or 1 can (14 ounces) tomatoes, chopped and drained in a strainer for 1 hour
- ½ teaspoon salt (more to taste)
- Pinch sugar
- Freshly ground black pepper
- 1½ teaspoons dried oregano, or 1 tablespoon slivered fresh basil leaves
- Optional toppings: thinly sliced red or yellow bell peppers; thinly sliced onion; sliced mushrooms; imported black olives, pitted and cut in half if desired; sliced artichoke hearts; drained, rinsed capers

1. Set a baking stone on the center rack and heat the oven to 450°F. Brush the pizza dough with 1 tablespoon of the oil. Sprinkle on the Parmesan.

2. Mix together the garlic, tomatoes, salt, sugar, and pepper and spread over the pizza. Sprinkle on the oregano.

Or, for a more intense sauce, do not brush the pizza dough with oil. Instead, heat 1 tablespoon of the olive oil in a large, heavy nonstick pan over medium heat and add the garlic. When it begins to sizzle, after 30 seconds to a minute, add the tomatoes, salt, sugar, and pepper. If you are using dried oregano, add it now. Cook, stirring often, until the tomatoes cook down slightly, about 10 minutes. Taste and adjust seasoning. If you are using fresh basil, stir it in now. Spread the sauce over the pizza.

3. Scatter any or all of the optional toppings over the tomato sauce. Drizzle on the remaining tablespoon of oil.

4. Place the pizza pan on the stone. Bake for 12 minutes. Pull out the lower rack of the oven and carefully slide the pizza from the pan onto the lower rack. Return to the oven for 1 minute to get a nice crisp brown bottom on the crust. Slide the pizza back onto the pan, or onto a paddle, and serve.

VARIATION

You can also use Pomí marinara sauce for this pizza if you happen to have a carton on hand. Measure out 1½ cups and pulse in a food processor a few times to make a coarse purée.

PIZZA MARGHERITA

Italy • Makes one 12- to 14-inch pizza

This is a classic cheese and tomato pizza, with a modest amount of tomatoes and a generous amount of fresh mozzarella.

- 2 tablespoons extra virgin olive oil
- 1 to 2 garlic cloves (to taste), minced
- 1 pound ripe tomatoes, peeled, seeded, chopped, and drained in a strainer for 30 minutes; or 1 can (14 ounces) tomatoes, chopped and drained in a strainer for 1 hour
- ½ teaspoon salt (more to taste)
- Pinch sugar
- One 12- to 14-inch pizza crust (page 56), ready for the oven
- ½ pound fresh mozzarella, preferably buffalo mozzarella, thinly sliced
- 1 tablespoon slivered fresh basil leaves

1. Place a baking stone on the center rack and heat the oven to 450°F.

2. Heat 1 tablespoon of the olive oil in a large, heavy nonstick pan over medium heat and add the garlic. When it begins to sizzle, after 30 seconds to a minute, add the tomatoes, salt, and sugar. Cook, stirring often, until the tomatoes cook down slightly, about 10 minutes. Taste and adjust the seasoning.

3. Spread the sauce over the pizza dough. Top with the mozzarella and the basil. Drizzle on the remaining 1 tablespoon oil.

4. Place the pizza pan on the stone. Bake for 12 minutes. Pull out the lower rack of the oven and carefully slide the pizza from the pan onto the lower rack. Return to the oven for 1 minute to get a nice crisp brown bottom on the crust. Slide the pizza back onto the pan, or onto a paddle, and serve.

ADVANCE PREPARATION: The pizza dough can be rolled out and stored, ready to go, in the refrigerator or freezer hours before you're ready to assemble the pizza and bake. The tomato sauce will keep for 3 or 4 days in the refrigerator.

PIZZA WITH MOZZARELLA AND CHERRY TOMATOES: Substitute 20 cherry tomatoes for the chopped tomatoes, garlic, salt, and sugar. Lightly brush the dough with olive oil and top with the cheese. Distribute the cherry tomato halves over the cheese, cut side down. Drizzle on 1 tablespoon olive oil and bake as in Pizza Margherita, opposite. Remove from the oven, sprinkle on the basil, and serve.

• Make the Pizza with Mozzarella and Cherry Tomatoes variation above. Add 16 small zucchini flowers and intersperse them with the tomatoes.

• In Italy, they do not always cook the tomatoes first. If you wish, just mix together the tomatoes, garlic, salt, and sugar. Brush the crust with olive oil and spread the tomatoes over in an even layer. Proceed with the recipe.

• Add any of the additions listed with Pizza Marinara with Tomatoes and Garlic (page 57). Scatter over the tomato sauce before drizzling on the final tablespoon of oil. Bake as directed.

• Substitute a handful of wild arugula leaves for the basil.

• Substitute goat cheese for some or all of the mozzarella.

PIZZA WITH TOMATO, EGGPLANT, AND MOZZARELLA

Italy • **Makes one 12- to 14-inch pizza**

Eggplant is a standard pizza topping all over Italy. I like to spread a thin layer of tomato sauce on the dough and top first with mozzarella, then with eggplant slices that have already been cooked.

> 1 small eggplant, thinly sliced
>
> Salt
>
> 3 tablespoons extra virgin olive oil
>
> ½ cup Basic Tomato Sauce (page 78) or commercial marinara sauce
>
> One 12- to 14-inch pizza crust (page 56 or page 57), ready for the oven
>
> 6 ounces mozzarella, thinly sliced
>
> 2 to 3 tablespoons freshly grated Parmesan
>
> ½ to 1 teaspoon dried oregano (to taste)
>
> Hot red pepper flakes (optional)

1. Sprinkle the eggplant slices generously with salt and let sit in a colander in the sink for 30 minutes to an hour. Press down on the eggplant, then pat dry with paper towels.

2. Heat 2 tablespoons of the oil in a large nonstick frying pan over medium-high heat and cook the eggplant slices on both sides until lightly browned.

3. Place a baking stone on the center rack and heat the oven to 450°F.

4. Spread the tomato sauce in an even layer over the pizza dough. Top with the mozzarella, then with the eggplant slices. Sprinkle the Parmesan, oregano, and red pepper flakes over the eggplant, and drizzle on the remaining 1 tablespoon olive oil.

5. Place the pizza pan on the stone. Bake for 15 to 20 minutes, depending on the thickness of the crust. Pull out the lower rack of the oven and carefully slide the pizza from the pan onto the lower rack. Return to the oven for 1 minute to get a nice crisp brown bottom on the crust. Slide the pizza back onto the pan, or onto a paddle, and serve.

ADVANCE PREPARATION: The pizza dough can be rolled out and stored, ready to go, in the refrigerator or freezer hours before you're ready to assemble the pizza and bake. The cooked eggplant slices and the tomato sauce will keep for a few days in the refrigerator.

VARIATION

Substitute ½ to ¾ pound sliced zucchini for the eggplant. No need to salt the zucchini before cooking.

PIZZA WITH MUSHROOMS AND ARTICHOKE HEARTS

Italy • Makes one 12- to 14-inch pizza

I saw this white pizza in pizzerias all over Rome. The mushrooms and artichoke hearts are sautéed in olive oil with garlic and fresh thyme, and spread over a mozzarella-topped crust.

3 tablespoons extra virgin olive oil

¼ pound mushrooms, sliced

2 garlic cloves, minced

5 or 6 baby artichoke hearts, quartered (use frozen or canned if desired)

Salt and freshly ground pepper

1 teaspoon fresh thyme leaves

One 12- to 14-inch pizza crust (page 56 or page 57), ready for the oven

6 ounces mozzarella, thinly sliced

¼ cup freshly grated Parmesan

1 teaspoon dried oregano

1. Set a baking stone on the center rack and heat the oven to 450°F.

2. Heat 1 tablespoon of the olive oil in a large nonstick skillet over medium heat and add the mushrooms. Cook, stirring often, until tender, about 5 minutes. Add the garlic, artichoke hearts, salt, pepper, and thyme, and continue to cook, stirring often, until the vegetables are fragrant and very lightly browned, about 5 more minutes. Remove from the heat, taste, and adjust seasonings.

3. Line the pizza dough with slices of mozzarella and top with the mushrooms and artichoke hearts. Sprinkle on the Parmesan and oregano. Drizzle on the remaining 2 tablespoons olive oil.

4. Place the pizza pan on the stone. Bake for 15 to 20 minutes, depending on the thickness of the crust. Pull out the lower rack of the oven and carefully slide the pizza from the pan onto the lower rack. Return to the oven for 1 minute to get a nice crisp brown bottom on the crust. Slide the pizza back onto the pan, or onto a paddle, and serve.

ADVANCE PREPARATION: The pizza dough can be rolled out and stored, ready to go, in the refrigerator or freezer hours before you're ready to assemble the pizza and bake. You can make the topping through Step 2 hours or even a day ahead of assembling the pizza. Keep in the refrigerator if you're making it more than a couple of hours ahead.

VARIATION

MUSHROOM AND FENNEL TOPPING: Substitute 1 medium fennel bulb, trimmed, cored, and finely chopped, for the artichoke hearts. Cook them in the olive oil for about 5 minutes before adding the mushrooms, and proceed with the recipe.

PIZZA WITH PEPPERS, TOMATO SAUCE, AND MOZZARELLA

Italy • Makes one 12- to 14-inch pizza

Sweet peppers are a favorite pizza topping of mine. If you have peperonata (page 85) on hand, you can make this topping in an instant. You could also substitute roasted peppers (page 84) for the sautéed peppers.

2 tablespoons extra virgin olive oil

1 large or 2 medium yellow or red bell peppers, or a mix, thinly sliced

1 to 2 garlic cloves (to taste), minced

Salt and freshly ground pepper

½ cup Basic Tomato Sauce (page 78) or commercial marinara sauce

One 12- to 14-inch pizza crust (page 56 or page 57), ready for the oven

5 or 6 ounces mozzarella, thinly sliced

2 teaspoons fresh thyme leaves

1. Set a baking stone on the center rack and heat the oven to 450°F.

2. Heat 1 tablespoon of the olive oil over medium heat in a medium nonstick skillet. Add the bell peppers and sauté until they begin to soften, about 3 minutes. Add the garlic, salt, and ground pepper, and cook for another 3 minutes, until the peppers are just tender. Adjust seasoning and remove from the heat.

3. Spread the tomato sauce over the pizza dough. Top with slices of mozzarella. Distribute the peppers over the mozzarella and sprinkle with the thyme. Drizzle the remaining 1 tablespoon olive oil over the top.

4. Place the pizza pan on the stone. Bake the pizza for 15 to 20 minutes, depending on the thickness of the crust. Pull out the lower rack of the oven and carefully slide the pizza from the pan onto the lower rack. Return to the oven for 1 minute to get a nice crisp brown bottom on the crust. Slide the pizza back onto the pan, or onto a paddle, and serve.

ADVANCE PREPARATION: The pizza dough can be rolled out and stored, ready to go, in the refrigerator or freezer hours before you're ready to assemble the pizza and bake. The peppers can be cooked a day ahead. The tomato sauce will keep for 3 to 5 days in the refrigerator.

VARIATION

ONION AND PEPPER TOPPING: Add 1 or 2 onions, thinly sliced, to the recipe. Cook them until tender in 2 tablespoons extra virgin olive oil, then add the peppers and proceed with the recipe.

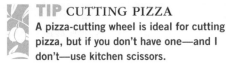 **TIP** CUTTING PIZZA
A pizza-cutting wheel is ideal for cutting pizza, but if you don't have one—and I don't—use kitchen scissors.

PIZZA WITH TOMATO SAUCE, MOZZARELLA, AND ARUGULA

Italy • **Makes one 12- to 14-inch pizza**

This is a pizza I've enjoyed all over Italy, but especially in the region of Puglia, where wild *rucola* is a popular green. The arugula is scattered over the pizza when it comes from the oven, making one dish out of pizza and salad.

> ¾ cup Basic Tomato Sauce (page 78) or commercial marinara sauce
>
> One 12- to 14-inch pizza crust (page 56 or page 57), ready for the oven
>
> 6 to 8 basil leaves, slivered
>
> 6 ounces mozzarella, thinly sliced
>
> Salt and freshly ground pepper
>
> 1 tablespoon extra virgin olive oil
>
> A handful or two of wild arugula, or coarsely chopped baby arugula leaves

1. Set a baking stone on the center rack and heat the oven to 450°F.

2. Spread the tomato sauce on the pizza dough, then the basil and cheese. Sprinkle with salt and pepper, and drizzle on the olive oil.

3. Place the pizza pan on the stone. Bake the pizza for 15 to 20 minutes, depending on the thickness of the crust. Pull out the lower rack of the oven and carefully slide the pizza from the pan onto the lower rack. Return to the oven for 1 minute to get a nice crisp brown bottom on the crust. Slide the pizza back onto the pan, or onto a paddle. Scatter the arugula on top and serve.

ADVANCE PREPARATION: The pizza dough can be rolled out and stored, ready to go, in the refrigerator or freezer hours before you're ready to assemble the pizza and bake. The tomato sauce will keep for 3 to 5 days in the refrigerator.

VARIATION

Substitute goat cheese for 2 to 3 ounces of the mozzarella.

"WHITE" PIZZA (Pizza Bianca)

Italy • **Makes one 12- to 14-inch pizza**

White pizza is a simple snack, pizza dough topped with olive oil, sea salt, and garlic. A sprinkle of chopped fresh rosemary or oregano completes the mix. The crispy pizza is ubiquitous in Rome, a favorite midmorning snack for schoolchildren.

> One 12- to 14-inch pizza crust (page 56 or 57), ready for the oven
>
> 2 tablespoons extra virgin olive oil
>
> ¾ teaspoon coarse sea salt
>
> 1 garlic clove, sliced in very thin slivers
>
> 1 tablespoon chopped fresh rosemary or oregano (or 2 teaspoons dried oregano)

1. Set a baking stone on the center rack and heat the oven to 425°F.

2. Brush the pizza crust with olive oil and sprinkle with the salt, garlic, and herbs. Set the pizza pan on the stone and bake for 12 to 15 minutes, until crisp. Pull out the lower rack of the oven and carefully slide the pizza from the pan onto the lower rack. Return to the oven for 1 minute to get a nice crisp brown bottom on the crust. Slide the pizza back onto the pan, or onto a paddle, and serve hot or at room temperature.

ADVANCE PREPARATION: There's no sauce to make the crust soggy, so this holds up well for a few hours.

VARIATION

If you don't want the pizza to be quite as crisp, use the thicker crust variation on page 57 and bake for 20 to 25 minutes.

PIZZA WITH TOMATO SAUCE AND POTATOES

Italy • **Makes one 12- to 14-inch pizza**

Pizza topped with potatoes might sound like carbs on carbs to some of you, but I can assure you, it is a wonderful thing. If you can slice the cooked potatoes very thin (but not so thin that they fall apart), your pizza will be all the better for it.

> ½ pound red-skinned potatoes or other waxy potatoes, scrubbed
>
> Salt
>
> ½ cup Basic Tomato Sauce (page 78) or commercial marinara sauce
>
> One 12- to 14-inch pizza crust (page 56 or 57), ready for the oven
>
> Freshly ground pepper
>
> 1 tablespoon chopped fresh rosemary (or 1 teaspoon crumbled dried) or 2 teaspoons dried oregano
>
> ¼ cup freshly grated Parmesan
>
> 2 tablespoons extra virgin olive oil

1. Place the potatoes in a medium saucepan and cover with water by 2 inches. Add 1 teaspoon salt and bring to a gentle boil. Cover partially and simmer the potatoes until just tender when pierced with a knife, 15 to 20 minutes, depending on their size. Drain and rinse with cold water. When cool enough to handle, slice thin.

2. Set a baking stone on the center rack and heat the oven to 450°F.

3. Spread the tomato sauce over the pizza dough and top with the sliced potatoes. Season generously with salt and pepper, and sprinkle on the rosemary and Parmesan. Drizzle on the olive oil.

4. Place the pizza pan on the stone. Bake for 12 to 15 minutes, depending on the thickness of the crust. Pull out the lower rack of the oven and carefully slide the pizza from the pan onto the lower rack. Return to the oven for 1 minute to get a nice crisp brown bottom on the crust. Slide the pizza back onto the pan, or onto a paddle, and serve hot or at room temperature.

ADVANCE PREPARATION: The cooked potatoes and the tomato sauce will keep for a few days in the refrigerator.

VARIATION

Add 6 ounces mozzarella, thinly sliced. Spread the tomato sauce in an even layer over the crust. Top with the mozzarella, then with the potatoes, and proceed with the recipe.

PROVENÇAL ONION PIZZA (Pissaladière)
France • Makes one 12- to 14-inch pizza

This is a signature Provençal dish from Nice and its environs—a pizza spread with a thick, sweet layer of onions that have been cooked slowly until caramelized. The authentic version, which is not vegetarian, is garnished with anchovies. (Indeed, the name *pissaladière* is derived from the Niçoise word *pissalat* or *pissala,* which is a paste made from anchovies and olive oil seasoned with cloves, thyme, and bay leaf. The condiment was traditionally brushed over the onions, a practice that evolved into the anchovy and olive garnish we see today.) Use sweet onions if you can for this. If you can't get them, just make sure to cook the onions you use for a long time, to draw out their sugars.

- **3 tablespoons extra virgin olive oil**
- **2 pounds sweet yellow onions, finely chopped**
- **Salt and freshly ground pepper**
- **3 garlic cloves, minced**
- **½ bay leaf**
- **2 teaspoons fresh thyme leaves (or 1 teaspoon dried)**
- **1 tablespoon capers, drained, rinsed, and puréed in a mortar and pestle or a mini processor**
- **One 12- to 14-inch pizza crust (page 56), ready for the oven**
- **20 to 24 whole Niçoise olives**

1. Set a baking stone on the center rack and heat the oven to 475°F.

2. Heat 2 tablespoons of the olive oil in a large, heavy nonstick skillet over medium-low heat. Add the onions and cook, stirring, until they begin to sizzle and soften, about 3 minutes. Add a generous pinch of salt, some pepper, and the garlic, bay leaf, and thyme. Stir everything together, reduce the heat to low, cover, and cook slowly for 45 minutes, stirring often. The onions should melt down to a purée. If they begin to stick to the pan, add a few tablespoons of water. Stir in the capers, taste, and adjust seasonings. If there is liquid in the pan, cook over medium heat, uncovered, until it evaporates. Discard the bay leaf.

3. Brush the remaining 1 tablespoon oil over the pizza dough. Spread the onions over the dough in an even layer. Dot with the olives.

4. Place the pizza pan on the stone. Bake for 15 to 20 minutes, until the edges of the crust are brown and the onions are beginning to brown. Pull out the lower rack of the oven and carefully slide the pizza from the pan onto the lower rack. Return to the oven for 1 minute to get a nice crisp brown bottom on the crust. Slide the pizza back onto the pan, or onto a paddle, and serve hot or at room temperature.

ADVANCE PREPARATION: The onion topping can be made a day ahead of time and held in the refrigerator. The pizza dough can be rolled out and stored, ready to go, in the refrigerator or freezer hours before you're ready to assemble the pizza and bake.

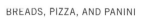

CALZONE WITH TOMATO AND KALE FILLING

Italy • **Makes 6 calzone**

A calzone is a pizza pocket, and in theory anything that tastes good on top of a pizza would taste good inside a calzone. But there are other possibilities as well, foods like greens that might burn and dry out if baked on top of a pizza. These calzone have a southern Italian flavor, with the slightly spicy tomato sauce and greens combination. They make a great late fall/winter meal.

> 1 generous bunch black kale (*cavolo nero*) or curly kale
>
> Salt
>
> 1¾ pounds fresh tomatoes, cored and peeled; or 1 can (28 ounces) tomatoes with juice
>
> 2 tablespoons extra virgin olive oil
>
> 1 medium onion, finely chopped
>
> 2 large garlic cloves, minced or put through a press
>
> 1 sprig fresh oregano, the leaves stripped from the stem (or ½ teaspoon dried)
>
> Pinch sugar (about ⅛ teaspoon)
>
> Freshly ground pepper
>
> Pinch hot red pepper flakes
>
> 4 ounces Pecorino Romano, grated (1 cup)
>
> 1 batch Pizza Dough (page 56), prepared through Step 3

1. Bring a large pot of water to a boil while you prepare the kale: Strip the leaves from the stems and wash thoroughly in several changes of water. When the water comes to a boil, add 1 tablespoon salt and the kale. Boil for 4 minutes (from the time the water returns to a boil). Transfer to a bowl of cold water, drain, and squeeze dry. Chop the kale into slivers and set aside.

2. Place the tomatoes in a food processor fitted with the steel blade and pulse 10 to 15 times, until they are crushed but not puréed.

3. Combine the oil and onion in a large, heavy nonstick skillet and cook over medium heat, stirring occasionally, until the onion is translucent, about 5 minutes. Add some salt and continue to cook, stirring occasionally, until the onion is quite tender but not colored, about 10 minutes. Add the garlic and stir together for a minute or two, until very fragrant, then stir in the tomatoes, oregano, sugar, additional salt, and pepper. Cook over medium heat, stirring now and again, until the tomatoes have cooked down and smell fragrant, 15 to 20 minutes. Stir in the pepper flakes and the kale. Taste and adjust seasoning. Remove from the heat and stir in the cheese. Taste again for seasoning.

4. Set a baking stone on the center rack and heat the oven to 450°F.

5. Punch down the dough and divide it into 6 equal pieces. Roll each piece into a thin circle. Place a spoonful of filling on half of a circle, leaving a border around the edge, and fold the other half over. Do not overfill. Pinch the edges of the half-moon-shaped envelope together, and squeeze at intervals between thumbs and fingers to create a pretty fluted edge.

6. Place the calzone on cornmeal- or semolina-dusted baking sheets, or on a baker's peel. Slide the calzone onto the baking stone from the peel, or place the baking sheets directly in the oven on top of the baking stone. Bake for 20 to 25 minutes, until browned. Serve hot.

ADVANCE PREPARATION: The blanched kale will keep for 4 or 5 days in a covered bowl in the refrigerator. The filling will keep for a few days in the refrigerator. The calzone can be frozen before baking, and transferred directly from the freezer to a hot oven. They can also be frozen after baking. Thaw and reheat in the oven, not the microwave, to get a crisp crust.

GRILLED ZUCCHINI, GOAT CHEESE, AND MINT PANINI
Italy

FOR EACH PANINI

½ medium zucchini, sliced on the diagonal

Olive oil for brushing

Salt and freshly ground pepper

2 thick slices country bread

1 ounce goat cheese

A few mint leaves, chopped

1. Heat a panini grill. Brush the zucchini slices with olive oil, season with salt and pepper, and place on the grill. Close the grill and grill for 2 to 3 minutes, just until translucent. Transfer to a plate.

2. Spread each slice of bread with cheese. Sprinkle the mint on the bottom slice. Top with the zucchini and the top slice of bread. Brush the outsides of the sandwich with olive oil and grill until nicely toasted.

ADVANCE PREPARATION: The zucchini can be roasted and the panini assembled several hours before grilling.

ABOUT PANINI

Today in the United States, with the proliferation of panini grills, Italian sandwiches are all the rage. In our home, we screen movies once a month, and the movie night always begins with a selection of these panini, served buffet-style on paper plates.

Panini grills are the grilling equivalent of electric waffle irons, two-sided hinged grills that fit easily onto a countertop. You can grill a sandwich between the two nonstick grill plates in minutes. I also use my panini grill for vegetables like peppers, eggplant, and zucchini. I particularly like to use it for eggplant and zucchini slices because it requires half the oil that I'd use if I fried the vegetables, and it only takes 2 minutes.

EGGPLANT AND RED PEPPER PANINI
Italy

FOR EACH PANINI

2 to 4 (½-inch-thick) slices eggplant (depending on the size of the eggplant)

Salt

Olive oil for brushing

1 tablespoon Pesto Genovese (page 74) or commercial pesto

2 thick slices country bread

½ to ¾ roasted red bell pepper (page 84; see Note)

Freshly ground pepper

3 heaped tablespoons grated cheese, such as mozzarella, fontina, provolone, Parmesan, or a combination

Note: *If I don't have roasted peppers on hand, I'll just brush pepper slices with oil and grill them in the panini grill.*

1. Sprinkle the eggplant slices with salt and let sit for 30 minutes. Pat dry and brush lightly with olive oil.

2. Heat a panini grill and place the eggplant slices on it in an even layer. Grill for 3 minutes, until cooked through and nicely marked by the grill. Transfer to a plate.

3. Spread a little pesto on the bottom slice of bread. Top with a layer of eggplant slices, then a layer of roasted pepper slices. Sprinkle with ground pepper. Top with the grated cheese and the other slice of bread. Brush the outsides of the sandwich with olive oil. Grill for 5 minutes, or until the bread is nicely toasted and the cheese has melted. Cut into halves or thirds, depending on the size of the bread. Serve hot.

ADVANCE PREPARATION: The eggplant can be grilled and the panini assembled several hours before grilling the panini.

VARIATION

EGGPLANT AND TOMATO PANINI: Substitute sliced tomatoes for the roasted peppers.

ARTICHOKE HEART AND RED PEPPER PANINI

Italy

FOR EACH PANINI

2 tablespoons extra virgin olive oil

1 medium garlic clove, minced

2 or 3 canned or thawed frozen artichoke hearts, sliced ½ inch thick

½ teaspoon fresh thyme leaves or a pinch of dried thyme

Salt and freshly ground pepper

2 thick slices country bread

3 tablespoons grated Gruyère cheese

½ to ¾ roasted bell pepper (page 84) or 2 or 3 slices tomato

1. Heat 1 tablespoon of the olive oil in a large, heavy skillet over medium heat and add the garlic. Cook, stirring, until fragrant, about 30 seconds, and add the artichoke hearts. Stir for a minute or two, just until the artichoke hearts are coated with oil. Season with thyme, salt, and pepper. Remove from the heat.

2. Heat a panini grill. For each panini, brush 2 slices of bread with olive oil. Top 1 slice with a layer of artichoke hearts. Sprinkle on the cheese. Top with the peppers and cover with the second slice of bread. Brush the outsides of the sandwich with olive oil.

3. Grill for 5 minutes, or until the cheese has melted and the bread is toasty.

ADVANCE PREPARATION: The artichoke hearts can be prepared through Step 1 several hours before assembling the panini. The panini can be assembled several hours before grilling.

GREENS AND FONTINA PANINI

Italy • **Makes 8 panini**

Salt

1 pound stemmed and washed sturdy greens, such as kale, chard, turnip greens, or mustard greens (for convenience, I buy the 1-pound bags of washed, stemmed greens)

2 tablespoons olive oil, plus additional for brushing

2 garlic cloves, minced

Freshly ground pepper

16 slices country bread or 16 squares Focaccia (page 43)

4 ounces fontina, or a mixture of fontina and mozzarella, grated

1. Bring a large pot of water to a boil and add a generous amount of salt and the greens. Bring the water back to a boil and boil for 1 to 4 minutes, depending on the sturdiness of the greens. Swiss chard takes a couple of minutes, kale and turnip greens and mustard greens 3 or 4 minutes. Transfer to a bowl of ice-cold water to cool for a few minutes, then drain and squeeze out excess water. Chop coarsely.

2. Heat the olive oil in a large, heavy skillet over medium heat and add the garlic. Cook, stirring, until the garlic is fragrant, about 30 seconds, and stir in the greens. Toss together to coat with oil and season to taste with salt and pepper. Remove from the heat.

3. Heat a panini grill. For each panini, brush 2 slices of bread with olive oil. Top 1 slice with some greens and top the greens with some cheese. Top with the remaining bread. Brush the outside of the sandwich with olive oil. Grill for 5 minutes, until the cheese has melted and the bread is toasty.

ADVANCE PREPARATION: You can prepare the greens through Step 2 several hours or even a day ahead of assembling the panini.

MUSHROOM AND GRUYÈRE PANINI

Italy • **Makes 4 panini**

> ¼ cup olive oil, plus additional for brushing
>
> ½ pound button mushrooms or cremini mushrooms, sliced
>
> 2 garlic cloves, minced
>
> Salt and freshly ground pepper
>
> 1 teaspoon fresh thyme leaves
>
> 8 slices country bread
>
> 6 ounces grated or sliced Gruyère cheese

1. Heat the oil in a large nonstick skillet over medium-high heat and add the mushrooms. Sauté until light brown and beginning to soften, about 3 minutes, and add the garlic. Stir for about 30 seconds, and add salt, pepper, and the thyme. Reduce the heat to medium and cook, stirring, until the mushrooms are tender, about 5 minutes. Remove from the heat. Taste and adjust seasonings.

2. Heat a panini grill. For each panini, brush a slice of bread with olive oil and top with a layer of mushrooms. Top the mushrooms with cheese and add the top piece of bread. Brush the outsides of the sandwich with olive oil. Grill in the panini grill for 5 minutes, or until the cheese is melted and the bread is toasty.

ADVANCE PREPARATION: The mushrooms can be prepared through Step 1 up to 2 days before assembling the panini. The panini can be assembled several hours before grilling.

BABY SPINACH AND FONTINA PANINI

Italy • **Makes 4 panini**

> 1 bag (6 ounces) baby spinach
>
> 1 tablespoon olive oil, plus additional for brushing
>
> 1 garlic clove, minced
>
> Salt and freshly ground pepper
>
> 8 slices country bread
>
> 2 tablespoons unsalted butter, softened
>
> 4 to 6 ounces grated fontina, or a mix of fontina and Parmesan, or a pregrated Mediterranean mix

1. Place the baby spinach in a bowl. Bring a pot of water to a boil and pour over the spinach. Let sit for about 30 seconds, then drain and squeeze dry.

2. Heat the olive oil over medium heat in a medium-size nonstick skillet and add the garlic. Cook for 30 seconds, or until fragrant. Stir in the spinach, toss together, and remove from the heat. Season to taste with salt and pepper.

3. Heat a panini grill. Spread all of the bread slices with butter. Top 4 slices with the spinach, top the spinach with the cheese, then another slice of bread. Brush the outsides of the sandwich lightly with olive oil. Grill in the panini grill for 5 minutes, until the cheese melts and the bread is toasty.

ADVANCE PREPARATION: The spinach can be prepared and the panini assembled several hours before grilling the panini.

VARIATION

Add the cooked mushroom preparation from the Mushroom and Gruyère Panini (at left). Toss with the spinach and proceed as above.

Sauces, Dressings, and Condiments

If I had to choose one word that applies to most of the sauces and condiments in the Mediterranean, it would be "big." Mediterranean sauces have big flavors. Practically without exception, these big flavors begin with garlic and end with olive oil. In between, there may be basil or other fresh herbs like cilantro or parsley, tomatoes and/or roasted sweet or hot peppers, olives or nuts, sesame paste and/or yogurt. In the more pungent sauces and condiments, the garlic is raw, mashed to a paste in a mortar and pestle before other ingredients are added. If the sauce is cooked, the big flavors are coaxed out of the ingredients through gentle cooking in olive oil on top of the stove, or by roasting in the oven or over hot coals.

Many sauces and condiments from the Mediterranean—*romesco* sauce from Spain, for example, Italian pesto, a walnut-thickened version of Greek skordalia—are thickened with nuts. The nuts contribute wonderful, complex textures and rich flavors. In Turkey and the Middle East, many of the sauces are tahini-based or made with thickened yogurt, and served with signature dishes like falafel, or simply with pita bread or vegetables.

Sauces and condiments in the Mediterranean have traditionally been used to preserve a season's bounty so that it could be enjoyed year-round. If you make pesto in the spring and summer, when basil is at its peak, and keep it covered with olive oil in the refrigerator, it will last for a very long time. So will the ripe red peppers that fill the markets at summer's end, once roasted and covered with olive oil. If you make tomato sauce when tomatoes are in season, and freeze it in plastic bags, you can have an evocative dinner in January in the time it takes to cook pasta and thaw the sauce in your microwave.

Sauces were also used to bring flavor to foods that were otherwise plain. At the traditional meatless meal served on Christmas Eve in Provence, boiled vegetables and salt cod were served with a pungent garlic mayonnaise (aïoli), and the resulting meal has evolved into a feast. Provence has a tradition in which otherwise bland beans, grains, and vegetables are tossed with vinaigrette and served as part of a nourishing meal that begins with a bowl of the broth in which they were cooked.

Entire meals can revolve around a *romesco* sauce (page 71) in Spain, or an aïoli (page 72) in the South of France. Indeed, I have been told by many a Catalan that the thing they love most about their grilled spring onion feast called *calçotada* is the *romesco* sauce that they eat, by the spoonful, with the onions. I certainly would jump at any opportunity to make and eat this pungent condiment, a mixture of almonds or hazelnuts, roasted sweet red peppers and tomatoes, garlic and toasted bread, all ground together and seasoned with paprika and sherry vinegar, olive oil, and hot pepper.

Some of these condiments, like the roasted peppers on page 84, the peperonata on page 85, and the *samfaina* on page 72, are foods in and of themselves, as at home served as a side dish or spooned onto a bruschetta or into a halved tomato, or even eaten on their own as an appetizer, as they are embellishing a serving of pasta or a piece of fish. Indeed, in addition to the recipes in this chapter, there are several recipes in the Little Foods chapter that could also be considered sauces or condiments. They can be served on their own, but also work as an accompaniment to other foods. These include tapenade and its variations on pages 121 to 122, and the Greek cucumber and yogurt salad called *tzatziki* in Greece and *cacik* in Turkey (page 106). Some soups, too, like the Spanish *salmorejo* on page 166, can also double as sauces.

ROMESCO SAUCE

Spain • **Makes about 2 cups**

Romesco is a thick, pungent nut-based sauce that is most often served with fish in Spain. It's also the dipping sauce for grilled spring onions called *calçots*, a Catalan specialty. Vegetarians use it as a topping for crostini or bruschetta, as an incredible condiment for beans, grains, or vegetables, and to thicken and augment the flavor of soups and stews. It is one of my all-time favorite foods. Because I toast rather than fry the bread that helps thicken the sauce, my version is lighter—but no less rich-tasting—than the authentic sauce.

1 large red bell pepper (about ½ pound)

3 medium tomatoes or 4 plum tomatoes (about ¾ pound)

2 large garlic cloves, peeled

¼ cup toasted almonds, or a combination of almonds and skinned roasted hazelnuts

2 thick slices (about 2 ounces) baguette or country style bread, lightly toasted

1 to 2 teaspoons chile powder or hot red pepper flakes (to taste; pepper flakes are hotter)

1 tablespoon chopped fresh flat-leaf parsley

1 teaspoon sweet paprika

1 to 1½ teaspoons salt

Freshly ground pepper

2 tablespoons sherry vinegar

¼ cup extra virgin olive oil

1. Place the oven rack at the highest level and heat the broiler. Place the bell pepper on a foil-covered baking sheet and broil, turning every 3 minutes or so, until uniformly charred. Place in a plastic bag, twist the bag shut, and cool. When the pepper is cool enough to handle, remove the charred skin (you can do this under running water), cut the pepper in half lengthwise, and remove the core, seeds, and membranes.

2. While waiting for the pepper to cool, place the tomatoes on the baking sheet and broil for 2 to 4 minutes, until charred on one side. Turn over and broil on the other side for 2 to 4 minutes, until charred. Remove from the heat, transfer to a bowl, and cool. Peel and core.

3. Turn on a food processor fitted with the steel blade and drop in the garlic cloves. When the garlic is chopped and adheres to the sides of the bowl, stop the machine and scrape down the sides. Add the almonds, bread, and chile powder, and process to a paste. Scrape down the sides of the bowl and add the bell pepper, tomatoes, parsley, paprika, salt, and ground pepper. Process until smooth. With the machine running, add the vinegar and olive oil in a slow stream. Process until well amalgamated, then scrape into a bowl. Taste and adjust seasoning, adding salt or chile powder as desired. If possible, allow the sauce to stand for an hour at room temperature before using.

ADVANCE PREPARATION: Romesco keeps for several days in the refrigerator; the garlic will become more pungent.

SPANISH PEPPERS

Spain is known for its sweet red peppers, the most famous being the small piquillos, which are roasted in the fields right after they're picked. Another popular pepper is the ñora pepper, a small, round, intensely sweet, and mildly spicy pepper that is always dried and is used to make Spanish paprika. The ñora is the pepper that is traditionally used in Catalan *romesco* sauce. In my adaptation of the authentic recipe, I've achieved a sweet/hot flavor by combining a large red bell pepper with chile powder or flakes and sweet paprika.

CATALAN RATATOUILLE (Samfaina)
Spain • Serves 6

Samfaina is a very well-cooked Catalan ratatouille that is used as a sauce. It's typically served with salt cod, rabbit, or chicken. For vegetarians it works beautifully as a topping for bruschetta or grilled polenta, or as a vegetable side dish.

The trick to making *samfaina* is to allow it to cook until the vegetables collapse and melt together into a sort of marmalade. It takes about 3 hours of quiet bubbling to reach the desired consistency, so make it on a day when you're going to be around for a few hours. Use a heavy enameled cast-iron casserole for this, or, even better, an earthenware casserole with a lid.

- ¾ pound (1 medium) eggplant, peeled and diced very small
- Salt
- ¼ cup extra virgin olive oil
- ¼ cup water
- 2 red bell peppers, peeled, seeded, and thinly sliced or diced
- 1 green bell pepper, peeled, seeded, and thinly sliced or diced
- 3 medium onions, very finely chopped
- 1 medium zucchini, peeled and very finely chopped
- 4 large garlic cloves, minced
- Freshly ground black pepper
- 1 pound very ripe tomatoes, peeled, seeded, and chopped; or 1 can (14 ounces) tomatoes, drained

1. Lay the eggplant pieces on some paper towels and sprinkle with salt. Drain for 30 minutes, then pat dry with paper towels.

2. Place the eggplant, olive oil, water, bell peppers, onions, zucchini, and garlic in an enameled cast-iron Dutch oven or an earthenware casserole set over a flame-tamer. Add 1 teaspoon salt and pepper to taste. Reduce the heat to low, cover, and cook until soft, about 1 hour, stirring gently and occasionally. Add the tomatoes, cover again, and cook until the mixture has reduced to a thick relish, 2 to 3 hours, stirring occasionally. Add tablespoons of water as needed if the juices have evaporated and the vegetables aren't done. In my experience, the opposite happens; the vegetables will release a lot of liquid as they cook. At the end of cooking, turn up the heat to boil off some of this liquid. Cool before serving.

ADVANCE PREPARATION: This benefits from being made a day ahead, and will keep for about 5 days in the refrigerator.

PROVENÇAL AND CATALAN GARLIC MAYONNAISE (Aïoli)
France and Spain • Makes 1½ cups

Aïoli is the quintessential Provençal condiment. It's a very pungent garlic mayonnaise that in its home country contains more garlic than the version opposite—which is already pretty garlicky. There is a meatless tradition on Fridays in Provence called *aïoli monstre* (page 293), or "huge aïoli": a feast of boiled vegetables and salt cod accompanied by copious amounts of aïoli.

In Catalonia, garlic mayonnaise—originally made without the egg but in modern times evolved into something more like this version—is traditionally eaten as an accompaniment to grilled spring onions and snails at a feast called the *cargolada*. It's also an indispensable accompaniment to paella (page 325).

In fact, aïoli requires no feast. It's easy enough to make, and wonderful with all sorts of vegetables, like greens, steamed artichokes, and asparagus. All it requires is a taste for raw garlic.

The egg yolks are traditional, but the whole egg and white work fine in the food processor version. Although most Mediterranean cooks use only olive oil for their aïoli, you will have an easier time building a stable mayonnaise if you use half canola oil and half olive oil (it has to do with the structure of the oil), and begin with the canola oil.

3 to 4 large garlic cloves (to taste), cut in half

½ teaspoon salt (more to taste)

½ cup canola oil

2 free-range, organic egg yolks (or 1 whole egg and 1 egg white)

½ cup extra virgin olive oil

1. Whether or not you are using a mortar and pestle for the mayonnaise, begin by grinding the garlic and salt together with 1 tablespoon of the canola oil to a smooth paste in a mortar and pestle.

2. If continuing the sauce in a mortar and pestle (use for egg yolks only; this is the traditional method, and will result in a very silky, creamy aïoli if you do it correctly): Add the egg yolks to the paste in the mortar and pestle and beat with the pestle until smooth. Measure the canola oil into a measuring cup with a spout and, drip by drip, work the oil into the egg yolks, gently but constantly stirring in one direction with the pestle or with a whisk. As the mayonnaise begins to emulsify, you can begin adding the oil in a steady stream, but the stream must be a thin one, and you must stir constantly but not too fast. When all of the canola oil has been added, add the olive oil in the same way. When all of the olive oil has been added and the mayonnaise is thick, taste and adjust salt. Refrigerate until ready to use.

If continuing the sauce in a food processor: Place the egg yolks or egg and egg white in the food processor fitted with the steel blade. Turn on, and begin drizzling in the canola oil in a thin stream. Add the olive oil in the same way. When all of the oil has been added, stop the processor and scrape in the garlic paste. Process for a few seconds, until well mixed into the mayonnaise. Taste and adjust salt. Refrigerate until ready to use.

ADVANCE PREPARATION: This should not be made too many hours ahead, because the garlic will become too strong and acrid. However, you can always make the mayonnaise (which is, after all, the time-consuming element in this recipe) several hours or even a day ahead. Mash the garlic shortly before serving, then work into the mayonnaise.

SPICY GARLIC MAYONNAISE (Rouille)
France • **Makes about 1¼ cups**

Rouille is a spicy, saffrony garlic mayonnaise. The name is derived from the French word for "rust," which is the color of the sauce. The spice comes from ground cayenne, or a dried red pepper that is pounded with the garlic.

Rouille is traditionally served on croutons with fish soup. It will make just as wonderful an accompaniment to any of the hearty vegetarian "bouillabaisses" (pages 156 to 158) in the Soups chapter.

I can make my rouille in a mortar and pestle, as many cooks do in Provence, because I have a big heavy marble one, which works much better than my wooden one. But a food processor works fine, and it's a lot easier. The food processor version is also fluffier than the mortar and pestle version. However, do use the mortar and pestle to make your garlic purée. Otherwise you'll get bits of garlic in your mayonnaise, and the pungency won't be right.

3 to 4 large garlic cloves (to taste), cut in half

½ teaspoon salt (more to taste)

2 generous pinches saffron

¼ teaspoon cayenne; or 1 dried hot red pepper, seeded

½ cup canola oil

2 free-range, organic egg yolks (or 1 whole egg and 1 egg white)

½ cup extra virgin olive oil

1. Whether or not you are using a mortar and pestle for the mayonnaise, begin by grinding the garlic, salt, saffron, and cayenne together with 1 tablespoon of the canola oil to a smooth paste in a mortar and pestle.

2. If continuing the sauce in a mortar and pestle (for egg yolks only): Add the egg yolks to the paste in the mortar and pestle and beat with the pestle until smooth. Gradually drizzle in the remaining canola oil, a drip or two at a time, and continue to stir constantly in one direction. When all of the canola oil has been added, begin adding the olive oil. As the mayonnaise begins to emulsify you can begin adding the oil in a steady stream, but stir constantly. When all of the oil has been added and the mayonnaise is thick, taste and adjust salt. Refrigerate until ready to use.

If continuing the sauce in a food processor: Place the egg yolks or egg and egg white in a food processor fitted with the steel blade. Turn on, and begin drizzling in the canola oil in a thin stream. Add the olive oil in the same way. When all of the oil has been added, stop the processor and scrape in the garlic paste. Process for a few seconds, until well mixed into the mayonnaise. Taste and adjust salt. Refrigerate until ready to use.

ADVANCE PREPARATION: Rouille should not be made too many hours ahead, because the garlic will become too strong. However, you can always make the mayonnaise (which is, after all, the time-consuming element in this recipe) several hours or even a day ahead. Mash the garlic and other ingredients shortly before serving, then work into the mayonnaise.

PESTO GENOVESE

Italy • **Makes about 1 cup**

I have a recipe scribbled in one of my many kitchen notebooks called *Really Good Pesto,* and this is it. You probably already know and love pesto, the classic basil paste/sauce that hails from the Ligurian coast of Italy and is now popular all over the world. How can it not be? It has such a heady flavor, all that basil, pounded or blended with garlic and pine nuts and bound with olive oil and cheese. You may be used to making your own pesto, or perhaps not, as it's easy to find it ready-made. But

MAKING PESTO: MORTAR AND PESTLE OR FOOD PROCESSOR?

When it comes to making pesto, most cooks and aficionados insist that the sauce must be made in a mortar and pestle so that the flavorful oils in the basil leaves can be properly released. Fred Plotkin, in his excellent and scholarly *Recipes from Paradise,* tells us that "a mortar and pestle mashes while the food processor or blender grinds. The flavors of herbs and nuts, their oils and essences, are released in a unique way that cannot be equaled in a machine." Clifford Wright says that the food processor is "too brutal: the scent of the basil needs to be coaxed from the leaf in a mortar."

Mr. Plotkin insists that it should only take about 20 minutes to make pesto in a mortar and pestle. I have made it several times this way, but it always takes more than 20 minutes. I try to be gentle while I grind and press firmly down on the leaves, so that I mash them rather than turn them into liquid, but I can never seem to avoid extracting a lot of juice from the leaves. In the end I always feel that I've spent a great deal of energy to create what always turns out to be a smaller amount of pesto than I'd expected. In short, I find making pesto in a mortar and pestle difficult. And because of that, I began to find over time that I was making pesto less and less often, and allowing my generous basil plants to bolt because I couldn't use them up quickly enough.

Then one day, with a lot of basil on hand, I decided I was going to tackle this problem, and came up with a compromise method. The purists will turn up their noses, because I do use the processor; but the fact is, this is "really good pesto." I begin with the mortar and pestle, which I use for the garlic, salt, and pine nuts. These I add to the basil once it's been finely chopped in the food processor. I process them all together while slowly adding the olive oil. Then I mix in the cheese. The pesto I end up with, in no time, is plenty fragrant, and I don't end up with basil juice and garlic aroma all over my arms and clothes. This is pesto I can make every day, which in fact I just about do during the summer when my basil plants go wild.

I have never been able to locate a commercially made pesto that didn't have an acrid garlic aftertaste, so I never buy it. Try this recipe, and you may never buy it again either.

It's of utmost importance that you use excellent ingredients for this. The olive oil should be extra virgin, one that has a mild/sweet flavor rather than an assertive one; the cheese must be imported, and freshly grated; and the garlic cloves should be plump and juicy. You can use the small-leaved Genoese basil that the Italians use for this, or you can use the large-leaf basil that's easy to find in the United States.

> 2 cups fresh basil leaves (no stems)
>
> 1 to 2 plump garlic cloves (to taste), cut in half lengthwise
>
> ¼ (rounded) teaspoon sea salt (more to taste)
>
> ⅓ to ½ cup extra virgin olive oil (to taste)
>
> 2 tablespoons pine nuts
>
> 2 tablespoons freshly grated pecorino
>
> ¼ cup freshly grated Parmesan (to taste)
>
> Freshly ground pepper

1. Place the basil leaves in the bowl of a food processor fitted with the steel blade and pulse until finely chopped. Scrape down the sides of the bowl.

2. In a mortar and pestle, combine the garlic, salt, and 1 tablespoon of the olive oil, and mash the garlic. Add the pine nuts and mash until you have a smooth paste.

3. Scrape the garlic paste into the food processor with the basil. Turn on the machine and process until the ingredients are mixed and adhering to the sides of the bowl. Scrape down the bowl. Turn on the machine and slowly drizzle in the remaining olive oil. Continue to process until the mixture is smooth and homogeneous. Add the cheeses and pepper to taste and pulse until everything is amalgamated. Taste and adjust salt.

4. If not using right away, scrape the pesto into a clean glass jar. Cover with about ¼ inch of olive oil, and refrigerate. Every time you use some of the pesto, replenish the olive oil.

ADVANCE PREPARATION: You can make pesto weeks before using it and store it in the refrigerator. Make sure that there is a good ¼ inch of olive oil covering the surface. You can freeze pesto, but some say that freezing robs it of its delicacy. I prefer to keep mine in the refrigerator.

ARUGULA PESTO

Italy • Makes about 1 cup

This is popular in the southern Italian region of Puglia, where it is tossed with pasta, often along with tomato sauce (see the recipe on page 78). This pesto has a slightly bitter, deeply vegetal flavor and a bright green hue that doesn't fade like the green of basil does. I can eat this by the spoonful, and often do, piled onto toasted country bread, a marvelous bruschetta. Grated ricotta salata is particularly nice sprinkled on top.

> 2 garlic cloves, cut in half lengthwise
>
> 2 tablespoons pine nuts or coarsely chopped walnuts
>
> 1 bunch (4 ounces) arugula, stemmed, washed, and dried
>
> ¼ teaspoon salt (more to taste)
>
> ⅓ cup extra virgin olive oil
>
> ⅓ cup freshly grated Parmesan
>
> 3 tablespoons freshly grated pecorino

Turn on a food processor fitted with the steel blade and drop in the garlic cloves. When they are chopped and adhering to the sides, stop the machine, scrape down the sides of the bowl, and add the pine nuts. Process until finely ground. Scrape down the bowl again and add the arugula and the salt. Pulse until the arugula is finely chopped, then process while you slowly drizzle in the olive oil. When the mixture is smooth, stop the machine and scrape out into a bowl. Stir in the cheeses and combine well. Use as you would use Pesto Genovese (opposite page).

ADVANCE PREPARATION: Cover the top with a film of olive oil, and this will keep in the refrigerator for a few weeks.

PISTOU

France • **Makes about 1 cup**

Pistou is the Niçoise version of Pesto Genovese (page 74), and is most often used as a final enrichment for vegetable soup (as in Soupe au Pistou, page 155). Unlike its Italian cousin, *pistou* is not made with pine nuts, so it has a different texture. It also contains more cheese, and it can include a tomato.

> 2 to 4 large garlic cloves (to taste), peeled
>
> 2 cups tightly packed fresh basil leaves
>
> ¼ to ½ teaspoon salt (to taste)
>
> ⅓ cup extra virgin olive oil
>
> 1 small tomato, peeled, seeded, and chopped (optional)
>
> 1 cup freshly grated Parmesan, or a mixture of Gruyère and Parmesan
>
> Freshly ground pepper

If making the *pistou* in a food processor: Turn on a processor fitted with the steel blade and drop in the garlic. When the garlic is chopped and adhering to the sides of the bowl, scrape down the sides, add the basil and salt, and process until finely chopped. Scrape down the sides once more and drizzle in the olive oil with the machine running, then drop in the tomato. Continue to process to a paste. Scrape into a bowl and stir in the Parmesan. Add pepper, taste, and adjust salt.

If making the *pistou* in a mortar and pestle: Grind the garlic with salt and 1 tablespoon of the olive oil to a paste. Add the basil, a handful at a time, and pound and grind the basil to a paste. Add the optional tomato and work into a paste with the basil. Drop by drop, work in the remaining olive oil. Stir in the cheese. Add pepper, taste, and adjust salt.

ADVANCE PREPARATION: Without the tomato, this (like pesto) will keep in the refrigerator for a few weeks if covered with olive oil. If you have included the tomato, it will keep for about 5 days.

USES FOR PESTO

Here are just a few of my favorite ways to use pesto:

Pasta with pesto: Pesto should be served at room-temperature, and never heated. You can warm it, though, by adding a tablespoon or two of the boiling water the pasta cooks in just before draining the pasta. Plan on 1 to 2 tablespoons pesto per serving of pasta. That's all you'll need for a fragrant coating of this heavenly sauce. If you use too much, the sauce will be too heavy and the pasta will be gummy.

Soup with pesto: Stir 1 to 3 teaspoons per serving into Minestrone (page 146) or Soupe au Pistou (page 155), or other vegetable or bean soups.

Crostini with pesto: Spread over crostini or bruschetta.

Eggs stuffed with pesto: A wonderful appetizer. See the recipe on page 131.

Rice with pesto: Stir into rice or risotto. You could use this mixture as a stuffing for vegetables.

Meat or fish with pesto: Use as a condiment for meat or fish.

Pizza or focaccia with pesto: Dollop onto pizza or focaccia.

LIGURIAN WALNUT SAUCE

Italy • **Makes about 1½ cups**

Walnut-based sauces can be found throughout the Mediterranean, from Turkey to Greece to Italy. According to food writer Fred Plotkin, this signature sauce from the Liguria region of Italy appeared in ancient Persian cuisine, and was probably adapted during the Middle Ages by the Genoese, when Genoa was a powerful trading city-state. The rich sauce certainly resembles Turkish Tarator Sauce (page 81). It is the classic accompaniment to the Ligurian ravioli called *pansôti,* which are filled with a mixture of greens and herbs (Ravioli with Greens, Herbs, and Ricotta, page 207), but is also wonderful with other types of pasta, like orecchiette. (If using as a sauce for pasta, thin out with the cooking water from the pasta until the mixture reaches the desired consistency.) It is also delicious with simply cooked vegetables like beets or greens, or spread onto bread or crostini. This recipe is adapted from the one in Fred Plotkin's *Recipes from Paradise*.

> 1 garlic clove, cut in half
>
> ½ teaspoon salt (more to taste)
>
> ¼ cup extra virgin olive oil
>
> 2 tablespoons bread crumbs
>
> 1¾ cups shelled walnuts
>
> 3 tablespoons freshly grated Parmesan
>
> ⅔ cup fresh ricotta cheese diluted with
>   2 tablespoons warm water

If making the sauce in a mortar and pestle: Mash together the garlic and salt with 1 teaspoon of the olive oil until the garlic is puréed. Add the bread crumbs and, a handful at a time, add the walnuts and grind to a paste. Stir in the Parmesan and ricotta and blend well. Gradually stir in the remaining olive oil and stir until smooth and homogenous. Taste and add salt as desired.

If making the sauce in a food processor: Turn on a processor fitted with the steel blade and drop in the garlic. When the garlic is chopped and adhering to the sides of the bowl, scrape down the sides, add the bread crumbs and walnuts, and process to a paste. Scrape into a bowl. Stir in the Parmesan, salt, and ricotta and blend well. Gradually stir in the olive oil and stir until smooth and homogeneous. Taste and add salt as desired.

ADVANCE PREPARATION: This will keep for about 3 days in a covered container in the refrigerator. But the fresher it is, the better.

BÉCHAMEL
France • Makes 2 cups

A béchamel is simply a cream sauce, though there is rarely cream in it. What causes it to be creamy and rich is the suspension of a flour and butter (or oil) paste, or *roux*, in a liquid, which is milk in a classic béchamel, but can also be stock. Italians and French use béchamel (*besciamella* in Italian) in gratins and lasagnas (which are really a kind of gratin). In this book, sometimes the ingredients and procedure for the béchamel will be in the recipe, because of variations in quantity needed and ingredients. Other recipes will refer to this one.

> 2 tablespoons unsalted butter
>
> 2 tablespoons unbleached all-purpose flour
>   (3 tablespoons for a thicker sauce)
>
> 2 cups milk (regular, low-fat, or fat-free),
>   warm or at room temperature but not hot
>
> Salt and freshly ground pepper

Melt the butter in a heavy, medium saucepan over medium-low heat. Add the flour and cook, stirring, for about 3 minutes, until smooth and bubbling but not browned. Whisk in the milk and bring to a simmer. Turn the heat to very low and simmer, stirring often with a whisk, for 20 minutes, until the sauce has thickened and lost its raw flour taste. Season with salt and pepper.

ADVANCE PREPARATION: You can make a béchamel up to a day ahead of using it, and keep it in the refrigerator. If you lay a sheet of plastic or wax paper directly on the top, there

MAKING A ROUX-THICKENED SAUCE

When you make a roux-thickened sauce, it's important that the liquid you add to the roux not be too hot. If it is, the roux won't have time to disperse in the liquid before the mixture comes to a boil, and you'll get lumps. The béchamel needs to simmer for 20 minutes in order to achieve a smooth, silky texture.

is less chance that a skin will form. But even if it does, you can get rid of it by whisking vigorously when you reheat the béchamel. Then the sauce should be as smooth as it was when you made it.

VARIATION

OLIVE OIL BÉCHAMEL: In traditional Provençal cooking, béchamel was usually made with olive oil. Olive oil works beautifully, and makes a sauce that is especially appropriate for lusty Provençal gratins. Just substitute olive oil, tablespoon for tablespoon, for the butter. Heat over medium heat, then add the flour and proceed as directed in the basic Béchamel (previous page).

MANY TOMATO SAUCES

There are so many ways to make a tomato sauce. I use fresh tomatoes only during the summer, when they're ripe and sweet. Throughout most of the year, canned tomatoes are so much better. When the wonderful heirlooms abound in the farmers' market, I rarely want to cook them, so I'm more likely to toss my pasta with uncooked tomato sauce (Fresh Tomato Concassée and Almond, Basil, and Tomato Sauce, opposite page). However, in mid- and late-summer, when every tomato grower sells his less-than-beautiful ones at a discount, take advantage of this and make sauce. Freeze what you don't use.

Tomato sauce can be as straightforward as tomatoes, olive oil, and salt. Onion and garlic deepen the flavor. Usually I make a quick sauce with only garlic, tomatoes, olive oil, and salt (Quicker Basic Tomato Sauce, opposite page). Dried herbs like thyme and oregano make an earthy, rustic sauce. Fresh basil will sweeten the flavor and add a peppery dimension. If using dried herbs such as oregano or thyme (or both), use ½ to 1 teaspoon per pound of tomatoes (to taste), and add them along with the tomatoes. Fresh basil sprigs can be cooked along with the sauce. Chopped fresh herbs should be added at the end of cooking.

BASIC TOMATO SAUCE (Marinara Sauce)

Italy • **Makes about 2½ cups, enough for 8 generous pasta servings (canned tomatoes will yield more, about 3 cups)**

- 2 tablespoons extra virgin olive oil
- 1 medium onion, chopped
- 3 to 4 garlic cloves (to taste), minced or thinly sliced
- 3 pounds ripe tomatoes, quartered (or cut into sixths if very large); or 2 cans (28 ounces) diced tomatoes, with juice
- ¼ teaspoon sugar
- A few sprigs fresh basil or 2 teaspoons fresh thyme leaves
- Salt

1. In a large nonstick frying pan or 3-quart saucepan over medium heat, heat the oil and add the onion. Cook, stirring often, until tender and golden, 8 to 10 minutes. Add the garlic and cook, stirring, until fragrant, about 1 minute. Add the tomatoes, sugar, basil, and salt, and bring to a boil. Reduce the heat to medium-low and simmer, stirring often, until thick. My favorite description of the consistency of the tomato sauce when it's ready is chef Mario Batali's: Simmer the tomatoes until they are "as thick as hot cereal." If you are using canned tomatoes or pulpy plum tomatoes, this will usually take about 30 minutes. However, if the tomatoes are very juicy, it may take up to 1 hour for them to cook down. The sauce will be very sweet. Taste and adjust seasonings.

2. If you used fresh, quartered tomatoes, put the sauce through a food mill fitted with the medium blade. If you used canned tomatoes but want a sauce with a smooth, even texture, pulse in a food processor fitted with the steel blade.

ADVANCE PREPARATION: Tomato sauce keeps well. You can hold it in the refrigerator for about 5 days, and freeze it for a few months. Portion it into small zipper bags and flatten it out to save room in your freezer; then you can thaw as many portions as you need at a time.

QUICKER BASIC TOMATO SAUCE

Variation of Basic Tomato Sauce

>   2 tablespoons extra virgin olive oil
>
>   3 to 4 garlic cloves (to taste), minced or thinly sliced
>
>   2 cans (28 ounces) diced tomatoes, with juice
>
>   ¼ teaspoon sugar
>
>   Salt
>
>   A few sprigs fresh basil, if available
>
>   2 tablespoons slivered fresh basil (optional)

Heat the oil in a large nonstick skillet over medium heat and add the garlic. As soon as it begins to color and smell fragrant, add the tomatoes, sugar, salt, and basil sprigs. Stir and turn up the heat. When the tomatoes begin to bubble, reduce the heat to medium and cook, stirring often, until thick and fragrant, 20 to 30 minutes. Stir in the slivered basil and cook for another couple of minutes. Remove from the heat, taste, and adjust seasoning. If you want a smooth texture, put through a food mill or pulse in a food processor fitted with the steel blade.

VARIATION

SOUTHERN TOMATO SAUCE: To either of the versions above, add ¼ to ½ teaspoon hot red pepper flakes. Add to the pan along with the garlic, and proceed with the recipe.

FRESH TOMATO CONCASSÉE

France • **Makes 3 cups**

I make this luscious uncooked tomato sauce for pasta right through the summer, when tomatoes abound in my garden and they're so sweet I don't even want to cook them. This also makes a great topping for bruschetta.

>   2 pounds sweet, ripe tomatoes, peeled, seeded, and finely chopped
>
>   Salt and freshly ground pepper
>
>   1 to 2 teaspoons balsamic vinegar (to taste; optional)

>   1 to 2 garlic cloves (to taste), minced or put through a press
>
>   2 tablespoons extra virgin olive oil
>
>   2 to 4 tablespoons slivered fresh basil (to taste)

Combine all of the ingredients in a large bowl. Let sit for about 15 minutes or longer to allow the flavors to emerge. Taste and adjust seasoning. Serve at room temperature.

ADVANCE PREPARATION: The *concassée* can be made several hours ahead of serving.

ALMOND, BASIL, AND TOMATO SAUCE

Italy • **Makes 1½ cups, enough for ¾ pound of pasta**

Some of the most interesting food in the Mediterranean comes from Sicily. Greeks, Romans, Arabs, and Normans have occupied the island, strategically situated between Italy and North Africa, at one time or another. The Arab influence is particularly evident in Sicily's cuisine, and the almonds in this sauce are a testament to that. They give this garlicky sauce, which is also known as *pesto Siciliano,* a marvelous texture. The sauce can be served with pasta, as a topping for bruschetta, or as an accompaniment to grilled meat, fish, or eggplant or other vegetables. I adapted the recipe from Clifford Wright's in *A Mediterranean Feast.*

>   3 to 6 large garlic cloves, finely chopped
>
>   4 large fresh basil leaves
>
>   ¼ cup blanched whole almonds
>
>   ½ teaspoon salt (more to taste)
>
>   2 tablespoons extra virgin olive oil
>
>   1 pound ripe tomatoes, preferably plum tomatoes, peeled, seeded, and drained

If making the sauce in a mortar and pestle: Combine the garlic, basil, almonds, salt, and 1 tablespoon of the olive oil and crush with the pestle to a paste. Transfer to a large bowl, add the tomatoes, and continue to crush with the pestle until chunky and well amalgamated. Work in the remaining 1 tablespoon olive oil. Taste and adjust salt. ▶

If making the sauce in a food processor: Turn on the processor fitted with the steel blade and drop in the garlic cloves. When the garlic is chopped and adhering to the sides of the bowl, stop the machine and scrape down the sides. Add the basil, almonds, and salt, and process until you have a paste. Add the tomatoes and olive oil and pulse until chunky and well amalgamated. Taste and adjust salt. Serve at room temperature.

ADVANCE PREPARATION: You can make this sauce several hours before serving.

GARLIC AND POTATO PURÉE (Skordalia)
Greece • **Makes 1½ cups**

Skordalia is Greece's answer to aïoli, a pungent purée made with garlic, potatoes, and olive oil. The sauce is served with fish, and it's great with vegetables—traditionally it's served with a beet salad (see the variation to Beet and Beet Greens Salad on page 94).

Before potatoes arrived in Europe after the discovery of the Americas, skordalia was made with stale bread and garlic, and in some villages it still is. I think it's best when made with a combination. In Macedonia and Cephalonia, skordalia is made with walnuts. Do not attempt to make this in a food processor because the potatoes will become gummy. The addition of yogurt here is not traditional; the idea comes from Nancy Harmon Jenkins (in *The Mediterranean Diet Cookbook*), and I like the way it lightens the skordalia. If you find the flavor too tart, you can omit the yogurt. I particularly like the variation made with walnuts that follows the recipe.

¾ **pound russet or Yukon gold potatoes, peeled**
Salt
¼ **cup drained yogurt (page 21; optional)**
3 to 4 garlic cloves (to taste), halved
½ **cup extra virgin olive oil**
1 cup cubed country bread, preferably stale

2 **tablespoons fresh lemon juice (more to taste)**
2 **to 4 tablespoons red wine vinegar (to taste)**

1. Place the potatoes in a saucepan and cover with water. Add ½ teaspoon salt and bring slowly to a boil over medium heat. Cover partially, reduce the heat, and simmer until the potatoes are tender all the way through when pierced with a skewer. Drain, return the potatoes to the pot, and cover tightly. Set aside for 5 minutes. Mash the potatoes through a potato ricer, a food mill, or in a standing mixer fitted with the paddle attachment. Stir in the yogurt.

2. Mash the garlic to a paste in a mortar and pestle with ¼ teaspoon salt and 1 tablespoon of the olive oil.

3. Moisten the bread with water, then squeeze dry. Add to the garlic and grind together, then stir into the potatoes. Gradually add the remaining olive oil, stirring all the while with a fork or a pestle. Add the lemon juice, vinegar, and salt to taste. The mixture should be like loose mashed potatoes. Taste and adjust lemon juice, vinegar, and salt. Transfer to a bowl and chill until ready to serve. If the mixture stiffens up, thin out with a little olive oil or water.

ADVANCE PREPARATION: Skordalia will keep for about 3 days in the refrigerator, but it will become quite pungent, and it will stiffen up. It's best to eat it soon after you make it.

VARIATION

This version made with walnuts is from northern Greece and the Balkans. Substitute 1 cup coarsely chopped walnuts for the bread. Grind the walnuts in the mortar after you've made the garlic paste, and work in as directed in Step 3. If you wish, substitute 1 tablespoon walnut oil for 1 tablespoon of the olive oil.

PINE NUT TARATOR SAUCE
Middle East • **Makes 1 cup**

This is much like the walnut variation of skordalia (opposite page), with bread standing in for potatoes. In many places in Turkey, the same sauce would be made with walnuts (see the variation below). Serve with Deep-Fried Cauliflower (page 101) or any cooked vegetable of your choice.

> ½ cup pine nuts
>
> 2 garlic cloves, peeled
>
> ½ teaspoon salt
>
> ½ cup extra virgin olive oil
>
> 4 slices French or Italian bread (2 ounces), crusts removed, soaked in water, and squeezed dry
>
> 2 to 4 tablespoons white wine vinegar or lemon juice (to taste)

1. If making the sauce in a mortar and pestle: Mash the pine nuts, garlic, salt, and 1 tablespoon of the olive oil until mashed to a paste. Add the bread and mash together, then work in the remaining olive oil and the vinegar.

If making the sauce in a blender: Combine half the pine nuts, all of the garlic, all of the salt, and half the bread in a blender and pulse together. Add half the olive oil and pulse together for a few seconds. Add the remaining pine nuts, bread, olive oil, and the vinegar, and blend until smooth. Scrape down the sides of the blender jar as necessary.

2. Scrape the sauce into a bowl, taste, and adjust salt. Cover and refrigerate for 1 hour or longer.

ADVANCE PREPARATION: Make this up to a day ahead. It will be more pungent by the next day.

VARIATION

TURKISH TARATOR SAUCE: Substitute ¾ cup coarsely chopped walnuts for the pine nuts. Substitute 2 tablespoons walnut oil for 2 tablespoons of the olive oil.

PURÉEING GARLIC IN A MORTAR AND PESTLE

When you mash garlic in a mortar and pestle, resist the temptation to pound the garlic with the pestle. Pounding releases the volatile compounds, and the resulting flavors will be too sharp. Always add a little salt to the mortar, to help break down the garlic, along with a spoonful of oil, which will absorb the volatile oils as you break it down. You have to pound it a little bit to begin the process, but rather than lifting your arm high above the bowl and coming down hard on the garlic cloves, use more of a wrist action. With several short pulses with the pestle, your garlic cloves will begin to break up. Then, grind them against the sides and bottom of the bowl, rubbing and pressing down at the same time, until you have a smooth purée.

YOGURT AND MINT SPREAD
Turkey • **Makes 1 cup**

This is served as an accompaniment to bread in Turkey, and is often part of a *meze* spread. I think it goes nicely with rice and bulgur as well. According to Turkish food writer Ghillie Basan, the dish should not be made with spearmint. Use fresh or dried peppermint instead.

> 2 to 3 garlic cloves (to taste), peeled
>
> ¼ teaspoon salt
>
> 1 tablespoon extra virgin olive oil
>
> 1 cup drained yogurt (page 21)
>
> 1 small bunch fresh peppermint, chopped, or 1 tablespoon dried mint

Grind the garlic, salt, and olive oil to a paste in a mortar and pestle. Stir into the yogurt along with the mint. Add salt to taste and serve.

ADVANCE PREPARATION: This is best when eaten shortly after being mixed together.

VARIATION

Substitute chopped fresh dill for the mint.

OIL AND VINEGAR DRESSING
Italy • **Makes ⅔ cup**

Long drives in the United States make me pine for Italy. Every gas station I have ever stopped at along the *autostrada* has a decent cafeteria-style restaurant. Salads are always available, with the full range of vinegars and olive oil on every table for dressing them. The Italians dress their salads simply, with good vinegar and olive oil, and just the right amount of salt. If your ingredients are good, that's all you need.

> 2 tablespoons red wine vinegar or sherry vinegar (or less, to taste)
>
> 1 teaspoon good-quality balsamic vinegar (optional)
>
> ¼ to ½ teaspoon salt (be generous)
>
> ½ cup extra virgin olive oil

Mix together the vinegars and salt until the salt has dissolved. Whisk in the oil. This is enough for a big salad that will serve 8.

VARIATION

Substitute lemon juice for half or all of the vinegar.

VINAIGRETTE TO KEEP IN THE REFRIGERATOR
France • **Makes 1½ cups**

I use this vinaigrette for the salads I eat every night for dinner. I like to keep it on hand in the refrigerator, so that salads only take as long to make as it takes to wash lettuce. Not that it takes a long time to make a vinaigrette. I keep it in a squeeze bottle.

> ¼ cup sherry vinegar or wine vinegar (more to taste)
>
> 1 tablespoon balsamic vinegar
>
> Salt
>
> 1 to 3 teaspoons Dijon mustard (to taste)
>
> 1 cup extra virgin olive oil
>
> 1 medium or large garlic clove, peeled

1. Whisk together the vinegars, salt, and mustard. Whisk in the olive oil.

2. Cut the garlic clove into thin slices, cutting down to the root end but not through it, and place in a jar or squeeze bottle. If using a jar, separate the slices and impale on a toothpick, leaving space between the slices. Pour the dressing over the garlic and let sit for an hour at room temperature, or up to a week or longer in the refrigerator. Use as needed, shaking well before each use.

ADVANCE PREPARATION: The dressing doesn't deteriorate much over time because the garlic is sliced, and flavors the mixture slowly, without making it too pungent. You can make it as far ahead as you wish. It will keep well for a week or 10 days. If the olive oil hardens in the refrigerator, simply bring the dressing to room temperature and shake the jar well before using.

WALNUT VINAIGRETTE
France • **Makes ½ cup**

In the Hautes-Alpes of northern Provence, olive trees give way to walnut trees, so walnut oil is the oil used to season food there. It has a wonderful nutty flavor and goes particularly well with bitter lettuces like endive and frisée. Because it's quite strong, I use it in conjunction with olive oil or canola oil.

> 2 tablespoons red wine vinegar or sherry vinegar
>
> 1 teaspoon balsamic vinegar (optional)
>
> Salt and freshly ground pepper
>
> 1 teaspoon Dijon mustard (optional)
>
> 1 small garlic clove, minced or put through a press (optional)
>
> ¼ cup extra virgin olive or canola oil
>
> 2 to 3 tablespoons walnut oil (to taste)

Stir together the vinegars, salt, pepper, mustard, and garlic. Whisk in the oils. Keep in a jar until you're ready to toss your salad. Shake or stir before using.

ADVANCE PREPARATION: This will keep for a few days in the refrigerator, though the garlic flavor will become more pronounced.

TAHINI DRESSING
Turkey • **Makes ⅔ cup**

This popular Turkish dressing is good drizzled over a tomato salad, as well as with steamed vegetables. It's thinner than the other tahini sauces in this chapter.

> 3 tablespoons tahini
>
> ¼ cup water
>
> 2 tablespoons fresh lemon juice
>
> 1 to 2 garlic cloves (to taste), mashed to a paste in a mortar and pestle with ¼ teaspoon salt
>
> ½ teaspoon freshly ground cumin seeds
>
> Salt and freshly ground pepper or Aleppo pepper

Mix together the tahini, water, lemon juice, garlic paste, cumin, salt, and pepper. Thin out with water if the dressing is too thick to pour.

ADVANCE PREPARATION: This will be good for a couple of days in the refrigerator, but it will thicken and become more pungent. Thin out with water as desired.

 TIP BUYING TAHINI
When you add lemon juice to tahini, the tahini stiffens up. It therefore helps to begin with a tahini that is fairly runny, the type you will find in Middle Eastern markets. The tahini will relax and thin out when you add water to it, so don't let the initial thickening alarm you.

TAHINI GARLIC SAUCE
Middle East • **Makes 1½ to 2 cups**

This sauce bears the name of its main ingredient, tahini. I've always found the mixture of garlic, lemon juice, and tahini addictive. You'll find it on the Middle Eastern *meze* table, as a dipping sauce for Deep-Fried Cauliflower (page 101), or as a dressing for salads. It accompanies *kofte* of all kinds, Falafel (page 104), and shawarma. I like to dip pita bread in it as well.

> 2 to 3 garlic cloves (to taste), cut in half
>
> Salt
>
> 1 cup tahini
>
> ½ cup fresh lemon juice (more to taste)
>
> Pinch hot red pepper flakes (more to taste; optional)
>
> Chopped fresh flat-leaf parsley

Mash the garlic cloves to a paste with ¼ teaspoon salt in a mortar and pestle. Transfer to a bowl and whisk in the tahini. Whisk in the lemon juice. The mixture will stiffen up. Gradually whisk in water until the sauce has the consistency of thick cream (or runny yogurt); you may need as much as ¾ cup water. If you want a tangier sauce, add more lemon juice. Add the red pepper flakes and salt to taste. Garnish with parsley and serve.

ADVANCE PREPARATION: Tightly covered, the sauce keeps in the refrigerator for a week, but the fresher it is, the better. It will thicken as it sits. Thin out each time with water or water and lemon juice.

VARIATION

You can make this into a salad dressing by thinning out further with water.

PARSLEY SAUCE
Middle East • Makes 2 cups

This goes well with everything the Tahini Garlic Sauce (page 83) goes with—salads, fried cauliflower, pita bread, *kofte,* falafel, and fish.

> 2 to 3 garlic cloves (to taste), cut in half
>
> Salt
>
> 1 cup tahini
>
> ½ cup fresh lemon juice (more to taste)
>
> 1 cup finely chopped fresh flat-leaf parsley
>
> 1 small tomato, peeled, seeded, and chopped (optional)
>
> Pinch hot red pepper flakes (more to taste; optional)

Mash the garlic to a paste with ¼ teaspoon salt in a mortar and pestle. Transfer to a bowl and whisk in the tahini. Whisk in the lemon juice. The mixture will stiffen up. Gradually whisk in water until the sauce has the consistency of thick cream (or runny yogurt); you may need as much as ¾ cup water. Stir in the parsley, tomato, and hot pepper flakes. Taste and adjust salt and lemon juice, and serve.

ADVANCE PREPARATION: The color won't be as nice because the acid in the lemon juice will dull the green of the parsley, but the sauce will taste good for 3 or 4 days. Keep in the refrigerator.

ROASTED OR GRILLED PEPPERS
Serves 4

There are many ways to roast peppers. You can roast them under a broiler or over a flame, or grill them over coals. The method I use most often, however, is oven-roasting. It's neater, and you don't have to watch the peppers very closely. I also think it yields more juice than grilling. The method you use will depend partly on how you plan to use the peppers. Oven-roasted peppers will be softer than grilled peppers. Oven-roasting also works best with fleshy peppers, which are the kind we typically find in American markets. However, I will usually use the burner method when I have only one pepper to grill.

> 4 medium red, green, or yellow bell peppers
>
> Salt and freshly ground pepper
>
> 2 tablespoons extra virgin olive oil

OPTIONAL SEASONINGS

> 1 or 2 garlic cloves (to taste), minced or put through a press
>
> 1 tablespoon red wine vinegar or sherry vinegar
>
> 2 tablespoons slivered fresh basil

1. Heat the oven to 400°F. Line a baking sheet with foil. Place the peppers on the foil and roast for 30 to 45 minutes, using tongs to turn the peppers every 10 minutes. The peppers are done when their skins are brown and puffed. They won't be black the way they are when you grill them.

2. Transfer the peppers to a bowl. Cover the bowl with a plate or plastic and cool for 30 minutes.

3. Carefully remove the skins and seeds from the peppers, holding them over the bowl so you don't lose any of the liquid. Cut into strips if desired, place in another bowl, and toss with salt and pepper. Strain in the juice, add the olive oil, and toss again. Refrigerate until ready to use. If you wish, toss with the optional seasonings shortly before serving.

ADVANCE PREPARATION: Roasted or grilled peppers are good keepers. If you cover them with olive oil, they'll keep in the refrigerator for several weeks. If you don't care to do that, you can still keep them for about 5 days.

VARIATIONS

USING A BURNER: Light a gas burner and place the peppers directly over the flame. As soon as one section has blackened, use tongs to turn the peppers and expose another section to the flame. Continue to turn until each pepper is blackened completely. Proceed with Step 2 of the recipe. You may need to run the pepper briefly under the faucet to rinse off the final bits of charred skin. If so, pat dry with paper towels.

USING THE BROILER: Heat the broiler, with the rack in the highest position. Cover a baking sheet with foil. Grill the peppers under the broiler, turning them every 3 minutes or so, until uniformly charred. Proceed with Step 2 of the recipe.

USING A GRILL: Prepare a hot grill. Roast the peppers over the coals, turning them as they blacken. Proceed with Step 2 of the recipe.

STEWED PEPPERS AND TOMATOES
(Peperonata)
Italy • Makes 4 cups

Onions, peppers, and tomatoes all add a dimension of sweetness to this marvelous, versatile sauce. The peppers for this are sometimes roasted first, and most recipes call for them to be sliced. However, if you dice them you'll get a sauce-like mixture that makes a great topping for pizza, pasta, polenta, and bruschetta. It can also be stirred into beaten eggs for an omelet or piperade (page 179), or into rice.

> 2 tablespoons extra virgin olive oil
>
> 1 medium onion, chopped
>
> 2 garlic cloves, minced
>
> 1½ pounds red and/or yellow bell peppers, thinly sliced or chopped
>
> 1 can (14 ounces) diced tomatoes, lightly drained
>
> Salt and freshly ground pepper

1. Heat the olive oil in a large nonstick skillet or heavy casserole over medium heat and add the onion. Cook, stirring, until tender, about 5 minutes. Add the garlic and peppers. Cook, stirring often, until the peppers are tender, about 10 minutes.

2. Add the tomatoes and salt and pepper to taste, and bring to a simmer. Simmer, stirring from time to time, until the tomatoes have cooked down somewhat, about 10 minutes. Cover, reduce the heat, and simmer another 10 to 15 minutes, until the mixture is thick and fragrant. Taste and adjust seasoning.

ADVANCE PREPARATION: Peperonata will keep for about 5 days in the refrigerator, with no deterioration in its flavor.

VARIATIONS

• If you substitute 1 or 2 green peppers for 1 or 2 of the yellow peppers, you'll get a savory/smoky flavor that is more reminiscent of Spanish or Balkan food than Italian, and very delicious. I've made the dish using canned roasted tomatoes, which also add smoke to the flavor.

• You can also add 1 or 2 hot peppers, such as serranos, for a spicy peperonata.

GREMOLATA
Italy • Makes about ¼ cup

This classic Italian seasoning—a mixture of minced garlic, parsley, and lemon zest—is wonderful with pasta, with roasted and grilled vegetables, and especially with pan-cooked mushrooms.

> 1 to 2 garlic cloves (to taste), finely minced
>
> ¼ cup finely minced fresh flat-leaf parsley
>
> 2 teaspoons grated lemon zest

Toss together all of the ingredients. Add to dishes shortly before serving.

ADVANCE PREPARATION: Gremolata shouldn't be made more than an hour or two ahead because the garlic will become very pungent.

CHERMOULA

Morocco • **Makes about 1 cup**

This unforgettable sauce should be as popular as pesto, but it is far from as well known. In Morocco, it is traditionally served with fish. I like to serve it with roasted cauliflower (page 275), grilled eggplant, roasted winter squash, and steamed carrots.

> 1⅓ cups roughly chopped fresh cilantro
>
> ⅔ cup roughly chopped fresh flat-leaf parsley
>
> 3 to 4 garlic cloves (to taste), peeled
>
> Salt
>
> 5 tablespoons extra virgin olive oil
>
> 2 teaspoons cumin seeds, ground
>
> 1 teaspoon sweet paprika
>
> ½ teaspoon coriander seeds, ground
>
> ⅛ teaspoon cayenne
>
> ¼ cup fresh lemon juice

1. Place the cilantro and parsley in a food processor fitted with the steel blade and chop very fine. (You can also do this on a cutting board). You should have 1 cup finely chopped herbs.

2. Grind the garlic to a paste with ¾ teaspoon salt and 1 tablespoon of the olive oil in a mortar and pestle. Add a small handful of the chopped herbs and gently but firmly grind until the herbs begin to dissolve, then add another handful. When all of the herbs have been mashed, work in the spices, remaining 4 tablespoons olive oil, and the lemon juice. Taste and adjust seasoning.

ADVANCE PREPARATION: This sauce is best when it is freshest, but you can pour a film of olive oil over the top and keep it for a few days in a jar in the refrigerator.

HARISSA

Tunisia • **Makes 1 cup**

Harissa is a fiery paste that is added to soups and stews, and even to salads, and it's essential for most of the Tunisian recipes in this book. This recipe was given to me a long time ago by Clifford Wright, and I never change it.

> 2 ounces dried guajillo chiles, or a combination of guajillos and other hot dried chiles
>
> 2 ounces dried Anaheim or pasilla chiles
>
> 5 garlic cloves, peeled
>
> ½ teaspoon caraway seeds, ground
>
> ¼ teaspoon coriander seeds, ground
>
> 1½ teaspoons salt
>
> 2 tablespoons extra virgin olive oil, plus additional for topping

1. Wearing rubber gloves, take the stems off the chiles and remove and discard the seeds. Place the chiles in a bowl and cover with hot or boiling water. Place a small plate or a lid over the chiles to keep them submerged in the water. Soak for 1 hour, then drain over a bowl. Reserve the soaking water.

2. Turn on a food processor fitted with the steel blade and drop in the garlic. When it is all chopped and adhering to the sides of the bowl, stop the machine and scrape down the sides. Add the drained chiles, spices, and salt. Process until everything is chopped. Stop the machine and scrape down the sides. With the machine running, add 2 tablespoons of the soaking water and the olive oil. Process until the mixture is smooth, stopping to scrape down the sides if necessary. Add more water if necessary.

3. Transfer the sauce to a jar. Wipe the inside edges of the jar with a paper towel, then pour on a film of olive oil to cover the harissa. Top with a lid and refrigerate.

ADVANCE PREPARATION: As long as you keep the top well covered with olive oil, so that air can't get in, your harissa will keep for 6 weeks in the refrigerator.

SAUCES, DRESSINGS, AND CONDIMENTS

PRESERVED LEMONS

North Africa • **Makes 1 pint or 1 quart**

Lemons preserved in a salt brine are a staple ingredient in North African cooking. They are used as both a condiment and as an ingredient in tagines and salads. Thin-skinned lemons are best for preserving; Meyer lemons, the sweet-tasting, light orange–hued lemons from California, are particularly well suited. Because a little preserved lemon goes a long way, you needn't pickle too many at a time, but you need enough to tightly pack the jar you are using. I've seen many different recipes for preserved lemons and tried several of them. They all seem to work. This is how I do it.

6 to 12 organic lemons, preferably organic Meyer lemons, or enough to fill a wide-mouth 1-pint or 1-quart jar

Sea salt or kosher salt

Fresh lemon juice

1. Sterilize your jar by submerging it in boiling water for a minute. Very carefully lift the jar out of the water using tongs (or a jar lifter, if you have one). Tip the water in the jar out of the jar into the pot as you remove it, so that you don't get scalded. Drain the jar on a clean dish towel, top down.

2. Quarter each lemon lengthwise from the pointed (bud) end down to within about ½ inch of the stem end, making sure to keep the lemon intact. Pack the cut lemons with salt. Place the lemons in the jar, packing as many as will fit. Add lemon juice to completely cover the lemons, then sprinkle 2 tablespoons salt over the top and cover tightly. Set in a cool place or in the refrigerator (that's where I keep mine) for at least 3 weeks. The lemons are ready when they have softened. To use, simply remove from the jar, rinse, and slice or chop as directed.

ADVANCE PREPARATION: These will keep for at least 6 months. Store them in the refrigerator. If a film develops, just rinse it off.

Little Foods: Starters, Snacks, Meze, and More

Any vegetarian who has traveled knows how to get around European, Middle Eastern, or North African restaurants without eating meat. At first it might seem daunting, but once you figure out that you can make a wonderful meal out of starters, tapas, and *meze*, you understand how enjoyable and easy it can be.

The Mediterranean is renowned for its "little foods": tapas from Spain; antipasti and *merende* from Italy; Provençal hors d'oeuvres, snacks, and salads; and *meze* from the eastern and southern Mediterranean. Indeed, if it weren't for all of the other recipes I wanted to include in this volume, I could have collected enough vegetarian "little foods" recipes here to fill a book, and a large one at that, because these dishes are among my favorites in the collective Mediterranean repertoire.

People in Mediterranean countries like to socialize in public places, to linger. Given a table or bar, a beverage, and people, plates of food inevitably materialize. A small plate of olives and a few squares of fresh white cheese can last as long as a *meze* feast of *tzatziki* and phyllo triangles, fried potatoes with oregano, Greek salad, zucchini fritters, and spinach pie—as long as people want to stay. Inevitably, the food will be replenished, more sherry or ouzo or strong mint tea will be poured, and conversations will continue.

In Italy, *antipasto* refers to the appetizer course (the word means "before the *meal*"—*pasto*—not, as some people think, "before the pasta"). According to food writer Clifford Wright, this tradition has developed only over the last 50 years. It's not that the foods served as antipasti in Italy did not exist before that; it's just that menus did not group them as a course. In some restaurants the antipasto course is enough to constitute a meal, whether or not you are vegetarian. Consider the *antipasti misti della casa* that we ordered at a small restaurant called L'Orso 80, in Rome near the Piazza Navona. This is what came to our table, an ample meal for four people: two kinds of eggplant, one sliced, grilled, and seasoned with pepperoncini and olive oil, and the other cut into chunks and cooked in olive oil; cauliflower with capers, parsley, and vinegar; balls of ultra-fresh mozzarella; celery with Emmenthaler; stewed fennel; borlotti beans with tomato sauce; roasted peppers; really good flat bread; and *supplì al telefono* (deep-fried cheese-filled rice balls).

The Italians also have a tradition called *merende,* little meals that people eat at midmorning and late afternoon. Walk through any Italian city in the afternoon and you will see schoolchildren rushing into pizza shops to buy their afternoon slice of *pizza bianca,* spinach torta, or panini. They could be described as "snacks," but what snacks these are!

Of course, before we became enamored with the foods of the Mediterranean in the United States, our notion of pre-dinner tidbits was founded in the French tradition of the hors d'oeuvre, which means, literally, "outside the work," the work here meaning the menu. In Provence, hors d'oeuvres, are not elaborate; just one or two small dishes—some olives and roasted almonds, a plate of perfect tiny radishes, some croutons spread with tapenade or brandade—are likely to accompany an aperitif before a meal. These little foods are among the most fundamental foods of southern France.

Salads are another story. In restaurants, they tend to be served as a first course, whereas in homes the salad normally follows the main dish. Mesclun is the king of the Provençal salads. It's difficult to believe that this mix of tender, pungent, bitter, and mild young salad greens was not too long ago unique to the *pays Niçois.* Traditional Niçoise mesclun consists of nine or ten different greens, including red- and green-tipped oak leaf lettuce, arugula, radicchio, frisée, chervil, dandelion greens, and mâche. Now packaged "spring mix" lettuces are available in every supermarket produce department, and we're all the better for it.

Provence also brings more substantial salads to our tables, like Farro Salad (page 112) and Couscous "Tabbouleh" (page 97). Some of these are modern salads; others are traditional, growing out of an Haute Provençal custom called the *bajano.* Vegetables, beans, and grains were cooked in salted water, and then dressed with a garlicky vinaigrette. The cooking water was eaten as a soup. Nothing goes to waste in good peasant cuisine.

ROASTED SALTED ALMONDS WITH CAYENNE
France • **Makes 2 cups**

Although this particular recipe comes from Provence, you could just as easily find the almonds in North Africa. One of my French recipes instructs the cook to "grill the almonds in a very hot oven until they sing."

> **2 cups almonds, with or without skins**
>
> **Salt**
>
> **Cayenne**

1. Heat the oven to 350°F.

2. Toss the almonds with salt and cayenne to taste, and place on a baking sheet. Roast until they begin to crackle, 5 to 10 minutes. Be careful when you open the oven door, because the capsicum in the cayenne is quite volatile, so avoid breathing in, and be careful of your eyes. Remove from the heat and cool.

ADVANCE PREPARATION: Keep the roasted almonds in an airtight container in the freezer and they're good for weeks.

APRICOT YOGURT DIP
Greece and Turkey • **Makes 2 cups, serving 8**

This wonderful garlicky yogurt dip with dried apricots is served with grilled meats in Greece and Turkey. But it goes equally well with rice pilaf, which is how I suggest you serve it. Or just serve it with bread as part of a *meze*.

> **2 cups drained yogurt (page 21)**
>
> **10 dried apricots, finely chopped**
>
> **1 to 2 garlic cloves (to taste), puréed with a little salt in a mortar and pestle.**

Combine all of the ingredients in a serving bowl.

ADVANCE PREPARATION: This dip keeps for a few days in the refrigerator, but the garlic becomes very pungent. You can mix together the apricots and yogurt, then add the garlic shortly before serving if you want to get ahead.

WHITE BEAN "BRANDADE"
France • **Makes about 3 cups**

Brandade, a creamy purée of salt cod, is a signature Provençal dish. This version—without the fish—is considered a "poor man's brandade." In Marseille, the dish is often garnished with pressed dried tuna roe (*poutargue,* or *bottarga*). I sprinkle chopped sage, rosemary, or parsley over mine.

> **2 garlic cloves**
>
> **Salt**
>
> **4 tablespoons extra virgin olive oil**
>
> **2 cans (15½ ounces each) white beans (cannellini or navy), drained and rinsed**
>
> **¼ cup milk (more as needed)**
>
> **2 tablespoons fresh lemon juice**
>
> **Freshly ground white pepper**
>
> **1 tablespoon chopped fresh sage, rosemary, or parsley**
>
> **Crostini (page 135), pita triangles, or crudités**

1. In a mortar and pestle, purée the garlic with ½ teaspoon salt and 1 tablespoon of the olive oil.

2. Purée the white beans with the mashed garlic in a food processor fitted with the steel blade. With the machine running, add the remaining 3 tablespoons olive oil, the milk, and lemon juice. Add pepper to taste and adjust the salt. The consistency should be like hummus. If the purée is too stiff, thin out with more milk. Taste and adjust seasoning.

3. Transfer to a serving bowl or platter. Sprinkle with the herbs. Serve warm or room temperature, with crostini, pita triangles, or crudités.

ADVANCE PREPARATION: The brandade will keep for about 5 days in the refrigerator. It will become thicker with time. Thin out as desired with milk.

READY-MADE SNACKS AND STARTERS

During the 12 years I lived in Paris, I operated a "Supper Club" in my apartment. These were paying dinners that I held monthly for about two dozen people, a cross between a salon and a dinner party. I would spend three days cooking for my dinners, and my preparations always included buying and cleaning a few bunches of radishes, buying luscious Nyons olives at the Provençal food shop around the corner, and toasting almonds. I would set these tidbits out on pretty plates here and there in my living room, and then I would be able to relax as I finalized my preparations in the kitchen. My guests, I knew, would feel welcome, looked after, because there would be something to eat, simply but beautifully presented, waiting for them when they arrived.

This may be a cookbook, but I can't begin this chapter without a discussion of little foods that are served throughout the Mediterranean that require no cooking. Somebody—a farmer, an olive mill worker, a cheese maker, perhaps—has done the work for you. These are foods to keep on hand in your refrigerator or your pantry, so that no guest ever arrives at your home without the possibility of wonderful-tasting sustenance.

Olives

Have you ever been hungry and eaten an olive? Try it if you haven't. One olive is an energy-rich food, and incredibly satisfying, especially if you're hungry. I have not been in a Mediterranean country where olives were not part of the edible landscape, especially as snacks, *meze,* and with aperitifs. Not having a jar or can of imported olives in my pantry makes me feel downright insecure, not about my own hunger, but about the potential hunger of a guest. To see the wide range of olives now available in the United States, read the discussion of olives and olive oil on pages 15 to 17.

Cheese

In France, cheese is strictly reserved for the course that follows the main course or the salad. It is often served in place of dessert. A Frenchman would never dream of serving cheese before the meal, as Americans have become accustomed to doing.

But throughout the rest of the Mediterranean, cheese is often served as a preamble to a meal or as part of a *meze*. It will usually be only one kind—small squares of fresh white cheese or feta, or a bowl of fresh cheese to spread on croutons. In Italy, you might be served slivers of aged Parmesan, ultra-fresh mozzarella balls, slivers of pecorino to eat with raw fava beans, or a few slices of provolone to chew on with your sausage. In Spain, you could be served a plate of thin, triangular slices of Manchego cheese, perhaps accompanied by Serrano ham. The trick here is moderation. Cheese should whet the appetite, not cut it.

Nuts

I am not talking about big bowls of addictive peanuts here. The nuts you might find on a Mediterranean table are likely to be roasted almonds or pistachios, served in a small bowl.

Melon

The melons that are routinely served throughout Spain and Provence are unbelievably sweet and juicy. Those that I ate most often in Spain were light green, served as often as not with Serrano ham, but you can always serve the melon without the ham, perhaps with just salt and pepper. Provence is famous for its small, round orange-fleshed Cavaillon melons, which taste like the most intense, juicy cantaloupes imaginable. Christine Picasso, my "French mother" and godmother to my son, Liam, serves platters of them, with ripe figs, every day before lunch and dinner when we visit her in Provence in the summer.

Radishes

If you are lucky enough to have farmers at your farmers' market who grow those beautiful small French radishes, take advantage of them, especially when you're planning a dinner party. Any kind of radish will do, though. Bring them home, scrub them if necessary, and trim off the greens. Make them into flowers if you wish by cutting "petals" down each side of the radish, from the root end to just above the stem end. Place them in a bowl of water in the refrigerator, and the petals will open out. Radishes in water will keep in the refrigerator for several days, and they're great to pull out for guests.

Lupini Beans

Pickled yellow lupini beans are usually brined and sold in jars and served as a snack, like olives, throughout the Mediterranean.

Olive Paste

Though nothing that you can get in a jar will match the tapenades you can make (pages 121 to 122), there are some good ones to be found. They should be as simple as possible, and the only oil you should see listed on the label is olive oil.

Red Pepper Purée (Ajvar)

This is made in the Balkan countries, and some of the imported brands I've tasted are quite good. Sometimes they're made with peppers only, sometimes with a mixture of peppers and eggplant (these are still bright orange-red). Very nice on croutons or with pita bread.

Sun-Dried Tomatoes

Good imported sun-dried tomatoes in olive oil make a wonderful snack, with mozzarella cheese or good bread. Zingermans (www.zingermans.com) imports a delicious one from Sicily.

Piquillo Pimientos

These are the sweetest of red peppers from Spain, nothing like any red pepper you've ever tasted. Keep a jar on hand to serve as an hors d'oeuvre. Wonderful on crostini or bruschetta (page 135), or just as is, drizzled with a little sherry vinegar and olive oil and sprinkled with sea salt.

Sicilian Caponata

Although I have a caponata recipe on page 276, there is at least one excellent imported jarred caponata that you can find through Zingermans.com. I always like to have something like that in my pantry for surprise guests.

BEET AND BEET GREENS SALAD
Greece and France • **Serves 4 to 6**

The Greeks serve beets with their greens as a side dish or part of a *meze*. It's a combination that can be dressed simply, with lemon juice and olive oil, or with a skordalia sauce on the side or spooned over the top (see the variation). I also like to serve this with a vinaigrette. The vinaigrette isn't the Greek way, it's more Provençal, but I love it.

> 1 large or 2 small bunches beets, with their greens
>
> Salt
>
> 2 tablespoons red wine vinegar or sherry vinegar
>
> 1 teaspoon balsamic vinegar
>
> 1 small garlic clove, minced or put through a press
>
> Freshly ground pepper
>
> 7 tablespoons extra virgin olive oil
>
> Juice of ½ lemon

1. Heat the oven to 425°F. Cut the greens off the beets, leaving about ½ inch of the stems attached. Scrub the beets and place in a baking dish or ovenproof casserole. Add about ¼ inch water, cover tightly with a lid or foil, and roast until the beets are tender, 35 to 40 minutes. Cool. If not using right away, refrigerate in a covered bowl.

2. Bring a large pot of water to a boil while you stem and wash the greens. Add 1 tablespoon salt to the water and blanch the greens for 1 or 2 minutes. Transfer the greens to a bowl of cold water, then drain and squeeze out the water. Chop coarsely.

3. Mix together the vinegars, garlic, salt and pepper to taste, and 6 tablespoons of the olive oil. When the beets are cool enough to handle, trim the ends off, slip off their skins, cut in half, then slice into half-moons. Toss with the dressing.

4. Toss the beet greens with the lemon juice, salt and pepper to taste, and the remaining 1 tablespoon olive oil. Line a platter with the greens, top with the beets, and serve.

ADVANCE PREPARATION: Cooked beets will keep for about 5 days in the refrigerator. Cooked beet greens will keep for about 3 days, and can be reheated.

VARIATIONS

BEET AND BEET GREENS SALAD WITH SKORDALIA: Make the vinaigrette without the garlic. The greens need not be tossed with oil and lemon juice. Serve the beets and beet greens with a bowl of Skordalia (made with walnuts, page 80) on the side, for guests to spoon onto the beets and greens.

● Add 1 tablespoon chopped fresh tarragon and toss with the beets before topping the greens.

● Substitute ½ cup Vinaigrette (page 82) for the vinegar and olive oil.

BEET AND YOGURT SALAD
Turkey • **Serves 4**

This colorful pink salad is just one of many Turkish vegetable salads that combine cooked vegetables with thick, garlicky yogurt. The beets are first marinated in a mixture of vinegar, sugar, and olive oil, and I love the sweet and pungent contrast of flavors. In Turkey, white wine vinegar or cider vinegar would be used. I like to use sherry vinegar.

> 4 medium beets, roasted (see Beet and Beet Greens Salad, left)
>
> 1½ tablespoons sherry vinegar
>
> 1 teaspoon sugar
>
> 2 tablespoons extra virgin olive oil
>
> Salt and freshly ground pepper
>
> 2 garlic cloves, puréed in a mortar and pestle with a pinch of salt
>
> ½ cup drained yogurt (page 21)
>
> 2 to 3 tablespoons minced fresh dill

1. Peel the roasted beets, preferably while still warm. Cut in half lengthwise, then slice crosswise into half-moons. Stir together the vinegar, sugar, olive oil, and salt and pepper to taste. Toss with the warm beets and marinate for 2 to 3 hours at room temperature or in the refrigerator.

2. Mix together the garlic and yogurt. Stir in half the dill and salt and pepper to taste. Drain the beets and stir some of the marinade into the yogurt (to taste). Toss the yogurt with the beets, or arrange the beets on a platter and spoon the yogurt over the top. Sprinkle on the remaining dill and serve.

ADVANCE PREPARATION: The beets can be roasted and marinated 4 or 5 days ahead.

VARIATION

LEBANESE BEETS WITH YOGURT: A very similar preparation is popular in the Middle East. Include the beet greens in the salad (see Beet and Beet Greens Salad on the opposite page). Line a platter with the cooked greens and the sliced beets. Marinating the beets is optional. Increase the yogurt to 1½ cups and omit the dill. Mix the yogurt with the garlic and spoon over the beets. Sprinkle with 2 tablespoons slivered fresh mint leaves.

SPICY BEET SALAD
Tunisia • **Serves 4**

This Tunisian rendition of a beet salad is slightly picante because of the harissa in the dressing. I love to eat it with a piece of feta; the salty, creamy cheese combines beautifully with the hot and sweet beets.

> 4 medium beets, roasted (see Beet and Beet Greens Salad, opposite page)
>
> 3 scallions, chopped
>
> 1 garlic clove, minced or put through a press
>
> ½ teaspoon harissa (more to taste)
>
> 1½ tablespoons red wine vinegar or sherry vinegar
>
> ¼ cup extra virgin olive oil
>
> 2 tablespoons chopped fresh flat-leaf parsley
>
> Salt and freshly ground pepper

Peel the beets and cut into small dice. Toss with the scallions, garlic, harissa, vinegar, olive oil, parsley, and salt and pepper to taste. Taste and adjust seasonings. Serve right away, or chill for a few hours.

ADVANCE PREPARATION: The roasted beets will keep for about 5 days in the refrigerator. You can prepare the salad a day ahead, but wait until serving before tossing with the parsley. Salad leftovers will be good for 3 or 4 days. They're delicious with feta cheese.

NORTH AFRICAN BEET SALAD
This variation of Spicy Beet Salad is a much simpler beet salad than the Tunisian version.

> 1 bunch beets, roasted (see Beet and Beet Greens Salad, opposite page)
>
> 1 tablespoon vinegar
>
> 2 tablespoons fresh lemon juice
>
> 1 to 2 teaspoons ground cumin seeds (to taste)
>
> Salt and freshly ground pepper
>
> ⅓ cup extra virgin olive oil
>
> 2 tablespoons chopped fresh flat-leaf parsley

Peel the roasted beets and slice. Toss with the remaining ingredients and serve.

SMALL BULGUR PATTIES (Kisir)
Turkey • **Serves 4 to 6**

Not all patties, or *kofte,* are made with meat. Throughout the Middle East, cooks also make this wonderful appetizer out of bulgur. I think it makes a lovely side dish as well. This recipe is based on one by Ghillie Basan, from *Classic Turkish Cookery.*

> ½ cup bulgur
>
> 4 scallions, finely chopped
>
> 2 to 4 garlic cloves (to taste), minced
>
> 1 serrano chile pepper, seeded and chopped
>
> 2 tablespoons tomato purée
>
> 1 tablespoon extra virgin olive oil
>
> 2 tablespoons chopped fresh flat-leaf parsley
>
> 2 tablespoons chopped fresh mint
>
> Salt and freshly ground pepper
>
> 12 small romaine or butter lettuce leaves
>
> 1 lemon, halved

1. Place the bulgur in a bowl and pour on boiling water to cover by ½ inch. Let sit for 1 hour. Drain through a cheesecloth-lined strainer and press the bulgur against the strainer to squeeze out excess water. In a bowl, combine the bulgur, scallions, garlic, serrano pepper, tomato purée, olive oil, parsley, mint, and salt and pepper to taste. Moisten your hands and knead the mixture for a couple of minutes, then allow to sit for 15 to 30 minutes, or until ready to serve.

2. With moistened fingers, form the bulgur mixture into 12 bite-size balls, pressing an indentation into the middle of each. Place on a lettuce leaf, squeeze some lemon juice into the indentations, and serve.

ADVANCE PREPARATION: You can make the patties a day ahead and keep in the refrigerator, but don't put them in the lettuce until you're ready to serve.

VARIATIONS

• Instead of lemon juice, drizzle a little bit of pomegranate molasses into the indentation of each ball.

• In the spring, when I get green garlic at the farmers' market, I use a bulb of it, finely chopped, in place of the scallions.

TABBOULEH

Lebanon • **Serves 6 to 8**

If you've ever eaten tabbouleh in a Lebanese restaurant, you know that the real thing is nothing like the salad that is passed off as tabbouleh at salad bars and deli counters and prepared salad coolers in American supermarkets. Lebanese tabbouleh is a lemony herb salad (mostly parsley) with a little bit of bulgur, not a bulgur salad with herbs. Along with *fattoush,* it is my absolute favorite Middle Eastern salad.

The authentic way to eat tabbouleh is by scooping it up with romaine lettuce leaves, but I feel just fine about using a fork. Make a lunch out of tabbouleh, with a piece of Syrian cheese or feta and some pita bread.

½ cup fine bulgur

1 garlic clove, minced (optional)

Juice of 3 to 4 large lemons (to taste)

6 cups chopped fresh flat-leaf parsley (from 6 large bunches)

1 cup chopped fresh mint (from 1 large bunch)

1 pound ripe tomatoes, very finely chopped

1 bunch scallions, white and light green parts, finely chopped

Salt and freshly ground pepper

½ cup extra virgin olive oil

1 bunch romaine lettuce, leaves separated

1 bunch scallions, cut into 1-inch lengths, for serving

1. Place the bulgur in a bowl and cover with boiling water by ½ inch. Soak for 20 minutes, until slightly softened. Drain through a cheesecloth-lined strainer and press the bulgur against the strainer to squeeze out excess water. Transfer to a large bowl and toss with the garlic, lemon juice, herbs, tomatoes, chopped scallions, and salt and pepper to taste (be generous with the salt). Leave at room temperature or in the refrigerator for 2 to

PREPARING PARSLEY

Parsley has tough stems, which is why, tedious as it may be, you need to pick off the leaves when the ingredient is called for. Put on some music, undo your bunch of parsley, and pick the leaves away from the stems. You can use the stems in a bouquet garni for soup. Place the leaves in a salad spinner and swish around in cold water to release any sand that may be adhering to them. Transfer to the basket and spin dry. Wrap in paper towels until ready to use.

To chop, either place the parsley in a wide glass and use scissors, pointing the scissors straight down into the glass. Or chop, one handful at a time, on a cutting board with a chef's knife. Keep in a bowl lined with paper towels in the refrigerator, covered well, for 1 or 2 days.

3 hours so that the bulgur can continue to absorb liquid and swell.

2. Add the olive oil, toss together, taste, and adjust seasonings. The tabbouleh should taste really lemony. Add more lemon juice if it doesn't. Serve with the lettuce leaves and cut scallions, which can be enclosed in the lettuce leaves with the tabbouleh.

ADVANCE PREPARATION: Tabbouleh will keep for a day in the refrigerator, though the bright green color will fade because of the lemon juice.

COUSCOUS "TABBOULEH"
France • Serves 4 to 6

This passes as tabbouleh in Provence, but it's more like a couscous salad with lots of parsley and mint or cilantro. It's very pretty and is as welcome on a *meze* table as real tabbouleh.

1 cup couscous

¾ teaspoon salt

½ teaspoon ground cumin

½ cup fresh lemon juice

1 cup water

¼ cup extra virgin olive oil

2 cups finely chopped fresh flat-leaf parsley

¼ cup finely chopped fresh mint or cilantro

4 scallions, white and light green parts, minced

1 red bell pepper, seeded and finely chopped

1 pound tomatoes, finely chopped

Small romaine lettuce leaves

1. Put the couscous in a bowl and toss with the salt and cumin. Mix together ¼ cup of the lemon juice and the water and pour over the couscous. Let sit for 30 minutes, stirring from time to time or rubbing the couscous between your fingers and thumbs to prevent it from lumping.

2. Cover the bowl with plastic and microwave the couscous on 100 percent power for 1 minute. Carefully remove the plastic. Stir in the remaining lemon juice and the olive oil, and cool. Toss with

the parsley, mint, scallions, bell pepper, and tomatoes. Taste and adjust seasonings. Refrigerate until ready to serve. Serve, using the romaine lettuce leaves as scoopers.

ADVANCE PREPARATION: The salad will hold for several hours in the refrigerator.

ANDALUSIAN CABBAGE SALAD
Spain • Serves 4 to 6

Clifford Wright, in his classic book *A Mediterranean Feast,* writes about the Arab influence on the cooking of the European Mediterranean. One of the many recipes in his book is for a very simple Syrian cabbage salad, in which the shredded Savoy cabbage is heavily salted and left to sit for an hour, then rinsed of the salt and tossed with olive oil, garlic, and lemon juice. He prefaces the recipe with the words: "The Arabs favored cool salads in the hot and arid climate of Syria." I thought of Cliff's recipe and those words on a stifling July afternoon in Granada, when I ate this salad at a small bar/restaurant next to my hotel, the Reina Cristina.

1 small Savoy cabbage or green cabbage (about 1¼ pounds), outer leaves discarded, the remainder cored and shredded

2 tablespoons sea salt (more to taste)

2 large garlic cloves (more to taste), finely chopped

2 tablespoons fresh lemon juice

6 tablespoons extra virgin olive oil

A handful imported black olives, pitted if desired

1. In a large bowl, toss the cabbage with the salt. Let sit for 1 hour.

2. Rinse the cabbage in several changes of water: Fill the bowl and swish the cabbage around, then drain. Do this several times. Then place the cabbage in a colander and rinse thoroughly. Taste to make sure that it is not too salty; if it is, rinse again. Place in the bowl and cover with ice water. Let sit for 15 minutes, then drain. ▶

3. Toss the cabbage with the garlic, lemon juice, and olive oil. Taste and adjust seasonings. Garnish with the olives and serve.

ADVANCE PREPARATION: You can cover and refrigerate this salad for 2 to 3 hours before serving it.

VARIATIONS

MIDDLE EASTERN CABBAGE SALAD WITH LEMON AND DILL: Add to the above recipe ¼ to ½ cup chopped fresh dill, to taste. Toss with the cabbage along with the dressing.

MIDDLE EASTERN CABBAGE SALAD WITH YOGURT, LEMON, AND DILL: Use only 2 tablespoons olive oil, and add ¼ to ½ cup chopped dill and ½ cup drained yogurt (page 21).

NORTH AFRICAN CARROT "COMPOTE"
(Ajlūk)
Algeria and Tunisia • Serves 4

This dish is typical of the Jews of Algeria and Tunisia. It makes a marvelous *meze,* but could also be served on its own as a starter, with lettuce leaves and flat bread. You could also serve it as a side dish, though this isn't the way it would be served in Tunisia.

    1 pound carrots, peeled and thickly sliced

    1 large russet potato (about ½ pound), peeled and diced

    2 tablespoons plus 1 teaspoon fresh lemon juice

    2 tablespoons plus 1 teaspoon extra virgin olive oil

    1 to 2 garlic cloves (to taste), mashed to a paste with ½ teaspoon salt in a mortar and pestle

    1 teaspoon freshly ground caraway seeds

    ¾ teaspoon freshly ground coriander seeds

    ½ teaspoon Harissa (page 86 or commercial)

    Imported black olives

    Romaine lettuce leaves

    Flat bread

1. Steam the carrots and potato until very soft, 15 to 20 minutes. Mash in a mortar and pestle or put

through a ricer. Stir in 2 tablespoons of the lemon juice and 2 tablespoons of the olive oil. Add the garlic paste, caraway, coriander, and harissa. Taste and adjust salt.

2. Mound the purée on a platter or in a wide bowl. Run a fork down the sides. Mix together the remaining lemon juice and olive oil and drizzle over the purée. Decorate with olives, surround with lettuce leaves, and serve with warm flat bread.

ADVANCE PREPARATION: The compote keeps for about 3 days in the refrigerator, but I'm sure you'll finish it at one sitting.

VARIATIONS

ZUCCHINI AJLŪK: The same compote can be made with zucchini. Substitute equal amounts zucchini or other summer squash for the carrots. You can omit the potato for a lighter mixture.

WINTER SQUASH AJLŪK: Substitute roasted winter squash (such as butternut squash or kabocha) for the steamed carrots. Heat the oven to 425°F. Pierce the squash with the tip of a paring knife in a few places and place on a foil-lined baking sheet. Roast for 30 minutes. Cool until you can handle it easily, then cut in half and remove the seeds. Brush the foil with oil. Return the squash to the foil, cut side down. Roast another 30 minutes, or until the squash is tender and easily pierced with a knife. Cool, then peel and proceed with the recipe.

EGGPLANT AJLŪK: Omit the potato. Substitute 1½ pounds grilled or roasted eggplant for the steamed carrots. Pierce 2 medium eggplants in several places with the tip of a knife and grill until charred and tender all the way through. Transfer to a colander set in the sink or over a bowl and drain for 15 minutes. (Or cut the eggplants in half lengthwise and score each half down to, but not through, the skin. Place cut side down on an oiled foil-covered baking sheet and roast in a 450°F oven until tender all the way through, 20 to 30 minutes. Lay the eggplant halves cut side down in a colander set in the sink or over a bowl and drain for 15 minutes.) Peel the eggplant and proceed with the recipe. Stir in a minced red bell pepper if desired.

CARROT SALAD (Ommok Houria)
Tunisia • Serves 4

This spicy blend of cooked carrots seasoned with caraway and harissa is one of the most popular salads in Tunisia. A similar dish from Morocco is seasoned with cumin and omits the harissa.

- 1 pound carrots, peeled and thinly sliced or cut into 3-inch spears
- 2 tablespoons extra virgin olive oil
- 2 garlic cloves, minced
- ½ teaspoon salt (or to taste)
- ½ teaspoon freshly ground pepper
- ½ to 1 teaspoon freshly ground caraway seeds (to taste)
- ¼ to ½ teaspoon Harissa (page 86 or commercial)
- 3 tablespoons chopped fresh flat-leaf parsley
- 2 tablespoons fresh lemon juice (more to taste)
- Imported black olives, such as kalamata, or preferably oil-cured olives
- 2 large eggs, hard-cooked and cut in wedges or slices (optional)

1. Either steam the carrots or simmer them in lightly salted water to cover until tender, 5 to 10 minutes. Drain.

2. Heat the olive oil in a large nonstick frying pan over medium heat and add the carrots, garlic, salt, pepper, caraway, and harissa. Stir together for about 3 minutes, until the carrots are nicely coated with the mixture. Add the parsley, toss, and transfer to a salad bowl. Toss with the lemon juice. Taste and correct seasonings. Garnish with olives and, if you wish, sliced hard-cooked eggs. Serve at room temperature.

ADVANCE PREPARATION: The carrots can be cooked a day or two ahead. It's best to finish them with the spices and lemon juice on the day you're serving. However, leftovers will be good for a few days.

MARINATED CARROTS
Italy • Serves 4 to 8

People who insist they don't like cooked carrots become immediate converts with this dish. It's one of my son's lunchbox favorites. It's a great thing to make with carrots that have been around in the refrigerator a little too long. Even better when they're sturdy and sweet.

In the authentic Italian version of this dish, the carrots are cooked in olive oil before being doused with vinegar and tossed with garlic and mint. I prefer to steam the carrots for a lighter dish. And I like them equally with or without the garlic and/or mint.

- 1 pound carrots, peeled, quartered lengthwise, and cut into 2- or 3-inch lengths
- 2 tablespoons sherry vinegar
- 2 tablespoons extra virgin olive oil
- Salt, preferably coarse sea salt

Steam the carrots for 5 to 6 minutes, until just tender. Refresh with cold water and toss with the vinegar, olive oil, and salt to taste. Cool, then serve at room temperature or cold.

ADVANCE PREPARATION: The prepared carrots keep well in the refrigerator for a week, but I'm sure they won't last that long.

VARIATIONS

- Add 1 finely minced or pressed garlic clove and toss with the cooked carrots, salt, vinegar, and olive oil.
- Add 1 to 2 tablespoons finely chopped fresh mint.

MASHED CARROTS WITH GARLICKY YOGURT

Turkey • **Serves 4**

People of the southern and eastern Mediterranean have wonderful ways with cooked carrots, which are served as *meze* and as salads. Versions of this dish, called *havuç ezmesi,* exist throughout Turkey. The carrots are cooked and mashed, and served with a pungent, garlicky yogurt sauce. It resembles carrot dishes from North Africa (pages 98 to 99), notably the compote (*ajlūk*) from Algeria and Tunisia, and Tunisian and Moroccan *ommok houria.* For the best texture, use a mortar and pestle or fork to mash the carrots.

> 1 pound carrots, peeled and sliced
>
> 1 teaspoon caraway seeds, lightly crushed
>
> 2 tablespoons extra virgin olive oil
>
> 2 to 3 tablespoons fresh lemon juice (to taste)
>
> Salt and freshly ground pepper
>
> 1 to 2 garlic cloves (to taste), peeled
>
> ⅓ cup drained yogurt (page 21)
>
> 1 tablespoon chopped fresh mint
>
> 1 tablespoon chopped fresh dill

1. Steam the carrots until quite tender, about 15 minutes. Transfer to a food processor fitted with the steel blade, a large mortar and pestle, or a bowl, and coarsely purée (use a fork if you're not using a food processor or a mortar and pestle). Add the caraway seeds, olive oil, 2 tablespoons of the lemon juice, and salt and pepper to taste. Mix together. The purée should retain some texture.

2. Mash the garlic to a paste with ½ teaspoon salt in a mortar and pestle. Stir into the yogurt. Add 2 to 3 teaspoons lemon juice if desired, and the chopped herbs.

3. Transfer the carrot mixture to a plate or a wide bowl. Make a well in the center. Fill the well with the yogurt sauce and serve warm.

ADVANCE PREPARATION: Since this dish is best served warm, make it close to serving time. You can prepare the ingredients hours ahead.

CAULIFLOWER À LA GRECQUE

France • **Serves 4**

I have never seen this dish in Greece, nor have I seen it in a Greek cookbook, but vegetables prepared in this way are served all over France.

The coriander seeds stand out as the defining seasoning here. Though most are strained out, I like to throw some back in with the vegetables because I enjoy the intense direct flavor when I crunch down on a seed. I can pinpoint my food memory's awareness of this spice to my first food trip to France, and specifically to a dish that I was served at the Paris restaurant L'Ambroisie.

> 1 tablespoon white wine vinegar or distilled white vinegar
>
> 1 medium cauliflower, broken into florets
>
> Salt
>
> ⅓ cup fresh lemon juice
>
> ½ cup dry white wine
>
> 2 teaspoons coriander seeds
>
> 2 teaspoons fennel seeds
>
> 1 teaspoon black peppercorns
>
> 2 sprigs fresh thyme
>
> 1 bay leaf
>
> ⅓ cup extra virgin olive oil
>
> ¾ cup water

1. Fill a bowl with water and add the vinegar. Drop in the cauliflower florets, swish them around, and drain. Bring a large pot of generously salted water to a boil and add the cauliflower. Boil 5 minutes and transfer to a bowl of cold water. Leave for a few minutes and drain.

2. In a large, heavy nonreactive soup pot or Dutch oven, combine the lemon juice, white wine, coriander seeds, fennel seeds, peppercorns, thyme, bay leaf, olive oil, and water. Bring to a boil and boil for 5 minutes. Add the cauliflower, reduce to a simmer, and simmer for 7 minutes. Remove the cauliflower, season with salt, and transfer to a platter or wide bowl. Strain the cooking liquid and return it to the pot. Bring to a simmer and reduce by half. Pour it over the cauliflower and cool.

Before throwing out the contents of the strainer, toss a teaspoon of the seeds over the cauliflower. Serve at room temperature or cold.

ADVANCE PREPARATION: This is an excellent keeper. You can make it up to 5 days before you serve it.

CAULIFLOWER WITH CAPERS, PARSLEY, AND VINEGAR
Italy • Serves 4 to 6

I've re-created this dish from a memory of one of the most extensive antipasti I've ever eaten, at the Ristorante L'Orso 80, not far from the Piazza Navona, in Rome. Even if you think you don't like cauliflower, you should try this; the vegetable comes alive when tossed with the savory, pungent marinade.

> Salt
>
> 1 large or 2 small or medium cauliflowers, broken into florets
>
> 2 garlic cloves, minced
>
> ¼ cup chopped fresh flat-leaf parsley
>
> ¼ cup capers, drained and rinsed
>
> 3 tablespoons white wine vinegar or champagne vinegar
>
> 7 tablespoons extra virgin olive oil
>
> Freshly ground pepper

1. Bring a large pot of water to a boil. Add a generous amount of salt and the cauliflower. Cook for 5 to 8 minutes, or until tender. Transfer to a bowl of ice-cold water, then drain.

2. In a large bowl, mix together the garlic, parsley, capers, vinegar, and olive oil. Season to taste with salt and pepper. Add the cauliflower and toss together. Let marinate, stirring from time to time, for 30 minutes if possible before serving. Taste and adjust seasoning before serving. Serve warm, cold, or at room temperature, with plenty of Italian bread for soaking up the marinade.

ADVANCE PREPARATION: This dish keeps well in the refrigerator for up to 5 days. You should replenish the parsley, which will have faded after a day.

DEEP-FRIED CAULIFLOWER
Middle East • Serves 6

My absolute favorite Middle Eastern restaurant in Los Angeles is Sunnin, a hole in the wall on Westwood Boulevard. I like to go there for lunch and order *meze,* which is served on paper plates with plastic utensils. Everything they make is good; I always order hummus and baba gannouj, tabbouleh, and *fattoush.* My big indulgence here is their fried cauliflower, which they serve with a tahini sauce. Much as I shun most deep-fried food, I cannot resist this.

> Salt
>
> 1 medium cauliflower, broken into florets
>
> 6 cups peanut, vegetable, or canola oil for deep-frying
>
> Tahini Garlic Sauce (page 83) or Parsley Sauce (page 84)

1. Bring a large pot of generously salted water to a boil. When the water reaches a boil, add the cauliflower and parboil for 4 minutes. Transfer to a bowl of ice water, then drain thoroughly. Pat the florets completely dry with paper towels.

2. Heat the oil in a deep-fryer, wok, or large saucepan to 360° to 375°F. Drop in the cauliflower, a few florets at a time, and deep-fry to a golden brown, turning the florets in the oil so they cook evenly. This should take no more than 3 minutes. Remove with a deep-fry skimmer or a slotted spoon and drain briefly on paper towels. Set the florets on a rack and sprinkle with salt. When all of the florets have been cooked, arrange on a platter and serve at once, with your choice of sauce.

ADVANCE PREPARATION: The cauliflower can be blanched several hours or even a day ahead and held in the refrigerator. Make sure to blot dry before frying.

PROVENÇAL CHICK PEA SALAD
France • Serves 4 to 6

Recipes for chick pea salads in older Provençal cookbooks are rather plain, the chick peas simply tossed with vinaigrette and parsley. I like to add a little color, so I add red bell pepper, and in season I might add a couple of chopped heirloom tomatoes from my garden. You can use canned chick peas, or soak and cook dried ones.

FOR THE SALAD

1 pound dried chick peas, picked over, rinsed, and soaked in 8 cups water for 6 hours or overnight; or 3 cans chick peas (15 ounces each), drained and rinsed

8 cups water (if using dried chick peas)

Salt

½ cup chopped fresh flat-leaf parsley

1 small red bell pepper, chopped

1 small green bell pepper, chopped

2 medium tomatoes, diced (optional)

FOR THE DRESSING

3 tablespoons fresh lemon juice

1 tablespoon red wine vinegar

1 to 2 garlic cloves (to taste), minced or put through a press

Salt and freshly ground pepper

½ cup extra virgin olive oil

1. *Make the salad:* If using dried chick peas, drain and transfer to a large saucepan or pot. Add the water and bring to a boil. Reduce the heat, cover, and simmer for 1 hour. Add 2 teaspoons salt, or more to taste, and continue to simmer until tender, 30 minutes to 1 hour. Drain.

2. Toss the cooked or canned chick peas with the parsley, bell peppers, and tomatoes.

3. *Make the dressing:* Whisk together the lemon juice, vinegar, garlic, salt, pepper, and olive oil.

4. Pour the dressing over the chick peas and toss. Serve warm, at room temperature, or chilled.

ADVANCE PREPARATION: The cooked chick peas will keep for about 5 days in the refrigerator. The salad can be assembled several hours before you wish to serve it. Keep in the refrigerator.

VARIATION

Omit the lemon juice and use 3 tablespoons vinegar in all.

CHICK PEA AND BULGUR SALAD
Middle East • Serves 6 to 8

This salad is substantial enough to eat for a light lunch or dinner, but you can also serve small portions as part of a *meze*. It's sort of like a beefed-up tabbouleh, with lots of parsley and mint. The hint of cinnamon adds a flavor that is unmistakably Middle Eastern.

¾ cup medium or coarse bulgur

Salt

2½ cups cooked chick peas

1 bunch scallions, white and most of the green parts, chopped

2 tablespoons minced fresh mint

5 tablespoons minced fresh flat-leaf parsley

¼ teaspoon ground cinnamon

2 plum tomatoes, finely chopped (optional)

¼ cup fresh lemon juice

⅓ cup extra virgin olive oil

Freshly ground pepper

Romaine lettuce leaves for scooping

1. Place the bulgur in a bowl, toss with ½ teaspoon salt, and pour on hot water to cover by an inch. Let sit for 20 minutes, then drain through a cheesecloth-lined sieve. Press the bulgur against the sieve to release water.

2. Toss the bulgur with the chick peas, scallions, mint, parsley, cinnamon, tomatoes, lemon juice, oil, and pepper to taste. Taste and adjust salt. Cover and allow to stand for about 30 minutes before serving, so that the flavors will emerge.

Toss again and serve in a bowl or on a platter, surrounded by the lettuce leaves.

ADVANCE PREPARATION: You can make this several hours before serving. The reconstituted bulgur and the cooked chick peas will keep for 5 days in the refrigerator.

VARIATION

In the spring, when I can buy green garlic at the farmers' market, I substitute it for the scallions. I use 1 large or 2 small bulbs, finely chopped.

HUMMUS

Middle East • Makes about 2 cups

Hummus, or *hummus bi tahini*, is everywhere. But the hummus you bring home in a container from your supermarket is lacking in the fresh, earthy flavor that you get from the real stuff. In a pinch you can make hummus with canned chick peas, but the flavor of peas that you cook yourself is richer, and a food processor makes the final preparation go very quickly. Traditional garnishes for hummus include pine nuts, finely chopped fresh mint leaves and whole mint leaves, sumac, and pomegranate seeds.

    1 heaped cup dried chick peas, picked over,
        rinsed, and soaked in 4 cups water
        for 6 hours or overnight

    4 cups water

    Salt

    2 large garlic cloves, peeled

    ½ teaspoon ground cumin

    ¼ cup fresh lemon juice

    ¼ cup extra virgin olive oil

    3 tablespoons tahini, stirred if the oil has
        separated

    Broth from the beans, water, or plain yogurt
        as desired

    FOR OPTIONAL GARNISH

    2 tablespoons pine nuts

    3 tablespoons chopped fresh mint

    Fresh mint leaves

    2 tablespoons pomegranate seeds or small
        imported black olives

    Warm pita triangles

1. Drain the chick peas and combine with the water in a large saucepan or pot. Bring to a boil, reduce the heat, and simmer for 1 hour. Add salt to taste (1 to 2 teaspoons) and continue to simmer until tender, about 1 hour. Remove from the heat and drain through a colander or strainer set over a bowl.

2. Turn on a food processor fitted with the steel blade and drop in the garlic. Process until the garlic adheres to the sides of the bowl. Turn off the machine and scrape down the sides of the bowl. Add the chick peas and cumin. Process to a coarse purée and scrape down the sides of the bowl.

3. Combine the lemon juice and olive oil, and with the machine running, pour into the processor. Add the tahini and process until the hummus is smooth. If the mixture seems thick or dry, thin out with liquid from the beans, water, or yogurt. Season generously with salt. Scrape into a bowl or mound onto a platter. Top with any of the garnishes. Serve with warm pita triangles.

ADVANCE PREPARATION: You can make the hummus a day ahead. Don't garnish it until ready to serve.

LEFTOVERS: Hummus will keep for 3 or 4 days in a covered container in the refrigerator.

VARIATION

Hummus is a delightful topping for crudités. Put the hummus in a pastry bag fitted with a medium star tip, and pipe onto cucumber rounds, squares of red pepper, and into cherry tomatoes.

TURKISH HUMMUS (Humus)
Turkey • Makes 2 cups

In Turkey, hummus is made without the tahini used in Middle Eastern versions. This makes for a lighter version, pungent with garlic and lemon juice and savory with cumin.

> 1 cup dried chick peas, picked over, rinsed, and soaked in 4 cups water for 6 hours or overnight; or 2 cups drained and rinsed canned chick peas
>
> 4 cups water (if using dried chick peas)
>
> Salt
>
> 2 to 4 garlic cloves (to taste)
>
> 1 teaspoon ground cumin seeds
>
> 4 tablespoons extra virgin olive oil
>
> 3 tablespoons fresh lemon juice (more to taste)
>
> 3 tablespoons drained yogurt (page 21)
>
> ½ teaspoon Aleppo pepper

1. If using dried chick peas, drain and combine with the water in a large saucepan or pot. Bring to a boil, reduce the heat, and simmer for 1 hour. Add salt to taste (about 2 teaspoons) and continue to simmer until tender, about 1 hour. Drain.

2. Turn on a food processor fitted with the steel blade and drop in the garlic. Process until the garlic adheres to the sides of the bowl. Turn off the machine and scrape down the sides of the bowl. Add the cooked or canned chick peas and cumin and process to a coarse purée.

3. Combine 3 tablespoons of the olive oil, the lemon juice, and yogurt, and add to the chick peas. Process until the mixture is smooth. Season generously with salt and more lemon juice if you want. Scrape into a bowl. Drizzle on the remaining 1 tablespoon olive oil and sprinkle with the Aleppo pepper.

ADVANCE PREPARATION: Hummus can be made a day ahead. Don't garnish it with the olive oil or red pepper until ready to serve. Leftovers will keep for 3 or 4 days in the refrigerator.

BAKED HUMMUS WITH PINE NUTS
Variation of Turkish Hummus

This hummus is made with tahini, then topped with pine nuts and melted butter, and baked. You can serve it with warm pita or any bread of your choice.

1. Heat the oven to 400°F. Substitute tahini for the yogurt. Make as directed at left, but don't add the garnishes. Scrape into a lightly oiled baking dish.

2. Melt 1 tablespoon unsalted butter in a small pan and add 1 tablespoon pine nuts and ½ teaspoon Aleppo pepper. Stir together, then spoon over the hummus.

3. Bake for 20 minutes, then serve hot with pita bread.

FALAFEL
Middle East • Serves 6 to 8 as a main dish or 10 to 12 as a *meze*

Here's another deep-fried food I love. Anyone who likes Middle Eastern food is familiar with falafel, called *ta'amia* in Egypt, the deep-fried rissoles made with soaked fava beans and/or chick peas. This is the hamburger of the Levantine Middle East, a street food and *meze* that is as popular in Lebanon, Syria, Israel, and Jordan as it is in Egypt, where it originated. When I was in Cairo, there were vendors on every other street corner, their *ta'amia* batter in big tubs and oil bubbling in large pans.

There are many recipes for falafel; those that have more Egyptian influences are fragrant with cilantro, parsley, spices, and garlic. When you make the batter, make sure to allow the elements to drain well before mixing, because if the batter is wet, the rissoles won't hold together when you fry them. I soak the beans 2 days ahead, and make up the batter the day before I'm serving the falafel. You'll also have time if you make the batter early in the day, but don't leave it for the last minute.

1 head garlic (about 15 cloves), minced

1 large onion, finely chopped

Salt

1½ cups dried yellow fava beans, picked over, rinsed, and soaked in water to cover by at least an inch for 12 hours or overnight

½ cup dried chick peas, picked over, rinsed, and soaked in water to cover by at least an inch for 12 hours or overnight

½ cup chopped fresh cilantro

½ cup chopped fresh flat-leaf parsley

2 tablespoons unbleached all-purpose flour

½ teaspoon freshly ground black pepper

1 teaspoon freshly ground coriander seeds

1 teaspoon freshly ground cumin seeds

1 teaspoon ground allspice

½ teaspoon ground cinnamon

½ teaspoon ground red pepper or cayenne

½ teaspoon baking soda

1 tablespoon baking powder

6 cups vegetable or canola oil for deep-frying

FOR SERVING

Arab bread or pita

Tahini Garlic Sauce (page 83) or Parsley Sauce (page 84)

Chopped tomatoes and cucumbers

Sliced radishes

Store-bought pickled turnips and cucumbers (optional)

Romaine lettuce leaves, torn into pieces

1. Place the garlic and onion in a strainer, salt lightly, and drain over a bowl for 2 hours. Press against the strainer to extract more liquid.

2. Drain the fava beans and chick peas, and place on paper towels to dry for 30 minutes.

3. Combine the garlic, onion, fava beans, chick peas, cilantro, parsley, flour, black pepper, coriander, cumin, allspice, cinnamon, red pepper, baking soda, baking powder, and 1½ tablespoons salt in a large bowl and stir well. Transfer, in batches, to a food processor fitted with the steel blade. Pulse until the ingredients are ground and the batter is fairly smooth. Scrape back into the bowl and stir together again.

4. Line a large strainer with cheesecloth and place over a bowl. Scrape the batter into the strainer and drain for 1 hour or longer. You should now have a coarse batter that is stiff enough to hold together when you shape the falafel.

5. Line a baking sheet with paper towels. Use a tablespoon to scoop up slightly larger than walnut-size portions of the batter and shape into a ball with moistened hands, then flatten slightly and shape like a hockey puck, about 2 inches in diameter and ½ inch thick. Place on the baking sheet. Continue to shape the falafel until all of the batter is used up, keeping your hands moistened. Place the baking sheet in the refrigerator for 30 minutes or longer so the falafel will stiffen up.

6. Heat the oil in a large, wide saucepan, wok, or deep fryer to 360° to 375°F. Cook the falafel a few at a time, being careful not to crowd the pan. When they bob to the surface, flip them over using a skimmer or a slotted spoon. Fry to a dark golden brown, 3 to 4 minutes. Drain on a paper towel–lined baking sheet, or on a rack. Serve hot, wrapped in Arab bread, with the sauces and garnishes.

ADVANCE PREPARATION: You can make the batter and shape the falafel a day or two before frying the patties. Keep in the refrigerator.

TZATZIKI
Greece • **Serves 6**

I have never been in a Greek restaurant or taverna and not ordered this garlicky cucumber and yogurt combination, the Greek version of Turkish *cacik* (below).

> 1 long English cucumber, peeled and grated on the large holes of a box grater (or use a food processor)
>
> Salt
>
> 2 to 3 garlic cloves (to taste), peeled
>
> 2 tablespoons extra virgin olive oil
>
> 1½ cups drained yogurt (about 4 cups undrained) (page 21)
>
> 1 to 2 tablespoons chopped fresh mint or dill
>
> 1 tablespoon red wine vinegar

1. Sprinkle the cucumber generously with salt, toss, and place in a colander in the sink. Let sit for 30 minutes. Rinse and squeeze out water.

2. Combine the garlic cloves, 1 tablespoon of the olive oil, and ¼ teaspoon salt in a mortar and pestle and grind to a paste.

3. Toss the cucumber with the garlic paste, yogurt, mint, vinegar, and remaining 1 tablespoon oil. Taste and adjust salt and garlic. Refrigerate until ready to serve.

ADVANCE PREPARATION: Don't make this too far ahead, because the cucumbers will continue to release water into the *tzatziki* and the bright flavors will fade.

TURKISH CUCUMBER AND YOGURT SALAD (Cacik)
Turkey • **Serves 4**

Cacik is the Turkish cousin of the Greek *tzatziki* (above). It can be served as a soup or as a salad. In Turkey, it traditionally accompanies meat. I think it's irresistible on its own, or as an accompaniment to pilaf.

> 1 English cucumber or 3 Persian cucumbers, finely chopped
>
> Salt
>
> 2 cups drained yogurt (page 21)
>
> 2 to 3 garlic cloves (to taste), mashed in a mortar and pestle with ¼ teaspoon salt
>
> 2 to 4 tablespoons (to taste) chopped fresh mint
>
> Freshly ground pepper

1. Toss the cucumber with a generous amount of salt and drain in a colander in the sink for 15 minutes. Rinse and drain on paper towels.

2. Mix together the yogurt, garlic, mint, and salt and pepper to taste. Stir in the cucumber. Adjust seasonings and serve.

VARIATIONS

● Substitute dill for the mint.

● Add ¼ to ½ cup finely chopped walnuts.

● Add 1 tablespoon fresh lemon juice.

● Substitute 2 hearts of romaine lettuce, cut in chiffonade (crosswise slivers), for the cucumber.

● To serve as a soup, place a couple of ice cubes in each of 4 bowls. If you wish, thin out the cucumber-yogurt mixture with a little water, and spoon into the bowls.

MARINATED EGGPLANT
Italy • **Serves 4 to 6**

The Italians can turn any vegetable into a refreshing appetite-whetter. This dish, meant to be part of an antipasto platter, is one of the simpler Mediterranean eggplant dishes. The eggplant is cooked briefly in salted boiling water, then tossed with vinegar, salt, olive oil, and garlic. It's one of the few Mediterranean eggplant dishes wherein the eggplant isn't fried or grilled.

Salt

1 large eggplant (1 to 1½ pounds), cut into 1-inch cubes

2 tablespoons white wine vinegar or red wine vinegar

1 garlic clove, minced

½ teaspoon dried oregano

Freshly ground pepper

⅓ cup extra virgin olive oil

1. Bring a large pot of water to a boil. Salt it generously and drop in the eggplant. Reduce the heat and simmer for 5 to 10 minutes, until the eggplant is cooked through but still holds its shape. Using a slotted spoon or skimmer, transfer to a bowl of cold water, then drain well. Place the eggplant on a few layers of paper towels and pat dry.

2. In a bowl, mix together the vinegar, garlic, oregano, and salt and pepper to taste. Add the cooked eggplant and toss to coat. Cover and refrigerate for 1 hour.

3. Shortly before serving, remove from the refrigerator and toss with the olive oil. Serve at room temperature with toothpicks.

ADVANCE PREPARATION: The marinated eggplant will keep for about a week in the refrigerator.

VARIATION

In Step 3, add 1 tablespoon capers, drained and rinsed; 1 tablespoon slivered fresh basil or 2 teaspoons chopped fresh mint; and 1 roasted red bell pepper, cut in strips or squares. Toss with the eggplant, along with the olive oil, just before serving.

SAUTÉED EGGPLANT WITH TOMATOES AND BALSAMIC VINEGAR

Italy • **Serves 4 as a side dish or 6 to 8 as an antipasto**

I ate this sweet and pungent eggplant dish in Puglia, at a farm restaurant high up in the Gargano hills above the Adriatic. Of the many Italian eggplant antipasti, this is one of my favorites.

1 large eggplant, cut into 1-inch dice

8 cups water

Salt

2 tablespoons extra virgin olive oil

1 small onion, sliced

4 garlic cloves, minced

Freshly ground pepper

1 tablespoon balsamic vinegar

1 can (14 ounces) chopped tomatoes, with juice

4 fresh basil leaves, slivered

1. Place the eggplant in a large, wide bowl. Pour in the water, add ¼ cup salt, and stir together. Cover with a plate and place a weight, such as a can of tomatoes, on top of the plate to keep the eggplant submerged. Soak the eggplant in the salted water for 1 to 2 hours. Drain and pat dry.

2. Heat the oil in a large nonstick skillet over medium heat and add the onion. Cook, stirring often, until tender, about 5 minutes. Stir in the garlic and cook for 30 seconds to a minute, until fragrant. Add the eggplant and turn the heat to medium-high. Cook, stirring often, until the eggplant is browned and just about tender, about 10 minutes. Season with salt and pepper.

3. Add the balsamic vinegar and stir for a minute, then add the tomatoes. When the tomatoes begin to cook quickly, reduce the heat to medium. Cook, stirring often, for 10 minutes, until the tomatoes have cooked down a bit. Cover the pan, reduce the heat to medium-low, and continue to cook for another 5 to 10 minutes, until the eggplant is very tender and the mixture is thick. Taste and adjust seasonings. Stir in the basil.

4. Transfer to a serving dish. Cool slightly and serve. This is excellent at room temperature.

ADVANCE PREPARATION: This dish is even better the day after you make it, and it will keep very well for about 5 days in the refrigerator.

GRILLED EGGPLANT
WITH HOT RED PEPPER FLAKES

Italy • **Serves 6**

Small Japanese eggplants will be very sweet and tasty in this dish, but it's delicious with any eggplant. If you have a panini grill, use it here.

> 2 pounds eggplant, preferably Japanese
>
> 6 tablespoons extra virgin olive oil
>
> Salt
>
> ½ teaspoon hot red pepper flakes (more to taste)
>
> 2 tablespoons chopped fresh mint

1. Prepare a grill, or heat a panini grill or electric griddle.

2. Cut the eggplants into lengthwise slices about ¼ inch thick. Brush with olive oil, using about 4 tablespoons of the oil. Sprinkle with salt.

3. Grill the eggplant slices for 2 to 3 minutes on each side, until nicely browned and cooked through. (This will only take about 3 minutes in a panini grill.) Remove from the heat and toss with the remaining 2 tablespoons olive oil. Place in a bowl and cover tightly so that the eggplant will continue to soften. Leave for 15 minutes, then arrange on a platter and sprinkle with the red pepper flakes and mint. Taste, sprinkle with salt if desired, and serve.

ADVANCE PREPARATION: You can make this dish several hours before serving. The flavors will intensify. It keeps well and will continue to taste great for about 3 days.

MEZE

In the eastern and southern Mediterranean, beginning in Greece and moving clockwise around the Mediterranean basin, there is a class of foods, a way of eating, really, that stands alone. These are *meze* (also known as *mezza, meza, maza, mazza, mezethes, mezedes*), the "little foods" of the Greek, Turkish, and Arab table that are laid before guests not to open their appetites, as typical French hors d'oeuvres might do, but to feed them. They need to be fed primarily because they are guests; also because they are socializing with other people. They may be drinking ouzo or glasses of wine or beer, and people cannot do that without food; or they may be sitting down to a meal, and that meal will include, or be wholly defined by, *meze.*

The Greeks categorize certain *meze* as *kraso-mezedes*—which go with wine—and others as *ouzomezedes*—which go with ouzo. But in truth, most *meze* go with both, and they go well with beer, raki, arak, and mineral water as well. It's common to see people around a table late in the afternoon, shaded from the sun and deep in conversation, with a few plates of olives, feta, and cucumbers on the table; but I have also made many an evening meal of *meze* in Greek tavernas.

The word *meze* does not usually stand alone, but goes hand in hand with the word *table.* The *meze* table is an offering. It is not a first course, but a way of sharing small dishes of food with others. In Greece, the *meze* table might include several salads or dips, such as Tzatziki (page 106), Beet and Beet Greens Salad with Skordalia (page 94), and Split Pea Purée (page 123); a selection of fritters like Zucchini Fritters (page 130), some crisp baked phyllo triangles (pages 137 to 141), and some stuffed grape leaves (page 114). Or there might be something as simple as a plate of olives, some eggs, sliced feta, and sliced cucumber. In the Middle East, the *meze* table invariably includes Hummus (page 104), Baba Gannouj (page 110), Tabbouleh (page 96), and Fattoush (page 128).

For such little dishes, these foods have very big flavors. They are the dishes that most attract me to these cuisines. And for a vegetarian, they're definitely dishes to return to again and again.

EGGPLANT SLICES
WITH TOMATO SAUCE AND FETA
Greece • **Serves 4 to 6**

Sliced eggplant sprinkled with feta is standard taverna fare in Greece. I like it best when the slices are first topped with a tomato sauce. You can fry, roast, or grill the eggplant slices. My favorite method is using a panini grill. Frying in olive oil is the traditional Greek method.

> 1 medium or large eggplant, cut into ⅓-inch-thick slices
>
> Salt
>
> ¼ cup extra virgin olive oil
>
> 1½ cups Basic Tomato Sauce (page 78) or commercial marinara sauce
>
> ½ cup crumbled feta (about 3 ounces)
>
> 2 tablespoons chopped fresh flat-leaf parsley

1. Sprinkle the eggplant slices generously with salt and place in a colander to drain for 1 hour. Squeeze out water and pat dry with paper towels.

2. To roast the eggplant: Heat the oven to 425°F. Place the eggplant slices on an oiled baking sheet and brush with some of the olive oil. Bake for 20 minutes, or until lightly browned and soft all the way through. Remove from the heat.

To grill the eggplant: Heat a panini grill or an outdoor grill and brush the eggplant slices with olive oil on both sides. Grill for 2 to 3 minutes in a panini grill, 2 minutes on each side in an outdoor grill, or until tender.

3. Heat the broiler, with the rack at the lowest position. Place the eggplant in a shallow baking dish or on an ovenproof platter. Top with the tomato sauce and sprinkle on the feta. Drizzle on the remaining olive oil and place under the broiler for about 1 minute, until the cheese begins to melt. Remove from the heat, sprinkle with the parsley, and serve.

ADVANCE PREPARATION: The eggplant slices can be cooked up to a day ahead. Hold in the refrigerator, covered.

ROASTED EGGPLANT SALAD
WITH FETA AND GREEN PEPPERS
Greece • **Serves 4 to 6**

The textures of the chopped pepper and red onion against the creamy chopped eggplant make this luscious dish unique among eggplant salads. This version has less oil and feta than the traditional Greek salad.

> 1½ pounds (about 2 medium) eggplants
>
> 2 tablespoons fresh lemon juice
>
> Salt and freshly ground pepper
>
> Pinch cayenne (optional)
>
> ¼ cup extra virgin olive oil
>
> 1 small or medium red onion, finely chopped and soaked for 5 to 10 minutes in cold water, then drained and rinsed
>
> 1 medium green bell pepper, finely chopped
>
> 1 medium tomato, peeled, seeded, and chopped
>
> 1 or 2 garlic cloves (to taste), minced or put through a press
>
> ½ cup crumbled feta (about 3 ounces)

1. Rinse the eggplants and pat dry. Prepare a medium-hot fire in a grill or heat the broiler. Broil or grill the eggplants about 6 inches from the heat, turning often, until the eggplants are soft and the skins are uniformly charred. Remove and place in a covered bowl until cool enough to handle.

2. Cut the eggplants in half lengthwise. Scoop the flesh out and discard the skins. Chop the eggplant, discarding as many seeds as you can, and place in a bowl. Add the lemon juice, salt, ground pepper, cayenne, and olive oil, and toss together. Add the onion, bell pepper, tomato, garlic, and feta, toss again, and serve.

ADVANCE PREPARATION: The eggplants can be roasted and tossed with the olive oil and lemon juice a day or two ahead.

GRILLED EGGPLANT PURÉE WITH MINT AND ALMONDS
Middle East • Serves 4

This is unlike any of the other Middle Eastern eggplant purées I've encountered. It's seasoned with fresh mint, lemon juice, and pomegranate syrup. Coarsely chopped almonds add marvelous texture. The pomegranate molasses adds a purplish tint to the purée and an unmistakable sweet and sour taste. If possible, serve the purée while still warm. I've based it on a recipe by Ghillie Basan from *Classic Turkish Cookery*.

- 1 pound eggplant (1 large or 2 long Japanese)
- 2 garlic cloves, mashed in a mortar and pestle with a generous pinch salt
- 3 tablespoons drained yogurt (page 21)
- 2 tablespoons fresh lemon juice
- 2 to 3 teaspoons (to taste) pomegranate molasses
- 2 to 3 tablespoons toasted almonds, coarsely chopped
- 2 to 4 tablespoons (to taste) finely chopped fresh mint, plus mint leaves for garnish
- Salt and freshly ground pepper
- Whole toasted almonds for garnish
- Flat bread or sliced baguette

1. Prepare a grill and grill the eggplant, turning every so often, until completely charred and softened. Alternatively, grill the eggplant over a gas flame or under a broiler, turning until uniformly charred and tender. Cool. When you can handle the eggplant, either cut in half lengthwise and scoop out the flesh, or simply lift off the skin and cut away the stem.

2. Purée the eggplant in a food processor fitted with the steel blade or in a bowl with a fork. Add the garlic, yogurt, lemon juice, molasses, chopped almonds, and chopped mint, and mix together. Add salt and pepper, taste and adjust seasonings.

3. Transfer to a serving bowl, garnish with almonds and mint, and serve with flat bread or sliced baguette.

ADVANCE PREPARATION: The purée is best served warm, but you can grill the eggplant several hours ahead and reheat it in a warm oven for about 20 minutes.

LEFTOVERS: Any leftovers are good for a few days.

BABA GANNOUJ
Middle East • Serves 6

Baba gannouj is *the* signature Middle Eastern eggplant purée, and is now well known in the United States. It's rarely absent on a *meze* table, and with reason. The mixture of smoky grilled eggplant and tahini is addictive.

- 2 pounds eggplants (2 large or 3 medium)
- ¼ cup fresh lemon juice (more to taste)
- ¼ cup tahini, stirred if oil has separated
- 2 garlic cloves, peeled
- ¾ teaspoon salt
- Extra virgin olive oil
- Chopped fresh flat-leaf parsley
- Imported black olives
- Pomegranate seeds (optional)
- Warm Arab bread

EGGPLANT AND SMOKE

Eggplant has more of an affinity for smoke than any other vegetable. Mediterranean cooks understand this, and from Greece to Morocco you'll find wonderful grilled eggplant dishes. The eggplant is grilled until it blackens and collapses, by which time the flesh is infused with the smoke from the coals that cooked it. The vegetable is then peeled and mashed into a moist purée. Garlic and olive oil always come into the picture, but what happens next is a function of where you are. A Greek will take mashed roasted eggplant and toss it with chopped peppers, tomatoes, red onions, and feta. A Turk will add thick yogurt and mint, maybe finely chopped almonds, whereas a Lebanese or Syrian cook will blend the eggplant with tahini for baba gannouj.

EGGPLANT: TO SALT OR NOT TO SALT

The notion that eggplant must be salted before cooking to draw out the bitter juices has been handed down from mother to daughter, cook to cook, for generations. But according to Russ Parsons, produce expert extraordinaire, eggplant is not bitter ("... even though," as he says in his latest book, *How to Pick a Peach*, "they have every right to be after everything that has been said about them."). But salting eggplants does make a difference if you're frying them: Because the salt pulls water out of the cells, the eggplants absorb oil more easily during cooking, resulting in the wonderful creamy texture that makes fried eggplant so enjoyable.

1. To grill the eggplant: Prepare a hot gas or charcoal grill. Pierce the eggplants in several places with a fork and place over the hot coals. Grill until blackened all over.

To roast the eggplant: Place on a foil-covered baking sheet and roast in a 425°F oven for 35 to 45 minutes, until thoroughly tender. The flavor of the baba gannouj will not be as smoky.

2. Place the grilled eggplant in a colander in the sink to cool and drain. Peel and discard the black skins, cut off the stems, and let the eggplants sit in the colander for another 15 to 30 minutes.

3. Purée the eggplant in a food processor fitted with the steel blade. Stir together the lemon juice and tahini. In a mortar and pestle, mash the garlic to a paste with the salt. Add the tahini-lemon mixture and the garlic paste to the food processor and blend with the eggplant. If the mixture is too thick, thin out with a little water. Taste and adjust salt.

4. Mound the purée on a platter, and drizzle on some olive oil. Sprinkle with parsley, olives, and pomegranate seeds. Serve with Arab bread.

ADVANCE PREPARATION: The baba gannouj can be made several hours ahead.

GRILLED EGGPLANT AND PEPPER SALAD

Morocco • Serves 4

I ate this salad often in Morocco, and never tired of it. It's utterly simple. The flavors come from the grilling and the vegetables themselves. It's best if you can find narrow Japanese eggplants for this.

- 2 pounds Japanese eggplants
- 2 medium green bell peppers
- 6 mildly hot red chile peppers, such as Anaheims
- Salt
- 2 tablespoons fresh lemon or lime juice
- 2 to 4 tablespoons extra virgin olive oil
- 1 teaspoon mashed garlic (1 plump clove; optional)

1. Heat the broiler or prepare a hot grill. Pierce the eggplants in several places with the tip of a knife. If broiling, line a baking sheet with foil and place close to the flame. Broil or grill the eggplants, bell peppers, and chile peppers, turning them every 4 to 5 minutes, until blackened all over and soft. The hot peppers will be done first, then the bell peppers, then the eggplants. Remove the peppers as they are done, place in a bowl, and cover tightly with plastic or with a plate. Let sit for 20 to 30 minutes. When the eggplants are done, transfer to a colander set in the sink and drain for 30 minutes.

2. Peel and seed the peppers, then cut into small dice. Peel, stem, and chop the eggplant. Toss with the peppers. Add salt to taste, the lemon juice, olive oil, and optional garlic. Stir together well.

VARIATIONS

TUNISIAN FLAVORS: Add a couple of tablespoons chopped cilantro and/or parsley. Season with ½ teaspoon crushed or ground cumin seeds.

TURKISH FLAVORS: Add a couple of tablespoons of chopped fresh mint and/or dill.

FARRO SALAD
France • Serves 4

In Provence, this is made with *épautre,* which is closer to farro than to wheat berries. But wheat berries will do if you can't get farro. It's a great, substantial salad to keep on hand in the refrigerator.

    1 cup farro or wheat berries, rinsed

    4 cups water

    Salt

    ⅓ cup fresh lemon juice

    4 medium tomatoes, cut into small dice

    1 medium cucumber, peeled, seeded, and cut
        into small dice

    1 medium red bell pepper, diced

    1 medium green bell pepper, diced

    ⅓ cup extra virgin olive oil

    1 to 2 tablespoons chopped fresh mint

    3 tablespoons chopped fresh flat-leaf parsley

    Freshly ground pepper

1. Combine the farro with the water in a saucepan and bring to a boil. Add 1 teaspoon salt, reduce the heat, cover, and simmer until the farro is tender, 30 to 40 minutes, stirring from time to time. (Wheat berries will probably take 45 to 60 minutes.) Remove from the heat and allow the grains to swell in the cooking water for 10 minutes, then drain.

2. Toss the farro with the lemon juice. Add the tomatoes, cucumber, bell peppers, olive oil, mint, parsley, and salt and pepper to taste. Refrigerate until ready to serve, or serve at once.

ADVANCE PREPARATION: This salad keeps well for several hours in the refrigerator. Once cooked, the farro will keep for 3 or 4 days in the refrigerator.

GIANT FAVAS WITH MINT
Spain • Serves 6

This is a classic Spanish tapa, but one I'd never had before reveling in it at Bar Pilar, a famous tapas bar in Valencia. You can find dried fava beans, the ones with the brown skins, in Middle Eastern markets, where you are also bound to find mint by the bundle. The idea here is to savor the beans one by one: Squeeze the bean out of the skin and into your mouth, and dip chunks of bread into the luscious, minty broth.

    1 pound dried fava beans, with skins, soaked
        in water to cover for 6 hours or overnight
        and drained

    1 onion, chopped

    4 garlic cloves, minced

    8 cups water

    1 generous bunch fresh mint

    Salt

    2 tablespoons chopped fresh mint for garnish

1. Put the beans in a bean pot or Dutch oven. Add the onion, garlic, and water. Bring to a boil, reduce the heat, and simmer for 1 hour. Add the bunch of mint and a generous amount of salt, 2 to 3 teaspoons, and continue to simmer for another hour, until the beans are tender and delicious.

2. Set a colander over a bowl and drain the beans. Remove the mint sprigs and place the beans in an earthenware baking dish or casserole. Return the broth to a saucepan and bring to a boil. Reduce until thick and fragrant. Taste and adjust seasonings. Pour over the beans, sprinkle on the chopped fresh mint, and serve.

ADVANCE PREPARATION: The prepared favas will keep for about 5 days in the refrigerator. Reheat gently.

FRESH FAVA BEAN PURÉE
Morocco • **Makes about 2 cups**

This is much like a fava bean version of hummus. Springtime in Los Angeles sees me running to the market every week to buy fava beans. Shelling and skinning them takes time, but it is so worth the effort. This is the kind of dish you might want to make when you have some friends around to help skin the beans. Then again, it is just the sort of fava bean preparation that will not suffer from being made with frozen double-shelled favas.

> 3 pounds fresh fava beans, shelled, or ½ pound frozen double-shelled favas, thawed
>
> 2 garlic cloves, mashed with ¾ teaspoon salt to a paste in a mortar and pestle
>
> 1 teaspoon freshly ground cumin seeds
>
> 1 tablespoon fresh lemon juice (more to taste)
>
> ¼ cup plus 1 tablespoon extra virgin olive oil
>
> Salt
>
> Black olives and/or small cherry tomatoes
>
> Warm pita triangles

1. If you are using fresh favas: Bring a large pot of salted water to a boil. Fill a large bowl with ice water. Drop the shelled fava beans into the boiling water and boil for 5 minutes. Drain and transfer immediately to the cold water. Cool for several minutes, then use your thumbnail to open up the skin at the spot where the bean attached to the pod, then gently squeeze out the bean.

2. Place the beans in a food processor fitted with the steel blade. Add the garlic paste and cumin. With the machine running, add the lemon juice and ¼ cup of the olive oil in a slow stream. Process to a smooth purée. Scrape down the sides of the bowl and adjust seasoning. Add salt if desired.

3. Mound the purée onto a platter. Using a fork, make furrows down the sides of the purée. Drizzle the remaining 1 tablespoon olive oil over the top. Garnish with olives and/or tomatoes, and serve with warm triangles of pita bread.

ADVANCE PREPARATION: This purée will keep for 3 to 5 days in the refrigerator. The color will be less vivid after a day.

TAPAS

Tapas are the little foods of Spain that are served at bars from about noon until about 3 in the afternoon (before lunch), then again from about 7 to 10 at night (before dinner). In Spain people do not go out with the intention of dining on tapas (though that in fact is what sometimes happens). They go out to socialize, to have conversations, to flirt, to have a drink. Tapas originated in Andalusia, where sherry is made. There are different theories as to how the tradition came about, but it's my hunch that it came about because people needed to nibble on something while sipping the fortified wine.

A Spanish bar is a lively place, where people from all walks of life and of all ages congregate. They talk about everything under the sun while sipping sherry, or beer, or cava, or Basque white wine poured into small glasses from a flask raised high in the air. They may stand at the bar, eating mussels and dropping the shells on the floor, or sit at a table with a group of friends. Small plates of food are set out, and somehow the barman and the diners keep track of the tab. One category of tapas, called *pinchos,* are so called because they are served with a toothpick (*pinchar* means "to prick"). As you eat your tapas you leave the toothpick on the plate, and the barman counts up the toothpicks to figure your bill. Spanish tortillas (pages 176 to 179) are often cut into squares and served on toothpicks, as are little canapés. The two other categories of tapas are small finger foods (*cosas de picar*—"things to nibble") like olives and almonds; and hot, saucy foods that come in small earthenware casseroles, called *cazuelas.* Giant Favas with Mint (opposite) is just such a dish.

FAVA BEAN SALAD

Algeria • **Serves 4 to 6**

This is a lemony mix of fresh favas and herbs, either cilantro or parsley. Like most fava bean dishes, it's pretty addictive. Unless you have a bunch of friends to sit around shelling and skinning the beans with you—which can be a pleasant enough activity if you have a nice chilled bottle of rosé wine to sip as you work—it will be well worth your money to find frozen shelled and skinned fava beans.

6 pounds fresh fava beans, shelled and skinned (page 113); or 1 pound frozen double-shelled favas, thawed

1 cup water

Salt

4 tablespoons extra virgin olive oil

4 tablespoons chopped fresh cilantro or flat-leaf parsley

1 garlic clove, mashed to a paste with ¼ teaspoon salt in a mortar and pestle

3 tablespoons fresh lemon juice

¼ teaspoon paprika

Freshly ground pepper

A handful imported black olives

Place the fava beans in a saucepan or Dutch oven with the water and ½ teaspoon salt. Bring to a simmer, add 2 tablespoons of the olive oil, and simmer for 10 minutes, until the favas are just tender and most of the water has boiled off. Add 3 tablespoons of the cilantro, the garlic paste, lemon juice, paprika, and remaining 2 tablespoons olive oil. Cover and simmer for 3 to 5 minutes. The beans should be tender and fragrant with the seasonings. Transfer to a bowl, add pepper to taste, and adjust salt. Cool and serve, garnished with olives and the remaining 1 tablespoon cilantro.

ADVANCE PREPARATION: Although the color of the favas will fade, the salad will remain delicious for a few days in the refrigerator. If you want to get ahead, skin the favas up to 2 days ahead and keep in a covered bowl in the refrigerator.

GRAPE LEAVES STUFFED WITH RICE, ONIONS, AND HERBS (Dolmades)

Greece • **Makes about 36, serving 8**

Everybody loves *dolmades*, stuffed grape leaves. They are labor-intensive, so make them with friends. Once made, they'll last quite a while in the refrigerator, and can be pulled out at a moment's notice for an hors d'oeuvre to serve with drinks, a quick lunch, or a snack. The herbs inside the *dolmades*, and the lemon juice that saturates them as they cook, are the key here.

1 jar (16 ounces) grape leaves packed in brine

6 tablespoons extra virgin olive oil

1 large red or white onion, finely chopped

1 cup finely chopped scallions

2 to 3 garlic cloves (to taste), minced

1¼ cups long-grain rice, rinsed and drained

½ cup chopped fresh dill

⅓ cup finely chopped fresh mint

½ cup finely chopped fresh flat-leaf parsley

Salt and freshly ground pepper

Juice of 2 large lemons, strained

1 lemon, sliced

1. Carefully unroll the grape leaves and rinse well under cold water. Bring a large pot of water to a boil and blanch the leaves, a few at a time, for 2 to 3 minutes. Transfer to a bowl of cold water, then drain and rinse once more with cold water. Drain again and set aside.

2. Heat 2 tablespoons of the olive oil in a large nonstick skillet over medium-low heat and add the onion and scallions. Cook, stirring, until tender but not browned, 5 to 8 minutes. Add the garlic, stir, and add the rice. Stir for a minute or two, then remove from the heat. Toss with the herbs, salt (about 1 teaspoon), and pepper. Stir in 2 tablespoons olive oil.

3. Separate any torn grape leaves from the blanched leaves. Oil a wide, deep sauté pan or a pasta pot and line with a thin layer of the torn leaves.

4. Place a few grape leaves on your work surface, vein side up and with the stems facing you. Snip off the stems. Place about 2 teaspoons filling on the bottom center of each leaf. Fold the sides over, then roll up tightly, tucking in the sides as you go. Place seam side down in the pan, fitting them in snug layers. Drizzle on the remaining 2 tablespoons olive oil and pour on the lemon juice. Barely cover with water, and top with a layer of lemon slices.

5. Cover the *dolmades* with a round of parchment paper and place a plate over the paper to weight them during cooking (this will keep them from opening). Bring to a simmer, cover, and simmer over low heat for 45 minutes to 1 hour, until the grape leaves are tender and the rice is cooked. Remove from the heat and carefully remove the *dolmades* from the water with a slotted spoon or tongs. Drain on a rack set over a sheet pan. Serve warm or cold.

ADVANCE PREPARATION: The grape leaves will keep for a week in the refrigerator. Place them on a plate and cover tightly with plastic wrap, or store in a sealed plastic container.

WARM GOAT CHEESE SALAD
France • **Serves 6**

This classic salad made its way out of Provence and into the kitchens of goat cheese aficionados everywhere decades ago. There are different ways to heat the fresh rounds of goat cheese; my friend Christine breads the rounds and quickly fries them in a nonstick pan. I prefer to marinate the rounds in olive oil with herbs and place them in a high oven until they begin to bubble. You can cut the rounds from a log of goat cheese, or use hockey-puck-shaped disks and cut them horizontally in half to get ½-inch rounds. The important thing is to use goat cheese that is fresh and creamy, and not too tart. Mesclun—a mix of baby salad greens—is a traditional bed for the hot, luscious cheese, but I like to use frisée if I can find it.

12 rounds fresh goat cheese, about ½ inch thick

4 sprigs fresh thyme

¼ cup extra virgin olive oil

12 Crostini (page 135)

1 teaspoon fresh thyme leaves

½ teaspoon chopped fresh rosemary (optional)

Freshly ground pepper

2 heads frisée, leaves separated (about 5 cups); or 5 cups mixed baby lettuces

1 small bunch chervil (if available), stems trimmed; or 1 tablespoon chopped fresh herbs, such as parsley, tarragon, or chives

1 red bell pepper, very thinly sliced

½ cup Vinaigrette (page 82)

Small French radishes (optional)

1. Place the rounds of goat cheese in a baking dish in a single layer. Place the thyme sprigs on top and drizzle on the olive oil. Cover and set aside for 1 hour or longer, turning the disks from time to time.

2. Heat the oven to 425°F. Place the crostini on a baking sheet and top with the goat cheese. Sprinkle with thyme and rosemary, and grind on some pepper. Bake for 5 to 6 minutes, until the cheese is beginning to bubble.

3. Meanwhile, toss the frisée, chervil, and bell pepper in a bowl with the vinaigrette. Distribute among 6 salad plates. Top each salad with 2 goat cheese croutons, garnish if you wish with radishes, and serve.

ADVANCE PREPARATION: You can make the crostini a day in advance, and marinate the cheese for up to a day. The lettuce can be washed, dried, and held in plastic bags in the refrigerator overnight. The vinaigrette will keep for a week in the refrigerator.

HEARTS OF ROMAINE
AND TOMATO SALAD

Spain • **Serves 4**

I spent several days in Malàga with my close friend Christine Picasso, who founded the exquisite Museo Picasso in that city, birthplace of the painter, her father-in-law. We spent our days in the museum and our evenings at humble restaurants at the beach, where we ate grilled sardines, squid, and shrimp sprinkled with sea salt and drizzled with olive oil. This was always preceded by the simplest of salads, hearts of romaine and wedges of tomato arranged on a platter, doused with good Spanish olive oil and sherry vinegar, and sprinkled with coarse sea salt. We would regale ourselves with the salad and finish by sopping up the oil and vinegar with thick slices of country bread. Use a good-quality sea salt for this, or even better, fleur de sel.

> 4 hearts of romaine, quartered, washed, and dried
>
> 2 medium or 4 small tomatoes, cut into wedges
>
> 1 tablespoon sherry vinegar
>
> 3 to 5 tablespoons extra virgin olive oil (to taste)
>
> Coarse sea salt or fleur de sel

Arrange the hearts of romaine and the tomatoes on a platter. Whisk together the vinegar and olive oil and pour over the vegetables. Sprinkle liberally with the salt and serve.

ADVANCE PREPARATION: You can prep the vegetables hours ahead, but dress them just before serving.

VARIATION

Sprinkle the vegetables with minced fresh parsley, marjoram, or thyme leaves.

SHREDDED ROMAINE
AND RADISH SALAD

Turkey • **Serves 4**

This is a beautiful salad, with bits of pink radish peeking through the pale green romaine. Romaine lettuce, which is called *cos lettuce* in England, is said to come from the Greek island of Kos, and is one of the oldest varieties of cultivated lettuce.

> 1 large head romaine lettuce, or 2 hearts of romaine, leaves separated
>
> 1 bunch scallions, white and light green parts only, finely chopped
>
> 8 red radishes, cut in half lengthwise, then sliced into half-moons
>
> 1 tablespoon chopped fresh dill
>
> 2 tablespoons fresh lemon juice, or 1 tablespoon lemon juice and 1 tablespoon red wine vinegar or sherry vinegar
>
> ⅓ cup extra virgin olive oil
>
> 1 garlic clove, minced or put through a press (optional)
>
> Salt and freshly ground pepper
>
> A handful imported black olives

1. Wash and dry the lettuce leaves, stack, and seal tightly in a zipper bag. Refrigerate for 1 hour, until very crisp. Cut the stacked leaves crosswise into ½-inch slivers. Place in a salad bowl with the scallions, radishes, and dill.

2. Mix together the lemon juice, olive oil, garlic, and salt and pepper to taste. Just before serving, stir again and toss with the salad. Garnish with olives and serve.

ADVANCE PREPARATION: The lettuce and radishes can be all ready to toss and refrigerated for hours before serving.

LEFTOVERS: I would not normally recommend day-old salad, and certainly not for a dinner party. But personally, I think this becomes a nice new kind of slaw, seasoned with the dill, and I enjoy eating it for dinner the night after I've made it.

SALAD WITH WARM GOAT CHEESE AND BASIL SAUCE
France • Serves 4

This warm goat cheese salad is one of the most renowned of the many wonderful toast traditions in Provence. It boasts a sort of liquid pesto that is drizzled onto the warm cheese just before serving the salad. The basil in Provence tends to be the small-leafed variety, which has a more peppery flavor than the larger, sweeter Genoese basil.

- A generous handful basil leaves
- ½ cup extra virgin olive oil
- 4 slices country bread, toasted and rubbed with a cut garlic clove
- 4 (¾-inch-thick) slices goat cheese from a log; or 2 round goat cheeses, each cut in half horizontally
- 1 large or 2 small heads leaf lettuce, or 5 cups mixed baby salad greens
- 2 tablespoons fresh lemon juice
- Salt and freshly ground pepper

1. In a mortar and pestle, mash the basil and work in enough of the olive oil, about ¼ cup, to make a runny paste. Let sit for about 1 hour.

2. Heat the oven to 450°F. Place the toast on a baking sheet and top with the rounds of goat cheese. Bake until the cheese begins to melt and bubble, about 8 minutes. Drizzle on enough of the basil paste to coat.

3. Place the lettuce in a bowl. Whisk together the lemon juice, remaining oil, and salt and pepper to taste, and toss with the lettuce. Distribute among 4 plates. Place a cheese toast on each salad and serve.

ADVANCE PREPARATION: You can make the basil paste and the dressing hours before you serve the salad. Hold at room temperature.

LEEKS COOKED IN WHITE WINE
Croatia and Bulgaria • Serves 4 to 6

I've had plenty of forgettable leeks à la vinaigrette in France, but this dish will make anyone who feels so-so about leeks pay attention to the vegetable. I like to serve this heavenly mixture of leeks, olive oil, wine, and garlic as a starter.

- 6 medium leeks (about 2½ pounds)
- Salt
- 2 tablespoons extra virgin olive oil
- 1 cup dry white wine, such as pinot grigio or sauvignon blanc
- Freshly ground pepper
- 4 large garlic cloves, minced
- 2 tablespoons chopped fresh flat-leaf parsley
- A handful imported black olives

1. Cut the ends and the dark green leaves off the leeks, then cut the leeks in half lengthwise. Place in a bowl of cold water for 10 minutes, then run under the faucet to remove any sand that may be lingering in between the layers. Cut into 2-inch pieces.

2. Bring a saucepan of water to a boil. Add a teaspoon of salt and the leeks. Parboil for 2 minutes and drain.

3. Spoon the olive oil into a wide nonreactive skillet and place the leeks in the skillet in an even layer. Pour in the wine, add ½ teaspoon salt, pepper to taste, and the garlic. Bring to a boil, cover, and reduce the heat to low. Simmer for 30 to 45 minutes, until the leeks are very tender but still intact and most of the liquid has evaporated.

4. Remove from the heat and allow the leeks to cool in the juices left in the pan. Transfer to a serving dish. Taste and adjust seasonings. Sprinkle on the parsley, garnish with olives, and serve.

ADVANCE PREPARATION: The leeks will keep for a day or two in the refrigerator. Reheat or bring to room temperature before serving.

MESCLUN SALAD
France • **Serves 4**

Mesclun salad goes by the name spring greens or mixed baby lettuces in this country. It is widely available, which is a wonderful thing. What isn't so wonderful is that most restaurants dress these delicate greens with super-sweet balsamic dressing, drowning out the wonderful nuances of all the different young lettuces and herbs. A touch of balsamic is okay; it contrasts nicely with the bitterness of some of the lettuces. But I do mean a touch. Also, you don't want to drown your delicate leaves in dressing, which is why there isn't much of it here. If you can get your hands on some chervil for this, you will create a salad with the real taste of a Niçoise mesclun salad.

- 1 tablespoon red wine vinegar or sherry vinegar
- ¾ teaspoon balsamic vinegar (optional)
- 1 small garlic clove, minced or put through a press (optional)
- Salt and freshly ground pepper
- ¼ cup extra virgin olive oil
- 5 to 6 ounces mixed baby salad greens
- A handful fresh herbs (such as chervil, tarragon, parsley, and/or chives), chopped

Whisk together the vinegars, garlic, and salt and pepper to taste in a bowl or measuring cup. Whisk in the olive oil. Toss with the greens and herbs just before serving.

ADVANCE PREPARATION: You can make the dressing as far ahead as a day or two. In that case, instead of crushing or pressing your garlic, cut it into slivers without cutting through the root end, and marinate it in the dressing. Then remove it before tossing the salad.

PURSLANE SALAD
Greece • **Serves 4 to 6**

Purslane—a succulent with small, almost juicy leaves and thick stems—is a popular salad green in the eastern Mediterranean. It's a healthy superfood, packed with phytochemicals and vitamins, and it has a marvelous texture and flavor. I wish it were more available here; I find it from time to time in the farmers' market, and rush home to make this salad, which is inspired by one I ate in Greece, at Popy's taverna on Ikaria.

- 1 generous bunch purslane, thick stems cut away (about 4 cups)
- 1 small cucumber, chopped
- ¼ cup kalamata olives, pitted and chopped
- 1 tablespoon red wine vinegar or white wine vinegar
- 2 tablespoons fresh lemon juice
- 1 or 2 garlic cloves (to taste), minced or put through a press
- ½ cup extra virgin olive oil
- Salt and freshly ground pepper
- 1 tablespoon brine from the olives (optional)

Toss together the purslane, cucumber, and olives. Whisk together the vinegar, lemon juice, garlic, olive oil, and salt and pepper to taste. If desired, whisk in 1 tablespoon of the brine from the olives. Toss with the salad and serve.

ADVANCE PREPARATION: This salad can be assembled and refrigerated for several hours. Toss just before serving.

LEFTOVERS: Due to the succulent nature of the purslane, leftovers won't get too soggy.

SUMMER SALAD
Greece • Serves 6

From the Adriatic shores of Croatia through the Greek mainland and out through the islands, this is the summer salad par excellence. It's also the salad I make daily throughout my California summer. I have a generous tomato garden full of heirlooms—which are ripe from the end of June through September—and wonderful farmers' markets for peppers, onions, and delicate Persian cucumbers. In Greece, sometimes the oil and vinegar are given to you to administer, sometimes the salad has already been doused.

- 1 small red onion, cut into half-moons
- 2 tablespoons plus 2 teaspoons red wine vinegar or sherry vinegar
- 5 medium or large ripe tomatoes, cut into wedges, and if large, the wedges cut in half crosswise
- ½ English cucumber, or 1 Persian cucumber, or 1 regular cucumber, peeled if thick-skinned or waxed, cut in half lengthwise, then sliced into half-moons about ⅓ inch thick
- 1 large green or yellow bell pepper, seeded and cut into strips or rings
- 4 ounces feta, cut into 1-inch squares or crumbled
- Salt and freshly ground pepper
- 6 tablespoons extra virgin olive oil
- 2 to 3 tablespoons chopped fresh mint or 1 teaspoon dried oregano
- 12 to 18 imported Greek black olives, such as kalamatas or Amphissas

1. Place the onion in a bowl and cover with cold water. Add 2 teaspoons of the vinegar and let sit for 10 to 15 minutes or up to 1 hour. Drain and rinse.

TIP RAW ONIONS
Soaking raw onions in water, sometimes with a little vinegar, then rinsing them, will wash away some of the acrid flavor that remains in your mouth for hours after you've eaten them. I use this technique for salsas and all sorts of dishes that call for raw onions.

2. Toss together the onion, tomatoes, cucumber, and bell pepper. Add the feta and toss again. Season with salt and pepper to taste. Add the oil, the remaining 2 tablespoons vinegar, and the herbs, and toss again. Taste, adjust the seasonings, sprinkle on the olives, and serve.

ADVANCE PREPARATION: You can assemble the salad hours before adding the seasonings, vinegar, and olive oil. If you salt the salad too long before serving, it will become watery as the salt draws out the juices from the vegetables.

VARIATIONS

In Croatia, this salad might include a few hot chiles, such as serranos, roasted and cut into strips or chopped. Chopped parsley might also be included, and the bell peppers are sometimes roasted.

LENTIL SALAD
Egypt • Serves 6

I was introduced to this salad by my friend and colleague Clifford Wright, and it is one of my favorite lentil preparations. The lentils are seasoned with lots of garlic, ground cumin, ground coriander, ground cardamom, and ground fenugreek, and the spices have an almost Indian flavor. The trick is not to overcook the lentils, so that they stay al dente. I've adapted this recipe from Cliff's, published in *Little Foods of the Mediterranean*.

- 5 tablespoons extra virgin olive oil
- 2 to 3 large garlic cloves (to taste), minced or put through a press
- ¾ teaspoon freshly ground cumin seeds
- ¾ teaspoon freshly ground coriander seeds
- ¼ teaspoon freshly ground cardamom seeds
- ½ teaspoon ground fenugreek seeds
- 1½ cups brown or green lentils, picked over and rinsed
- Salt and freshly ground pepper
- 2 tablespoons chopped fresh cilantro
- 1 tablespoon lemon juice (optional; more to taste)

1. Combine 3 tablespoons of the olive oil and the garlic in a small frying pan or saucepan over medium heat. When the garlic begins to sizzle, add the spices. Stir together for about 30 seconds, then remove from the heat and set aside.

2. Place the lentils in a medium saucepan, cover by 1 inch with water, and bring to a boil. Add 1 teaspoon salt, reduce the heat, and cook just until the lentils are al dente, about 25 minutes. Drain and toss at once with the garlic and spices, pepper to taste, cilantro, and lemon juice if desired. Taste and adjust salt. Transfer to a serving platter, drizzle the remaining 2 tablespoons olive oil over the top, and serve warm or at room temperature.

ADVANCE PREPARATION: This keeps for 4 days in the refrigerator. Warm and drizzle on more olive oil before serving.

MUSHROOMS IN GARLIC SAUCE
(Mushrooms al Ajillo)
Spain • **Serves 4**

This is one of my favorite tapas. It comes in several renditions. In southern Spain, the mushrooms might be spiced with chile pepper, and sliced before cooking. At tapas bars in Madrid, the sauce might be thickened with flour and the mushrooms left whole. I like to leave the mushrooms whole or cut them in half or quarters if large. You can serve them from plates with toothpicks, but they also make a very nice side dish.

> 2 tablespoons extra virgin olive oil
>
> 3 garlic cloves, minced
>
> 1 small dried red chile, crumbled, or ¼ to ½ teaspoon hot red pepper flakes
>
> 1½ pounds button mushrooms, wiped clean, stems trimmed, and cut in half or quarters, if large
>
> Salt
>
> ½ cup dry white wine or fino sherry
>
> Freshly ground pepper
>
> 1 tablespoon fresh lemon juice
>
> 2 tablespoons chopped fresh flat-leaf parsley

Heat the oil in a large, heavy nonstick skillet over medium heat and add the garlic and red chile. When the garlic begins to sizzle, after about 30 seconds, add the mushrooms and sprinkle with salt. Cook, stirring, until the mushrooms begin to release liquid, 3 to 5 minutes, then add the white wine. Continue to cook over medium heat, stirring from time to time, until the liquid has just about evaporated, 5 to 10 minutes. Season with salt and pepper, stir in the lemon juice and parsley, and remove from the heat. Serve hot or warm.

ADVANCE PREPARATION: You can make these a day ahead and reheat. Add the parsley and lemon juice when you reheat.

MARINATED MUSHROOMS
Italy • **Serves 4 to 6**

Marinated mushrooms are always a pleasing item on an antipasto platter. I like to fill a bowl with these and place them on the coffee table with other nibbles, like olives, toasted almonds, radishes, and marinated carrots (page 99); they always disappear before dinner is served.

> ⅔ cup extra virgin olive oil
>
> ½ cup water
>
> ⅓ cup fresh lemon juice
>
> 2 tablespoons sherry vinegar or champagne vinegar
>
> 1 bay leaf
>
> 2 garlic cloves, crushed
>
> 6 whole black peppercorns
>
> ½ teaspoon salt
>
> 1 pound small mushrooms, cleaned, stems trimmed

1. In a large nonreactive skillet or wide saucepan, combine the olive oil, water, lemon juice, vinegar, bay leaf, garlic, peppercorns, and salt, and bring to a boil. Reduce the heat, cover, and simmer for 15 minutes. Strain through a sieve set over a bowl, then return the strained marinade to the pan. Bring back to a simmer over medium-low heat and add the mushrooms. Simmer, turning the mush-

rooms over once or twice, for 5 minutes, until just cooked through. Turn off the heat and allow the mushrooms to cool in the marinade.

2. Transfer the mushrooms with the marinade to a stainless-steel bowl, cover, and refrigerate for 1 hour or more.

3. To serve, remove from the marinade with a slotted spoon, place in a serving bowl or on a platter, and have toothpicks and napkins close by.

ADVANCE PREPARATION: You can make these 3 to 4 days ahead.

VARIATION

Sprinkle the mushrooms with chopped fresh herbs, such as parsley, chervil, or marjoram, when you serve them.

MUSHROOM AND CELERY SALAD
Italy • **Serves 4**

I've been making this salad for years, long before I learned that it's popular in the Veneto region. I made it whenever I had a bunch of celery languishing in the refrigerator—almost instinctively. The combination of textures is wonderful.

In Italy, this would be made with a wild mushroom called *ovuli,* which describes their size and shape (egglike). Creminis will be fine. It's best to use the inner stalks of celery for this salad.

- ½ pound cremini mushrooms, cleaned, stems trimmed, and very thinly sliced
- 4 celery stalks, from the heart of the celery, very thinly sliced
- 2 tablespoons chopped fresh flat-leaf parsley
- Salt and freshly ground pepper
- 2 tablespoons fresh lemon juice
- ⅓ cup extra virgin olive oil
- 2 ounces shaved Parmesan

Toss together the mushrooms, celery, and parsley. Salt and pepper generously. Mix together the lemon juice and olive oil, and toss with the vegetables. Just before serving, toss again with the Parmesan.

ADVANCE PREPARATION: The salad can be assembled hours before tossing with the dressing and the Parmesan.

VARIATION

For a truly luxurious salad, add 1 white truffle, shaved. Reduce the lemon juice to 1 tablespoon.

TAPENADE
France • **Makes about 1½ cups**

This isn't quite an authentic tapenade because it doesn't contain the anchovies that season so many Provençal dishes. If you eat anchovies, add about 4 fillets, well rinsed, along with the olives. But if you don't, you won't miss them.

The dish is a signature of Provence, made with the fleshy Nyons olives that grow in the northern part of the region. Nyons olives are hard to find here, so look for a dark black olive with a moist, not too salty flesh. I find kalamatas a little too metallic tasting. Amphissa olives from Greece are the closest in texture, though they are a light color and don't make as pretty a tapenade as the dark black olives make. If you can't find Amphissas, use any black olives from France or North Africa.

- 2 large garlic cloves, cut in half
- ½ pound imported black olives (see the headnote), pitted
- 1½ tablespoons capers, drained and rinsed
- 1 teaspoon fresh thyme leaves (or ½ teaspoon dried)
- 1 teaspoon chopped fresh rosemary (or ½ teaspoon dried)
- 1 teaspoon Dijon mustard
- 2 tablespoons fresh lemon juice
- 2 tablespoons extra virgin olive oil
- Freshly ground black pepper (lots)
- Chopped fresh rosemary or thyme for garnish

Turn on a food processor fitted with the steel blade and drop in the garlic. When it is chopped and adhering to the sides of the bowl, turn off the processor and scrape down the sides of the bowl. Add the olives, capers, thyme, rosemary, and mustard, and purée until fairly smooth. Add the lemon juice, olive oil, and pepper, and process until you have a smooth paste. Scrape into an attractive serving bowl, garnish with herbs, and serve.

ADVANCE PREPARATION: This keeps for 2 weeks in the refrigerator.

VARIATIONS

GREEN OLIVE TAPENADE: Substitute imported green olives for the black olives.

GREEN OLIVE AND ALMOND TAPENADE: Substitute 1¼ cups green olives and ¼ cup blanched almonds for the black olives. Grind the almonds along with the olives.

 **TIP** PITTING OLIVES
I find the easiest way to do this is to lay a few at a time on my work surface and crush them with the flat side of a knife. Then pull the pit out. You can also use a cherry pitter, but I think the knife method is more efficient. Be sure to throw away the pits, and not to put them in with the olives.

ORANGE AND OLIVE SALAD
North Africa • Serves 6

The first time I had this salad I was in Provence, not Tunisia or Morocco (though I subsequently ate the salad in North Africa). Lulu Peyraud, proprietress of the famous Bandol winery Domaine Tempier, served it to me and a dozen others at a lunch for the grape pickers. Lulu is an exceptional Provençal cook, but she's interested in all good food from the Mediterranean. She served this with a squid ragout. In North Africa, it would be one of several small dishes served at the beginning of a feast.

> 8 navel oranges, peeled, white pith removed, and sliced
>
> ½ cup imported black olives, pitted and halved
>
> 1 red onion, sliced very thin and soaked for 10 minutes in water with 1 teaspoon vinegar

> 3 tablespoons fresh lemon juice
>
> ½ to 1 teaspoon freshly ground cumin seeds (to taste)
>
> Salt and freshly ground pepper
>
> 6 tablespoons extra virgin olive oil

1. Line a platter or a wide bowl with the orange slices. Scatter the olives over the oranges. Drain the onion and distribute over the oranges.

2. Whisk together the lemon juice, cumin, salt, pepper, and olive oil. Pour over the oranges and serve.

ADVANCE PREPARATION: You can assemble the platter several hours before you dress and serve the salad.

BLACK-EYED PEA SALAD
Greece • Serves 4 to 6

According to Greek food writer Diane Kochilas, the Greeks love black-eyed peas, at least those who have no memory of World War II, when for many they were the only food around. This recipe, funnily enough, is much like a Southwestern black-eyed pea salad that I make every year for New Year's Day good luck.

> 1½ cups black-eyed peas
>
> 1 bay leaf
>
> Salt
>
> 6 tablespoons extra virgin olive oil
>
> 1 small red bell pepper, diced
>
> 2 plump garlic cloves, minced
>
> 1 teaspoon cumin seeds, lightly crushed in a mortar
>
> ¼ teaspoon mustard seeds
>
> 1 red onion, halved, sliced, soaked for 10 minutes in water with 1 teaspoon vinegar, then drained and rinsed (optional)
>
> 2 tablespoons chopped fresh dill (more to taste)
>
> 2 tablespoons chopped fresh flat-leaf parsley
>
> 2 tablespoons red wine vinegar
>
> Freshly ground pepper

1. Place the beans in a pot with the bay leaf and cover with water by 2 to 3 inches. Bring to a boil, reduce the heat, and simmer gently for 30 minutes. Add 1 teaspoon salt and continue to simmer gently until tender but not mushy, another 15 to 20 minutes. Drain through a colander set over a bowl. Transfer the black-eyed peas to a salad bowl. Discard the bay leaf

2. Meanwhile, heat a medium skillet over medium-high heat and add 2 tablespoons of the oil. When it is hot, add the bell pepper and cook, stirring often, until just crisp-tender, 2 to 3 minutes. Add the garlic, cumin seeds, and mustard seeds, and stir together for another minute or two, until the garlic is fragrant. Remove from the heat and toss with the black-eyed peas. Cool to room temperature, or chill.

3. Just before serving, add the onion, dill, parsley, vinegar, the remaining 4 tablespoons olive oil, and pepper to taste, and toss together. Taste and adjust seasonings. Add some broth from the beans if you want the mixture to be moister.

ADVANCE PREPARATION: You can make the dish through Step 2 up to 3 days before you wish to serve. Keep well covered in the refrigerator. Proceed with Step 3 shortly before serving.

VARIATION

BLACK-EYED PEA SALAD WITH FETA: This makes the dish a little more substantial. Before serving, crumble 2 to 3 ounces feta over the top of the salad.

SPLIT PEA PURÉE (Fava)

Greece • Serves 6 as a *meze* or 4 as a more substantial dish

This is known as *fava* in Greece, even though it's made with yellow split peas. But it does in fact resemble the purée of split fava beans that you find all over Puglia, in Italy. *Fava* needs time—you need to cook the split peas until they fall apart and thicken, then let them settle for a while, to get a thick purée, which you'll top with chopped onion, a drizzle of olive oil, and a squeeze of lemon juice (the classic topping)—or with a mixture of chopped tomato, scallions, capers, vinegar, and olive oil (as they do in Santorini). As usual, my version is not as rich as the authentic dish, being more sparse when it comes to the quantity of olive oil. But it's delicious nonetheless.

FOR THE PURÉE

4 tablespoons extra virgin olive oil

1 medium red onion, finely chopped

2 garlic cloves, minced or put through a press

1 heaped cup yellow split peas, rinsed and drained

1 bay leaf

Salt

1 to 2 tablespoons red wine vinegar (to taste)

FOR THE CLASSIC TOPPING

1 small red onion, thinly sliced or chopped, soaked for 5 to 10 minutes in cold water, then drained and rinsed

1 tablespoon extra virgin olive oil

Juice of ½ lemon

FOR THE SANTORINI TOPPING

3 scallions or 1 small onion, chopped, soaked for 5 to 10 minutes in cold water, then drained and rinsed

1 garlic clove, minced

1 large ripe tomato, finely chopped or grated on the large holes of a box grater

2 tablespoons capers (more to taste), rinsed and drained

2 tablespoons sherry vinegar

2 to 3 tablespoons extra virgin olive oil (to taste)

1. *Make the purée:* Heat 2 tablespoons of the olive oil in a heavy, medium casserole or saucepan over medium heat and add the onion. Cook, stirring, until tender, then add the garlic. Cook, stirring, until fragrant, about 30 seconds, and add the peas. Stir together to coat the split peas with oil, then add the bay leaf and enough water to cover by 2 inches. Bring to a boil. Reduce the heat, cover, and simmer for 1 hour. Add a generous amount of salt (1 to 2 teaspoons, to taste). Continue to simmer, uncovered, for another 30 minutes to 1 hour, until the split peas have broken down to a coarse purée. Turn off the heat, taste, and adjust the salt, and stir in the remaining 2 tablespoons olive oil and the vinegar. Place a towel over the pot and let sit until the peas have thickened into a stiff mass, about 1 hour. Mound onto a platter. Discard the bay leaf.

2. *If making the classic topping:* Scatter the scallions over the purée, drizzle on the olive oil and lemon juice, and serve.

If making the Santorini topping: Mix together the scallions, garlic, tomato, capers, vinegar, and olive oil. Spoon over the purée and serve.

ADVANCE PREPARATION: The *fava* will keep for 5 days in the refrigerator.

VARIATIONS

• You could also sprinkle this with, or stir in, a couple of tablespoons chopped or slivered mint leaves, oregano, marjoram, or parsley.

• You can make a cooked version of the Santorini topping: Heat 1 tablespoon of the oil in a medium skillet over medium heat and add the scallions. Cook, stirring, until tender, 3 to 5 minutes. Add the garlic and cook until fragrant. Add the tomato and cook, stirring, until it cooks down and thickens slightly, about 5 minutes. Stir in the capers, vinegar, remaining olive oil, and salt to taste. Remove from the heat. Spoon over the thickened split peas and drizzle with more olive oil if desired.

ROASTED PEPPER SALAD WITH LETTUCE AND TOMATO
Spain • **Serves 4**

I've never tasted red peppers sweeter than the piquillo peppers of Spain, but the thin-skinned red peppers called *lipstick peppers* that I can get at late-summer farmers' markets in Los Angeles, are

a close second. If you can get piquillos or lipstick peppers, I recommend them for this salad. Otherwise, use regular red bell peppers.

> 1½ pounds red or red and yellow peppers (see headnote), roasted and peeled (page 84)
>
> 2 tablespoons sherry vinegar
>
> 1 to 2 garlic cloves (to taste), minced or put through a press
>
> 6 tablespoons extra virgin olive oil
>
> Salt
>
> 1 small head leaf lettuce or romaine
>
> 1 pound tomatoes, cut into wedges

1. Cut the peppers into ½-inch strips. Mix together the vinegar, garlic, olive oil, and salt to taste. Toss half of the dressing with the peppers.

2. Tear the lettuce into bite-size pieces and toss with the tomatoes and remaining dressing. Line the outside rim of a platter or a wide bowl with the lettuce and tomatoes. Fill with the peppers. Serve at room temperature or slightly chilled.

ADVANCE PREPARATION: The roasted peppers will keep for about 5 days in the refrigerator, and for a week if you toss them with the dressing.

RED PEPPER PURÉE
The Balkans • **Makes about 1 cup**

Refugees from the countries that once made up Yugoslavia pine for *ajvar,* the red pepper relish that varies in heat from region to region, country to country. I can see why. Keep it on hand in the refrigerator to spread on croutons and panini.

> 2 pounds (4 large or 6 medium) fleshy red bell peppers, roasted (page 84)
>
> 2 to 3 hot chiles, preferably red ones
>
> 2 tablespoons tomato paste
>
> 1¼ teaspoons salt (more to taste)
>
> ¼ cup water
>
> 2 garlic cloves, cut in half
>
> 4 tablespoons extra virgin olive oil

1. Peel the roasted peppers and remove the seeds and membranes over a bowl to catch juices. Transfer the peppers and juices to a food processor fitted with the steel blade.

2. Roast the chiles over a burner flame, or under the broiler, until charred. Transfer to a bowl, cover tightly, and cool. Wearing plastic gloves, peel and seed the chiles. Add to the food processor, along with the tomato paste and 1 teaspoon of the salt. Process until finely chopped. With the machine running, add the water and process until smooth.

3. Place the garlic and remaining ¼ teaspoon salt in a mortar and pestle along with 1 tablespoon of the olive oil, and mash until you have a smooth purée.

4. Heat 2 tablespoons of the olive oil over medium heat in a medium nonstick skillet and add the garlic purée. Cook for about 30 seconds, then stir in the pepper purée. Bring to a simmer and cook, stirring, until the purée is quite thick. Stir in the remaining 1 tablespoon olive oil, taste, and adjust salt.

5. Remove from the heat, cool, and transfer to a jar. Place a thin film of olive oil over the top if storing.

ADVANCE PREPARATION: The purée will keep for 2 weeks in the refrigerator. Keep it covered with a thin film of olive oil.

VARIATION

EGGPLANT AND RED PEPPER PURÉE: Substitute 1 pound eggplant (1 large) for 1 pound of the peppers. Heat the oven to 450°F. Oil a baking sheet with olive oil. Cut the eggplant in half lengthwise, then, with the point of a knife, score them down to the skin but not through it. Place cut side down on the oiled baking sheet and bake for 30 minutes, until thoroughly softened and beginning to collapse. Remove from the oven and place cut side down in a colander in the sink. Drain and cool for 30 minutes. Remove the seeds and skin. Purée in the food processor with the peppers and other ingredients and proceed with the recipe, adding 1 tablespoon red wine vinegar when you add the water.

GRILLED PEPPER SALAD
Turkey • Serves 4

This is a very simple *meze* (I like it as a side dish as well). The standard Turkish condiment—thickened yogurt mixed with puréed garlic, salt, and lemon juice—is all that is needed, but olive oil is also welcome. It's nice to eat this warm, because the warm, smoky peppers contrast so nicely with the cold, tart yogurt. But if you have some roasted peppers in the refrigerator, nothing should stop you from serving them with this topping.

In Turkey, long, slightly hot, light green carliston peppers are used. If you can find something like these in your farmers' market—Hungarian wax peppers or mild Anaheims—they'll be great. But sweet bell peppers are also good.

24 small, narrow, slightly hot or sweet peppers (see headnote), or 4 sweet bell peppers (red, yellow, green, or a mixture)

½ cup drained yogurt (page 21)

2 to 4 tablespoons fresh lemon juice (to taste)

2 to 4 garlic cloves (to taste), mashed in a mortar and pestle with a generous pinch salt

Salt and freshly ground pepper

1. Grill the peppers over coals, under the broiler, or over a gas flame until blackened. Remove from the heat and place in a bowl. Cover the bowl with plastic wrap and let sit for 15 minutes.

2. Skin the peppers, cut in half, and remove the seeds and membranes. Cut larger bell peppers lengthwise into quarters. Place on a platter or individual plates.

3. Mix together the yogurt, lemon juice, garlic, and salt and pepper to taste. Spoon over the warm peppers and serve.

ADVANCE PREPARATION: Roasted peppers will keep for a week in the refrigerator. They will continue to release liquid, which they can marinate in. Pour it off and warm the peppers before serving, or serve them at room temperature with the topping.

MUHAMMARA
Middle East • **Makes 2 cups**

This dip is one of the prize dishes of the Middle East. It may not be on the tip of your tongue, like hummus or baba gannouj, but go to any Lebanese or Syrian restaurant that has an extensive *meze* table, and you will find it. And you won't believe how wonderful it is. It's made with walnuts, peppers, tomato paste, and bread crumbs, seasoned with Aleppo pepper and cumin and pomegranate molasses. Serve it with warm Arab bread. Make the dip a day (or more) before you wish to serve it for the best flavor.

> 1 pound (2 large) red bell peppers
>
> ¼ pound walnuts
>
> 4 teaspoons tomato paste
>
> ¾ cup fresh bread crumbs
>
> 3 tablespoons extra virgin olive oil (more to taste)
>
> 1½ tablespoons pomegranate molasses
>
> 1 tablespoon fresh lemon juice
>
> 1 teaspoon Aleppo pepper
>
> 1 teaspoon freshly ground cumin seeds
>
> ½ teaspoon sugar
>
> ½ to ¾ teaspoon salt (to taste)

1. Roast the peppers over a gas flame, over coals, or under a broiler, turning the peppers with tongs, until completely charred. Transfer to a bowl and cover tightly with a plate or with foil. Cool for 15 to 30 minutes. Slip off the charred skins and rinse briefly with cold water. Quarter the peppers and remove the seeds and membranes. Drain in a colander for 15 minutes.

2. Place the peppers in a food processor fitted with the steel blade and pulse several times, until they are reduced to a pulp. Add the walnuts and pulse together several times. Scrape down the sides of the bowl, then add the tomato paste, bread crumbs, olive oil, pomegranate molasses, lemon juice, Aleppo pepper, cumin, sugar, and salt. Process into a paste, scraping down the processor from time to time. Taste and adjust salt. If desired,

thin out with a little more olive oil. Refrigerate until close to serving time, then bring to room temperature to serve.

ADVANCE PREPARATION: This dip will keep for 2 weeks in the refrigerator if tightly covered.

GRILLED PEPPER SALAD (Mechwya)
Tunisia • **Serves 4 to 8**

There are many variations on *mechwya,* a grilled vegetable (mainly peppers) salad from Tunisia. I love this one, which is slightly picante with its mix of sweet and hot peppers, and beautiful as well, served from a colorful bowl with flat bread for sopping up the juices.

> 3 bell peppers, preferably a mixture of red and green or red, yellow, and green
>
> 2 hot peppers, such as Anaheim or Fresno
>
> 3 tomatoes
>
> 1 or 2 garlic cloves (to taste), peeled
>
> ½ teaspoon salt
>
> ½ teaspoon freshly ground caraway seeds or Tabil (page 24)
>
> 2 tablespoons fresh lemon juice
>
> ¼ cup extra virgin olive oil
>
> Imported black olives

1. Grill the bell and hot peppers over a hot grill or a gas flame, or under the broiler, until charred. Place in a bowl and cover with a plate or with foil. Cool until you can handle them, then peel and seed. Cut in quarters or halves and drain in a colander set over the sink for 10 minutes. Chop coarsely.

2. Grill the tomatoes over a hot grill or under the broiler, turning after 2 to 3 minutes, until the skin is charred. Place in a bowl and cool until you can handle them. Peel, seed, and chop coarsely.

3. Purée the garlic with the salt and caraway in a mortar and pestle. Add the tomatoes and peppers, and gently mash together. The vegetables should not break down to a purée; you should be able to distinguish pieces of pepper, though the tomatoes may be mashed. Stir together the lemon juice and olive oil, and toss half of it with the vegetables. Drizzle as much of the rest as you wish over the top. Decorate with olives and serve.

ADVANCE PREPARATION: This salad only gets better with time, so make it up to a day ahead, but don't arrange it in a bowl or on a platter or decorate it until you're ready to serve. Adjust seasoning first, then garnish and serve.

SPINACH WITH YOGURT AND PINE NUTS

Turkey • **Serves 2 to 3**

This recipe shows the respect with which the Turks cook spinach. All you need to do to wilt baby spinach is place it in a bowl and pour on boiling water. Let it sit for a minute or two, then drain, rinse, and squeeze out the water.

FOR THE DRESSING

3 tablespoons drained yogurt (page 21)

1 to 2 garlic cloves (to taste), mashed to a paste with salt in a mortar and pestle

2 teaspoons fresh lemon juice (more to taste)

Salt

FOR THE SPINACH

10 ounces baby spinach

1 tablespoon extra virgin olive oil

1 small red onion, finely chopped

½ teaspoon sugar

¾ teaspoon cumin seeds, crushed or ground

1 teaspoon currants, chopped

1 tablespoon pine nuts

½ teaspoon Aleppo pepper

Salt and freshly ground pepper

Pita or Arab bread for serving

1. *Make the dressing:* Mix together the yogurt, garlic, and lemon juice. Season to taste with salt. Set aside.

2. *Make the spinach:* Place the spinach in a bowl and pour on boiling water to cover. Let sit for a couple of minutes, then drain, rinse with cold water, and squeeze dry. Chop the spinach.

3. Heat the olive oil in a medium skillet over medium heat. Add the onion, sugar, and cumin seeds, and cook, stirring, until tender, about 5 minutes. Stir in the currants, pine nuts, and Aleppo pepper. Cook for 2 minutes. Add the spinach, toss together well, and season to taste with salt and pepper. Transfer to a serving dish.

4. Pour the dressing over the spinach and serve at once, with pita bread or Arab bread.

ADVANCE PREPARATION: You can make this dish through Step 3 several hours before serving. Reheat gently on top of the stove, and proceed with the recipe.

SWISS CHARD STALK AND TAHINI DIP

Middle East • **Serves 6 to 10**

This ingenious Middle Eastern dish is another example of how Mediterranean cooks never let a thing go to waste. I learned it from Clifford Wright, Mediterranean food scholar par excellence, great cook, and close friend. I don't let the Middle Eastern origins of this dish dictate my menu; rather, whenever I'm using thick-stemmed Swiss chard leaves for another dish, be it Italian, Provençal, Spanish, Middle Eastern, or North African, I save the stems for this luscious appetizer. Serve it with warm Arab bread or toasted pita triangles.

1 pound Swiss chard stalks, coarsely chopped

2 to 4 garlic cloves (to taste), mashed in a mortar and pestle with a big pinch salt

½ cup tahini

¼ to ½ cup fresh lemon juice (to taste)

Salt

1 tablespoon extra virgin olive oil

¼ cup toasted pine nuts

1 tablespoon finely chopped fresh mint (optional)

1. Boil the chard stalks in salted water or steam until tender when pierced with a fork, 15 to 20 minutes. Drain well and transfer to a food processor fitted with the steel blade.

2. Add the garlic to the chard and process until smooth. Add the tahini and process until smooth. With the machine running, add the lemon juice and ½ teaspoon salt. Taste and adjust seasonings.

3. Transfer the dip to a wide bowl or platter. Drizzle on the olive oil and garnish with the pine nuts and mint.

ADVANCE PREPARATION: This dip will be good for about 3 days, but the fresher it is, the better.

WARM TOMATOES WITH GOAT CHEESE
France • **Serves 4**

Goat cheese is *the* cheese of Provence. You will find it in every market, small or large, and you will find people making it in every village. If you can't find small individual rounds for filling the tomatoes, crumble or slice the cheese from a larger log.

- 4 medium tomatoes
- 4 small fresh goat cheeses or 4 (1-inch-thick) rounds cut from a log
- 4 slices country bread, lightly toasted and rubbed with a cut garlic clove
- 1 teaspoon chopped fresh thyme, or a combination of thyme, rosemary, and savory (or ½ teaspoon herbes de Provence)
- 2 tablespoons extra virgin olive oil
- 4 black or green olives, pitted (optional)

1. Set the rack about 3 inches from the heat source and heat the broiler.

2. Cut the tomatoes in half across the equator and scoop out the seeds and flesh from the middle. Place a goat cheese in each tomato shell (or crumble in goat cheese to fill the tomatoes). Place each tomato on a slice of toast. Sprinkle with the herbs. Drizzle the olive oil over the top. Place on a baking sheet and run under the broiler for 2 to 5 minutes,

until the cheese has melted and begun to brown. Remove from the heat, place an olive on each serving if you like, and serve.

ADVANCE PREPARATION: You can assemble the tomatoes several hours before heating under the broiler. Shortly before serving, place the tomatoes on the toasts, sprinkle with the herbs, and drizzle with the oil.

FATTOUSH (Bread and Vegetable Salad)
Middle East • **Serves 10 as a meze or 6 as a more substantial dish**

Fattoush vies with tabbouleh as one of my favorite Middle Eastern salads. Give me bread soaked with salad dressing any time and I'll be happy. The name of this salad indicates that the dish is made with stale pita or flat bread (*fatta*). It's just one of many Arab dishes that use crumbled up flat bread or pita. The bread is traditionally fried, but I toast it to cut down on fat. Then it's tossed with salad vegetables (cucumbers, tomatoes, romaine lettuce, scallions), herbs, and greens, and dressed with lemon juice and olive oil. I have seen various greens called for in *fattoush,* including arugula, watercress, chickweed, and purslane. Use what you can get. But make sure you include plenty of parsley and mint. You'll also need sumac, which intensifies the lemony flavor of the salad. You can find sumac in Middle Eastern markets.

- 1 large garlic clove, minced (optional)
- ¼ cup fresh lemon juice
- ½ cup extra virgin olive oil
- ¼ teaspoon salt (more to taste)
- Freshly ground black pepper
- 1 pound tomatoes, coarsely chopped
- 1 English cucumber or 3 Persian cucumbers, cut in half lengthwise, then into half-moon slices
- 1 bunch scallions, sliced
- ½ cup chopped fresh flat-leaf parsley
- ¼ cup slivered fresh mint leaves
- 1 romaine lettuce heart (the lighter, inner leaves), cut into ½-inch-wide chiffonade

1 small bunch arugula, stemmed and coarsely chopped

1 bunch watercress or purslane, coarsely chopped

6 large radishes, sliced into half-moons

1 tablespoon sumac

Three 6-inch pocket breads, homemade (page 50) or commercial, quartered, split open, and toasted until crisp

Note: *You can substitute an additional romaine heart for the arugula and purslane.*

1. Combine the garlic, lemon juice, olive oil, salt, and pepper to taste in a small bowl.

2. Toss the tomatoes, cucumber, scallions, parsley, mint, romaine, arugula, watercress, radishes, and sumac together in a large bowl.

3. Just before serving, add the dressing to the vegetables and toss together. Crumble in the pita bread and toss again. Taste, adjust seasonings, and serve.

ADVANCE PREPARATION: You can prep the vegetables and toast the bread hours before composing the salad. But do not toss the salad until just before serving.

PANZANELLA (Italian Bread Salad)
Italy • Serves 6

Here's another ingenious Mediterranean use of stale bread—combining it with ripe tomatoes for a delicious salad.

1 pound stale country bread or baguette, cut into cubes (about 7 cups)

1 small red onion, sliced very thin

1 pound tomatoes, chopped

2 tablespoons chopped fresh basil

2 tablespoons chopped fresh flat-leaf parsley

¼ cup red wine vinegar or sherry vinegar

1 large garlic clove, minced or crushed in a mortar and pestle

Salt and freshly ground pepper

½ cup extra virgin olive oil

1. Place the bread in a bowl and cover with the onion. Pour on cold water to cover and let sit for 20 minutes. Lift the onions off the bread and rinse them in a strainer. Drain the bread and squeeze out excess water (the bread will fall apart). Transfer the onions and bread to a salad bowl.

2. Add the tomatoes, basil, and parsley to the bowl. Mix the vinegar, garlic, salt, pepper, and olive oil, and toss with the bread mixture. Cover and refrigerate for 1 hour or longer before serving.

ADVANCE PREPARATION: This salad can be assembled several hours before you wish to serve it.

GRILLED ZUCCHINI SLICES
Italy • Serves 4

This beautiful Italian country starter is as simple as can be, but it's always a hit. Cut thin, lengthwise zucchini slices, grill them, sprinkle with salt, olive oil, and parsley, and serve.

1 pound zucchini, or zucchini and long yellow squash

2 to 3 tablespoons extra virgin olive oil

Salt and freshly ground pepper

2 tablespoons chopped fresh flat-leaf parsley

1. Prepare a grill. Slice the squash lengthwise or on the bias into thin, long strips. Brush with olive oil, season with salt and pepper, and grill for about 3 minutes on each side, until tender but intact. Transfer to a platter and sprinkle with additional salt if desired.

2. Just before serving, drizzle with a little more olive oil and sprinkle with the parsley.

ADVANCE PREPARATION: This is good served at room temperature, so you can grill the zucchini ahead. It will hold for a couple of hours.

VARIATION

Sprinkle the zucchini with hot red pepper flakes before or after grilling.

DIANE KOCHILAS'S ZUCCHINI FRITTERS
Greece • **Serves 6 to 8**

Most of the tavernas I went to in Greece served zucchini fritters, and no two were the same. A version I ate at the Tsiri Taverna in Athens were floury, and I liked them very much; but I had more success with this herby bread crumb version, which I learned from cookbook author Diane Kochilas when I took her classes in Ikaria. In Greece, these would be part of a *meze*. I think they make a nice side dish as well.

The key here is to make sure the zucchini is squeezed of all of its water. Large, overdeveloped zucchini are said to be less watery, and the seeds from big zucchini have a lot of nice texture.

> Salt
>
> 2 pounds large zucchini, grated on the big holes of a box grater or in a food processor
>
> 2 large eggs
>
> ½ cup chopped mixed fresh herbs, such as fennel fronds, dill, mint, and parsley (I like to use mostly dill)
>
> 1 tablespoon ground cumin
>
> 1 cup fresh or dry bread crumbs (more as necessary)
>
> 1 cup crumbled feta
>
> Freshly ground pepper
>
> Pure olive oil for frying
>
> Unbleached all-purpose flour for dredging
>
> Tzatziki (page 106) or plain Greek yogurt for serving (optional)

1. Salt the zucchini generously and drain in a colander for 1 hour, tossing and squeezing the zucchini from time to time. Take up handfuls of zucchini and squeeze out all of the moisture. Or wrap the zucchini in a clean dish towel and squeeze out the water by twisting at both ends.

2. In a large bowl, beat the eggs and add the zucchini, herbs, cumin, bread crumbs, feta, and salt and pepper to taste. Mix together well. Take up a small handful of the batter, and if it presses neatly into a patty, it is the right consistency. If it seems wet, add more bread crumbs or a few tablespoons

flour. When the batter has the right consistency, cover the bowl with plastic wrap and refrigerate for 1 hour or longer. The batter will stiffen; if the zucchini weeps, pour off the liquid.

3. Heat 1 inch of olive oil in a large frying pan. Meanwhile, take up heaped tablespoons of the zucchini batter and form balls or patties. Lightly dredge in the flour.

4. When the oil is rippling, or about 275°F, fry the fritters in batches until golden brown, turning once with a spider or slotted spoon. Remove from the oil and drain briefly on a rack. Serve with *tzatziki* if desired.

ADVANCE PREPARATION: The batter can be assembled up to a day before you make and fry the fritters.

VARIATION

These are the zucchini fritters we had in Athens. They were more doughy (and consequently heavier) than Diane's, but they were delicious: Substitute ½ cup chopped fresh dill for the mixed herbs and substitute flour for the some or all bread crumbs.

EGGS AND VEGETABLES STUFFED WITH TAPENADE
Serves 6 to 8

You can blend tapenade with hard-cooked egg yolks to make a marvelous filling not just for eggs but for vegetables as well. I make platters of these for buffets, and also serve them as part of a Provençal hors d'oeuvre plate.

> 6 large eggs, hard-cooked
>
> 1 recipe Tapenade (page 121)
>
> Salt
>
> 6 small tomatoes or 24 cherry tomatoes
>
> 3 small zucchini, cut in half lengthwise, then cut into 3-inch lengths
>
> 2 red bell peppers, cut into wide 2-inch-long strips
>
> Lemon wedges, chopped fresh parsley, rosemary sprigs, and radishes for garnish

1. Peel the hard-cooked eggs, cut them in half lengthwise, and carefully remove the yolks. Combine the yolks and the tapenade in a food processor fitted with the steel blade, or in a mortar and pestle, and blend together until smooth. Taste and season with salt.

2. If using small tomatoes, cut them in half across the equator, scoop out the seeds, salt lightly, and reverse on a rack over the sink or over a baking sheet to drain for 15 minutes. If using cherry tomatoes, cut off the tops and carefully scoop out some of the pulp.

3. Bring a large pot of generously salted water to a boil and drop in the zucchini. Parboil for 3 minutes and transfer to a bowl of ice-cold water. Drain and carefully scoop out the seeds, using a spoon to create a channel down the middle of each piece.

4. Using a spoon or a piping bag, fill or top the tomatoes, egg whites, zucchini, and bell pepper pieces with the tapenade. Arrange on a platter. Garnish with lemon wedges, chopped fresh parsley, rosemary sprigs, and radishes.

ADVANCE PREPARATION: The egg yolks make this dish more perishable than tapenade made without them, but the enriched tapenade will still hold for 4 or 5 days in the refrigerator, in a covered container. You can prepare the eggs and vegetables several hours before you wish to serve them, and hold them in the refrigerator on a platter, covered, or in plastic bags.

EGGS FILLED WITH PESTO
Serves 6

I don't know why I'd never thought of this before working on this book. For years I've used tapenade for my deviled eggs, but pesto also makes a great filling.

> 6 large eggs, hard-cooked
>
> ½ cup Pesto Genovese (page 74)
>
> Salt and freshly ground pepper
>
> Olive oil for drizzling
>
> Freshly grated Parmesan for sprinkling

1. Peel the eggs and slice them in half lengthwise. Remove the yolks, discard 3 of them, and mash the other 3 with the pesto, either in a food processor fitted with the steel blade or in a mortar and pestle.

2. Spoon the enriched pesto into the egg whites. Season with salt and pepper. Arrange on a platter and drizzle with a little olive oil. Sprinkle with a little Parmesan just before serving.

ADVANCE PREPARATION: The eggs and filling can be made a day or two ahead. Stir the filling to refresh the color before filling the eggs.

GRILLED MOZZARELLA IN RADICCHIO BUNDLES
Italy • Serves 4

This southern Italian dish, beautiful packets of grilled cheese, makes a marvelous starter. The warm, almost sweet mozzarella contrasts beautifully with the bitter radicchio.

> Salt
>
> 2 good-size heads radicchio, leaves separated
>
> 8 ounces fresh mozzarella
>
> Coarse sea salt and freshly ground pepper
>
> 2 teaspoons fresh thyme leaves
>
> 2 teaspoons chopped fresh rosemary
>
> 2 tablespoons extra virgin olive oil
>
> 2 tablespoons chopped fresh flat-leaf parsley
>
> ¼ cup Vinaigrette (page 82) or Oil and Vinegar Dressing (page 82)

1. Prepare a grill, or heat a gas or electric grill to high. Cut 8 pieces of kitchen string, each about 10 inches long, and soak them in a bowl of water while you prepare the bundles.

2. Bring a large pot of water to a boil and add a generous amount of salt. Using tongs, dip half the radicchio leaves into the water 1 leaf at a time for 5 seconds, and transfer immediately to a bowl of ice water. Drain and blot dry with paper towels.

▶

3. Cut the mozzarella into 8 thick slices, then cut each slice in half, so that the pieces are small enough to wrap in the leaves. Place each piece of mozzarella on a leaf. Sprinkle with a little sea salt and freshly ground pepper, and the fresh thyme and rosemary. Drizzle on a teaspoon of olive oil. Wrap each leaf around the cheese, enclosing it completely. Tie up with the soaked kitchen string. Brush the bundles with the remaining olive oil.

4. Break up the remaining radicchio and toss with the parsley and vinaigrette. Divide the salad among 4 plates.

5. Grill the bundles for 2 minutes on each side, until the radicchio is browned and water from the cheese is beginning to ooze out. Do not be alarmed if the bundles smoke. Transfer to the salad-lined plates and serve.

ADVANCE PREPARATION: The bundles can be prepared several hours before grilling and serving. Hold in the refrigerator.

GRILLED FETA IN GRAPE LEAVES
Turkey • Serves 4

In this Turkish specialty, a square of feta is enclosed in a grape vine leaf, speared with a kebab skewer, and grilled. The pungent leaf becomes crisp while the cheese begins to melt, and it's a wonderful combination to pop into your mouth.

> 16 grape leaves packed in brine
>
> 8 ounces firm feta, cut into 16 (1-inch) squares
>
> Extra virgin olive oil for brushing

1. Prepare a grill. Carefully unroll the grape leaves and rinse well under cold water. Bring a large pot of water to a boil and blanch the leaves, a few at a time, for 2 to 3 minutes. Transfer to a bowl of cold water, then drain and rinse once more with cold water. Pat dry. Set aside.

2. Place a leaf on your work surface, vein side up and with the stem facing you. Snip off the stem. Place a square of feta on the leaf. Fold the bottom up over the feta, then fold in the sides and roll up

tightly, tucking in the sides as you go. Run a skewer through the middle. Continue until all of the leaves are filled, placing 3 or 4 stuffed leaves on each skewer. Brush the packets with olive oil.

3. Grill, turning often, until the grape leaves are crispy and the cheese inside is bubbling, about 4 minutes. Serve hot.

ADVANCE PREPARATION: You can assemble the grape leaf and feta packages several hours before grilling. Keep in the refrigerator.

FRICO
Italy • Serves 8

Frico is a marvelous snack from the Friuli–Venezia Giulia region of Italy. The traditional cheese for frico is a cow's milk cheese called Montasio, which has been aged anywhere from 16 months to 3 years. If you can't find Montasio (it's sold in many Italian markets), you can make frico with freshly grated Parmigiano-Reggiano or Asiago, provided the cheese is not dried out.

It takes some practice to make frico; the trick is cooking the lacy wafer of cheese just until it's crisp, but removing it from the pan before it turns brown, when it will take on a bitter, burnt-cheese flavor. Once you get the knack, it's easy, and it's a very popular snack. Do not use a microplane to grate the cheese; it will be too fine if you do. A hand-held Mouli grater works very nicely, producing long strands of cheese.

> Extra virgin olive oil or olive oil spray
>
> 1 pound Montasio, Asiago, or Parmesan cheese, coarsely grated

METHOD 1

This results in large, curled frico. You break off pieces leisurely as you sip a glass of nice white Friulian wine.

Brush or spray a 10-inch nonstick skillet with a very small amount of olive oil. Heat the pan over medium heat. When the pan is hot, sprinkle a handful or two of the cheese over the pan in a single layer. It should look like a cheese crêpe. Reduce the heat to low and, using the back of a fork, push down on the frico in several places to force the fat out. Once the frico is firm, flip it over with a spatula and cook on the other side, pressing down again with a fork. The frico is done when it is firm and ever so slightly golden. Transfer to a plate and stand a clean wine bottle in the middle. Pull the edges up around the sides of the wine bottle, then remove the wine bottle and allow to cool. Or, keeping it simple, just allow the frico to cool flat.

METHOD 2

These frico are smaller and can be stuffed.

Follow the directions in Method 1, but use a 7-inch nonstick pan. When the frico is done, place over a clean empty tomato paste can or shot glass and fold down the sides to form a cup. Cool, then lift the frico off the can or cup.

ADVANCE PREPARATION: The only thing you can do in advance here is grate the cheese. If made too far ahead, frico loses its crisp texture.

DEEP-FRIED RICE AND MOZZARELLA BALLS (Supplì al Telefono)

Italy • **Makes 20 to 24**

These are called *arancini* ("little oranges") in Sicily and *supplì al telefono* in Rome. *Supplì al telefono* means "telephone wires," which is what the hot mozzarella looks like when the balls are broken open and the cheese pulls into thin strings.

I'm usually not a big fan of deep-fried foods, but these I can't resist. *Supplì* are a wonderful way to use up leftover risotto. Authentic Roman *supplì* usually contain prosciutto, but I prefer this vegetarian version, which is really all about cheese and rice. I've based this recipe on one (which isn't vegetarian) by Carol Field, from *Italy in Small Bites*.

FOR THE RISOTTO

6 cups Simple Vegetable Broth (page 145)

2 tablespoons extra virgin olive oil

1 tablespoon unsalted butter

1 medium onion, finely chopped

2 cups Arborio, Carnaroli, or Vialone Nano rice

Pinch saffron

½ cup freshly grated Parmesan

Salt and freshly ground pepper

FOR THE SUPPLÌ

3 large eggs

½ pound mozzarella, diced or grated

½ cup freshly grated Parmesan (optional)

3 tablespoons minced fresh flat-leaf parsley

Salt and freshly ground pepper

2 cups fine dried bread crumbs

Pure olive oil or peanut oil for deep-frying

1. *Make the risotto:* In a saucepan, bring the broth to a simmer, with a ladle nearby or in the pot. Make sure that it is well seasoned with salt.

2. Heat the olive oil and butter in a wide, heavy nonstick skillet over medium heat. Add the onion and cook gently until it is just tender; do not brown. Add the rice and stir just until the grains become separate and coated with oil, about 2 minutes. Crush the saffron between your fingers and add to the rice. Begin adding the simmering broth, a couple of ladlefuls (about ½ cup) at a time. The broth should just cover the rice and should be bubbling, not too slowly but not too quickly. Cook, stirring and adding broth as it is absorbed, until the rice is cooked al dente, 20 to 25 minutes. Add

TIP SUCCESSFUL SUPPLÌ
The key to successful *supplì* is to make them small, and not to squeeze the rice around the filling. They should be the size of an egg (if you make them oval-shaped) or a small lime (if you make them round). If you squeeze the rice to close up the balls they will be too compact and heavy. Use a light hand.

the Parmesan and salt and pepper with the last ladleful of broth. Taste and adjust seasonings. Transfer to a baking sheet and cool for 2 hours, or refrigerate in a covered bowl overnight.

3. *Make the supplì:* Beat 1 of the eggs and stir into the cooled rice. In another bowl, mix together the cheeses, parsley, and salt and pepper to taste. Line a baking sheet with parchment.

4. Moisten your hands with water. Scoop up a handful of rice, about the size of a small lime or egg (about 1½ tablespoons), and spread it in your hand so that it's about ½ inch thick. Make an indentation in the center and fill with a generous pinch of the cheese mixture. Add a little more rice to cover the cavity, then gently close your hand to enclose the filling, and shape the rice into a ball or an oval. Take care not to squeeze, so that the rice is not too compacted. Place the ball on the parchment-lined baking sheet and continue to make the *supplì* until all of the rice and filling are used up. Keep your hands moistened to prevent the rice from sticking.

5. Beat the remaining 2 eggs in a bowl and season with salt and pepper. Place the bread crumbs in another bowl or on a sheet of parchment. Dip a rice ball into the eggs and roll around to coat thoroughly. Now dip into the bread crumbs and roll around to evenly coat. Return to the parchment-lined baking sheet. When all of the balls have been breaded, refrigerate for 10 to 15 minutes while you heat the oil.

6. In a deep frying pan, a wok, a deep fryer, or a wide saucepan, heat at least 3 inches of oil to 375°F. One at a time, lower 3 or 4 rice balls into the oil using a skimmer or a spider. (Cook only 3 or 4 at a time so that you don't crowd the pan.) Fry until golden brown, about 4 minutes, flipping them over halfway through if they don't appear to be browning evenly. Repeat with the remaining balls, letting the oil come back to 375°F between batches. Drain briefly on paper towels. These should be served hot and eaten with the hands, breaking them open so that the cheese pulls into strands.

ADVANCE PREPARATION: You can assemble the rice balls up to a day before you deep-fry them. The risotto can be made up to 4 days ahead.

LEFTOVERS: Any leftovers can be reheated in a 325°F oven or toaster oven for 10 to 15 minutes, though they will lose their crispness (they still taste good).

BRUSCHETTA AND CROSTINI

Bruschetta are thick slices of country bread lightly toasted or grilled, then rubbed with garlic, drizzled with olive oil, and sprinkled with sea salt. Crostini are thinner slices, often cut from a baguette, that are toasted, grilled, or fried; rubbed with garlic (or not); brushed with oil (or not); and topped. Whereas crostini are almost always served as appetizers, or tossed in salads, or floated on soups, you can make a meal out of bruschetta topped with something substantial; see Toppings for Bruschetta and Crostini on page 136. Both bruschetta and crostini are wonderful vehicles for just about any type of spread, and that something doesn't have to be Italian.

Just when you think you have nothing to serve with the glass of white wine you've just offered your friends who dropped in unexpectedly, look in your refrigerator. If you have bread and olive oil, even if the bread is a little stale (actually, all the better), you have the makings for bruschetta or crostini. That little bit of leftover pesto in the jar on the door would be perfect with either. Hummus (page 103), Baba Gannouj (page 110), Balkan Red Pepper Purée (page 124), Tapenade (page 121), roasted red peppers (page 84), and Fresh Tomato Concassée (page 79) are all good candidates.

BRUSCHETTA

Italy • **Serves 4 to 6**

The bread to use for bruschetta is a porous-textured, chewy, crusty country loaf. It should be thickly sliced, ½ to ¾ inch, and drizzled with a high-quality extra virgin olive oil.

> **6 (½- to ¾-inch-thick) slices country bread**
>
> **1 large garlic clove, cut in half**
>
> **3 tablespoons extra virgin olive oil for drizzling**
>
> **Sea salt or fleur de sel**

Toast the bread in a toaster oven, on a grill, or under a broiler just until lightly browned. Remove from the heat and rub vigorously with the cut side of the garlic. Cut the slices of bread in half and drizzle with the olive oil. Sprinkle on the salt and serve.

ADVANCE PREPARATION: You should serve bruschetta warm if possible, so don't make them too far in advance.

CROSTINI

Italy • **Serves 8 to 10**

These Italian croutons differ from bruschetta because they are thinner, smaller slices, and more thoroughly toasted, until they're hard all the way through. They can be made several hours ahead because they needn't be served hot. If you're making a lot of crostini, it's easiest to lay them on a sheet pan and toast them in a hot oven. But you can also use the grill or broiler, or the toaster.

In France and elsewhere in the Mediterranean, these toasts would be called *croutons* and often would be fried in butter. I prefer this lighter version as a garnish for soups and stews.

> **1 baguette, either Italian or French,
>   sliced ½ inch thick; or 8 slices country
>   bread, sliced ½ inch thick, then cut into
>   3 × 3-inch pieces**
>
> **Extra virgin olive oil**
>
> **1 garlic clove, cut in half**

Heat the oven to 400°F. Place the slices of bread on a baking sheet and brush with olive oil. Bake for 5 minutes and flip the bread slices over. Bake another 5 minutes, or until the slices are lightly browned. Alternatively, toast the bread in a toaster oven or grill over coals, then brush with the oil. Rub with the garlic. Serve with the topping of your choice, or use for soups or salads.

ADVANCE PREPARATION: Crostini can be prepared several hours ahead. Wrap in foil.

CATALAN BREAD WITH TOMATO

Spain • **Serves 2 to 4**

This signature dish of Catalonia, which goes by the Catalan name *pa amb tomàquet,* is as ubiquitous as olive oil in that part of Spain. If you have good bread and a ripe, or even almost ripe (but in-season), tomato, you can enjoy this any time of day, including at breakfast.

> **4 (½- to ¾-inch-thick) slices country bread**
>
> **1 medium tomato, cut in half crosswise**
>
> **Extra virgin olive oil for drizzling**
>
> **Salt, preferably coarse sea salt**

Toast the bread lightly. Rub with the cut side of the tomato, squeezing the tomato as you rub the bread. Drizzle on a little olive oil and sprinkle with salt.

ADVANCE PREPARATION: This is a dish you'll want to make and eat. It's the immediate flavor of that freshly cut tomato with the olive oil that's so good.

VARIATION

Once the bread is toasted, rub it with a cut clove of garlic. Then rub with the tomato, drizzle on the oil, and sprinkle with salt.

TOPPINGS FOR BRUSCHETTA AND CROSTINI

You can easily make a meal of bruschetta or crostini. Here are some of my favorite toppings for both:

For Bruschetta

Marinara Sauce and Parmesan: Top the bruschetta generously with warm Marinara Sauce (page 78), sprinkle with grated Parmesan, and serve on a plate.

Mushrooms: Heat mushrooms—pick from Wild Mushroom Ragout (page 285), Mushrooms al Ajillo (page 120), or Sautéed Mushrooms with Gremolata (page 284)—and place a generous spoonful on each bruschetta. Sprinkle with freshly grated Parmesan and serve.

Pan-Cooked Greens and Fontina: Top bruschetta with some pan-cooked greens (page 66). Sprinkle on some grated fontina. Place in a 350°F oven until the cheese melts, or run quickly under the broiler. Serve hot.

Grilled Tomato: I have a vivid memory of this bruschetta, which was served at the Monte Sacro *azienda agrituristica* in the Gargano region of Puglia. The bread was perfectly grilled and brushed with exquisite olive oil, then topped with a quickly grilled plum tomato half and some fresh basil. It's best if you make the bruschetta on a grill. Then cut plum tomatoes in half lengthwise, brush with olive oil, and place cut side down on the grill for 3 minutes. Remove from the heat and place cut side up on the bruschetta. Sprinkle with sea salt and slivered fresh basil or chopped fresh parsley or oregano.

Grilled Tomato and Mozzarella: Follow the above recipe, except top the bruschetta with a slice of fresh mozzarella cheese, and then with the grilled tomato.

Fresh Tomato Concassée: Top with a generous spoonful of Concassée (page 79) and a few slivers of Parmesan.

White Bean "Brandade": I like to warm the brandade (page 91) first. Spoon it onto the bruschetta and sprinkle with slivered or finely chopped fresh sage leaves or chopped fresh parsley.

Provençal Tomato and Bean Ragout: Warm the ragout (page 303) and spoon onto bruschetta. If you wish, sprinkle with grated Parmesan and chopped fresh basil, parsley, or oregano.

Fresh Tomatoes, Arugula, and Olives: I enjoyed this bruschetta all over the southern Italian region of Puglia, where it is called *Ciaredda*. According to food writer Carol Field, it is a signature bruschetta of Lecce, a beautiful baroque city in the heel of the Italian boot. Eat what you can't get onto the bread as a delicious salad: Toss together 1 tightly packed cup arugula leaves torn into small pieces, 1 large or 2 medium tomatoes (peeled, seeded, and diced), 18 imported black olives (pitted), and ¼ cup slivered Parmesan. Dress with 2 teaspoons red wine vinegar (or sherry vinegar) and 2 tablespoons extra virgin olive oil. Top the bruschetta with the salad. Add salt as desired.

Peperonata: Place a heaped spoonful of peperonata (page 85) on each bruschetta. If you wish, sprinkle with a little grated Parmesan or pecorino.

For Crostini

Tapenade: See page 121

Hummus: See page 103

Baba Gannouj: See page 110

White Bean "Brandade": See page 91

Balkan Red Pepper Purée: See page 124

Muhammara: See page 126

Pesto Genovese: See page 74

Arugula Pesto: See page 75

Roasted Peppers: See page 84

Fresh Fava Bean Purée: See page 113

CRETAN BARLEY RUSKS WITH TOMATO TOPPING

Greece • **Serves 4**

The Greeks use rusks—twice-baked breads—for a number of dishes. I love this tradition; there are shops that sell huge selections of the rusks, piled high and beautiful, all over Athens. They're made from different types of flour, including barley, wheat, chick peas, and rye. This recipe is the Greek answer to bruschetta, with a savory uncooked tomato topping. Vassilis Kochilas, husband of Greek food authority Diane Kochilas, made this for me one July day, with tomatoes from their garden in the village of Cristos Raches.

> 4 large Greek barley rusks (available in Greek markets), or homemade rusks
>
> 2 large, firm, ripe tomatoes (1 pound), grated on the big holes of a box grater
>
> 1 to 2 tablespoons capers, rinsed
>
> 1 garlic clove, minced or put through a press
>
> 1 small red onion, finely chopped and rinsed with cold water
>
> ¼ cup chopped kalamata olives
>
> 1 tablespoon chopped fresh dill
>
> Salt
>
> ⅓ cup extra virgin olive oil
>
> 2 ounces feta, crumbled (½ cup)
>
> 2 teaspoons dried oregano

1. One by one, sprinkle the rusks with cold water until softened but not soggy. Tap off the water and set the rusks on a platter.

2. Toss together the tomatoes, capers, garlic, onion, olives, dill, and salt to taste.

3. Drizzle 1 tablespoon olive oil over each of the rusks. Top with the tomato mixture. Sprinkle on the cheese and oregano, and drizzle on the remaining olive oil.

ADVANCE PREPARATION: The tomato topping can be made several hours before topping the rusks.

MAKING RUSKS WITH THE BREAD YOU HAVE ON HAND

I want you to try the Cretan Barley Rusks with Tomato Topping even if you don't have access to Greek rusks and don't want to make your own from scratch. If your oven has a pilot light, you don't even have to turn it on. If it doesn't, put the oven on the lowest setting. Cut a loaf of country bread into thick slices and place them on a baking sheet. Place in the oven for 10 hours, until the bread is completely dry. Cool and store in plastic bags.

CHEESE AND HERB PHYLLO TRIANGLES

Greece • **Makes about 4 dozen**

The Greeks make wonderful *mezedes* using phyllo. (You can find these paper-thin sheets of dough, usually packaged in 1-pound boxes, in the freezer section of many supermarkets, Greek and Middle Eastern markets, and gourmet shops.) They cut the phyllo into strips, brush the strips with butter and/or olive oil, dollop on a spoonful of filling, and encase the filling in the strips by folding the strip over the filling on the diagonal, then over itself until the entire strip is folded into a tidy bite-size triangle. This is baked until crisp and golden and served hot. Any number of fillings can be used, including any of the Greek pie fillings on page 227. The cheese filling below is classic.

> 2 large eggs, beaten
>
> 1½ cups Greek Myzithra or fresh ricotta cheese
>
> 4 ounces feta, crumbled (1 cup)
>
> ½ cup grated kefalotyri cheese (a mixture of half Parmesan and half Pecorino Romano cheese can be substituted)
>
> ¼ cup chopped fresh dill
>
> Salt and freshly ground pepper
>
> 2 tablespoons unsalted butter
>
> 2 tablespoons extra virgin olive oil
>
> ½ pound phyllo dough (see Note on page 138)

Note: *Phyllo comes in 1-pound packets. You'll only need ½ pound for this recipe and the two that follow. Unwrap your dough and take out half the sheets. Refold the remaining ½ pound, wrap tightly in a double thickness of plastic wrap and aluminum foil, and freeze. I have seen phyllo dough in ½-pound packets, but the sheets are cut too small, so buy the 1-pound packets.*

1. Beat the eggs in a mixing bowl. Add the Myzithra, feta, kefalotyri, dill, and salt and pepper to taste. Mix together well.

2. Heat the oven to 350°F. Oil one or two baking sheets, or cover with parchment. Melt the butter with the olive oil.

3. Cover the phyllo dough with a clean dish towel, and place a second, damp towel on top. To make the triangles, take a sheet of phyllo, lay it down horizontally on your work surface, and cut into strips 2½ inches wide. Cover the strips you aren't working with, and the rest of the phyllo, with a damp towel. Brush one strip with the butter–olive oil mixture. Place a teaspoonful of filling on the strip about an inch down from the top, lift a corner of the pastry, and fold over the filling diagonally until the shorter edge of the strip meets the longer edge. Now fold the triangle of covered filling down toward you, and continue folding over and down at right angles until you reach the end of the strip. Seal the end, brush with more melted butter and olive oil, and place on the baking sheet. Continue filling all of the triangles in this way. If any phyllo is left over, discard it, as it will dry out quickly.

4. Bake for 20 minutes, or until golden brown. Serve hot.

ADVANCE PREPARATION: The assembled triangles can be covered tightly with plastic and refrigerated overnight, or frozen for several weeks. Transfer directly from the freezer to the oven without thawing. Add 5 minutes to the baking time.

CHEESE AND WINTER SQUASH PHYLLO TRIANGLES

Greece • **Makes about 4 dozen**

I had a small butternut squash lying around the house, and some phyllo dough left over from a pie that I'd made. With feta and kefalotyri on hand in the refrigerator, it wasn't difficult to come up with these beautiful, cheesy triangles.

> 1 small butternut squash (about ¾ pound)
>
> 1 large egg
>
> 2 ounces feta, crumbled (about ½ cup)
>
> ¼ cup grated kefalotyri or Parmesan
>
> ¾ teaspoon dried mint
>
> Salt and freshly ground pepper
>
> 2 tablespoons unsalted butter
>
> 2 tablespoons extra virgin olive oil
>
> ½ pound phyllo dough (see Note at left)

1. Heat the oven to 425°F. Pierce the butternut squash with the tip of a paring knife in a few places and place on a foil-lined baking sheet. Bake for 30 minutes, remove from the heat, and cool until you can handle it easily. Cut the squash in half and remove the seeds. Brush the foil with oil. Return the squash to the foil, cut side down. Bake another 30 minutes, or until the squash is tender and easily pierced with a knife. Cool slightly, then peel and mash the squash with a fork. Turn the oven down to 350°F.

2. Beat the egg in a medium bowl. Add the squash, feta, kefalotyri, mint, and salt and pepper to taste.

3. Oil baking sheets or line with parchment. Melt the butter with the olive oil.

4. To make the triangles, take a sheet of phyllo, lay it down horizontally on your work surface, and cut into strips 2½ inches wide. Cover the strips you aren't working with, and the rest of the phyllo, with a damp towel. Brush 1 strip with the butter–olive oil mixture. Place a teaspoonful of filling on the strip about an inch down from the top, lift a

corner of the pastry, and fold over the filling diagonally until the shorter edge of the strip meets the longer edge. Now fold the triangle of covered filling down toward you, and continue folding over and down at right angles until you reach the end of the strip. Seal the end, brush with more melted butter and olive oil, and place on the baking sheet. Continue filling all of the triangles in this way. If any phyllo is left over, discard it, as it will dry out quickly.

5. Bake for 20 minutes, or until golden brown. Serve hot.

ADVANCE PREPARATION: The assembled triangles can be covered tightly with plastic and refrigerated overnight, or frozen for several weeks. Transfer directly from the freezer to the oven without thawing. Add 5 minutes to the baking time.

MUSHROOM AND FETA PHYLLO TRIANGLES

Greece • **Makes about 4 dozen**

This is a filling I created by combining some leftover mushroom ragout with feta.

- ½ ounce (about ½ cup) dried porcini mushrooms
- 3 cups boiling water
- 4 tablespoons extra virgin olive oil
- 1 shallot, chopped
- 2 garlic cloves, minced
- 6 ounces cremini or white mushrooms, cleaned, trimmed, and sliced ¼ inch thick
- 6 ounces oyster mushrooms, trimmed and torn into pieces
- Salt
- 1 teaspoon unbleached all-purpose flour
- ¼ cup dry white wine
- 2 tablespoons chopped fresh flat-leaf parsley
- Freshly ground pepper
- 6 ounces (about 1½ cups) crumbled feta
- 2 tablespoons unsalted butter
- ½ pound phyllo dough (see Note, opposite page)

 **TIP** CUTTING PHYLLO
The Greeks make their triangles by cutting long strips along the length of phyllo dough. I cut strips along the shorter edge. I find that this gives me sufficient dough for a nicely wrapped turnover, and I can get more triangles out of a package of phyllo this way.

1. Place the dried mushrooms in a large Pyrex measuring cup and add the boiling water. Soak for 30 minutes. Place a strainer over a bowl, line it with cheesecloth or paper towels, and drain the mushrooms. Squeeze the mushrooms over the strainer to extract all the flavorful juices. Then rinse the mushrooms, away from the bowl with the soaking liquid, until they are free of sand. Squeeze dry. If very large, chop coarsely. Set aside. Measure out 2 cups of the soaking liquid and set aside.

2. Heat 2 tablespoons of the olive oil in a large, heavy nonstick skillet over medium heat and add the shallot. Cook, stirring often, until tender, about 3 minutes. Add the garlic, stir, and cook for about 30 seconds, then add the cremini and oyster mushrooms and about ½ teaspoon salt. Cook, stirring often, until the mushrooms begin to soften and sweat, about 5 minutes. Add the flour and cook, stirring, for 2 or 3 minutes. Add the reconstituted dried mushrooms and the wine and turn the heat to high. Cook, stirring, until the liquid boils down and glazes the mushrooms, 5 minutes. Add the mushroom soaking liquid. Bring to a simmer, add salt to taste, and cook over medium-high heat, stirring often, until the mushrooms are thoroughly tender and fragrant and the surrounding broth has reduced by a little more than half, 10 to 15 minutes. Stir in the parsley and remove from the heat. Stir in some freshly ground pepper, taste, and adjust salt. Stir in the feta. Keep warm.

3. Heat the oven to 350°F. Oil baking sheets or line with parchment. Melt the butter with the remaining 2 tablespoons olive oil.

4. To make the triangles, take a sheet of phyllo, lay it down horizontally on your work surface and

MORE LITTLE FOODS

In addition to the selection of recipes included in this chapter, many of the other dishes in this book can be eaten as starters, tapas, *meze,* and antipasti. Most notable are the omelets, the pizzas, the savory tarts and gratins, and some of the vegetable and bean dishes.

Other Dishes from Spain

Tortilla Española (page 176)

Bar Pilar's Tortilla Española (page 177)

Tortilla Murciana (page 178)

Sweet Green Pepper Tortilla from Murcia (page 178)

Spicy Potatoes with Aïoli (page 288)

Stuffed Lipstick Peppers (page 287)

Pisto (page 293)

Other Dishes from Italy and France

Any of the omelets or frittatas (pages 175 to 193)

Any of the pizzas (pages 57 to 63); cut them into 16 pieces rather than 8

Spinach and Ricotta Torta (page 235)

Focaccia (page 43)

Ratatouille (pages 295 to 299)

Tian Niçois (page 298)

Caponata (page 276)

Stewed Eggplant and Onions (page 276)

Asparagus with Parmesan (page 271)

Braised Fennel with Parmesan (page 282)

Sautéed Mushrooms with Gremolata (page 284)

Wild Mushroom Ragout (page 285)

Wild Mushrooms with Tomatoes and Basil (page 286)

Other Dishes from Greece and Turkey

Mashed Black-Eyed Peas with Garlic Purée (page 306)

Fried Potatoes with Tomatoes and Oregano (page 291)

Potato and Olive Stew (page 291)

Sautéed Peppers with Tomatoes (page 288)

Greek Stewed Green Beans with Tomato (page 272)

Soufiko (page 300)

Fassoulia (page 305)

Stuffed Eggplants (page 279)

Türlü (page 299)

Imam Bayildi (page 278)

Any of the Greek pies (pages 230 to 245), cut in very small portions

Baked Spicy Feta (page 198)

Saganaki (page 198)

Other Dishes from North Africa

Tunisian Eggplant Omelet (page 190)

Baked Potato, Onion, and Parsley Omelet (page 192)

Tunisian Bell Pepper, Tomato, and Potato Omelet (page 193)

Tunisian Carrot and Parsley Omelet (page 193)

Chakchouka (page 194)

cut into strips 2½ inches wide. Cover the strips you aren't working with, and the rest of the phyllo, with a damp towel. Brush one strip with the butter-olive oil mixture. Place a teaspoonful of filling on the strip about an inch down from the top, lift a corner of the pastry, and fold over the filling diagonally until the shorter edge of the strip meets the longer edge. Now fold the triangle of covered filling down toward you, and continue folding over and down at right angles until you reach the end of the strip. Seal the end, brush with more melted butter and olive oil, and place on the baking sheet. Continue filling all of the triangles in this way. If any phyllo is left over, discard it, as it will dry out quickly.

5. Bake for 20 minutes, or until golden brown. Serve hot.

ADVANCE PREPARATION: The assembled triangles can be covered tightly with plastic and refrigerated overnight, or frozen for several weeks. Transfer directly from the freezer to the oven without thawing. Add 5 minutes to the baking time.

Soups

When I travel in the Mediterranean, I take a lot of photographs of food in markets. One of my favorites from my most recent travels, taken in the Campo de' Fiori in Rome, is a close-up of a mixture of fresh borlotti beans and cut-up vegetables—carrots, zucchini, greens—sold by the kilo as minestrone. The vegetables were so beautiful that—though I knew I couldn't—I wanted to gather up handfuls of the mix; they looked like they'd feel wonderful in my hands. But I also understood they would come into their own when simmered with other aromatics in a big pot of water, and served up as soup with Parmesan sprinkled over the top.

There is a saying in Provence: *La soupo tapo un trau* ("soup plugs up a hole"), and throughout the Mediterranean, the peasant meal has historically consisted of soup and little else. Until recent times, this meant, simply, a vegetable (or garlic in the case of the garlic soups) cooked in water. In Provence, the word *soup* referred to pieces of bread that were moistened with the bouillon in which vegetables or beans had been cooked. The word evolved and over time came to mean the contents of the soup pot. And the contents of the soup pot have evolved into rich, complex, nourishing soups, minestrones, and bouillabaisses, many of which you will find in this chapter.

Bread is still an important element in many Mediterranean soups. Leftover minestrone is combined with stale bread to make the Tuscan specialty ribolitta; tomatoes and bread are combined into a savory Tuscan pap called *pappa al pomodoro*. Bread gives cold Spanish gazpacho its singular texture, and thick garlic croutons add substance to Majorcan bread and vegetable soup and the vegetable bouillabaisses of Provence.

As rich and satisfying as a minestrone is, it is also emblematic of peasant cooking, or *cucina povera,* the cooking of the poor. When it comes to drawing maximum flavor out of little, poor cooks have always been the most ingenious. They had little or no meat to work with, but with seasonal vegetables, beans, herbs, a rind of Parmesan for flavor, and pasta or rice or bread to bind it all together, they could create a delicious meal in a bowl that was truly sustaining.

Many of the soups that you'll find in this chapter are just such hearty bean and vegetable soups, and they make perfect high-protein, one-dish meals. Although minestrones tend to be long-simmering and require a certain amount of vegetable prep, there are some that require little time or forethought. I'm thinking specifically of the lentil soups, which cook quickly. If I have lentils in my cupboard, I know that I have dinner.

Other hearty soups that can easily make a satisfying dinner include those to which eggs are added at the end of cooking. The eggs are poached in the soup and served, usually, on croutons in each bowl. You break up the poached egg as you eat your soup and the yolk oozes into the soup; it's a luscious, nourishing sensation.

Mediterranean soups can also be cooling, refreshing, and light. It's not surprising that cold gazpachos are part of the Andalusian gastronomic landscape. Summers there can be blazing hot, and nothing is more refreshing than a serving of gazpacho, poured from a cold pitcher into a glass full of ice cubes.

There are of course many Mediterranean soups that we won't see in a vegetarian cookbook. Some soups are based on chicken stock, and when I felt that the stock was integral to the soup, I did not attempt a substitution. I am thinking of the famous Greek egg-lemon soup, and several chicken soups from the Middle East. But there are more than enough recipes here to keep you and your family extremely well fed and happy.

SIMPLE VEGETABLE BROTH

Makes 7 cups

This is a very simple, sweet-tasting broth in which the vegetables are just thrown into the pot. No need to roast them first, unless you want a darker, more intensely flavored broth. The base includes lots of carrots for sweetness and garlic for depth of flavor.

- 1 onion, quartered
- 4 carrots, thickly sliced
- 1 celery stalk, sliced
- 4 to 8 garlic cloves (to taste), crushed
- 1 leek, white and light green parts, cleaned and sliced
- Vegetable trimmings such as chard stalks, sliced; parsley stems; leek greens, cleaned and sliced; mushroom stems; scallion trimmings
- 8 cups water
- Salt

Combine the onion, carrots, celery, garlic, leek, and trimmings in a large soup pot, pasta pot, or Dutch oven. Pour in the water and add salt to taste, about 2 teaspoons. Bring to a boil. Reduce the heat, cover partially, and simmer gently for 30 minutes or longer. Strain through a fine strainer.

ADVANCE PREPARATION: This broth is best used within a day of being made, but you can freeze it.

GARLIC BROTH

Makes 7 cups

This is a full-bodied broth that is the closest a vegetarian broth can get to chicken broth. When you simmer the garlic, its flavor sweetens and the pungency dissipates—as long as you don't simmer it for too long. If you add vegetable bouillon cubes to this, which will deepen the flavor, make sure to shop for a brand that is not full of additives and contains no hydrogenated vegetable oil.

VEGETABLE TRIMMINGS FOR BROTH

Vegetable trimmings are the parts of the vegetable that you usually throw away—like the dark outer leaves of leeks, carrot tops, mushroom stems, parsley stems, asparagus ends, and scallion tops. These add flavor to a vegetable broth. Sometimes they can even be the base of the broth. I don't hold on to them as a matter of course, but if I know I'm going to be making a vegetable broth, I'll keep trimmings in the refrigerator for a day or two to add to it. Sometimes I'll be inspired to make a soup or a broth just because I have trimmings—like asparagus ends or leek greens—left over from another dish.

I first published this recipe nearly 30 years ago, in my first cookbook, *The Vegetarian Feast.* My cooking has matured a lot since then, but this broth has never lost its appeal.

- 2 heads garlic, separated into cloves and peeled
- 2 vegetable bouillon cubes (optional)
- 2 tablespoons extra virgin olive oil
- 1 bay leaf
- 2 sprigs fresh thyme
- 2 sprigs fresh flat-leaf parsley
- 8 cups water
- 2 teaspoons salt

Combine the garlic, bouillon cubes, oil, bay leaf, thyme, and parsley in a large saucepan or soup pot. Pour in the water and add the salt. Bring to a boil, reduce the heat, cover partially, and simmer for 45 minutes. Taste and adjust salt. Strain and discard the solids. If not using right away, cool and chill or freeze.

ADVANCE PREPARATION: The broth can be frozen and it can be made a day ahead, but it's best if used right away.

MINESTRONE

Italy • Serves 6

Some of the many versions of minestrone call for meat stock; others, like this, rely on plain old water. Like all "big soups," this one will taste even better the day after you make it; but don't add the pasta or bright green vegetables until shortly before serving.

2 tablespoons extra virgin olive oil

2 medium onions, chopped

2 large or 3 medium leeks, white and light green parts only, cleaned and sliced

2 medium carrots, chopped

2 celery stalks, chopped

Salt

6 large garlic cloves, minced or put through a press

½ small head green cabbage, shredded (about 4 cups)

8 cups water

2 medium potatoes (a waxy variety, such as a red-skinned), scrubbed and diced

2 medium turnips, peeled and diced

1 can (14 ounces) tomatoes, seeded and chopped, with juice

1 teaspoon chopped fresh oregano (or ½ teaspoon dried)

1 Parmesan rind

A few sprigs each fresh thyme and parsley

1 bay leaf

1 can (15 ounces) cannellini or borlotti beans, drained and rinsed

1 pound fresh fava beans, shelled

1 pound fresh peas, shelled, or 1 cup thawed frozen peas

½ pound green beans, cut into 1-inch lengths

¼ pound Tuscan kale (*cavolo nero*), turnip greens, or Swiss chard, stemmed, washed well, and shredded or chopped (about 2 cups)

½ cup soup pasta, such as elbow macaroni, small shells, or broken spaghetti

Freshly ground pepper

¼ cup chopped fresh parsley

6 tablespoons freshly grated Parmesan

1. Heat the olive oil in a large, heavy soup pot or Dutch oven over medium-low heat and add the onions. Cook, stirring, until they begin to soften, and add the leeks. Cook, stirring, for about 5 minutes, until tender and translucent but not browned. Add the carrots and celery and a generous pinch of salt, and continue to cook, stirring often, for 5 to 10 minutes, until the vegetables are tender and fragrant. Stir in the garlic and cabbage, add a little more salt, and cook for about 5 minutes, until the cabbage has wilted. Add the water, potatoes, turnips, tomatoes, and oregano, and bring to a boil. Tie the Parmesan rind, thyme and parsley sprigs, and bay leaf together with kitchen string (or in a piece of cheesecloth) and add to the pot. Add salt (at least 2 teaspoons), reduce the heat to low, cover, and simmer for 45 minutes. Stir in the canned beans.

2. While the soup is simmering, blanch the green vegetables: Bring a pot of water to a boil, drop in the shelled favas, and boil for 1 minute. Transfer to a bowl of cold water with a skimmer or slotted spoon. Drain and slip off the skins. Set aside. Bring the water in the pot back to a boil, then add a teaspoon of salt and the fresh peas and green beans. Boil for 5 minutes, until just tender but still bright green. Remove with a slotted spoon or skimmer, refresh with cold water, and set aside with the favas. Retain the cooking water in case you want to thin out the soup later.

3. Add the kale and the pasta to the soup and simmer another 10 minutes, or until the pasta is cooked al dente. Stir the cooked or thawed peas, favas, and green beans into the soup. Grind in some pepper and taste. Does the soup taste vivid? Does it need more salt (probably)? Or garlic? It should be savory and rich-tasting. Adjust seasonings as necessary. If it seems too thick, thin out with a little cooking water from the green vegetables.

4. Remove the bouquet garni from the soup, stir in the chopped parsley, and remove from the heat. Serve in wide soup bowls, with a tablespoon of Parmesan sprinkled over the top.

ADVANCE PREPARATION: The soup can be made through Step 1 a day or two ahead. It improves overnight. The green vegetables can be blanched a day or two ahead and kept in the refrigerator in a covered bowl. Add them to the soup shortly before serving. The finished soup will keep for 3 or 4 days in the refrigerator, and it benefits from being cooked a day ahead of time. However, the pasta will absorb more liquid, so the soup will require thinning out. If you're making the soup ahead, add the pasta and green vegetables to the soup on the day you are serving it.

LEFTOVERS: Turn leftovers into another dish by making the Ribolitta that follows.

THE POWER OF STALE BREAD

I never throw out a stale loaf of bread. To me it just represents an opportunity for a new dish. It could be a soup, salad, or a main dish. Here are some you'll find in this book:

Panzanella (Italian Bread Salad, page 129)

Fattoush (page 128)

Tuscan Bread and Tomato Soup (Pappa al Pomodoro, page 148)

Ribolitta (page 147)

Gazpacho (page 165)

Strata and variations (pages 196 to 197)

Chick Pea Fattet (page 308)

RIBOLITTA
Italy • Serves 2

In Tuscany, the typical way to transform leftover bean and vegetable soup into a new, thoroughly enjoyable meal—and one that is the ultimate comfort food—is to heat it with dry or toasted bread and blend this up to make something between a pap and a soup. This is called *ribolitta,* which means "reboiled." You can make ribolitta with other types of vegetable or bean and vegetable soups. This one is based on Faith Willinger's formula in *Red, White & Greens,* though hers is made with a winter bean and vegetable soup.

> 3 to 4 thick slices good-quality artisanal country bread
> 2½ cups leftover Minestrone (opposite page)
> Salt and freshly ground pepper
> Extra virgin olive oil for drizzling

1. Heat the oven to 325°F. Place the bread on the rack and toast until dry but not browned, 20 to 25 minutes.

2. Heat the soup in a saucepan or soup pot. Remove ½ cup of the beans and vegetables. Bring the remaining soup to a simmer, then submerge the bread in the soup and take the pan off the heat. Let stand for 20 minutes, until the bread is soft. Blend, using a hand-held blender or the pulse action of a food processor. Return to the pot, add the beans and vegetables you set aside, and heat through. The ribolitta should have the consistency of oatmeal. Dilute with water as necessary. Taste and adjust salt and pepper. Spoon the ribolitta into bowls or onto soup plates, drizzle olive oil over each serving, and serve.

ADVANCE PREPARATION: Ribolitta will stiffen up considerably if you make it too far in advance. If you do make it in advance, thin it out as desired with water or broth, and adjust salt.

TUSCAN BREAD AND TOMATO SOUP
(Pappa al Pomodoro)

Italy • Serves 4 to 6

Pappa means "pap," which is what this soup is. Like ribolitta, a more heavenly pap there has never been. I can still recall the flavor and texture of the first *pappa al pomodoro* I ever tasted. It was in New York, not Italy, about 30 years ago. The restaurant was Da Silvano, an Italian place on Sixth Avenue in Greenwich Village. The humble mixture tasted luxurious: There was just enough garlic, basil, and salt to bring the tomatoes, star of the dish, very much to life. Although the soup is traditionally made with unsalted Tuscan bread, it works beautifully with any country bread. More proof that bread, however stale, need never go to waste.

- 2 tablespoons extra virgin olive oil
- 1 small onion, chopped
- 4 garlic cloves, minced or put through a press
- 1½ pounds ripe tomatoes, peeled, seeded, and chopped; or 1 can (28 ounces) tomatoes, with juice
- 2 tablespoons tomato paste
- Pinch sugar
- ¼ teaspoon hot red pepper flakes
- Salt and freshly ground pepper
- 1 pound stale country bread, crusts removed, cut into cubes (about 7 cups)
- 4 cups water
- 2 to 3 tablespoons slivered fresh basil

1. Heat the oil in a large, heavy soup pot over medium-low heat. Add the onion and cook, stirring, until tender, about 5 minutes. Add the garlic and cook, stirring, for about a minute, until fragrant. Add the tomatoes, tomato paste, sugar, red pepper flakes, and salt and pepper to taste, and cook, stirring occasionally, until the tomatoes have cooked down and smell fragrant and wonderful, about 10 minutes.

2. Stir the bread cubes into the tomatoes. Add the water, half the basil, and about 1 teaspoon salt. Simmer, stirring and mashing the bread, for about 10 minutes, until the soup is thick. Stir in the remaining basil and taste and adjust seasoning. Serve hot, warm, or at room temperature.

ADVANCE PREPARATION: This soup can be made a day ahead, and will be even more flavorful the second day.

KALE MINESTRONE

Italy • Serves 6

This winter soup is perfect during that long season when it seems that the only vegetables you can find at the farmers' markets are cabbage and kale.

- 2 tablespoons extra virgin olive oil
- 1 large onion, finely chopped
- 1 carrot, finely chopped
- 2 tablespoons chopped fresh flat-leaf parsley
- 4 garlic cloves, minced or put through a press
- 1 can (14 ounces) tomatoes, seeded and chopped, with juice
- ¼ medium cabbage, cored and shredded
- ½ pound (1 heaped cup) dried white beans, picked over, rinsed, soaked in water to cover for 6 hours or overnight, and drained
- 6 cups water
- 1 Parmesan rind
- 1 bay leaf
- Salt
- ½ cup rice (long-grain or Arborio)
- 1 large bunch kale (about ¾ pound), stemmed and coarsely chopped
- Freshly ground pepper
- ¼ cup freshly grated Parmesan

1. Heat the oil in a soup pot over medium heat and add the onion, carrot, and parsley. Cook, stirring often, until the mixture is fragrant and the vegetables tender, about 10 minutes. Stir in half the minced garlic and cook, stirring, for another minute or so, until the garlic begins to smell fragrant. Add the tomatoes and their liquid and cook, stirring occasionally, for 5 to 10 minutes, until the tomatoes have cooked down a bit. Add the cabbage, stir together for a couple of minutes, until the cabbage begins to wilt, then add the drained beans, water, Parmesan rind, and bay leaf. Bring to a boil, reduce the heat to low, cover partially, and simmer for 1 to 1½ hours, until the beans are tender.

2. Add the remaining chopped garlic, salt (2 teaspoons or more), the rice, and kale, cover partially, and continue to simmer another 30 minutes to 1 hour, until the beans are thoroughly cooked and the soup very fragrant. Add pepper, taste, and adjust salt. Remove the Parmesan rind and bay leaf.

3. Serve, topping each bowl with a spoonful of Parmesan.

ADVANCE PREPARATION: This minestrone keeps for a few days in the refrigerator and freezes well. Bring back to a simmer and serve. It will benefit from being made ahead.

PARMESAN RINDS FOR SOUP

Parmesan rinds, that hard part of a block of Parmesan that you pay for but can't eat, are a secret ingredient in many of my soups. Simmered in a bouquet garni, they add a rich, smoky flavor, almost a meaty dimension, to a soup. They are the vegetarian equivalent of a ham bone. When I reach the end of my Parmesan, rather than throw out the rind, I put it in a plastic container or bag and keep it in the cheese drawer of my refrigerator. It can become as hard as stone, but that won't diminish its flavoring potential when added to a soup. Cut your rinds into 2- or 3-inch lengths and keep them on hand for months.

LENTIL MINESTRONE WITH GREENS
Italy • Serves 4 to 6

This is as warming, filling, and comforting a winter soup as you can get. The greens, added towards the end of cooking, make a great partner for the lentils, and you really have every nutrient I can think of in one bowl. If you make this soup a day ahead, don't add the pasta or rice, or the greens, until you reheat before serving.

2 tablespoons extra virgin olive oil

1 small onion, chopped

1 large or 2 small carrots, minced (about ¾ cup)

4 large garlic cloves, minced or put through a press

1 can (14 ounces) tomatoes, seeded and chopped, with juice

½ teaspoon dried thyme (or 1 teaspoon fresh leaves)

½ teaspoon dried oregano

¾ pound (about 1½ cups) lentils, picked over and rinsed

8 cups water

1 Parmesan rind

A few sprigs each fresh parsley and thyme

1 bay leaf

A few pinches cayenne

Salt

Freshly ground pepper

½ pound Swiss chard, stalks removed, leaves washed and chopped (2 cups, tightly packed)

½ cup soup pasta (such as elbow macaroni, small shells, or tubetti) or Arborio rice

2 tablespoons chopped fresh flat-leaf parsley

¼ cup freshly grated Parmesan

1. Heat the oil in a heavy soup pot or Dutch oven over medium-low heat and add the onion and carrot. Cook, stirring, until the vegetables are tender, about 5 minutes or a little longer, and stir in the garlic. Cook, stirring, just until the garlic smells fragrant and is beginning to color, about 1 minute,

OLD WORLD BEANS, NEW WORLD BEANS

Dried beans—both the ancient varieties that have been around for thousands of years (lentils, chick peas, fava beans), and the New World beans that arrived after the discovery of the Americas in the 15th century—are popular throughout the Mediterranean world.

Lentils and Chick Peas

Lentils and chick peas have both been cultivated for thousands of years in the Mediterranean, and they are represented in just about every cuisine.

Lentils come in four varieties—brown, green, red, and black (also called beluga because they call to mind caviar). Brown lentils are used in soups, stews, pilafs, and side dishes. Green and black lentils are used primarily in salads and side dishes, and red lentils, which fall apart when cooked and change in hue from bright orange to dark yellow, are used almost entirely in soups.

As you can see from the recipes in this book, I use lentils for soups more than anything else, though you'll also find at least one lentil salad (page 119). Lentils are very quick-cooking (35 to 40 minutes), require no soaking, and have a distinct, wonderful earthy flavor that seems to appeal to people of all ages. They marry wonderfully with a vinaigrette, and if you eat meat, you'll enjoy them with sausages.

Where would we be without chick peas? They are probably most well known here as the base for hummus, but they also appear in salads and stews and soups from Spain to Turkey, through the Middle East and North Africa. They lend themselves to every Mediterranean flavor palette, from the olive oil, garlic, and lemon juice of southern Europe to the more exotic spices of Turkey, the Middle East, and North Africa (cumin and coriander; caraway, cilantro, mint, and chile). In Provence, chick pea flour is made into the wonderful polenta-like pancakes called *socca* and thicker polenta fritters called *panisses* (it's *pannelle* in Sicily). Their earthy flavor is unmistakable, their texture substantial and satisfying.

Black-Eyed Peas

It may come as a surprise to you that these beans, which we associate with the American South, are popular in Greece, Turkey, and the Middle East. They have been cultivated in the Mediterranean since Roman times, and were probably brought there from Africa, where they have been grown for thousands of years. According to food historians, black-eyed peas probably came to North America from the Mediterranean, and to South America from Africa via the slave trade. The beans are used in wonderful salads and stews in the Mediterranean. The Greeks have a wonderful dish of Mashed Black-Eyed Peas with Garlic Purée (page 306), and they cook them with lots of fennel in a stew (page 306).

New World Beans

White beans are popular all around the Mediterranean basin, particularly in France, Italy, the Balkans, and Greece, where they show up in soups, stews, salads, and starters. In southern France, they appear in the famous cassoulet of the Languedoc, and they're blended up into a purée called *Poor Man's Brandade* (page 91) in Provence. White beans love tomatoes, another New World food, and show up with them in soups and stews and tagines, and in the famous Italian mixture of pasta and beans called Pasta e Fagioli (page 218).

Borlotti beans, with their speckled red and white pods, are very popular in Italy and also in Provence, where they're called *haricots écossais*. They're eaten both fresh and dried, and they have an affinity for garlic, olive oil, and tomatoes. These are the beans you will find in the Provençal version of minestrone, Soupe au Pistou (page 155).

The other New World bean that shows up in Mediterranean cooking is the lima bean. It's not everywhere—in Spain and Greece, for the most part, although occasionally it will show up in a North African tagine. There are two varieties, one small and more delicate, one large. The giant white beans that are cooked for *meze* in Greece, and in hearty stews in Spain, are limas.

and stir in the tomatoes, thyme, and oregano. Turn the heat to medium and bring to a simmer. Cook, stirring often, for about 10 minutes, until the tomatoes have cooked down somewhat and smell fragrant. Stir in the lentils and water and bring to a boil.

2. Tie the Parmesan rind, parsley and thyme sprigs, and bay leaf together with kitchen string (or in a piece of cheesecloth). Add to the soup. Add the cayenne, reduce the heat, cover, and simmer for 30 minutes. Add salt, about 2 teaspoons to begin with (you will probably add more later), and simmer another 15 to 30 minutes, until the lentils are tender and the broth fragrant.

3. Add pepper to the soup and stir in the chard and pasta. Continue to simmer another 10 to 15 minutes, until the pasta is cooked through. Taste. Is there enough salt? Garlic? Adjust seasonings and remove the Parmesan rind bundle. Stir in the parsley. Serve, topping each bowlful with a generous sprinkle of Parmesan cheese.

ADVANCE PREPARATION: The soup can be made through Step 2 up to 4 days before you serve. It will thicken. You can thin it out with water to taste. Bring back to a simmer and proceed with the recipe.

LEFTOVERS: The thickened soup makes a delicious topping for bruschetta. Cut thick slices of good, crusty country bread, toast them, and rub with a cut clove of garlic. Warm the leftover soup (don't thin it), place on top of the bread, sprinkle on a little Parmesan, and serve.

ISTRIAN MINESTRONE (Manestra)
Croatia • **Serves 6 to 8**

My friend Mira Furlan, a Croatian actress who, with her husband Goran Gajic, had to leave their home when Croatia and Serbia were at war in the 1990s, pines for this soup, which is called *manestra* in Croatia. When we were together in Istria, a magical region of Croatia not far from the Italian border, she and Goran took me to a wonderful

agriturismo restaurant called Alla Beccaccia. Mira saw this soup simmering in the kitchen, and she requested it as a starter to our amazing meal. What makes this unusual is the combination of beans and corn; it is really Old World meeting the New.

The recipe I've developed is not authentic: Real *manestra* is flavored with a prosciutto bone, which simmers with the beans. "How could I achieve a similar cured flavor?" I pondered as I enjoyed my soup on that beautiful day in July. My solution is to include several rinds of Parmesan in my bouquet garni. It's not prosciutto, but it gives the soup a great depth of flavor. When I made the soup at home for Mira and Goran, they approved.

¾ pound (1½ cups) dried borlotti beans, pink beans, or pinto beans, picked over, rinsed, and soaked in 8 cups water overnight or for 6 hours

1 large onion, chopped

4 garlic cloves, minced or put through a press

8 cups water

4 Parmesan rinds (about 4 ounces)

1 bay leaf

A few sprigs each fresh thyme and parsley

Salt and freshly ground pepper

Leaves from 1 bunch fresh flat-leaf parsley (about ¾ cup)

3 tablespoons extra virgin olive oil

1 medium carrot, chopped

1 can (14 ounces) tomatoes

¾ pound starchy potatoes (russets or Yukon golds), peeled and diced

2 cups fresh corn kernels

2 tablespoons slivered fresh basil (optional)

Freshly grated Parmesan

1. Drain the beans and combine with half of the chopped onion, half of the garlic, and the water in a large soup pot. Bring to a boil. Meanwhile, tie the Parmesan rinds, bay leaf, thyme sprigs, and parsley sprigs together in a piece of cheesecloth and add to the pot. Reduce the heat, cover, and simmer for 1 hour. Add 2 teaspoons salt and freshly ground pepper to taste. ▶

2. In a mortar and pestle, mash together the remaining garlic and ¼ teaspoon salt. Add the parsley leaves and continue to mash together until you have a paste. Work in 2 tablespoons of the olive oil.

3. Heat the remaining 1 tablespoon of oil in a nonstick skillet over medium heat and add the remaining onion and the carrot. Cook, stirring, until tender, about 5 minutes, and stir in the garlic-parsley paste. Cook, stirring, for a couple of minutes, until fragrant, and stir in the tomatoes and ½ teaspoon salt. Cook until the tomatoes thicken slightly and smell fragrant, about 10 minutes.

4. Stir the tomato mixture into the beans. Add the potatoes and simmer for 30 minutes to 1 hour, until the beans are tender, the potatoes are falling apart, and the broth is very fragrant. Taste and adjust seasonings. Pull out the cheesecloth bag, press it against the side of the pot to expel broth, and discard.

5. Stir the corn into the soup and simmer for 10 minutes, until tender and fragrant. Stir in the basil, if using. Taste and adjust seasonings. Serve hot, passing a bowl of grated Parmesan for people to spoon on.

ADVANCE PREPARATION: This soup is even better a day after you make it. It will keep for 5 days in the refrigerator and freezes well.

VARIATION

Add ½ cup soup pasta, such as small shells or macaroni, to the soup along with the corn. The soup will be thicker. If you are making it ahead, don't add the pasta until shortly before serving, or it will swell and soften too much.

CABBAGE AND WHITE BEAN MINESTRONE

Italy • Serves 4 to 6

This soup makes a tasty and hearty winter dinner. Like other soups with pasta, you can make it ahead, but don't add the pasta until shortly before serving.

- 2 tablespoons extra virgin olive oil
- 1 large onion, finely chopped
- 1 carrot, finely chopped
- 1 celery stalk, finely chopped
- 2 tablespoons chopped fresh flat-leaf parsley
- 5 garlic cloves, 4 minced or put through a press, 1 cut in half
- 1 can (14 ounces) tomatoes, seeded and chopped, with juice
- 1½ pounds cabbage, cored and coarsely chopped
- ½ pound (1 heaped cup) dried white beans, picked over, rinsed, soaked in water to cover for 6 hours or overnight, and drained
- 8 cups water
- 1 Parmesan rind
- 1 bay leaf
- Salt and freshly ground pepper
- ½ cup elbow macaroni or small shells
- 4 to 6 thick slices country bread
- ¼ cup freshly grated Parmesan

1. Heat the oil in a soup pot over medium heat and add the onion, carrot, celery, and parsley. Cook, stirring often, until the mixture is fragrant and the vegetables tender, about 10 minutes. Stir in half the minced garlic and cook, stirring, for another minute or so, until the garlic begins to smell fragrant. Add the tomatoes and cook, stirring occasionally, for 5 to 10 minutes, until they have cooked down a bit. Add the cabbage, stir for a minute, then add the drained beans, water, Parmesan rind, and bay leaf. Bring to a boil, reduce the heat to low, cover partially, and simmer for 1 hour, or until the beans are just about tender.

2. Add the remaining minced garlic and salt (2 teaspoons or more), cover, and simmer another 30 minutes to 1 hour, until the beans are thoroughly cooked and the soup very fragrant. Add pepper, taste, and adjust salt. Remove the Parmesan rind and bay leaf.

3. Add the pasta and cook until the pasta is al dente, 5 to 10 minutes.

4. Meanwhile, toast the bread and rub each slice with the cut side of the halved clove of garlic. Place a crouton in each bowl and ladle on the soup. Top each bowl with a spoonful of Parmesan and serve.

ADVANCE PREPARATION: The soup can be made a day ahead through Step 2 and refrigerated. Bring back to a simmer and proceed with the recipe. It keeps for a few days in the refrigerator and freezes well.

LEFTOVERS: Continue to enjoy leftovers as a soup until you run out, or transform the soup into Ribolitta (page 147).

TUSCAN BEAN AND FARRO SOUP WITH CABBAGE AND WINTER SQUASH

Italy • **Serves 6**

This big soup, based on a Lynne Rossetto Kasper recipe from *The Italian Country Table,* is multidimensional, with layers of sweet and savory, earthy and herbal and vegetal flavors, chewy and soft textures.

Farro is an ancient whole wheat grain that is still popular in Tuscany. It's a softer, gentler, and quicker-cooking wheat than our domestic whole wheat berries, and has a sweet flavor that Kasper aptly describes as tasting "like barley and hazelnuts." This soup was my introduction to the grain, and it sold me on it.

FOR THE SOUP

½ cup imported Italian farro

10 cups water

Salt

1 tablespoon extra virgin olive oil

1 medium onion, chopped

1 medium carrot, chopped

1 small celery stalk, with leaves, chopped

2 teaspoons chopped fresh sage

3 large garlic cloves, minced or put through a press

1 pound green cabbage, cored and shredded

½ pound (1 heaped cup) dried borlotti or pinto beans, picked over, rinsed, soaked in water to cover overnight or for 6 hours, and drained

1 pound butternut squash, peeled, seeded, and diced (about 2 cups)

1 Parmesan rind

Freshly ground pepper

Freshly grated Parmesan

FOR THE SOFRITO

1 tablespoon extra virgin olive oil

3 large garlic cloves, minced or put through a press

Generous ½ teaspoon dried rosemary, crumbled

1 can (14 ounces) tomatoes, chopped, with juice

Salt

1. *Make the soup:* Combine the farro and 2 cups of the water in a medium saucepan and bring to a boil. Reduce the heat, cover, and simmer until tender, about 40 minutes. Stir in ¼ teaspoon salt and remove from the heat. If there is water left in the pan, drain it. Set aside. ▶

SOFRITO

Sofrito is a mixture of aromatic ingredients that are cooked in oil or fat and added to a dish. Cooking the *sofrito* can be the beginning step in a recipe, but here the *sofrito* is stirred into the soup after the beans have cooked, and then simmered with it for another half hour, with incredibly heady results. The *sofrito* traditionally includes a pork product like pancetta, but a vegetarian version is no less aromatic.

2. Meanwhile, heat the olive oil in a large, heavy soup pot or Dutch oven over medium heat and cook the onion until it begins to soften, about 3 minutes. Add the carrot, celery, and sage and continue to cook, stirring, until the vegetables are tender, 8 to 10 minutes. Add the garlic and cook, stirring, until fragrant, about 1 minute. Add the cabbage and ½ teaspoon salt and cook, stirring often, until the cabbage is limp, about 10 minutes. Add the drained beans, squash, Parmesan rind, and the remaining 8 cups water, or enough to cover the solids by 2 inches. Bring to a boil, reduce the heat, and simmer for 1 hour. Add salt to taste and simmer another 30 minutes, or until the beans are tender. Discard the Parmesan rind. Ladle out 2 cups of the beans and vegetables with a small amount of broth and purée in a blender or food processor fitted with the steel blade (if using a blender, do this in batches to avoid hot soup splashing). Return to the pot.

3. *Make the sofrito:* While the soup is simmering, heat the oil in a medium nonstick skillet over medium heat and add the garlic and rosemary. Cook until fragrant, about 30 seconds, and stir in the tomatoes. Add salt and cook, stirring often, until the tomatoes have cooked down and the *sofrito* is thick and delicious and beginning to stick to the pan, 10 to 15 minutes.

4. Stir the *sofrito* into the soup. Continue to simmer for another 30 minutes. By now it should be incredibly aromatic. Stir in the farro. Taste and adjust salt, and add lots of freshly ground pepper. Serve with freshly grated Parmesan.

ADVANCE PREPARATION: This soup involves three different procedures, and any or all of them can be done up to 3 days ahead of serving the soup: The farro can be cooked, the soup can be cooked, and the *sofrito* can be made and stirred into the soup if desired. The finished soup keeps well and gets even better over 2 or 3 days.

STRACCIATELLA

Italy • **Serves 3 as a light supper or 4 as a first course**

This light, classic Roman soup is perfect for kicking off a dinner party. Follow it with a substantial dish like one of the lasagnas on pages 221 to 222. You could also make it for a light supper, accompanied by a salad of one kind or another. The soup is of the egg drop variety; eggs are beaten with a small amount of semolina flour and Parmesan, and stirred into the simmering broth shortly before you serve it. The egg-semolina mixture cooks up into little rag-like shards, the *stracciatella* ("little rags") that the soup is named for.

If you are using broccoli florets as the vegetable, you'll want to simmer them for a couple of minutes in the broth before adding the egg mixture. Spinach, however, can be added along with the eggs.

> 4 cups Simple Vegetable Broth (page 145)
>   or Garlic Broth (page 145)
>
> Salt
>
> 2 large eggs
>
> 1 tablespoon semolina flour
>
> ¼ cup freshly grated Parmesan

> **OPTIONAL VEGETABLE**
>
> 1 good-size broccoli crown (about 6 ounces), florets sliced about ½ inch thick
> or
> ¼ pound spinach, stemmed, cleaned, and cut in slivers, or baby spinach

1. Reserve ¼ cup of the broth and bring the rest to a simmer in a saucepan. Taste and adjust salt. If there is any visible fat, skim it away.

2. Beat the eggs in a bowl and stir in the reserved ¼ cup broth, the semolina, and the cheese.

3. If using broccoli, add it to the broth and simmer for 2 to 3 minutes, until tender but still bright green. Add the little bits of the florets that crumbled onto your cutting surface to the egg mixture.

If using spinach, add it to the broth.

4. Drizzle the egg mixture into the broth, scraping all of it in with a rubber spatula. At this point, you can either stir the soup vigorously with a fork, then reduce the heat and let the soup cook at a bare simmer for another minute without stirring, or you can stir very slowly with a wooden spoon, paddling it back and forth until the little "rags" form. Serve at once.

ADVANCE PREPARATION: The broth can be made weeks ahead and frozen, or a day ahead and refrigerated. If making the asparagus variation below, the asparagus can be cooked and held hours ahead of serving the soup.

VARIATIONS

STRACCIATELLA WITH ASPARAGUS: Substitute ¾ pound asparagus for the spinach or broccoli. Trim the asparagus and slice it about ½ inch thick. Use the trimmings for your vegetable broth. Before adding the egg mixture, bring the broth to a boil and add the asparagus. Cook for 3 to 4 minutes, until just tender. Remove from the broth and shock in a bowl of ice water. Drain and distribute among 4 soup bowls. Measure your broth and add enough to make 4 cups, as some may have evaporated when you cooked the asparagus. Taste and adjust seasonings. Proceed with the recipe, beginning at Step 2.

LEMON STRACCIATELLA: This is based on a southern Italian wedding soup. The semolina is absent, there is more Parmigiano-Reggiano cheese, and there is lemon zest. You could also include the green vegetable here. Make the egg mixture with 2 large eggs, 4 ounces finely grated Parmesan, the grated zest of half a large lemon, a pinch of freshly grated nutmeg, and 2 tablespoons broth. With the broth at a bare simmer, stir in the egg mixture. Using a fork, stir with long strokes for about 15 seconds, then leave the mixture at a bare simmer for 1 minute. Serve at once.

SOUPE AU PISTOU

France • **Serves 8 generously**

This big spring vegetable soup from Provence is much like an Italian minestrone, but the enrichment comes at the end rather than at the beginning.

Instead of cooking aromatics in oil before adding water and vegetables, here everything is just thrown into the pot and cooked until the vegetables are tender and the broth fragrant. Then, just before the soup is served, a rich Provençal pesto (*pistou*) is stirred in. *Pistou* differs from pesto in its consistency—there are no pine nuts—and the occasional inclusion of a tomato. It's a heady mixture.

If you're lucky enough to find fresh cranberry beans at your farmers' market, use them. If not, use all dried white beans.

FOR THE SOUP

1 cup dried white beans, picked over, rinsed, soaked in water to cover for 6 hours or overnight, and drained (increase to 2 cups white beans if fresh cranberry beans, below, are unavailable)

8 cups water

1 large onion, chopped

6 to 8 large garlic cloves, minced or put through a press

A bouquet garni made with a few sprigs each fresh thyme and parsley, a Parmesan rind, and a bay leaf

½ pound green beans, or ¼ pound green beans and ¼ pound yellow wax beans, trimmed and broken into 1-inch pieces

2 medium zucchini (about ½ pound), scrubbed and diced

1 pound fresh cranberry beans, shelled (if available)

2 large carrots, chopped

2 celery stalks, chopped

2 leeks, white and light green parts only, cleaned and sliced

2 medium turnips, peeled and diced

1 pound red-skinned potatoes, diced

1 pound tomatoes, peeled, seeded, and chopped; or 1 can (14 ounces) tomatoes with juice

Salt

½ cup soup pasta, such as macaroni or small shells

Freshly ground pepper

½ cup freshly grated Parmesan or Gruyère

FOR THE PISTOU

2 to 4 large garlic cloves (to taste), peeled

2 cups tightly packed fresh basil leaves

Rounded ¼ teaspoon salt (more to taste)

⅓ cup extra virgin olive oil

1 small tomato, peeled, seeded, and chopped (optional)

¼ to ½ teaspoon salt (to taste)

1 cup freshly grated Parmesan, or a mixture of Gruyère and Parmesan

Freshly ground pepper

1. *Make the soup:* Combine the drained white beans and the water in a large, heavy soup pot. Bring to a boil. Skim off any foam, then add the onion, 2 of the garlic cloves, and the bouquet garni. Reduce the heat, cover, and simmer for 1 hour.

2. Set aside half the green beans and half the zucchini. Add the remaining beans, zucchini, and garlic to the soup pot along with the cranberry beans, carrots, celery, leeks, turnips, potatoes, and tomatoes. Bring back to a boil. Add salt (be generous), reduce the heat, cover, and simmer for 1 hour. Taste and adjust the seasonings.

3. While the soup is simmering, bring a pot of water to a boil, add 1 teaspoon salt and the reserved zucchini, and cook for 3 or 4 minutes, just until bright on the outside and translucent. Transfer from the pot with a slotted spoon or deep-fry skimmer to a bowl of ice cold water. Drain and set aside. Bring the water back to a boil and drop in the reserved green beans. Cook for 5 minutes, until tender and bright. Transfer to a bowl of ice-cold water. Drain and set aside with the zucchini.

4. *Make the pistou while the soup simmers:* If making the *pistou* in a food processor: Turn on the processor fitted with the steel blade and drop in the garlic. When the garlic is chopped and adhering to the sides of the bowl, stop the machine. Scrape down the sides of the bowl, add the basil and salt, and process until finely chopped. Scrape down the sides once more. With the machine running, drizzle in the oil, then drop in the tomato, if using. Process to a paste. Add the salt, then stir in the cheese and pepper.

If making the *pistou* in a mortar and pestle: Mash the garlic to a paste with the salt. Add the basil, a handful at a time, and pound and grind the basil to a paste. Add the tomato and work into a paste with the basil. Work in the olive oil drop by drop. Stir in the cheese and pepper.

5. About 10 minutes before serving, add the pasta to the simmering soup and cook until al dente, 5 to 10 minutes. Add pepper, taste, and adjust salt. Stir the blanched zucchini and green beans into the soup and heat through. Discard the bouquet garni.

6. To serve, you can stir the *pistou* into the soup before serving, place a dollop of *pistou* in each bowl of soup and stir in, or pass the *pistou* in a bowl and let people stir in their own. Pass additional Parmesan or Gruyère for sprinkling.

ADVANCE PREPARATION: The soup can be made through Step 2 up to 3 days ahead, and definitely benefits from being made a day ahead. Refrigerate overnight, then bring back to a simmer and proceed with the recipe. The blanched zucchini and green beans will keep for 2 or 3 days in a covered bowl in the refrigerator. Soupe au Pistou will keep for about 5 days in the refrigerator. You'll lose the brightness of the vegetables, and the soup will thicken because of the pasta.

LEFTOVERS: If you wish to transform leftovers into something else, see the recipe for Ribolitta on page 147.

BOUILLABAISSE OF FRESH PEAS
France • Serves 4

In our house, fresh shelled peas rarely get as far as a cooking pot. My son, Liam, and I tend to shell them and eat them like candy. But if you can possibly manage to resist eating the peas right out of the pods, use them for this incredibly sweet soup from Provence. There is a peasant tradition in this Mediterranean region of France of making "poor man's bouillabaisse" with vegetables (see also the

Spinach Bouillabaisse, right, and the Tomato, Egg, and Bread Bouillabaisse on page 158); it's the saffron that gives the French license to call it a bouillabaisse. For this soup, only fresh peas will work; don't try it with frozen.

2 tablespoons extra virgin olive oil

1 medium onion, chopped

1 pound Yukon gold potatoes, scrubbed and sliced

4 large garlic cloves, minced

4 cups freshly shelled peas (about 4 pounds in the pod)

Generous pinch saffron

6 cups water

Salt and freshly ground pepper

4 large eggs

4 thick garlic croutons (Crostini, page 135)

3 tablespoons chopped fresh flat-leaf parsley, or a mixture of parsley, tarragon, and chives

Rouille (page 73), optional

1. Heat the oil in a heavy soup pot over medium heat and add the onion. Cook, stirring, until tender, about 5 minutes, and add the potatoes and garlic. Cook, stirring, until the garlic begins to smell fragrant, about 1 minute, and add the peas and crumble in the saffron. Stir together for a minute, then add the water and about 2 teaspoons salt. Bring to a boil, reduce the heat, cover, and simmer for 30 minutes, until the vegetables are tender and the broth sweet. Taste, adjust salt, and add pepper.

2. Have the soup at a bare simmer. One by one, break each egg into a teacup, then tip into the soup. Poach the eggs for 4 to 5 minutes, until just set. Place a crouton in each bowl and, using a skimmer or a slotted spoon, scoop out a poached egg and place it on top. Stir the herbs into the soup, then ladle the soup into the bowls. Serve at once, passing the rouille at the table for people to add if they wish.

ADVANCE PREPARATION: You can have the peas shelled and ready hours ahead of time, but the soup is best served right away.

SPINACH BOUILLABAISSE
France • Serves 4 generously

This soup comes from Provence, where many hearty soups that feature potatoes, saffron, and a poached egg are called *bouillabaisse.*

16 cups (4 quarts) water

Salt

2½ pounds fresh spinach, stemmed

1 tablespoon extra virgin olive oil, plus additional for drizzling

2 leeks, white and light green parts only, cleaned and sliced, or 1 onion, chopped

4 to 6 garlic cloves (to taste), minced

1 pound red-skinned potatoes, scrubbed, peeled if desired, and sliced

A bouquet garni made with a bay leaf and a few sprigs each fresh thyme and parsley

A generous pinch saffron

Freshly ground pepper

4 large eggs

4 thick slices bread, toasted and rubbed with garlic

½ cup grated Gruyère cheese

1. Bring the water to a boil in a large pot. Add 1 tablespoon salt and the spinach. Blanch just until wilted, less than a minute. Using a slotted spoon, transfer the spinach to a bowl of cold water. Let sit for a couple of minutes, drain, and squeeze out the water. Chop coarsely and set aside. Measure out 6 cups of the cooking water and set aside.

2. Heat 1 tablespoon olive oil in a large, heavy soup pot or Dutch oven over medium heat and add the leeks. Cook, stirring often, until tender and translucent, about 5 minutes, and add the garlic. Cook, stirring, for another minute or so, until fragrant. Add the spinach and stir together for a few seconds, then add the potatoes, the 6 cups reserved blanching water, and the bouquet garni. Bring to a boil and crumble in the saffron. Reduce the heat to a simmer, cover, and simmer for 15 minutes, or until the potatoes are tender. Taste and adjust salt. Add pepper. Discard the bouquet garni. ▶

3. Have the soup at a bare simmer. One by one, break each egg into a teacup, then tip into the soup. Poach the eggs for 4 to 5 minutes, until just set. Place a crouton in each bowl and, using a skimmer or a slotted spoon, scoop out a poached egg and place it on top. Ladle the soup into the bowls. Sprinkle on the cheese and drizzle on a little olive oil. Serve.

ADVANCE PREPARATION: You can make this through Step 2 a day ahead.

VARIATION

GREENS BOUILLABAISSE: Substitute sturdier greens for the spinach. Kale, Swiss chard, and turnip greens are all good candidates. Blanch them for a longer time, 2 to 4 minutes, until tender. Proceed with the recipe. If you can find greens that are already stemmed, washed, and packaged, a 1-pound bag will be sufficient. I actually prefer this version to the one with spinach, because the leftovers hold up better.

TOMATO, EGG, AND BREAD BOUILLABAISSE

France • Serves 4 generously

This amazingly simple Provençal soup defines comfort food. Bread is sustenance throughout the Mediterranean, and stale bread has many delicious uses. Both Portugal, where it's called Stone Soup, and Provence have versions of this. And if you looked, you'd probably find something similar in Spain, Greece, and Italy—wherever there are good ripe tomatoes, olive oil, potatoes, eggs, crusty country bread, and a legacy of poverty. Saffron and garlic infuse the broth and give the potatoes a beautiful hue. The eggs, poached right in the soup and served up in each bowlful, enrich the dish and make each serving all the more sustaining. Use large, wide soup bowls for this.

  2 tablespoons extra virgin olive oil

  1 large onion, thinly sliced

  2 large garlic cloves (more to taste), minced or put through a press

1 pound ripe tomatoes, peeled, seeded, and chopped

Salt

2 tablespoons chopped fresh flat-leaf parsley, plus additional for garnish

1 bay leaf

¼ teaspoon paprika

4 cups water

1 pound red-skinned potatoes, peeled if desired and sliced

A generous pinch saffron

Freshly ground pepper

4 large eggs

4 to 8 thick slices stale or lightly toasted country bread, rubbed with garlic

1. Heat the olive oil in a large, heavy soup pot or casserole over medium heat and add the onion. Cook, stirring, until tender, about 5 minutes. Add the garlic and stir for about a minute, until fragrant. Add the tomatoes, salt to taste, and the parsley, bay leaf, and paprika, and cook, stirring from time to time, for 10 minutes, until the tomatoes have cooked down a bit and smell fragrant. Add the water and potatoes, and bring to a boil. Add more salt and crumble in the saffron. Reduce the heat, cover, and simmer for 20 to 25 minutes, or until the potatoes are tender. Taste, adjust the salt, and add pepper. Discard the bay leaf.

2. Have the soup at a bare simmer. One by one, break each egg into a teacup, then tip into the soup. Poach the eggs for 4 to 5 minutes, until just set. Place a piece or two of bread in each bowl and, using a skimmer or a slotted spoon, scoop out a poached egg and place it on top. Ladle the soup into the bowls. Sprinkle on parsley and serve.

ADVANCE PREPARATION: The soup can be made through Step 1 a day ahead and refrigerated. Bring back to a simmer and proceed with the recipe.

PROVENÇAL WHEAT BERRY SOUP

France • Serves 6 to 8

This is my version of a hearty Provençal harvest soup, *soupe d'epautre.* The wheat berries used are actually spelt, more commonly known here by the Italian name, *farro.* The grains are softer than the wheat berries we find in whole foods stores, with a wonderful earthy flavor; you can find them in Italian delis and gourmet markets. In the traditional *soupe d'epautre,* the grain is simmered with a mutton, prosciutto, or ham bone. I use Parmesan rinds to enrich the flavor in this vegetarian version.

2 cups farro, rinsed

1 ounce (about 1 cup) dried porcini mushrooms

2 cups boiling water

1 tablespoon extra virgin olive oil

1 onion, chopped

½ pound carrots, chopped

2 celery stalks with leaves, chopped

½ pound cabbage, shredded or finely chopped

1 teaspoon each chopped fresh rosemary and
    thyme (or ½ teaspoon crumbled dried)

4 large garlic cloves, minced or put through
    a press

A bouquet garni made with a bay leaf, a few
    sprigs each fresh thyme and parsley, and
    4 Parmesan rinds tied in a cheesecloth

2 tablespoons tomato paste

10 cups water

Salt and freshly ground pepper

1 can (15 ounces) white beans or borlotti
    beans, drained and rinsed

¼ cup chopped fresh flat-leaf parsley

½ cup grated Gruyère cheese (Parmesan can be
    substituted)

1. Soak the farro in water to cover for 1 hour or longer. Drain.

2. Meanwhile, place the dried mushrooms in a bowl or Pyrex measuring cup and pour on the boiling water. Let sit for 15 to 30 minutes, until the mushrooms are softened. Drain the mushrooms through a cheesecloth-lined strainer set over a bowl. Press down on the mushrooms to release all the liquid, then rinse them in several changes of water to rid of sand. Chop coarsely and set aside.

3. Heat the oil in a large, heavy soup pot or Dutch oven over medium heat and add the onion. Cook, stirring, for 3 to 5 minutes, until it begins to soften. Add the carrots, celery, cabbage, and rosemary and thyme, cover, reduce the heat to medium-low, and cook, stirring often, for 5 to 10 minutes, until the vegetables are fragrant and tender enough to pierce with the tip of a knife. Add the garlic and cook, stirring, for a minute, until fragrant, then add the soaked mushrooms and their liquid, the farro, bouquet garni, tomato paste, and water. Bring to a boil, add salt (at least 2 teaspoons, eventually more), reduce the heat, cover, and simmer for 1 hour, until the farro is tender and the soup fragrant. If you feel that it is too thick, thin out with more water. Add pepper and adjust salt. Remove the bouquet garni and stir in the beans and parsley. Heat through and serve, passing the cheese for sprinkling.

ADVANCE PREPARATION: The soup can be made a day or two ahead, but don't add the parsley. If it thickens too much overnight, add a little water and reheat. Adjust seasonings. Add parsley just before serving.

PROVENÇAL CHICK PEA SOUP
France • **Serves 4 to 6**

You'll find chick peas throughout the Mediterranean, picking up different seasonings in different places. In Provence, you're most likely to find them in a soup fragrant with olive oil and garlic, like this one, or in a salad like the one on page 102. This thick, hearty soup makes a filling meal with a green salad and some crusty bread.

> 1 pound dried chick peas, picked over, rinsed, soaked in water to cover for 6 hours or overnight, and drained
>
> 8 cups water
>
> 1 large leek, white and light green parts only, cleaned and chopped
>
> 4 to 6 garlic cloves (to taste), minced
>
> 1 can (14 ounces) chopped tomatoes, drained
>
> A bouquet garni made with 1 bay leaf, a few sprigs each fresh parsley and thyme, and a Parmesan rind
>
> Salt and freshly ground pepper
>
> 1 tablespoon extra virgin olive oil, plus additional for drizzling
>
> ¼ cup chopped fresh flat-leaf parsley
>
> 8 to 12 garlic croutons (Crostini, page 135)

1. Place the chick peas in a large soup pot, add the water, and bring to a boil. Skim off any foam, then add the leek, garlic, tomatoes, and bouquet garni. Cover, reduce the heat, and simmer for 1 hour.

2. Add 2 teaspoons salt to the beans and simmer for another hour, until the chick peas are thoroughly tender. Add pepper, taste, and adjust salt. Remove the bouquet garni.

3. Using a hand-held blender, purée the soup coarsely. You can also put it through the medium blade of a food mill, or pulse in a food processor. It should retain some texture. Return to the pot and stir in 1 tablespoon olive oil and the parsley; taste and adjust seasoning.

4. Heat the soup through and serve, floating a couple of garlic croutons in each bowl and drizzling on a little stream of olive oil.

ADVANCE PREPARATION: This soup keeps well for about 4 days. It will continue to thicken, so you may want to thin it out with water.

LENTIL SOUP WITH GOAT CHEESE
France • **Serves 6**

This lentil soup is a simple one, just lentils, onion, garlic, and seasonings. But it's garnished with goat cheese, which melts into the soup and adds a wonderful deep, earthy flavor.

> 1 tablespoon extra virgin olive oil
>
> 1 medium onion, chopped
>
> 4 garlic cloves, minced
>
> 1 pound (2 heaped cups) lentils, picked over and rinsed
>
> 8 cups water
>
> A bouquet garni made with a bay leaf, a few sprigs each fresh thyme and parsley, and a Parmesan rind
>
> Salt and freshly ground pepper
>
> 2 to 3 tablespoons chopped fresh flat-leaf parsley (to taste)
>
> 4 ounces fresh goat cheese, cut in thin slices or crumbled
>
> 12 thin garlic croutons (Crostini, page 135)

1. Heat the olive oil in a large, heavy soup pot or Dutch oven over medium heat and add the onion. Cook, stirring, until tender, about 5 minutes. Stir in the garlic and cook, stirring, for 30 seconds to 1 minute, until fragrant. Add the lentils, water, and bouquet garni, and bring to a boil. Reduce the heat, cover, and simmer for 30 minutes.

2. Stir in salt (2 teaspoons or more) and pepper. Cover and continue to simmer for another 15 to 30 minutes, until the lentils are thoroughly tender and the broth fragrant. Remove the bouquet garni.

3. Using a hand-held blender, purée the soup coarsely. Taste and adjust seasonings. Stir in the parsley. Serve, floating a slice of goat cheese or a handful of the cheese if it's crumbled, and a crouton or two in each bowl.

ADVANCE PREPARATION: You can make the soup up to a day or two ahead. You will probably need to thin it out to your taste with water.

PROVENÇAL LENTIL AND TOMATO SOUP
France • Serves 4

If you have lentils in your kitchen, you have dinner. Time and time again I turn to this quick-cooking, richly flavored legume when I'm in a quandary as to what to make. There are so many ways to approach a lentil soup, as evidenced by the many variations you find throughout the Mediterranean—and in this book!

- 1 cup lentils, picked over and rinsed
- 4 garlic cloves, peeled
- 1 bay leaf
- 5 cups water
- 3 tablespoons extra virgin olive oil
- 2 medium onions, chopped
- 1 celery stalk, chopped
- 2 large, ripe tomatoes, peeled, seeded, and chopped; or 1 can (14 ounces) tomatoes, chopped, with juice
- 1 sprig fresh thyme
- A handful fresh basil leaves, slivered or chopped
- Salt and freshly ground pepper
- ½ cup elbow macaroni or other soup pasta
- ¼ cup freshly grated Parmesan or Gruyère

1. Place the lentils in a saucepan or soup pot with 1 of the garlic cloves and the bay leaf. Add 4 cups of the water and bring to a boil. Reduce the heat, cover, and simmer for 20 minutes. Drain through a strainer set over a bowl. Rinse the lentils with cold water and set aside, along with the cooking water. Discard the bay leaf.

2. Mash the cooked garlic clove with the remaining 3 garlic cloves in a mortar and pestle. Set aside.

3. Heat 2 tablespoons of the oil in a heavy soup pot or Dutch oven over medium heat and add the onions and celery. Cook, stirring, until tender, about 5 minutes. Add the tomatoes, mashed garlic, and the lentils, and cook, stirring, for 5 minutes. Add the cooking water from the lentils along with the remaining 1 cup water, the thyme, a few basil leaves, and salt and pepper to taste. Bring to a simmer, cover, and simmer for 30 minutes over low heat. The lentils should be tender but intact, the broth fragrant. Add the pasta and continue to cook another 5 to 10 minutes, until the pasta is tender. Taste and adjust seasoning. Add the remaining basil and 1 tablespoon olive oil. Serve with Parmesan or Gruyère for sprinkling.

ADVANCE PREPARATION: This soup tastes even better the day after you make it, but don't add the pasta. Bring back to a simmer, cook the pasta in the soup as directed, and serve.

LEFTOVERS: The soup will keep for about 5 days.

GARLIC SOUP
France • Serves 4

Whenever anybody insists that they don't have time to cook, this simple soup is my retort. A Provençal saying goes *"Aïgo boulïdo sauva la vida"* ("Boiled garlic saves lives"), and indeed, the soup is recommended as a cure for everything from hangovers to stomach ailments to colds. It's truly the chicken soup of Provence. In my home it's much more than that—it's dinner, especially on those days when the cupboard may be on the bare side. There are many ways to make a meal out of this, as indicated in all of the variations that follow.

In the authentic version, the garlic cloves are merely crushed, then simmered. I tend to chop them or put them through a press, to get a little more punch. If you want a milder soup, then do it the Provençal way.

6 cups water

4 to 6 garlic cloves (to taste), minced, put
   through a press, or crushed

1 bay leaf

1 sprig fresh sage or thyme

1½ to 2 teaspoons salt (more to taste)

Freshly ground pepper

2 egg yolks or 1 whole large egg

1 tablespoon extra virgin olive oil

1 tablespoon chopped fresh flat-leaf parsley

4 thick garlic croutons (Crostini, page 135)

¼ cup freshly grated Gruyère or Parmesan

1. In a soup pot, combine the water, garlic, bay leaf, sage, and salt, and bring to a boil. Reduce the heat, cover, and simmer for 20 minutes. Add a few twists of pepper, taste, and adjust seasonings.

2. Beat the egg yolks or egg and the olive oil together in a bowl. Stir in 1 ladleful of the hot soup. Turn off the heat under the soup and stir in the tempered egg. Add the parsley. Discard the bay leaf.

3. Place a crouton in each soup bowl and ladle in the soup. Top with a tablespoon of Gruyère or Parmesan and serve.

ADVANCE PREPARATION: This is best made close to serving time, and it takes so little time that there's really not much need to get a jump on it.

VARIATIONS

There are many ways to turn this humble broth into a more substantial soup, which is what I always do if it's going to be dinner:

- Increase the water to 7 cups, and simmer 1 cup pasta (soup pasta, broken vermicelli, or fusilli) in the soup until al dente before enriching with the egg yolks. You may have to adjust the salt.

- Increase the water to 7 cups. Add ¾ pound sliced red-skinned potatoes and simmer with the garlic until tender before enriching with the egg yolks. You may have to adjust the salt.

- Add ½ pound broken up broccoli florets or green beans to the soup and simmer for 5 to 10 minutes before enriching with egg yolks.

- Add 1 cup skinned, shelled fresh fava beans (page 113) to the soup and simmer for 5 to 10 minutes before enriching with egg yolks.

AN ODE TO GARLIC SOUP

L'oulo canto sus lou fiò:
Oh! La bono aigo-boulido!
Entre li dous grand cafiò
Lando, lando regalido!
Nòsti gent vènon dina,
Arrena.
Un brout de sàuvi dins l'oulo
Reviscoulo
Lou crestian …

The soup pot sings on the hearth:
Oh! The good garlic soup!
Between the two big andirons
Burn, joyous flame!
Our tired people are coming to dine.
From one sprig of sage in the pot
The Christian will draw strength …

From *Lis Isclo d'Or* by *Frédéric Mistral*

PROVENÇAL WINTER SQUASH SOUP
France • Serves 4

This is an everyday soup in homes all over Provence. It can be seasoned with thyme or sage, thickened with rice or potatoes. Any type of winter squash will do; if you use a dense squash like butternut, the soup will be thicker. If it seems too thick, just thin out with water or milk.

2 pounds winter squash, such as butternut,
   kabocha, hubbard, or a combination

2 tablespoons extra virgin olive oil

ROASTING WINTER SQUASH

Roasting the squash before making the soup is far from traditional: Ovens did not exist in most Provençal peasant homes until recent times. But one day I just didn't feel like peeling the hard squash, so I put it in the oven for a while, then peeled it when it had softened up. I kept the juices and added them to the water so that I wouldn't lose any sweet flavor. And ever since, that's the way I've been working with winter squash destined to be puréed with the rest of the soup.

- 1 medium onion, chopped
- 3 large garlic cloves, minced
- 2 teaspoons fresh thyme leaves or chopped fresh sage
- 1 medium Yukon gold or russet potato, peeled and diced; or ⅓ cup rice
- 6 cups water
- 1 bay leaf
- Salt and freshly ground pepper
- ¼ cup chopped fresh flat-leaf parsley

1. Heat the oven to 375°F. Cut the squash in half lengthwise and scoop out the seeds. Cover a baking sheet with foil, lightly oil the foil with olive oil, and place the squash halves on top, cut side down. Roast for 30 minutes, or until you are able to pierce the skin easily with a fork. It should not be tender all the way through. Cool. Collect any juices from the pan and set aside in a bowl. When the squash is cool enough to handle, peel and dice it.

2. Heat the oil in a heavy soup pot or Dutch oven over medium heat. Add the onion and cook, stirring, until tender, about 5 minutes. Add the garlic and stir for 30 seconds to 1 minute, until fragrant. Stir in the squash, thyme, and potatoes. Add the water, any juices from roasting the squash, the bay leaf, and about 2 teaspoons salt. Bring to a boil, reduce the heat, cover, and simmer for 30 minutes to 1 hour, until the squash is tender and the broth fragrant.

3. Discard the bay leaf. Using a hand-held blender or a food mill fitted with the medium blade, purée the soup. Taste and adjust salt, and add lots of freshly ground pepper. Stir in the parsley and serve.

ADVANCE PREPARATION: This soup will hold up well, on top of the stove or in the refrigerator, for several hours. Don't stir in the parsley until just before serving.

VEGETABLE SOUP WITH CHICK PEAS AND SPINACH (Potaje de Vigilia)

Spain • **Serves 6 to 8**

The Andalusians call this soup *potaje de vigilia,* or "fasting soup." Fasting here refers to its vegetarian nature, as it would have been eaten on Christian days of abstinence, when meat was forbidden. Actually, there's nothing meager about it. It makes a substantial meal. In the authentic recipe, which I came across in Clifford Wright's *Mediterranean Vegetables,* the croutons are fried in olive oil. To cut down on oil, I toast the bread.

- 1 cup dried chick peas, picked over, rinsed, soaked in water to cover for 6 hours or overnight, and drained
- 6 cups water
- Salt
- 4 slices baguette
- 1½ tablespoons sherry vinegar
- 2 tablespoons extra virgin olive oil
- 1 medium onion, chopped
- 3 garlic cloves, minced
- 2 medium ripe tomatoes, peeled, seeded, and chopped; or 1 cup chopped canned tomatoes, with juice
- 2 teaspoons paprika
- 1 pound potatoes (russets or Yukon golds), peeled and diced
- Freshly ground pepper
- 1 pound spinach, stemmed and coarsely chopped
- 3 tablespoons pine nuts (optional)

¼ cup finely chopped fresh flat-leaf parsley

Pinch saffron, crumbled

1 large egg, hard-cooked and chopped

1. Combine the drained chick peas and 4 cups of the water in a large saucepan. Bring to a boil, reduce the heat, cover, and simmer for 1 hour. Add 1 teaspoon salt and continue to simmer until tender, 30 minutes to 1 hour.

2. Toast the bread until golden and tear it into smaller pieces. Place in a small bowl and douse with the vinegar. Set aside.

3. Heat the oil in a heavy soup pot over medium heat and add the onion. Cook, stirring, until it begins to soften, about 3 minutes. Add one-third of the garlic, the tomatoes, and the paprika, and cook, stirring often, until the tomatoes cook down to a thick paste, 10 to 15 minutes.

4. Add the chick peas with their liquid, the potatoes, another teaspoon of salt, pepper, and the remaining 2 cups water. Bring to a boil, reduce the heat to low, and simmer until the potatoes are tender, about 30 minutes. Stir in the spinach and simmer another 10 minutes. Taste and adjust seasoning.

5. Add the remaining garlic, the soaked bread, pine nuts, parsley, saffron, and hard-cooked egg to the soup. Stir once, turn off the heat, and let the soup rest for 10 minutes. Serve hot.

ADVANCE PREPARATION: You can make this soup through Step 4 up to a day ahead of serving. You might want to hold off adding the spinach until you reheat, if you want it to have a nice color. Bring the soup to a simmer and proceed with Step 5.

CASTILIAN GARLIC SOUP WITH PAPRIKA AND SAFFRON
Spain • Serves 4

This recipe calls to mind a garlic soup I ate in Spain many years ago, at the start of a 5-week drive through Europe that began in Madrid. My friend Franci and I covered a lot of ground in a small white Fiat. On the first leg of our journey, we drove north from Madrid to Santander, on the Atlantic coast. It was a long drive, with a break for lunch somewhere in the vicinity of Bilbao, long before there was a famous art museum there. I ate this soup for lunch, and I never forgot it. The recipe is a classic one, adapted from Penelope Casas's recipe in *The Foods and Wines of Spain*.

2 tablespoons extra virgin olive oil

6 plump garlic cloves, peeled and cut in half lengthwise

1 tablespoon paprika

½ teaspoon ground cumin

Pinch cayenne

6 cups water

Salt

Pinch saffron, crumbled

4 large eggs

4 (½-inch-thick) slices crusty country bread, toasted

1 tablespoon chopped fresh flat-leaf parsley

Freshly grated Parmesan (optional)

1. Heat the oil in a heavy soup pot or 2-quart saucepan, or (preferably) an earthenware pot set on a flame tamer, over low heat. Add the garlic and cook gently, stirring often, until tender and golden, about 12 minutes. Stir in the paprika, cumin, and cayenne, then remove the pot from the heat and, using a fork, the back of your spoon, or a pestle, crush the garlic cloves. Add the water, stir, and return to the heat. Bring to a simmer, add salt to taste (1½ to 2 teaspoons) and the saffron, cover, and simmer gently for 20 minutes. Taste and adjust seasonings.

2. Shortly before serving, break the eggs, one by one, into a teacup, then tip into the soup. The broth should be barely simmering. Cover and cook for 4 to 5 minutes, just until the whites set. Place a piece of toast in each soup bowl. Lift out an egg and place on top of the bread. Ladle in the soup. Sprinkle with parsley and Parmesan, and serve.

ADVANCE PREPARATION: You can make the soup through Step 1 several hours before you wish to serve it. Reheat gently and proceed with Step 2.

GAZPACHO
Spain • Serves 4

When I went to Spain 20 years ago, I ate gazpacho everywhere I went, and it was always different— not so much in flavor, but the garnishes varied. But when I spent time in Andalusia in the summer of 2005, the gazpacho varied little from restaurant to restaurant. I was glad of this, because it was always wonderful, as you'll see when you try this. It was July, and hot, and the gazpacho was served from big glass pitchers, poured into glasses, over ice, without garnishes. You'll love the little kick that a mere slice of onion and a couple of garlic cloves give to the soup. Otherwise, it's really about tomatoes. Give me stale bread and ripe tomatoes, and I'll make a drinkable salad any time.

> 2 thick slices stale French bread, crusts removed (about 1 ounce)
>
> 1 pound ripe tomatoes, peeled and roughly chopped
>
> 2 to 4 garlic cloves (to taste), peeled
>
> 1 slice red or white onion, coarsely chopped and rinsed with cold water
>
> 2 tablespoons extra virgin olive oil
>
> 1 to 2 tablespoons sherry vinegar or red wine vinegar (to taste)
>
> ½ to 1 teaspoon sweet paprika (to taste)
>
> Salt and freshly ground pepper
>
> ½ to 1 cup ice water, depending on how thick you want your soup to be

OPTIONAL GARNISHES

> ½ cup finely chopped, seeded cucumber (more to taste)
>
> ½ cup finely chopped, seeded tomato (more to taste)
>
> ¼ cup chopped fresh basil or parsley
>
> ½ cup finely chopped green bell pepper
>
> ½ cup small croutons (Crostini, page 135)
>
> 1 large egg, hard-cooked and finely chopped

1. Place the bread in a bowl and sprinkle with enough water to soften it. Let sit for 5 minutes, until soft enough to squeeze, and squeeze out the water.

2. Combine the bread, tomatoes, garlic, onion, olive oil, vinegar, paprika, and salt and pepper in a blender and blend until smooth. Taste and adjust seasonings. Pour into a bowl or pitcher, thin out as desired with water, cover, and chill for several hours.

3. Meanwhile, if using garnishes, place them in small bowls on a platter. Serve the soup in glasses over ice if it's a very hot day and you aren't serving garnishes (I like to serve it this way with drinks, before we sit down to dinner). Otherwise, serve it in bowls and pass the tray of garnishes.

ADVANCE PREPARATION: You can make the soup a day ahead.

GAZPACHO IN THE NEW SPANISH KITCHEN

As classic as the above recipe for gazpacho is, and as consistently as I ate it all over Spain, there is a revolutionary movement going on in haute cuisine in this country. Avant-garde chefs are adding all sorts of unexpected ingredients to the classic base, including cherries and watermelon, mangoes, anchovies, and sardines!

COLD TOMATO AND ROASTED PEPPER SOUP (Salmorejo)

Spain • **Serves 4 to 6**

This Andalusian soup is a first cousin of Gazpacho (page 165), which is to say it's a true expression of ripe tomatoes seasoned with vinegar and olive oil. Only ripe, in-season tomatoes will do. *Salmorejo* is traditionally garnished with hard-cooked eggs, herbs, and Serrano ham. If you're not vegetarian you might try it this way, but it's perfectly delicious, and refreshing as only gazpacho can be, without the ham.

>   2½ pounds ripe red tomatoes, peeled, seeded, and roughly chopped
>
>   1 large green bell pepper, roasted (page 84), peeled, seeded, and chopped
>
>   5 ounces stale French bread, broken into small pieces
>
>   2 garlic cloves, minced
>
>   1 to 2 tablespoons sherry vinegar (to taste)
>
>   2 tablespoons extra virgin olive oil
>
>   Salt and freshly ground pepper
>
>   1 cup cold water
>
>   2 or 3 large eggs, hard-cooked
>
>   2 tablespoons chopped fresh herbs, such as parsley, chives, tarragon, or basil, alone or in combination

1. In a large bowl, combine the tomatoes, bell pepper, bread, garlic, vinegar, and olive oil. Salt and pepper generously, toss together, cover, and refrigerate for 2 hours. Add the water and about ½ teaspoon salt.

2. In batches, transfer the mixture to a blender and purée. If you wish, thin out with more cold water. The soup should be thick. Taste and adjust seasonings. Refrigerate until ready to serve.

3. Cut the eggs into tiny dice. Toss with the herbs and season with salt and pepper. Ladle the soup into bowls, sprinkle each serving with the chopped eggs and herbs, and serve.

ADVANCE PREPARATION: You can make this soup several hours before you serve it (you will have to give yourself at least 2 hours for the soup to chill properly). You could prep all of the produce a day ahead. Roasted peppers will keep for a week in the refrigerator. If you do have some on hand, include any juices that have accumulated in the bowl.

WHITE GAZPACHO WITH GRAPES

Spain • **Serves 4 to 6**

A mixture of puréed almonds, bread, and garlic, this gazpacho is said to come from Màlaga, although I didn't see it on too many menus in that city. It's incredibly refreshing, and a nice change from the classic tomato gazpacho.

>   ⅔ cup blanched almonds
>
>   2 medium garlic cloves, peeled
>
>   1 to 1½ teaspoons salt (to taste)
>
>   4 slices stale white bread, crusts removed, soaked in water until soft, then squeezed (about ½ to ⅔ cup, once the water is squeezed out)
>
>   2 tablespoons sherry vinegar or red wine vinegar
>
>   3½ cups ice water
>
>   ¼ cup extra virgin olive oil
>
>   30 seedless grapes, halved

1. Place the almonds, garlic, and salt in a food processor fitted with the steel blade or in a blender jar. Pulse until finely chopped. Add the bread, vinegar, and ½ cup of the ice water and blend until smooth. With the blender on, stream in the olive oil and continue to blend until smooth. Transfer to a bowl and whisk in the remaining ice water. Taste and add salt or vinegar as desired. Refrigerate for an hour or more.

2. Ladle the soup into bowls, garnish with the grapes, and serve.

ADVANCE PREPARATION: This soup can be made a day ahead. It will taste more pungent on the second day.

ICED CUCUMBER SOUP WITH WALNUTS
The Balkans • Serves 4 to 6

This Turkish and Bulgarian soup has variations all over the Balkans. The Greek version would not include the walnuts. It's a refreshing soup, pungent with garlic and with wonderful texture because of the walnuts.

FOR THE SOUP

4 garlic cloves, peeled

Salt

⅔ cup shelled walnuts

3 slices French or Italian bread, crusts removed, soaked in water, then squeezed

2 tablespoons walnut oil or extra virgin olive oil, or 1 tablespoon each

2 cups drained yogurt (page 21)

½ cup ice water, preferably spring water

1 tablespoon white wine vinegar or fresh lemon juice

1 English cucumber, about 10 inches long, or 3 Persian cucumbers, cut into tiny dice

Ice cubes (optional)

FOR GARNISH

⅓ cup finely chopped walnuts

Olive oil (optional)

2 tablespoons finely chopped fresh dill

Lemon wedges

1. Place the garlic in a mortar with ½ teaspoon salt and mash to a paste.

2. If making the soup in a mortar and pestle: Add the walnuts, a handful at a time, and mash to a paste with the garlic. Add the bread and work into the paste. Work in the oil, a little at a time. Transfer to a large bowl and stir in the yogurt.

   If making the soup in a food processor: Pulse the walnuts in a food processor fitted with the steel blade until finely ground. Add the bread and pulse until the mixture has been reduced to a paste. Add the mashed garlic and process until blended. Add the oil with the machine running.

Add the yogurt and pulse until everything is well blended. Transfer to a bowl.

3. Stir in the ice water and vinegar. Add salt to taste. Chill for 1 hour or longer.

4. Season the cucumber lightly with salt and add to the soup base. Stir.

5. If you wish, place an ice cube in each bowl. Ladle in the soup. Top with chopped walnuts, a drizzle of olive oil if desired, and a sprinkling of dill. Pass the lemon wedges.

ADVANCE PREPARATION: You can make this several hours before serving it. Keep the soup base and the cucumbers refrigerated separately. The longer it sits, the more pungent it will become.

WHITE BEAN SOUP
The Balkans • Serves 4

This is a beautiful bean soup, with flecks of red pepper, tomato, carrot, and bright green parsley and mint. It's slightly picante because of the hot red pepper flakes.

½ pound (1 heaped cup) dried white beans, such as navy beans or cannellini, picked over, rinsed, soaked in water to cover for 6 hours or overnight, and drained

5 cups water

1 bay leaf

Salt and freshly ground pepper

2 tablespoons extra virgin olive oil

1 large onion, finely chopped

3 large garlic cloves, minced

1 large red bell pepper, diced

1 large carrot, diced

1 medium parsnip, peeled, cored, and diced

1 teaspoon paprika

½ teaspoon hot red pepper flakes

A bouquet garni made with 5 fresh parsley sprigs and 5 fresh mint sprigs

2 tablespoons chopped fresh-flat leaf parsley

2 tablespoons chopped fresh mint

1. Combine the drained beans, water, and bay leaf in a large saucepan. Bring to a boil, skim off any foam, and reduce the heat. Cover and simmer for 1 hour, until the beans are just tender. Add salt to taste (about 2 teaspoons) and freshly ground pepper.

2. Heat the olive oil in a heavy soup pot or Dutch oven over medium heat and add the onion. Cook, stirring, until tender, and add the garlic, bell pepper, carrot, and parsnip. Cook, stirring, until the garlic is fragrant, about 1 minute. Add the beans with their liquid, the paprika, red pepper flakes, and bouquet garni, and bring back to a boil. Reduce the heat, cover, and simmer for 30 minutes, until the beans and vegetables are tender and the broth aromatic. Taste and adjust salt. Remove the bouquet garni and bay leaf and stir in the chopped parsley and mint. Serve hot.

ADVANCE PREPARATION: The soup keeps for 3 or 4 days in the refrigerator. It's best if you add the mint and parsley just before serving.

MAJORCAN BREAD AND VEGETABLE SOUP

Spain • **Serves 4 generously**

Called a *sopa* in Majorca, this is a thick soup in which day-old bread soaks up much of the broth. The broth is so delicious, you might just want to eat the bread on the side. But with the bread this is definitely a one-dish meal. Add a poached egg to it if you want something even more substantial.

- 3 tablespoons extra virgin olive oil
- 1 bunch scallions, white and light green parts only, chopped
- 1 small onion, chopped
- 5 garlic cloves, 4 minced, 1 cut in half
- 1 green bell pepper, finely chopped
- ½ pound zucchini, chopped
- 2 tablespoons minced fresh flat-leaf parsley
- ½ pound tomatoes, peeled, seeded, and chopped

- ¾ pound cabbage, cored and coarsely chopped
- 2 artichoke hearts, each cut into sixths (page 267), optional; or canned, in brine
- Salt and freshly ground pepper
- 5 cups Simple Vegetable Broth (page 145) or water
- ½ pound green beans, trimmed and broken in half if very long
- 12 slices country bread, stale or lightly toasted

1. Heat 2 tablespoons of the oil in a large oven-proof casserole over medium heat and add the scallions and onion. When they begin to soften, after about 3 minutes, stir in the minced garlic, bell pepper, zucchini, and parsley, stir together for a minute or two, then cover and reduce the heat to low. Cook for 15 minutes, stirring occasionally. Add the tomatoes, turn the heat to medium-high, and cook, stirring, for 5 minutes. Add the cabbage, artichoke hearts, and salt and pepper to taste. Cover, reduce the heat to low, and simmer for 15 minutes. Add the broth, bring to a boil, and stir in the green beans. Reduce the heat, cover, and simmer for 20 minutes. Taste and adjust seasonings.

2. Heat the oven to 450°F. Rub both sides of the bread with the cut clove of garlic. Slide half the bread under the vegetables, ladling broth and vegetables over the slices so that they are submerged, and place the remaining bread on top. (If you don't mind washing out another pot, you could place the first layer of bread in a large earthenware casserole, ladle in the soup, then top with the second layer of bread.) Drizzle with the remaining 1 tablespoon olive oil and bake for 10 minutes. Serve hot or warm.

ADVANCE PREPARATION: The soup can be prepared through Step 1 three days before serving and kept in the refrigerator. The beans will lose color, but not flavor. The broth just gets better.

TOMATO SOUP WITH CILANTRO AND VERMICELLI

North Africa • Serves 4

When I lived in Paris, I used to get the most wonderful facials from a beautician named Malika. Malika's mother was Tunisian, and she had taught her to make this tomato soup, which Malika called, simply, *coriander soup*. It's essentially a spicy tomato soup, with lots and lots of cilantro, and vermicelli added at the end. The authentic version would undoubtedly contain meat, either mutton, beef, or dried salted meat used to flavor soups and stews. I've always made this vegetarian version.

- 1 generous bunch cilantro
- 1 tablespoon extra virgin olive oil
- 1 medium onion, chopped
- 1 tablespoon sweet paprika
- ½ teaspoon freshly ground cumin seeds
- 4 garlic cloves, minced
- 1 can (28 ounces) crushed tomatoes in purée
- 4 cups water
- Salt and freshly ground pepper
- ½ cup broken vermicelli
- Juice of 1 lime (optional)

1. Separate about 12 sprigs of cilantro from the bunch and tie the rest into a bundle. Chop the 12 sprigs and set aside.

2. Heat the olive oil in a large soup pot or Dutch oven over medium heat and add the onion. Cook, stirring, until tender, about 5 minutes, and add the paprika, cumin, and half the garlic. Cook, stirring, for about a minute, until fragrant, and add the tomatoes. Cook, stirring from time to time, until the tomatoes cook down a bit and smell very fragrant, about 10 minutes. Add the water, the remaining garlic, the cilantro bunch, and salt to taste, about 2 teaspoons. Bring to a simmer, reduce the heat, and simmer for 30 minutes.

3. Discard the cilantro bunch. Add freshly ground pepper, taste, and adjust salt. Add the vermicelli. Cook until the vermicelli is tender, about 5 minutes.

Stir in the chopped cilantro and the lime juice if using. Correct seasoning again and serve.

ADVANCE PREPARATION: The soup can be made a day or two ahead, but don't add the vermicelli until shortly before serving.

BEAN AND VEGETABLE SOUP WITH PASTINA

Tunisia • Serves 4 to 6

Algerian and Tunisian cooks like to use small, round pasta, which they call *plombs* (pellets). Plombs are the same as Italian soup pasta (pastina), specifically *acini di pepe*. They also use a large, spherical couscous, referred to as *gros couscous* in French, and often labeled *toasted pasta balls, moghrabiya,* or *Israeli couscous* in some American gourmet groceries. You can use either, though it's easier to find the pasta. The authentic Algerian soup would be flavored with preserved meat jerky and mutton fat or *smen* (fermented butter). Olive oil and no meat will, however, do just fine. This recipe is adapted from a recipe in Kitty Morse's *The Vegetarian Table: North Africa.*

- 1 bunch cilantro
- 2 tablespoons extra virgin olive oil, plus additional for drizzling
- 1 large or 2 medium onions, chopped
- 4 garlic cloves, minced
- 1 tablespoon sweet paprika
- 1 teaspoon ground turmeric
- 1 cup dried shelled fava beans, soaked in 4 cups water for 6 hours or overnight and drained
- 1 cup dried white beans or chick peas, picked over, rinsed, soaked in 4 cups water for 6 hours or overnight, and drained
- 8 cups water
- 1 can (28 ounces) crushed tomatoes in purée
- 2 carrots, sliced
- ½ pound winter squash or waxy potatoes, peeled and diced
- Salt and freshly ground pepper

1 to 2 teaspoons harissa (to taste)

1 package (10 ounces) frozen baby lima beans

½ cup acini di pepe or large couscous

2 tablespoons chopped fresh mint

Lemon or lime wedges

1. Tie half the cilantro sprigs into a bundle and chop the rest. Set aside the chopped cilantro.

2. Heat the oil in a large bean pot or Dutch oven over medium heat and add the onion. Cook, stirring, until tender, about 5 minutes, and add the garlic, paprika, and turmeric. Stir for about a minute, until fragrant, and add the fava beans, white beans, water, and tomatoes. Bring to a boil, add the cilantro bundle, reduce the heat, cover, and simmer for 1 hour. Add the carrots and squash, a generous amount of salt, some pepper, and the harissa, and continue to simmer for another hour. Taste and adjust salt.

3. Add the lima beans and pasta to the soup and simmer, stirring occasionally, until both are tender. Discard the cilantro bundle. Stir in the chopped cilantro and the mint, adjust salt, and serve. Drizzle on some olive oil if desired and garnish with lemon or lime wedges.

ADVANCE PREPARATION: This soup gets better overnight, but don't add the pasta or the chopped cilantro and mint until shortly before serving. You may need to thin out with water.

CHICK PEA BREAKFAST SOUP (Leblebi)
Tunisia • Serves 4

This is the hearty Tunisian soup (some call it a stew) called *leblebi* that is traditionally eaten for breakfast. The soup itself is a pretty simple bowl of chick peas flavored with onion, garlic, harissa, and olive oil, but it's embellished, like Andalusian gazpacho, with any number of garnishes. These can look beautiful on a buffet, and make for a fun meal.

1 pound dried chick peas, picked over, rinsed, soaked in 8 cups water for 6 hours or overnight, and drained

8 cups water

1 tablespoon extra virgin olive oil

1 onion, chopped

4 large garlic cloves, minced or put through a press

2 heaped teaspoons cumin seeds, ground

2 tablespoons harissa

Salt

2 to 4 tablespoons fresh lemon juice (to taste)

FOR GARNISH

You'll want enough to fill small bowls or ramekins that you can set on a tray:

Lemon wedges

Coarse sea salt

Harissa (page 86 or commercial)

Chopped fresh tomatoes

Chopped green and red bell peppers

2 large eggs, hard-cooked and chopped

Rinsed capers

Sliced pickled turnips

Freshly ground cumin

Finely chopped fresh flat-leaf parsley

Finely chopped fresh cilantro

Sliced Preserved Lemons (page 87)

Croutons or sliced stale bread

Thinly sliced scallions, both white and green parts

Extra virgin olive oil

1. Combine the drained chick peas and water in a large, heavy soup pot or Dutch oven. Bring to a boil, reduce the heat, cover, and simmer for 1 hour.

2. Meanwhile, heat the oil in a medium nonstick frying pan over medium heat and add the onion. Cook, stirring, until tender, about 5 minutes. Stir in the garlic and cumin and stir for 30 seconds to a minute, until the garlic smells fragrant. Stir the mixture into the simmering beans.

3. After the chick peas have cooked for 1 hour, stir in the harissa and salt (2 teaspoons or more). Cover and cook for another 30 minutes to 1 hour, until the chick peas are very tender and the broth fragrant. Add lemon juice, taste, and adjust salt.

4. Serve the soup, passing your choice of garnishes on a large tray, or have them laid out on a buffet. Stir the garnishes into the soup and enjoy.

ADVANCE PREPARATION: The finished soup will taste great for 3 to 4 days. Keep in the refrigerator. You will want to refresh the condiments each time you serve.

LEFTOVERS: The cooked chick peas will keep for 4 to 5 days in the refrigerator, and can be turned into a leftover *leblebi* salad: Drain the chick peas, toss with condiments of your choice, and season with lemon juice, olive oil, garlic, salt, pepper, and cumin.

HEARTY BEAN, CHARD, AND VERMICELLI SOUP (Hlelem)
Tunisia • Serves 4

Hlelem is one of my favorite Tunisian dishes, a thick mixed bean soup that I would gladly make every week.

    2 tablespoons extra virgin olive oil
    1 medium onion, chopped
    4 garlic cloves, minced
    1 celery stalk, with leaves, chopped
    1 cup dried chick peas, picked over, rinsed, soaked in 4 cups water overnight, and drained
    1 cup giant white dried lima beans, soaked in 4 cups water overnight and drained; or 1 can butter or large lima beans, drained
    6 cups water
    1 can (6 ounces) tomato paste
    Salt
    1 pound Swiss chard, with stems, chopped
    ½ cup chopped fresh flat-leaf parsley
    ½ cup broken vermicelli
    2 to 3 teaspoons Harissa (page 86 or commercial)
    Freshly ground pepper
    Lemon wedges

Heat the olive oil in a large, heavy bean pot or Dutch oven over medium heat and add the onion. Cook, stirring, until tender, about 5 minutes, and add the garlic and celery. Cook, stirring, for a minute, until the garlic is fragrant. Add the chick peas, lima beans, water, and tomato paste. Bring to a boil, reduce the heat, cover, and simmer for 1 hour. Add salt (about 2 teaspoons) and the chard and parsley. Cover and simmer for another 30 minutes to 1 hour, until the broth is fragrant and the beans and vegetables tender. Stir in the vermicelli and simmer until tender. Add the harissa and pepper, taste, and adjust salt. Serve with lemon wedges.

ADVANCE PREPARATION: This can be made a day ahead. The flavors will improve overnight. Wait until the day you serve it to add the vermicelli.

Eggs and Cheese

One of my favorite Spanish paintings is Diego Velázquez's *Old Woman Frying Eggs* (1618), which hangs in the National Gallery of Scotland. An old woman sits at a small brazier, cooking two eggs in olive oil in a glazed *cazuela,* while a boy holding a melon and a carafe of wine looks on. She holds an egg in one beautiful hand, a wooden spoon that looks just like many of my own in the other. Beside her on a table are an onion and some shallots, a brass mortar and pestle, and a jug of olive oil, all that is needed for this simple meal. My eye falls first on the woman's beautifully lit face, worn but exquisite; then on the two profoundly yellow eggs in the *cazuela.* The whites are set, indicating that the eggs are just about ready to eat, which is perhaps why the boy has appeared with the melon and the wine. This might be all that there *was* to eat for these peasants in 17th-century Spain. Meager rations, but nutritionally you could do a lot worse. And they were sure to taste good.

Eggs, an inexpensive source of protein in countries where protein could be scarce, have always been an important food in the Mediterranean. One of the signature dishes of Spain,

173

for example, is a simple potato and onion omelet called *tortilla española* (a *tortilla* in Spain is a frittata or flat omelet, and should not be confused with the Mexican flat bread of the same name). *Tortilla española* is served as a tapa in bars all over the country, and is eaten by many families as a quick light meal. In the Valencia province of Spain, where the Arabs introduced elaborate irrigated vegetable gardens called *huertas*, the tortilla is a protein-rich vehicle for all sorts of vegetables.

It was customary in Provence for farmers and hunters to carry flat omelets—filled with tomatoes in summer, onions or chard at other times of year—when they went off for the day to work. In the fall, the woods are busy with people hunting for mushrooms, and those wild mushrooms invariably go into luscious omelets. Eggs are also the perfect vehicle for truffles, the gastronomic jewel of the Mediterranean. If you are lucky enough to come by a black or white truffle in the late fall or early winter, immediately enclose it with a few eggs in a jar. The intense and volatile aroma of the truffle will penetrate the eggshells. Crack the eggs, grate the truffle into the eggs, and make a simple rolled omelet. It will make you swoon.

You also find wonderful egg dishes in Middle Eastern and Tunisian cuisines. Tunisian cooking has different categories of egg dishes, all of which involve cooking vegetables, herbs, and spices, adding eggs, and continuing to cook until the eggs set. One type of Tunisian egg dish is called *ujjah* (eggs), another *tajin,* and the third, which is baked in the oven, is *makhouda.* They are all akin to the Italian frittata or Spanish tortilla, and indeed were probably introduced to Tunisia by the Spaniards in the Middle Ages.

Omelets, however, are not the only dishes you'll find in this chapter. Cheese is vital to the cuisines of the Mediterranean. Since it so often goes into egg dishes, I've devoted these pages to both ingredients. But some of the recipes, like the Greek fried cheese called *saganaki,* feature cheese alone.

These dishes are incredibly versatile. They can be served as starters or be the main event. They're as welcome at lunch as they are at dinner, and here, where we love to brunch, they are perfect for that meal too.

MASTER FRITTATA

Here's the basic technique for making the frittatas and omelets in this chapter. You can adapt it easily to serve 1 or 10. You'll find I often refer to this recipe.

> 2 to 10 large eggs
>
> Salt and freshly ground pepper
>
> 1 to 3 tablespoons low-fat milk
>
> Filling of your choice (page 176)
>
> 1 tablespoon extra virgin olive oil

1. Beat the eggs in a large bowl. Stir in salt (use ½ teaspoon salt for 8 to 10 eggs), pepper, milk, and the filling.

2. Heat the olive oil in a heavy nonstick skillet (see Frittatas by Any Name, right, for information about pan sizes) over medium-high heat. Hold your hand above it; it should feel hot. Drop a bit of egg into the pan, and if it sizzles and cooks at once, the pan is ready. (The reason it must be hot is that you want the eggs to form a cooked surface on the bottom of the pan immediately. You will be lifting this gently with a spatula and shaking and tilting the pan so that the uncooked eggs run underneath and the frittata cooks layer by layer.) Pour in the egg mixture. Swirl the pan to distribute the eggs and filling evenly over the surface. Shake the pan gently, tilting it slightly with one hand while lifting up the edges of the frittata with the spatula in your other hand, to let the eggs run underneath during the first few minutes of cooking.

A 2-egg frittata will be done quickly, with just the tilting of the pan and letting the eggs run underneath until it is no longer or only slightly moist on the top. Once it is set, slip it out of the pan onto a plate. It's fine to leave the top a little runny.

A larger frittata must be covered and cooked over low heat once you've cooked it for the first few minutes, tilting the pan as described above. Once the bottom layers have set, reduce the heat to low, cover (use a pizza pan if you don't have a lid that will fit your skillet), and cook for 5 to 10

In Spain it's a tortilla, in France an omelet, and in Italy a frittata. Whatever the name, it's a flat omelet, and it's filled with something luscious. You can make a 2-egg frittata for one person using an 8-inch omelet pan; a 6- to 8-egg frittata, which will serve 4 to 6 people, in a 10-inch pan; or a 10-egg frittata, which will serve 6 to 10 people, in a 12-inch pan. Since the larger frittatas will go under the broiler, the pan should be ovenproof. You'll really appreciate your nonstick cookware when you make these.

The traditional method for making a flat omelet involved cooking the eggs on one side until set, then sliding the omelet onto a plate and flipping it over into the pan to cook on the other side. Now that most cooks have broilers, you don't have to go through that sometimes tricky maneuver to finish your omelet; you can slip it under the broiler for a few minutes instead.

Throughout the Mediterranean, flat omelets are routinely served at room temperature. They can be slightly runny on the top or firm.

minutes, depending on the number of eggs, shaking the pan gently every once in a while. From time to time, remove the lid and loosen the bottom of the frittata with a wooden spatula, tilting the pan, so that the bottom doesn't burn. It will, however, turn a deep golden brown. This is fine. The eggs should be just about set; cook a few minutes longer if they're not.

3. The largest frittatas usually require finishing underneath the broiler and cooling in the pan before serving.

Heat the broiler. When all but the top layer of the frittata is set, finish 3 to 4 inches under the broiler for 1 to 3 minutes, watching very carefully to make sure the top doesn't burn (it should brown slightly, and it will puff under the broiler). Remove from the heat, shake the pan to make sure the frittata isn't sticking (it will slide around a bit in the nonstick pan), and cool for at least 5 minutes and up to 15. Loosen the edges with a wooden or plastic spatula. Carefully slide from the pan onto a large, round platter. Cut in wedges and serve.

ADVANCE PREPARATION: Frittatas can be made a few hours ahead and served at room temperature. They're good cold, and make great picnic or lunchbox fare. If serving the next day, cool to room temperature, cover with plastic, then foil, and refrigerate. They'll keep for about 3 days in the refrigerator.

FRITTATA FILLINGS

As the recipes that follow illustrate, the possibilities for frittata fillings are endless. In addition to those in these pages, here are some of my other favorites:

Red pepper, onion, and peas: For 10 eggs, sauté 1 medium onion in 1 tablespoon olive oil until tender. Add 2 minced garlic cloves and 1 chopped large red bell pepper and continue to cook until the pepper is tender, about 8 minutes longer. Season with salt and pepper. Add 1 cup thawed frozen peas to the mix and stir into the eggs.

Asparagus: Cut ¾ pound asparagus into 1-inch pieces and steam for 5 minutes. Stir into the eggs along with ¼ cup chopped fresh herbs, such as parsley, tarragon, chives, or dill. This is enough for 6 to 8 eggs.

Cooked spinach or other greens: Chop 1 to 2 cups blanched spinach or greens and sauté with 1 to 2 minced garlic cloves in 1 tablespoon olive oil, just until heated through. Season with salt and pepper. This is enough for 6 to 10 eggs.

Leftover risotto: Use any of the recipes on pages 316 to 324. Stir leftovers into the beaten eggs.

SPANISH OMELET WITH POTATOES AND ONIONS (Tortilla Española)

Spain • **Serves 3 to 4 as a main dish or 6 to 8 as a tapa**

This classic omelet of Spain is all about four ingredients: eggs, potatoes, onion, and olive oil. I've seen recipes that call for as much as a cup of olive oil and as little as 2 tablespoons. I think ¼ cup is a happy medium, enough to cook the potatoes and onions, then the frittata, without saturating everything. But I have a lower-fat method as well, which follows. Not authentic but tasty. The classic pan for this is a straight-sided, well-seasoned cast-iron skillet. But a heavy nonstick pan works well too, and that's what I use.

> ¼ cup extra virgin olive oil
>
> 1 medium onion, finely chopped
>
> 3 medium potatoes, preferably Yukon golds or russets, peeled and either thinly sliced or diced
>
> Salt and freshly ground pepper
>
> 6 large eggs

1. Heat the olive oil in a 10-inch straight-sided cast-iron skillet, or in a heavy ovenproof 10-inch nonstick frying pan, over medium heat. Add the onion and cook, stirring, until tender but not browned, about 5 minutes. Add the potatoes and cook, stirring, until tender when pierced with a fork, about 10 minutes. Season generously with salt and pepper. Using a slotted spoon, remove the potatoes and onion from the pan and transfer to a bowl to cool slightly while you beat the eggs. Do not turn off the heat under the pan.

2. Heat the broiler. Beat the eggs in a bowl and add about ½ teaspoon salt and a generous amount of pepper. Stir in the potatoes and onion, then scrape the eggs and vegetables back into the pan. Shake the pan gently while you lift the edges of the omelet as the eggs set. When the bottom of the omelet has set, turn the heat to low and cover the pan. Cook gently for 10 minutes. Uncover the pan and slide under the broiler to set the top. Remove from the heat.

3. Let the tortilla set in the pan for a few minutes, then slide out onto a serving plate. Cool to room temperature or serve hot.

ADVANCE PREPARATION: *Tortilla española* is usually served at room temperature, so you can make this hours before serving. You can even make it a day ahead and refrigerate it. Allow it to come to room temperature before serving.

VARIATION

LOWER-FAT SPANISH TORTILLA: Steam the potatoes until tender, about 10 minutes, and cool slightly in a bowl. Sauté the onions in 1 tablespoon olive oil, then add to the potatoes. Heat 1 tablespoon olive oil in the pan over medium heat and proceed with the recipe at Step 2.

BAR PILAR'S TORTILLA ESPAÑOLA

Spain • **Serves 3 to 4 as a main dish, or 6 to 8 as a tapa**

The *tortilla española* at the Bar Pilar, a wonderful tapas bar in Valencia, comes to the table hot, in a small cast-iron pan. It looks almost like a little soufflé, with a domed top and a puffy interior. After many attempts to make a traditional *tortilla española* that looked like the Bar Pilar version, I came up with this. Instead of frying the potatoes, I boil them and put them through a ricer into the eggs along with sautéed onions. After setting the bottom of the tortilla in a cast-iron skillet on top of the stove, I put it in a 350°F oven, which gives it the puff and texture I remember from the Bar Pilar. I don't know if this is how they do it at all. I'm sure they don't add the parsley that I've added here for color. In any case, it's a delicious Spanish omelet.

¾ **pound Yukon gold or russet potatoes, peeled and quartered if large**

Salt

2 to 3 tablespoons extra virgin olive oil (to taste)

1 medium onion, finely chopped

Freshly ground pepper

6 large eggs

2 tablespoons finely chopped fresh flat-leaf parsley

1. Place the potatoes in a medium saucepan and cover with water. Add 1 teaspoon salt and bring to a boil over medium-high heat. Reduce the heat to medium and boil gently, partly covered, until tender, 20 to 30 minutes, depending on the size of the potatoes. Drain and return the potatoes to the pot. Cover tightly and allow the potatoes to steam for 10 minutes while you prepare the remaining ingredients.

2. Heat the oven to 350°F. Heat 1 or 2 tablespoons olive oil in a heavy 10-inch cast-iron or ovenproof nonstick skillet over medium-low heat. Add the onion and cook gently until translucent and tender, about 5 minutes. Remove the onion from the pan with a slotted spoon and transfer to a bowl. Don't clean the pan.

3. Put the potatoes through a ricer or food mill into the bowl with the onion. Sprinkle with salt and pepper. Add another tablespoon of olive oil to the pan. Turn the heat up to medium-high.

4. Beat the eggs with about ½ teaspoon salt and a generous amount of pepper. Stir in the potatoes and onion, and the parsley, then scrape the mixture into the pan. Shake the pan gently while you lift the edges of the tortilla as the eggs set. When the bottom of the tortilla has set, place the pan in the oven. Bake for 20 minutes, or until set all the way through and a little puffed.

5. Remove from the oven and allow to sit for a few minutes before sliding onto a serving dish. Or serve hot from the pan.

ADVANCE PREPARATION: If you are planning to serve this cold or at room temperature, you could make it several hours to a day ahead. You can cook the potatoes up to a day ahead, but don't rice them until you're ready to make the omelet.

TORTILLA MURCIANA

Spain • **Serves 4 to 6**

This is a typical flat omelet from Murcia, the southern Spanish province between Valencia and Andalusia, a land of market gardens called *huertas*. The vegetable omelets here reflect the seasons. This one is clearly a summer dish. Serve it hot or at room temperature, as a tapa (as it would be served in Spain) or a light lunch or supper.

> 1 small Japanese eggplant (about 6 ounces), peeled and diced
>
> 3 tablespoons extra virgin olive oil
>
> 1 small onion, finely chopped
>
> 1 green bell pepper, chopped
>
> 1 small zucchini, cut in half lengthwise, seeded, and diced
>
> 1 large ripe tomato (½ pound), peeled, seeded, and chopped
>
> 1 tablespoon chopped fresh basil
>
> Salt
>
> 8 large eggs
>
> Freshly ground pepper

1. Heat the oven to 450°F. Place the eggplant on a baking sheet and toss with 1 tablespoon of the olive oil. Bake for 15 minutes, until softened and browned.

2. Heat the remaining 2 tablespoons oil in a 10- or 12-inch ovenproof nonstick skillet over medium heat and add the onion and bell pepper. Cook, stirring, until they soften and begin to color, about 10 minutes. Add the eggplant and zucchini and cook, stirring, until the zucchini softens and begins to color, about 8 minutes. Add the tomato, basil, and salt to taste, and cook, stirring often, until the mixture begins to thicken, 3 to 5 minutes. Taste and adjust seasonings.

3. Heat the broiler. Beat the eggs until frothy and season with a scant ½ teaspoon salt and pepper to taste. Turn the heat under the pan to medium-high and pour in the eggs. Shake the pan and lift the edges of the eggs as they set, tilting the pan to distribute them and let them run underneath the mixture. When the eggs have just about set, transfer the pan to the broiler, about 3 inches from the heat. Broil until the top of the tortilla is set, 1 to 3 minutes, then cool in the pan. Slide the tortilla onto a plate or platter. Cut into wedges and serve.

ADVANCE PREPARATION: If you're serving this dish at room temperature, you can make it several hours ahead. The filling will keep for 3 or 4 days in the refrigerator. Reheat in the pan and proceed with the recipe.

SWEET GREEN PEPPER TORTILLA FROM MURCIA

Spain • **Serves 4 to 6**

This is another tortilla from the Spanish province of Murcia. When you cook green peppers for a while in olive oil, they become very sweet. In the summer I find thin-skinned bell peppers at the farmers' markets that resemble more closely the peppers used in Spain. Use the regular bell peppers from the supermarket if you don't have access to the thin-skinned variety.

> 4 green bell peppers or thin-skinned sweet peppers from the farmers' market
>
> 8 large eggs
>
> Salt and freshly ground pepper
>
> ½ teaspoon freshly ground cumin seeds
>
> Pinch cayenne
>
> 2 tablespoons extra virgin olive oil
>
> 2 garlic cloves, minced
>
> 1 tablespoon chopped fresh basil
>
> ½ cup shredded Manchego cheese
>
> Paprika for dusting

1. Heat the oven to 425°F. Line a baking sheet with aluminum foil and lightly oil the foil. Place the peppers on the baking sheet and roast, turning the peppers every 10 minutes until the skins are puffed and browned, about 30 minutes. Remove from the heat and transfer to a bowl. Cover tightly with plastic and cool. Peel, seed, and dice the peppers.

2. In a medium bowl, beat the eggs until frothy and season with a scant ½ teaspoon salt, pepper to taste, the cumin, and cayenne. Set aside. Heat the olive oil in a 10-inch ovenproof nonstick skillet over medium heat and add the diced peppers. Cook, stirring, for 3 minutes. Add the garlic and continue to cook, stirring, until the mixture is very tender and fragrant, about 5 minutes. Season with salt and pepper and stir in the basil.

3. Heat the broiler. Pour the eggs into the hot pan with the peppers. Shake the pan and lift the edges of the eggs as they set, tilting the pan to distribute them and to let them run underneath the mixture. When the eggs have just about set, sprinkle the cheese over the top and transfer the pan to the broiler, about 3 inches from the heat. Broil until the top of the tortilla is set, 1 to 2 minutes. Sprinkle the top with paprika. Cool the tortilla in the pan, then slide onto a plate or platter. Cut into wedges and serve

ADVANCE PREPARATION: You can make the pepper filling for this omelet 3 or 4 days ahead, and reheat in the pan before proceeding with the recipe. If you are serving the tortilla at room temperature, you can make it several hours ahead of time.

SCRAMBLED EGGS WITH PEPPERS
(Piperade)
France and Spain • **Serves 4**

The authentic version of this traditional Basque dish contains Bayonne ham, but my vegetarian version would not be mistaken for another dish. The word *piperade* refers both to this classic egg dish and to the pepper sauce (much like the Italian Peperonata, page 85) that typically accompanies fish, meat, or eggs in the Basque region of France and Spain.

> 2 tablespoons extra virgin olive oil
>
> 1 medium onion, finely chopped
>
> 2 large green bell peppers or thin-skinned sweet peppers from the farmers' market, seeded and cut into thin strips

> 1 large red bell pepper or thin-skinned red pepper from the farmer's market, seeded and cut into thin strips
>
> 1 serrano or jalapeño chile pepper, seeded and minced
>
> 2 large garlic cloves, minced
>
> Salt
>
> 2 pounds tomatoes, peeled, seeded, and chopped; or 1 can (28 ounces) tomatoes, drained and chopped
>
> Pinch sugar
>
> 1 teaspoon fresh thyme leaves (or ½ teaspoon dried)
>
> 6 to 8 large eggs
>
> Freshly ground pepper

1. Heat the olive oil in a large nonstick skillet over medium heat and add the onion. Cook, stirring, until tender, about 5 minutes, and add the bell peppers, chile, and garlic. Stir together until the garlic begins to smell fragrant, about 1 minute, and add about ¾ teaspoon salt. Continue to cook, stirring often, for about 10 minutes, until the peppers are quite soft. Add the tomatoes, sugar, and thyme, bring to a simmer, reduce the heat to low, and cook uncovered for 1 hour, stirring often. The mixture should be very thick and quite sweet.

2. Beat the eggs in a bowl, then add ½ teaspoon salt and pepper to taste. Add to the bell pepper mixture. Cook, stirring over low heat, until the eggs are just set but still creamy. Remove from the heat, divide among 4 plates, and serve.

ADVANCE PREPARATION: The pepper mixture will keep for a week in the refrigerator. Reheat in a pan on top of the stove and proceed with the recipe.

Alla Beccaccia

July 24, 2005
Istria

We arrived here by boat from Venice, a four-hour crossing across the Adriatic to Pula. Our friends Mira and Goran with their son Marko, a classmate of Liam's, met us at the boat. The next day they took us to eat lunch at an azienda agrituristica *called Alla Beccaccia, near Fazana. Pino and Jadranka Radolovich have created a beautiful restaurant in a restored barn. The ceiling is pitched above wooden beams; the terrace, where we ate, is covered. I can imagine eating there in the fall, inside by the large hearth.*

Jadranka does the cooking. She's of Slovenian descent, but when they opened their bed-and-breakfast, most of the tourists who came were Italian, and she liked what they made in the kitchen a lot more than the Slovenian food she had grown up with. So she learned from her guests.

We sat down under the arbor and Pino brought us the traditional Istrian brandy called biska, *which is made with mistletoe and has a smooth, herbal flavor. It's the traditional Croatian way to begin a meal, and it went down nicely. So did Pino's honey brandy, which tasted very much of honey, with a strong alcohol kick.*

After our drink, Pino brought out a wooden platter of local cheeses. Skuta is a fresh sheep's cheese, very much like the fresh goat's cheese we had in Greece, but milder. There was also a kashkaval (a delicious hard sheep's cheese) and olives. We drizzled the farm's olive oil over the cheese, and over the gorgeous, peppery wild arugula that was piled into the middle of the platter.

For me the high point of the meal was the next course, a platter of scrambled eggs with wild asparagus. It wasn't the season for wild asparagus, but in the spring they gather the pencil-thin, grass-like shoots and freeze all that they don't eat. The eggs are yellow-orange, cooked in lots of butter with the gorgeous bits of asparagus. The dish, called fritaija, *presumably related to the Italian frittata, was the ultimate luxury.*

ASPARAGUS WITH SCRAMBLED EGGS
Italy • Serves 4

Asparagus is a particularly beloved vegetable in the Veneto region of Italy, where it is served topped with an egg sauce made from hard-cooked eggs, lemon juice, olive oil, parsley, and sometimes capers (at right) and anchovies. Another preparation, which I like even better, pairs the asparagus with creamy scrambled eggs, which are piled on top of the cooked asparagus like a soft, fluffy blanket. In the Mediterranean, the asparagus might be the thick-skinned white variety, which must first be peeled; the green variety, which we are used to; or thin-stemmed wild asparagus like the type we reveled in with our scrambled eggs at Alla Beccaccia in Istria.

I prefer to cook my asparagus in a steamer, but you can also boil the stems in generously salted boiling water. This makes a particularly comforting family supper, particularly when you serve it with toasted country bread.

> 1 pound asparagus tips (2 pounds, trimmed and peeled if using thick green stalks or white stalks)
>
> 2 tablespoons unsalted butter
>
> 4 to 8 large eggs
>
> 1 to 3 teaspoons milk
>
> ¼ to ½ teaspoon salt
>
> Freshly ground pepper
>
> 1 tablespoon snipped chives (optional)

1. Steam the asparagus over boiling water until tender, about 5 minutes. Rinse briefly with cold water and keep warm.

2. Melt the butter in a medium or large nonstick frying pan (depending on the number of eggs you are scrambling) over medium-low heat. Beat together the eggs, milk, salt, and pepper. When the butter is beginning to bubble, add the eggs. Cook slowly, stirring, until the eggs are just set but still creamy. Stir in the chives and remove from the heat.

3. Place the asparagus on a platter or on individual serving plates and spoon the eggs on top. Serve immediately.

ADVANCE PREPARATION: You can cook the asparagus several hours ahead, but you'll need to reheat the spears by submerging them for about 30 seconds in simmering water. Proceed then with Step 2.

ASPARAGUS WITH EGG SAUCE
Italy • Serves 4

My starting point for this dish is a recipe in Clifford Wright's *Mediterranean Vegetables*. Although anchovies are a key ingredient in the authentic sauce, a purely vegetarian rendition, without the anchovies, is pungent and excellent. Serve this as a starter.

> 1 pound asparagus (white or green)
>
> 2 large eggs, hard-cooked
>
> 2 to 3 teaspoons fresh lemon juice (to taste)
>
> 2 to 3 tablespoons extra virgin olive oil (to taste)
>
> 2 teaspoons capers, rinsed and chopped
>
> Salt and freshly ground pepper

1. Trim the asparagus, and—if the stalks are thick, or if you're using white asparagus—peel the bottoms. Steam over boiling water for 5 to 8 minutes, until tender. You could also cook the asparagus in salted boiling water for the same amount of time. Transfer to a bowl of ice water and drain.

2. Cut the eggs in half and put the yolks through a sieve. Mince the whites. Mix together the yolks, lemon juice, olive oil, and capers. Stir in half the whites and season with salt and pepper.

3. Place the asparagus on a platter and cover with the sauce. Sprinkle the remaining egg whites around the spears or over the sauce. Serve at room temperature.

ADVANCE PREPARATION: You can make this recipe several hours ahead, through Step 2. The egg sauce will keep for a couple of days in the refrigerator.

WILD MUSHROOM FRITTATA

Italy • Serves 4

If you are lucky enough to be just about anywhere in the Mediterranean in the fall, you will have plenty of opportunities to eat wild mushrooms. Frittatas make a wonderful vehicle for them. We can get many different types of wild mushrooms at whole foods stores, supermarkets, and farmers' markets.

> 2 tablespoons plus 1 teaspoon extra virgin olive oil
>
> ¾ pound wild mushrooms, such as chanterelles, oyster mushrooms, or porcinis, stems trimmed, torn in half or into quarters if very large
>
> 2 garlic cloves, minced or put through a press
>
> 1 teaspoon fresh thyme leaves
>
> 2 tablespoons chopped fresh flat-leaf parsley
>
> Salt and freshly ground pepper
>
> 8 large eggs
>
> 2 tablespoons milk

1. Heat 1 tablespoon of the olive oil in a large heavy skillet over medium-high heat until hot. Add the mushrooms and sear, tossing them in the pan for about 8 minutes. Turn the heat to medium, add 1 teaspoon oil and the garlic, thyme, parsley, and salt and pepper to taste. Cook, stirring, for another 2 or 3 minutes, until the mushrooms are tender and fragrant. Remove from the heat, taste, and adjust seasoning.

2. Heat the broiler. Heat a heavy ovenproof 10-inch nonstick skillet over medium-high heat. Meanwhile, beat the eggs and milk together in a large bowl. Stir in ½ teaspoon salt, some pepper, and the mushrooms. Add the remaining 1 tablespoon oil to the pan, and when it is hot, add the eggs and mushrooms. Shake the pan and lift the edges of the eggs as they set, tilting the pan to distribute them and let them run underneath the mixture. When the eggs have just about set, transfer the pan to the broiler, about 3 inches from the heat. Broil until the top of the tortilla is set, 1 to 3 minutes. Remove from the heat and serve hot or warm.

VARIATION

Substitute 2 cups Wild Mushroom Ragout (page 285) and 2 tablespoons parsley for the wild mushrooms, garlic, thyme, and parsley. Stir into the eggs and cook as directed. The Mushroom Ragout will keep for 3 or 4 days in the refrigerator.

TRUFFLE OMELET

France • Serves 2

I have made several journeys to a small, unassuming restaurant called La Beaugravière, in Mondragon, just off the Autoroute in the Rhône Valley, in order to eat chef Guy Jullien's truffle omelet. Monsieur Jullien is passionate about truffles, and he doesn't skimp when he adds them to the various truffle dishes he has on the menu. I have always felt, though, that eggs, more than any other food, allow the truffle to express itself the most completely.

This omelet is rolled, not flat. And you will need to plan a day or two ahead to give yourself time to perfume the eggs with the truffle.

> 1 medium fresh truffle (1 to 2 ounces)
>
> 4 large eggs
>
> Salt and freshly ground pepper
>
> 4 teaspoons milk
>
> 4 teaspoons unsalted butter or extra virgin olive oil

1. Put the truffle and eggs in a large jar, close it tightly, and refrigerate for a day or more.

2. Break 2 of the eggs into a bowl and beat with a fork or a whisk until frothy. Add salt and pepper to taste and 2 teaspoons milk. Grate half the truffle into the eggs and mix well.

3. Heat an 8-inch omelet pan over medium-high heat. Add 2 teaspoons of the butter or olive oil. When the butter stops foaming, or the oil feels hot when you hold your hand above it, pour in the eggs, scraping every last bit into the pan. Swirl the pan to distribute the eggs evenly over the surface.

Shake the pan gently, tilting it slightly with one hand while lifting up the edges of the omelet with the spatula in your other hand, to let the eggs run underneath during the few minutes of cooking. As soon as the eggs are set on the bottom, jerk the pan quickly away from you then back toward you so that the omelet folds over on itself. Tilt the pan and roll the omelet out onto a plate.

4. Repeat with the remaining eggs, milk, and truffle, and serve.

ADVANCE PREPARATION: This is one of the few omelets in this chapter that is best eaten hot. It's a last-minute dish.

RICOTTA FRITTATA WITH FRESH HERBS
Italy • Serves 4 to 6

On a very hot day in Puglia, we drove up into the mountains from the coast of the Gargano Promontory. Our destination was an *azienda agrituristica* called Monte Sacro. As we rounded a hairpin turn at the summit of the narrow road, we were stopped by a herd of the largest cows I had ever seen, all wearing bells the size of a small child's head. They ambled casually across the road while we took pictures, then we continued on our way until we reached the farm, where well-shaded tables were set for the day's lunch. The view, and the breeze on this steamy day, were restorative in themselves. Slices of this fluffy ricotta frittata were already on the table, and Liam, then 7, gobbled them up. For this frittata, try to find fresh, good-quality ricotta in an Italian market.

6 large eggs

Salt and freshly ground pepper

1 cup fresh ricotta cheese

1 garlic clove, minced

1 tablespoon chopped fresh marjoram, parsley, or mint

2 tablespoons extra virgin olive oil

1. Heat the broiler. In a medium bowl, beat together the eggs, salt, pepper, ricotta, garlic, and herbs.

2. Heat the olive oil in an ovenproof 10-inch skillet over medium-high heat. When the oil is hot, pour in the egg mixture. Jiggle and tilt the pan and lift the edges of the mixture so that the eggs can run underneath. Reduce the heat to low and cover. Cook for 10 minutes, or until just about set. Run the pan under the broiler, 3 to 4 inches from the heat, until set and browned on the top (just a few minutes at most).

3. Slide the frittata onto a wide plate or platter. Serve hot, cool, or at room temperature.

ADVANCE PREPARATION: This frittata keeps well. If you need to get a jump on a menu, make it a day ahead and refrigerate.

VARIATIONS

RICOTTA FRITTATA WITH ZUCCHINI: Mix up the eggs and other ingredients as directed. Heat 1 tablespoon of the oil in the pan over medium heat, and when it is hot, add 1 small or medium zucchini, finely chopped. Cook, stirring often, until tender, about 8 minutes. Season to taste with salt. Add the remaining 1 tablespoon olive oil to the pan, turn up the heat to medium-high, and pour in the egg mixture. Jiggle and tilt the pan to distribute the zucchini through the eggs, and lift the edges of the mixture so that the eggs can run underneath. Reduce the heat to low and cover. Proceed as directed.

RICOTTA FRITTATA WITH ASPARAGUS: Trim the ends off ¾ pound asparagus and cut the asparagus into ½-inch pieces. Place in a steamer above boiling water and steam for 5 minutes. Remove from the heat, rinse with cold water, and drain on paper towels. Stir into the egg and ricotta mixture and proceed with the recipe.

LARGE RATATOUILLE OMELET
France • **Makes 4 servings**

One Sunday afternoon when I was living in Paris, I had a surprise visit from my friend and colleague Deborah Madison. It was wonderful to see her, and we made a date for dinner the next night. I assumed she and her husband, Patrick, would want to go out, it being Paris. We met at a café, and after a glass of wine Deborah said, "So, what have you prepared for us?" At a loss, I said that I'd assumed they'd want to go out, but it would be no trouble to whip up dinner. I knew I had some ratatouille in the refrigerator, and eggs, and salad makings. This is the omelet I made. It was only years later that Deborah admitted to me that there is one food she has an aversion to, and that's eggs!

> 1 cup (or more) leftover Ratatouille (page 296)
>
> 8 large eggs
>
> Salt and freshly ground pepper
>
> 2 tablespoons milk
>
> 2 tablespoons extra virgin olive oil

1. If the ratatouille has a lot of liquid, place in a colander set over a bowl and drain for 15 to 30 minutes. Beat the eggs well and stir in the salt, pepper, and milk. Stir in the ratatouille.

2. Heat the broiler. Heat the olive oil in a heavy ovenproof 10- or 12-inch nonstick skillet over medium-high heat. Hold your hand above it; it should feel hot. Drop a bit of egg into the pan, and if it sizzles and cooks at once, the pan is ready. Pour in the egg mixture. Swirl the pan to distribute the eggs and filling evenly over the surface. Shake the pan gently, tilting it slightly with one hand while lifting up the edges of the frittata with a wooden or plastic spatula in your other hand to let the eggs run underneath during the first few minutes of cooking. Reduce the heat to low, cover (use a pizza pan if you don't have a lid that will fit your skillet), and cook for 10 minutes, shaking the pan gently every once in a while. From time to time, remove the lid and loosen the bottom of the

omelet with the spatula, tilting the pan so that the bottom doesn't burn. It will, however, turn a deep golden brown. The eggs should be just about set; cook a few minutes longer if they're not.

3. Finish the omelet 3 to 4 inches under the broiler for 2 to 3 minutes, watching very carefully to make sure the top doesn't burn (it should brown slightly, and it will puff under the broiler). Remove from the heat, shaking the pan to make sure the omelet isn't sticking (it will slide around a bit in the nonstick pan). Cool for at least 5 minutes and up to 15, then loosen the edges with the spatula. Carefully slide from the pan onto a large, round platter. Serve hot, warm, or at room temperature.

ADVANCE PREPARATION: Ratatouille keeps well for about 5 days in the refrigerator. The omelet can be made several hours before you serve it.

INDIVIDUAL EGGPLANT AND TOMATO FRITTATA
Italy • **Serves 1**

This is a dish to make with leftovers: If you have a little tomato sauce, not enough for a pasta dish, an omelet is a good place for it. The same goes with leftover eggplant slices. If you want to make it without leftovers and you have a panini grill, the slices can be ready in about 2 minutes.

> 2 large eggs
>
> 1 teaspoon milk
>
> Salt and freshly ground pepper
>
> 2 or 3 grilled eggplant slices, quartered
>
> 1 tablespoon Basic Tomato Sauce (page 78)
>   or commercial marinara sauce
>
> 1 garlic clove, minced or put through a press
>
> A few leaves fresh basil, torn into small pieces
>
> 1 tablespoon extra virgin olive oil

1. Heat an 8-inch omelet pan over medium-high heat. Meanwhile, beat the eggs in a bowl. Add the milk, salt and pepper, eggplant, tomato sauce, garlic, and basil.

2. Add the olive oil to the hot pan. Wait until it ripples, then pour in the egg mixture. Cook, shaking the pan and lifting up the edges of the eggs with a spatula, then tilting the pan to allow the eggs to run underneath.

3. When the frittata is set, slide it onto a plate. Place the pan over the plate, hold the two together, and reverse the frittata back into the pan to brown on the other side. Cook for less than a minute, then slide out and serve. This can also be served at room temperature.

ADVANCE PREPARATION: The eggplant can be grilled and the tomato sauce prepared a few days before you make this.

PROVENÇAL FLAT ONION OMELET
France • Serves 6

Sticking cloves into the onions and soaking them in water doused with vinegar makes them very mild. You can skip or shorten the step for a more pungent omelet.

> 1 pound white onions, peeled
>
> Whole cloves
>
> 2 tablespoons red wine vinegar
>
> 2 tablespoons extra virgin olive oil
>
> Salt and freshly ground black pepper
>
> 10 large eggs
>
> 3 tablespoons milk

1. Cut the onions in half and stick each half with a clove. Place in a bowl and cover with water. Add the vinegar and soak for 1 hour to half a day. Drain, discard the cloves, pat dry, and mince.

2. Heat 1 tablespoon of the olive oil in a heavy 12-inch nonstick skillet over medium-low heat. Add the onions and cook, stirring often, for 10 minutes, until slightly golden but not browned. Remove from the heat. Season with salt and pepper.

3. Beat the eggs in a bowl and add the milk, about ½ teaspoon salt, and freshly ground pepper. Stir in the onions. Clean and dry your pan. Using the remaining 1 tablespoon olive oil, make 1 large

PROVENÇAL FLAT OMELETS

Farmworkers in Provence traditionally carried cold flat omelets to work with them, to eat during their long days in the fields. Indeed, the Provençal name for the onion omelet I've included is *la meissouneiro,* "the harvester's omelet." I was really impressed by all of the different omelets I found in this region of France. The idea that they were just as good cold as hot, and eminently portable, was a revelation to me.

omelet or several smaller omelets, following the directions in the Master Frittata recipe on page 175. Serve hot or cold.

ADVANCE PREPARATION: You can cook the onions several hours before you make the omelet(s). The omelet(s) can be made several hours or even a day ahead if serving cold.

PROVENÇAL FLAT TOMATO OMELET
France • Serves 4

Here's one thing you can do in late summer, when the markets and your gardens abound with tomatoes. Only sweet, ripe tomatoes will work for this beautiful orange/yellow creation.

> 2 to 3 tablespoons extra virgin olive oil (as needed)
>
> 4 large garlic cloves, minced
>
> 3 pounds ripe tomatoes, peeled, seeded, and chopped
>
> 2 pinches sugar
>
> Salt and freshly ground pepper
>
> 8 large eggs
>
> 3 tablespoons slivered fresh basil

1. Heat 1 tablespoon of the oil in a large nonstick skillet over medium heat and add the garlic. Cook, stirring, until it begins to sizzle and smell fragrant, and add the tomatoes, sugar, and salt. Bring to a simmer and cook, stirring often, for about 20 minutes, until the tomatoes have cooked down and are beginning to stick to the pan. Add pepper and adjust salt. Cool for 10 minutes.

2. Beat the eggs in a bowl and add ½ teaspoon salt and a generous amount of pepper. Stir in the tomato sauce and basil. Clean and dry your pan.

3. Using the remaining oil, make 1 large or several individual omelets, following the directions in the Master Frittata recipe on page 175.

ADVANCE PREPARATION: The tomato sauce will keep for 3 to 5 days in the refrigerator. Bring to room temperature or warm it before adding to the eggs. The omelet(s) can be made several hours or even a day ahead if serving cold.

VARIATION

Uncooked tomatoes also make a wonderful filling for an omelet. Use 1½ pounds ripe red tomatoes. Cut them in half crosswise, sprinkle with salt, and drain cut side down on a rack above a baking pan or sink for 30 minutes. Chop half the tomatoes and toss in a bowl with 1 to 2 minced garlic cloves (to taste), salt to taste, and 2 tablespoons chopped fresh basil. Slice the remaining tomatoes in rounds. Stir the chopped tomatoes into the eggs and proceed as directed. Once the bottom of the omelet has set, top with the sliced tomatoes and finish as directed.

PROVENÇAL FLAT SORREL OMELET
France • **Serves 4**

Sorrel is one of those greens, very sharp tasting and acidic, that you may be at a loss for what to do with if you see it in a farmers' market. This is one of the best ways to use it that I can think of. The mild, creamy eggs contrast so nicely with the tangy sorrel.

What distinguishes this from other French sorrel omelets is the copious amount of garlic. You can also make one large omelet, but it's easier to achieve the slightly runny consistency that I like if you make individual omelets. This omelet is best served hot.

½ pound (about 5 cups) fresh sorrel, stemmed

8 large eggs

4 garlic cloves, preferably fresh green garlic, minced

Salt and freshly ground pepper

2 tablespoons extra virgin olive oil

1. Heat a 10- or 12-inch nonstick skillet over medium-high heat and add the sorrel. Stir until the leaves wilt, which will happen in a couple of minutes. The color will change from bright dark green to olive. Remove from the heat and chop coarsely.

2. For each omelet, beat 2 eggs and stir in a quarter of the minced garlic, a couple of tablespoons of chopped sorrel, and salt and pepper to taste. Heat about 1½ teaspoons olive oil in an 8-inch nonstick omelet pan over medium-high heat. Make the omelets following the directions for individual omelets in the Master Frittata recipe on page 175; leave the tops slightly runny. Serve at once.

ADVANCE PREPARATION: You can prepare the sorrel through Step 1 several hours or even a day before you make the omelets.

PROVENÇAL FLAT SWISS CHARD OMELET (Truccha)
France • **Serves 4 as a main dish or 6 as a starter**

Truccha is the signature omelet of Provence and my favorite of all of the omelets of this region. It's packed with Swiss chard and lots of garlic. When I worked at La Mère Besson restaurant in Cannes, they made so many of these that there was one man in the kitchen whose job was just to stem and blanch chard. He spent entire mornings every day at this task. At the restaurant they didn't cook the garlic first, as I do here, they just threw it into the eggs, and the omelets were very garlicky indeed.

The amount of greens you use for this omelet is flexible. Don't hesitate to pack the omelet, but on the other hand, feel free to make it with as little as one small bunch of greens, blanched and chopped.

And other greens—beet greens, for example, or spinach—will work equally well.

Salt

½ to 1 pound Swiss chard, stemmed

2 tablespoons extra virgin olive oil

2 garlic cloves, minced

Freshly ground pepper

8 large eggs

2 tablespoons milk

1. Heat a large pot of water over high heat. When the water comes to a boil, add a generous tablespoon of salt and the greens. Cook for about 2 minutes, until tender, and transfer to a bowl of ice water. Let sit for a few minutes, then drain, squeeze dry, and chop.

2. Heat 1 tablespoon of the oil in a 10-inch nonstick skillet over medium heat and add the garlic. Cook, stirring, until fragrant, 30 seconds to 1 minute, then stir in the chard. Cook, stirring, for about 1 minute, until coated with oil. Season to taste with salt and pepper and remove from the heat.

3. Beat the eggs in a bowl, stir in ½ teaspoon salt, pepper to taste, the milk, and the cooked greens.

4. Clean and dry your pan and heat the remaining 1 tablespoon oil over medium-high heat. Cook, following the directions in the Master Frittata recipe on page 175 for 1 large omelet or for several individual omelets. Carefully slide from the pan onto a large, round platter. Cut into wedges and serve.

ADVANCE PREPARATION: The greens can be prepared through Step 1 or Step 2 several hours or even a day or two ahead. The *truccha* can be made a few hours ahead and served at room temperature.

BAKED ARTICHOKE HEART OMELET
(Tortino)
Italy • Serves 4

This Italian baked omelet is one of those satisfying dinners that you can throw together without much thought—if you have frozen artichoke hearts in your freezer (which I highly recommend). Or make it with fresh tiny artichokes to announce the arrival of spring.

1 pound baby artichokes, trimmed (see page 267); or 1 package (12 ounces) frozen artichoke hearts, thawed

2 tablespoons extra virgin olive oil

1 to 2 garlic cloves, minced (optional)

Salt and freshly ground pepper

8 large eggs

1 tablespoon minced fresh flat-leaf parsley

1 tablespoon freshly grated Parmesan

1. Heat the oven to 400°F. Oil a 2-quart baking dish.

2. If using fresh artichokes, bring a pot of generously salted water to a boil and add the artichokes. Reduce the heat and boil gently for 10 minutes. Transfer to a bowl of cold water, drain, and quarter the artichokes.

3. Heat the oil in a large, heavy skillet over medium-high heat and add the artichokes. Cook, stirring often, until golden brown, 5 to 8 minutes. Add the garlic and cook for another 30 seconds to a minute, until fragrant. Season with salt and pepper, and spread in an even layer in the baking dish.

4. Beat the eggs and add the parsley, ½ teaspoon salt, and pepper to taste. Pour over the artichokes. Bake for 20 to 30 minutes, until the omelet is firm and lightly browned. Remove from the heat and immediately sprinkle on the Parmesan. Serve hot or warm.

ADVANCE PREPARATION: If you're serving this omelet warm, you can make it an hour or two ahead of time. You can make it through Step 3 several hours ahead.

POACHED EGGS WITH TZATZIKI

Greece • **Serves 4**

This simple, satisfying dish from northeastern Greece can be eaten for a light lunch or supper, or for breakfast if you don't mind garlic first thing in the morning.

> 1 teaspoon vinegar
>
> 4 large eggs
>
> 1 cup Tzatziki (page 106; omit dill or mint and vinegar)
>
> Paprika
>
> Salt and freshly ground pepper

1. Bring a skillet full of water to a simmer and add the vinegar. Carefully break 1 egg at a time into a teacup, then tip into the water. Poach for 4 minutes, until set. Remove with a slotted spoon and drain on kitchen towels.

2. Spoon ¼ cup *tzatziki* onto each of 4 plates and sprinkle with paprika. Make a depression in the center with the back of your spoon, and top with an egg. Season with salt and pepper, and serve.

ADVANCE PREPARATION: The *tzatziki* can be made a few hours ahead.

POACHED EGGS WITH GARLIC SAUCE

Turkey • **Serves 4**

In this Turkish version of the Greek poached egg recipe, a simple garlic and yogurt sauce replaces the *tzatziki*. You can also fry the eggs for this dish. Serve with Greek Country Bread (page 47), Turkish Country Bread (page 49), or Soft Turkish Pocket Bread (page 50).

> 2 garlic cloves
>
> Salt
>
> ½ cup drained yogurt (page 21)
>
> Freshly ground pepper
>
> 2 teaspoons unsalted butter
>
> ¼ to ½ teaspoon Turkish red pepper or Aleppo pepper (to taste)

> 1 teaspoon vinegar
>
> 4 large eggs
>
> Bread (see headnote)

1. Mash the garlic in a mortar and pestle with ¼ teaspoon salt until you have a smooth paste. Stir into the yogurt. Add ground pepper to taste and adjust salt.

2. Melt the butter and add the red pepper.

3. Bring a skillet full of water to a simmer and add the vinegar. Carefully break 1 egg at a time into a teacup, then tip into the water. Poach for 4 minutes, until set.

4. Remove with a slotted spoon and drain on paper towels. Transfer each egg to a plate or bowl. Season with salt and pepper. Spoon a tablespoon of the yogurt over the top of each egg and drizzle on the seasoned butter. Serve with bread, passing the remaining yogurt in a bowl.

ADVANCE PREPARATION: The yogurt sauce can be made a few hours ahead.

BAKED VEGETABLE OMELET

Greece • **Serves 4**

You know this omelet hails from the eastern Mediterranean when you taste the dill and mint. It has a wonderful, fluffy texture, which is always the case when you combine yogurt with eggs.

> 3 tablespoons olive oil
>
> 1 bunch scallions, white and light green parts, chopped
>
> 2 garlic cloves, minced
>
> 1 pound zucchini, diced
>
> Salt and freshly ground pepper
>
> ⅓ cup chopped fresh dill
>
> 2 tablespoons chopped fresh mint
>
> 8 large eggs
>
> 3 tablespoons drained yogurt (page 21)
>
> ¼ cup freshly grated kefalotyri cheese or Parmesan

1. Heat the oven to 400°F. Oil a 2-quart baking dish with 1 tablespoon of the olive oil.

2. Heat the remaining 2 tablespoons oil in a large, heavy skillet over medium heat. Add the scallions and cook, stirring, until tender, about 3 minutes. Add the garlic, stir until fragrant, about 30 seconds, and add the zucchini. Cook, stirring, until tender, about 10 minutes. Season to taste with salt and pepper, and continue to cook until any liquid in the pan has evaporated. Stir in the dill and mint. Remove from the heat.

3. Heat the baking dish in the oven for 5 minutes, while you beat the eggs in a large bowl. Season with ½ teaspoon salt and freshly ground pepper to taste. Whisk in the yogurt and cheese. Stir in the zucchini mixture. Pour into the heated baking dish and place in the oven. Immediately turn the heat down to 275°F. Bake for 30 to 40 minutes, until set. Serve hot, warm, or at room temperature.

ADVANCE PREPARATION: The zucchini can be prepared through Step 2 as far as a day ahead.

VARIATION

You can also cook this omelet in a pan on top of the stove. Follow the directions in the Master Frittata recipe on page 175.

SCRAMBLED EGGS WITH TOMATOES AND FETA

Greece • **Serves 2 as a light supper or 4 as a starter**

Greeks are a late-night people, especially in the summer, when the villages begin to come alive at around 10 or 11 at night, once the torpor of the afternoon has dissipated. When Liam, Rachel, and I visited Diane Kochilas's ancestral island, Ikaria, we adjusted our body clocks to this rhythm. It was not unusual to find Liam and Diane's son Yiorgos thoroughly engrossed in a game of tag at 1 a.m. And it wasn't unusual for me to arrive at Diane's house at 11 the next morning and find her kids finishing up their breakfast, which was sometimes this delicious dish of eggs scrambled with tomatoes from the garden. I love to serve this dish for supper. Serve with Greek Country Bread (page 47), Turkish Country Bread (page 49), or Soft Turkish Pocket Bread (page 50).

> 1 pound ripe tomatoes, peeled if desired, seeded, and finely chopped
>
> 1 tablespoon olive oil
>
> 1 garlic clove, minced (optional)
>
> 2 teaspoons finely chopped fresh mint, oregano, parsley, or thyme
>
> Salt and freshly ground pepper
>
> 4 large eggs
>
> 1 to 2 ounces (¼ to ½ cup) crumbled feta (to taste)
>
> Bread (see headnote)

1. Drain the tomatoes in a strainer set over a bowl for 15 minutes. Heat the oil in a medium nonstick skillet over medium heat and add the garlic. Cook, stirring, until fragrant, about 30 seconds, and add the tomatoes. Cook, stirring, until they cook down and thicken a little bit, about 5 minutes. Turn up the heat and let some of the liquid in the pan boil off. Stir in the herbs. Add salt and pepper to taste.

2. Beat the eggs in a bowl and season with salt and pepper. Add the cheese and pour into the pan. Reduce the heat to medium-low. Stir everything together until the eggs set. Let sit off the heat for 5 minutes. Serve hot or warm, with fresh bread.

ADVANCE PREPARATION: You can cook the tomatoes through Step 1 several hours before continuing with Step 2. Reheat gently, then proceed with the eggs. Unlike regular scrambled eggs, these taste good at room temperature. They firm up in a nice way.

PERSIAN HERB OMELET

Iran • **Serves 6**

Although Iran is not on the Mediterranean, Persian cooking has been a very important influence on the food of the Mediterranean, and I wanted to include a few of my favorite recipes, like this omelet. Herb omelets are popular in Iran, where they are called *coucou*, or *kookoo*. The green omelet is a traditional Persian New Year's dish, symbolizing fruitfulness and prosperity.

Give the herbs some time to soak and swell in the eggs before you cook the omelet. The traditional omelet contains red piquant berries called barberries (*zereshk* in Persian), which are available in Iranian markets. These should be soaked for 10 minutes before using, then drained. I've made this ingredient optional, however, because I want you to make this whether or not you can find the barberries. Like other flat omelets, this can be served hot or at room temperature, which makes it transportable.

1 tablespoon barberries (optional)

10 large eggs

½ teaspoon baking soda

1 teaspoon unbleached all-purpose flour

¾ teaspoon salt

¼ teaspoon freshly ground black pepper

⅓ cup finely chopped walnuts

1¼ cups chopped fresh flat-leaf parsley

½ cup chopped chives or scallions (white and light green parts only)

⅓ cup chopped fresh cilantro

⅔ cup chopped fresh dill

2 tablespoons extra virgin olive oil or unsalted butter

Greek Country Bread (page 47) or Turkish Country Bread (page 49)

Drained yogurt (page 21)

1. In a small bowl, cover the barberries with water and soak for 10 minutes. Drain and rinse.

2. Beat the eggs in a large bowl and stir in the barberries, baking soda, flour, salt, pepper, walnuts, parsley, chives, cilantro, and dill. Let sit for 30 minutes.

3. Heat the oven to 350°F. Add the oil to a 12-inch round earthenware baking dish or 3-quart gratin dish and spread it around evenly. Heat the dish in the oven for 5 minutes, or until a drop of egg sizzles when drizzled into the dish. Scrape in the egg mixture. Bake for 35 to 45 minutes, until set. Serve hot or cold, with bread and yogurt.

ADVANCE PREPARATION: Since this omelet is good cold as well as hot, it can be made up to a day ahead.

TUNISIAN EGGPLANT OMELET

Tunisia • **Serves 4 to 6**

You can see how the French influence, in the form of Gruyère cheese, has crept into this classic Tunisian *makhouda* (the French occupied Tunisia from 1881 to 1956). But this would never be confused with a European omelet.

1 large eggplant (1 to 1½ pounds)

1 tablespoon extra virgin olive oil

1 medium onion, finely chopped

1 medium red bell pepper, diced

8 large eggs

½ bunch fresh flat-leaf parsley, minced

2 to 4 garlic cloves (to taste), minced or put through a press

⅛ teaspoon rose water, or 1 teaspoon ground dried rosebuds

Salt

¼ teaspoon freshly ground pepper

⅛ teaspoon ground cinnamon

¼ pound Gruyère cheese, grated or cut into small cubes (1 cup, tightly packed)

Harissa (page 86 or commercial; optional)

1. Heat the oven to 450°F. Cut the eggplant in half lengthwise and score down the middle, being careful not to cut through the skin. Oil a baking sheet and place the eggplant on it, cut side down. Bake for 20 minutes, or until the skin has begun to

Cheese-Making with Lefteris and Diamanto

July 15, 2005
Ikaria

Today Diane took us to the home and farm of Lefteris and Diamanto Plaka, who welcomed us into their home, fed us wonderful meze, *let us milk their goats, and showed us how they make cheese.*

A fire is already burning in the living room hearth when we arrive at the farm. Lefteris feeds olive branches into the flames, while Diamanto serves us luscious lemon spoon sweets with glasses of water. When the fire is very hot, she sets a large pot of goat's milk, about 5 quarts, over the flame and brings the milk to a boil. As the milk heats up, she stirs in 5 teaspoons of salt, one for each quart of milk. Once the milk reaches a boil, she takes it off the heat and lets it cool down until it is tepid. Then she stirs in the rennet. With a spoon, she cuts up the curd, and heats the milk again so that the curds and whey will separate.

Diamanto next lines a strainer with thick cheesecloth and sets it over a bowl. She strains the milk through the cheesecloth, gathers up the cloth, knots it at the top, and hangs it over the sink, where the curds will continue to drip until all of the whey has run off. What will remain in the cheesecloth is 2½ to 3 pounds of beautiful white cheese, which the Ikarians call kathoura.

Watching the cheese-making is a prelude to a midmorning feast of mezedes, *which Lefteris and Diamanto serve with their powerful homemade grappa. We eat cucumbers and tomatoes from the garden (sprinkled with sea salt), home-cured olives, feta, hard-cooked eggs, and cured fish. Diamanto brings out the most wonderful fried zucchini sticks; simply fried in abundant olive oil, they're like zucchini French fries. She serves us fried peppers and eggplant, potatoes and radishes.*

Fortified, we walk out to see the goats. Everywhere I look there is something growing. Tomatoes are starting in little flats, strawberries are growing in pots and cans, squash, cucumbers, and melon are growing on vines, figs are ripening on trees. The goats are adorable, some young, some older. Diamanto's son snags a mother goat and her baby, has the baby nurse for a few minutes to stimulate the mother's milk production, then one by one, we each get a turn milking. From now on, every time I eat a piece of feta, I will think about my moment with the goat and her udder.

TUNISIAN OMELETS

They are called many things—*aijjahs* and *eggahs*, *makuda*, *makhouda*, *maquda*, and *makbuba*, and *tagine*. According to food historian Clifford Wright, the word *maquda* is derived from the Arabic word meaning "to congeal." Whatever the name, they are all variations on the frittata, spiced up (usually) with a little harissa or cayenne or both, filled with vegetables, often with tuna as well. Some of the Tunisian omelets are filled not only with cooked vegetables, but also with chopped hard-cooked eggs. Eggs within eggs. They are all very easy to make. They're usually baked in an earthenware baking dish, and can be served warm or at room temperature.

shrivel and the eggplant has softened. Transfer to a colander, cut side down, and drain for 30 minutes. Turn the oven down to 350°F. Carefully peel the eggplant and cut into dice.

2. Heat the olive oil in a large, heavy nonstick skillet over medium heat and add the onion and bell pepper. Cook, stirring often, until tender, 5 to 10 minutes. Stir in the eggplant and cook for another minute, stirring. Remove from the heat.

3. In a large bowl, beat the eggs and add the parsley, garlic, rose water, about ½ teaspoon salt, the pepper, and cinnamon. Stir in the eggplant filling and the cheese, and if you want a spicy dish, add about 1 teaspoon harissa.

4. Oil a 2-quart earthenware baking dish, preferably a round one, and pour in the egg mixture. Bake for 30 minutes, until golden brown and set. Cool for 10 minutes or longer, and serve hot or at room temperature, cut into wedges or squares.

ADVANCE PREPARATION: In Tunisia, this would be served at room temperature. You can make it several hours or even a day before you wish to serve it. The eggplant filling will keep in the refrigerator for 3 or 4 days.

BAKED POTATO, ONION, AND PARSLEY OMELET
Tunisia • **Serves 4 to 6**

Potato and onion omelets are not unique to Spain, though the Spanish version is somewhat of a national dish. In this spicy Tunisian *makhouda*, which is no doubt related to the *tortilla española* (page 176), the cooked potatoes are riced before being stirred into the eggs with the onion and parsley. The omelet is baked in an earthenware dish, and can be served warm or at room temperature.

> 1 pound Yukon gold potatoes, peeled
>
> Salt
>
> 2 tablespoons extra virgin olive oil
>
> 1 medium onion, finely chopped
>
> Leaves from 1 bunch fresh flat-leaf parsley, chopped
>
> 8 large eggs
>
> ½ teaspoon cayenne (more to taste) or 1 teaspoon Harissa (page 86 or commercial)
>
> ½ teaspoon freshly ground black pepper

1. Place the potatoes in a pot and cover with water by 2 inches. Add 1 teaspoon salt and bring to a boil over medium heat. Reduce the heat and boil gently until the potatoes are tender all the way through, about 20 minutes. Drain, return to the pot, and cover. Let sit for 5 minutes, then put through a potato ricer, a food mill, or a strainer. Set aside.

2. Heat the oil in a medium skillet over medium heat and add the onion. Cook, stirring, until it begins to soften, about 3 minutes, and add the parsley. Cook, stirring, until the onion is tender, about 5 minutes. Cool slightly.

3. Heat the oven to 350°F. Generously oil a 2-quart baking dish, preferably a round earthenware one. Place in the oven for 5 minutes.

4. Meanwhile, beat the eggs in a large bowl and stir in ½ teaspoon salt, the cayenne, and the black pepper. Add the potatoes and onion-parsley mixture and mix well. Scrape into the heated baking

dish and bake for 30 minutes, or until the omelet is set and a knife inserted in the center comes out clean. Serve warm or at room temperature.

ADVANCE PREPARATION: Since this omelet can be served at room temperature, you could make it several hours ahead of serving.

BELL PEPPER, TOMATO, AND POTATO OMELET

Tunisia • **Serves 4 to 6**

This garlicky dish is more of a vegetable stew with eggs stirred in at the end of cooking than a frittata filled with vegetables. It is said to have its roots in Tunisian Jewish cookery.

> 2 tablespoons extra virgin olive oil
>
> 1 small onion, finely chopped
>
> ½ pound red-skinned potatoes, diced
>
> ½ pound green bell peppers, sliced
>
> 4 garlic cloves, puréed in a mortar and pestle with ½ teaspoon salt
>
> ½ pound tomatoes, peeled, seeded, and diced
>
> Freshly ground pepper
>
> ½ teaspoon freshly ground caraway seeds
>
> ½ teaspoon freshly ground coriander seeds
>
> ½ teaspoon cayenne (more to taste) or 1 teaspoon Harissa (page 86 or commercial)
>
> 3 tablespoons water
>
> Salt
>
> 8 large eggs

1. Heat the oil in a 10-inch nonstick skillet over medium heat and add the onion. Cook, stirring, until it begins to soften, about 3 minutes. Add the potatoes and bell peppers. Cook, stirring, until the peppers begin to soften, about 5 minutes, and stir in the garlic. Cook, stirring, until fragrant, about 1 minute, and add the tomatoes, pepper, caraway, coriander, cayenne, and water. Stir together. Bring to a simmer, reduce the heat to medium-low, cover, and cook, stirring often, for 1 hour, adding salt to taste after the first 15 minutes. When the mixture is very fragrant and tender, taste and adjust the seasonings.

2. Beat the eggs in a bowl and season with ½ teaspoon salt. Stir the eggs into the vegetables and shake the skillet to distribute them evenly through the pan. Cover and continue to cook until the eggs have set, about 10 minutes. Remove from the heat and serve warm or at room temperature.

ADVANCE PREPARATION: The vegetable mixture can be made a day ahead. Reheat and proceed with Step 2. The finished omelet can be made a few hours ahead if serving at room temperature.

CARROT AND PARSLEY OMELET

Tunisia • **Serves 4 to 6**

This *makhouda* is an example of a Tunisian omelet that contains eggs within eggs. It's quite spicy, with lots of harissa and ground caraway.

> 1 pound carrots, sliced
>
> 1 tablespoon freshly ground caraway seeds
>
> 1 tablespoon Harissa (page 86 or commercial)
>
> 4 large garlic cloves, minced
>
> Salt and freshly ground pepper
>
> 8 large eggs
>
> 2 large eggs, hard-cooked and finely chopped
>
> ¼ cup chopped fresh flat-leaf parsley
>
> 1 tablespoon extra virgin olive oil

1. Either steam the carrots or cook them until tender in a pot of salted boiling water. It should take about 20 minutes to get them thoroughly tender. Mash with a fork or pulse in a food processor fitted with the steel blade until coarsely puréed. Stir in the caraway seeds, harissa, garlic, and salt and pepper to taste, and combine well.

2. Beat the 8 eggs in a medium bowl and add ½ teaspoon salt. Stir in the carrot mixture, the chopped hard-cooked eggs, and the parsley.

3. Heat the oil in a 10-inch nonstick skillet over medium-high heat. When the oil is hot, scrape in the egg mixture. Cook, following the directions in the Master Frittata recipe on page 175. Finish under the broiler if necessary. Remove from the heat, slide out onto a platter if desired, and serve warm or at room temperature.

ADVANCE PREPARATION: You can make the carrot filling a day ahead and keep it in the refrigerator. The omelet can be made several hours ahead if it's to be served at room temperature.

VARIATION

TUNISIAN CAULIFLOWER OMELET: Substitute cauliflower, broken into florets, for the carrots. Or use a combination of cauliflower and carrots. Just keep total weight at 1 pound. The cauliflower will be tender after 10 minutes of steaming.

NORTH AFRICAN FRIED PEPPER STEW WITH EGGS (Chakchouka)

Algeria and Tunisia • **Serves 6 as a main dish or 8 as a starter without the eggs**

Many cooks define *chakchouka* (or *shakhshuka*) as a salad, but I think of it more as a stew. It is a classic Algerian and Tunisian dish, with many variations. It can be served as an appetizer without the eggs, but I think it makes a splendid main dish with the eggs. You can use an assortment of peppers for this; *chakchouka* should have some heat, but the degree of heat can match your own taste for it. This one is mildly hot. If you want a spicier dish, add a jalapeño or serrano pepper to the mix.

> 2 tablespoons extra virgin olive oil
>
> 1 large onion, thinly sliced
>
> 2 large green bell peppers, seeded and sliced
>
> 2 large red bell peppers, seeded and sliced
>
> 2 green Anaheim peppers, seeded and diced
>
> 4 garlic cloves, minced
>
> 1 to 2 teaspoons Harissa (page 86 or commercial; to taste)
>
> 1 teaspoon Tabil (page 24), plus additional for serving

> Salt and freshly ground pepper
>
> 1½ pounds plum tomatoes, chopped
>
> ¼ cup chopped fresh flat-leaf parsley
>
> 4 large eggs
>
> Moroccan Flat Bread (page 54)

1. Heat the oil in a large nonstick skillet, or in an earthenware casserole set on a flame tamer, over medium heat. Add the onion and cook, stirring often, until golden, about 10 minutes. Add the bell peppers and cook, stirring often, until they begin to soften, about 5 minutes. Add the garlic and cook, stirring, until fragrant, about a minute. Stir in the harissa, tabil, and salt and pepper, then add the tomatoes. Cover partially and cook, stirring from time to time, until the tomatoes have cooked down to a chunky purée, 20 to 25 minutes. Stir in all but 2 teaspoons of the parsley, taste, and adjust seasonings.

Note: *If you are using an earthenware casserole, the cooking times will be longer. It will take about 10 minutes for the peppers to soften, and 30 to 40 minutes for the mixture to cook down.*

2. With the back of your spoon, make 4 depressions in the vegetables. Break an egg into each depression. Cover and cook for 5 to 6 minutes, until the eggs are set. Sprinkle the eggs with salt, the remaining parsley, and, if you wish, tabil, and serve with bread.

ADVANCE PREPARATION: This stew can be made a few days ahead through Step 1, and it will taste even better on the second day.

VARIATION

TURKISH MENEMEM: This Turkish vegetable ragout with eggs is virtually identical, but spiced differently. Omit the harissa and the tabil from the above recipe, and cook as directed. Serve with thickened yogurt seasoned with crushed garlic, Turkish red pepper (*kirmizi biber;* page 26) or Aleppo pepper (page 25), and salt and freshly ground black pepper.

HOMEMADE RICOTTA CHEESE

Italy • **Makes 4 cups**

If you have never eaten fresh ricotta cheese, then I urge you to try this, even if you only try it once, so that you can taste the difference between the fresh product and the commercial one. Fresh ricotta has a luscious, rich flavor and light texture that commercially available varieties do not have (there are usually gums and stabilizers added to commercial brands). If you are lucky enough to have a real Italian deli in your neighborhood (or a Trader Joe's, which sells an excellent brand of fresh ricotta), you will probably have access to fresh ricotta; even if you don't see it in the dairy case, it's worth asking for in the cheese department.

To make this you will need an instant-read thermometer, preferably the digital kind that you can set to go off when it has reached the desired temperature; a large pot; and a strainer or colander lined with a double thickness of cheesecloth. That said, making ricotta is incredibly easy.

> 4 cups whole milk
>
> 4 cups goat's milk (if unavailable, substitute 4 cups whole milk)
>
> 2 cups buttermilk
>
> 2 cups whole-milk or goat's milk yogurt
>
> 1 cup heavy cream (preferably not ultra-pasteurized)
>
> 3 tablespoons white wine vinegar or fresh lemon juice

1. Line a strainer or colander with a double thickness of cheesecloth and set over a pot or bowl.

2. Pour the whole milk, goat's milk, buttermilk, yogurt, heavy cream, and vinegar into a large pot and place over low heat. Insert a thermometer and heat the mixture until the temperature reaches 194°F. At this point the milk will curdle.

3. Carefully ladle the curdled milk into the cheesecloth–lined strainer or colander. Pour out the liquid in the bowl (the whey) and set the strainer or colander back over the bowl. Place in the refrigerator and leave to drain for 2 to 12 hours.

4. Transfer the ricotta to a container and store, tightly covered, in the refrigerator.

ADVANCE PREPARATION: The ricotta will keep for a week in the refrigerator.

SFORMATO WITH RICOTTA AND GREENS

Italy • **Serves 6**

This is much like a timbale or gratin, though a *sformato* can be light and puffy (see the variation). The egg whites and yolks are beaten separately to give the mixture some lift, but with the ricotta and all the greens, this one isn't light and airy like a French soufflé. I like to use those bags of mixed Southern greens that I find in my supermarket and Trader Joe's. The greens are already washed and stemmed, which makes things pretty simple in the kitchen and yields quite a lot of cooked greens. This is one of the rare dishes in my Mediterranean repertoire for which I recommend butter over olive oil.

> Salt
>
> 1 pound mixed stemmed greens (leaves only), washed
>
> 1 tablespoon unsalted butter
>
> ½ onion, minced
>
> Freshly ground pepper
>
> 1¾ cups Homemade Ricotta Cheese (left) or 1 container (15 ounces) commercial ricotta
>
> 4 large eggs, separated, plus 2 egg whites
>
> 1 cup plus 2 tablespoons freshly grated Parmesan
>
> 2 tablespoons fresh marjoram, torn or roughly chopped (or 1 teaspoon dried oregano)

1. Set a rack in the lower third of the oven and heat the oven to 375°F. Butter a 2-quart soufflé dish. ▶

2. Bring a large pot of water to a boil, then add a tablespoon of salt and the greens. Blanch for 2 minutes and transfer to a bowl of cold water. Drain, squeeze dry, and chop fine. You should have about 1½ cups chopped blanched greens.

3. Heat the butter in a heavy nonstick pan over medium heat and add the onion. Cook, stirring, until tender and just beginning to color, 5 to 8 minutes. Stir in the greens. Cook, stirring, for a couple of minutes, until coated with butter and fragrant. Season with salt and pepper and remove from the heat.

4. Beat the ricotta and egg yolks together in a large bowl. Stir in the greens mixture, 1 cup of the Parmesan, and the marjoram. Season to taste with salt and pepper—begin with ½ teaspoon salt and adjust to taste.

5. Beat all 6 egg whites to medium-stiff peaks. Stir one-quarter of the beaten whites into the ricotta mixture, then gently fold in the rest. Scrape into the soufflé dish. Sprinkle the remaining 2 tablespoons Parmesan over the top. Bake for 50 minutes, until slightly puffed, firm, and lightly browned. Serve hot, warm, or at room temperature. The hot *sformato* will be runny in the center, but will firm up if you allow it to cool.

ADVANCE PREPARATION: You can prepare the greens through Step 3 up to a day before assembling and baking the *sformato*.

VARIATION

You can make a lighter, more soufflé-like version of this if you reduce the greens to ½ pound.

SAVORY BREAD PUDDINGS (STRATAS)

People throughout the Mediterranean turn stale bread into delicious meals in many different ways. The Italians make these savory bread puddings called *stratas*. When my baguettes and country breads go stale and hard, I know that this is going to be on my dinner table. There are many reasons I love this comforting, easy dish, not the least of which is the fact that I hate throwing out food. And there are many ways to make a strata; mine are not as rich as many.

BASIC STRATA

Italy • **Serves 4 to 6**

This is the simplest and arguably the most comforting of stratas, made with eggs, milk, cheese, and bread.

- ½ pound stale bread, sliced about ½ inch thick (see Note)
- 1 large garlic clove, cut in half
- ¾ cup grated Gruyère cheese
- 4 large eggs
- 2 cups milk (less with the variations that follow)
- Salt and freshly ground pepper

Note: *If your bread is too hard to slice, dip it in milk for about half a minute, then you'll be able to slice or cut it. If your bread is long and narrow, like a baguette or a ciabatta, you can just cut it in half down the middle, then cut sandwich-size pieces.*

1. Heat the oven to 350°F. Oil or butter a 2-quart baking dish or gratin. If the bread is soft, toast it lightly. Rub all the slices, front and back, with the cut clove of garlic. Layer half of the slices in the baking dish. Top with half the cheese. Repeat the layers.

2. Beat together the eggs and milk. Add ½ teaspoon salt and a few twists of pepper and pour over the bread. Bake for 40 to 50 minutes, until puffed and browned. Serve hot or warm.

ADVANCE PREPARATION: The bread and cheese layers for this recipe, and for all of the variations that follow, can be assembled hours before beating together the eggs and milk and completing the casserole.

LEFTOVERS: Strata keeps well in the refrigerator for about 3 days and can be reheated in the microwave.

STRATA WITH MUSHROOMS AND SAGE

For this variation of Basic Strata, prepare the recipe, adding the following:

1 pound mushrooms, sliced

1 tablespoon extra virgin olive oil

2 garlic cloves, minced or put through a press

2 to 3 tablespoons chopped fresh sage leaves

1. Heat a large nonstick skillet over medium heat and add the mushrooms and a generous pinch of salt. Cook, stirring, until the mushrooms begin to release water. Continue to cook until they've softened and most of the liquid has evaporated, 5 to 8 minutes. Add the olive oil and the garlic, and cook, stirring, for another minute, until the garlic is fragrant. Add the sage, stir, and season with salt and pepper. Pour off any liquid remaining in the pan into a 2-cup Pyrex measuring cup.

2. Proceed with the Basic Strata recipe, adding half the mushrooms to the first layer of bread before adding the cheese, and topping the second layer with the remaining mushrooms. Beat the eggs, and add the salt and pepper. Add enough milk to the cup with the mushroom liquid to make 2 cups, and beat together with the eggs. Pour over the bread and bake as directed.

STRATA WITH TOMATOES AND THYME

For this variation of Basic Strata, prepare the recipe, adding the following:

1 pound fresh tomatoes, sliced; or 1 can (14 ounces) tomatoes, drained and sliced

1 teaspoon fresh thyme (or ½ teaspoon dried)

Substitute ¼ cup of grated Parmesan for ¼ cup of the Gruyère (so you have ½ cup Gruyère and ¼ cup Parmesan)

1. Layer half of the prepared bread slices in the baking dish. Top with half the tomato slices. If any garlic remains after rubbing the bread, mince it and scatter over the tomatoes. Sprinkle the tomato slices with salt, pepper, and thyme, and top with half the cheese. Repeat the layers.

2. Beat together the eggs, salt, pepper, and milk as directed, pour over the bread, and bake.

STRATA WITH GREENS, OR WITH TOMATOES AND GREENS

For this variation of Basic Strata or Strata with Tomatoes and Thyme, prepare the recipe, adding the following:

1 pound greens, such as Swiss chard, beet greens, kale, or spinach

1 tablespoon extra virgin olive oil

1 or 2 garlic cloves (to taste), minced or put through a press

1. Bring a large pot of water to a boil and add 1 tablespoon salt and the greens. Blanch for 2 minutes, until just tender. (If using spinach, just blanch for 20 seconds.) Transfer immediately to a bowl of cold water, then drain, squeeze out water, and coarsely chop. Heat the olive oil in a large nonstick skillet over medium heat and add the garlic. Cook, stirring, for about 30 seconds, just until it begins to color. Add the greens and toss together until coated with oil, 30 seconds to 1 minute. Remove from the heat and season with salt and pepper.

2. If adding to the basic recipe, divide the greens in half and layer over the bread before adding the cheese, or the cheese and tomatoes.

BAKED SPICY FETA

Greece • **Serves 6**

This was one of my very favorite *mezedes* when I visited Greece. The feta would come to the table hot, just beginning to ooze around the edges, and topped with spicy red pepper and olive oil. Sometimes the feta was mildly seasoned, sometimes quite hot. Diane Kochilas's version, which we made at her cooking class, was quite spicy. This one is milder. Diane specifies tinned feta because it is sold in blocks and is easier to cut into slices than barrel-aged feta. You can find this type of feta in Greek and Middle Eastern markets.

> 1 pound Greek tinned feta or Telemes cheese
>
> 4 tablespoons extra virgin olive oil
>
> Scant ¾ teaspoon cayenne (more or less to taste)
>
> 3 teaspoons dried Greek oregano
>
> Lemon wedges

1. Heat the oven to 375°F. Cut the feta into 6 equal squares. Cut six 8-inch squares of aluminum and brush each with olive oil. Place a piece of cheese on each square. Drizzle 2 teaspoons of oil over each piece of cheese and sprinkle with cayenne and ½ teaspoon oregano. Fold up the edges of the aluminum and crimp together to seal. Place on a baking sheet.

2. Bake the feta packages for 10 minutes, or just until the feta begins to melt. Remove from the heat, cut open each packet, sprinkle with a little bit of lemon juice, and serve hot in the packets.

ADVANCE PREPARATION: You can prepare the feta packets hours before you bake them. Hold in the refrigerator.

GREEK FRIED CHEESE (Saganaki)

Greece • **Serves 4**

This is another popular Greek *meze,* made with hard cheese like kefalograviera or kefalotyri. Haloumi will work too, and so will other hard yellow cheeses, like kashkaval or even Gruyère or Cheddar. The cheese is very lightly floured, then seared in butter or olive oil in a pan called a *saganaki pan.* Definitely not Mediterranean Light, but you don't eat much of it either.

> ½ pound kefalograviera, kefalotyri, haloumi, or other hard yellow cheese
>
> Unbleached all-purpose flour
>
> Freshly ground pepper
>
> About ¼ cup extra virgin olive oil or unsalted butter
>
> Lemon wedges

1. Cut the cheese into 3 × ½-inch pieces. Rinse briefly with water, then dredge very lightly in the flour and season with pepper.

2. Heat the oil in a medium heavy skillet over medium-high heat until very hot, almost smoking. Add the cheese, a few pieces at a time, and cook on both sides for 2 to 3 minutes, until lightly browned and beginning to soften. It should not melt. Remove from the heat and serve with lemon wedges.

ADVANCE PREPARATION: You can prepare the cheese through Step 1 an hour or so before cooking it.

CHEESE SOUFFLÉ WITH TRUFFLES
(Soufflé aux Truffes)

France • **Serves 4**

Christine Picasso always makes sure to have a few of the season's truffles in the freezer at her house in Provence, and when people are around over Christmas and New Year's, she pulls them out and invariably makes this luxurious soufflé. The soufflé is the ultimate expression of eggs and cheese together, and when infused with the heady scent of truffles, it's enough to make you swoon. Try to remember to enclose the eggs and the truffle in a jar for a couple of days before you make this.

FOR THE SOUFFLÉ

1 medium or large fresh truffle (1 to 2 ounces)

6 large eggs

1 recipe Béchamel (page 77), made with 3 tablespoons flour

1 tablespoon softened butter for the soufflé dish

¼ cup freshly grated Parmesan

1 cup grated Gruyère cheese

2 large egg whites

⅛ teaspoon cream of tartar

Pinch of salt

1. Put the truffle and eggs in a large jar or container, close it tightly, and refrigerate for a day or more.

2. Make the béchamel, following the instructions on page 77. Make sure that the béchamel is adequately seasoned.

3. Separate the eggs. One by one, beat the egg yolks into the béchamel. Grate the truffle or finely mince, and stir into the béchamel. Transfer to a large bowl and set aside.

4. Set the oven rack in the lowest position. Heat the oven to 375°F. Smear the inside of a 2-quart soufflé dish with 1 tablespoon softened butter and sprinkle in 2 tablespoons of the Parmesan. Tap and tilt the dish to distribute the cheese evenly over the sides. Combine the remaining Parmesan with the Gruyère.

5. Place the 8 egg whites in the bowl of a standing mixer, or use a large bowl and balloon whisk or a hand-held mixer, and begin beating at medium-low speed. When the egg whites begin to foam, add the cream of tartar and the pinch of salt. Beat until the whites form satiny peaks that hold their shape when lifted with the spatula or beater. Be careful not to overbeat. The peaks should be stiff but not dry.

6. Using a balloon whisk or a rubber scraper, stir one-quarter of the beaten egg whites into the béchamel to lighten it. Carefully fold in the remaining egg whites, along with the grated cheese, adding a handful of cheese every time you fold the egg whites and turn the bowl. Fold until the mixture is homogenous and all the cheese has been added, working rapidly but with a light hand.

7. Carefully scrape the soufflé mixture into the soufflé dish. Set the dish on a baking sheet, and bake for 25 to 30 minutes, until puffed and browned. Serve at once, spooning the runny middle part over the fluffy outer section with each portion.

ADVANCE PREPARATION: The béchamel can be made a day ahead (cover with plastic wrap, placing the wrap directly on top of the sauce to prevent a skin from forming). Reheat over medium-low heat and whisk well before proceeding with the recipe.

Note: *Another way to get an intense truffle flavor is to keep the truffle in butter for a few days and use the butter for the béchamel. Restaurants do this, but restaurants use a lot more butter than I do in my kitchen.*

Pasta

I've zeroed in on Italy in this chapter. Not that you can't find pasta elsewhere in the Mediterranean, like France and Greece and the Middle East, but Italy is practically synonymous with pasta, and as every vegetarian who has been there knows, you don't have to try hard to find meatless sauces and combinations.

I wanted to find pasta dishes I'd never had before for this book, so I went looking for them in southern Italy. If you ever get it in your head that you know everything there is to know about pasta, go to a region of Italy you've never visited before. When I went to Puglia, a region where produce is prominent in the cuisine, I was almost flummoxed by the pastas I'd never seen on a menu. I knew all about the little ear-shaped noodles called orecchiette, which are tossed with a sauce made from broccoli rabe, and sure enough I found that dish on many menus; but I also found orecchiette tossed with luscious tomato sauce, and with tomato sauce and arugula. I wasn't at all familiar with strozzapreti, a thick, chewy pasta that looks like a twisted towel that was on menus everywhere, often (to confuse me even more) with another name, like gemelli ("twins") or casareccia ("twists") because they resemble two pieces of pasta that have been twisted together. The same thing happened in Sicily, where I discovered the hollow spaghetti-like pasta called bucatini or perciatelli. In Abruzzo, the province just north of Puglia, I encountered wonderful versions of spaghetti alla chitarra, hand-made pasta that is cut on a frame with a set of strings that looks like the neck of a guitar. It was tossed with arugula pesto and tomato sauce, and I've re-created the dish for you, though you won't have to make your own pasta for it.

Pasta is the most well-known of the foods that the Italians call *primi,* or first courses. Soups, risottos, polenta, and gnocchi also fall within this category. Not that you can't have only pasta as your meal when you travel in Italy; that is common too. But if you are sitting down to a traditional Italian dinner, the first course will likely be a small serving of pasta tossed with just enough sauce to coat the noodles, but not so much that there is any left on the plate when you finish. Cheese is sprinkled on at the table, in judicious amounts so as not to weigh down the noodles.

Here, especially for everyday cooking, pasta is more likely to be the main event, and that's how I am assuming you are going to approach these recipes. Serve any of these dishes with a salad and some crusty bread, and you will have eaten a wonderful meal.

There are two categories of pasta in Italy, *pastasciutta*, which is dried pasta; and *pasta fresca,* fresh pasta. Fresh pasta is cut into noodles and served with sauce, or layered for lasagna, or cut into squares, triangles, or circles and filled with something. Fresh pasta is also lightly sauced, often with little more than butter, broth, cream, or a light tomato sauce. Fresh pasta is a specialty of the region of Emilia-Romagna, but it is available everywhere in Italy.

Dried pasta comes in an endless variety of shapes, some of which are made only in specific regions of the country. Orecchiette, for example, is a specialty of Puglia. Cavatelli (aka cavateddi, cavatieddi) are curled pastas found throughout the south. Pizzoccheri is buckwheat pasta found in Lombardy. If you want to learn more about regional pasta specialties, I highly recommend Fred Plotkin's *Italy for the Gourmet Traveller.*

Another *primi,* gnocchi—feather-light dumplings made with potatoes and flour—are served with sauces the same way pasta is, and I've included a few recipes in this chapter. Potato gnocchi have ridged surfaces that catch the sauce, and they can be truly heavenly. Semolina gnocchi, much loved in Rome, are disk-shaped gnocchi made with semolina, milk, egg yolks, and Parmigiana-Reggiano. Layered in a baking dish and baked with butter and cheese, they're a true indulgence.

These recipes represent just a smattering of the many meatless pasta dishes you can find in Italy, but they will certainly whet your appetite. Beyond what you have here, keep in mind that practically any cooked vegetable can be tossed with pasta, olive oil, and a little cheese, and with that you'll have a meal.

A SMALL CATALOGUE OF PASTA

The list that follows is by no means exhaustive. It covers the pasta you will encounter in this book, as well as many types that you are likely to come across if you travel in Italy or dine in good Italian restaurants outside of Italy.

Long Pasta

Bucatini (perciatelli): Long, hollow, spaghetti-like strands, like straws. Popular in southern Italian cuisines, it goes well with robust sauces.

Bucatoni: Fatter bucatini, more tube-like.

Capellini (angel hair): Very thin, delicate strands. Cooks quickly and should be served with very light sauces.

Fettuccine: Flat ribbons about ¼ inch wide.

Linguine: Very narrow ribbons, sort of like flat spaghetti.

Maccheroni (or spaghetti) alla chitarra: Fresh pasta cut into thin strips by pressing them through steel wires that look like the strings of a guitar. A specialty of Abruzzo.

Pappardelle: Wide, flat ribbons about ¾ to 1 inch wide, and most often made from fresh egg pasta.

Pizzoccheri: Buckwheat pasta typical of the Valtellina region of Lombardy. Usually served in a rich mixture of cabbage, potatoes, garlic, and melted cheese.

Spaghetti: We all know what this is. Very sturdy, a good vehicle for many types of sauces, especially tomato sauce and pesto.

Spaghettini: Thin spaghetti, thicker than angel hair but thinner than regular spaghetti.

Spaghettoni: Thick spaghetti.

Tagliarini, tagliolini: Very thin, flat ribbons.

Tagliatelle: Flat ribbons similar to fettuccine, sometimes wider. Called *picagge* in Liguria.

Trenette: Thick, narrow ribbons.

Vermicelli: Very thin, fine spaghetti, often sold broken up for soup.

Tubular Pastas (Maccheroni)

Garganelli: The only tubular pasta handmade from fresh egg pasta dough, these are tubes rolled on the diagonal, with a ridged edge.

Macaroni: The American name for small, tubular semicircles, known also as elbow macaroni.

Maccheroni: This refers to all types of tubular pasta.

Penne: The most widely used tubular pasta, these are named after pens, because of the "nib," or pointed end. They can be smooth (*lisce*) or ridged (*rigata*).

Rigatoni: Large, ridged tubes with an appealing chewy texture.

Other Pasta Shapes

Conchiglie: Tiny "conch shells," used in soups. Large, ridged shells are called *conchiglioni*.

Farfalle: Bow ties or butterflies.

Fusilli: Corkscrew pasta, short spiral shapes. Long spiral pasta is called *fusilli lunghi* or *fusilli col buco*.

Orecchiette: "Little ears." Small, ridged, slightly domed pasta disks. A specialty of Puglia, where they are still made by hand from eggless pasta.

Radiatore: A short, ridged pasta that looks like a little radiator.

Rotelle: "Cartwheels"—they look like little wheels.

Strozzapreti: The name means "priest stranglers," so called, legend has it, because a gluttonous priest once choked on this pasta, which looks like a twisted towel with one long crease. It's a thick, chewy pasta, widespread in southern Italy. Strozzapreti can also be called gemelli ("twins") or casareccia ("twists") because they resemble two pieces of pasta twisted together.

Filled, Layered, and Baked Pasta

Agnolotti (agnoli): Large, filled pasta, square or half-moon shaped.

Cannelloni, manicotti: Rectangular sheets of pasta that are rolled around a filling and baked with a sauce.

Lasagna: Flat, wide sheets of pasta that are layered with fillings.

Ravioli: Square stuffed pasta.

Pansôti: Triangular stuffed pasta parcels from the Italian Riviera (see page 207). The name means "little bellies." Pansôti are traditionally filled with a mixture of five greens and ricotta, and served with walnut sauce.

Tortellini, tortelli: Small half-moon-shaped ravioli that are pinched together at two corners.

Tortelloni: Large "hat-shaped" filled pasta made by pulling together the corners of filled pasta triangles. Cappelleti are small hat-shaped pasta.

FRESH PASTA DOUGH
Makes enough for 6 generous servings

Every once in a while I get a hankering for home-made ravioli. There is simply nothing like it, time-consuming though it may be. This basic pasta dough can be used for ravioli or any other fresh pasta, such as fettuccine or spaghetti alla chitarra. I recommend you use a food processor to mix the dough.

> 3 scant cups unbleached all-purpose flour; or for a firmer dough, use half fine semolina flour, half unbleached all-purpose
>
> ¾ teaspoon salt
>
> 3 large eggs
>
> 2 to 3 tablespoons water

1. Place the flour and salt in the bowl of a food processor fitted with the steel blade, and pulse a few times to combine. Add the eggs and 2 table-spoons water, and process until the dough comes together into a ball. If it seems dry, add another tablespoon of water.

2. Transfer the dough to a lightly floured work surface. Knead by hand for a few minutes, until you have a smooth ball. Wrap in plastic and let rest on the counter for 30 minutes to 1 hour.

3. To roll out the dough using a pasta roller, cut the dough into 4 equal pieces. Keep the other pieces covered with plastic while you roll out one piece at a time. Set the rollers at the widest opening. Flatten the first piece of dough into a thick strip no wider than the machine, to enable it to pass through the rollers. If necessary, dust the pasta very lightly with flour or semolina. Run the pasta through the machine. Fold in thirds, crosswise, and run through the machine again. Repeat this procedure two more times, until the dough is smooth and somewhat elastic. Set the machine to the next smaller opening and run the dough through the rollers twice.

4. Continue rolling and stretching the dough, using the smaller opening each time, until the next to the last or the last opening is reached, dusting lightly with flour only as necessary. (The strip of dough will be long. If you don't have enough space on your worktable, halfway through the rolling process cut the strip of dough in half and continue to work with each piece separately, keeping the unused dough covered with plastic or a damp towel).

5. Shape and cut the pasta as directed in your recipe.

ADVANCE PREPARATION: Once cut, you can leave pasta to dry completely. Dried pasta can be stored in a covered jar for months, just like commercial pasta. If you don't dry it out and wish to keep it overnight in the refrigerator, dust with semolina and place in freezer bags. You can also freeze fresh pasta for a couple of months.

HALF-MOON RAVIOLI WITH WINTER SQUASH FILLING
Italy • **Serves 6**

When I served this ravioli at a dinner party, my friend Marguerite said: "My mouth is so happy!" Yours will be too; it is really one of the most wonderful of all the Italian ravioli. In Italy, where all winter squash is referred to as *pumpkin,* it would be called *pumpkin ravioli.* I use butternut squash, which is incredibly sweet and has a great buttery texture.

> 2½ pounds butternut squash (1 large)
>
> 1 egg yolk
>
> ½ cup ground toasted almonds
>
> 2 teaspoons minced fresh sage
>
> ¾ cup freshly grated Parmesan, plus additional for serving
>
> Salt
>
> ¼ teaspoon freshly ground pepper
>
> ¼ teaspoon freshly grated nutmeg
>
> 1 recipe Fresh Pasta Dough (at left)
>
> 3 cups Simple Vegetable Broth (page 145)
>
> 4 tablespoons (½ stick) unsalted butter
>
> 2 tablespoons slivered fresh sage

HOW TO COOK PASTA

Because it's extremely important that you use 5 to 6 quarts of generously salted water for every pound of pasta that you cook, you need to have a big pot for cooking it. A pasta pot with an insert is nice, but any big pot will do. For every 6 quarts of water add 1 to 2 tablespoons of salt once the water comes to a boil. Drop in the pasta. You can do this gradually or all at once. I like adding long pasta gradually to the water, because it helps prevent the strands from sticking to each other. Other shapes, like orecchiette and fusilli, can be added all at once. Some people cover their pot until the water comes back to the boil (it will stop when you add the pasta), but I rarely bother, though I do stir the pasta occasionally as the water is coming back to a boil.

Each type of pasta requires a different amount of time in boiling water before it reaches the al dente stage. Al dente pasta is supple, and you can bite through it, but it resists the bite slightly. It is firm "to the tooth," which is what *al dente* means in Italian. Most packages indicate the time, but if yours doesn't, you'll have to test it when you think it's just about ready. In fact, even if the cooking time is given, I like to test my pasta about 1 minute before the indicated time, especially if the pasta isn't imported from Italy. Take out a piece or a strand with tongs, run it under cold water so you don't burn your mouth, and bite. Fresh pasta will be ready within minutes, as soon as it comes to the surface of the water.

While the pasta is cooking, you need to heat the bowl it will be served from, or the plates it will be served on. If there's a hot sauce, I like to toss my pasta in the pan with my sauce, which heats the pasta through while you toss it. If I'm not using a hot sauce, I heat my bowl by ladling some of the pasta cooking water into it and letting it sit while the pasta cooks. In some recipes, you'll be using some of the pasta cooking water to toss with the noodles, which adds a wonderful flavor dimension as well as thinning the sauce and heating the noodles. So before you drain pasta, always remove some of the water. (This is when a basket insert comes in handy, because the water stays in the pot.)

There are two other important rules when it comes to cooking pasta:

Don't add oil to the cooking water. It will just make the pasta slippery, and then the sauce won't adhere to it properly.

Don't rinse the pasta when you drain it. Toss immediately with the sauce, or with olive oil or butter and cheese.

1. Heat the oven to 425°F. Pierce the butternut squash in a few places and place on a foil-lined baking sheet. Roast for 30 minutes, then cool until you can handle it easily. Cut the squash in half and remove the seeds. Oil the foil and return the squash to the foil, cut side down. Roast until the squash can be easily pierced with a knife, about 30 minutes. Cool slightly, then peel. Mash with a fork or in a food processor fitted with the steel blade. You should have 2 cups of purée.

2. In a food processor fitted with the steel blade, or in a large bowl, mix together the mashed squash, egg yolk, ground almonds, minced sage, Parmesan, salt, pepper, and nutmeg.

3. Roll out the dough and fill the ravioli following the directions on page 206. Instead of cutting squares, cut half-moon shapes. Freeze as directed on page 206, until ready to serve.

4. In a medium saucepan, reduce the broth by half. Heat the butter in a large frying pan over medium heat, and when sizzling, add the slivered sage. Cook, stirring, for a couple of minutes, and stir in the reduced broth. Keep warm. ▶

5. Bring a large pot of water to a rolling boil and add 1 tablespoon salt. Reduce the heat slightly so that the water is boiling gently. Add the ravioli and cook just until they float to the surface, about 4 minutes once the water returns to a gentle boil, turning the ravioli over halfway through. With a skimmer or slotted spoon, transfer to the frying pan. Toss with the sauce and serve, passing additional Parmesan.

ADVANCE PREPARATION: You can make the filling up to 3 days before you make the ravioli. The filled ravioli can be frozen (see below) for a couple of months.

SHAPING RAVIOLI

Roll out one-fourth of the dough at a time to get long, wide strips. Beat together 1 egg with 1 tablespoon water; brush the strips with the egg wash.

Place teaspoons of filling along the length of the dough, spacing them about 2 inches apart along the bottom half of each strip. Fold the top half of the strip over to cover the mounds of filling. Press down around each mound to secure the filling and make sure there are no air pockets.

Using a ravioli wheel or a sharp knife, trim the length of the folded strip of pasta on each side, then cut between each mound.

Cover a baking sheet with parchment and dust the parchment with semolina. Place the ravioli on the baking sheet. It doesn't take long for the pasta to become soggy, so I put my ravioli in the freezer right away (which also clears up counter space). Once the ravioli are frozen, you can transfer them to freezer bags for long-term storage. Transfer directly from the freezer to a pot of boiling salted water to cook.

RAVIOLI WITH BEET GREENS AND RICOTTA

Italy • **Serves 4**

We call this *pink ravioli* at our house, because the beet greens always bleed into the ricotta, resulting in a luscious pink filling. If you don't want to spend the time making ravioli, make the equally delicious lasagna (opposite page), or use wonton wrappers for the ravioli instead of pasta dough.

FOR THE FILLING

Salt

2 large bunches beet greens, about 1½ pounds (see Note)

2 cups fresh ricotta cheese

2 large eggs

¼ cup finely chopped fresh flat-leaf parsley

Pinch freshly grated nutmeg

½ cup freshly grated Parmesan, plus additional for serving

1 recipe Fresh Pasta Dough (page 204)

½ recipe Basic Tomato Sauce (page 78) or extra virgin olive oil for serving

Note: *Red chard will also make a pink ravioli filling. Chard is more robust than beet greens and doesn't lose as much volume when you blanch it. One pound should suffice to get 1½ cups chopped blanched chard. Other greens, such as green chard or kale, can also be substituted for the beet greens, but the ravioli won't be pink.*

1. *Make the filling:* Bring a large pot of water to a boil. Add 1 tablespoon salt and the greens. Cook for 2 minutes, until tender, then use a skimmer or slotted spoon to transfer to a bowl of cold water. Drain and squeeze out water. Chop fine. You should have about 1½ cups chopped greens.

2. Blend the ricotta in a food processor fitted with the steel blade. Add the eggs and blend until smooth, then scrape into a bowl. Stir in the greens, parsley, nutmeg, salt, and the Parmesan. Taste and adjust salt.

PASTA

3. *Make the ravioli:* Roll out the dough and fill and cut the ravioli following the directions on page 206.

4. Heat the tomato sauce if using. Bring a large pot of water to a rolling boil and add 1 tablespoon salt. Reduce the heat slightly so that the water is boiling gently. Add the ravioli and cook for about 4 minutes once the water returns to a gentle boil, turning the ravioli over halfway through. With a skimmer or slotted spoon, transfer to a warm serving dish or plates. Top with sauce or douse with olive oil, sprinkle with Parmesan, and serve.

ADVANCE PREPARATION: You could make the filling while the pasta dough is resting. Or you can cook the greens up to 3 days ahead and keep them in a covered bowl in the refrigerator. The entire filling will keep for a day in the refrigerator.

BEET GREEN LASAGNA

For this variation to Ravioli with Beet Greens and Ricotta, in addition to the filling, you'll need:

> 2 cups Béchamel (page 77)
>
> 8 ounces no-boil lasagna noodles
>
> ½ cup freshly grated Parmesan

1. Heat the oven to 350°F. Butter or oil a 2-quart lasagna dish or baking dish. Spoon a thin layer of béchamel over the bottom of the dish. Top with a layer of noodles. Cover the noodles with a thin layer of béchamel, spread a layer of the filling over the béchamel, and sprinkle on some Parmesan. Making sure you have enough béchamel and Parmesan set aside to complete the lasagna, repeat the layers until the filling is used up. End with a layer of pasta covered with a layer of béchamel and a sprinkling of Parmesan. Cover tightly with foil.

2. Bake for 30 minutes, until the pasta has softened and the béchamel is bubbling. Remove the foil and bake another 5 to 10 minutes, until the top begins to brown. Let the lasagna sit for 5 minutes, then serve.

ADVANCE PREPARATION: The lasagna can be assembled up to a day ahead and held in the refrigerator. However, cover with plastic rather than foil for storing, to avoid a reaction with the greens.

RAVIOLI WITH GREENS, HERBS, AND RICOTTA (Pansôti)
Italy • **Serves 6**

Fresh pasta filled with local herbs, ricotta, and greens shows up in one form or another from Nice through the Italian boot. In Liguria, the dish is called *pansôti,* which means "potbellied," because the ravioli, usually triangular, are stuffed so full. The Ligurian mixture of greens and herbs can include beet greens, borage, spinach, watercress, arugula, fennel, chicory, parsley, marjoram, nettles, chervil, Swiss chard, and basil. I am certainly not going to recommend that you hunt for all of these, but try to have a mixture of at least one or two cooked greens and two or three different chopped herbs.

The Ligurian version of this dish is always served with walnut sauce. A simple tomato sauce will also work well.

> Salt
>
> 5 cups stemmed mixed greens, such as spinach (see Note), beet greens, Swiss chard, chicory, Savoy cabbage, nettles (about ½ pound)
>
> 1 cup mixed finely chopped fresh herbs, such as parsley, chervil, marjoram, basil, fennel, arugula
>
> 2 cups fresh ricotta cheese
>
> 1 large egg, beaten
>
> Freshly grated nutmeg
>
> ½ cup freshly grated Parmesan, plus additional for serving
>
> Freshly ground pepper
>
> 1 recipe Fresh Pasta Dough (page 204)
>
> ½ recipe Ligurian Walnut Sauce (page 76) or Basic Tomato Sauce (page 78) for serving

Note: *If you use baby spinach, all you need to do is pour boiling water over it to blanch it.*

1. Bring a large pot of water to a boil. Add a heaped tablespoon of salt and parboil the greens (other than spinach) for about 2 minutes, just until tender. Transfer to a bowl of ice water, then drain and squeeze out excess water. Chop very fine. Combine with the herbs in a mixing bowl. Add the ricotta, egg, nutmeg, Parmesan, and salt and freshly ground pepper to taste.

2. One sheet at a time, roll out the dough and fill and cut the ravioli as directed on page 206.

3. Warm the walnut sauce or tomato sauce. Bring a large pot of water to a rolling boil and add 1 tablespoon salt. Reduce the heat slightly so that the water is boiling gently. Add the ravioli and cook for about 4 minutes once the water returns to a gentle boil, turning the ravioli over halfway through. With a skimmer or slotted spoon, transfer to warmed serving dish or plates.

4. If you are using the walnut sauce, thin it with a little of the pasta water. Top the ravioli with walnut sauce or tomato sauce and serve.

ADVANCE PREPARATION: You can prep the greens for the filling up to 2 days ahead of making it. The filling will hold a day in the refrigerator. The ravioli can be frozen for a couple of months.

POTATO AND MINT RAVIOLI
Italy • Serves 4 to 6

This was on the menu at a vegetarian restaurant (yes, vegetarian!) in Rome. Most of the food at the restaurant was disappointing. (If you're vegetarian, you're better off eating at traditional Italian restaurants when you're in Italy. You'll find plenty to eat on a typical Italian menu.) But these ravioli were good, and it wasn't surprising to find them on a Roman menu, because the Romans love mint. The potatoes and mint are a beguiling combination.

1¼ pounds Yukon gold potatoes, peeled, and quartered if large

Salt

¼ to ½ cup milk

⅓ to ½ cup freshly grated Parmesan (to taste), plus additional for serving

Freshly ground pepper

2 tablespoons extra virgin olive oil

1 large or 2 medium garlic cloves, minced

4 tablespoons finely chopped fresh mint

⅔ recipe Fresh Pasta Dough (page 204)

1 recipe Basic Tomato Sauce (page 78) or extra virgin olive oil for serving

1. Boil the potatoes gently in salted water until tender, 25 to 30 minutes. Drain and return to the pot. Cover the pot and steam the potatoes for 5 minutes. Transfer to a standing mixer fitted with the paddle, or to a bowl, and mash at low speed or with a potato masher. Beat in the milk gradually, until the potatoes reach a smooth consistency. Beat in the Parmesan and season generously with salt and pepper.

2. Heat 1 tablespoon of the olive oil in a small skillet over medium heat and add the garlic. Cook, stirring, until fragrant, 30 seconds to 1 minute. Stir into the potatoes along with 2½ tablespoons of the chopped mint and the remaining 1 tablespoon olive oil. Taste and adjust seasonings.

3. Roll out the dough and fill and cut the ravioli as directed on page 206.

4. Warm the tomato sauce if using. Bring a large pot of water to a rolling boil and add 1 tablespoon salt. Reduce the heat slightly so that the water is boiling gently. Add the ravioli and cook just until they float to the surface, about 4 minutes once the water returns to a gentle boil, turning the ravioli over halfway through. With a skimmer or slotted spoon, transfer to a serving dish or plates. Top with the warm tomato sauce or douse with olive oil. Sprinkle with the remaining 1½ tablespoons chopped mint and serve, passing additional Parmesan.

ADVANCE PREPARATION: You can make the filling several hours before filling the pasta. The filled ravioli can be frozen and kept in freezer bags for up to 2 months.

An Italian Truck Stop

July 29, 2005
Autostrada A14

Today was the first day of our journey from Bologna down the Adriatic coast of Italy. Our destination was Puglia, the heel of the boot. We drove about halfway, stopping for the night in Francaville, near Pescara.

We set out from Bologna in our VW Golf a little before noon. By the time we reached Ancona we were ready for lunch, so we pulled off the autostrada *to fill up with gas at a servizio, then parked and went into their* Fini Grill *for a bite to eat. The self-serve restaurant was packed.*

In the middle of the room there was a cold buffet with platters of arugula and radicchio, sliced red and yellow peppers, tomato wedges, and cooked green beans. Next to the salads and vegetables were assorted cheese plates, bowls of fresh buffalo mozzarella, and cold pastas. Behind the counter across from the buffet, women were taking orders for hot dishes—pastizio, tortelloni with tomato sauce, grilled swordfish, steak, and contorni *(vegetable dishes) like roasted zucchini and eggplant.*

Rachel and I put together salad and cheese plates, ordered some eggplant and zucchini, and got some rigatoni with ragù Bolognese for Liam. I looked around for salad dressing and caught sight of a table full of condiments: there were several bottles of extra virgin olive oil and a selection of vinegars, including Prosecco vinegar, red wine vinegar, and balsamic. There were sea salt and pepper mills, and some freshly grated Parmesan.

We ate our lunch happily, slowly, as other traveling families came and went. Afterwards I ordered an espresso, hoping it would keep me from becoming sleepy after such a nice lunch. As I sipped the good coffee, I had to keep reminding myself that we were at a gas station.

GARGANELLI WITH MUSHROOM SAUCE

Italy • **Serves 4**

Garganelli are ridged handmade tubular pasta. Squares of pasta are cut, rolled around a tube, then against a ridged surface. They are lovely, and I was happy to see them on menus in Bologna, where they are most often served with wild mushrooms. You can find dried garganelli in many gourmet groceries. One good brand is Rustichella d'Abruzzo.

> 1 ounce (about 1 cup) dried porcini mushrooms
>
> 3 cups boiling water
>
> 2 tablespoons extra virgin olive oil
>
> 1 shallot, chopped
>
> 2 garlic cloves, minced
>
> ¾ pound button mushrooms, trimmed and sliced ¼ inch thick
>
> ¾ pound oyster mushrooms, trimmed and torn into pieces
>
> Salt
>
> 1 tablespoon unbleached all-purpose flour
>
> ½ cup dry white wine
>
> 2 tablespoons chopped fresh flat-leaf parsley
>
> Freshly ground pepper
>
> 12 ounces garganelli or penne rigati
>
> Freshly grated Parmesan

1. Place the dried mushrooms in a Pyrex measuring cup and pour in the boiling water. Let soak for 30 minutes. Place a strainer over a bowl, line it with cheesecloth or paper towels, and drain the mushrooms. Squeeze the mushrooms over the strainer to extract all the flavorful juices. Then rinse the mushrooms, away from the bowl with the soaking liquid, until they are free of sand. Squeeze dry and, if very large, chop coarsely. Set aside. Measure out 2 cups of the soaking liquid and set aside.

2. Heat the olive oil in a large, heavy nonstick skillet over medium heat and add the shallot. Cook, stirring often, until tender, about 3 minutes. Add the garlic, stir together for about 30 seconds, then add the button and oyster mushrooms and about ½ teaspoon salt. Cook, stirring often, until the mushrooms begin to soften, about 5 minutes. Add the flour and cook, stirring, for 2 or 3 minutes. Add the reconstituted dried mushrooms and the wine and turn the heat to high. Cook, stirring, until the liquid boils down and glazes the mushrooms, about 5 minutes. Add the mushroom soaking liquid. Bring to a simmer, add salt to taste, and cook over medium-high heat, stirring often, until the mushrooms are thoroughly tender and fragrant and the surrounding broth has reduced by a little more than half, about 20 minutes. Stir in the parsley and remove from the heat. Stir in some freshly ground pepper, taste, and adjust salt. Keep warm.

3. Bring a large pot of water to a boil, add a generous amount of salt, and cook the pasta until al dente. Drain and toss with the mushrooms. Serve with Parmesan.

ADVANCE PREPARATION: The mushroom sauce will keep well in the refrigerator for about 3 days. Reheat gently on top of the stove, and if necessary, thin out with some of the pasta water.

HOMEMADE GARGANELLI

You can make your own garganelli using the Fresh Pasta Dough on page 204.

Roll the dough out into wide strips, then cut the strips into 1½-inch squares. Turn a square so that the point is facing you. Place a pencil or a small round wooden spoon handle horizontally on the bottom of the diamond and roll it up. Press the pencil down on a ridged surface, such as a comb or a gnocchi board, to get the ridged surface. Slide the pencil out from the pasta and dry the pasta on a floured kitchen towel for 30 minutes before cooking.

ORECCHIETTE WITH UNCOOKED TOMATOES AND ARUGULA

Italy • **Serves 4 to 6**

If you go to Puglia in the summer, you will find something like this on menus all over the region. I came back from a summer trip to this region of Italy, my suitcase packed with different types of Pugliese pasta, to a garden full of cherry tomatoes. What else could I make? Try to find peppery wild arugula for this.

> 1 pound cherry tomatoes, quartered
>
> 1 plump garlic clove (more to taste), minced
>
> Salt (I like to use a very good coarse sea salt or fleur de sel for this)
>
> 1 teaspoon balsamic vinegar (optional)
>
> 1 cup chopped fresh arugula
>
> 2 heaped tablespoons chopped fresh basil
>
> ¼ cup extra virgin olive oil
>
> ¾ to 1 pound orecchiette
>
> ½ cup freshly grated ricotta salata or Parmesan

1. Combine the cherry tomatoes, garlic, salt, balsamic vinegar, arugula, basil, and olive oil in a wide pasta bowl. Let sit for 30 minutes. Taste and adjust seasonings.

2. Bring a large pot of water to a rolling boil. Add a generous amount of salt and the pasta. Cook until al dente. Drain, toss with the tomatoes, sprinkle on the cheese, and serve.

ADVANCE PREPARATION: You can make the sauce a few hours ahead. Keep at room temperature.

ORECCHIETTE WITH BROCCOLI RABE

Italy • **Serves 4**

Orecchiette with broccoli rabe is a classic Pugliese dish, one of the signature dishes of the region. When I crave this and I can't get broccoli rabe, I make it with other greens, which I buy already stemmed and washed at my local Trader Joe's.

> 1 pound broccoli rabe or other greens, such as kale, chard, mustard greens, turnip greens, or a mix
>
> Salt
>
> 2 tablespoons extra virgin olive oil
>
> 2 garlic cloves, minced
>
> ¼ to ½ teaspoon hot red pepper flakes (to taste)
>
> ¾ pound orecchiette
>
> ½ cup grated ricotta salata, Parmesan, or a mix of Pecorino Romano and Parmesan

1. If using broccoli rabe, cut away the tough stem ends and wash well. If using greens, stem and wash in at least two changes of water. Bring a large pot of water to a boil. Season generously with salt and add the greens or the broccoli rabe. Cook for 2 to 4 minutes, until tender, and transfer using a spider or a slotted spoon to a bowl of ice-cold water. Let sit for a few minutes and drain. Squeeze out water and chop fine. Save the water for cooking the pasta.

2. Heat the oil in a medium nonstick skillet over medium heat and add the garlic and red pepper flakes. Cook until the garlic smells fragrant, 30 seconds to a minute, and add the greens. Toss together for a minute, season to taste with salt, and remove from the heat but keep warm.

3. Bring the water back to a boil and add the orecchiette. Cook until al dente. Stir 3 or 4 tablespoons of the pasta water into the greens. Drain the pasta and toss with the greens and cheese. Serve at once.

ADVANCE PREPARATION: The greens can be prepared through Step 2 a couple of days ahead of time and refrigerated. Reheat before tossing with the pasta.

ORECCHIETTE WITH RAW AND COOKED TOMATO SAUCE

Italy • **Serves 4**

In Puglia, time and again you'll find orecchiette served with tomato sauce. Sometimes the sauce is thick, sometimes very light. In one of my favorite versions, the orecchiette was topped with a thick tomato ragù, then an uncooked tomato mixture. You can serve this in winter using canned tomatoes. If you don't want it to be spicy, omit the red pepper flakes, which are characteristic of Pugliese cuisine but not essential.

> ½ pound sweet fresh ripe tomatoes, peeled, seeded, and chopped; plus 2 pounds ripe tomatoes, quartered (or cut in sixths if the tomatoes are very large), or 1 can (28 ounces) tomatoes, with juice
>
> Salt
>
> 3 garlic cloves, minced or thinly sliced
>
> 3 tablespoons extra virgin olive oil
>
> 1 medium onion, chopped
>
> ¼ teaspoon hot red pepper flakes (more to taste; optional)
>
> ¼ teaspoon sugar
>
> A few sprigs fresh basil
>
> 2 sprigs fresh thyme
>
> ¾ pound orecchiette
>
> Parmesan, Pecorino Romano, or ricotta salata

1. Toss the ½ pound chopped fresh tomatoes with salt to taste, one-third of the garlic, and 1 tablespoon of the olive oil. Set aside while you make the sauce.

2. Heat the remaining 2 tablespoons oil in a wide nonstick frying pan or 3-quart saucepan over medium heat and add the onion. Cook, stirring often, until tender and golden, about 8 minutes. Add the remaining garlic and cook, stirring, until fragrant, about 1 minute. Add the quartered or canned tomatoes, red pepper, sugar, basil, thyme, and salt to taste, and bring to a boil. Reduce the heat to medium-low and simmer, stirring often, until thick. If you are using canned tomatoes or pulpy plum tomatoes, this will usually take about

20 minutes. However, if the tomatoes are very juicy, it may take up to 45 minutes for them to cook down. The sauce will be very sweet. Taste and adjust seasonings.

3. If using fresh quartered tomatoes, put the sauce through the medium blade of a food mill. If using canned tomatoes but want a sauce with a smooth, even texture, remove the basil and thyme sprigs and pulse in a food processor fitted with the steel blade. You can also mash the sauce with the back of a spoon. Return to the pan, add another sprig of basil, or some chopped leaves if you wish, and heat through.

4. Bring a large pot of water to a boil and add 1 tablespoon salt. Add the pasta and cook until al dente. Drain and toss with the warm tomato sauce and the uncooked tomatoes. Serve with Parmesan, pecorino, or ricotta salata.

ADVANCE PREPARATION: The sauce, without the uncooked tomatoes, will keep for 3 or 4 days in the refrigerator and freezes well.

VARIATION

Add ½ cup fresh ricotta to the above recipe. Spoon a tablespoon of the cooking water from the pasta into the ricotta, then toss with the tomato sauce and pasta as directed.

PASTA WITH UNCOOKED TOMATOES, BASIL, CAPERS, OLIVES, AND FETA

Serves 4

I'm reluctant to cook my heirloom tomatoes. They are so sweet and juicy that my summer pasta sauces tend to be uncooked, like this one. There's so much flavor here, I don't even use garlic (but you can—see the variation that follows).

> 2 tablespoons extra virgin olive oil
>
> 3 cups chopped fresh ripe tomatoes or halved cherry tomatoes
>
> 1½ tablespoons capers, rinsed
>
> ½ cup halved or chopped black Italian or Greek olives, such as Gaeta or kalamata

3 tablespoons minced fresh flat-leaf parsley

¼ cup minced fresh basil

Salt and freshly ground pepper

¾ pound penne or fusilli

2 ounces feta, crumbled (about ½ cup)

1. Combine the olive oil, tomatoes, capers, olives, parsley, basil, salt, and pepper in a large bowl and let sit for 30 minutes or longer.

2. Bring a large pot of water to a boil. Add a heaped tablespoon of salt and the pasta. Cook until al dente, drain, and toss at once with the tomato sauce and feta. Serve hot or at room temperature.

ADVANCE PREPARATION: This sauce becomes even better if it sits for an hour or so. If you want the basil to maintain its vivid color, leave it out until just before serving.

VARIATION

Add 1 garlic clove, finely minced or put through a press, to the sauce.

PASTA WITH LIGURIAN ARTICHOKE SAUCE

Italy • Serves 4 to 6

This recipe, based on one from Fred Plotkin's *Recipes from Paradise*, shows just how ingenious the Italians are in their use of vegetables. Just by cooking thinly sliced artichokes in olive oil with a little garlic and onion, you come up with a delicious accompaniment to pasta. The sauce also makes a great topping for bruschetta. Make it in the spring, when tender artichokes hit the market. But be sure to trim all of the outer leaves away; it's just the tender parts that you'll be using here.

Juice of 1 lemon

4 medium artichokes

2 tablespoons extra virgin olive oil

1 small onion, preferably a spring onion, minced

1 to 2 garlic cloves (to taste), minced

⅓ cup dry white wine

¼ cup water

Salt

1 tablespoon minced fresh flat-leaf parsley

¾ to 1 pound fettuccine or linguine

Freshly grated Parmesan

1. Fill a bowl with water and add the lemon juice. Cut away the stems and tops of the artichokes, and break off all of the tough outer leaves until you get to the tender, pale green ones. Quarter the artichokes, cut away the chokes, and slice very thin. Add them to the bowl of lemon water as you cut them, to prevent discoloration.

2. Heat the olive oil in a nonstick skillet or heavy pot over medium heat and add the onion. Cook, stirring, until translucent, 3 to 5 minutes, and add the garlic. Cook, stirring, until fragrant, about 1 minute. Drain the artichokes and add to the pan. Cook, stirring, until coated with oil. Add the wine and water, and bring to a boil. Reduce the heat, add salt to taste, cover, and simmer for 15 minutes, until the artichokes are tender. If the pan dries out, add more water. Add the parsley, taste, and adjust seasonings. Keep warm while you cook the pasta.

3. Bring a large pot of water to a boil and add a generous amount of salt. Cook the pasta until al dente. Add ¼ cup of the cooking water to the artichokes. Drain the pasta and toss with the artichoke sauce. Serve, passing Parmesan to sprinkle on top.

ADVANCE PREPARATION: You can make the sauce through Step 2 up to 2 days ahead. Keep in the refrigerator and reheat gently on top of the stove.

VARIATION

You can make more of a purée out of this sauce. Cool slightly, then pound in a mortar and pestle or pulse gently in a food processor, so that it retains some texture. Serve as a bruschetta topping.

PENNE WITH ASPARAGUS AND EGGS
Italy • Serves 4

This richly textured pasta recipe comes from the mountainous part of the mostly flat Puglia, which borders on Molise and Campania to the north. It is adapted from a recipe in Clifford Wright's *Mediterranean Vegetables*. It's important to toss the pasta and other ingredients immediately after cooking, because it's the heat from the pasta that cooks the eggs.

> Salt
>
> 1 pound asparagus, trimmed and cut into 1-inch lengths
>
> 2 tablespoons extra virgin olive oil
>
> 2 garlic cloves, lightly crushed
>
> 1 can (14 ounces) crushed tomatoes; or 1 pound fresh tomatoes, peeled, seeded, and finely chopped
>
> Freshly ground pepper
>
> 2 large eggs
>
> ¼ cup freshly grated Pecorino Romano
>
> ¾ pound penne

1. Bring a large pot of water to a boil and add a generous amount of salt. Add the asparagus and cook for 4 to 5 minutes, until tender. Using a spider or a slotted spoon, transfer to a bowl of ice water. Cool, then drain and set aside. Cover the pot to keep the water hot.

2. Heat the olive oil and garlic cloves together in a medium skillet over medium-high heat until the garlic begins to color. Remove the garlic, add the tomatoes, and cook, stirring frequently, until cooked down slightly and fragrant, about 10 minutes. Stir in the asparagus. Season to taste with salt and pepper. Keep warm.

3. Beat the eggs in a large pasta bowl and add a generous amount of coarsely ground pepper. Stir in half the pecorino.

4. Bring the water in the pot back to a rolling boil and add the penne. Cook until al dente, drain, and toss immediately with the eggs. Add the hot tomato sauce and toss again. Serve at once, passing the remaining pecorino in a bowl.

ADVANCE PREPARATION: You can make this through Step 2 a few hours before finishing the dish. Leave at room temperature and reheat gently before proceeding with Step 3.

PERCIATELLI WITH TOMATO SAUCE AND RICOTTA
Italy • Serves 4 to 6

Perciatelli is a long, tubular pasta, a bit like hollow spaghetti. It's popular in Sicily and Calabria. Use the freshest ricotta you can get for this. Peas (my variation) add an extra dimension.

> 2 tablespoons extra virgin olive oil
>
> 1 small or ½ medium onion, chopped (about ⅔ cup)
>
> 1 garlic clove, minced
>
> 3 cups peeled, finely diced tomatoes (fresh or canned)
>
> Pinch sugar
>
> Salt
>
> 2 tablespoons chopped fresh basil
>
> ½ pound fresh ricotta cheese (about 1 cup)
>
> 1 pound perciatelli
>
> 1 cup cooked fresh or thawed frozen peas
>
> Freshly grated Parmesan

1. Heat the olive oil over medium heat in a large, wide nonstick skillet and add the onion. Cook, stirring often, until tender and translucent, about 5 minutes. Add the garlic and cook, stirring, for about 1 minute, until fragrant. Stir in the tomatoes and sugar and cook over medium heat, stirring often, until they have cooked down and smell fragrant, about 10 minutes. Season to taste with salt and stir in the basil. Transfer ½ cup of the sauce to a bowl, add the ricotta, and stir to mix. Keep the remaining sauce warm.

2. Bring a large pot of water to a boil. Add a generous amount of salt and the pasta. Cook until al dente, or, if you prefer to do as the Sicilians do,

until tender. Drain and transfer to a wide pasta bowl or platter. Pour on the tomato sauce. Top with the ricotta mixture and the peas. Sprinkle on some Parmesan and bring to the table. Toss and serve, passing more Parmesan at the table.

ADVANCE PREPARATION: You can prepare the tomato sauce several hours before you cook the pasta. Reheat gently.

SPAGHETTI ALLA CHITARRA WITH ARUGULA PESTO AND TOMATO SAUCE

Italy • **Serves 4 to 6**

Spaghetti alla chitarra is the most famous pasta from Abruzzo, the region of southern Italy that sits above the ankle and below the calf of the boot, just north of Puglia. *Alla chitarra* means "guitar style," so named because the fresh egg noodles are made by pressing pasta strips through steel wires that are anchored across a box, like guitar strings. On this side of the ocean, I use linguine, and it's just fine. The pasta is tossed with a slightly picante tomato sauce and marvelous arugula pesto.

1½ cups Southern Tomato Sauce (page 79)

Salt

¾ to 1 pound spaghetti alla chitarra, linguine, or tagliatelle

½ to ¾ cup Arugula Pesto (to taste; page 75), at room temperature or slightly warm

⅓ cup grated ricotta salata

Bring a large pot of water to a boil while you heat the tomato sauce gently in a saucepan. Add a generous amount of salt to the pasta water and cook the pasta until al dente. Stir 1 to 2 tablespoons of the pasta water into the pesto. Drain the pasta, transfer to a warm pasta bowl, and toss with the tomato sauce. Spoon the pesto on top and sprinkle with the ricotta salata. Present the beautiful pasta, then toss again to distribute the pesto through the noodles. Serve at once.

ADVANCE PREPARATION: The tomato sauce will keep for a few days in the refrigerator. The arugula pesto will keep for a few weeks if covered with a film of olive oil.

SPAGHETTI WITH BLACK PEPPER AND PECORINO

Italy • **Serves 4 to 6**

It wasn't in Rome that I first encountered this classic Roman pasta, but in an Italian restaurant in Beverly Hills called Enoteca Drago. So utterly simple, yet so compelling. This is definitely one of those recipes to put in your "there is always dinner in the larder" folder. David Downie, whose wonderful book *Cooking the Roman Way* is one of my absolute favorite Mediterranean cookbooks, gives very sound advice in the introduction to his recipe for this dish (upon which mine is based): He says that the trick to making the dish work is "to dilute the cheese and pepper with 1 tablespoon of pasta water per serving, and to amalgamate the ingredients in the pot the pasta water was boiled in."

Salt

¾ to 1 pound spaghetti

2 tablespoons extra virgin olive oil

1 to 2 teaspoons freshly ground black pepper (to taste)

1½ cups freshly grated Pecorino Romano

1. Bring a large pot of water to a boil and add a tablespoon or two of salt. Cook the pasta until al dente. Ladle out ½ cup of the cooking water and reserve.

2. Drain the pasta and return at once to the pot along with the reserved cooking water and olive oil. Gradually add the pepper and half the cheese while you toss the pasta in the pot. Serve in warm bowls, passing the remaining cheese in a bowl.

VARIATION

Add 1 cup fresh or thawed frozen peas. If using fresh peas, cook along with the pasta. If using frozen, add to the pasta water a minute or so before draining the pasta.

FUSILLI WITH TOMATO SAUCE, CAULIFLOWER, AND OLIVES

Serves 4

The marriage of cauliflower and olives is a Mediterranean match made in heaven. You find it often, in Greek stews, Tunisian tagines, Italian pastas. You can use other pastas for this dish, such as penne rigata, spaghetti, or perciatelli.

½ medium head cauliflower

2 tablespoons extra virgin olive oil

Salt

2 to 4 garlic cloves (to taste), peeled

¼ to ½ teaspoon hot red pepper flakes (to taste)

12 kalamata olives, pitted and cut in half lengthwise

1 cup Basic Tomato Sauce (page 78)

¾ pound fusilli

2 ounces feta, crumbled

1. Place the cauliflower cut side down on your cutting board and slice ¼ inch thick. Heat the olive oil in a large nonstick skillet over medium heat. Add the cauliflower and cook, shaking the pan often or stirring, until it begins to sizzle and brown around the edges, about 5 minutes. Add salt to taste, the garlic, and red pepper flakes and continue to cook, stirring, for another 2 to 3 minutes, until the garlic is fragrant and the cauliflower crisp-tender. Taste to make sure the cauliflower is well seasoned. Stir in the olives and tomato sauce and turn the heat to low, or turn off the heat if not serving right away.

2. Bring a large pot of water to a rolling boil and add a tablespoon or two of salt and the pasta. Cook until al dente, drain, and toss with the cauliflower sauce. Sprinkle feta over the top and serve at once.

ADVANCE PREPARATION: The recipe can be made through Step 1 as far ahead of time as a day. Keep in the refrigerator overnight, or on the stove for a few hours.

STROZZAPRETI WITH WILD ARUGULA AND WILD ASPARAGUS

Croatia • **Serves 4 to 6**

This is inspired by an Istrian dish that I ate at a wonderful *agrituristico* restaurant called Alla Beccaccia, near Fažana. We tasted many wonderful pasta dishes there, all made with farm ingredients. One pasta, a dumpling-like noodle called *pljukanci,* was tossed with arugula, homemade prosciutto, and a creamy sauce, which I think was simply ricotta and butter. Another pasta called *fuzi* was tossed with asparagus, home-cured prosciutto, and homemade sausage. I've combined the vegetarian elements of both recipes here and used the southern Italian pasta called strozzapreti, which most resembles the *pljukanci.*

Salt

¾ pound wild asparagus or ½ pound regular asparagus, tough ends trimmed, cut into 1-inch lengths

¾ to 1 pound strozzapreti

½ cup fresh ricotta cheese

2 tablespoons extra virgin olive oil

1 bunch (about 2 ounces) wild arugula (available at farmers' markets)

⅓ cup freshly grated Parmesan

Freshly ground pepper

1. Bring a large pot of water to a boil and add a generous amount of salt. Add the asparagus, cook for 2 minutes, and transfer with a spider or slotted spoon to a bowl of cold water. Drain and set aside.

2. Bring the water back to a boil and add the pasta. Cook until al dente. Stir 2 tablespoons of the pasta cooking water into the ricotta. Drain the pasta and toss at once with the asparagus, ricotta, olive oil, arugula, Parmesan, and pepper to taste. Serve hot.

ADVANCE PREPARATION: Have everything prepped and ready to go hours ahead of time, then throw together this pasta at the last minute.

TRENETTE WITH PESTO, GREEN BEANS, AND POTATOES

Italy • **Serves 6**

This is the classic Ligurian pesto dish. Trenette are narrow, flat pasta strands, much like fettuccine or tagliatelle (either can be substituted) but narrower. The potatoes may be surprising to you if you aren't familiar with this dish, and you may look askance at the combination, especially if you eschew carbs. But the combination is classic, the slippery texture of the pasta contrasting nicely with the drier texture of the potatoes, which soak up oil and flavor. The green beans add beautiful color and crunch.

> ¾ pound creamer or red-skinned potatoes, scrubbed
>
> Salt
>
> 1 cup trimmed haricots verts or broken green beans
>
> 1 recipe Pesto Genovese (page 74)
>
> 1 pound trenette, fettuccine, or tagliatelle
>
> Freshly grated Parmesan

1. Place the potatoes in a saucepan and cover with salted water. Bring to a boil, reduce the heat, cover partially, and boil gently until tender, about 20 minutes. Drain and cut into halves if very small, quarters if medium-small.

2. Bring a large pot of water to a boil. Add 2 tablespoons salt and the green beans. Boil for 4 minutes, until tender. Transfer the beans with a spider or slotted spoon to a bowl of ice water. Let sit for a minute, then drain.

3. Place the pesto in a large, wide serving bowl. Bring the water back to a boil and cook the pasta until al dente. Stir 1 to 2 tablespoons of the pasta water into the pesto. Drain the pasta and transfer to the bowl along with the potatoes and green beans. Toss everything together and serve with Parmesan for sprinkling.

ADVANCE PREPARATION: The pesto can be made a week or two ahead and refrigerated.

WHOLE WHEAT SPAGHETTI WITH GREEN BEANS AND TOMATO SAUCE

Italy • **Serves 4 to 6**

I ate this at a restaurant in Ostuni, in Puglia, on a hot summer night. The spaghetti was a rustic whole wheat spaghetti, which I have since found in my local Italian market, where it's called *spaghetti integrale*. The dish is a breeze, relying as it does on the best of local ingredients.

> Salt
>
> A handful green beans, trimmed and broken in half if long
>
> 1⅓ to 1½ cups Basic Tomato Sauce (page 78) or any good commercial marinara sauce
>
> ¾ to 1 pound whole wheat spaghetti
>
> ½ cup grated ricotta salata or Parmesan

1. Bring a large pot of water to a boil, salt generously, and add the beans. Cook for 5 minutes, until tender. Transfer with a spider or slotted spoon to a bowl of ice water, let sit for a minute, and drain. Save the water for the pasta.

2. Heat the sauce in a wide frying pan or saucepan.

3. Bring the water back to a boil and cook the pasta until al dente. Drain and toss with the sauce and beans. Sprinkle with the cheese and serve.

ADVANCE PREPARATION: The beans can be cooked and chilled hours or even a day ahead. Just before draining the pasta, drop the green beans into the cooking water to reheat, and drain with the pasta. The tomato sauce will keep for 3 or 4 days in the refrigerator. Reheat on top of the stove.

LAGANARI WITH EGGPLANT, TOMATO SAUCE, AND OREGANO

Italy • **Serves 4 to 6**

Laganari are thick, flat handmade noodles typical of the cuisine of Puglia. This dish was served at an extraordinary seven-course dinner I had at Il Frantoio, an olive farm near Ostuni. As laganari aren't easy to find outside of Puglia, I recommend tagliatelle or fettuccine—or spaghetti. You could also use pappardelle. In the summer, you can find the small Italian white and purple eggplants at some farmers' markets. If you grow your own oregano, use the pretty purple flowers as a garnish.

    1 pound small white and purple eggplants

    Salt

    3 tablespoons extra virgin olive oil

    1½ cups Southern Tomato Sauce
        (page 79)

    ¾ to 1 pound laganari, tagliatelle, or fettuccine

    1 to 2 tablespoons fresh oregano (to taste),
        plus oregano flowers or sprigs for garnish

    ½ cup freshly grated Pecorino Romano, ricotta
        salata, Parmesan, or a combination

1. If you are working with small eggplants, not more than 3 inches long, trim the ends and cut them into 1-inch-thick wedges. If the eggplants are a little bigger than this, cut them crosswise first, then into wedges. Sprinkle with salt and allow to sit for 30 minutes. Pat dry.

2. Heat a large, heavy nonstick or well-seasoned skillet over medium-high heat. Add the olive oil, and when it begins to ripple, add the eggplant. Cook, stirring often, until the edges are nicely browned and the eggplant thoroughly softened, about 10 minutes. Add the tomato sauce, stir, and heat through. Remove from the heat and keep warm.

3. Bring a large pot of water to a boil, add a generous tablespoon of salt, and cook the pasta until al dente. Drain and toss with the tomato sauce–eggplant mixture and the oregano leaves. Serve, garnishing each serving with an oregano flower or sprig. Pass the cheese for sprinkling on top.

ADVANCE PREPARATION: You can make the sauce up to 3 days ahead and reheat.

VARIATION

The sauce and eggplant combination is so good, you could serve it alone without the pasta as a *meze* or antipasto.

PASTA WITH BEANS (Pasta e Fagiole)

Italy • **Serves 4 generously**

This Italian classic is often listed as a soup on restaurant menus. I like to make it as a thick stew. I tweak my recipe all the time, as this is a dish with many interpretations; but it always boils down to a gutsy, hearty, tomatoey mixture of pasta and beans.

    1 tablespoon extra virgin olive oil

    1 medium or large onion, chopped

    1 generous teaspoon chopped fresh rosemary
        (or ½ teaspoon crumbled dried)

    2 to 4 large garlic cloves (to taste), minced
        or put through a press

    1 can (28 ounces) tomatoes, with juice,
        chopped

    Salt and freshly ground pepper

    ½ pound dried white or borlotti beans,
        picked over, rinsed, soaked in 4 cups water
        for 6 hours or overnight, and drained

    1 heaped tablespoon tomato paste

    1 small dried red pepper or ¼ to ½ teaspoon
        hot red pepper flakes

    A bouquet garni made with a bay leaf,
        1 Parmesan rind, and a few sprigs each
        fresh thyme and parsley

    6 cups water

    ½ pound elbow macaroni, penne, or fusilli

    2 to 3 tablespoons chopped fresh flat-leaf
        parsley (to taste)

    1 to 2 tablespoons chopped fresh basil
        (to taste; optional)

    ½ cup freshly grated Parmesan

1. Heat the oil in a large, heavy casserole or Dutch oven over medium heat and add the onion. Cook, stirring, until just tender, about 5 minutes. Add the rosemary and garlic, and stir together for another minute, until the garlic is fragrant. Stir in the tomatoes, add some salt and pepper, and cook, partially covered, for 15 minutes, stirring often, until the tomatoes have cooked down and the mixture is very fragrant.

2. Add the beans, tomato paste, hot pepper, bouquet garni, and water. Bring to a boil, reduce the heat, cover, and simmer for 1 hour. Add salt to taste (1 to 2 teaspoons), cover, and simmer another 30 minutes to 1 hour, until the beans are tender. Remove the bouquet garni.

3. Ten to 15 minutes before serving, stir the pasta into the simmering beans. When it is cooked al dente, taste and adjust seasonings. Stir in the parsley and basil, and serve, passing the Parmesan in a bowl.

ADVANCE PREPARATION: You can make the dish through Step 2 a day or two ahead. Refrigerate, then bring back to a simmer, stirring often, before continuing. Add water if necessary. The finished dish will keep for about 4 days in the refrigerator, but the pasta will continue to soften and swell, reducing the amount of liquid in the stew.

LEFTOVERS: Use leftovers to make **MACARONI WITH BEANS AND CHEESE:** Heat the oven to 350°F. Oil a gratin or baking dish, the size of which is determined by how much *pasta e fagiole* you have left over. Toss leftovers with ¼ to ½ cup freshly grated Parmesan cheese, or a mixture of Parmesan and Gruyère, and spoon into the dish. Sprinkle 2 tablespoons bread crumbs over the top, and drizzle on a tablespoon of olive oil. Bake for 25 to 35 minutes, until the top is browned and the mixture is sizzling.

PASTA WITH TOMATOES, BEANS, AND FETA

Greece • **Serves 4 to 6**

This recipe is more Greek than Italian. I make it at least once a week during tomato season, when I'm loath to cook my sweet homegrown tomatoes. Use rigatoni or penne, and either favas, green beans, or Italian flat beans.

> Salt
>
> 3 pounds fresh fava beans, shelled and skinned (page 113); or ¾ pound green beans or Italian flat beans, trimmed and cut into 2-inch lengths
>
> 1¼ pounds ripe tomatoes, peeled and chopped
>
> 2 garlic cloves, minced
>
> 2 to 3 tablespoons extra virgin olive oil (to taste)
>
> ½ to 1 teaspoon balsamic vinegar (optional)
>
> 2 tablespoons chopped fresh mint or basil
>
> Freshly ground pepper
>
> 1 pound rigatoni or penne
>
> ½ cup crumbled feta

1. Bring a large pot of water to a rolling boil. Add a generous amount of salt and the beans. Boil favas for 1 minute, then remove from the pot with a spider or slotted spoon and shock in a bowl of ice water. Boil green beans for 5 minutes (6 to 7 minutes for flat green beans), until just tender, and transfer with a spider to a bowl of ice water. Cool for a few minutes, then drain. Save the water for the pasta.

2. In a large pasta bowl, toss together the tomatoes, garlic, olive oil, vinegar, mint, and salt and pepper to taste. Add the beans, toss together, and allow to sit at room temperature for 30 minutes to an hour. Taste and adjust seasonings.

3. Bring the salted water back to a boil and add the pasta. Cook until al dente, drain, and toss with the tomato mixture. Add the feta, toss again, and serve at once.

ADVANCE PREPARATION: You can cook the favas or green beans a day ahead and keep in the refrigerator. The tomato mixture can be made several hours before you cook the pasta.

BAKED EGGPLANT STUFFED WITH PASTA

Italy • Serves 4

This was my favorite dish at Osteria Piazzetta Cattedrale, a very nice restaurant in Ostuni that was recommended by the staff at Il Frantoio, the olive farm in Puglia where I spent a few idyllic days in August 2005. The pasta used in Puglia is strozzapreti or gemelli, a toothsome pasta that you can find in Italian markets.

> 4 small or 2 large eggplants
>
> Salt
>
> Extra virgin olive oil
>
> Freshly ground pepper
>
> 6 ounces strozzapreti
>
> 1½ cups Southern Tomato Sauce (page 79)
>
> ½ cup freshly grated Parmesan, or a combination of Parmesan and Pecorino Romano, or ricotta salata

1. Cut the eggplants lengthwise in half. Using a spoon, scoop out a small hollow in each half, about 1 inch in from the edges. Use the flesh for another purpose, such as a dip or mixed vegetable stew. Salt the eggplant and let sit for 30 minutes. Pat dry.

2. Heat the oven to 425°F. Brush the eggplants generously with olive oil and place cut side down in an oiled baking dish. Bake for 30 to 40 minutes, until tender all the way through when pierced with a knife (the eggplants should hold their shape, however). Remove from the oven and flip the eggplants over. Season with salt and pepper. Reduce the heat to 350°F.

3. While the eggplant is cooking, cook the pasta in a large pot of boiling salted water. It should be slightly more al dente than normal—cooked about 2 minutes less than instructed on the package. Drain and toss with 1 cup of the tomato sauce. Place the pasta mixture in the eggplant hollows and top with the remaining tomato sauce and the cheese. Brush the dull side of a sheet of aluminum foil with olive oil and cover the dish. Return to the oven and bake for 30 to 40 minutes, until the egg-

plant is thoroughly tender and the cheese melted and beginning to color. Serve hot.

ADVANCE PREPARATION: The tomato sauce can be made 4 to 5 days ahead. The dish can be assembled hours before baking and held in the refrigerator. Make sure not to overcook the pasta.

MACARONI WITH TOMATO SAUCE AND GOAT CHEESE

Serves 4 to 6

Although I think of this grown-up style macaroni as a summer dish, to make when tomatoes are at their peak, the truth is, it's equally delicious when you use canned tomatoes for the sauce. The goat cheese gives the dish the creaminess that a béchamel gives a standard macaroni & cheese.

> Salt
>
> ½ pound penne or elbow macaroni
>
> 2 tablespoons extra virgin olive oil
>
> 2 to 3 large garlic cloves (to taste), minced or put through a press
>
> 2 pounds fresh tomatoes, quartered; or 3 cans (14 ounces each) tomatoes, drained of all but about ½ cup of the juice
>
> ⅛ teaspoon sugar
>
> 4 ounces soft, mild goat cheese
>
> ½ cup freshly grated Parmesan
>
> 2 tablespoons slivered fresh basil
>
> Freshly ground pepper
>
> ½ cup bread crumbs

1. Heat the oven to 350°F. Oil a 2-quart baking dish or gratin with olive oil.

2. Bring a large pot of water to a boil, add 1 tablespoon salt and the pasta, and cook until just al dente. Do not overcook. Drain and transfer to a large bowl.

3. Meanwhile, heat 1 tablespoon of the oil over medium heat in a large, heavy nonstick skillet and add the garlic. When the garlic just begins to color, after about 30 seconds, add the tomatoes, sugar, and salt (about ½ teaspoon). Cook, stirring often, for 20 to 25 minutes, until the tomatoes are cooked down and fragrant. Remove from the heat and pass through the medium blade of a food mill. Stir in the goat cheese and Parmesan and combine well. Add the fresh basil and pepper (a few grinds of the mill). Taste and adjust salt. Toss with the pasta, then scrape into the baking dish.

4. Toss the bread crumbs with the remaining tablespoon olive oil and sprinkle over the top of the macaroni. Bake until the bread crumbs are lightly browned, about 30 minutes. Let stand for 5 to 10 minutes before serving.

ADVANCE PREPARATION: You can make the tomato sauce (Step 3) up to 3 days ahead and keep it in the refrigerator, or freeze it for several months. Reheat and stir in the cheese just before tossing with the pasta. The assembled macaroni will keep for several hours outside of the refrigerator, and can be covered and refrigerated for up to 3 days before baking.

MUSHROOM LASAGNA

Serves 6

My lasagna-making life changed forever when I discovered no-boil lasagna noodles. Before, it was an event, because I always made the pasta. Even when you don't make the pasta, having to cook the noodles can mean the difference between not making lasagna regularly and making it. This richly flavored lasagna combines a béchamel with my standard mushroom ragout and Parmesan cheese. It's a true crowd-pleaser.

FOR THE MUSHROOMS

- 1 ounce (about 1 cup) dried porcini mushrooms
- 2 cups boiling water
- 2 tablespoons extra virgin olive oil
- 1 medium onion, chopped
- 4 garlic cloves, minced or put through a press
- ¾ pound white or cremini mushrooms, trimmed and sliced ¼ inch thick
- ¾ pound oyster mushrooms, trimmed and torn into pieces

Salt

- ½ cup fruity red wine, such as a Côtes du Rhône
- 2 teaspoons chopped fresh rosemary (or 1 teaspoon crumbled dried)
- 2 teaspoons chopped fresh sage or ¼ cup chopped fresh flat-leaf parsley

Freshly ground pepper

FOR THE BÉCHAMEL

- 3 tablespoons unsalted butter
- 3 tablespoons sifted unbleached all-purpose flour
- 3 cups milk (can use low-fat milk)
- Salt and freshly ground pepper
- Freshly grated nutmeg

FOR THE LASAGNA

- ½ pound no-bake lasagna noodles
- 1 cup freshly grated Parmesan
- Unsalted butter (optional)

1. *Make the mushrooms:* Place the dried mushrooms in a Pyrex measuring cup and pour on the boiling water. Let soak for 30 minutes. Place a strainer over a bowl, line it with cheesecloth or paper towels, and drain the mushrooms. Squeeze the mushrooms over the strainer to extract all the flavorful juices. Then rinse the mushrooms, away from the bowl with the soaking liquid, until they are free of sand. Squeeze dry and, if very large, chop coarsely. Set aside. Measure out 1½ cups of the soaking liquid and set aside.

2. Heat the olive oil in a large, heavy nonstick skillet over medium heat and add the onion. Cook, stirring often, until tender, about 5 minutes. Add half the garlic, stir together for about 30 seconds, then add the white and oyster mushrooms and about 1 teaspoon salt. Cook, stirring often, until the mushrooms begin to soften and sweat, about 5 minutes. Add the reconstituted dried mushrooms and the wine and turn the heat to high. Cook, stirring, until the liquid boils down and glazes the mushrooms, 5 to 10 minutes. Add the remaining

garlic, the rosemary, and sage and stir in the mush-room soaking liquid. Bring to a simmer, add salt, and cook over medium-high heat, stirring often, until the mushrooms are thoroughly tender and fragrant and the surrounding broth has reduced by a little more than half, 10 to 15 minutes. Remove from the heat, stir in some freshly ground pepper, taste, and adjust salt.

3. *Make the béchamel:* Melt the butter in a heavy saucepan over medium-low heat. Add the flour and cook, stirring, for a couple of minutes, until smooth and bubbling. Whisk in the milk and bring to a simmer. Simmer, stirring, for 15 to 20 minutes, until the sauce has thickened and lost its raw flour taste. Season with salt, pepper, and a pinch of nut-meg. The béchamel isn't meant to be very thick.

4. *Assemble the lasagna:* Heat the oven to 350°F. Oil or butter a 2-quart rectangular baking dish. Reserve about 6 tablespoons each béchamel and Parmesan for the top layer of the lasagna. Spread a thin layer of béchamel over the bottom of the bak-ing dish. Arrange a layer of lasagna noodles over the béchamel and spread a thin layer of béchamel over the noodles. Top with a thin layer of mush-rooms and a sprinkling of Parmesan. Repeat the layers until all but one layer of pasta and the béchamel and cheese that you set aside is used up. Add a last layer of pasta, cover the top with the béchamel that you set aside, and finally, the cheese. Dot with butter if you wish. Cover the pasta with foil (if you have not buttered the top of the pasta, lightly oil or butter the dull side of the foil).

5. Bake for 30 minutes. Remove the foil and bake another 10 to 15 minutes, until the top begins to brown. Serve hot or warm.

ADVANCE PREPARATION: The mushroom filling can be made up to 4 days before assembling and baking the lasa-gna. The béchamel can be made a day ahead. Whisk well and reheat gently before assembling the lasagna. The assem-bled lasagna can be tightly covered and refrigerated for a day before baking.

LASAGNA WITH GREENS AND TOMATO SAUCE
Italy • Serves 6 to 8

Not to be confused with "green lasagna" (*lasagna verde*), in this recipe it's the filling, not the noo-dles, that is green. Here in California, I use the 1-pound bags of already washed and stemmed sturdy greens that I buy at my local Trader Joe's, and I often use Pomì marinara, the one brand that is as good as homemade. With no-boil lasagna noodles, this means that the dish is fairly quick to make. This lasagna is delicious in both its north-ern Italian and southern Italian versions, the northern Italian being a pure white and green, with béchamel sauce standing in for the tomato sauce of the southern rendition.

> Salt
>
> 1 pound stemmed and cleaned greens, such as kale, turnip greens, or Swiss chard
>
> 2 tablespoons extra virgin olive oil
>
> 2 large garlic cloves, minced
>
> Freshly ground pepper
>
> 1 pound fresh ricotta cheese
>
> 1¼ cups freshly grated Parmesan, tightly packed
>
> Freshly grated nutmeg
>
> 2½ cups Béchamel (page 77) or Marinara Sauce (page 78 or commercial)
>
> ½ pound no-boil lasagna noodles
>
> 1 tablespoon unsalted butter

1. Bring a large pot of water to a boil, add a gener-ous tablespoon of salt, and the greens. Blanch for 2 to 3 minutes, until tender. Transfer to a bowl of ice water, cool for a minute, then drain and squeeze dry. You should have a little over 2 cups cooked greens.

2. Heat the olive oil in a large, heavy skillet over medium-high heat and add the garlic. Cook, stir-ring, until fragrant, about 1 minute, and stir in the greens. Cook, stirring, for 2 to 3 minutes, until fragrant, tender, coated with oil, and infused with garlic. Season to taste with salt and pepper.

3. Chop the greens mixture very fine with a chef's knife, or by pulsing in a food processor fitted with the steel blade. Transfer to a bowl and stir in the ricotta and ½ cup of the Parmesan. Season to taste with salt, pepper, and a little bit of nutmeg. Set aside.

4. Heat the oven to 350°F. Butter or oil a 2-quart lasagna dish or baking dish. Spoon a thin layer of béchamel or tomato sauce over the bottom of the dish. Top with a layer of noodles. Cover the noodles with a thin layer of béchamel or tomato sauce, spread a layer of the filling over the sauce, and sprinkle on some Parmesan. Making sure you have enough sauce and Parmesan set aside to complete the lasagna, repeat the layers until the filling is used up (½ pound of noodles usually gives me 4 layers). End with a layer of pasta covered with a layer of sauce and a sprinkling of Parmesan. Dot with the butter. Cover tightly with foil.

5. Bake for 30 minutes, until the pasta has softened and the sauce is bubbling. Remove the foil and bake another 5 to 10 minutes, until the top begins to brown. Remove from the oven, allow to sit for 5 minutes, then serve.

ADVANCE PREPARATION: The lasagna can be assembled up to a day ahead and held in the refrigerator. However, cover with plastic rather than foil, to avoid a reaction with the greens.

VARIATION

QUICKER FREE-FORM LASAGNA WITH GREENS: Once, when I had 1 hour total to prepare a dinner for friends and had a gift of greens on hand, I simply prepared the greens as directed above, blanching them and cooking them with garlic, but dispensed with the béchamel. I cooked the lasagna noodles (they only took 3 or 4 minutes), and tossed together the noodles, the ricotta mixed with a little of the pasta cooking water to melt and thin it out, greens, and grated cheeses. The greens remain brighter than in the assembled and baked lasagna, and for this reason you might like this free-form variation even better.

GNOCCHI
Italy • Serves 6

Gnocchi are little potato dumplings, popular throughout Italy and also in Nice. You probably won't make these every day, as they require some time, but they're actually quite easy. If you do make them, you'll be spoiled. I like to serve gnocchi with Basic Tomato Sauce (page 78) or Southern Tomato Sauce (page 79) and Parmesan.

> 2 pounds starchy potatoes, such as russet, scrubbed
>
> Salt
>
> 1⅓ cups unbleached all-purpose flour (more as needed)
>
> 1 extra-large egg yolk
>
> ¼ cup extra virgin olive oil

1. Cover the potatoes with water in a large saucepan, add a little salt, and bring to a boil. Reduce the heat to medium and boil gently until tender, about 40 minutes. Drain and return to the pot. Cover and let steam in the dry pot off heat for 5 to 10 minutes.

2. While the potatoes are still warm, peel and pass them through a potato ricer or the medium blade of a food mill into a large bowl.

3. Make a well in the center of your mashed potatoes and sprinkle the flour all over evenly. Place the egg yolk and 1 teaspoon salt in the middle of the well and beat together with a fork. Now, using the fork, begin to sweep flour and potatoes into the center of the well and incorporate them. When the yolk and all of the flour has been incorporated into the potatoes, shape the dough into a ball and gently knead for 4 or 5 minutes, until smooth. If necessary, add flour to your hands and your work surface. The dough shouldn't be sticky, but you must be careful that you don't add too much flour or the gnocchi will be heavy.

4. Divide the gnocchi dough into 6 pieces. Roll out each piece into a rope about ¾ inch in diameter, and cut the rope into 1-inch pieces. Keeping your hands floured, either gently press each piece against the inside curve of a fork so that you have a thumb print on one side and ridges on the other, or roll the dumplings down the back of the fork to make a ridged cylinder. Place on a parchment-lined baking sheet and cover with a towel as you continue to shape the gnocchi.

5. Bring a large pot of water to a boil and add 1 tablespoon salt. Set up a bowl of ice water next to your cooking area. In batches, drop the gnocchi into the boiling water and cook until they float to the surface, 1 to 3 minutes. With a skimmer or a slotted spoon, transfer immediately to the ice water. Continue to cook the gnocchi, replenishing ice in the water bath if necessary. When all of the gnocchi have been cooked and cooled, drain and toss in a bowl with the olive oil.

6. Reheat gently in a pan or in a medium oven, or directly in the sauce with which you are serving.

Note: *If serving the gnocchi with tomato sauce, heat the tomato sauce in a large skillet. Omit the water bath, and transfer the gnocchi directly from the cooking water to the tomato sauce. Toss together and serve, with freshly grated Parmesan.*

ADVANCE PREPARATION: You can cook and cool the gnocchi, drain, toss them with the oil, and keep in the refrigerator, covered, for up to 2 days. Cooked gnocchi can also be frozen. Toss with the oil first.

GNOCCHI WITH EGGPLANT AND PEPPERS

Italy • Serves 4 to 6

There's an unprepossessing hotel in Mattinata, on the Gargano Promontory of Puglia, that happens to have a first-rate restaurant called La Rucola. We were only there for a night, and I would have loved to stay longer, just to try everything on the menu. One thing we did eat was a gnocchi dish, the gnocchi tossed with seared eggplant and peppers spiced with hot red pepper and enriched with squares of provolone cheese. Months later, my

mouth is happy when I think of it. I must confess that I usually buy gnocchi ready-made, but the gnocchi you make yourself are always lighter.

> 1½ pounds eggplant, cut into ¾-inch dice
>
> Salt
>
> 4 tablespoons extra virgin olive oil
>
> ¾ pound red bell peppers, cut into ½-inch squares
>
> 2 garlic cloves, minced
>
> ¼ teaspoon hot red pepper flakes
>
> 1 teaspoon fresh thyme leaves
>
> Freshly ground pepper
>
> 1 recipe Gnocchi (prepared through Step 4, page 223) or 1 pound commercial gnocchi
>
> 2 ounces provolone or mozzarella, cut into ½-inch squares; or ½ cup grated ricotta salata

1. Sprinkle the eggplant with salt and let sit for 30 minutes. Rinse and pat dry.

2. Heat a large, heavy nonstick frying pan over medium-high heat until hot. Add 2 tablespoons of the olive oil, and when it is hot and swirls easily in the pan, add the eggplant. Cook, tossing or stirring, until lightly browned and just about cooked through, about 8 minutes. Season with salt.

3. Add another 1 tablespoon oil and the bell peppers. Cook, stirring or tossing often, until the peppers are just about tender, about 5 minutes. Stir in the garlic, red pepper flakes, and thyme, and continue to cook, stirring, until the garlic is fragrant, about 1 minute. Add salt and pepper to taste, reduce the heat to medium-low, and cover. Continue to cook for another 5 minutes, until the vegetables have given off some liquid and the liquid is bubbling.

4. Bring a large pot of water to a boil and add 1 tablespoon salt. Set up a bowl of ice water next to your cooking area. In batches, drop the gnocchi into the boiling water and cook until they float to the surface, 1 to 3 minutes. With a skimmer or a slotted spoon, transfer immediately to the ice water.

Continue to cook the gnocchi, replenishing ice in the water bath if necessary. When all of the gnocchi have been cooked and cooled, drain and toss in the pan with the eggplant and peppers, adding the remaining 1 tablespoon olive oil and the cheese. Heat through and serve.

ADVANCE PREPARATION: You can make this dish several hours or even a day in advance. Reheat gently on top of the stove.

VARIATION

You can also serve the vegetable mixture with dried pasta or polenta, or as is, as a side dish or an appetizer.

BAKED SEMOLINA GNOCCHI WITH BUTTER AND PARMESAN

Italy • **Serves 6**

I loved to cook long before I know that I would *become* a cook, just as I loved Mediterranean food long before I discovered the Mediterranean. Somewhere in the back of my mind, I knew I had once written a recipe for this, which I had tested and liked so much that it stayed in my head for decades. I thought it might be in an old manuscript I had once put together, before my life took me to France. Sure enough, I found it there, and it was almost exactly the recipe I'm giving you here.

These gnocchi are flat disks made from a polenta-like mixture of semolina, milk, cheese, butter, and egg yolks. It's a Roman dish, rich by Mediterranean standards, that's at once comforting and luscious.

> 4 cups milk (whole milk is traditional, but I see no reason why you shouldn't use 2% or even 1% if you wish)
>
> 1 teaspoon salt
>
> 1¼ cups semolina (Cream of Wheat)
>
> 6 tablespoons unsalted butter

> 2 egg yolks
>
> 1¾ cups freshly grated Parmesan

1. In a large, heavy saucepan over medium heat, bring the milk to just under a boil. Lower the heat, add the salt, and carefully add the semolina in a thin, slow stream, stirring constantly with a wooden spoon. Stir over low heat with a wooden spoon, as you would polenta, for 10 minutes.

2. Remove the pan from the heat and stir in 4 tablespoons of the butter, the yolks, and 1 cup of the cheese. Stir rapidly, so that the egg doesn't coagulate, until the ingredients are well blended.

3. Moisten a large marble slab (or a plastic or Formica surface) with cold water. Scrape the semolina out of the pan and onto the work surface, and with an offset spatula or the side of a large knife, spread in an even layer about ½ inch thick. Dip the spatula or knife into cold water occasionally to facilitate the process. Let the semolina cool completely, about 30 minutes.

4. Heat the oven to 400°F. Butter a 2-quart baking dish generously. Moisten a 2-inch round cookie cutter or the rim of a glass, and cut the semolina into circles. Make a layer of gnocchi in the dish, with the edges slightly overlapping. Sprinkle with some of the remaining Parmesan and dot with some of the remaining butter. Make a second layer, dotting with butter and sprinkling with Parmesan, and repeat until all of the gnocchi are used up. Make sure to overlap the disks slightly. Use the excess bits of gnocchi to fill in spaces.

5. Bake for 15 to 20 minutes, until the top begins to brown. To finish browning the top, place under the broiler for a minute. Allow to settle for a few minutes, until the butter stops sizzling, then serve with any remaining cheese on the side.

ADVANCE PREPARATION: You can make this recipe through Step 4 a day ahead of time.

Savory Pies and Gratins

Walk into any *traiteur,* or food shop, in Nice and you'll find an impressive display of *tourtes aux legumes,* vegetable tortes. In spring and summer, they could be filled with squash and tomatoes, ratatouille, eggplant and tomatoes, or greens. As the weather cools, winter squash will replace summer squash, and greens like Swiss chard will predominate. The pies may be double-crusted, bound with rice and a small amount of egg and cheese; or they could be single-crusted, quiche-like tarts whose vegetable fillings are bound with custard.

The variety of savory pies in Greece is truly astounding. All over the country, pies are made with spinach or greens—often the wild greens that grow in the countryside—and with cheese. Then, from region to region and from village to village, there are specialties. Greeks make pumpkin *pitas* (pita is the Greek word for "pie") and leek *pitas,* fennel *pitas* and zucchini pies, onion pies and olive pies, and all manner of cheese pies. In Epirus, the region of Greece that is most widely recognized for its pies, they make, among others, a lentil pie and a milk and pasta pie.

Greek *pitas* are made with homemade phyllo, which is rolled thin and layered like commercial phyllo. The number of layers varies from region to region, though in these recipes I've been pretty consistent. Sometimes the dough is rolled into long ropes and coiled into large, round pans. Other pies are shaped into individual coils. Homemade Greek phyllo is not as thin and paper-like as commercial phyllo or, for that matter, the Bosnian strudel dough that is used for savory pies in that country.

Bosnian pies, also called *pitta* (but with two Ts instead of one), are another revelation. The delicate homemade strudel dough that Bosnian women learn to make as young girls is pulled like Austrian strudel dough, a legacy of the Austro-Hungarian Empire that still has culinary traces in the Balkans.

The pies you find throughout the Mediterranean are filled with variations on the same vegetable themes. What distinguishes one country's pies from another's are the type of crusts used, the cheeses, and the seasonings. The Greeks use abundant herbs, notably dill, parsley, and mint. Their winter squash and leek pie, redolent with mint and leeks and baked in a crisp phyllo crust, would never be confused with Provençal pumpkin torte, earthy with sage and bound with rice. The best known Greek pie with spinach filling, spanakopita is packed with feta and seasoned with parsley and dill, whereas an Italian or Provençal greens torte, baked in a yeasted olive oil crust, will include Gruyère or Parmesan and local herbs like thyme and rosemary.

I've included vegetable gratins with pies because most gratins could as easily be baked inside a crust as not. Gratins get their name from the French word *gratter*, "to scratch" or "to scrape." The word originally referred to the crusty bits that stick to the sides and bottom of a baked dish, which are so delicious to scrape away and eat. Now the word refers to a baked dish that browns on the top and sides as it cooks in the oven, what we might call a casserole. The French call the oval baking dishes used for such dishes *gratins* as well. If cheese or a béchamel is spread over a baked food (or a soup like onion soup) and then browned in the oven, it is a *gratinée*.

But the French don't have the monopoly on gratins. Eggplant Parmesan is a gratin, as is Greek moussaka. Lasagna and the other baked pasta dishes in the Pasta chapter are gratins. When topped with a sauce and cheese and browned in the oven, polenta could also be called a gratin, as could crusty baked Balkan rice pilafs.

Gratins and tarts are great keepers. They both make terrific vegetarian main dishes, and gratins especially can be easily and quickly assembled. They're great cold, and leftovers are terrific in lunch boxes, or cut into small diamond shapes and served as hors d'oeuvres. If there are kids in your family who are reluctant to eat vegetables, the recipes in this chapter might provide you with a subversive (and delicious) way to slip them into their diets.

YEASTED OLIVE OIL PASTRY

Makes enough for one 10- or 11-inch double-crusted torte, one galette, or two 10-inch tarts

Yeasted crusts are delicate and tasty, and much easier to manipulate than short crusts, as they don't crack and tear. Roll this thin so it doesn't become too bready.

> 2 teaspoons active dry yeast
>
> ½ cup lukewarm water
>
> ½ teaspoon sugar
>
> 1 large egg, at room temperature, beaten
>
> ¼ cup extra virgin olive oil
>
> 2 cups unbleached all-purpose flour (more as needed)
>
> ¾ teaspoon salt

1. Dissolve the yeast in the water, add the sugar, and allow to sit until creamy, about 5 minutes. Beat in the egg and olive oil. Combine the flour and salt, and stir into the yeast mixture. You can use a bowl and wooden spoon for this, or a mixer with the paddle. Work the dough until it comes together in a coherent mass, adding flour as necessary. Turn out onto a lightly floured surface and knead for a few minutes, adding flour as necessary, until the dough is smooth; do not overwork. Shape into a ball. Place in a lightly oiled bowl, cover tightly with plastic wrap, and allow the dough to rise in a draft-free spot until doubled, about 1 hour.

2. Turn the dough out onto a lightly floured surface, gently knead a couple of times, and cut into 2 equal pieces (or as directed in the recipe). Shape each piece into a ball. Cover the dough loosely with plastic wrap and let rest for 5 minutes. Then roll out into thin rounds, as directed in the recipe, and use to line lightly oiled pans. If not using right away, freeze the dough to prevent it from rising and becoming too bready. The dough can be transferred directly from the freezer to the oven.

ADVANCE PREPARATION: You can make the dough a day ahead and refrigerate. Once rolled out, the dough will keep for a month in the freezer, well wrapped.

VARIATION

Substitute ½ cup whole wheat flour for ½ cup of the all-purpose flour.

GREEK PIE CRUST

Greece • Makes enough for one 10-inch double-crusted pie

This is the crust I learned from Diane Kochilas, at her wonderful Greek cooking school in Ikaria, an island in the northeast Aegean. It works equally well with all-purpose flour as it does with half all-purpose and half whole wheat or whole wheat pastry flour. The whole wheat version has a nuttier flavor.

> 2¼ cups unbleached all-purpose flour; or 1¼ cups all-purpose and 1 cup whole wheat or whole wheat pastry flour; plus all-purpose flour as necessary for rolling out the dough
>
> ¾ teaspoon salt
>
> ¼ cup extra virgin olive oil
>
> 1 tablespoon red wine vinegar, lemon juice, or ouzo
>
> ¾ cup water

1. If making the dough by hand: In a bowl, mix together the flour and salt. Make a well in the center and add the olive oil, vinegar, and water, and mix with a fork just until the dough comes together.

If using a food processor fitted with the steel blade or an electric mixer fitted with the paddle attachment: Mix together the flour and salt. With the machine running, add the olive oil, then the vinegar and water. The dough should come together in a ball. Do not overwork.

2. Turn the dough out onto a lightly floured surface and knead just until smooth, no longer than a minute. If you have used a food processor or mixer, this will entail just a quick shaping of the dough into a ball. Divide the dough in half. Press each half into a circle about 4 inches in diameter. Dust with flour if the dough is sticky. Wrap tightly in plastic and place in a plastic bag. Let rest for 1 hour at room temperature, or up to 3 days in the refrigerator.

3. Roll out each piece of dough on a lightly floured surface to a thin 12-inch round, dusting both sides of the dough with all-purpose flour as necessary to prevent it from sticking to the surface or to your rolling pin. Spray or brush a tart or pie pan with olive or vegetable oil. Line the pan with one round of the dough, fill with the filling of your choice, then top with the second sheet of dough. Pinch the edges together and make a few slits in the top. Bake as directed in the recipe.

ADVANCE PREPARATION: The dough will keep for 3 days in the refrigerator and can be frozen for several months. Roll it out before you freeze it.

DEEP-DISH EGGPLANT TORTA
Serves 8

This is really a molded eggplant Parmesan in a crust. It slices beautifully and is great for a vegetarian showcase main dish. It's time-consuming, but you can make all or part of it well before you wish to serve it. It looks beautiful on a buffet.

> Salt
>
> 3 to 3½ pounds eggplants (3 large), cut into ⅓-inch-thick slices
>
> Olive oil
>
> 2 to 3 large garlic cloves (to taste), minced or put through a press
>
> 3 pounds tomatoes, quartered; or 2 cans (28 ounces each) tomatoes, drained of all but about ½ cup of the juice
>
> ⅛ teaspoon sugar
>
> 1 tablespoon tomato paste
>
> 2 to 3 tablespoons slivered fresh basil leaves (to taste)

> Freshly ground pepper
>
> 1 recipe Yeasted Olive Oil Pastry (page 229)
>
> 4 large eggs, beaten
>
> 6 ounces mozzarella, sliced thin if fresh, otherwise grated
>
> ½ cup fresh bread crumbs
>
> 1 heaped cup freshly grated Parmesan

1. Salt the eggplant slices and let stand for 30 minutes. Heat the oven to 450°F.

2. Heat 1 tablespoon olive oil in a large, heavy non-stick skillet over medium heat and add the garlic. When it just begins to color, after about 30 seconds, add the tomatoes, sugar, tomato paste, and salt to taste. Cook, stirring often, for 20 to 25 minutes, until the tomatoes are cooked down and fragrant. Pass through a food mill fitted with the medium blade. Stir in the basil and add pepper, a few grinds of the mill. Taste and adjust seasonings.

3. Rinse the eggplant slices and blot dry. Generously oil baking sheets with olive oil. Place the eggplant rounds on the baking sheets and brush the tops with olive oil. Bake until lightly browned and tender, 10 to 15 minutes. Turn the oven down to 375°F.

4. Oil a 10-inch springform pan or cake pan. Roll out two-thirds of the dough to a large, thin round and line the pan, making sure that there is some overhang all the way around the edge. Brush the bottom and inside of the crust with some of the beaten eggs. Arrange one-third of the eggplant over the crust, with the pieces slightly overlapping. Top with one-third of the mozzarella, then one-third of the tomato sauce, and one-third of the bread crumbs and Parmesan. Repeat the layers two more times, ending with the tomato sauce, bread crumbs, and Parmesan. Pour in all but 2 tablespoons of the beaten eggs; they should sink into the filling.

5. Roll the remaining dough into a 10-inch round and place it over the top of the torte. Fold over the overhanging edge and pinch an attractive lip around the rim. Brush the top crust with the

A PIE BY ANY OTHER NAME

They are called pies; tarts and tortes and tortas; galettes; and *pitas* and *pittas*. All of them are savory pies. The differences between one and another mainly have to do with the amount and type of crust and the size and shape of the pie.

Tarts are single-crusted pies; tortes and tortas are double-crusted and can be made either in a regular pie pan, a cake pan, or a springform pan. Galettes are free-form, made with one round of dough whose edge is pulled up over the filling, gathered at the top, and baked on a baking sheet. *Pitas* and *pittas* are pies from Greece and the Balkans, respectively. They're usually made with phyllo dough, in a cake pan or straight-sided tart pan.

But the fillings and crusts are interchangeable. If you want to make one of the pies in this chapter that calls for phyllo dough but you don't have the phyllo, use the Yeasted Olive Oil Pastry on page 229. Or vice versa. If you're making a torte but want to make it as a free-form pie rather than line a pan and then roll out a top crust, you could roll out all the dough at once and make a galette, as long as your filling isn't too runny.

reserved beaten eggs. Bake for 50 minutes to 1 hour, until golden brown. Cool on a rack for 15 to 30 minutes. Serve hot or at room temperature, in wedges.

ADVANCE PREPARATION: The tomato sauce will keep for 3 or 4 days in the refrigerator and can be frozen for a few months. The torta can be assembled and refrigerated or frozen for a day before baking. The finished torta will hold for several hours.

LEFTOVERS: The torta will be good for about 5 days, although the bottom crust will probably get soggy after a while. Eat it for lunch or dinner until there is no more left. You can warm it up in a low oven or a microwave, or just eat it right from the refrigerator.

LIGURIAN ARTICHOKE AND GREENS TORTA

Italy • **Serves 6 to 8**

Greens and artichokes are a recurring theme in Mediterranean cooking. This *torta* has a particularly rich and satisfying filling, creamy with ricotta, savory with Parmesan, and with hard-cooked eggs hidden between the crusts.

- 1 recipe Yeasted Olive Oil Pastry (page 229)
- 6 small artichokes, trimmed; or 1 package (12 ounces) frozen artichoke hearts, thawed and chopped
- Juice of 1 lemon, if using fresh artichokes
- 1 pound beet greens, chard, or broccoli rabe, or 1½ pounds spinach, stemmed
- Salt
- 2 tablespoons extra virgin olive oil
- ½ onion, minced
- 1 plump garlic clove, minced
- Freshly ground pepper
- 2 large eggs, beaten
- 1¾ cups Homemade Ricotta Cheese (page 195) or 1 container (15 ounces) commercial ricotta
- 1¼ cups freshly grated Parmesan
- 2 tablespoons roughly chopped fresh marjoram or 1 teaspoon dried oregano
- 1 teaspoon unbleached all-purpose flour
- 2 large eggs, hard-cooked and cut into quarters
- 1 egg yolk beaten with 1 tablespoon water

1. Heat the oven to 375°F. Roll out half the pastry and use to line an oiled 10-inch tart pan.

2. If you are using fresh artichokes, fill a bowl with water and add the lemon juice. Cut the artichokes in half, remove any choke, and cut into thin slices; place in the lemon water.

3. If using greens, chard, or broccoli rabe: Bring a large pot of water to a boil, add 1 tablespoon salt, and the greens. Blanch for 1 to 2 minutes only and transfer with a spider or slotted spoon to a bowl of cold water. Drain, squeeze dry, and chop coarsely. You should have about 2 cups. If using spinach:

Place the leaves in a bowl and cover with boiling water. Let sit for 1 minute, then drain and squeeze out water.

4. Bring a large pot of water to a boil and add 1 tablespoon salt, or bring the greens water back to a boil. Drop in the sliced fresh artichokes. Boil for 2 to 3 minutes, until just tender. Transfer with a spider to a bowl of cold water, drain, and squeeze out excess water. Chop coarsely. (There's no need to blanch thawed frozen artichokes.)

5. Heat the oil in a heavy nonstick pan over medium heat and add the onion. Cook, stirring, until translucent, 3 to 5 minutes, and stir in the artichokes. Cook, stirring, until lightly browned, 5 to 10 minutes. Add the garlic and cook, stirring, until fragrant, 30 seconds to 1 minute. Stir in the greens. Cook, stirring, for 1 minute, until coated with oil and fragrant. Season the vegetables with salt and pepper and remove from the heat.

6. Beat together the eggs and ricotta. Stir in the vegetables, Parmesan, marjoram, flour, and salt and pepper to taste (begin with ½ teaspoon salt and adjust to taste). Spread half the filling over the pie crust. Sprinkle the quartered eggs here and there, and top with the remaining filling. Roll out the top crust and place over the filling. Crimp the edges of the bottom and top crust together. Brush the crust with the egg wash. Slash in a few places. Bake for 40 to 50 minutes, until nicely browned. Cool on a rack for 15 minutes before serving, or serve at room temperature.

ADVANCE PREPARATION: The cooked greens and artichokes will keep for about 3 days in the refrigerator. The torta can be assembled and baked several hours before serving.

GREENS AND POTATO TORTA OR GALETTE

Serves 6

This luscious pie works well with a number of greens—chard, broccoli rabe, beet greens, spinach—whatever looks best in the market. It's quite dramatic as a galette, equally delicious put together as a torta. Serve it hot or at room temperature. It's an excellent keeper.

¾ pound small potatoes, such as baby Yukon golds or red-skinned potatoes, peeled

Salt

2 to 2½ pounds chard, beet greens, broccoli rabe, or spinach, stemmed

2 tablespoons extra virgin olive oil

1 medium or large onion, chopped

2 large garlic cloves, minced

½ cup chopped fresh flat-leaf parsley

2 tablespoons chopped fresh basil

Freshly ground pepper

1 cup Homemade Ricotta Cheese (page 195) or commercial ricotta

2 large eggs, beaten

2 tablespoons milk

½ cup tightly packed grated Gruyère cheese

¼ cup freshly grated Parmesan

Freshly grated nutmeg

1 recipe Yeasted Olive Oil Pastry (page 229)

1. Place the potatoes and 2 teaspoons salt in a large pot of water (you'll be cooking the greens in the same water) and bring to a boil. Reduce the heat to medium, cover partially, and boil the potatoes for 20 minutes, until tender when pierced with a knife.

2. When the potatoes are done, remove from the water with a spider or slotted spoon and set aside until cool enough to handle, then cut into ½-inch slices. Bring the water back to a rolling boil and add another teaspoon salt and the greens. Blanch for about 2 minutes, until just tender. Transfer with a spider to a bowl of cold water. Drain and squeeze

dry. It is not necessary to remove every drop of water. Chop coarsely and set aside.

3. Heat the olive oil in a large nonstick skillet over medium heat. Add the onion and cook, stirring, until tender, about 5 minutes. Stir in the garlic and cook, stirring, until fragrant, 30 seconds to 1 minute. Stir in the greens, potatoes, and herbs, and gently toss together. Season to taste with salt and pepper, and transfer to a large bowl.

4. In a food processor fitted with the steel blade, process the ricotta until smooth. Scrape down the sides. Set aside 2 tablespoons of the beaten egg. Add the remaining egg to the processor along with the milk. Process until smooth, then scrape out into the bowl with the greens and potatoes. Stir in the Gruyère and Parmesan, add more salt and pepper and a pinch of nutmeg, and combine everything thoroughly. Taste and adjust seasonings.

5. Heat the oven to 375°F. Gently punch down the dough.

6. If making a galette: Roll the pastry into a large, thin circle about 16 inches in diameter. Transfer to an oiled baking sheet. Top with the filling, leaving a 2½-inch edge, and fold the edge in over the filling, draping folds all the way around. There will be an opening in the center.

If making a torta: Oil a 10-inch pie plate, springform pan, or tart pan with a removable bottom. Roll out two-thirds of the pastry to a thin circle and line the pan, easing the pastry into the edges. There should be some overhang. Scrape in the filling. Roll the remaining pastry to a 10-inch circle, and place on top of the filling. Fold the edge of the bottom crust over the top crust and crimp the dough all the way around the edge. Gently score the top crust with a paring knife.

7. Brush the torta or galette with the reserved egg. Bake for 45 to 50 minutes, or until the top is golden brown. Cool on a rack for at least 10 minutes before serving. Serve hot or warm.

ADVANCE PREPARATION: The potatoes and greens can be cooked up to 3 days ahead and held in the refrigerator in a covered bowl. The galette or torta can be assembled and baked several hours before you wish to serve it.

LEFTOVERS: This dish continues to taste terrific for 3 or 4 days, which makes for handy picnic or lunch fare, or an instant dinner, warmed in the oven or microwave.

MUSHROOMS AND GREENS TART
France • Serves 4 to 6

This is the type of dish that you'll find in food shops (*traiteurs*) along the Côte d'Azur. It can be eaten warm or at room temperature, and transports well. It's a great dish for a picnic.

½ recipe Yeasted Olive Oil Pastry (page 229)
Salt
1½ pounds greens, such as chard, stemmed
2 tablespoons extra virgin olive oil
1 shallot, minced
½ pound mushrooms, sliced
Freshly ground pepper
1 teaspoon finely chopped fresh rosemary
2 large garlic cloves, minced
3 large eggs
⅓ cup milk
½ cup tightly packed grated Gruyère cheese
¼ cup freshly grated Parmesan

1. Heat the oven to 375°F. Roll out the pastry and use it to line an oiled 10-inch tart pan with a removable bottom.

2. Bring a large pot of water to a boil, salt abundantly, and add the greens. Cook for 1 to 4 minutes, depending on the greens, until just tender. Transfer to a bowl of ice water, then drain and squeeze out water. Chop.

3. Heat the olive oil in a large nonstick skillet over medium heat and add the shallot. Cook, stirring, until tender, about 3 minutes. Add the mush-

rooms and cook, stirring often, until tender, about 8 minutes. Add salt and pepper to taste, the rosemary, and garlic. Cook for another minute. Add the greens and stir for another minute. Adjust seasonings.

4. Whisk together the eggs and milk. Add ½ teaspoon salt and stir in the cheeses and mushroom/greens mixture. Scrape into the pastry shell. Bake for 35 minutes, or until browned and sizzling. Serve hot, warm, or at room temperature.

ADVANCE PREPARATION: The mushrooms and greens can be prepared up to 3 days before assembling the tart. The tart will keep for 3 to 4 days in the refrigerator.

VARIATION

MUSHROOM AND GREENS GRATIN: Omit the crust. Oil a 2-quart gratin or baking dish and scrape in the filling. Bake as directed.

PROVENÇAL ZUCCHINI AND GREENS TORTE
France • **Serves 6 to 8**

This is a gorgeous double-crusted savory torte, packed with vegetables, texture, and flavor. The filling could as easily be used for a gratin (see the variation that follows) if you don't feel like putting it into the easy-to-work-with and satisfying pastry. It's important to cut the zucchini into very small dice, about ¼ or ⅓ inch, for the best texture and look. You can use a number of greens for this—spinach, chard, and beet greens are all good choices. You can prepare the filling for this while the dough is rising.

> Salt
>
> 1 pound greens, such as chard, beet greens, or spinach, stemmed
>
> 2 tablespoons extra virgin olive oil
>
> 1 medium onion, finely chopped
>
> 2 pounds zucchini, cut into small dice (¼ to ⅓ inch)

> 2 to 3 large garlic cloves (to taste), minced or put through a press
>
> ½ cup chopped fresh flat-leaf parsley
>
> 1 teaspoon fresh thyme (or ½ teaspoon dried)
>
> 1 to 2 teaspoons chopped fresh rosemary (or ½ to 1 teaspoon crumbled dried)
>
> Freshly ground pepper
>
> 3 large eggs
>
> ½ cup Arborio or medium-grain rice, cooked (opposite page)
>
> ½ cup tightly packed grated Gruyère cheese
>
> 1 recipe Yeasted Olive Oil Pastry (page 229)

1. Bring a large pot of water to a boil. Add 1 tablespoon salt and the greens. Blanch for 2 minutes, until just tender. Using a slotted spoon or deep-fry skimmer, transfer to a bowl of cold water, then drain. Squeeze out excess water and chop. Set aside.

2. Heat the olive oil in a large nonstick skillet over medium heat and add the onion. Cook, stirring, until tender, about 5 minutes, and stir in the zucchini. Season to taste with salt, and cook, stirring, until just tender and still bright green, about 8 minutes. Stir in the garlic and cook until fragrant, about 1 minute. Stir in the greens, parsley, thyme, and rosemary, toss everything together, and remove from the heat. Taste and season with salt and pepper.

3. Beat the eggs in a large bowl and reserve 2 tablespoons for brushing the crust. Stir in ¼ to ½ teaspoon salt (to taste), the zucchini mixture, rice, and Gruyère. Mix everything together, add lots of pepper, taste once more, and adjust seasoning.

4. Heat the oven to 375°F. Oil a 10- or 12-inch tart pan or springform pan. Roll out two-thirds of the pastry and use to line the pan, with the edge of the dough overhanging. Scrape in the filling. Roll out the remaining pastry to fit the pan and place on top of the filling. Crimp the edges of the top and bottom together. Cut 4 or 5 small slits in the top crust with a sharp knife and brush with the reserved beaten egg. Bake for 40 to 50 minutes,

COOKING ARBORIO RICE FOR PIES

You can cook the Arborio rice in much the same way you would cook pasta. Bring 2 quarts water to a boil in a saucepan. Add 2 teaspoons salt and the rice. Boil for 15 minutes, until the rice is tender. Drain through a strainer and set aside.

until golden brown. Cool on a rack for at least 10 minutes before serving (preferably longer). This can also be served at room temperature.

ADVANCE PREPARATION: The blanched greens will keep for 3 or 4 days in the refrigerator in a covered bowl. The finished torte keeps for a few days in the refrigerator, and it makes a great leftover. Take wedges to work for enviable lunches.

VARIATION

ZUCCHINI AND GREENS GRATIN: Omit the crust. Oil a 2-quart gratin dish and scrape in the filling. Mix ¼ cup bread crumbs with 1 tablespoon extra virgin olive oil and sprinkle over the top. Bake for 40 to 45 minutes in a 375°F oven, until the top is nicely browned.

SPINACH AND RICOTTA TORTA

Italy • Serves 12 to 16

When I was in Rome, I found myself returning again and again to Il Fornaio bakery near the Campo de' Fiori, just to look at all of their breads, focaccia, and especially their savory tortas. This *torta ricotta e spinaci,* laid out in a sheet pan with a lattice crust over the top, was the most inviting item there. It's beautiful on a buffet, makes great picnic or lunch box fare, and is a perfect light supper.

> 1½ recipes Yeasted Olive Oil Pastry (page 229)
> Salt
> 2½ pounds fresh spinach, stemmed
> 1 tablespoon extra virgin olive oil

> 1 medium red onion, finely chopped
> 2 garlic cloves, minced
> 1 large egg
> 1 pound fresh ricotta cheese
> ½ cup freshly grated Parmesan
> Freshly ground pepper
> 1 large egg beaten with 1 tablespoon water

1. Roll three-quarters of the pastry into a 15 × 19-inch rectangle. Fit the pastry into an oiled half-sheet pan (12½ × 17½ inches). Shape a lip around the edge. Set aside.

2. Bring a large pot of water to a boil. Add a generous amount of salt and the spinach. Remove from the water immediately—in less than half a minute—and transfer to a bowl of ice water. Drain and squeeze dry. Chop medium-fine.

3. Heat the oil in a large nonstick skillet over medium heat. Add the onion and cook, stirring often, until tender, about 5 minutes. Stir in the garlic and cook for another minute, until fragrant. Stir in the spinach and remove from the heat.

4. Heat the oven to 375°F. Beat the egg in a large bowl and beat in the ricotta. Stir in the spinach mixture and the Parmesan and season with salt and pepper to taste. Spread over the crust in an even layer. Roll the remaining pastry thin and cut into ½-inch-wide strips. Place half the strips over the spinach on the diagonal about 3 inches apart. Place the remaining strips on top, on the opposite diagonal, to form a lattice. Brush the lattice and the edge of the crust with the egg wash. Bake for 30 minutes, until the crust is golden brown.

ADVANCE PREPARATION: The filling can be made a day ahead and refrigerated. The pastry can be made ahead, rolled out, and frozen, or refrigerated overnight.

SPRING ONION, GARLIC, AND GREENS TART

Serves 4 to 6

If you've never seen the plump, juicy heads of green garlic that hit Mediterranean markets (and California markets too) in the spring, you've got a real treat in store. Combine the garlic with gently cooked spring onions—those small green onions that you might confuse with scallions, except they're bigger than scallions, and bulbous—and irresistibly generous bunches of Swiss chard that you'll also find at spring farmers' markets. Make this as a tart or a gratin (see the variation that follows).

>   Salt
>
>   2½ to 3 pounds Swiss chard, stemmed and
>   washed thoroughly
>
>   ½ recipe Yeasted Olive Oil Pastry (page 229)
>
>   2 tablespoons extra virgin olive oil
>
>   1 pound spring onions, bulbs and light green
>   parts of the tops only, chopped
>
>   ½ head green garlic, cloves (if the garlic has
>   begun to form them) separated, peeled, and
>   minced; or 4 garlic cloves, minced
>
>   Freshly ground pepper
>
>   3 large eggs, beaten
>
>   ½ cup milk
>
>   ½ cup grated Gruyère cheese
>
>   ¼ cup freshly grated Parmesan

1. Bring a large pot of water to a boil. Add 1 tablespoon salt and the greens. Blanch for 2 minutes, or until just tender, and transfer to a bowl of cold water. Drain and squeeze out water. Chop coarsely and set aside.

2. Heat the oven to 375°F. Oil a 10-inch tart pan. Roll out the pastry and use to line the pan.

3. Heat the olive oil in a large, heavy nonstick frying pan over medium heat and add the spring onions. Cook, stirring often, until tender and fragrant, 5 to 8 minutes. Stir in the garlic and cook for 2 minutes or so, just until fragrant. Add the chopped greens and stir together. Season with salt and pepper. Remove from the heat and set aside.

4. Beat the eggs in a medium bowl. Beat in the milk and ½ teaspoon salt, then stir in the greens and onions. Add plenty of pepper and stir in the cheeses. Scrape the filling into the pastry shell. Bake for 30 to 40 minutes, until firm and beginning to brown on top. Serve hot, warm, or at room temperature.

ADVANCE PREPARATION: The greens can be blanched and chopped up to 3 days ahead and kept in a covered bowl in the refrigerator. Step 3 can also be completed several hours before you assemble the gratin or tart, and the vegetables held at room temperature. The tart can be made several hours before serving. Reheat in a 325°F oven for 15 minutes if desired.

VARIATION

SPRING ONION, GARLIC, AND GREENS GRATIN: Omit the crust. Oil a 2-quart gratin dish and scrape in the filling. Bake as directed above.

CABBAGE GALETTE

France • **Serves 6 to 8**

This Provençal galette puts cabbage to wonderful use. The cabbage is cooked gently with onion and garlic, seasoned with dill, and enriched with eggs and Gruyère or feta. You can use regular white cabbage or Savoy cabbage.

>   2 tablespoons extra virgin olive oil
>
>   1 medium onion, chopped
>
>   2 large garlic cloves, minced or put through
>   a press
>
>   Salt
>
>   1 small (1½ to 1¾ pounds) cabbage, cored
>   and chopped
>
>   3 to 4 tablespoons chopped fresh dill (to taste)
>
>   Freshly ground pepper
>
>   2 large eggs, hard-cooked and chopped
>
>   2 large eggs, beaten
>
>   ¾ cup packed grated Gruyère cheese or
>   crumbled feta
>
>   1 recipe Yeasted Olive Oil Pastry (page 229)

1. Heat the olive oil in a large, wide, heavy non-stick skillet over medium heat and add the onion. Cook, stirring often, until beginning to color, about 10 minutes. Add the garlic and some salt, cook another minute, then stir in the cabbage. Cook, stirring often, for 15 minutes, adding salt to taste about halfway through. The cabbage should be cooked down and fragrant but still have some color. Stir in the dill, pepper, and hard-cooked eggs. Remove from the heat.

2. Reserve 2 tablespoons of the beaten eggs for brushing the galette. Combine the remaining beaten eggs, cabbage mixture, cheese, and ½ teaspoon salt in a large bowl and mix together well. Taste and adjust seasonings.

3. Heat the oven to 375°F. Roll the pastry out into a large, thin circle about 16 inches in diameter. Transfer to an oiled baking sheet. Top with the filling, leaving a 2½-inch edge. If the egg runs out over the edge of the dough, just sweep it back over the cabbage, then fold the edge in over the filling, draping folds all the way around. Brush the exposed pastry with the reserved egg.

4. Bake for 45 to 50 minutes, until the crust is golden brown. Cool for at least 10 minutes before serving. Serve hot or warm.

ADVANCE PREPARATION: The filling, without the beaten eggs, can be made 1 or 2 days ahead and kept in a covered bowl in the refrigerator.

LEFTOVERS: The galette will continue to taste terrific for 3 or 4 days after it's made. This makes it handy picnic or lunch fare, and an instant dinner, warmed in the oven or microwave.

PROVENÇAL PUMPKIN TORTE
France • Serves 6

Seasoned with fresh sage, this wonderful torte is one of winter squash's favorite companions.

> 2 to 2½ pounds winter squash, seeds and membranes scraped away, the flesh cut into large pieces (see Note)
>
> 2 tablespoons extra virgin olive oil
>
> 1 large onion, chopped
>
> 3 large garlic cloves, minced or put through a press
>
> ½ cup Arborio or medium-grain rice, cooked (see page 235)
>
> 2 tablespoons chopped fresh sage
>
> 2 tablespoons chopped fresh flat-leaf parsley
>
> ½ cup grated Gruyère cheese
>
> ¼ cup freshly grated Parmesan
>
> Salt and freshly ground pepper
>
> 3 large eggs, beaten
>
> 1 recipe Yeasted Olive Oil Pastry (page 229)

Note: *If using butternut, cut in half crosswise, just above the bulbous bottom part, then cut these halves into lengthwise quarters and scrape away the seeds and membranes.*

1. Steam the squash over boiling water for 15 to 20 minutes, until tender. Drain and cool in a colander for 15 minutes (butternut squash will not be watery). Peel, place in a bowl, and mash with a fork, large wooden spoon, potato masher, or pestle.

2. Heat the oil in a heavy nonstick skillet over medium heat and add the onion. Cook, stirring, until tender, about 5 minutes, and stir in the garlic. Cook for another minute or two, until fragrant. Remove from the heat and toss with the squash, rice, sage, parsley, cheeses, salt, and pepper. Reserve 2 tablespoons of the beaten eggs and stir the rest into the filling. Taste and adjust seasonings.

3. Heat the oven to 375°F. Oil a 10- or 12-inch tart pan or springform pan. Roll out two-thirds of the

pastry and line the pan, with the edge of the dough overhanging. Scrape in the filling. Roll out the remaining pastry, top the torte, then crimp the edges of the top and bottom together. Cut 4 small slits in the top crust with a sharp knife and brush with the reserved beaten eggs. Bake for 45 to 50 minutes, until golden brown. Cool on a rack for at least 10 minutes before serving. This can also be served at room temperature.

ADVANCE PREPARATION: The squash can be cooked and mashed 3 or 4 days ahead and kept in the refrigerator in a covered bowl. The filling will keep for 2 or 3 days in the refrigerator.

LEFTOVERS: The tart will keep for a few days in the refrigerator. Serve it warm or at room temperature.

VARIATIONS

PUMPKIN GRATIN: Omit the crust. Oil a 2-quart gratin dish with extra virgin olive oil. Place the filling in the gratin, drizzle with 1 tablespoon olive oil, and bake at 375°F until light brown on the top and edge, about 40 minutes.

PUMPKIN GALETTE: Do not divide the dough. Roll out to 1 large circle and make a galette, following the directions in the Cabbage Galette recipe on page 236.

FENNEL AND SCALLION PIE
Greece • Serves 6

This is a classic Greek country *pita*. Leeks are traditional, but one day I found that I had a lot of fennel and scallions in my refrigerator, and decided to throw them together with the feta I always keep on hand. I used dried dill because I didn't have any fresh. What resulted tasted wonderful, and no less Greek than the classic.

> 5 tablespoons extra virgin olive oil
>
> 1 medium onion, chopped
>
> 2 pounds fennel, trimmed, quartered, cored, and chopped (about 5 cups)
>
> 2 bunches scallions, both white and green parts, chopped

Salt and freshly ground pepper

3 large eggs

6 ounces feta, crumbled (about 1½ cups)

½ cup chopped fresh dill (or 1 to 2 tablespoons dried; to taste)

⅔ cup chopped fresh flat-leaf parsley

12 sheets phyllo dough (see Note)

Note: *In Los Angeles, I can buy a thicker, richer phyllo dough made in Bosnia. I use less of it, 5 or 6 layers on the bottom, 3 or 4 on the top.*

WORKING WITH PHYLLO

Because phyllo dough is so thin, it can dry out quickly once it's exposed to air, and that makes it almost impossible to work with, because it cracks and crumbles when you try to manipulate it.

Most phyllo comes frozen in long 1-pound packages. Don't buy the smaller sheets that are sold in smaller boxes, as they're not quite large enough for these recipes. Thaw the phyllo overnight in the refrigerator, not at room temperature. If the dough thaws too quickly, it will sweat and the sheets will stick together.

Open up the package of phyllo and unfold the sheets of dough. Remove the number of sheets your recipe calls for, and fold the remaining dough back up. Wrap tightly in plastic, then in foil. Either refrigerate or freeze.

Lay your phyllo dough out on a work surface and cover completely with a kitchen towel. Moisten another kitchen towel and place it on top of the dry one. This will prevent your phyllo from drying out. Remove one sheet at a time from under the towels, following the recipe.

My recipes in this chapter all call for brushing the phyllo with olive oil as you layer the sheets, but you could substitute melted butter, or a mixture of olive oil and melted butter. Whatever you do use, you need to brush the phyllo dough so that it will crisp as it bakes.

1. Heat 2 tablespoons of the olive oil in a large nonstick skillet over medium heat and add the onion. Cook, stirring often, until just tender, about 4 minutes, then add the fennel and scallions. Cook, stirring often, until the vegetables are tender and fragrant, 8 to 10 minutes. Season to taste with salt and pepper, and remove from the heat.

2. Beat the eggs in a large bowl. Crumble in the feta and stir in the cooked vegetables, dill, and parsley. Combine well. Taste and adjust salt and pepper.

3. Heat the oven to 350°F. Oil a 10- or 12-inch tart pan. Place the remaining 3 tablespoons olive oil in a small bowl. Layer 7 sheets of phyllo dough in the tart pan, placing them not quite evenly on top of each other so that the edges fan out around the edge of the pan and brushing each sheet with olive oil before adding the next sheet. Top with the vegetable mixture. Fold the edges of the dough over the filling and brush with olive oil. Layer 5 more sheets of dough over the top, brushing each sheet and fanning them out as you did with the bottom sheets. Stuff the edges into the side of the pan. Brush the top with olive oil. Pierce the top of the pie in several places with a sharp knife.

4. Bake for 50 minutes to 1 hour, until the top is golden brown. Serve hot or at room temperature.

ADVANCE PREPARATION: You can cook the fennel and onions a day or two ahead and keep them in a covered bowl in the refrigerator. You can make the filling hours or even a day before assembling the pie, and keep in the refrigerator. The pie can be assembled, covered tightly with plastic, and refrigerated for a day.

GREENS AND SWEET ONION PIE
Greece • Serves 6

The Greeks forage for their greens, and use a mixture for their pies. You can use a mix of greens, or just one type. When I use beet greens for this, the beets go into a salad, the greens into the luscious pie.

Salt

2 to 2½ pounds greens, such as beet greens, red or green chard, or spinach, stemmed

2 tablespoons extra virgin olive oil, plus additional if using phyllo

2 cups chopped sweet onions, such as Vidalia

2 large garlic cloves, minced or put through a press

¼ cup chopped fresh dill

¼ cup chopped fresh flat-leaf parsley

3 large eggs, beaten

4 ounces feta, crumbled (about 1 cup)

Freshly ground pepper

1 recipe Greek Pie Crust (page 229), or Yeasted Olive Oil Pastry (page 229), or 12 sheets phyllo dough

1. Bring a large pot of water to a boil. Add 1 tablespoon salt and the greens. Blanch for 2 minutes, until just tender. Using a slotted spoon or deep-fry skimmer, transfer to a bowl of cold water, then drain. Squeeze out excess water and chop. Set aside.

2. Heat the oven to 375°F. Oil a 10-inch ceramic pie or tart pan (I like to use a ceramic dish for this). Heat the olive oil in a large nonstick skillet over medium heat and add the onions. Cook, stirring often, until tender but not browned, about 5 minutes. Add the garlic and cook, stirring, for another 30 seconds to 1 minute, until the garlic is fragrant. Stir in the greens and herbs and stir for a minute, until the greens are coated with oil. Remove from the heat.

3. Reserve 2 tablespoons of the beaten eggs for brushing the crust (if making the pie with pastry). Crumble or blend the feta into the remaining eggs

in a large bowl. Add the greens mixture, toss, and season to taste with salt and pepper.

4. If making the pie with pastry: Roll out two-thirds of the pastry and use to line the pie dish. Scrape in the filling. Roll out the remaining pastry and place over the filling. Crimp the bottom and top edges together, then pinch an attractive fluted edge all the way around the rim of the pie. Brush the top with the reserved beaten eggs and make a few slashes in the top crust so that steam can escape as the pie bakes.

If making the pie with phyllo: Line the pie dish with 7 sheets of phyllo, brushing each sheet with olive oil and turning the dish after each addition so that the edges of the phyllo drape evenly over the edge of the dish. Scrape in the filling. Fold the draped edges in over the filling, then layer the remaining 5 pieces on top, brushing each piece with olive oil. Stuff the edges into the side of the pan. Brush the top with oil and pierce in a few places with the tip of a knife.

5. Bake for 40 to 50 minutes, until the crust is golden. Serve hot, warm, or at room temperature.

ADVANCE PREPARATION: The blanched greens will keep in the refrigerator in a covered bowl for 3 or 4 days. You can assemble the pie several hours before baking and keep in the refrigerator, or freeze. Transfer directly from the freezer to the preheated oven, and increase the baking time by about 10 minutes.

LEFTOVERS: The pie keeps for a few days, but you must keep recrisping the phyllo if using. This is easily done, either in a low oven (250° to 300°F) for 10 to 20 minutes, or in a hot oven that has just been turned off for 5 to 10 minutes.

WINTER SQUASH PIE WITH BULGUR AND FETA
Greece • Serves 4 to 6

The Greeks do many versions of savory pumpkin pie, some in phyllo dough, some in pie dough. For this one I've used a yeasted dough, which truth to tell, you'd be more likely to find in Italy or Provence. But I love its light, almost flaky texture. Butternut squash is a variety of winter squash that you're more likely to find in America than Europe, but I choose to use it here because it's so sweet, and holds its shape nicely, which makes the pie very pretty when you cut into it. I also think the mint highlights the sweet flavors of the squash. Roasting the whole squash for 30 minutes facilitates peeling.

1 good-size butternut squash (1½ to 2 pounds)

Salt and freshly ground pepper

2 tablespoons extra virgin olive oil

3 tablespoons fine bulgur

¼ cup warm water

1 onion, finely chopped

PUMPKIN BY ANY OTHER NAME

Throughout the Mediterranean, winter squash—usually referred to there as *pumpkin*—is used in luscious gratins and pies, and also in filled pastas. The place determines the seasoning; in Greece, the winter squash pies are fragrant with mint, whereas France and Italy favor sage.

The huge orange squash that is often used in the Mediterranean does resemble overgrown, bulbous pumpkins. But the flesh is thicker and denser than that of our pumpkins. When I make savory pumpkin pies and gratins, I like to use butternut squash, which has such a sweet flavor and dense texture. But other winter squash will also work. At the farmers' market you might find kabocha squash or hubbards, and in the supermarket you'll find banana squash, usually cut up.

4 large eggs

2 ounces feta, crumbled (about ¼ cup)

2 teaspoons dried mint

½ recipe Yeasted Olive Oil Pastry (page 229)

1. Heat the oven to 375°F. Pierce the squash in a few places. Place on a foil-lined baking sheet and roast for 30 minutes, until it begins to soften. Remove from the oven, cool for about 10 minutes, then, using a towel to steady the squash without burning your hands, cut in half lengthwise. Scrape out the seeds, peel, and cut into ½-inch dice. Place the diced squash in a roasting pan or baking dish, season with salt and pepper, and toss with 1 tablespoon of the olive oil. Cover the dish with foil and return to the oven for 30 minutes, until the squash is tender. Stir the squash every 10 minutes to ensure even roasting. Leave the oven on.

2. Meanwhile, place the bulgur in a bowl and cover with the warm water. Let sit until the bulgur is tender and has absorbed all of the water, about 15 minutes. Stir the bulgur and set aside.

3. Heat the remaining 1 tablespoon olive oil in a skillet over medium heat. Add the onion and cook, stirring often, until tender and translucent, about 5 minutes. Remove from the heat.

4. Beat the eggs in a large bowl and crumble in the feta. Stir in the bulgur, onion, roasted squash, dried mint, ½ teaspoon salt, and some pepper.

5. Roll out the pastry to a 14-inch round. Fit into an oiled 10-inch tart pan. Pinch an attractive lip around the edge. Scrape the filling into the pie shell. Bake for 30 to 40 minutes, until firm and beginning to brown on the top. Serve hot, warm, or at room temperature.

ADVANCE PREPARATION: The squash can be cooked and the bulgur reconstituted up to 3 days ahead, and kept in the refrigerator in a covered bowl. The filling will keep for 2 or 3 days in the refrigerator.

WINTER SQUASH AND LEEK PIE
Greece • Serves 6

I first ate a Greek savory pumpkin pie, in phyllo pastry, at a conference on Greek gastronomy organized by the Oldways Preservation Trust and the International Olive Oil Council. People from all over Greece were brought in from their villages to make local specialties in a market setting for the lunches at the conference. I found myself back at the booth with the vegetable pies over and over again.

2½ pounds winter squash (1 large or 2 smaller butternut squash), seeds and membranes scraped away, cut into large pieces (see Note)

½ cup chopped fresh flat-leaf parsley

¼ cup chopped fresh mint

¼ teaspoon freshly grated nutmeg

4 ounces feta, crumbled (about 1 cup)

½ cup freshly grated Parmesan

2 tablespoons extra virgin olive oil, plus additional for brushing

3 large leeks (about 1½ pounds), white and light green parts only, washed well and chopped

2 large garlic cloves, minced or put through a press

3 large eggs, beaten

Salt and freshly ground pepper

12 sheets phyllo dough

Note: *If using butternut, cut in half crosswise, just above the bulbous bottom part, then cut these halves into lengthwise quarters and scrape away the seeds and membranes.*

1. Steam the squash over boiling water for 15 to 20 minutes, until tender. Drain and cool in a colander for another 15 minutes (butternut squash will not be watery). Peel and place in a bowl. Mash with a fork, large wooden spoon, potato masher, or pestle. Stir in the herbs, nutmeg, and cheeses.

▶

2. Heat the olive oil in a large, heavy nonstick frying pan over medium heat and add the leeks. Cook, stirring, until tender and just beginning to color, 5 to 10 minutes. Add the garlic and continue to cook for another minute, until fragrant. Add the leek mixture to the squash. Reserve 2 tablespoons of the beaten eggs for brushing the tart. Mix the remaining eggs into the squash. Season to taste with salt and pepper.

3. Heat the oven to 375°F. Brush a 10- or 12-inch tart pan with olive oil and layer in 7 sheets of phyllo dough, placing them not quite evenly on top of each other so that the edges overlap the sides of the pan all the way around and brushing each sheet with olive oil before adding the next. Scrape in the filling, fold the dough edges in, and brush with olive oil. Layer 5 more sheets of dough over the top, brushing each sheet with olive oil. Stuff the edges into the side of the pan. Brush the top with the reserved egg. Pierce the top of the pie in several places with a sharp knife. Bake for 40 to 50 minutes, until the top is golden brown. Serve warm or at room temperature.

ADVANCE PREPARATION: The squash can be cooked and mashed 3 or 4 days ahead and kept in the refrigerator in a covered bowl. The filling will keep for 2 or 3 days in the refrigerator.

LEFTOVERS: The tart keeps for a few days, but you must keep recrisping the phyllo. This is easily done, either in a low oven (250° to 300°F) for 10 to 20 minutes, or in a hot oven that has just been turned off for 5 to 10 minutes.

VARIATIONS

You can also make this as a galette or a double-crusted tart, using 1 recipe for either the Greek Pie Crust (page 229) or Yeasted Olive Oil Pastry (page 229).

ZUCCHINI AND HERB PIE
Greece • Serves 8 to 10

I've had many versions of this pie. The one that stands out in my memory was a simple, thin *pita*, incredibly fragrant with dill, that I shared with my sister-in-law Margaret and her twin sister, Deborah, in a taverna overlooking the sea in Ikaria. We were hungry, having hiked for 2 hours in the hot sun like mad dogs and Englishmen. But now we were on a shady terrace, the beach below us, eating Greek salad and this luscious pie. Along with the shredded zucchini, it contained what I thought were bits of shredded carrots. Diane Kochilas's recipe, which we cooked the next night, called for chopped zucchini flowers, and now I'm wondering if this was what looked to me (and tasted like) carrots. I give you the choice here.

Diane and her assistant, Yioula, say it's better to use big, older zucchini for this, as they contain less water than the younger squash. Whichever you use, make sure to give yourself the extra hour that the zucchini needs to drain. This recipe has about half as much olive oil as a Greek recipe would have; it still tastes Greek to me.

- 3 pounds zucchini, ends trimmed
- Salt
- 3 tablespoons extra virgin olive oil, plus additional for brushing
- 2 large onions, finely chopped
- 5 to 6 squash blossoms, finely chopped, or 1 medium carrot, shredded
- 1 cup finely chopped wild fennel or dill, or a combination
- ½ cup chopped fresh mint
- ½ cup chopped fresh flat-leaf parsley
- Leaves from 5 to 6 sprigs fresh oregano, finely chopped (optional)
- 7 ounces crumbled feta (about 1¾ cups)
- 2 large eggs, beaten
- Freshly ground pepper
- Greek Pie Crust (page 229)

1. Grate the zucchini in a food processor or on the large holes of a box grater. Place in a large colander, salt generously, and let drain for 1 hour, pressing down occasionally to squeeze out liquid. After an hour, take up handfuls and squeeze out moisture (or wrap in a kitchen towel and twist the towel). Place in a bowl.

2. Heat 2 tablespoons of the oil in a large skillet over medium heat and add the onions. Cook, stirring, until tender, about 8 minutes. Add to the zucchini. Stir in the remaining 1 tablespoon olive oil, the squash blossoms, herbs, feta, eggs, pepper, and additional salt to taste.

3. Heat the oven to 350°F. Oil a 10- or 12-inch pie or tart pan. Divide the dough 2 equal pieces. Roll out the first piece to a circle 2 inches wider than the pan. Line the pan with the pastry and brush with olive oil. Scrape in the filling. Roll out the remaining pastry to the size of the pan. Place over the filling. Press the edges of the top and bottom layers of dough together and roll in to form an attractive lip around the edge. Score the top in a few places with the tip of a knife and brush with olive oil. Bake for 1 hour, until the pastry is golden. Cool on a rack to room temperature. Slice in wedges and serve.

ADVANCE PREPARATION: You can make the filling a day ahead. The pie can be assembled and baked several hours before serving.

SUMMER SQUASH

Zucchini is the best-known summer squash, and it will work for any of the summer squash recipes here. But if you shop at a farmers' market, try some of the other varieties on offer. These might include pale green marrow squash, which taper toward the stem end and tend to have a denser flesh than zucchini; long, narrow *cocozelle*, an Italian squash with a richer flavor; yellow crookneck squash, which are bulbous at one end; yellow straight-necked squash; flat, scalloped pattypan squash; and the round *Ronde de Nice*, which have a firm dense flesh and a mild flavor.

SPANAKOPITA

Greece • Serves 6

This is just one version of the popular Greek spinach pie. Like the other Greek classic, moussaka (page 258), spanakopita has been badly done too many times in too many mediocre Greek restaurants (both here and in Greece). This one is alive with flavors of the Greek countryside—dill, rosemary, thyme, parsley—and it's packed with spinach.

- 2¼ pounds fresh spinach, stemmed
- 2 tablespoons extra virgin olive oil, plus additional for brushing
- 3 large leeks, white and light green parts only, washed well and thinly sliced
- Leaves from 1 bunch fresh flat-leaf parsley, chopped
- 2 tablespoons chopped fresh rosemary (or 2 teaspoons crumbled dried)
- ¼ cup chopped fresh dill
- 1½ teaspoons fresh thyme leaves (or ¾ teaspoon dried)
- 3 large eggs, beaten
- 6 ounces feta, crumbled (about 1½ cups)
- Salt and freshly ground pepper
- ¼ teaspoon freshly grated nutmeg
- 12 sheets phyllo dough
- 1 egg white, lightly beaten

1. Wilt the spinach in a large nonaluminum frying pan over medium-high heat with the water left on the leaves after washing. Transfer to a colander, rinse with cold water, and press out as much water as possible. Then wrap in a towel and squeeze out more water. Chop fairly fine and set aside.

2. Heat the oven to 375°F. Heat the olive oil in a large, heavy nonstick skillet over medium heat and add the leeks. Cook, stirring often, for about 10 minutes, until softened and just beginning to brown. Add the spinach and stir until the spinach is coated with oil.

3. Scrape the spinach and leeks into a large bowl. Stir in the parsley, rosemary, dill, thyme, eggs, feta, salt, pepper, and nutmeg. Taste and adjust seasonings.

4. Brush a 10- or 12-inch tart pan with olive oil and layer in 7 sheets of phyllo dough, placing them not quite evenly on top of each other so that the edges overlap the sides of the pan all the way around and brushing each sheet with olive oil before adding the next. Scrape in the filling. Fold the edges of the dough over the spinach mixture and brush with olive oil. Layer 5 more sheets of dough over the top, brushing each sheet with olive oil. Stuff the edges into the sides of the pan. Brush the top with beaten egg white. Pierce the top of the pie in several places with a sharp knife. Bake for 45 to 50 minutes, until the top is golden brown. Serve hot or at room temperature.

ADVANCE PREPARATION: The wilted spinach will keep for 3 or 4 days in the refrigerator. You can make the recipe through Step 2 several hours or a day ahead. Keep on top of the stove or in the refrigerator in a covered bowl. The Spanakopita can be assembled a few hours before you bake it, and held in or out of the refrigerator.

LEFTOVERS: Spanakopita keeps for a few days, but you must keep recrisping the phyllo if using. This is easily done, either in a low oven (250° to 300°F) for 10 to 20 minutes, or in a hot oven that has just been turned off for 5 to 10 minutes.

CLEANING LEEKS

Because leeks are buried deep within the ground (which is what keeps the bottoms white), they tend to be quite gritty and must be cleaned thoroughly before using. The most efficient way to do this is to trim off the root ends, then cut the leeks in half lengthwise, exposing all of the layers. Place in a bowl of ice cold water for about 10 minutes. Then run the leeks under the faucet, holding them under the stream and shuffling the layers so that the water will run through and wash out any dirt that has loosened from the layers.

POTATO PITTA
Bosnia • Serves 8 to 10

This is my adaptation of the wonderful potato pie I learned to make from Amra Slipac at the Aroma Café in Los Angeles (see page 247). I include sour cream in the filling, to add a little moisture. I'm not about to make my own strudel dough, as Amra does, so my version is made with commercial phyllo. I can still make the coils, but the dough is more brittle than Amra's delicate strudel dough. Still, nobody complains about this rendition of a Bosnian classic.

> 2 pounds potatoes, such as russets or Yukon golds (see Note), peeled
>
> 1½ medium onions, cut into small dice
>
> Salt and freshly ground pepper
>
> ½ cup sour cream (reduced-fat is fine)
>
> 1 pound phyllo dough
>
> Extra virgin olive oil for brushing

Note: *Amra says you can use any type of potato, but you have to cut very small dice. I use baking potatoes, which have a lovely soft texture.*

1. Heat the oven to 400°F. Spray a 12-inch tart pan or cake pan with cooking spray and line with parchment. Spray the parchment.

2. Cut the potatoes into very small dice, about ¼ inch. As you work, put the diced potatoes into a bowl of cold water so they won't discolor. You can also put the onions in the water; they will have a milder flavor.

3. When all of the potatoes are done, drain in a colander. Add the onions to the colander and season abundantly with salt (about 1 tablespoon) and pepper (½ to 1 teaspoon). Add the sour cream and toss together well. Keep the mixture in the colander, and set the colander in a bowl or in the sink. The potatoes and onions will continue to leach water.

4. Place a sheet of phyllo horizontally on your work surface (with the long edge closest to you). Brush lightly with olive oil and top with another sheet of phyllo dough. Fold in half horizontally, with the folded edge at the bottom. Brush with a little more oil, then, leaving a 2-inch border on the bottom and sides, and a wider border on the top, spread ½ cup of the filling along the length of the phyllo. Fold the ends in over the filling, then fold the bottom edge over and carefully roll up into a cylinder about 1 inch thick. Place seam side down along the edge of the pan. Continue to wrap the filling and coil the ropes into the pan, starting each cylinder where the last one left off, until the entire pan is filled. If there is still filling and phyllo, start another, smaller coil in another pan, or make a little pie.

5. When the pie is assembled, brush the top with olive oil. Bake on the lower rack of the oven for 20 minutes. Transfer to the middle rack and bake an additional 30 minutes, until nicely browned. Cool on a rack for at least 10 minutes before serving. You can serve this hot or warm. To serve, lift out pieces of the coil for each person.

ADVANCE PREPARATION: The pie should be baked once it's assembled so that the dough doesn't become too soggy.

LEFTOVERS: I think the *pitta* keeps well for a few days once baked, and can easily be recrisped in a low oven (250° to 300°F) for 10 to 20 minutes. Amra probably wouldn't agree, though; she wants you to eat it all the day it's made.

VARIATIONS

- Add 2 tablespoons chopped fresh dill to the filling.
- Add 1 cup grated Gruyère cheese or ½ cup Parmesan to the filling.

COILED SUMMER SQUASH PITTA
Bosnia • Serves 8 to 10

Amra Slipac, who taught me how to make the potato *pitta,* told me that summer squash is also used for this dish. "The best is a type we grew in Bosnia, a round squash that isn't watery." Ronde de Nice fits this bill, as do other firm summer squash. I recommend salting the squash first, to draw out water so that it doesn't sweat too much into the phyllo.

> 2½ to 2¾ pounds firm summer squash, such as Ronde de Nice or pattypan
>
> 1 medium onion, cut into small dice
>
> Salt
>
> 2 plump garlic cloves, minced
>
> ¼ cup finely chopped fresh flat-leaf parsley, dill, or mint, or a combination
>
> Freshly ground pepper
>
> ¾ cup crumbled feta or grated kashkaval
>
> 1 pound phyllo dough
>
> Extra virgin olive oil for brushing

1. Cut the squash into very small dice, about ¼ inch. Toss in a colander with the onions and a generous amount of salt, about 1 tablespoon, and drain over a bowl for 1 hour.

2. Working in batches, wrap the squash and onion in a towel and squeeze to press out water. Transfer to a bowl.

3. Heat the oven to 375°F. Spray a 12-inch tart pan or cake pan with cooking spray and line with parchment. Spray the parchment. Toss the zucchini and onion with the garlic, herbs, salt and pepper, and the cheese.

4. Place a sheet of phyllo horizontally on your work surface (with the long edge closest to you). Brush lightly with olive oil and top with another piece of phyllo dough. Fold in half horizontally, with the folded edge at the bottom. Brush with a little more oil, then, leaving a 2-inch border on the bottom and sides, and a wider border on the top, spread ½ cup of the filling along the length of the phyllo. Fold the ends up over the filling, then fold the bottom edge over and carefully roll up into a cylinder about 1 inch thick. Place seam side down along the edge of the pan. Continue to wrap the filling and coil the ropes into the pan, starting each cylinder where the last one left off, until the entire pan is filled. If there is still filling and phyllo, start another, smaller coil in another pan, or make a little pie.

5. When the pie is assembled, brush the top with olive oil. Bake on the middle rack for 45 to 50 minutes, until nicely browned. Cool on a rack for at least 10 minutes before serving. You can serve this hot or warm. To serve, lift out pieces of the coil for each person.

ADVANCE PREPARATION: This pie should be baked once it's assembled so that the dough doesn't become too soggy. But you can prepare the squash and onion through Step 2 a day ahead and keep in the refrigerator.

LEFTOVERS: Like the Potato Pitta (page 244), this also keeps well for a few days once baked, and can easily be recrisped in a low oven (250° to 300°F) for 10 to 20 minutes. Again, Amra probably wouldn't agree with me, since she wants you to eat it all the day it's made.

EGGPLANT AND TOMATO GRATIN
(Bohemienne Gratinée)

France • **Serves 4**

This is like a Provençal version of eggplant Parmesan, but the eggplant and tomatoes are cooked together until they meld into a confit. In Provence, anchovies season the mixture, but you can omit them and obtain a truly delicious mixture with pure summer vegetable flavors.

> 2 pounds (2 large or 3 medium) eggplants
>
> Salt
>
> 3 tablespoons extra virgin olive oil
>
> 2 medium onions, thinly sliced
>
> 3 to 4 large garlic cloves (to taste), minced or put through a press

> 3 pounds ripe tomatoes, peeled, seeded, and chopped
>
> ⅛ teaspoon sugar
>
> 1 teaspoon fresh thyme leaves (or ½ teaspoon dried)
>
> Freshly ground pepper
>
> 2 tablespoons slivered fresh basil leaves
>
> 1 heaped tablespoon unbleached all-purpose flour
>
> 2 large eggs, beaten
>
> ¾ cup freshly grated Parmesan
>
> 2 tablespoons bread crumbs

1. Slice the eggplant about ⅓ inch thick and sprinkle with a generous amount of salt. Let sit for 30 minutes. Heat the oven to 500°F.

2. Blot the eggplant slices dry and cut them into dice. Toss with 1 tablespoon of the olive oil and place in a baking pan or on a baking sheet. Bake for 10 to 15 minutes, tossing every 5 minutes, until just about soft and beginning to brown.

3. Heat 1 tablespoon oil in a large, heavy nonstick skillet over medium heat and add the onions. Cook, stirring, until tender, about 5 minutes. Add the garlic and stir for another minute, until the garlic begins to color and smell fragrant. Stir in the eggplant, tomatoes, sugar, thyme, salt, and pepper. Reduce the heat to low, cover, and cook, stirring from time to time, for 1 to 1½ hours, until the mixture has cooked down to a thick, fragrant mixture. Taste and adjust seasonings.

4. Oil a 2-quart gratin dish and turn the oven down to 400°F. Stir the basil, flour, eggs, and ½ cup of the Parmesan into the eggplant mixture, then scrape into the gratin dish and top with the remaining Parmesan and the bread crumbs. Drizzle on the remaining 1 tablespoon oil. Bake for 20 to 30 minutes, until the top browns and the mixture is bubbling.

ADVANCE PREPARATION: You can make the dish through Step 3 up to 3 days ahead.

The Aroma Café

May 30, 2006
Los Angeles

In a little strip mall on the west side of Los Angeles sits the unassuming Aroma Café. From the outside it appears to be like many small coffee shops, but go around any time after 11 a.m. and you might feel displaced, like you'd been picked up and put down in the Balkans. In fact, the people you hear speaking Serbo-Croatian, enjoying their moment of relaxation during the day as Europeans do and Americans only imagine, are the ones who are displaced. They are from the republics of the former Yugoslavia—Bosnia and Herzegovina, Croatia, and Serbia. It seems so unlikely in today's unfriendly political climate, but during the 1990s, when their countries were being ripped apart by civil wars, they were offered visas and green cards, and ultimately citizenship, in the United States. Many were in mixed marriages, and their lives were truly imperiled.

Among the people in this group were the Slipacs, from Bagna Luka in Bosnia. Adem Slipac, an economist, came with his wife, Amra, their parents, and his young daughter, Senita, in 1992. They settled in Los Angeles, and while Adem was trying to figure out how a Bosnian economist with little English could find work in California, the women in the family, terrific cooks all, busied themselves making regional food and selling it to their homesick compatriots.

Word got around. Adem was soon looking for a space for a café, which he found just south of Pico Boulevard, not far from the family's home. When the Aroma Café opened, they had a ready-made clientele.

I knew nothing about the Aroma Café until a Sunday in December when I went with my son to his friend Marko's birthday party. Marko's parents are Croatian. His mother, Mira Furlan, is an actress, and had been as celebrated in Yugoslavia as any of our stars are here. But when war broke out between Serbia and Croatia, death threats replaced stellar reviews. Mira and her husband, Goran Gajic, a director, fled the country. They went to London, then to New York, and eventually they got work in Hollywood.

In their house, a kid's birthday party is just an excuse to have a lavish buffet for adults, and on their beautiful table were a number of exquisite pies made with homemade strudel dough, which was wrapped around the filling and coiled into beautiful rounds. Some were filled with spinach and cheese, others with cheese only. Then there was the one I liked the best, a savory pie unlike any I'd ever eaten in the Mediterranean. It was filled with potatoes, finely diced, seasoned only with onion, salt, and lots of pepper. There was something about the texture and the simplicity of the flavors, and the originality of it. I had to find out where this came from.

That's when I found out about the Aroma Café. Everybody at the party knew the place; it was their hangout. I went the next day, had Greek salad and a squash pitta *for lunch, and I have been going back ever since. When I go with Mira and Goran it's truly wonderful, because they know exactly what to order and we chat with Adam and Amra. After one of those dinners I asked if I could come and work with Amra, and learn from her how to make the potato* pitta. *They said any Monday or Tuesday afternoon would be fine.*

I have spent a fair amount of time in restaurant kitchens, and I have never been in one as clean and quiet as Amra's. I show up on a warm Tuesday in May, and Amra is ready for me in the kitchen. She is there with her mother, who sits in a chair with a large bowl into which she dices apples for strudel. The large worktable where Amra makes strudel dough (and everything else) is ready for us.

Amra gives me a bowl with 10 peeled potatoes and tells me to cut them into very small dice, about ¼ inch square. The diced potatoes go into a bowl of cold water, which is set aside while she pulls the strudel dough.

Watching people who grew up with pulling strudel dough is a wonder. They make it look so easy. Amra takes her pound of dough and places it on the cloth-covered table. She quietly rolls out the dough, rolling the long dowel along the dough, then rolling the dough up around the dowel and unrolling it, stretching it as she rolls. Before long the dough is a huge ⅛-inch-thick oval covering most of the table. She oils the surface of the dough, and lets it rest while she prepares the filling.

Amra drains the potatoes in a colander, then places the colander in a bowl. The mixing is done right in the colander, to allow the potatoes to continue to weep. With her hands, she mixes about 1½ chopped onions in with the 10 diced potatoes, then adds a generous amount of salt and black pepper. That's it.

Now back to the dough. She pulls the strudel dough, like I've learned to do with pastry chef Sherry Yard, until it is gossamer and thin, extending 6 to 8 inches over the edges of the table.

The potato filling is placed in two 2-inch-wide rows down each side, just in from the edges of the table. There is a space down the middle. Now, using the actual tablecloth to guide the dough, Amra lifts the dough at the edges and encloses the potato filling. She folds the ends in over the filling, then gently rolls up the strudel, turning the log over using the cloth, then rolling toward the center. She does the same on the other side. Once both sides meet in the center, she cuts down the middle, for two long ropes.

Amra heats the oven to 425°F and takes down a 15-inch round pan. She oils it generously. On the table, she begins to coil her potato strudel. She then transfers the beginning of this coil to the oiled pan and turns the pan while she feeds the strudel into it. The next piece begins where the first half left off, and eventually the coil fills the pan. The entire pie is brushed with oil, and it goes into the oven on the lower shelf. After 20 minutes Amra moves the pie to the center rack. In all, it will take about an hour before the coil is golden brown. It is unbelievable when it emerges from the oven, a fragrant golden coil with soft, moist potatoes inside.

It's so simple. The filling is just four ingredients: potatoes, onions, salt, pepper—nothing cooked before, baked to perfection. "We usually drink kefir (iced yogurt) with this," says Amra, "and we'll have a salad."

All this time Amra's mother has been quietly making dessert strudel, first the apple strudels, then four big cherry strudels. She drains jars of Morello cherries from Trader Joe's over a bowl. Meanwhile, she takes sheets of phyllo and extends them by echeloning about five layers, coating every two layers with oil. Then she distributes the cherries over the dough, sprinkles them with sugar and bread crumbs, folds the ends over, and rolls up the logs. This she bakes until golden.

Amra also makes a cheese pie that has been ordered for pick-up. With her hands, she mixes up the filling. About a pound of Bulgarian feta, which she likes for the tartness, two eggs, and a little milk to moisten. That's it.

The entire time that I've been in this calm kitchen I've been eyeing a tiered cooling rack filled with small, round flat breads set on wooden boards. I've had Amra's bread, and it is fantastic, with a crisp crust and a moist, spongy interior. They are the size of pitas, but not pocketed, and I'm eager to learn these as well. The trick, Amra tells me, is a very moist dough and a hot oven. I'll try this at home, but meanwhile I elicit a promise from her to call me the next time she's mixing dough. You will find the recipe for Amra's bread on page 47.

EGGPLANT PARMESAN

Italy • Serves 4 generously

This classic gratin is often heavy and oily, but it needn't be. I think of it as a summer dish, to make when eggplants and fresh tomatoes are at their height. However, since eggplants are available year-round in supermarkets and you can make a perfectly good tomato sauce with canned tomatoes, you can make it at any time of year. I like to use my panini grill to cook the eggplant slices. You can get by with a minimum of oil, and you get a lot of rich flavor with little effort.

Salt

2 pounds (about 2 large) eggplants, sliced into rounds about ⅓ inch thick

4 to 5 tablespoons extra virgin olive oil (as needed)

2 to 3 large garlic cloves (to taste), minced or put through a press

3 pounds tomatoes, quartered; or 2 cans (28 ounces each) tomatoes, drained of all but about ½ cup of the juice

⅛ teaspoon sugar

2 to 3 tablespoons slivered fresh basil leaves (to taste)

Freshly ground pepper

8 ounces fresh mozzarella, sliced

½ cup freshly grated Parmesan

¼ cup bread crumbs

1. Salt the eggplant slices generously and let stand for about 30 minutes.

2. Heat 1 tablespoon of the olive oil in a large, heavy nonstick skillet over medium heat and add the garlic. When the garlic is fragrant and just beginning to color, after about 30 seconds, add the tomatoes, sugar, and salt (about ¾ teaspoon). Cook, stirring often, for 20 to 25 minutes, until the tomatoes are cooked down and fragrant. Put through a food mill fitted with the medium blade. Stir in the basil and add pepper, a few grinds of the mill. Taste and adjust seasonings.

BREAD CRUMBS

I like to keep bread crumbs on hand in the freezer. To that end, I sometimes go out and buy a loaf of white bread, just to blend up in my food processor. I let the bread dry for a day, then break it up into pieces and pulse it in the food processor. I store the crumbs in a plastic bag or container in the freezer so that I always have them. I also make bread crumbs when I have a baguette or another loaf on hand that's going stale. Rarely do I distinguish between dry and fresh bread crumbs in a recipe.

3. Heat the oven to 500°F or heat a panini grill. Blot the eggplant slices dry and place on a baking sheet. Brush both sides of the eggplant slices with some of the olive oil. Bake in the oven until browned on the bottom and tender, 10 to 15 minutes, or grill in batches in the panini grill, 2 to 3 minutes per batch.

4. Turn down or heat the oven to 375°F. Oil a 2-quart gratin dish. Spoon a third of the tomato sauce over the bottom of the baking dish. Layer half the eggplant slices over the tomato sauce. Top with the mozzarella and spoon on another third of the tomato sauce. Sprinkle on half the Parmesan. Add the remaining eggplant in a layer, top with the remaining tomato sauce, and sprinkle on the remaining Parmesan. Sprinkle bread crumbs over the top and drizzle on 1 tablespoon olive oil. Bake for 30 minutes, until bubbling and browned on the top.

ADVANCE PREPARATION: The tomato sauce will keep in the refrigerator for 3 days, and freezes well for a couple of months. The gratin can be assembled a day or two ahead of time and baked just before serving. It also reheats well, if you need to bake it a few hours ahead.

LEFTOVERS: If you want to do something new with the leftovers, you could fill an omelet with spoonfuls of the gratin. It will be quite marvelous, almost decadent.

PROVENÇAL FENNEL AND TOMATO GRATIN

France • Serves 6

The longer you cook fennel, the sweeter it gets. For this gratin, you parboil the fennel first, then toss it with tomatoes and onions, and bake for an hour. What you get is a sweet and savory combination that is meltingly tender and tastes utterly Provençal (or, I might add, Italian). It's as good served at room temperature as it is right from the oven.

Salt

3 large or 6 small fennel bulbs (3 pounds), trimmed and quartered

Freshly ground pepper

2 pounds tomatoes

2 tablespoons extra virgin olive oil

1 onion, sliced

3 garlic cloves, minced

Sugar

2 teaspoons fresh thyme (or 1 teaspoon dried)

1 bay leaf

⅓ cup grated Gruyère cheese, or a mixture of Gruyère and Parmesan

1. Heat the oven to 375°F. Oil a 2- or 3-quart gratin dish. Bring a large pot of generously salted water to a boil and add the fennel. Boil for 5 minutes, until easily pierced with a knife. Transfer with a spider or slotted spoon to a bowl of cold water and cool for about 5 minutes. Drain and pat dry. Core the fennel quarters and slice crosswise about ¼ inch thick. Transfer to a large bowl and season to taste with salt and pepper.

2. Add the tomatoes to the boiling water, boil for 30 seconds, and transfer to a bowl of cold water. Drain and peel. Cut the tomatoes in half across the equator and squeeze out the seeds. Slice 2 of the tomatoes into rounds and chop the rest.

3. Heat 1 tablespoon of the olive oil in a large, heavy skillet over medium heat and add the onion. Cook, stirring, until tender, about 5 minutes. Add the garlic and cook, stirring, until fragrant, 30 seconds to 1 minute. Add the chopped tomatoes, season with salt, pepper, and a pinch of sugar, and cook, stirring occasionally, until the tomatoes have cooked down slightly and smell very fragrant, about 10 minutes. Toss with the fennel. Stir in the thyme and bay leaf. Taste and adjust salt and pepper.

4. Scrape the fennel and tomato mixture into the gratin dish. Top with the sliced tomatoes. Sprinkle the tomatoes with salt and pepper and a very small pinch of sugar. Bake the gratin for 45 minutes, until just beginning to brown.

5. Sprinkle the grated cheese over the top of the gratin in an even layer. Drizzle on the remaining 1 tablespoon olive oil. Bake an additional 15 minutes, until the top is beginning to brown. Serve hot, warm, or at room temperature.

ADVANCE PREPARATION: You can make this recipe through Step 4 up to a day ahead. Or you can make it through Step 5 several hours before serving and either reheat or serve warm or at room temperature. To reheat, place in a 325°F oven for 15 minutes.

POTATO AND MUSHROOM GRATIN
France • **Serves 6**

Fall in Provence and Italy means wild mushrooms. I've always had a weakness for potatoes and mushrooms in the same pot, and here they bake together into the most savory of gratins. The potatoes become infused with that earthy mushroom flavor, all the more so if you use wild ones, but with the dried porcini, even plain white mushrooms will produce a memorable dish. The robust flavors of this gratin make this taste and seem richer than it is.

1 ounce dried porcini mushrooms (about 1 cup)

2 cups boiling water

1 pound fresh mushrooms, preferably wild mushrooms such as oyster mushrooms, shiitake, or morels, cleaned, stems trimmed (remove stems if using shiitake), and thinly sliced

Salt

2 tablespoons extra virgin olive oil

3 large garlic cloves, minced or put through a press

2 teaspoons fresh thyme (or 1 teaspoon dried)

2 teaspoons chopped fresh sage (optional)

¼ cup dry white wine or red wine

Freshly ground pepper

2½ pounds russet or Yukon gold potatoes, peeled and thinly sliced

½ cup grated Gruyère cheese

¼ cup freshly grated Parmesan

2 cups milk

1. Place the dried mushrooms in a bowl or Pyrex measuring cup and pour on the boiling water. Let sit for 30 minutes. Drain through a cheesecloth-lined strainer over a bowl and squeeze the mushrooms over the strainer. Rinse the mushrooms thoroughly to remove the grit, squeeze dry, and chop coarsely. Set aside. Measure out 1 cup of the soaking liquid and set aside.

2. Heat a large nonstick skillet over medium-high heat and add the fresh mushrooms. Sprinkle with

salt and cook, stirring, until they begin to release liquid, 3 to 5 minutes. Cook in their own juices, stirring often, for 5 minutes, until just about tender. Turn the heat to high to cook off the juices in the pan, then turn it back down to medium and add the soaked dried mushrooms, olive oil, garlic, thyme, and sage. Continue to cook for another minute or two, until the mixture is fragrant. Add the wine and cook until the liquid in the pan has evaporated. Remove from the heat. Season with additional salt if desired, and pepper.

3. Heat the oven to 350°F. Butter a 3-quart baking dish or gratin dish, or rub with olive oil, and place on a half-sheet pan. Toss the potatoes and mushrooms together in a large bowl. Season with salt and pepper. Combine the Gruyère and Parmesan and add half to the bowl. Toss with the potato mixture and transfer to the baking dish. Combine the mushroom soaking liquid and the milk. Season with 1 teaspoon salt (more or less to taste) and grind in some pepper. Pour over the potatoes. Bake for 1 hour. Sprinkle the remaining cheese over the top and bake for another 30 to 45 minutes, until the top is nicely browned. Let sit for 10 minutes before serving.

ADVANCE PREPARATION: The mushrooms can be cooked several hours or even a day or two ahead. Refrigerate if holding for more than a couple of hours. The gratin is terrific reheated the next day; it will keep in the refrigerator for 3 or 4 days.

LEFTOVERS: If you have a small amount left over and want to stretch it into another meal, stir the leftover gratin into beaten eggs and make a delicious frittata (page 176).

PROVENÇAL SUMMER POTATO GRATIN
France • **Serves 4 to 6**

This potato gratin with onions and tomatoes is a nice departure from the classic creamy French *gratin dauphinois*.

2 garlic cloves

Extra virgin olive oil

2¼ pounds medium tomatoes, peeled

2 pounds russet or Yukon gold potatoes, scrubbed and sliced about ¼ inch thick

Salt and freshly ground pepper

2 teaspoons fresh thyme (or 1 teaspoon dried)

1 pound onions (2 medium), sliced about ¼ inch thick

1 bay leaf

1½ cups boiling water

12 imported black olives, pitted

1. Heat the oven to 375°F. Cut 1 of the garlic cloves in half and rub a 3-quart gratin or baking dish with the cut sides. Mince the remaining garlic and set aside. Oil the gratin dish with olive oil.

2. Slice 2 of the tomatoes into thin rounds and peel and chop the rest. Arrange half of the potato slices in the gratin dish, slightly overlapping the slices, and season generously with salt and pepper. Sprinkle on half of the thyme. Top with half of the onions. Season the onions and lay the bay leaf on top. Toss the chopped tomatoes and minced garlic together with salt and pepper to taste, and spoon over the onions. Repeat the layers of potatoes, thyme, and onions and top with the sliced tomatoes. Be sure to season each layer generously.

3. Season the boiling water with ½ teaspoon salt and ¼ teaspoon pepper and pour over the vegetables. Dot the top with olives and cover with foil. Bake for 45 minutes. Uncover and bake another 30 minutes, until most of the liquid has been absorbed by the potatoes and the gratin is lightly browned around the edges. Serve hot or warm.

ADVANCE PREPARATION: The gratin can be assembled several hours before you bake it.

VARIATIONS

• After baking for 1 hour, sprinkle ½ cup grated Gruyère, or a mixture of Gruyère and Parmesan, over the gratin. Bake uncovered until the cheese is bubbling and beginning to brown.

• Mix ½ cup tapenade into the tomatoes.

PROVENÇAL GREENS GRATIN
France • **Serves 4 to 6**

I start making this in December, when the greens abound in our Los Angeles farmers' markets. In Provence, it is more of a year-round dish because chard is a year-round green. The rice is a marvelous binder, adding texture and substance. If you're using chard, chop up the stems and add them to the onions. I usually use a mixture of greens, like the generous tops of the beets that I buy at the farmers' markets combined with Swiss chard.

Salt

2 generous bunches greens, stemmed (chop and reserve chard stems)

2 tablespoons extra virgin olive oil

1 medium onion, chopped

2 large garlic cloves, minced

3 large eggs

½ cup milk

Freshly ground pepper

½ cup tightly packed grated Gruyère cheese

½ cup long-grain or medium-grain rice, cooked (see Note)

½ cup chopped fresh flat-leaf parsley

2 tablespoons bread crumbs

Note: *To cook the rice, combine with 1 cup water and ¼ teaspoon salt in a saucepan. Bring to a boil, reduce the heat, cover, and simmer for 12 to 15 minutes, until all of the water has been absorbed. Remove from the heat, uncover, and place a clean dish towel over the top of the saucepan. Return the lid to the pan and let sit undisturbed for 10 minutes.*

1. Bring a large pot of water to a boil. Add 1 tablespoon salt and the greens. Blanch for 1 to 2 minutes, until just tender. Using a slotted spoon, transfer to a bowl of cold water, then drain and squeeze out excess water. Chop coarsely and set aside.

2. Heat the oven to 375°F. Oil a 2-quart gratin dish.

3. Heat 1 tablespoon of the olive oil in a large, heavy nonstick skillet over medium heat. Add the onion and cook, stirring often, until just about tender, 3 to 5 minutes. If using chard, add the chopped stems to the onion and cook, stirring, for 3 to 5 minutes, until just tender. Stir in the garlic and cook, stirring, for a minute or so, until fragrant. Add the chopped greens and stir everything together, then remove from the heat.

4. In a large bowl, beat the eggs and add the milk, ½ teaspoon salt, pepper to taste, and the cheese. Stir in the rice, parsley, and greens. Combine thoroughly and scrape into the baking dish. Sprinkle the bread crumbs over the top and drizzle on the remaining 1 tablespoon oil.

5. Bake for 30 to 40 minutes, until the top is lightly browned and the mixture is sizzling. Serve hot, warm, or at room temperature.

ADVANCE PREPARATION: This is a great keeper. You can do the dish in stages, preparing the greens up to 3 days ahead and keeping them in a covered bowl in the refrigerator. The cooked rice will also keep for 3 days. The gratin can be made a day ahead and reheated in a low oven for about 20 minutes.

LEFTOVERS: The cold gratin slices up beautifully and makes a great lunch.

PROVENÇAL KALE AND CABBAGE GRATIN

France • Serves 6

Gratins, or *tians,* as they're called in Provence (*tian* refers to the baking dish they're made in), were a revelation to me when I lived in France. Because they're bound with rice and eggs, they are sturdy enough to slice, and they can grace a starter plate as well as serve as the main attraction. They're also good to go, in a lunchbox. In Provence they're made with whatever vegetables are in season. This, then, would be a winter *tian.*

> 3 tablespoons extra virgin olive oil
> 1 medium onion, finely chopped
> 2 large garlic cloves, minced or put through a press
> 1 pound kale, preferably black kale (*cavolo nero*), leaves stripped from the stems and slivered
> Salt
> 1 small (1 pound) cabbage, either Savoy or green, quartered, cored, and slivered
> 6 leaves fresh sage, chopped
> Freshly ground pepper
> 2 large eggs
> ½ cup chopped fresh flat-leaf parsley
> ½ cup rice, preferably a short-grain rice like Arborio, cooked (see page 235)
> ½ cup grated Gruyère cheese
> ¼ cup freshly grated Parmesan
> 2 tablespoons bread crumbs

1. Heat the oven to 375°F. Oil a 2-quart gratin.

2. Heat 2 tablespoons of the olive oil in a large, heavy nonstick skillet over medium heat and add the onion. Cook, stirring often, until tender and translucent, about 5 minutes. Stir in the garlic and cook for another minute, until fragrant, then stir in the kale and about ½ teaspoon salt. Cook the kale in the liquid left on the leaves after washing until it begins to wilt. Stir often, and when most of the kale has wilted, add the cabbage, sage, and another ½ teaspoon salt. Cook, stirring, for 10 minutes, until the vegetables are wilted and fragrant but still have some texture. Add pepper, taste, and adjust salt.

3. Beat the eggs in a bowl and add the cooked vegetables, parsley, rice, and cheeses. Stir together well and scrape into the baking dish. Sprinkle the bread crumbs over the top and drizzle on the remaining 1 tablespoon olive oil. Bake for 30 to 40 minutes, until firm and browned on the top. Serve hot or warm.

ADVANCE PREPARATION: The entire dish can be made a day ahead and reheated. Or prepare the vegetables through Step 2 a day ahead and assemble the gratin the next day. It will keep for 4 or 5 days in the refrigerator.

CABBAGE, KALE, AND POTATO GRATIN
Serves 4 to 6

Cabbage, kale, and potatoes combine beautifully together in this comforting winter gratin. You won't have trouble pleasing everybody in the family with this; serve it as a main dish or side dish.

¾ pound starchy potatoes, such as russets or Yukon golds, sliced

Salt

1 pound cabbage, quartered, cored, and cut into ribbons

1 pound kale, stemmed

2 tablespoons extra virgin olive oil or butter, or 1 tablespoon each

2 garlic cloves, minced or put through a press

2 teaspoons fresh thyme (or 1 teaspoon crumbled dried)

Freshly ground pepper

¾ cup grated Gruyère cheese

3 large eggs

1½ cups milk

1. Heat the oven to 375°F. Butter or oil a 3-quart gratin dish.

2. Steam the potatoes for 5 to 10 minutes, until tender, and set aside.

3. Bring a large pot of water to a boil, then add 1 tablespoon salt and the cabbage. Boil for 3 minutes, until the cabbage is just tender, and transfer with a spider or slotted spoon to a bowl of cold water. Drain and set aside.

4. Bring the water back to a boil and add the kale. Cook for about 4 minutes, until tender, and transfer to a bowl of cold water. Drain, squeeze out water, and cut into strips.

5. Heat the oil in a large, heavy nonstick skillet over medium heat and add the garlic. Cook for about a minute, just until fragrant and beginning to change color. Stir in the cabbage, kale, and thyme. Cook, stirring, until coated with oil and fragrant. Stir in the potatoes and season the mixture generously with salt and pepper. Remove from the heat and stir in ½ cup of the cheese. Scrape into the gratin dish.

6. Beat together the eggs and milk. Add ½ teaspoon salt, some pepper, and the remaining ¼ cup cheese. Stir together and pour over the potato mixture. Bake for 40 minutes, until nicely browned. Serve hot or warm.

ADVANCE PREPARATION: The cabbage and kale can be blanched up to 3 days ahead and kept in a covered bowl in the refrigerator.

LEFTOVERS: The gratin will be delicious for up to 3 days. Reheat in a microwave or a low oven.

PROVENÇAL SUMMER SQUASH, RED PEPPER, AND TOMATO GRATIN
France • Serves 4 to 6

This gorgeous summer gratin, like many Provençal *tians,* includes rice as a binder. Any type of rice will do here, as will any type of green or yellow summer squash. It's good cold and makes a great lunch, main dish, or side dish.

3 tablespoons extra virgin olive oil

1 large or 2 small red onions, chopped

1 large red bell pepper, cut into ¼-inch dice

3 large garlic cloves, minced or put through a press

About 1¼ pounds summer squash, cut into ½-inch dice (4 cups)

Salt and freshly ground pepper

2 teaspoons fresh thyme (or 1 teaspoon crumbled dried)

½ cup rice, cooked

3 large eggs

½ cup milk (whole or low-fat)

¾ cup grated Gruyère cheese

¾ pound tomatoes, sliced

¼ cup bread crumbs

1. Heat the oven to 375°F. Oil a 2- to 2½-quart gratin. ▶

2. Heat 2 tablespoons of the olive oil in a large, heavy nonstick skillet over medium heat. Add the onion and cook, stirring often, until translucent, about 5 minutes. Add the bell pepper and continue to cook, stirring, until the pepper begins to soften, 3 to 5 minutes. Add the garlic, stir for about 30 seconds, until it begins to smell fragrant, and stir in the squash. Cook, stirring often, until the squash is translucent but not mushy, 5 to 10 minutes. Season with salt and pepper. Stir in the thyme and rice, and remove from the heat.

3. Beat the eggs in a large bowl. Beat in the milk, cheese, and ½ teaspoon salt. Stir in the cooked vegetables and combine well. Scrape into the gratin dish.

4. Cover the top of the gratin with the tomatoes in a single layer. Sprinkle the bread crumbs over the top. Drizzle on the remaining 1 tablespoon olive oil. Bake for 45 minutes, or until the top is browned and the gratin is sizzling. Allow to sit for at least 10 minutes before serving. Serve hot, warm, or at room temperature.

ADVANCE PREPARATION: The vegetables can be cooked through Step 2 several hours before you assemble the gratin. They can be held in the pan on top of the stove or refrigerated overnight. The finished gratin keeps well, for 3 or 4 days.

SUMMER SQUASH GRATIN
France • Serves 4 to 6

One August, vacationing at my friend Christine's house in Provence, I lugged a 3-foot-long dark green squash from the caretaker's garden to the house, wondering what could be done with it. "This is not an overgrown zucchini," Patricia, the caretaker's wife explained. "This is an heirloom squash with tiny seeds and flesh that's somewhere between that of a winter squash and a summer squash." It was extraordinary, very sweet, not at all watery, and robust. Here in the States we can sometimes get Ronde de Nice at farmers' markets. This round, light green summer squash has a texture that somewhat resembles the caretaker's 3-foot-long crooknecks. Use them if you find them, otherwise use young, firm zucchini and yellow squash. This is the simplest of gratins, and appeals to kids and grown-ups equally.

> 2 tablespoons extra virgin olive oil
>
> 1 medium onion, chopped
>
> 2 garlic cloves, minced
>
> 2 pounds summer squash (I recommend a mixture of green and yellow), sliced
>
> Salt and freshly ground pepper
>
> 2 tablespoons chopped fresh flat-leaf parsley
>
> 4 large eggs
>
> ½ cup milk (whole or low-fat)
>
> ¾ cup grated Gruyère cheese, or a mixture of Gruyère and Parmesan

1. Heat the oven to 375°F. Oil a 2-quart baking dish or gratin with olive oil.

2. Heat the olive oil in a large, heavy skillet over medium heat. Add the onion and cook, stirring often, until tender and translucent, 3 to 5 minutes. Stir in the garlic and cook, stirring, until fragrant, about a minute. Add the squash and turn the heat up slightly. Sauté the squash, stirring often or flipping in the pan, until translucent and just tender. Season to taste with salt and pepper and continue to cook for another minute or two. Stir in the parsley and remove from the heat.

3. Beat the eggs in a large bowl and add the milk. Add ½ teaspoon salt and some freshly ground pepper, then stir in the cooked squash mixture along with the cheese. Stir everything together well, then scrape into the baking dish. Bake for 35 to 40 minutes, until the gratin has set and the top has browned. Serve hot or warm.

ADVANCE PREPARATION: You can prepare the squash, through Step 2 several hours or even a day before you assemble the gratin. The baked gratin will hold well for a few hours. Reheat in a low oven if desired.

PURPLE CAULIFLOWER GRATIN
Italy • Serves 4 to 6

How can you resist a purple cauliflower? This is a simple gratin, the blanched cauliflower tossed with olive oil, seasoned with garlic, sprinkled with bread crumbs and cheese, and baked. In Puglia, where this vegetable is everywhere, that cheese would be Pecorino Romano; in my house I'll use that, or Parmesan, or (and this makes the dish more French than Italian) Gruyère, or a combination.

Salt

1 generous head purple (or white) cauliflower (1½ to 2 pounds), broken into florets

2 tablespoons extra virgin olive oil

2 garlic cloves, minced

2 tablespoons minced fresh flat-leaf parsley

Freshly ground pepper

¼ cup bread crumbs

½ cup freshly grated Pecorino Romano or Parmesan, or a combination

1. Heat the oven to 400°F. Oil a 2-quart baking dish or gratin dish. Bring a large pot of water to a boil. Add a tablespoon of salt and drop in the cauliflower. Boil for 5 minutes. Transfer the cauliflower to a bowl of cold water, let sit for a couple of minutes, then drain well.

2. Heat 1 tablespoon of the olive oil in a large, heavy skillet over medium heat and add the garlic. Cook, stirring, for about 30 seconds, until fragrant, and add the cauliflower and parsley. Stir together for about a minute and season generously with salt and pepper. Remove from the heat.

3. Mix together the remaining 1 tablespoon olive oil, bread crumbs, and cheese. Toss with the cauliflower, stirring well to coat, then transfer to the baking dish, scraping all of the bread crumbs over the cauliflower. Bake for 20 to 25 minutes, until the cheese is nicely browned. Serve hot or warm.

ADVANCE PREPARATION: The recipe can be prepared through Step 2 hours before assembling the gratin. Hold on top of the stove or in the refrigerator.

PROVENÇAL SWISS CHARD GRATIN
France • Serves 6

When we make dishes with chard, the stalks are so often cast away. But they're welcome in this Provençal gratin, whose many textures are only enhanced by the chopped stems.

1½ to 2 pounds Swiss chard

Salt

3 tablespoons extra virgin olive oil

1 medium onion, minced

3 large garlic cloves, minced or put through a press

Freshly ground pepper

3 large eggs

¾ cup grated Gruyère cheese

½ cup chopped fresh flat-leaf parsley

½ cup medium-grain or Arborio rice, cooked (see page 235)

1 teaspoon fresh thyme (or ½ teaspoon dried)

2 tablespoons bread crumbs

1. Bring a large pot of water to a boil while you clean the chard. Strip the leaves from the stalks, and hold on to the stalks. Wash the leaves and stalks in several rinses of water. When the water comes to a boil, add 1 tablespoon salt and the chard leaves. Blanch for about 2 minutes, just until tender. Using a deep-fry skimmer or slotted spoon, transfer to a bowl of cold water, then drain. Squeeze out water and chop medium-fine. You should have about 2 heaped cups (if you have more, that's fine). Trim both ends off the chard stalks, then dice.

2. Heat the oven to 375°F. Brush a 2- or 2½-quart baking or gratin dish with olive oil.

3. Heat 2 tablespoons of the oil in a large, heavy nonstick skillet over medium heat and add the onion. Cook, stirring, until tender, about 5 minutes. Add the diced chard stalks and a little salt and cook, stirring often, for 5 to 8 minutes, until the stalks are just tender. Add the garlic, stir together for a minute or so, until the garlic is fragrant, and stir in the chard leaves. Stir together for

30 seconds to a minute, just to blend the mixture and coat the leaves with oil. Season with salt and pepper, and remove from the heat.

4. Beat the eggs in a bowl. Stir in the chard, cheese, parsley, rice, and thyme. Stir together, taste, and add more salt and pepper if desired. Transfer to the baking dish. Sprinkle the bread crumbs over the top and drizzle on the remaining 1 tablespoon oil. Bake for 40 to 45 minutes, until firm and browned on the top. Cool for at least 10 minutes before serving. You can serve this warm or at room temperature.

ADVANCE PREPARATION: The blanched chard will keep for 3 or 4 days in the refrigerator in a covered bowl, and can be frozen in a freezer bag for a few months. The recipe can be prepared through Step 3 up to 2 days ahead. It can be completed several hours or even a day ahead and reheated for about 15 minutes in a 325°F oven, or served at room temperature.

LEFTOVERS: Any leftovers will keep for 3 or 4 days in the refrigerator.

VARIATION

Cook the mixture of chard leaves, onions, and chard stalks through Step 3. Rather than making a gratin, serve the greens as a side dish, or toss with pasta, olive oil, and Parmesan or Pecorino Romano for a wonderful main dish.

BALKAN-STYLE MOUSSAKA
The Balkans • Serves 6

You may think you don't like this Greek eggplant dish because cooks can be heavy-handed with it. Traditionally, the moussaka sauce contains beef or lamb, but during the Greek Orthodox fasting periods, such as Lent, the sauce is made without it. This tomato sauce, spiced with a little cinnamon, a pinch of allspice, and a few cloves, has complex, sweet and savory eastern Mediterranean flavors that you won't soon forget. The topping here is much lighter than the traditional Greek béchamel, which can be heavy, even gummy. Instead, it's a

light mixture of yogurt and eggs. You can spread the preparation of this dish over a couple of days, or put it together on a leisurely afternoon and bake it right before dinner.

FOR THE CASSEROLE

2 to 2½ pounds (2 large or 3 medium) eggplants

Salt

2 tablespoons extra virgin olive oil, plus additional for brushing

2 medium onions, chopped

2 large garlic cloves, minced or put through a press

2½ pounds tomatoes, peeled and chopped; or 3 cans (14 ounces each) tomatoes, with juice, chopped

1 heaped tablespoon tomato paste

½ teaspoon sweet paprika

Heaped ¼ teaspoon ground cinnamon

3 whole cloves

Pinch ground allspice (or 2 or 3 allspice berries, ground in a mortar and pestle)

½ teaspoon sugar

1 bay leaf

Salt and freshly ground pepper

½ cup chopped fresh flat-leaf parsley

FOR THE TOPPING

4 large eggs

1¼ cups plain yogurt

Salt and freshly ground pepper

Sweet paprika

½ cup freshly grated Parmesan, kefalotyri, or kashkaval cheese

1. *Make the casserole:* Slice the eggplants lengthwise about ⅓ inch thick. Salt the slices generously and place in a large bowl or colander for 30 minutes to 1 hour, the longer the better. Meanwhile, heat the oven to 450°F and oil baking sheets with olive oil.

2. Heat the olive oil in a large, heavy nonstick skillet over medium heat and add the onions. Cook,

stirring, until tender, about 5 minutes, and add the garlic. Cook, stirring, until fragrant, about a minute, and stir in the tomatoes, tomato paste, paprika, cinnamon, cloves, allspice, sugar, bay leaf, and salt. Bring to a simmer, reduce the heat to low, cover, and simmer for 20 to 30 minutes, stirring occasionally. The mixture should be thick and very fragrant. Stir in some pepper and remove from the heat. Taste and adjust salt. Discard the bay leaf, and the cloves if you can see them. When the mixture has cooled slightly, stir in the parsley.

3. Rinse the eggplant slices and pat dry with paper towels. Place on the oiled baking sheets and brush the tops with olive oil. Bake for 10 to 15 minutes, until lightly browned and cooked through. Transfer to a bowl. Turn the oven down to 350°F.

4. Oil a 3-quart baking dish or gratin dish. Make an even layer of half the eggplant over the bottom, pour on all of the tomato sauce, and spread evenly. Top with a layer of the remaining eggplant. Bake for 30 minutes.

5. *Make the topping:* Beat together the eggs and yogurt, season with salt (about ½ teaspoon), pepper, and a pinch of paprika, and pour over the eggplant. Sprinkle the cheese evenly over the top. Return to the oven and bake for another 25 to 30 minutes, until golden. Serve warm.

ADVANCE PREPARATION: The sauce can be made a couple of days ahead and kept in the refrigerator in a covered bowl. The assembled casserole, without the egg and yogurt topping, will keep for a couple of days in the refrigerator, or it can be frozen (without the topping). Bring to room temperature before baking.

LEFTOVERS: The moussaka will be good for 3 or 4 days. Reheat in a low oven or a microwave.

VARIATION

You can also cook the eggplant slices in a panini grill, following the directions in the Eggplant Parmesan recipe on page 250.

ZUCCHINI, POTATO, AND ARTICHOKE MOUSSAKA
Greece and the Balkans • Serves 6

A number of wonderful vegetarian dishes have evolved throughout Greece and the Balkans because there are many fasting days in the Greek Orthodox calendar, when no meat may be eaten. In this moussaka, layers of potato and zucchini slices stand in for eggplant.

FOR THE CASSEROLE

1½ pounds potatoes, such as Yukon golds

Salt

1¾ pounds zucchini

3 tablespoons extra virgin olive oil

2 medium onions, chopped

2 large garlic cloves, minced or put through a press

2 pounds tomatoes, peeled and chopped; or 1 can (28 ounces) tomatoes, with juice, chopped

1 heaped tablespoon tomato paste

½ teaspoon sweet paprika

Heaped ¼ teaspoon ground cinnamon

3 whole cloves

Pinch ground allspice (or 2 or 3 allspice berries, ground in a mortar and pestle)

½ teaspoon sugar

1 bay leaf

Salt and freshly ground pepper

½ cup chopped fresh flat-leaf parsley

1 can (15 ounces) artichoke hearts packed in water, drained and rinsed

FOR THE TOPPING

4 large eggs

1¼ cups plain yogurt

Salt and freshly ground pepper

Sweet paprika

½ cup freshly grated Parmesan, kefalotyri, or kashkaval cheese

1. *Make the casserole:* Heat the oven to 425°F. Oil baking sheets with olive oil. Slice the potatoes lengthwise in oval slices about ¼ inch thick. Place on the baking sheets, salt lightly, and bake for about 15 minutes, until they are just beginning to brown and can be easily pierced with a knife.

2. Slice the zucchini in lengthwise slices about ⅓ inch thick. Heat 2 tablespoons of the olive oil in a large nonstick skillet over medium-high heat and add the zucchini in a single layer (you will have to do this in batches). Cook for about 3 minutes, until lightly browned. Flip over and cook for another 3 minutes, until lightly browned. Transfer to a baking sheet lined with paper towels.

3. In the same skillet, heat the remaining 1 tablespoon olive oil over medium heat and add the onions. Cook, stirring, until tender, about 5 minutes, and add the garlic. Cook, stirring, until fragrant, about a minute, and stir in the tomatoes, tomato paste, paprika, cinnamon, cloves, allspice, sugar, bay leaf, and salt. Bring to a simmer, reduce the heat to low, cover, and simmer for 30 to 45 minutes, stirring occasionally. The mixture should be thick and very fragrant. Stir in pepper and remove from the heat. Taste and adjust salt. Discard the bay leaf, and the cloves if you can see them. When the mixture has cooled slightly, stir in the parsley.

4. Heat the oven to 350°F. Oil a 3-quart baking dish or gratin dish. Make an even layer of half the potatoes over the bottom. Top with half the zucchini. Pour on all the tomato sauce and spread out evenly. Top with all the artichoke hearts in a layer, then the remaining zucchini and, finally, the potatoes. Bake for 30 minutes.

5. *Make the topping:* Beat together the eggs and yogurt, season with salt (about ½ teaspoon), pepper, and a pinch of paprika, and pour over the top. Sprinkle on the cheese in an even layer. Bake for another 25 to 30 minutes, until golden. Serve warm.

ADVANCE PREPARATION: The tomato sauce (Step 3) will keep for 4 days in the refrigerator. The moussaka can be assembled a day or two before baking and refrigerated (without the egg and yogurt topping). It can also be frozen. Bring to room temperature before baking.

LEFTOVERS: The moussaka will keep for 3 to 4 days in the refrigerator. Reheat in a low oven or a microwave.

CABBAGE GRATIN
The Balkans • Serves 4

Even if you have very little interest in cooked cabbage, I urge you to try this Balkan casserole. The longer you cook cabbage, the sweeter it gets. Here it's cooked on top of the stove for 30 minutes, then baked in the gratin for another 50. The result is an incredibly sweet, caramelized dish that melts in your mouth. Tomatoes and red pepper add color and acidity to the dish.

> 2 tablespoons extra virgin olive oil
>
> 1 medium onion, finely chopped
>
> 1 medium red bell pepper, diced small
>
> 1 small cabbage, cored and finely chopped (about 8 cups)
>
> Salt
>
> 3 tablespoons water
>
> ⅔ cup canned tomatoes, chopped and drained
>
> 1 teaspoon paprika
>
> Freshly ground black pepper
>
> 3 plum tomatoes, sliced thin

1. Heat the oven to 350°F. Oil a 2-quart baking or gratin dish.

2. Heat 1 tablespoon of the olive oil in a large nonstick skillet over medium heat. Add the onion and bell pepper. Cook, stirring, until the vegetables begin to soften, about 3 minutes. Add the cabbage and about ½ teaspoon salt, stir together, cover, and reduce the heat to low. Cook, stirring occasionally, for 10 to 15 minutes, until the cabbage is tender and limp. Add the water, cover, and cook for another 15 minutes, until the cabbage is quite tender and its bright green color has faded. Stir in the chopped tomatoes, paprika, and lots of pepper.

3. Transfer the mixture to the baking dish. Arrange the sliced tomatoes over the top, sprinkle with salt and pepper, and drizzle on the remaining 1 tablespoon oil. Bake for 40 to 50 minutes, until the gratin is charred around the edges and the tomato slices are shriveled. Serve warm or at room temperature.

ADVANCE PREPARATION: This gratin can be made up to a day ahead and reheated for 15 to 20 minutes in a 300°F oven.

CAULIFLOWER GRATIN WITH FETA AND OLIVES
Greece • Serves 4 to 6

Cauliflower, olives, and feta are a match made in heaven. The Greeks know this and put that knowledge to delicious use.

1 large cauliflower (about 1½ pounds), broken into florets

¾ pound tomatoes, chopped

2 garlic cloves, minced or put through a press

1½ teaspoons fresh thyme leaves (or ½ teaspoon dried)

Salt

2 tablespoons extra virgin olive oil

2 tablespoons toasted pine nuts

12 kalamata olives, pitted and cut in half lengthwise

Freshly ground pepper

6 ounces feta, crumbled (about 1½ cups)

3 to 4 tablespoons milk (low-fat is fine)

¼ cup bread crumbs

1. Heat the oven to 375°F. Brush a 2-quart gratin dish with olive oil. Steam the cauliflower over boiling water for 6 minutes, until just tender.

2. Toss together the tomatoes, garlic, thyme, salt, and 1 tablespoon of the olive oil in a large bowl. Add the cauliflower, pine nuts, olives, and pepper, and toss together. Turn into the gratin dish.

3. Pulse the feta and milk together in a food processor until blended but still with some lumps of feta. Spoon over the cauliflower.

4. Toss together the bread crumbs and the remaining 1 tablespoon oil and sprinkle over the cheese. Bake for 35 to 40 minutes, until the top is lightly browned and the gratin is bubbling. Serve hot or warm.

ADVANCE PREPARATION: The gratin can be assembled hours before baking and held in or out of the refrigerator.

Vegetables and Beans

In a way, the title of this chapter is redundant, since the entire book is a collection of vegetable and bean recipes from the Mediterranean. My selections for this chapter, however, were not arbitrary. My intention is to show you how incredibly varied and wonderful the bean and vegetable dishes throughout the different regions of the Mediterranean can be, from simple side dishes like the Italian Carrots with Currants and Pine Nuts (page 275) to complex, hearty main dishes like the Turkish Chick Pea Stew (page 308). There are more recipes here than in any other chapter in the book, yet for every recipe I chose to include, there are anywhere from five to a dozen that I've left out.

From west to east and north to south, the same vegetables and beans are cultivated throughout the Mediterranean. The market photos I took while traveling through Spain, Italy, and Greece during the summer of 2005 are filled with inviting images of shiny purple eggplants, both large and small, red and green peppers, zucchini and round summer squash, squash blossoms, and everywhere, tomatoes. Green beans and Romano beans, arugula and basil, onions of all colors, and plump heads of garlic beckon shoppers. Only the language on the price tags tells me where I am.

But give those vegetables to a cook from Turkey or a cook from Spain, and the dish she will make with them will tell your taste buds immediately where you are. This is what is truly exciting about Mediterranean cookery; every country, even every region within those countries, has culinary traditions that have changed little over the years, and that distinguish the food of one place from that of another.

In Provence, for example, it goes without saying that the eggplants, zucchini, onions, peppers, and tomatoes in the beautiful market at Apt will be made into ratatouille, seasoned with thyme and bay leaf, possibly basil and oregano. The Catalan Spaniard may grill those same vegetables for an *escalivada*, whereas the Spaniard from La Mancha will make *pisto,* and the Turk will make *türlü,* seasoning it with crushed coriander seeds and mint. In Syria, the fresh spinach that is sautéed with garlic, pine nuts, and raisins in Catalonia, Provence, and Liguria will be seasoned with a mix of cinnamon, allspice, coriander, and nutmeg, and topped with thick yogurt. And so it goes.

Mediterranean vegetables are pan-fried and deep-fried, stewed, sautéed, roasted, and grilled. They're battered and they're stuffed with rice, which is sometimes combined with meat, other times with herbs, still others with pine nuts, raisins, and sweet spices. There's a whole category of Greek and Turkish vegetable cookery (which I have not paid too much attention to in these pages, even though they are important in both countries) known as *olive oil dishes.* These are dishes in which the vegetables are stewed for a long time in a great deal of olive oil, ½ to 1 cup. They can be truly delicious, but to my taste, even though you leave most of the olive oil behind when you serve the vegetables, they are heavy. I just don't like to cook with that much oil. I've adapted some of the dishes, like the Greek Artichoke and Fresh Fava Stew on page 269, to use much less oil than their authentic counterparts.

Another vegetable and bean theme I've noticed running through the Mediterranean culinary repertoire is the combination of greens and dried beans. Chick peas and greens are paired in dishes from Spain to Tunisia. The wonderful Dried Fava Beans and Greens on page 309, made with chicory, is a signature dish that you will find on every menu in Puglia. Elsewhere in Italy, you'll find white beans with chard, and lentils with kale. This is typical rustic peasant fare, with its roots in poverty, yet so delicious, nourishing, and comforting that you really can live on it.

ARTICHOKES À LA BARIGOULE
France • Serves 6

This savory Provençal stewed artichoke dish—juicy and sweet with lots of red peppers and tomatoes, garlic and sweet onion—is one of my all-time favorite Mediterranean dishes. The dish has many versions, some of which look nothing like this recipe. I've tried them all, but always go back to this one.

It's a dish that requires lots of paper napkins, because you are bound to use your fingers when you eat it.

- 1 lemon, cut in half
- 2 pounds baby artichokes (or globe artichokes if small ones are not available)
- 2 tablespoons extra virgin olive oil
- 1 large sweet onion, such as Vidalia or Maui, chopped; or 1 bunch spring onions, chopped
- 1 large or 2 small red bell peppers, diced
- Salt
- 4 large garlic cloves, minced or put through a press
- 1½ pounds tomatoes, peeled, seeded, and chopped; or 1 can (14 ounces) tomatoes, drained and chopped
- 1 teaspoon fresh thyme leaves (or ½ teaspoon dried)
- 1 bay leaf
- ¾ to 1 cup water
- Freshly ground pepper
- 2 to 4 tablespoons chopped fresh basil or flat-leaf parsley (to taste)

1. Using the lemon, prepare the artichokes by removing the tops, stems, and tough leaves (page 267). Cut small artichokes in half, large artichokes into quarters, and cut away the chokes. Immediately place in the bowl of lemon water.

2. Heat the oil in a large, heavy nonstick skillet or casserole over medium heat and add the onion. Cook, stirring, until tender, 3 to 5 minutes. Add the bell pepper and about ¼ teaspoon salt, and stir together for 3 to 5 minutes, until the pepper begins to soften. Add the garlic and stir for another minute, until the garlic is fragrant and has colored slightly. Add the tomatoes and a little more salt, and cook, stirring from time to time, for 5 to 10 minutes, until the tomatoes have cooked down slightly and smell fragrant. Drain the artichokes and add them to the skillet along with the thyme, bay leaf, and ¾ cup water, or enough so that the artichokes are halfway submerged in liquid, and bring to a simmer. Add salt and pepper, cover, and simmer for 30 to 40 minutes, until the artichokes are tender and the sauce fragrant. Check from time to time and add water if necessary. Taste and adjust salt and pepper. Stir in the basil. Discard the bay leaf. Serve hot, warm, or at room temperature.

ADVANCE PREPARATION: This dish keeps well for 3 or 4 days in the refrigerator.

VARIATION

ARTICHOKES À LA BARIGOULE WITH FAVA BEANS: In the spring, I use fava beans whenever I can. They make a beautiful addition to this dish. Add to the above recipe 1 pound fava beans. Shell them while the artichokes are simmering, then bring a small pot of water to a boil and drop in the favas. Boil for 1 minute, then transfer to a bowl of cold water. Drain and slip off the skins. Stir into the artichokes and simmer for 10 minutes, until tender but still bright green. Stir in the basil or parsley. Serve hot or at room temperature. The favas can be skinned a day ahead and held in the refrigerator.

STUFFED ARTICHOKES
Italy • Serves 4

Romans stuff their artichokes with a mixture of bread crumbs and herbs—usually mint and parsley—which may or may not be enriched with minced coppa (a lean cured pork sausage) and pancetta. In Puglia, the mixture might include beaten egg. The Romans braise their artichokes in a mixture of white wine and olive oil; cooks in Puglia use a tomato sauce (see the variation that follows).

I like to make stuffed artichokes when I find huge globes at the farmers' market. The artichokes in Italy are smaller than these.

1 lemon

4 globe artichokes

2 large eggs, lightly beaten

1 cup fresh bread crumbs

¼ cup chopped fresh flat-leaf parsley

2 tablespoons chopped fresh mint

3 garlic cloves, minced

¼ cup freshly grated Parmesan

Salt and freshly ground pepper

2 cups dry white wine

⅓ cup extra virgin olive oil

1. Using the lemon, prepare the artichokes by removing the tops, stems, and tough leaves (opposite page). Pull open each artichoke at the center, and using a melon baller or grapefruit spoon, scoop out the furry chokes. Immediately place in a bowl of lemon water.

2. Mix together the eggs, bread crumbs, chopped herbs, garlic, and cheese. Season to taste with salt and pepper. Remove the artichokes from the water, turn them upside down, and shake out excess water. Gently open out the leaves and place a heaped spoonful of filling in the center of each one. Close the leaves back over the filling and tuck any remaining filling between the leaves. Place in a heavy casserole or Dutch oven. Pour the wine around the artichokes and drizzle over the olive oil. Sprinkle with salt. Bring to a boil, then reduce the heat, cover, and simmer gently until very tender, about 1 hour. Cool slightly. Transfer the artichokes to a platter and pour on the pan juices. Serve warm.

ADVANCE PREPARATION: You can stuff the artichokes hours before you cook them, and hold in the refrigerator.

VARIATION

PUGLIESE STUFFED ARTICHOKES: Substitute 2 cups Basic Tomato Sauce (page 78) for the wine. Cook the artichokes in the tomato sauce, and spoon it over the finished artichokes before serving.

ROMAN-STYLE BRAISED BABY ARTICHOKES WITH PARSLEY AND MINT
Italy • **Serves 6**

This is not too different from the preceding recipe for stuffed artichokes. Since it would be a tedious business stuffing baby artichokes, I simply sprinkle the artichokes with the herbs. The braising medium is similar, but with more wine and more olive oil.

1 lemon, cut in half

2 pounds baby artichokes

Salt and freshly ground pepper

¼ cup minced fresh flat-leaf parsley

2 heaped tablespoons minced fresh spearmint

4 garlic cloves, minced

¾ cup extra virgin olive oil

1½ cups dry white wine, preferably Italian

½ cup water

1. Using the lemon and dropping the artichokes into lemon water as you finish, prepare the artichokes by removing the tops, stems, and tough leaves (opposite page).

2. Drain the artichokes and place them base side down and in a single layer in a Dutch oven or large skillet. Sprinkle with salt and pepper. Mix together the herbs, garlic, and 3 tablespoons of the olive oil. Place a spoonful on top of each artichoke. Drizzle 1 tablespoon olive oil over the artichokes, then pour the remaining ½ cup oil, the wine, and water around them. Bring to a boil, reduce the heat, cover, and simmer for 30 to 40 minutes, until the artichokes are tender. Serve hot or at room temperature.

ADVANCE PREPARATION: The cooked artichokes will keep for 5 days in the refrigerator and will be just as good on the fifth day as they were on the first.

ARTICHOKES

How the people of the Mediterranean figured out that the unopened flower buds of a thistle plant were edible, and deliciously so, is beyond me. But they did, to our great good fortune, and for over 500 years the plant has been a favorite vegetable, particularly in France, southern Italy, Greece, and the Middle East.

Outside of the Mediterranean, artichokes can be almost austere in their simplicity. They're steamed or boiled, and served with a hollandaise or mayonnaise or vinaigrette, to be eaten leaf by leaf until you reach the heart. But the small purple artichokes and larger globe artichokes that appear in spring markets throughout the Mediterranean (and here in California) inspire much more elaborate dishes, like Artichokes à la Barigoule (page 265), Provençal Artichoke, Mushroom, and Potato Ragout (page 268), Fritteda (page 268), and Roman-Style Braised Baby Artichokes with Parsley and Mint (page 266). Spain, France, Italy, Greece, and Turkey all have recipes for stuffed artichokes, of which the Italian recipe on page 265 is just one example. Artichokes and other spring vegetables like favas, peas, and spring onions meet up in ragouts like the Greek Artichoke and Fresh Fava Stew on page 269.

Many dishes are made using just the fleshy hearts, while others include the entire plant. Whether the whole plant or just the hearts will be used, artichokes must be prepared before cooking.

How to Prepare Artichokes

Fill a bowl with water and add to it the juice of ½ lemon. Have the other half of the lemon close by. Cut the stem off from the artichoke about ½ inch from the bottom and dip the cut end into the lemon water, or rub with the cut side of the lemon. Use a sharp chef's knife to cut off the top of the artichoke, about ½ inch down. Rub the cut end with the lemon. Break off and discard the tough bottom leaves until you get to the lighter green leaves.

If your recipe requires cooked artichoke hearts, then you can go right ahead and boil or steam the artichoke as is until a leaf comes away easily when pulled, about 45 minutes. Cool, then pull off the leaves (save them for another purpose, such as an appetizer platter before dinner) until the bottom is exposed. With a sharp paring knife, cut away the inner leaves and furry "chokes" attached to the heart, and discard.

If your recipe calls for the whole artichoke or cut-up artichokes, you will need to trim the leaves. Use kitchen scissors to cut the pointy end off each leaf. Rub the cut edges with lemon. Now cut the artichoke into halves or quarters and remove the chokes with your paring knife. As you cut each piece, transfer the piece to the bowl of lemon water, to prevent discoloration.

PROVENÇAL ARTICHOKE, MUSHROOM, AND POTATO RAGOUT

France • **Serves 4 to 6**

This robust Provençal dish is less of a spring and summer dish, and more of a comforting fall/winter meal.

> 1½ ounces (about 1½ cups) dried porcini mushrooms
>
> 3 cups boiling water
>
> 2 lemons
>
> 12 small or 6 medium or large artichokes
>
> 2 tablespoons extra virgin olive oil
>
> 1 large onion, thinly sliced
>
> 4 to 5 large garlic cloves (to taste), minced or put through a press
>
> 2 pounds red-skinned or Yukon gold potatoes, scrubbed and quartered
>
> ½ cup dry white wine
>
> 1 bay leaf
>
> 1 teaspoon fresh thyme leaves (or ½ teaspoon dried)
>
> Salt and freshly ground pepper
>
> ¼ cup chopped fresh flat-leaf parsley

1. Place the mushrooms in a bowl or large Pyrex measuring cup and pour over the boiling water. Let sit for 30 minutes.

2. Using one of the lemons, prepare the artichokes by removing the tops, stems, and tough leaves (page 267). Cut small artichokes in half, large artichokes into quarters, and cut away the chokes. Immediately place in a bowl of lemon water.

3. Place a strainer lined with cheesecloth or paper towels over a bowl and drain the mushrooms. Squeeze out liquid over the strainer, then rinse the mushrooms in several changes of water to rid them of grit. Chop coarsely and set aside. Add enough water to the soaking liquid to measure 3 cups. Set aside.

4. Heat the olive oil in a large, heavy casserole or nonstick skillet over medium heat. Add the onion and cook, stirring, until tender, about 5 minutes.

Add the garlic and mushrooms and cook, stirring, until fragrant, about 1 minute. Drain the artichokes and add with the potatoes, stir together for another minute, then stir in the wine. Bring to a boil and cook until most of the liquid is gone. Add the soaking liquid from the mushrooms, the bay leaf, thyme, salt, and pepper. Bring to a simmer, reduce the heat, cover, and simmer for 40 minutes, until the potatoes and artichokes are tender. Taste and adjust salt. Stir in 1 to 3 tablespoons lemon juice (to taste) and the parsley. Simmer uncovered for another few minutes—longer if you want to reduce the liquid. Taste and adjust seasonings. Discard the bay leaf. Serve hot or at room temperature.

ADVANCE PREPARATION: This dish can be made a day or two ahead and reheated.

LEFTOVERS: The ragout is good for 3 or 4 days.

SICILIAN SPRING VEGETABLE STEW (Fritteda)

Italy • **Serves 6**

This dish, known as *fritteda* in Sicily and *vignarola* in Rome, was introduced to me by my friend Clifford Wright, who knows just about everything there is to know about Mediterranean food. The authentic dish is made with scallions rather than spring onions; I use the green spring onions I find at the farmers' market at the same time of year that I find the first favas, sweet peas, and early baby artichokes. If you can't find tender young, small artichokes, I recommend using frozen artichoke hearts. You could also use frozen peas. Although this is traditionally cooked for a very long time, I hate to do that to peas and favas, so this version will be different from the *fritteda* you would eat in Sicily.

> 1 lemon
>
> 6 small young artichokes
>
> 2 tablespoons extra virgin olive oil
>
> ½ pound spring onions or scallions, white part only, finely chopped

1 medium fennel bulb, trimmed, quartered, cored, and chopped

⅔ cup water

Salt and freshly ground black pepper

Freshly grated nutmeg

3 pounds fresh fava beans, shelled and skinned (page 113)

3 pounds fresh peas in the pod, shelled (3 cups shelled peas or frozen peas)

IF SERVING COLD

4 fresh mint leaves, chopped

1 teaspoon red wine vinegar

1 tablespoon sugar

1. Using the lemon, prepare the artichokes by removing the tops, stems, and tough leaves (page 267). Quarter the artichokes, cut away the chokes, and slice about ½ inch thick. Immediately place in a bowl of lemon water.

2. Heat the oil in a large, heavy skillet or Dutch oven over medium heat. Add the onions and cook, stirring, until tender, 3 to 5 minutes. Drain the artichokes and add to the skillet along with the fennel. Cook, stirring, for 5 minutes, until the vegetables begin to soften. Add the water and salt to taste, and bring to a boil. Simmer for 5 minutes, then add pepper and a pinch of nutmeg. Cover and simmer for 20 minutes.

3. Check to see if the artichokes and fennel are tender. Add the favas and peas, and more water if the pan looks dry. Cover and simmer another 20 minutes, until all of the vegetables are tender. Taste and adjust salt and pepper. Serve hot or warm.

4. *If serving cold:* Stir in the mint, vinegar, and sugar and cool.

ADVANCE PREPARATION: The *fritteda* can be made a day ahead.

VARIATION

Add ½ pound small red-skinned potatoes, scrubbed and halved, when you add the artichokes and fennel.

WILD FENNEL

Wild fennel is an indispensable seasoning in the Greek kitchen. The feathery plant, which looks like dill, grows everywhere in the countryside. It loves California hillsides as well, and happens to grow in abundance on the grounds of my son's Los Angeles public school. Curious students and teachers are likely to find me gathering it every time I go up there. The fresh herb is not, however, sold in many markets. You can use fresh dill instead, when fennel is called for (a different flavor altogether), or you can buy bulb fennel and cut the fronds for the herb and use the bulb for another recipe, such as the Provençal Tomato Gratin on page 251.

ARTICHOKE AND FRESH FAVA STEW
Greece • Serves 6

This is a springtime dish in Greece, as it is for me in Los Angeles. It's a bit labor intensive, but worth it. Delectable young artichokes and fava beans hit my farmers' market in April and May and stick around into June here, and this is one dish I love to use them in. You could make the same dish substituting fresh peas for the favas. The dish resembles the Sicilian *fritteda* on page 268, which isn't surprising, given the widespread cultivation of these spring vegetables throughout the Mediterranean.

I can find baby artichokes at my local Trader Joe's markets as well as the farmers' markets. If you can't find them, use globe artichokes. If you're buying your ingredients at the farmers' market, you're also bound to find green garlic at this time of year.

The recipe that this is based on is an "olive oil" recipe, meaning that the vegetables are traditionally stewed in a great deal of olive oil, two or three times as much as here. I substitute some water for the olive oil.

2 lemons, halved

2 pounds baby artichokes (12 to 18, depending on the size) or 6 globe artichokes

4 tablespoons extra virgin olive oil

1 white onion or 1 bunch spring onions, chopped

3 large garlic cloves, minced; or 1 bulb spring garlic, skinned and minced

2 pounds fresh fava beans, shelled and skinned (page 113); or 1 cup fresh peas

1 teaspoon sugar (optional)

¼ cup chopped wild fennel, fennel fronds, or dill

Salt and freshly ground pepper

1. Using one of the lemons, prepare the artichokes by removing the tops, stems, and tough leaves (page 267). Cut baby artichokes in half; cut globe artichokes into sixths. Rub the cut sides with one of the cut lemon halves. Scoop or cut out the chokes with the tip of a paring knife, and immediately submerge the artichokes in lemon water.

2. Heat 2 tablespoons of the olive oil in a large, heavy casserole or Dutch oven over medium heat and add the onion. Cook, stirring, until tender, about 5 minutes, and add the garlic. Cook for a minute, stirring, until fragrant. Drain the artichokes and add to the stew along with the remaining 2 tablespoons olive oil, the skinned fava beans, sugar, fennel, and the juice of the remaining lemon. Add enough water to just cover everything and about 1 teaspoon salt. Bring to a simmer, cover, and simmer for 20 to 30 minutes, until the vegetables are tender and the broth fragrant.

3. Turn the heat to high and reduce the liquid in the pan by about a third. Stir in a generous amount of freshly ground pepper. Taste and adjust salt. Serve warm.

ADVANCE PREPARATION: You can prepare this a day or two ahead and reheat on top of the stove.

LEFTOVERS: The dish is good for 4 to 5 days. The color of the favas will fade, but the flavors won't.

ARTICHOKE AND POTATO STEW
Greece • Serves 4 to 6

This aromatic, slightly lemony dill- and mint-seasoned dish is equally delicious made with canned or fresh tomatoes. As always, this has much less olive oil than the authentic Greek dish, but not less flavor.

2 lemons

12 small or 6 medium or large artichokes

2 tablespoons extra virgin olive oil (more to taste)

1 medium red onion, chopped

4 garlic cloves, minced or put through a press

1½ pounds red-skinned potatoes, scrubbed and halved if small, quartered if large

1 pound plum tomatoes, peeled and chopped; or 1 can (14 ounces) tomatoes, drained and chopped

Salt

1 bay leaf

1 generous bunch fresh dill, chopped (about ½ cup, tightly packed)

¼ to ½ cup chopped fresh mint (to taste)

Freshly ground pepper

Crusty bread

Feta

1. Using one of the lemons, prepare the artichokes by removing the tops, stems, and tough leaves (page 267). Cut small artichokes in half, large artichokes into quarters, and cut away the chokes. Immediately place in lemon water.

2. Heat the oil in a large, heavy casserole or non-stick frying pan over medium heat. Add the onion and cook, stirring, until just about tender, 3 to 5 minutes. Add the garlic, stir together for a minute, until fragrant, and add the potatoes. Drain the artichokes, add to the pan, and stir until the vegetables are coated with oil. Add the tomatoes and a little salt, and cook, stirring often, until the tomatoes cook down slightly and smell fragrant. Add the bay leaf, salt, and enough water to just cover the vegetables, and bring to a simmer. Cover and simmer for 30 minutes, until the vegetables are just tender.

3. Stir in the dill and mint, and continue to cook for another 20 minutes. If the broth seems too watery, uncover and cook over high heat until the liquid reduces somewhat (there should be some juice). Add pepper, taste, and adjust salt. Stir in 1 to 3 tablespoons lemon juice, to taste. Discard the bay leaf. Serve hot or at room temperature, with thick slices of crusty country bread for soaking up the juice, and a slice of feta cheese.

ADVANCE PREPARATION: You can make the recipe through Step 2 two to three days ahead. The finished dish can be made a day ahead and refrigerated.

LEFTOVERS: You can enjoy the leftovers for 3 or 4 days.

ASPARAGUS WITH PARMESAN
(Asparagi alla Parmigiana)

Italy • **Serves 4 to 6**

This is one of Italy's great vegetable dishes. Years ago, I was alone in Florence, in the month of May, and took myself to a rather fancy restaurant, just so that I could eat this dish, which I saw on the menu that was posted outside the door. I can't remember what else I ate at that meal. But I do remember that at the next table there was another person dining alone. He was an elderly gentleman, and he was eating a large bowl of spring peas with a spoon; like me, he was reveling in the spring's bounty. Afterward, the waiter brought him a large bowl of cherries and set a bowl of water next to them. One by one, he dipped the cherries into the water to rinse them, clearly enjoying every one of them. I learned a lot from that man. How to enjoy dining alone, eating exactly what you want to eat, something that will be at its best at that very moment, and being in the moment with that food. This is something that people all over the Mediterranean know instinctively.

2 pounds fresh asparagus, trimmed

½ teaspoon salt

⅔ cup freshly grated Parmesan

3 tablespoons unsalted butter

1. Steam the asparagus or cook in generously salted boiling water for 5 minutes. If boiling, transfer to a bowl of ice water, then drain. If steaming, rinse with cold water.

2. Heat the oven to 425°F. Butter a rectangular or oval baking dish. Lay the asparagus in the dish in overlapping rows, with the tips of the second row overlapping the bottoms of the first row, so that all of the tips are exposed. Sprinkle the first row with salt and cheese before arranging the second row, then sprinkle the second row with salt and cheese. Dot with butter.

3. Bake the asparagus in the upper third of the oven for 15 minutes, or until the cheese is golden. Let sit for about 5 minutes before serving.

ADVANCE PREPARATION: You can cook the asparagus and assemble the casserole several hours before baking. You could also cook the asparagus a day ahead.

VARIATION

ASPARAGUS WITH PARMESAN AND EGGS: This makes a light supper or lunch. Make the Asparagus with Parmesan as directed. Meanwhile, poach or fry 4 to 8 eggs. Divide the asparagus among 4 plates and place 1 to 2 eggs on each serving. Drizzle any juices left in the asparagus pan over the eggs, grind on some pepper, and serve.

GARLIC GREEN BEANS

France • **Serves 4**

This Provençal way of sprucing up green beans is incredibly simple. They're cooked in salted boiling water, then finished in olive oil with lots of garlic and parsley.

> Salt
>
> 1 pound green beans, trimmed
>
> 1 to 2 tablespoons extra virgin olive oil (to taste)
>
> 1 to 3 garlic cloves (to taste), minced
>
> Freshly ground pepper
>
> 2 tablespoons chopped fresh flat-leaf parsley

1. Bring a large pot of water to a boil, then add a generous spoonful of salt and the beans. Cook for 4 to 5 minutes, until tender, and transfer to a bowl of ice water. Drain.

2. Heat the oil in a large, heavy nonstick skillet over medium heat and add the garlic. As soon as it begins to sizzle and smell good, after about 30 seconds to 1 minute, stir in the beans. Cook, stirring, for another 3 or 4 minutes, until the beans are coated with oil and cooked garlic. Season to taste with salt and pepper, stir in the parsley, and serve.

ADVANCE PREPARATION: You can make this through Step 1 hours or even a day before proceeding with Step 2.

STEWED GREEN BEANS WITH TOMATOES

Greece • **Serves 4 to 6**

When I was in Ikaria studying Greek cooking with Diane Kochilas, my son and his kid-sitter, Rachel, would go to the same taverna every day for lunch. Liam always ordered spaghetti, but he also liked the vegetable dishes Rachel sampled. This one was a particular favorite, which surprised me, as the green beans are cooked longer, and are therefore a less vivid green, than the green beans I blanch or steam at home. I'm actually surprised that I like them so much too. They're pretty addictive.

> 3 tablespoons extra virgin olive oil
>
> 1 large onion, chopped
>
> 2 large garlic cloves, minced
>
> 1 pound fresh green beans, trimmed
>
> 1 cup peeled, chopped tomatoes
>
> ½ cup water
>
> Salt and freshly ground pepper
>
> About ¼ cup chopped fresh mint, flat-leaf parsley, or dill (optional)
>
> 1 to 2 tablespoons red wine vinegar (to taste; optional)

Heat 2 tablespoons of the olive oil in a wide skillet or Dutch oven over medium heat and add the onion. Cook, stirring, until tender and translucent, about 8 minutes. Add the garlic and cook, stirring, for another minute, until fragrant. Stir in the green beans and remaining 1 tablespoon oil and toss to coat. Add the tomatoes and water. Bring to a simmer, add salt and pepper, cover, and simmer for 30 minutes, until the beans are tender and the mixture is stew-like. Serve hot or at room temperature. Stir in the mint and vinegar right before serving.

ADVANCE PREPARATION: This dish keeps well, and you don't have to worry about the beans fading, as they aren't bright anymore. The flavor, on the other hand, just gets brighter. It'll be good for about 4 days. Keep in the refrigerator.

BRAISED BROCCOLI WITH WHITE WINE
(Broccoli alla Romana)

Italy • **Serves 4 to 6**

I am not one to cook broccoli for a long time, but this southern Italian approach results in a marvelously savory dish that gives a new dimension to the vegetable.

> 2 tablespoons extra virgin olive oil
>
> 1 plump garlic clove, minced
>
> 1 generous bunch broccoli (about 2 pounds), broken into florets
>
> 1½ cups dry white wine
>
> Salt and freshly ground pepper

1. Heat the olive oil in a large nonstick skillet over medium-high heat. Add the garlic, stir for a few seconds, and add the broccoli florets. Reduce the heat to medium, toss the broccoli florets until they are coated with oil, and add the wine, salt, and pepper. Simmer uncovered, stirring from time to time, for 5 minutes. Cover and continue to simmer for another 10 to 15 minutes, until the broccoli is very tender and fragrant.

2. Using a slotted spoon, transfer the broccoli to a serving bowl or platter and keep warm. Bring the cooking liquid back to a boil and reduce to about ½ cup. Pour over the broccoli and serve.

ADVANCE PREPARATION: It's best not to prepare this dish ahead of time because the broccoli will continue to fade in the wine and become too limp.

SWEET AND SOUR CABBAGE

Italy • **Serves 4 to 6**

We might associate cabbage more with central European cuisines than with those of the Mediterranean. Yet it has played a major role there since the Middle Ages, when it was probably the most widely eaten vegetable. I've observed something interesting when I serve this dish to my son. Usually, he eats his vegetables last; but this one, because it's sweet, he gobbles up first.

> 2 tablespoons extra virgin olive oil
>
> 1 small onion, thinly sliced
>
> 1 medium cabbage, quartered, cored, and thinly sliced
>
> 3 large tomatoes, peeled, seeded, and chopped; or 1 can (14 ounces) tomatoes, with some juice from the can
>
> 2 tablespoons red or white wine vinegar
>
> 1 tablespoon sugar
>
> 1 to 2 teaspoons salt (to taste)
>
> Freshly ground black pepper

Heat the olive oil in a large nonstick skillet over medium heat and add the onion. Cook, stirring, until tender, about 5 minutes. Add the cabbage and cook, stirring, until it begins to wilt, about 5 minutes. Add the tomatoes, vinegar, sugar, salt, and pepper, stir together, and cook uncovered, stirring often, for 20 minutes, or until the cabbage is tender and fragrant. Taste and adjust seasonings. Serve hot or warm, as a starter or side dish.

ADVANCE PREPARATION: This dish will keep for 3 or 4 days in the refrigerator, and is even better the day after it's made.

PREPARING CABBAGE LEAVES FOR STUFFING

It's much easier to cook the cabbage before you try to separate the leaves. Bring a large pot of water to a boil, then add 1 tablespoon salt and the whole cabbage. Cook for about 20 minutes, until a skewer can be easily inserted into the center of the cabbage. Transfer the cabbage to a bowl of ice water and cool completely.

Take a sharp knife and cut out the core. Carefully separate the leaves. Cut out the hard, wide rib at the base of the large outer leaves.

STUFFED CABBAGE

Turkey • Serves 6 to 8

My friend John Lyons is a very talented gardener, and every once in a while he gives me an enormous cabbage from his garden. Cabbage is great for stuffing, and the Mediterranean has many recipes to choose from. Though the signature stuffed cabbage dishes from Nice and the Middle East use meat fillings, these fragrant stuffed cabbage leaves from Bursa, the first seat of the Ottoman dynasty, do not. They are filled with a rice and chestnut stuffing that's seasoned, like so many Turkish dishes, with cinnamon and allspice, dill and parsley.

2 tablespoons extra virgin olive oil

1 medium onion, finely chopped

4 garlic cloves, minced

1 teaspoon sugar

½ cup short-grained rice, rinsed under cold water until the water runs clear or soaked in cold water for 30 minutes

1 teaspoon ground allspice

1 teaspoon ground cinnamon

½ teaspoon salt (more to taste)

1¼ cups water

1½ cups vacuum-packed or canned shelled chestnuts, chopped

1 small bunch dill, thick stems removed, finely chopped, plus additional for serving

½ cup chopped fresh flat-leaf parsley

Freshly ground pepper

1 large head cabbage (2 to 4 pounds), leaves prepared for stuffing (page 273)

Juice of 1 lemon

2 tablespoons tomato paste

2 lemons, cut into wedges

1. Heat 1 tablespoon of the olive oil in a large skillet over medium heat and add the onion. Cook, stirring, until tender, 3 to 5 minutes. Add the garlic and sugar and cook, stirring, until the garlic is fragrant, about 1 minute. Add the rice, allspice, cinnamon, and salt. Stir together and add 1 cup of the water, or enough to barely cover the rice. Bring to a boil, reduce the heat to low, cover, and simmer until all of the liquid has been absorbed, about 20 minutes. Remove from the heat. Allow to sit for 10 minutes without disturbing.

2. Toss the rice and chestnuts together in a large bowl. Add the dill and parsley, taste, and season with salt and pepper. Lightly oil a heatproof casserole or a heavy skillet. Place a cabbage leaf on your work surface in front of you, with the wide, ribbed bottom closest to you. Place a heaped tablespoon of the rice mixture on top of the leaf. Roll the leaf over once and tuck in the sides. Continue to roll the leaf into a tight package. Place in the pan. Fill and roll the remaining leaves and pack them into the pan.

3. Mix together the remaining 1 tablespoon oil, lemon juice, and tomato paste with ¼ cup water. Pour over the cabbage rolls. Invert a plate over the cabbage rolls to weight them and keep them from opening up. Bring to a simmer over medium heat, reduce the heat, and cover. Simmer for 20 to 25 minutes, until the cabbage rolls are translucent. Remove from the heat and cool. Transfer to a platter, sprinkle with additional dill if desired, and serve with lemon wedges.

ADVANCE PREPARATION: The leaves can be stuffed a day ahead of time and held in the refrigerator. The filling will keep for a couple of days in the refrigerator.

VARIATIONS

STUFFED CABBAGE WITH EGG-LEMON SAUCE: Omit the tomato paste in the cooking water. Serve with this egg-lemon sauce: Place 2 egg yolks and 2 tablespoons fresh lemon juice in a bowl set over a pot of simmering water and beat until thick. Whisk in ½ cup cooking liquid from the cabbage and continue to beat until smooth and thick. Remove from the heat and season to taste with salt.

STUFFED CABBAGE WITH TAHINI SAUCE: Omit the tomato paste in the cooking liquid. Serve with this tahini sauce: Mix together 2 tablespoons tahini, ¼ cup cooking liquid from the cabbage, 2 tablespoons fresh lemon juice, and 1 to 2 garlic cloves mashed to a paste in a mortar and pestle with ¼ teaspoon salt. Season with salt and freshly ground pepper to taste.

CARROTS WITH CURRANTS AND PINE NUTS

Italy • Serves 6

Throughout the European Mediterranean, from Spain to the Ligurian coast of Italy, greens are cooked with currants and pine nuts (page 282). I'd never seen other vegetables handled in this manner until I came across this dish in a Venetian cookbook.

>   2 tablespoons extra virgin olive oil
>
>   1½ to 2 pounds carrots, sliced about ¼ inch thick
>
>   Salt and freshly ground pepper
>
>   ¼ cup currants or raisins
>
>   3 tablespoons toasted pine nuts
>
>   1½ tablespoons red wine vinegar

Heat the olive oil in a large skillet over medium-high heat and cook the carrots until lightly browned and tender, about 10 minutes. Season with salt and pepper. Add the currants and pine nuts, heat through, and stir in the vinegar. Taste and adjust seasonings, and serve.

ADVANCE PREPARATION: The dish can be made several hours before serving and reheated.

LEFTOVERS: Any leftovers can be eaten for a couple of days.

ROASTED CAULIFLOWER WITH CHERMOULA

Serves 4 to 6

When cauliflower is blanched, then tossed with olive oil and roasted, the edges brown and sweet flavors emerge. The intensely herbal, spicy Moroccan sauce that is usually served with fish makes the perfect foil for the subtle cauliflower.

>   Salt
>
>   1 large cauliflower, broken into florets
>
>   2 tablespoons extra virgin olive oil
>
>   Chermoula (page 86)

1. Bring a large pot of water to a boil. Add 1 teaspoon salt and the cauliflower. Blanch for 2 minutes and transfer to a bowl of ice water. Drain and blot dry.

2. Heat the oven to 400°F. Toss the cauliflower with the olive oil and salt it generously. Bake for 30 minutes, stirring from time to time, until tender and lightly browned. Serve hot, with the *chermoula sauce.*

ADVANCE PREPARATION: The blanched cauliflower will keep for a few days in the refrigerator.

VARIATIONS

CARROTS WITH CHERMOULA: Substitute 2 pounds carrots for the cauliflower. Slice the carrots about ½ inch thick on the diagonal. Steam for 5 to 10 minutes, until just tender. Remove from the heat, refresh with cold water, and toss with the *chermoula.* Serve hot or at room temperature.

WINTER SQUASH WITH CHERMOULA: Substitute 1 large butternut squash for the cauliflower. Peel, seed, and dice the squash. Toss with 1 tablespoon extra virgin olive oil, season with salt and pepper, and place on a lightly oiled baking sheet. Cover with foil and bake 30 to 40 minutes in a 375°F oven, until tender. Toss with the *chermoula.* Serve hot or warm.

STEWED EGGPLANT AND ONIONS

Italy • **Serves 6 to 8 as an antipasto**

Everywhere you travel in Italy, especially in the summer, you will find different eggplant dishes. I particularly like this one, served as one of many starters at an *azienda agrituristica*, or farm/hotel, in the hills of the Gargano National Park in Puglia.

> 2½ pounds (2 large) eggplants, cut into 1-inch dice
>
> Salt
>
> 4 tablespoons extra virgin olive oil
>
> 1 large onion, sliced
>
> 2 large garlic cloves, sliced
>
> 1 cup peeled, chopped tomatoes
>
> 1 tablespoon wine vinegar or sherry vinegar
>
> ½ cup water
>
> Chopped fresh basil or oregano (optional)

1. Sprinkle the eggplant with salt and allow to sit in a colander for 30 minutes. Pat dry.

2. Heat a large, well-seasoned skillet over medium-high heat. Add 3 tablespoons of the olive oil, and when it begins to ripple, add the eggplant. Cook, stirring often, until the edges are nicely browned and the eggplant thoroughly softened, about 10 minutes. Remove from the pan.

3. Add the remaining 1 tablespoon olive oil to the skillet, reduce the heat to medium, and add the onion. Cook, stirring often, until tender, about 8 minutes. Add the garlic, stir until fragrant, about 1 minute, and return the eggplant to the pan. Stir in the tomatoes, vinegar, water, and salt to taste. Bring to a simmer and cook for 15 minutes, until the tomatoes have broken down and the vegetables are soft. Taste and adjust seasonings. Serve warm or at room temperature, sprinkled with fresh basil or oregano if desired.

ADVANCE PREPARATION: This keeps well for 3 or 4 days in the refrigerator and will improve overnight.

CAPONATA

Italy • **Serves 6**

This Sicilian eggplant relish combines eggplant, celery, capers, and olives in a sweet-and-sour tomato sauce. The many influences on Sicily's cooking are evident here—the olive oil, olives, and capers; the Arab love of sweet-and-sour combinations (I have seen versions of this dish that contain raisins); and the introduction of New World foods (tomatoes and peppers) into the cuisine.

> 1½ pounds (about 1 large) eggplant, cut in half lengthwise
>
> 3 tablespoons extra virgin olive oil
>
> 1 medium onion, chopped
>
> 3 large garlic cloves, minced or put through a press
>
> 2 red bell peppers, cut into ½-inch squares
>
> Salt
>
> 1 can (14 ounces) crushed tomatoes in purée
>
> 2 tablespoons plus ¼ teaspoon sugar
>
> 3 celery stalks, sliced about ½ inch thick and blanched in a large pot of salted boiling water
>
> 3 heaped tablespoons capers, rinsed and drained
>
> ¼ cup coarsely chopped pitted green olives
>
> ¼ cup wine vinegar or sherry vinegar
>
> Freshly ground pepper

1. Heat the oven to 450°F. Line a baking sheet with foil and brush the foil lightly with olive oil. Score the cut sides of the eggplant halves with a small knife, cutting down to the skin but not through it. Place the eggplants on the baking sheet, cut side down, and bake for 20 minutes, until the eggplants collapse and the skins have begun to shrivel. Drain and cool, cut side down, in a colander over a plate. When cool enough to handle, pull off and discard the skin, scraping off any eggplant that adheres, and chop the eggplant. The eggplant should be soft and is not meant to hold its shape.

2. Heat 1 tablespoon of the olive oil in a large, heavy nonstick skillet over medium heat and add the onion. Cook, stirring, until tender but not browned, about 5 minutes, and add two-thirds of the garlic. Cook for a minute, until the garlic begins to smell fragrant, then add the bell peppers and about ¼ teaspoon salt. Cook, stirring, until just about tender, about 8 minutes. Add 1 tablespoon oil and the eggplant, and cook, stirring for another 5 minutes, until the vegetables are tender. The eggplant will fall apart, which is fine. Transfer to a bowl.

3. Add the remaining 1 tablespoon olive oil and the remaining garlic to the skillet. Cook for about 30 seconds, just until the garlic begins to color, and add the tomatoes, about ¼ teaspoon salt, and ¼ teaspoon sugar. Cook, stirring, for 5 to 10 minutes, until the tomatoes have cooked down somewhat—they should not be dry, however—and they smell fragrant. Return the eggplant mixture to the pan and stir together. Add the celery, capers, olives, vinegar, salt to taste, and remaining 2 tablespoons sugar. Reduce the heat to medium-low and cook, stirring often, for 15 to 30 minutes, until the vegetables are thoroughly tender and the caponata is quite thick, sweet, and fragrant. Season to taste with salt and pepper and cool to room temperature.

ADVANCE PREPARATION: Caponata gets better overnight, so make at least a day ahead if possible. It will keep for 3 to 5 days in the refrigerator.

TIP QUICK ROASTING EGGPLANT

Quick roasting eggplant, as you do in the Caponata recipe, has the same effect as the salting method for drawing out juices. When the eggplant comes out of the hot oven and cools, it releases its juices. It also has a nice roasted flavor and won't require a great amount of oil for cooking.

CHEESE-AND-VEGETABLE-STUFFED EGGPLANTS

Greece • **Serves 6 to 8**

This beautiful stuffed eggplant dish is based on the recipe that we learned in Diane Kochilas's cooking class in Ikaria, Greece. The Greek method is to fry the eggplants first in lots of olive oil, to soften them. My method is not Greek; it involves less oil and the results are delicious. I roast the eggplants to soften them, then fill and bake to finish the cooking. These make a delightful vegetarian main dish.

> 8 small eggplants (about ½ pound each), or 6 medium eggplants (about ¾ pound each)
>
> 2 tablespoons extra virgin olive oil, plus additional for brushing
>
> Salt
>
> 6 small or 3 large onions, chopped
>
> 4 to 6 garlic cloves (to taste), minced
>
> 2 pounds tomatoes, peeled and chopped
>
> Freshly ground pepper
>
> 1 cup chopped fresh flat-leaf parsley
>
> ½ pound kefalotyri cheese, cut into 1-inch cubes, plus ½ cup grated kefalotyri

1. Heat the oven to 425°F. Set the eggplants on your work surface. Leave the stems on and cut a hollow out of each eggplant, scooping out about one-third of the flesh. Leave enough flesh so that when the stuffed eggplant bakes, it will stay intact. Set aside the flesh for use in another dish.

2. Brush the eggplants, especially the cavity, with olive oil and place them cut side down on an oiled baking sheet. Bake for 30 to 40 minutes, until the eggplants are tender (but still hold their shape) and lightly browned. Flip the eggplants over and season generously with salt. Set aside. Turn the oven down to 375°F.

3. Heat 2 tablespoons olive oil in a large, wide skillet over medium heat and add the onions. Cook, stirring often, until tender, about 8 minutes, and add the garlic. Cook, stirring, until fragrant, about a minute, and add the tomatoes. Season with salt and pepper and cook gently, stirring occasionally, for about 8 minutes, until the tomatoes have cooked down slightly. Stir in the parsley, then taste and adjust seasonings.

4. Place 4 cubes of cheese (or as many as will fit in one layer) in the cavity of each eggplant. Top with a generous mound of the tomato-onion mixture. Sprinkle with grated cheese. Bake until the eggplants are thoroughly tender and the cheese has melted, about 30 minutes. If the cheese begins to brown before the eggplants are tender, cover with an oiled piece of foil.

ADVANCE PREPARATION: The eggplants can be roasted, the filling prepared, and the stuffed eggplants assembled hours, or even a day, before the final baking. Cover and hold in the refrigerator.

IMAM BAYILDI
Turkey • Serves 4

This is probably the most famous Turkish eggplant dish. The name means "the imam fainted," and refers to the fact that the imam's pleasure was so great when he ate this dish that he swooned. Another version of the story claims that the imam fainted when he learned how much expensive olive oil was used in the dish. No matter why the imam did swoon, the vegetables should be so soft that they melt in your mouth.

There are many recipes for *imam bayildi*. My technique for roasting the eggplant before filling it is one I developed so that I wouldn't have to use quite so much olive oil.

> 2 medium or 4 small eggplants, cut in half lengthwise
>
> 6 tablespoons extra virgin olive oil
>
> 1 large or 2 medium onions, sliced very thin
>
> 6 garlic cloves, minced
>
> 1½ pounds tomatoes, peeled and chopped
>
> ¼ cup finely chopped fresh flat-leaf parsley

> 2 tablespoons finely chopped fresh dill
>
> 2 tablespoons finely chopped fresh basil (optional)
>
> Salt
>
> 2½ teaspoons sugar
>
> ¼ cup water
>
> 2 tablespoons fresh lemon juice (optional)

1. Heat the oven to 450°F. Oil a baking sheet with olive oil. Make a slit down the middle of the cut sides of the halved eggplants, being careful not to cut through the skin. Place on the baking sheet, skin side up, and roast for 20 minutes, until the skin begins to shrivel. Drain, skin side up, in a colander over a plate for 30 minutes.

2. Meanwhile, heat 2 tablespoons of the olive oil in a large nonstick skillet over medium heat and add the onion. Cook, stirring often, until tender, about 5 minutes, and add the garlic. Cook, stirring, for 30 seconds to 1 minute, until fragrant. Transfer to a bowl. Add the tomatoes, herbs, 1 teaspoon salt, 1 teaspoon of the sugar, and 1 tablespoon oil.

3. Place the eggplants skin side down in the pan in which you cooked the onions. Season with salt. Fill the eggplants with the onion-tomato mixture. Mix together the remaining 3 tablespoons olive oil, the remaining 1½ teaspoons sugar, the water, and lemon juice. Drizzle over and around the eggplants. Cover the pan and place over low heat. Cook gently for 1½ hours, basting from time to time with the liquid in the pan and adding water to the pan if it becomes too dry. By the end of cooking, the eggplants should be practically flat and the liquid in the pan slightly caramelized. Spoon this juice over the eggplant. Cool in the pan and serve at room temperature.

ADVANCE PREPARATION: You can roast the eggplant through Step 1 and make the filling through Step 2 several hours before assembling and cooking the *imam bayildi*. Once cooked, the finished dish can sit for several hours, or be stored in the refrigerator overnight and brought back to room temperature before serving.

STUFFED EGGPLANTS (OR PEPPERS)

Turkey • **Serves 6 as a main dish or 8 to 10 as a *meze***

The typical Turkish stuffing for vegetables is a delicate rice mixture seasoned with allspice, cinnamon, parsley, and dill. It's sweet and savory and is fairly addictive. Once stuffed, the vegetables are gently cooked in water and oil. This is a beautiful dish to serve as part of a Middle Eastern buffet.

6 long, thin eggplants or medium red bell peppers

3 tablespoons extra virgin olive oil

1 large or 2 medium onions, finely chopped

2 tablespoons pine nuts

4 garlic cloves, minced

2 tablespoons currants, soaked for 5 minutes in hot water

1 teaspoon ground cinnamon

1 teaspoon ground allspice

1 teaspoon sugar

3 cups water

1¼ cups short-grain rice

Salt and freshly ground pepper

½ cup finely chopped fresh flat-leaf parsley

¼ cup finely chopped fresh dill

2 tablespoons fresh lemon juice (optional)

Lemon wedges

1. If making the dish with eggplants: Cut them in half crosswise and, using a paring knife, cut a cylinder around the inside, leaving about ¼ inch of flesh inside the skin. Using a spoon, scoop out the flesh, right down to the end of the eggplant. Set aside the flesh for use in another dish.

If making the dish with peppers: Cut off the tops, then remove and discard the seeds and membranes.

2. Heat 1 tablespoon of the olive oil in a large, wide saucepan or skillet over medium heat and add the onion and pine nuts. Cook, stirring, until the onion is tender and beginning to color, about 8 minutes, and add the garlic. Cook, stirring, until fragrant, 30 seconds to 1 minute, and stir in the currants, cinnamon, allspice, and sugar. Stir together, then add ½ cup water. Cook, stirring, until most of the liquid has evaporated, about 5 minutes. Add the rice, ¾ teaspoon salt, and some pepper. Add 2 cups water and bring to a boil. Reduce the heat and simmer, uncovered, until the liquid is absorbed, 10 to 15 minutes. Remove from the heat and cover the pan with a clean towel. Leave for 10 minutes, then stir in the herbs. Taste and adjust salt and pepper.

3. Sprinkle the insides of the eggplants with salt. Stuff the eggplants or peppers with the rice mixture. For peppers, replace the cap. Lay the eggplants, or stand the peppers, in a wide pan. Mix together the remaining ½ cup water, 2 tablespoons olive oil, and the lemon juice, and pour over and around the vegetables. Bring to a simmer, reduce the heat, and cover the pan. Simmer for 40 to 50 minutes, until there is no longer any liquid, just oil, in the pan and the vegetables are very tender. Uncover and cool in the pan.

4. If the eggplant halves are quite long, cut them in half. Arrange the vegetables on a platter, garnish with lemon wedges for squeezing over the vegetables, and serve.

ADVANCE PREPARATION: This is an excellent keeper, and since it should be served at room temperature, it's fine to make it a day ahead and refrigerate overnight. Bring back to room temperature before serving. You can also make up the rice filling a day before stuffing the vegetables.

ARAB EGGPLANT, TOMATO, AND CHICK PEA CASSEROLE

Middle East • **Serves 4 as a main dish or 6 as a side or** *meze*

This simple casserole is hearty and comforting. The eggplant is broiled (or grilled) before being layered with chick peas in tomato sauce, then the dish is baked. I've seen more than one name for this dish, and it goes without saying that there's more than one version. It should be served at room temperature with fresh Arab Bread (page 51), and always tastes best if made a day ahead.

- 1 pound (1 large or 2 medium) eggplants, peeled if desired, cut in half lengthwise, then sliced about ½ inch thick
- 2 tablespoons extra virgin olive oil, plus additional for brushing
- 1 large onion, chopped
- 2 to 4 garlic cloves (to taste), minced
- 1 can (28 ounces) chopped tomatoes, with juice
- 3 tablespoons tomato paste
- Salt and freshly ground pepper
- 1 can (15 ounces) chick peas, drained
- 3 tablespoons chopped fresh flat-leaf parsley

1. Set an oven rack about 2 inches from the heat source and heat the broiler. Oil a baking sheet with olive oil. Cover the baking sheet with the eggplant slices and brush each slice lightly with oil. Broil for 2 to 3 minutes, until lightly browned. Flip the slices over and broil another minute, until lightly browned on the other side and softened all the way through. Watch closely so the slices don't burn.

Note: *The eggplant slices can also be grilled over a medium-high fire for 2 to 3 minutes on each side; or in a panini grill for 2 to 3 minutes.*

2. Heat 2 tablespoons olive oil in a large, heavy saucepan over medium heat and add the onion. Cook, stirring often, until tender, about 5 minutes, and add the garlic. Cook, stirring, until the garlic is fragrant, about 1 minute, and add the tomatoes and tomato paste. Bring to a simmer, season with salt, and simmer, stirring often, for 20 to 25 min-utes, until the sauce is thick and fragrant. Add pepper, taste, and adjust salt. Stir in the chick peas.

3. Heat the oven to 350°F. Oil a 2-quart baking dish or gratin. Cover the bottom with one-third of the tomato–chick pea sauce and top with a layer of half the eggplant. Spoon half the remaining sauce over the eggplant, and repeat the layers.

4. Bake for 20 to 30 minutes, until bubbling. Remove from the heat and cool. Sprinkle on the parsley before serving warm.

ADVANCE PREPARATION: You can assemble this dish through Step 3 up to 2 days ahead and keep in the refrigerator.

LEFTOVERS: The casserole will be good for about 5 days.

FAVA BEAN AND POTATO STEW

Algeria • **Serves 4**

Many Mediterranean fava bean recipes, like the one I adapted this dish from, utilize the whole bean, provided it's tender. I have access to tender young favas at the Los Angeles farmers' markets, but truth to tell, I will never enjoy them in their pods, or even in their skins. There's just too much cellulose. So I always go through the process of shelling and skinning the beans. But it's worth it. This is a particularly tasty, comforting stew, especially when served with country bread or pita.

- 2 tablespoons extra virgin olive oil, plus additional for drizzling
- 2 medium onions, chopped
- 6 garlic cloves, minced
- 4 tablespoons chopped fresh flat-leaf parsley
- 4 tablespoons chopped fresh cilantro
- Salt
- 1 can (14 ounces) chopped tomatoes
- 2 pounds fresh fava beans, shelled and skinned (page 113)
- 1 pound potatoes, such as Yukon gold, diced
- 2 tablespoons tomato paste
- ¾ teaspoon ground cinnamon
- 1 tablespoon paprika

2 cups water

Freshly ground pepper

1. Heat the olive oil in a large skillet or Dutch oven over medium heat and add the onions. Cook, stirring, until tender, about 5 minutes. Add the garlic, 2 tablespoons of the parsley, 2 tablespoons of the cilantro, and about 1 teaspoon salt, and continue to cook, stirring, for another 1 or 2 minutes, until the mixture is very fragrant. Add the tomatoes and cook, stirring often, for 10 to 15 minutes, until the tomatoes have cooked down and smell fragrant.

2. Add the fava beans, potatoes, tomato paste, cinnamon, paprika, and the 2 cups water, or enough to just cover the vegetables, and bring to a simmer. Simmer for 20 minutes, or until the potatoes and favas are tender. Stir in the remaining 2 tablespoons parsley and 2 tablespoons cilantro, grind in some pepper, taste, and adjust salt. Drizzle on some olive oil and serve.

ADVANCE PREPARATION: You can make this dish up to a day ahead and reheat. Wait until you reheat before you add the remaining parsley and cilantro.

LEFTOVERS: The stew will continue to taste great for about 5 days.

FAVA BEANS

Fava beans are native to the eastern Mediterranean, and are popular throughout the region, particularly in southern Italy, Greece, and Spain. Fresh favas are a sign of spring throughout the region (and, I might add, in California), and you find dishes everywhere that show them off in conjunction with other spring vegetables, such as fresh peas, scallions, and baby artichokes (see the Artichoke and Fresh Fava Stew on page 269 and the Fritteda on page 268). One of the great springtime pleasures in Tuscany is eating raw young fava beans with Pecorino Toscano and a glass of red wine. In Provence, I've enjoyed a similar delightful ritual, without the cheese. You sit around with your aperitif, leisurely peeling the shelled beans and popping them into your mouth.

Dried fava beans, skinned and split, are also popular throughout the Mediterranean. One of the signature dishes of Puglia is Dried Fava Beans and Greens (page 309), a luscious, comforting dish that was on every menu I encountered in that region. The dried beans go into many North African soups and stews (pages 169 to 171) as well as salads, and they're a key ingredient in the Middle Eastern Falafel (page 104).

In California, my local farmers' markets begin offering favas in March, and I buy them every week, knowing that they will not be around for too long. They go into pastas and risottos, salads and soups. I don't mind shelling and skinning the beans; it's a leisurely task that is so worth the prize.

How to Prepare Favas

Once you shell the favas, you must remove their tough skins. Bring a couple of quarts of water to a boil in a medium saucepan. Prepare an ice bath. Drop the fava beans into the water and boil for 1 minute, then transfer to the ice water. Leave for a few minutes, then drain.

Use your thumbnail to open up the skin at the spot where the bean is attached to the pod, then gently squeeze out the bean. I find that the process goes quickly if I pick up a handful of beans, hold one between my thumb and forefinger, and use my other thumbnail to flick off the edge of the bean. I squeeze the bean out and catch it with my thumb and forefinger, then put it into the bowl I've placed on the work surface while dropping the skin with my other hand into my compost bucket.

BRAISED FENNEL WITH PARMESAN
Italy and France • **Serves 4 to 6**

Fennel is popular throughout the Mediterranean, but especially so in Italy. This simple braised fennel dish is also made in France, where Gruyère would be used rather than Parmesan. Sometimes fennel is difficult to find in the supermarket, but I always find it in Middle Eastern markets. Don't core the fennel until after you've cooked it in the boiling water. That way it will stay intact.

> Salt
>
> 2 pounds fennel bulbs, tough outer layers
>   removed, ends trimmed, the bulbs quartered
>
> Freshly ground pepper
>
> 2 tablespoons extra virgin olive oil
>
> ½ cup freshly grated Parmesan or
>   Gruyère cheese

1. Bring a large pot of generously salted water to a boil and add the fennel. Boil for 5 to 8 minutes, until tender. Transfer to a bowl of ice water. Reserve ½ cup of the cooking water. Using tongs so you don't burn your fingers, transfer the fennel to a cutting board and cut out the cores.

2. Heat the oven to 400°F. Oil a baking dish or gratin that is large enough to accommodate the fennel in a single layer. Place the fennel in the baking dish, season with salt and pepper, and drizzle with the olive oil. Pour the reserved cooking water into the dish. Cover with foil and bake for 20 minutes, until the fennel is quite tender.

3. Baste with any liquid that remains in the dish and reduce the heat to 325°F. Sprinkle on the cheese and bake, uncovered, for another 10 to 15 minutes, until the cheese has melted and begun to brown. Serve hot.

ADVANCE PREPARATION: You can make the dish through Step 2 several hours before you wish to serve it.

GREENS WITH CURRANTS AND PINE NUTS
Serves 4

This is a popular dish from Catalonia to Genoa. In Catalonia, you'll find the dish made with spinach; in Provence, with chard; and in Italy, with spinach or other greens. The Greeks do something like it too, using wild foraged greens. In Nice, this combination is sweetened and baked in a dessert crust for an intriguing sweet pastry. Of all the greens used in this dish, Swiss chard is my favorite.

> ⅓ cup currants, raisins, or golden raisins
>
> Salt
>
> 2 pounds greens, such as spinach, chard
>   (my preference), or beet greens, stemmed
>
> 2 tablespoons extra virgin olive oil
>
> 2 garlic cloves, minced
>
> ⅓ cup pine nuts
>
> Freshly ground pepper

1. Place the currants in a bowl and pour on hot water to cover. Soak for 10 minutes and drain.

2. Bring a large pot of water to a boil and add 1 heaped tablespoon salt and the greens. Cook for 1 to 2 minutes, until just tender (spinach will be ready in just 30 seconds). Transfer to a bowl of ice water and let sit for a few minutes. Drain and squeeze out as much water as you can. Chop coarsely.

3. Heat the oil in a large, heavy nonstick skillet over medium heat. Add the garlic, pine nuts, and currants, and cook, stirring, just until the garlic begins to smell fragrant and the pine nuts begin to color, about 1 minute. Add the chopped greens and toss until they are well coated with oil and heated through, 2 to 3 minutes. Season to taste with salt and pepper and serve, or cool and serve at room temperature.

ADVANCE PREPARATION: You can make this dish several hours before serving. Reheat gently on top of the stove if you want to serve it hot. The blanched greens will keep in a covered bowl in the refrigerator for 3 or 4 days.

KALE WITH GARLIC AND OLIVE OIL
Italy • **Serves 4**

The kale that I love to use for this recipe, a standard technique for any type of greens, is the black kale (*cavolo nero*) that I can get throughout the winter months at my farmers' markets. It's such a dark green that it's practically black, thus the name (though it's also known as dinosaur kale). If you can't find it, use regular kale, which is easy to get hold of in supermarkets, or Russian kale, also sold in farmers' markets.

> Salt
>
> 2 large bunches kale, preferably black kale (*cavolo nero*), stemmed
>
> 2 tablespoons extra virgin olive oil
>
> 2 garlic cloves, minced
>
> ¼ teaspoon hot red pepper flakes
>
> Freshly ground pepper
>
> 1 lemon, cut into wedges

1. Bring a large pot of water to a boil and add 1 to 2 tablespoons salt and the kale. Parboil for 2 to 4 minutes, until the kale is tender. Transfer immediately to a bowl of ice water, then drain, squeeze out the water, and chop coarsely.

2. Heat the oil in a large, heavy nonstick skillet over medium heat. Add the garlic and pepper flakes, and cook, stirring, until the garlic is fragrant and just begins to color, 30 to 60 seconds. Stir in the greens. Stir for a couple of minutes, until the kale is nicely seasoned with garlic and oil. Add salt and pepper to taste, and serve, passing lemon wedges to squeeze onto the greens.

ADVANCE PREPARATION: The blanched greens will keep in the refrigerator for about 3 days.

SPINACH WITH SPICES AND YOGURT
Syria • **Serves 6 as a side dish or 8 to 10 as a *meze***

There are several layers of flavor and texture going on here. The spinach is sautéed with spices—allspice, cinnamon, clove, coriander—then topped with a creamy, garlicky yogurt, which is in turn sprinkled with chopped walnuts.

I've adapted this heavenly dish from Clifford Wright's *Mediterranean Vegetables*. Serve it with Arab Bread (page 51) and a simple rice pilaf (pages 327 to 328).

> 2 pounds spinach, preferably leaf spinach, stemmed and wilted (page 284)
>
> 1 to 2 large garlic cloves (to taste), peeled
>
> Salt
>
> 2 tablespoons plus 1 teaspoon extra virgin olive oil
>
> 2 cups drained yogurt (page 21)
>
> ⅛ teaspoon ground allspice
>
> ⅛ teaspoon ground clove
>
> ⅛ teaspoon freshly grated nutmeg
>
> ⅛ teaspoon ground cinnamon
>
> 1 scant teaspoon coriander seeds or 1 teaspoon freshly ground coriander
>
> ½ cup chopped walnuts

1. Squeeze excess water out of the spinach and chop coarsely.

2. Mash the garlic to a paste with ½ teaspoon salt and 1 teaspoon of the olive oil in a mortar and pestle. Stir into the yogurt and set aside.

3. Heat the remaining 2 tablespoons olive oil in a wide, heavy skillet over medium heat and add the spices. Cook, stirring, until they begin to sizzle, and add the spinach. Cook, stirring, until heated through and coated with the oil and spices, 2 to 3 minutes. Transfer to a serving platter and spoon the yogurt over the top. Sprinkle with walnuts and serve.

ADVANCE PREPARATION: The spinach can be wilted up to 3 days ahead and kept in the refrigerator.

WILTING SPINACH

Spinach is so delicate that it takes very little in the way of cooking to soften it, and it will lose much of its volume once the leaves have wilted. You can wilt just-washed spinach simply by heating in a wide frying pan over high heat. As the water left on the leaves comes to a boil, the spinach will collapse. I find this somewhat inefficient if I have a large amount, because the leaves don't all cook down at the same time and the cooking can be uneven. If I am dealing with a large amount of spinach, I blanch it in a large pot of generously salted boiling water. The spinach wilts on contact with the water, and need only stay in for 10 to 20 seconds. I then immediately transfer it, using my Chinese deep-fry skimmer, to a bowl of ice water, and drain.

Another easy way to wilt spinach, especially if you don't have too much, or if you're working with baby spinach, is to put the spinach in a bowl and pour on boiling water to cover. Let sit for about 30 seconds, then drain and rinse with cold water. When I want to make a spinach dish in a hurry, I buy the washed, stemmed baby spinach and use this method.

After the spinach is wilted, it's important to squeeze out excess water before you proceed with a recipe. You can do this by the handful, or wrap the spinach in a towel, twist the towel, and squeeze over the sink. Your towel will absorb some of the green from the spinach, but it will wash out.

Wilted Spinach for 1: Two Ways

- Wilt 2 heaped cups baby spinach as described above. Drain and squeeze dry. Toss with a little extra virgin olive oil and fresh lemon juice if desired. Season with salt and serve.

- Wilt 2 heaped cups baby spinach as described above. Drain and squeeze dry. Heat 2 to 3 teaspoons extra virgin olive oil in a nonstick skillet over medium heat and add 1 minced garlic clove. Cook, stirring, until fragrant, 30 seconds to 1 minute. Stir in the spinach, season with salt and pepper, and toss until coated with oil and garlic. Serve.

SAUTÉED MUSHROOMS WITH GREMOLATA

Italy • **Serves 2 as a main course, 4 as a first course or side dish, or 12 as a topping for bruschetta**

As you can see from the yield above, this dish is extremely versatile. If I have some meaty wild mushrooms, or even nice cultivated ones, I sometimes make this and serve it on bruschetta for dinner. You can also use the mushrooms as a pizza topping.

> 2 tablespoons extra virgin olive oil
>
> 1 pound cultivated or wild mushrooms (such as shiitake, chanterelles, or oyster mushrooms, or a combination), trimmed and quartered if small, thickly sliced if large
>
> Salt
>
> 2 tablespoons dry white wine
>
> Freshly ground black pepper
>
> 1 recipe Gremolata (page 85)

1. Heat a large, heavy nonstick skillet over medium-high heat. Add 1 tablespoon of the olive oil, and when it's hot, add the mushrooms. Sear the mushrooms, stirring with a wooden spoon or tossing in the pan, until they are lightly browned and begin to exude their juices. Add salt to taste and the wine, and continue to cook, stirring or tossing the mushrooms in the pan, until the wine has just about evaporated and the mushrooms are glazed, 5 to 10 minutes.

2. Add the remaining 1 tablespoon oil, pepper to taste, and the gremolata. Cook, stirring, until fragrant, about 1 more minute. Taste and adjust salt. Serve hot.

ADVANCE PREPARATION: You can make this recipe through Step 1 hours in advance. Reheat over medium-high heat and proceed with Step 2.

WILD MUSHROOM RAGOUT
Provence and Italy • Serves 6

Mushrooms have been the vegetarian's meat stand-in for decades. They're hearty, savory, and for a vegetable, well, meaty. But in the Mediterranean, mushrooms are appreciated not as a meat substitute, but on their own merits. In the fall, you'll find people out in the forests from the Rock of Gibraltar to the far reaches of Turkey hunting for wild mushrooms. I've benefited from the fruits of these hunts, mostly in Provence and Italy. Here in the States I rely on the farmers' markets to provide me with wild mushrooms like girolles and other chanterelles; but I can find oyster mushrooms and shiitake in supermarkets. You can use all wild or a combination of wild and cultivated for this.

1 ounce (about 1 cup) dried porcini mushrooms

2 cups boiling water

2 tablespoons extra virgin olive oil

1 medium onion or 2 shallots, chopped

4 garlic cloves, minced or put through a press

1 pound button mushrooms, cleaned, trimmed, and sliced ½ inch thick

1 pound wild mushrooms, trimmed and brushed clean; or oyster mushrooms, trimmed and torn into pieces if very large

Salt

1 tablespoon unbleached all-purpose flour

½ cup fruity red wine, such as a Côtes du Rhône

2 teaspoons chopped fresh rosemary (or 1 teaspoon crumbled dried)

2 teaspoons chopped fresh sage

Freshly ground pepper

1. Place the dried mushrooms in a Pyrex measuring cup and pour on the boiling water. Let soak for 30 minutes. Place a strainer over a bowl, line it with cheesecloth or paper towels, and drain the mushrooms. Squeeze the mushrooms over the strainer to extract all the flavorful juices. Rinse the mushrooms, away from the bowl with the soaking liquid, until they are free of sand. Squeeze dry and, if very large, chop coarsely. Set aside. Measure out 1½ cups of the soaking liquid and set aside.

2. Heat the olive oil in a large, heavy nonstick skillet over medium heat and add the onion. Cook, stirring often, until tender, about 5 minutes. Add half the garlic, stir together for about 30 seconds, then add the button mushrooms, wild mushrooms, and about 1 teaspoon salt. Cook, stirring often, until the mushrooms begin to soften and exude their juices, about 5 minutes. Add the flour and continue to cook the mushrooms, stirring, until they have softened a little more and you can no longer see the flour, about 2 minutes. Add the reconstituted dried mushrooms and the wine and turn the heat to high. Cook, stirring, until the liquid boils down and glazes the mushrooms, 5 to 10 minutes. Add the remaining garlic, rosemary, and sage, stir together, and stir in the mushroom soaking liquid. Bring to a simmer, add salt to taste, and cook over medium-high heat, stirring often, until the mushrooms are thoroughly tender and fragrant and the surrounding broth is thick and gravy-like, 10 to 15 minutes. Remove from the heat, stir in some freshly ground pepper, taste, and adjust salt. Serve hot or warm.

ADVANCE PREPARATION: The ragout can be made up to 3 or 4 days before you wish to serve it. Reheat gently.

WILD MUSHROOMS

Here are some wild mushrooms used in the Mediterranean that are available in the United States, either in gourmet groceries, farmers' markets, Whole Foods stores, or online.

Porcini (cèpes in French): A large, luxurious, rich-tasting mushroom that is more often sold in its dried form.

Girolles or **Chanterelles:** A delicate yellow tuba-shaped mushroom with a longish stem and wonderful texture.

Morels: A small, smooth mushroom with a domed cap and creamy texture.

Trompettes de la Mort: Almost-black, thin-fleshed mushroom shaped like a trumpet.

Pleurottes: These thick, meaty mushrooms are cultivated and available now in most supermarkets.

WILD MUSHROOMS WITH TOMATOES AND BASIL

Italy • Serves 4

Porcini mushrooms with tomatoes and basil is a dish I encountered often on Italian menus, and one I could never resist. Sometimes it was part of a larger antipasto platter, other times it was a first course. I'm more likely to serve it as a main dish, spooned over polenta or tossed with pasta.

2 tablespoons extra virgin olive oil

1 medium onion or 2 shallots, chopped

3 to 4 garlic cloves (to taste), minced or put through a press

1 pound fresh porcini or other wild mushrooms (such as chanterelles, shiitake, or oyster mushrooms), cleaned, trimmed, and thickly sliced

Salt

¼ cup dry white wine

1 pound tomatoes, peeled, seeded, and chopped; or 1 can (14 ounces) tomatoes, drained and chopped

Pinch sugar

Freshly ground pepper

1 tablespoon slivered fresh basil

Heat the olive oil in a large, heavy nonstick skillet over medium heat and add the onion. Cook, stirring often, until tender, about 5 minutes. Add half the garlic, stir for about 30 seconds, then add the mushrooms. Turn up the heat to medium-high and cook the mushrooms, stirring, until they begin to brown, about 5 minutes. Add ½ teaspoon salt. Cook, stirring often, until the mushrooms begin to soften and exude their juices, about 5 minutes. Add the wine and turn the heat to high. Cook, stirring, until the liquid boils down and glazes the mushrooms, 5 to 10 minutes. Add the tomatoes, remaining garlic, sugar, and a little more salt. Reduce the heat to medium and cook, stirring often, until the tomatoes have cooked down and smell fragrant, about 15 minutes. Stir in some pepper and the basil, taste and adjust salt, and remove from the heat. Serve warm.

ADVANCE PREPARATION: This dish can be made up to 3 days before you serve it. If you're making it ahead, don't add the basil until you reheat the mushrooms.

VALENCIA-STYLE PEAS

Spain • Serves 4

I love peas so much that I rarely want to tinker with them. But this kind of tinkering is well worth it. The dish is startlingly sweet, with that hint of saffron that tells you it comes from Spain. One of the great things about it is that it works very well with frozen peas. This is adapted from a recipe by Penelope Casas.

2 garlic cloves, 1 peeled, 1 minced

Pinch saffron

Salt

1 tablespoon extra virgin olive oil

1 spring onion or 4 scallions, finely chopped (½ cup)

1½ cups fresh or frozen peas

2 tablespoons dry white wine

2 tablespoons water

2 sprigs fresh flat-leaf parsley

1 bay leaf

1½ teaspoons fresh thyme leaves (or ¼ teaspoon dried thyme)

Freshly ground pepper

1. Place the whole garlic clove in a mortar and pestle with the saffron and ¼ teaspoon salt. Mash to a paste. Set aside.

2. Heat the oil in a medium skillet or saucepan over medium heat and add the onion. Cook, stirring, until tender, about 3 minutes, and add the minced garlic. Cook, stirring, until fragrant, about 30 seconds, and add the peas. Cook for a minute, then stir in the wine, water, parsley, bay leaf, and thyme. Cover and simmer for 2 minutes.

3. Add the garlic-saffron paste to the peas, season with salt and pepper, cover, and simmer for 5 minutes more, until the peas are tender and the liquid evaporated. Remove the bay leaf and serve.

ADVANCE PREPARATION: It's best to make this recipe close to serving time. What is time-consuming is shelling the peas (if you're using fresh), and that can be done as far in advance as a day. Everything else can be prepped hours in advance.

SPRING PEAS WITH SUGAR

Italy • Serves 4 to 6

This Milanese recipe is meant to be prepared when peas are at their freshest, in the spring. My son, Liam, and I have a hard time seeing the peas from the pod to the pan when they're sweet like this; we tend to eat them like candy. But if you can resist, you won't regret it.

> 2 tablespoons unsalted butter
>
> 2 pounds fresh peas, shelled
>
> 1 cup water
>
> 1 teaspoon sugar
>
> Salt

Heat the butter in a large, wide skillet or saucepan over medium heat and add the peas. Cook, stirring, for 2 minutes. Add the water, sugar, and about ½ teaspoon salt. Bring to a boil and cook for about 2 minutes, until the peas begin to look shriveled. Reduce the heat and boil gently for another 5 minutes. Using a slotted spoon, remove the peas from the pan. Reduce whatever liquid remains in the pan to about 3 tablespoons. Toss with the peas, taste, adjust seasoning, and serve.

ADVANCE PREPARATION: I have made these peas a few hours ahead and reheated them. They were fine, but they're still best when served right away.

STUFFED LIPSTICK PEPPERS

Spain • Serves 6

When peppers are on the menu in Spain, be they stuffed or roasted or the star of a salad, they are usually the ultra-sweet, small, thin-skinned red piquillos. In recent years at the Santa Monica farmers' market, I've been able to find lipstick peppers, which are similar, if not the very same pepper, bright red and super-sweet. Unlike Greek- and Italian-style roasted bell peppers, these smaller lipstick-shaped peppers are stuffed through a slit in the side rather than from the top.

> 12 lipstick, piquillo, or other small, sweet red peppers
>
> 4 tablespoons extra virgin olive oil
>
> 2 garlic cloves, minced
>
> ½ cup chopped fresh flat-leaf parsley
>
> 2 cups fresh bread crumbs
>
> 1 cup grated Manchego cheese
>
> Salt and freshly ground pepper
>
> 1½ cups Basic Tomato Sauce (page 78)

1. Roast the peppers over a flame or on a grill until uniformly charred. Place in a plastic bag or in a covered bowl and cool. When cool enough to handle, remove all of the charred skin, rinse briefly, and pat dry.

2. Cut a slit down the side of each pepper, beginning at the stem end and stopping just before you get to the tip. Gently open the slit and remove the seeds and membranes, trying to keep the peppers intact. Set aside.

3. Heat 2 tablespoons of the olive oil in a large, nonstick skillet over medium heat and add the garlic. Cook, stirring, until fragrant, about 1 minute. Stir in the parsley and bread crumbs, and stir together until the bread crumbs are coated with oil and beginning to crisp. Remove from the heat and stir in the cheese. Season to taste with salt and pepper, and stir in 1 tablespoon olive oil. Cool slightly. Using a small spoon, stuff the peppers.

▶

4. Heat the oven to 350°F. Oil a baking dish large enough to accommodate the peppers in a single layer. Lay the peppers in the dish, slit side up. Drizzle on the remaining 1 tablespoon oil. Cover the baking dish with foil or a lid and bake the peppers for 20 minutes. Meanwhile, heat the tomato sauce.

5. Ladle the tomato sauce onto serving plates or a serving platter. Top with the stuffed peppers and serve.

ADVANCE PREPARATION: Roasted peppers will keep for about 5 days in the refrigerator. The peppers can be stuffed and held for a day or two in the refrigerator before baking.

SAUTÉED PEPPERS WITH TOMATOES
Greece • Serves 4 to 6

This is a kind of Greek peperonata, a savory mixture of peppers and tomatoes that is cooked in abundant olive oil. The Greeks use twice as much olive oil, easily, for this dish. But the dish works just fine with the amount I'm calling for here, which is still a lot for me. The peppers brown in the hot oil and taste almost as if they've been roasted. If you can find long thin-skinned sweet peppers at a farmers' market, you should use them. Otherwise, use a selection of bell peppers, quartered. Serve this as a part of a *meze* or as a side dish.

> ¼ cup extra virgin olive oil
>
> 2 pounds mixed red, yellow, and green bell peppers, quartered, seeded, and membranes removed; or long thin-skinned green peppers, halved and seeded
>
> Salt
>
> 4 garlic cloves, minced
>
> 1 cup peeled, chopped tomatoes
>
> 2 to 3 tablespoons chopped fresh flat-leaf parsley (to taste)

1. Heat the oil in a large nonstick frying pan over medium-high heat. When it is hot, add the peppers and cook, stirring often, until they begin to brown and soften, about 10 minutes. Reduce the heat to medium-low, cover, and continue to cook, stirring from time to time, until the peppers are nice and soft, and well browned, 5 to 10 more minutes, depending on the thickness of the peppers. Season to taste with salt.

2. Using tongs or a slotted spoon, transfer the peppers to a bowl. Add the garlic to the hot oil and cook until fragrant, about 30 seconds. Stir in the tomatoes and cook, stirring often, until they break down and thicken, about 10 minutes. Season with salt.

3. Add the peppers to the tomatoes and stir to combine well. Taste and adjust seasoning. Stir in the parsley and serve. Or cool and serve at room temperature.

ADVANCE PREPARATION: This pepper dish will keep for 3 days in the refrigerator. The flavors will ripen.

SPICY POTATOES WITH AÏOLI
Spain • Serves 6 to 8 as a tapa or 4 to 6 as a side dish

There's a wonderful tapas bar in Valencia called Bar Pilar, where I found myself night after night for dinner, ordering the same dishes. These fried potatoes could be described as decadent, with their rich layers of spicy tomato sauce, then garlicky aïoli (which the Catalans call *allioli*).

> 2 pounds potatoes, a medium-starchy type like Yukon golds
>
> 4 tablespoons extra virgin olive oil
>
> Salt and freshly ground pepper
>
> 1 garlic clove, crushed
>
> ½ dried red chile pepper, crushed; or ¼ teaspoon crushed hot red pepper flakes
>
> 1½ cups Basic Tomato Sauce (page 78)
>
> ¼ cup dry white wine
>
> Tabasco sauce (optional)
>
> ½ cup Aïoli (page 72)

1. Scrub or peel the potatoes, as you wish, and cut into wedges.

2. Heat 3 tablespoons of the oil in a large skillet over medium-high heat and add the potatoes. Brown well on all sides and season with salt and pepper. Reduce the heat to low, cover, and cook, shaking the pan and stirring the potatoes from time to time, until tender, 15 to 20 minutes. Taste and adjust seasoning.

3. Meanwhile, heat the remaining 1 tablespoon olive oil over medium heat in a medium skillet and add the garlic clove. Cook, stirring, until browned, and remove from the oil. Add the chile, stir for a few seconds, and add the tomato sauce, white wine, and a dash of Tabasco. Bring to a simmer and cook, stirring often, for 10 to 15 minutes, until thick. Taste and adjust seasoning.

4. Transfer the potatoes to a warm serving dish. Top with the tomato sauce, and top the tomato sauce with the aïoli. Serve hot.

ADVANCE PREPARATION: All of the elements of this dish can be done a few hours in advance and held separately. You can even do the tomato sauce a few days ahead. Shortly before serving, reheat the potatoes and the sauce and assemble as directed.

POTATOES WITH GREEN BEANS AND GARLIC

Spain • **Serves 4**

Here is more proof that the Spanish have an innate sense of what to do with potatoes. In this dish they're paired with green beans, garlic, and spring onions, and the dish is set off by bright wedges of hard-cooked eggs. I've enjoyed this as both a main dish and a side.

1 pound red-skinned potatoes, scrubbed and halved

Salt

¾ pound green beans, preferably flat beans, trimmed and broken in half

2 tablespoons extra virgin olive oil

1 bunch spring onions, bulb and light green parts only, chopped; or 1 medium onion, chopped

2 to 3 large garlic cloves (to taste), minced

Freshly ground pepper

2 large eggs, hard-cooked and cut into wedges

1. Steam the potatoes over 1 inch of boiling water for 15 minutes, until tender.

2. Bring a medium or large pot of water to a boil and add a generous spoonful of salt and the green beans. Boil for 4 to 5 minutes, until just tender. Transfer to a bowl of ice water and drain.

3. Heat the oil in a large nonstick skillet over medium heat and add the onions. Cook, stirring often, until tender, 5 to 8 minutes. Stir in the garlic and continue to cook for another minute or so, until the garlic is fragrant. Stir in the beans and cook, stirring, for 5 minutes, until quite tender and coated with oil but still bright green.

4. Gently stir in the potatoes, and add lots of salt and pepper. Scatter the egg wedges over the top, cover, reduce the heat to low, and cook another 10 minutes. Serve hot or warm.

ADVANCE PREPARATION: This dish can be made a few hours ahead and reheated. Don't add the egg wedges until you reheat the dish. The steamed potatoes and blanched beans (Steps 1 and 2) will both keep for 3 to 4 days in covered bowls in the refrigerator.

WHAT IS A RED-SKINNED POTATO, ANYWAY?

Red-skinned potatoes are the most common waxy variety of potato. Waxy potatoes hold their shape when cooked, so they're good for stews, soups, and salads, or other dishes where you don't want the potato to fall apart. White boiling potatoes—sometimes called creamers or long whites, depending on their size—have the same kind of starch and can be substituted when red-skinned potatoes are called for.

ROASTED POTATOES WITH ROSEMARY

Italy • Serves 4

Driving through Abruzzo on our way to the Gargano Promontory, we took a detour into the hills to the village of Laciano, hoping to get there in time for the market and to have a look at the church. But by the time we got there, the market was shutting down, and everybody seemed to have closed up shop and gone home for a siesta. It was a very hot Saturday afternoon, and I would have gladly slept as well. But we were hungry, so we looked for a trattoria. We wound up at a self-service canteen, very humdrum, and yet … there were beautiful big portions of buffalo mozzarella and tomatoes, the usual selection of vinegars and olive oil on the tables, big wedges of ripe, juicy watermelon, and hotel pans filled with the most luscious roasted potatoes and vegetables. Although most Italians would eat these savory vegetables with meat, I think they make a terrific accompaniment to egg dishes.

1½ to 2 pounds potatoes, any type (I like Yukon golds, fingerlings, and Dutch yellow), scrubbed and cut into uniform chunks, about 1½ inches wide

2 to 3 tablespoons extra virgin olive oil (enough to coat the potatoes)

Salt and freshly ground pepper

1 tablespoon chopped fresh rosemary (more to taste)

1. Heat the oven to 425°F. Pat the potato pieces dry with kitchen towels. Oil a large baking dish or baking sheet. Toss the potatoes with enough oil so that all of the pieces are coated. Salt generously and sprinkle with freshly ground pepper. Add the rosemary and toss again, then spread in an even layer in the baking dish.

2. Roast the potatoes until tender when pierced with a knife and lightly browned, 25 to 40 minutes. Stir from time to time to ensure even browning.

ADVANCE PREPARATION: The potatoes should be roasted right after you've prepped them, but once roasted they can sit for an hour or two and be reheated.

ROASTED POTATOES AND ROOT VEGETABLES WITH ROSEMARY

Italy • Serves 4 to 6

Root vegetables sweeten as they roast, and they go wonderfully with potatoes. It's so easy to just throw this dish together and put it into the oven. When I had these at the self-service trattoria in Laciano, even though the vegetables had been sitting out for some time, they were delicious.

When I make this, I like to use purple potatoes. They have a good texture for roasting and add wonderful color to the dish.

2½ pounds mixed root vegetables, such as carrots, parsnips, turnips, fennel, and shallots

1 head garlic, cloves separated

1 pound potatoes, scrubbed and quartered

Salt and freshly ground pepper

1 tablespoon chopped fresh rosemary

2 to 3 tablespoons extra virgin olive oil (enough to coat the vegetables)

1. Heat the oven to 425°F. Oil a baking sheet or baking dish large enough to fit all of the vegetables in a single layer. Peel the vegetables and cut into 1½-inch chunks. Toss with the garlic, potatoes, salt, pepper, rosemary, and olive oil until all of the vegetables are coated with oil.

2. Spread the vegetables in an even layer on the baking sheet. Place in the top third of the oven and roast for 20 minutes, stirring halfway through. Reduce the heat to 375°F and roast until lightly browned and tender all the way through when pierced with a knife, about 10 minutes. Remove from the heat and serve.

ADVANCE PREPARATION: The vegetables should be roasted right after they're prepped, but they can hold for a few hours once roasted. Reheat in a medium oven.

VEGETABLES AND BEANS

FRIED POTATOES WITH TOMATOES AND OREGANO

Greece • Serves 4 to 6

Liam referred to this luscious dish, a favorite in Greek tavernas, as "pizza potatoes." It's an apt description of fried potatoes topped with tomato sauce and oregano. In Greece, the potatoes are shallow-fried in abundant olive oil, much more than I use here—and I'm using a lot, for me! When you pour off the oil, you'll see that not all of it is absorbed.

⅓ cup extra virgin olive oil

4 medium potatoes, preferably Yukon golds, scrubbed, peeled if desired, and cut into thin wedges or ¼ × ½ × 2-inch sticks

Salt and freshly ground pepper

1½ teaspoons dried oregano

2 garlic cloves, minced

1 pound ripe, firm tomatoes, peeled, seeded, and chopped; or 1 can (14 ounces) chopped tomatoes, with juice

¼ cup crumbled feta (optional)

1. Heat the olive oil in a wide nonstick skillet over medium-high heat and add half the potatoes. Cook, turning, until nicely browned and cooked through, about 10 minutes. Season with salt, pepper, and ½ teaspoon of the oregano. Transfer with a slotted spoon to a serving dish or platter, leaving the oil in the pan. Cook the remaining potatoes, season them, and transfer to the serving dish.

2. Pour off all but 1 tablespoon of the oil and add the garlic to the skillet. Cook, stirring, until fragrant, 30 seconds to 1 minute. Add the tomatoes, season with salt, pepper, and the remaining ½ teaspoon oregano, and cook until the tomatoes thicken and smell fragrant, 5 to 10 minutes. Taste and adjust seasonings. Either pour the tomato sauce directly over the potatoes, or make a space in the middle of the serving dish and fill with the tomato sauce (for dipping). Sprinkle with feta if desired, and serve.

ADVANCE PREPARATION: This dish should be made as close as possible to serving time if you want the potatoes to stay crisp. However, you can cook the potatoes a few hours ahead and warm them in a 350°F oven for 15 to 20 minutes if you don't mind losing some of the crispiness.

POTATO AND OLIVE STEW

Greece • Serves 4 as a main dish or 6 as a side dish

This savory stew of potatoes, tomatoes, and kalamata olives is extremely comforting. It's from the Greek Ionian Islands; similar dishes are found in the Balkans, along the Adriatic. My rendition of this dish calls for considerably less olive oil than an authentic Greek recipe would use. Serve it as a main dish, with bread and feta, or as a side dish.

1½ pounds medium or small red-skinned potatoes, scrubbed

2 tablespoons extra virgin olive oil

Salt

2 large garlic cloves, minced

16 kalamata olives, pitted and left whole

1¼ cups canned chopped tomatoes, with juice

Freshly ground pepper

½ to 1 teaspoon dried oregano (to taste)

½ lemon

1 to 2 ounces feta (optional)

1. Cut the potatoes in half. If small and round, quarter them. If medium-size, cut each half into ½-inch-thick slices.

2. Heat a heavy casserole or Dutch oven over medium-high heat and add the olive oil. When it is hot, add the potatoes and cook, stirring, until coated with oil and sizzling. Salt the potatoes. Stir in the garlic, stir for about 30 seconds, until sizzling, and add the olives. Continue to cook for 2 or 3 minutes, stirring, until the mixture is fragrant. Add the tomatoes, salt (not too much at first because the salt from the olives will season the sauce), and pepper, and bring to a simmer. Cover, reduce the heat to low, and simmer for 30 to 40 minutes, until the potatoes are tender and the sauce thick. Taste and adjust the salt. Check the stew and stir often, adding water if the potatoes begin to stick to the pot.

3. Stir the oregano into the stew. Squeeze in a few drops of lemon juice, simmer a few more minutes, and serve. Top each serving with crumbled feta if you wish.

ADVANCE PREPARATION: You can make this dish several hours or even a day ahead of time and reheat. You might need to thin it out with a little water.

PAN-FRIED ZUCCHINI WITH MINT AND PEPPERONCINI

Italy • **Serves 4**

The Romans love zucchini. Although I first tasted this dish many years ago at a Sardinian restaurant in Rome, it's actually a traditional Roman Jewish recipe. Serve it on its own as a side dish, or toss the zucchini with pasta.

> 2 tablespoons extra virgin olive oil
>
> 4 garlic cloves, crushed
>
> 2 pounds zucchini, thinly sliced
>
> 1 small dried hot chile pepper (pepperoncini), crumbled; or ¼ teaspoon hot red pepper flakes
>
> 2 tablespoons white wine vinegar
>
> ¼ cup tightly packed minced fresh flat-leaf parsley
>
> ¼ cup tightly packed minced fresh basil or mint
>
> Salt, preferably kosher salt or coarse sea salt

1. Heat the olive oil in a large, heavy skillet over medium heat until it ripples and feels hot when you hold your hand above it. Add the garlic cloves and cook until golden and fragrant, 2 to 3 minutes. Remove the garlic and discard.

2. Add the zucchini and the chile pepper to the skillet, and cook, stirring, for 2 to 3 minutes, until the zucchini begins to look transparent in the middle and bright green on the outside. Add the vinegar and turn up the heat so that it boils. Boil for

1 to 2 minutes, or until the vinegar evaporates. Reduce the heat, cover, and simmer for 4 to 5 minutes, until the zucchini is tender. Stir in the herbs and salt, taste, and adjust seasonings. Serve hot or at room temperature.

ADVANCE PREPARATION: You can make this recipe a few hours ahead. Hold at room temperature or in the refrigerator.

LEFTOVERS: The leftovers will keep for a couple of days in the refrigerator. Use them as a filling in a frittata (page 176).

SAUTÉED ZUCCHINI AND RED PEPPERS
Serves 6

This simple sauté is one of those summer Mediterranean dishes that you'd see in Provence, Italy, or Spain, albeit cooked in more olive oil than I'm using here. Since zucchini and peppers are available year-round, you could brighten up a winter table with the dish. In season, try to get those sweet lipstick peppers that appear in farmers' markets in the fall. Otherwise, use a red bell pepper.

> 1 tablespoon extra virgin olive oil
>
> 1 red bell pepper or 2 lipstick peppers, diced a little smaller than the zucchini
>
> 1½ pounds zucchini, diced
>
> 1 to 2 garlic cloves (to taste), minced
>
> Salt and freshly ground pepper
>
> 1 tablespoon chopped fresh flat-leaf parsley, marjoram, or dill

Heat the olive oil in a large nonstick skillet over medium heat. Add the red pepper and cook, stirring, until just about tender, 5 minutes. Add the zucchini and garlic, and stir together for a minute. Add salt and pepper, and cook, stirring often, until the zucchini is tender but still bright, 8 to 10 minutes. Taste and adjust seasoning. Toss with the fresh herbs and serve.

ADVANCE PREPARATION: I have made this dish several hours before serving and reheated it with good results. But I prefer to serve it right away.

PAN-COOKED ZUCCHINI AND TOMATOES (Pisto)

Spain • Serves 6 generously

Pisto is a sort of ratatouille-like mixture, served as a tapa in southern Spain and usually as a side dish in central Spain. *Pisto Manchega,* from La Mancha, is traditionally served with eggs or chorizo.

Cook the dish for a long time so that the zucchini and tomatoes melt together. Serve with thick slices of toasted garlic bread, or with rice or eggs. Try also the variation at right, in which you stir eggs into the mixture just before serving. If you're making this to serve as a tapa, make half the quantity.

- 2 tablespoons extra virgin olive oil
- 2 medium onions, chopped
- 1 green bell pepper, diced
- 4 garlic cloves, minced
- 2 pounds zucchini, diced
- 2 pounds tomatoes, peeled, seeded, and chopped; or 1 can (28 ounces) tomatoes, drained and chopped
- ½ teaspoon sugar
- Salt
- ¼ cup water
- Freshly ground black pepper

Heat the oil in a large, heavy nonstick skillet over medium heat and add the onions. Cook, stirring often, until just about tender, about 5 minutes. Add the bell pepper and cook another 5 minutes, until the vegetables are soft. Add the garlic and cook, stirring, for a minute or two, until fragrant. Stir in the zucchini and toss together for a couple of minutes, until it is coated with oil and beginning to look translucent. Add the tomatoes, sugar, and a generous amount of salt, and increase the heat to medium-high. Cook, stirring often, for 5 to 10 minutes, until the tomatoes have cooked down slightly. Add the water, stir together, and reduce the heat to medium. Cook, uncovered, for 30 to 35 minutes, stirring often and pressing down on the zucchini with the back of a spoon, until the vegetables are soft and easy to mash. Keep pressing down on the mixture so that it thickens and the zucchini breaks down somewhat. Taste, adjust the salt, and add lots of pepper. Serve hot or warm.

ADVANCE PREPARATION: *Pisto* will keep for 3 or 4 days in the refrigerator. It will be better the day after you make it.

VARIATIONS

- Just before serving, heat the *pisto* and stir in 2 eggs, beaten with a little salt. Cook, stirring, until the eggs have set. They will thicken and add a velvety substance to the *pisto*.

- Heat the oven to 400°F. Transfer the cooked *pisto* to a lightly oiled baking dish. For each serving of *pisto*, make a depression with the back of a spoon in the top, and break an egg into the depression. Salt and pepper lightly. Place in the oven and bake until the eggs are set, about 6 minutes.

HUGE AÏOLI FEAST (Aïoli Monstre)

France • Serves 10

This is a garlicky feast to enjoy at any time of year, with vegetables that are in season. If you are a fish eater, then grill some fish to go along. But hard-cooked eggs and chick peas will do just fine for protein to accompany the vegetables. *Aïoli monstre,* also known as *le grand aïoli,* translates literally as "monster aïoli," and it's one of those great Provençal traditions. Like so many of the great Mediterranean eating traditions, it grew out of the Christian rituals of deprivation. Traditionally, it is eaten on Fridays, and before Christmas and Easter, when religious custom calls for meatless meals. Salt cod was allowed, and boiled vegetables. To make the meal substantial and give it some flavor, the pungent garlic mayonnaise was served alongside.

Make a party out of this meal. Fill platters with the vegetables and hard-cooked eggs, bowls with chick peas, and more bowls with aïoli. The wine to serve is a dry rosé, either from Provence or California. In Provence, a nap always follows the feast, aïoli being a known soporific.

Although it's traditional to boil the vegetables,

I steam some of them and simmer the rest. I always save the sweet bouillon from the vegetables to use as stock.

1 lemon, cut in half

5 globe artichokes

4 or 5 beets, with greens, scrubbed

8 medium leeks, white and light green parts only, trimmed, cut in half lengthwise, and cleaned

10 medium carrots, trimmed and cut in half lengthwise

6 medium turnips, peeled and quartered

4 small fennel bulbs, trimmed and quartered

Salt

¾ pound green beans, trimmed

12 medium potatoes, red-skinned or white, cut in half

4 or 5 medium zucchini or other summer squash, cut in half lengthwise and then into 3-inch pieces

1 small or medium head cauliflower, broken into florets

¾ pound asparagus, trimmed

10 large eggs, hard-cooked and halved or quartered

¾ pound dried chick peas, cooked (page 102); or 3 cans (15 ounces each) chick peas, drained and rinsed

A double batch Aïoli (page 72)

1. Using the lemon, prepare the artichokes by removing the stems, tops, and tough leaves (page 267). Cut the artichokes into quarters, and cut away the chokes. Steam over 1 inch of simmering water for 30 to 40 minutes, until the leaves pull away easily and the heart can be easily pierced with the tip of a knife. Set aside.

2. Roast the beets (see Beet and Beet Greens Salad, page 94) and set aside. Stem and clean the beet greens and set aside.

3. Place the leeks, carrots, turnips, and fennel in a large pot, fill with water, add 1 teaspoon salt, and bring to a boil. Reduce the heat to medium and simmer for 30 minutes, until the vegetables are tender when pierced with a knife. With a slotted spoon, transfer to a bowl of ice water, then drain and set aside. Bring the water back to a rolling boil, add a little more salt, then the green beans. Cook for 4 minutes, then shock in ice water. Blanch the beet greens in the boiling water for 1 to 2 minutes and shock in ice water. (Strain the liquid from the pot and use as vegetable stock.)

4. Steam the remaining vegetables until tender. The potatoes should take 20 to 30 minutes, the zucchini 8, the cauliflower 5 or 6, and the asparagus 4.

5. Arrange all the vegetables and the eggs on platters, the chick peas in a bowl, and the aïoli in several bowls. Serve at room temperature.

Or, to serve hot: Bring a large pot of water to a boil. In batches, dip the steamed vegetables into the water for 30 seconds, transfer to platters with a slotted spoon or skimmer, and serve with generous helpings of aïoli and lots of chilled dry rosé.

ADVANCE PREPARATION: All of the vegetables and the chick peas can be cooked ahead, even a day or two ahead. Reheat as instructed in Step 5. The aïoli should be made as close to serving time as is convenient.

VEGETABLES AND BEANS

RATATOUILLE & COMPANY

Mediterranean cuisines have long had an affinity for eggplant. The Arabs brought it from Persia in the 9th or 10th century, and by the 10th century it was well established in Spain and Sicily. In Turkey, eggplant is sometimes referred to as "poor man's meat," and indeed, it is a substantial food.

Because eggplant has an affinity for garlic, olive oil, onions, sweet peppers, summer squash, and especially tomatoes, and because all of these vegetables are summer vegetables and much loved throughout the region, it's no coincidence that just about every country in the Mediterranean has an eggplant stew in its repertoire that includes these other vegetables.

From Provence comes the best known of these stews, the famous ratatouille (page 296). For some reason, ratatouille made inroads into the American consciousness long before many other Mediterranean dishes were known here (I learned to make it in the late 1960s, and made it by the gallon when I was starting out as a caterer in the 1970s). Caponata (page 276), a Sicilian eggplant relish, is a sweet and sour dish that uniquely includes vinegar and sugar, celery, capers, and olives. The Greek dish *soufiko* (page 300) contains potatoes, but in other ways it is quite similar to ratatouille, with all of the vegetables cooked first in abundant olive oil and then finished together in one pot. *Türlü* (page 299), Turkey's famous stew, has all of the same summer vegetables, plus a few others, like green beans and sometimes okra, but how differently it's seasoned, with cinnamon and coriander seeds, paprika and fresh mint, vinegar and sugar.

Catalonia's answer to ratatouille is *samfaina* (known also as *xamfaina*), which many cooks like to simmer down to an almost marmalade consistency. *Samfaina* (page 72) is really regarded as a sauce, and has a presence in many other Catalan dishes, like salt cod with *samfaina,* and chicken with *samfaina.* Another Catalan eggplant and vegetable medley is called *escalivada. Escalivar* means "to cook in hot ashes," and the vegetables for *escalivada* are grilled before being combined. Spain also has its *pisto* (page 293), or *pisto a la plancha,* a vegetable medley that always includes summer squash and sometimes eggplant. *Pisto* is often enriched with eggs, as is the North African vegetable stew *chakchouka* (page 194).

Of course, each one of these dishes has many versions, depending on who's cooking. But no matter how they're prepared, and no matter what the seasonings, there are constants that run from Spain to North Africa: abundant olive oil, garlic and onions, eggplant and/or squash, tomatoes. They all speak to me of late summer, when these vegetables are at their peak.

TWO METHODS FOR ONE RATATOUILLE

France • **Serves 6**

Ratatouille can be long-simmering and intense, or it can be a quicker dish, with brighter colors and vivid flavors. I can't decide which I like better, so I'm including them both here. What is important—no matter which cooking method you choose—is that each separately cooked batch of vegetables be properly seasoned. And ratatouille always benefits from being made a day ahead, to give the flavors time to ripen.

Salt

1½ pounds (1 large) eggplant, cut into ½-inch cubes

3 tablespoons extra virgin olive oil

¾ pound (2 medium) onions, thinly sliced

¾ pound mixed red and yellow bell peppers, cut into ¾ × 1½-inch slices

4 to 6 large garlic cloves (to taste), minced or put through a press

Freshly ground pepper

1½ pounds mixed yellow squash and green zucchini, sliced about ½ inch thick (if very thick, cut in half lengthwise)

¾ pound tomatoes, peeled, seeded, and coarsely chopped

1 bay leaf

1 to 2 teaspoons fresh thyme leaves (or ½ to 1 teaspoon dried)

½ teaspoon dried oregano

2 to 4 tablespoons slivered or chopped fresh basil (to taste)

METHOD 1: LONG-COOKING RATATOUILLE

1. Salt the eggplant generously and place in a colander in the sink. Let sit for 30 minutes to 1 hour. Meanwhile, heat the oven to 450°F. Rinse the eggplant, pat dry, and place in a large casserole—large enough to hold all the ingredients, and preferably earthenware. Toss with 1 tablespoon of the olive oil. Roast for 15 to 20 minutes, tossing from time to time, until the eggplant is lightly browned and fragrant. Remove the casserole from the oven and turn the oven down to 350°F.

2. Heat 1 tablespoon oil in a large, heavy nonstick skillet over medium heat. Add the onions and cook, stirring often, until just about tender, about 5 minutes. Stir in the peppers and a generous pinch of salt. Cook, stirring often, until the peppers have softened and smell fragrant, 5 to 10 minutes. Stir in half the garlic and cook for another minute, then season with salt and pepper and transfer to the casserole with the eggplant. Heat the remaining 1 tablespoon oil in the skillet and add the squash, salt, and pepper. Cook, stirring, until the squash begins to look translucent, 5 to 10 minutes. Stir in the remaining garlic, stir together for a minute, or until fragrant, and transfer to the casserole. Add half the tomatoes, the bay leaf, thyme, oregano, and more salt to taste and toss everything together.

3. Cover and bake the ratatouille for 1 hour. Stir in the remaining tomatoes and continue to bake for another 30 minutes, until the vegetables are very soft and very fragrant. The ratatouille should be very juicy. For a really intense flavor, transfer the ratatouille to a colander set over a bowl. Let drain for 15 minutes. Pour the juices into a pan, bring to a boil, and reduce by half. Stir back into the ratatouille. Taste and season with salt and pepper. Discard the bay leaf. Serve warm or cold, preferably the next day. Stir in the basil shortly before serving.

METHOD 2: QUICKER RATATOUILLE

1. Salt the eggplant generously and place in a colander in the sink. Let sit for 30 minutes to 1 hour. Meanwhile, heat the oven to 450°F. Rinse the eggplant and pat dry, place in a large, heavy flameproof casserole, and toss with 1 tablespoon of the olive oil. Roast for 15 to 20 minutes, tossing from time to time, until the eggplant is lightly browned and fragrant. Remove the casserole from the oven.

2. Heat 1 tablespoon oil in a large, heavy nonstick skillet over medium heat. Add the onions and cook, stirring often, until just about tender, about 5 minutes. Stir in the peppers and a generous pinch of salt. Cook, stirring often, until the peppers have softened and smell fragrant, 5 to 10 minutes. Stir in half the garlic and cook for another minute, then season with salt and pepper and transfer to the casserole with the eggplant. Heat the remaining 1 tablespoon oil in the skillet and add the squash, salt, and pepper. Cook, stirring, until the squash is tender but still bright, 5 to 10 minutes. Stir in the remaining garlic, stir together for a minute, or until fragrant, and transfer to the casserole. Add the tomatoes, bay leaf, thyme, oregano, and more salt and pepper to taste, and toss everything together. Cook over medium-low heat until the vegetables begin to sizzle. Cover and cook, stirring often, for about 15 minutes, until the mixture is juicy and fragrant, the vegetables tender but still bright. Taste and adjust seasonings. Discard the bay leaf. Serve warm or cold, preferably the next day. Stir in the basil shortly before serving.

ADVANCE PREPARATION: Whichever cooking method you choose, your ratatouille will benefit from a day to mellow in the refrigerator. You can make the long-cooking ratatouille through Step 2 and let it stand for an hour or two, or longer in the refrigerator, before proceeding with Step 3.

LEFTOVERS: The leftovers will keep for 4 or 5 days. I like to eat them as a first course with a vinaigrette.

ONE MORE RATATOUILLE
France • **Serves 6**

Every time I think I've settled on the ratatouille recipe to end all ratatouille recipes, I find another irresistible one. So it was when I came across a recipe for a *tian Niçois,* a ratatouille gratin, by Provençal food writer Andrée Maureau, from her book *Tians et Petits Farcis.* The ratatouille that is the base for her gratin is marvelously sweet, and very simple to make. It stands alone beautifully, or you can transform it into a gratin.

> 1 pound eggplant, quartered lengthwise, then cut into ½-inch slices
>
> Salt
>
> 2 to 3 tablespoons extra virgin olive oil

> 1 pound onions, chopped
>
> 1 pound firm, ripe tomatoes, peeled, seeded, and chopped
>
> 2 large or 3 medium red bell peppers, or a mix of red and yellow, cut into 1-inch pieces
>
> 4 garlic cloves, minced
>
> 1 teaspoon chopped fresh rosemary
>
> 1 teaspoon fresh thyme leaves (or ½ teaspoon dried)
>
> Freshly ground pepper
>
> 1 pound zucchini, cut into large dice

1. Place the eggplant slices in a colander and sprinkle with salt. Let sit for 30 minutes to 1 hour. Rinse and pat dry.

2. Heat 2 tablespoons of the olive oil in a large, heavy nonstick skillet over medium heat and add the onions. Cook, stirring often, for 10 minutes, until very tender and fragrant. Add the tomatoes and cook, stirring, for 5 minutes. Add the eggplant and cook, stirring, for 5 minutes. Add the bell peppers, garlic, rosemary, thyme, and salt and pepper, stir together, cover, and cook gently, stirring often, for 45 minutes. Add the zucchini and more oil if necessary, and cook for another 20 to 30 minutes, until all of the vegetables are tender and the mixture is very fragrant. Taste and adjust seasoning.

3. If you wish, transfer the ratatouille to a colander set over a bowl and drain for 10 minutes. Place the juices in a saucepan, bring to a boil, and reduce by half. Stir back into the ratatouille. Serve hot, warm, or at room temperature.

ADVANCE PREPARATION: Ratatouille is always better the day after it's made.

LEFTOVERS: This ratatouille will keep for 3 to 5 days in the refrigerator and can be frozen for a couple of months, though the textures won't be as pleasing.

TIAN NIÇOIS

This gratin is a variation on One More Ratatouille (page 297) prepared through Step 2.

In addition, you'll need:

> 1 pound tomatoes, cut in half across the equator and seeded
>
> Salt and freshly ground pepper
>
> 2 tablespoons extra virgin olive oil
>
> 3 large eggs
>
> ½ cup milk
>
> ½ cup grated Gruyère cheese or Parmesan
>
> 2 tablespoons bread crumbs
>
> 20 imported black olives, pitted

1. Heat the oven to 400°F. Cover a baking sheet with foil and oil the foil. Sprinkle the tomatoes with salt and pepper, place on the baking sheet, and drizzle with 1 tablespoon of the olive oil. Roast for 20 minutes. Set aside.

2. Drain the ratatouille in a colander set over a bowl for 10 minutes. Oil a 2- or 3-quart baking dish or gratin.

3. Beat the eggs in a bowl and stir in the juices from the ratatouille, the milk, and half the cheese. Stir in the ratatouille, then scrape it all into the baking dish. Mix together the bread crumbs and remaining cheese and sprinkle over the top. Top with the roasted tomatoes and the olives. Drizzle on the remaining 1 tablespoon olive oil. Bake for 30 to 40 minutes, until browned and bubbling.

RATATOUILLE TART: The ingredients, with the exception of the bread crumbs, are the same as in the *tian,* above. Omit the bread crumbs and stir all of the cheese into the ratatouille, egg, and milk mixture. Heat the oven to 375°F. Line a 10-inch tart pan with Yeasted Olive Oil Pastry (page 229) or Greek Pie Crust (page 229). Scrape the ratatouille mixture into the crust, top with the roasted tomatoes and olives, and drizzle with 1 tablespoon olive oil. Bake for 30 to 40 minutes, until the tart is set and browned. Remove from the heat and cool for 10 to 15 minutes before cutting.

LIGURIAN RATATOUILLE

Italy • Serves 4

In the Italian Riviera, this is actually categorized as a sauce, and it's served with pasta or gnocchi. It's called *rattatuia,* which indicates just how fine the lines are between the cooking of the French and Italian Rivieras. There are probably many versions of this dish. Mine is inspired by Fred Plotkin, from *Recipes from Paradise.* What is interesting about this recipe, and a bit surprising, is that there are no onions in it, unlike most of the other ratatouille-like dishes. This makes for a slightly more delicate dish.

> 3 tablespoons extra virgin olive oil
>
> 1 medium red, yellow, or green bell pepper, cut into thin strips
>
> 2 tablespoons unbleached all-purpose flour
>
> Salt and freshly ground pepper
>
> 1 medium eggplant, diced; or 2 baby eggplants, thinly sliced
>
> 1 medium or 2 small zucchini, thinly sliced
>
> 1 medium or 2 small yellow squash, thinly sliced
>
> 1 pound tomatoes, peeled, seeded, and sliced
>
> 2 garlic cloves, cut in slivers
>
> 20 small or 12 large fresh basil leaves, slivered

1. Heat 1 tablespoon of the olive oil in a large skillet over medium heat and add the bell pepper. Cook, stirring, until tender, 5 to 8 minutes. Remove from the pan and set aside.

2. Season the flour with a little salt and pepper. Lightly flour the eggplant, zucchini, and yellow squash by tossing in the flour, then shaking off the excess.

3. Heat the remaining 2 tablespoons oil over medium heat until it swirls easily in the pan and add the eggplant, zucchini, and yellow squash. Cook, stirring or tossing in the pan, until very lightly browned, about 5 minutes. Add the tomatoes, garlic, half the basil, and the bell pepper, and stir together. Season with salt and pepper, reduce the heat to low, and cover partially. Simmer, stir-

ring often, 20 to 30 minutes, until the vegetables have cooked down and the mixture is thick. Stir in the remaining basil. Taste and adjust seasonings. Serve hot, warm, or cold.

ADVANCE PREPARATION: Like its French cousins, this ratatouille will taste even better if you serve it the day after you make it. It will keep for 3 to 5 days in the refrigerator.

TURKISH RATATOUILLE (Türlü)
Turkey • Serves 6

This is another summer vegetable stew, *türlü* in Turkish. The dish can be heavy with olive oil, or rely more on a mixture of water and tomato purée as a medium in which the vegetables cook. Needless to say, I prefer the latter, with enough olive oil nonetheless to give the dish great texture and flavor.

I know the list of ingredients is long, but each one has a worthwhile presence in the dish. Make it leisurely one day and serve it the next (and the next and the next) for best results. You can begin this in a pan and finish in an earthenware dish in the oven, or you can cook it entirely on top of the stove in a covered frying pan.

1 tablespoon tomato paste

1¼ cups water

1 tablespoon white wine vinegar or apple cider vinegar

1 teaspoon sugar

1 teaspoon ground cinnamon

1 teaspoon sweet paprika

4 tablespoons extra virgin olive oil

1 large eggplant, cut in half lengthwise and then sliced

Salt and freshly ground pepper

2 medium onions, sliced

4 large garlic cloves, minced

2 teaspoons coriander seeds, lightly crushed

2 green bell peppers, sliced

2 medium zucchini, sliced

4 ripe tomatoes, peeled, seeded, and sliced

2 bay leaves

⅓ to ½ cup chopped fresh flat-leaf parsley, plus additional for serving

¼ cup chopped fresh mint, plus additional for serving

¼ pound green beans, trimmed (optional; see Note)

¼ pound small okra, ends trimmed (optional)

Yogurt

Note: *If you are using green beans, they will be even more tender if you blanch them for 3 or 4 minutes before adding them to the baking dish.*

1. Stir together the tomato paste, water, vinegar, sugar, cinnamon, and paprika, and set aside. Heat the oven to 350°F. Oil a deep earthenware baking dish.

2. Heat 2 tablespoons of the oil in a large nonstick skillet over medium-high heat. Add the eggplant slices in one layer and cook until lightly browned. Using tongs or a spatula, turn over and cook the other sides until lightly browned. You will probably have to cook the eggplant in batches to avoid crowding the pan. Season with salt and pepper. Transfer to the baking dish.

3. Reduce the heat to medium, heat the remaining 2 tablespoons oil in the skillet, and add the onions. Cook, stirring often, until tender, 5 to 8 minutes, and stir in the garlic and coriander seeds. Cook, stirring, until the garlic is fragrant, about 1 minute, and add the green peppers and zucchini. Continue to cook, stirring often, until the vegetables are limp and the zucchini is just beginning to color, about 10 minutes. Season with salt and pepper, and scrape into the baking dish.

4. Add the tomato paste mixture to the pan, bring to a boil, and stir and scrape with a wooden spoon to deglaze. Add to the baking dish along with the tomatoes, bay leaves, parsley, mint, green beans, and okra. Season generously with salt and pepper, cover, and bake until the vegetables are very soft, about 1½ hours, stirring from time to time. Taste and adjust seasonings. Discard the bay leaves. ▶

If you have a large frying pan with a lid, you can cook this over low heat on top of the stove. Follow the directions on the previous page, but transfer the cooked ingredients to a bowl. Deglaze as instructed, then return all of the ingredients to the pan. Bring back to a simmer, cover, and simmer for 1 to 1½ hours, until the stew is very tender, stirring often. Taste and adjust seasonings. Discard the bay leaves.

5. Cool slightly before serving with yogurt and additional chopped fresh herbs.

LEFTOVERS: Use leftovers to make TÜRLÜ TOPPED WITH A FRIED EGG. Take the *türlü* out of the refrigerator and set it on the stove to come to room temperature a few hours before dinner. When you're ready to eat, fry an egg, sunny side up, and put it right on top of your serving of *türlü*. It makes a wonderful supper.

IKARIAN SUMMER VEGETABLE STEW (Soufiko)
Greece • Serves 6 to 8

Every Mediterranean region has at least one summer vegetable stew (with eggplant, tomatoes, peppers, zucchini), and Greece's is *soufiko*. It is distinguished from other ratatouille-like stews by the inclusion of potatoes, and the typical Greek seasonings—parsley, mint, oregano. Diane Kochilas, when teaching this dish at her summer cooking class in Ikaria, described it as a Zen dish, because you take a very long time with it, cooking each vegetable separately in olive oil, then layering them in a pot and cooking them some more. This is slow cooking at its best. By the time all of the vegetables are in the pot, you have been cooking for close to an hour, by which time you really are in a meditative state.

The dish requires a lot of olive oil, more than I am accustomed to using, but it's necessary here; how much you use is really determined by the size of your skillet. You want to coat it well for each vegetable.

2 medium eggplants, sliced about ¼ inch thick

4 medium zucchini, sliced about ¼ inch thick

2 large green bell peppers, cut into 1-inch strips

Salt

Extra virgin olive oil as needed (⅔ to ¾ cup)

2 large onions, chopped

3 garlic cloves, minced

3 large tomatoes, grated or peeled, seeded, and chopped

1 pound red-skinned potatoes, scrubbed and sliced about ¼ inch thick

Freshly ground pepper

4 tablespoons chopped fresh herbs, preferably a mix of mint, flat-leaf parsley, and oregano

1. Place the eggplant, zucchini, and peppers in separate bowls and sprinkle with salt. Let sit for 30 minutes to 1 hour. Remove from the bowls (pour off any liquid) and pat dry. Keep separate.

2. Heat 2 tablespoons olive oil over medium heat in a large, heavy nonstick skillet and add the onions. Cook, stirring often, until tender, about 8 minutes. Add the garlic and cook for another minute or two, until fragrant. Stir in the tomatoes and add salt to taste. Cook, stirring often, for about 10 minutes, until fragrant. Transfer to a bowl.

3. Film the bottom of a heavy casserole or Dutch oven with about 2 tablespoons oil. Spoon in about one-quarter of the tomato-onion mixture. Set aside.

4. Wipe your skillet clean and return to the heat. Add 2 tablespoons oil, and when it is hot, add the potatoes in one layer. Cook for about 4 minutes on each side, or until golden brown. Remove from the pan with tongs or a slotted spoon, holding the potatoes over the pan to allow oil to drip back in. Drain on paper towels, then place in a layer in the casserole. Season with salt and pepper and spoon another one-quarter of the tomato-onion mixture over the top. Sprinkle with 1 tablespoon of the herbs.

5. Add more olive oil to the pan if necessary and cook the eggplant until lightly browned on each

side. Remove from the pan with tongs and drain on paper towels. Sprinkle with salt and pepper (remember that the eggplant has been salted, so taste before you add more salt), and layer into the casserole. Spread another one-quarter of the tomato-onion mixture over the eggplant, and sprinkle with another 1 tablespoon of the herbs.

6. Add 2 more tablespoons oil to the pan and cook the zucchini until lightly browned on each side. Remove from the heat with tongs, drain briefly on paper towels, season with salt (taste first) and pepper, and layer into the casserole. Sprinkle with 1 tablespoon of the herbs.

7. Add 1 tablespoon oil to the pan if necessary and cook the peppers until just wilted, about 5 minutes. Remove from the pan and layer over the zucchini in the casserole. Season with salt and pepper. Spread the remaining tomato-onion mixture over the top, and sprinkle with the remaining 1 tablespoon herbs.

8. Place the casserole over medium heat and bring to a simmer. Cover, reduce the heat to low, and simmer for 30 to 45 minutes, checking from time to time to make sure nothing is sticking. If the potatoes begin to stick, pour in ½ cup water. The mixture should be incredibly fragrant and all the vegetables tender. Taste and adjust seasonings. Serve hot or at room temperature.

ADVANCE PREPARATION: This dish can be assembled a day ahead and refrigerated before the final simmer. The *soufiko* will keep for 3 or 4 days in the refrigerator.

VEGETABLE RAGOUT WITH CHICK PEAS, TURNIPS, AND GREENS
Tunisia • **Serves 6**

Here, slow-cooked greens take on a very comforting aspect. The stew is hearty and somewhat spicy, great for a vegetarian main dish. Serve it with couscous.

- ½ pound dried chick peas, picked over, rinsed, soaked in 4 cups water for 6 hours or overnight, and drained
- 5 cups water
- 2 tablespoons extra virgin olive oil
- 2 large onions, chopped
- 2 to 4 garlic cloves (to taste), minced or put through a press
- 1 pound greens (mustard, chard, turnip, kale, or a combination), stemmed and chopped
- Salt
- 2 teaspoons coriander seeds, ground in a spice mill
- ½ teaspoon caraway seeds, ground in a spice mill
- ½ teaspoon freshly ground pepper
- ½ to 1 teaspoon cayenne (to taste)
- 2 carrots, sliced
- ¾ pound turnips, peeled and cut into wedges
- 1 to 2 teaspoons Harissa (page 86 or commercial; more to taste)
- 1 tablespoon tomato paste
- ¼ cup chopped fresh flat-leaf parsley
- 1 to 2 tablespoons fresh lemon juice (to taste; optional)
- 1 bunch fresh cilantro, chopped

1. Combine the chick peas and 4 cups water in a large saucepan or pot. Bring to a boil, reduce the heat, cover, and simmer for 1 hour.

2. Heat the oil in a large, heavy soup pot or Dutch oven over medium heat and add the onions. Cook, stirring often, until softened and translucent, about 8 minutes. Stir in the garlic and cook together for another minute. Add the greens (with the water left on the leaves after washing) and ½ teaspoon

salt and cook, stirring, until they wilt. Stir in the ground coriander and caraway, the black pepper and cayenne, and mix well. Add the carrots and turnips, then pour in the chick peas with their broth. Add 1 cup water, or enough so that everything is well covered. Bring to a boil, add salt (1 to 2 teaspoons), the harissa, tomato paste, and parsley. Reduce the heat and simmer for 1 hour. Stir in the lemon juice and cilantro, and simmer another 10 minutes. Taste and add salt, cayenne, or harissa as desired.

ADVANCE PREPARATION: The chick peas can be cooked through Step 1 hours or even a day before you finish the ragout. The entire dish can be prepared a day ahead. It will be even better the next day. It will freeze for several months.

LEFTOVERS: You can enjoy this for 3 or 4 days, with couscous or rice, or just by itself.

SPICY VEGETABLE STEW WITH SWISS CHARD, FAVAS, AND POTATOES
Tunisia • **Serves 6**

This spicy stew is one of many *murshans*, Tunisian vegetable stews whose name, says food historian Clifford Wright, derives from a word that means "to nibble." The dish that this is adapted from traditionally calls for fresh black-eyed peas (see the variation; frozen might be easier to find), but I love to use fresh fava beans. Serve with couscous.

   2 tablespoons olive oil

   1 large red onion, finely chopped

   1 large leek, white and light green parts only, chopped

   4 garlic cloves, minced

   2 teaspoons freshly ground caraway seeds

   2 teaspoons freshly ground coriander seeds

   1 teaspoon freshly ground cumin seeds

   1 teaspoon Tabil (page 24)

   2 to 3 teaspoons Harissa (page 86 or commercial)

   4 plum tomatoes, peeled, seeded, and chopped; or 1 can (14 ounces) tomatoes, drained and chopped

   4 cups water

   ¾ pound Swiss chard, with stems, chopped

   1 pound red-skinned potatoes, diced

   Salt

   1 pound fresh fava beans, shelled and skinned (page 113)

   Leaves from 1 bunch fresh cilantro, chopped

1. Heat the olive oil in a large, heavy casserole, Dutch oven, or earthenware pot over medium heat and add the onion and leek. Cook, stirring, until they soften, about 5 minutes, and add the garlic. Stir together for about 1 minute, until fragrant, then turn up the heat to medium-high and add the caraway, coriander, cumin, tabil, and harissa. Cook, stirring, for about 30 seconds, then add the tomatoes. Cook, stirring, until the mixture is thick, about 5 minutes. Add the water, Swiss chard, potatoes, and a generous amount of salt. Bring to a boil, reduce the heat, and simmer for 1 hour.

2. Add the fava beans to the pot along with three-quarters of the cilantro and simmer for another 15 minutes. Taste and adjust salt. Sprinkle with the remaining cilantro and serve.

ADVANCE PREPARATION: This stew can easily be made a day ahead, and indeed will benefit from it. If you wish to retain some color in the favas, don't add them until you reheat the stew.

VARIATION

SPICY VEGETABLE STEW WITH SWISS CHARD, BLACK-EYED PEAS, AND POTATOES: Substitute fresh or frozen black-eyed peas for the fava beans. You will need to simmer the stew for another 30 minutes after you've added them in Step 2.

TOMATO AND BEAN RAGOUT
Italy and France • Serves 6

I've enjoyed beans stewed with tomatoes in Italy and Provence. In Italy, the dish might be part of an antipasto platter, or it could be served as a soup. In Provence, this ragout is a summer dish, made with fresh borlotti beans (they call them *écossais*) and tomatoes. I make it throughout the year, using fresh tomatoes in summer and canned in winter. If you can't find borlotti beans, try the dish with pintos, which are not too different. You can also use white beans. The ragout definitely benefits from being cooked a day or two ahead.

2 onions, peeled

2 whole cloves

1 pound (2 heaped cups) dried borlotti beans, pinto beans, or white beans, picked over, rinsed, and soaked in water to cover for 6 hours or overnight, then drained

8 cups water

4 to 6 large garlic cloves (to taste), minced or put through a press

A bouquet garni made with a few sprigs fresh thyme, a bay leaf, a couple fresh parsley sprigs, and a Parmesan rind

Salt

2 tablespoons extra virgin olive oil

2 pounds fresh tomatoes, peeled, seeded, and chopped; or 1 can (28 ounces) chopped tomatoes, with juice

1 tablespoon tomato paste

Pinch sugar

1 teaspoon fresh thyme (or ½ teaspoon dried) or 1 teaspoon dried oregano

Freshly ground pepper

2 to 3 tablespoons slivered fresh basil or chopped fresh flat-leaf parsley (to taste)

Bruschetta (page 135)

¼ to ½ cup grated Gruyère or Parmesan (optional)

1. Cut one of the onions in half and stick a clove into each half. Chop the other onion.

2. Combine the beans and water in a large pot. Bring to a boil and skim off any foam, then add the halved onion, half of the garlic, and the bouquet garni. Reduce the heat, cover, and simmer for 1 hour. Add salt to taste (2 teaspoons or more) and simmer for another 30 to 60 minutes, until the beans are tender but not mushy. Taste and adjust salt. Discard the bouquet garni and onion, and drain the beans over a bowl. Measure out 2½ cups of the cooking liquid and set aside. If you are making this in advance, refrigerate some more of the cooking liquid for thinning the sauce.

3. Heat 1 tablespoon of the olive oil in a large, heavy soup pot or casserole over medium heat and add the chopped onion. Cook, stirring, until tender, about 5 minutes. Add the remaining garlic and stir together until fragrant, 30 seconds to 1 minute. Add the tomatoes, tomato paste, sugar, thyme, and salt to taste. Cook, stirring occasionally, for 10 to 15 minutes, until the tomatoes have cooked down somewhat and smell very fragrant. Stir in the beans and the reserved 2½ cups cooking liquid. Bring to a simmer, cover, and cook over low heat for 30 minutes, until the ragout is thick and fragrant. Stir often so nothing sticks to the bottom of the pot. Add pepper, taste, and adjust salt.

4. Stir in the basil and simmer another minute. Drizzle on the remaining 1 tablespoon oil. Serve over bruschetta, with cheese sprinkled over the top if desired.

ADVANCE PREPARATION: The beans can be cooked a day or two ahead through Step 2. The entire dish benefits from being made 1 or 2 days ahead through Step 3. Bring back to a simmer before proceeding.

LEFTOVERS: The ragout will keep for a few days in the refrigerator. You may need to thin it out with water or liquid from the beans. You can serve the dish as a ragout the first night and as a smaller gratin the second (reduce the amount of bread crumbs and cheese in the variation that follows). You can also make *pasta e fagiole* by adding cooked pasta—2 or 3 ounces per serving—to the leftovers.

TOMATO AND BEAN GRATIN: Heat the oven to 400°F. Oil a 3-quart gratin or baking dish. Make the ragout as directed, but don't drizzle on the last tablespoon of oil. Spoon the ragout into the baking dish. Toss ½ cup bread crumbs with 1 tablespoon olive oil. Sprinkle in an even layer over the beans. Sprinkle on the cheese. Bake for 30 minutes, until the top is browned and the gratin is bubbling. Serve hot or warm.

WHITE BEAN AND CHARD RAGOUT

Italy • **Serves 6**

Beans with greens come in many, many configurations in the Mediterranean. This Italian dish would traditionally include a pork product, like pancetta or sausage, but makes a fine vegetarian dish, savory with tomatoes, garlic, and rosemary.

1 pound dried white beans, either Great Northerns or cannellini, picked over, rinsed, soaked in 8 cups water for 6 hours or overnight, and drained

7 cups water

1 large onion, chopped

4 to 6 garlic cloves (to taste), minced or put through a press

A bouquet garni made with a bay leaf, a few sprigs fresh parsley and thyme, and a Parmesan rind

Salt

2 tablespoons extra virgin olive oil

1 teaspoon crumbled dried rosemary

1 teaspoon fresh thyme leaves (or ½ teaspoon dried)

1 can (28 ounces) tomatoes, chopped, with juice; or 1½ pounds fresh ripe tomatoes, peeled, seeded, and chopped

1 generous bunch Swiss chard (¾ to 1 pound)

Freshly ground pepper

Freshly grated Parmesan

1. Combine the beans with the water, half the onion and garlic, and the bouquet garni in a large soup pot or Dutch oven. Bring to a boil, skim off any foam, reduce the heat, cover, and simmer for 1 hour. Season generously with salt.

2. While the beans are simmering, heat the oil in a large, heavy nonstick skillet over medium heat and add the remaining onion. Cook, stirring, until tender, about 5 minutes, and stir in the remaining garlic, the rosemary, and thyme. Cook for 30 seconds to 1 minute, until fragrant, and stir in the tomatoes. Add salt to taste and cook, stirring often, until the tomatoes have cooked down and the mixture is thick, beginning to stick to the pan, and delicious, 15 to 20 minutes.

3. When the beans have cooked for 1 hour, stir in the tomato sauce. Simmer for another 30 to 60 minutes, until the beans are tender and the broth very tasty.

4. Meanwhile, separate the chard leaves from the stems and wash both stems and leaves thoroughly. Slice the stems crosswise about ¼ inch thick and stir into the beans. Simmer for 10 to 15 minutes, until tender. Stack the chard leaves and cut them crosswise into slivers. Shortly before serving, stir the leaves into the beans. Simmer for 5 to 10 minutes, until tender but still bright. Discard the bouquet garni, add lots of fresh pepper, taste, and adjust salt. Serve, passing Parmesan to sprinkle on top.

ADVANCE PREPARATION: You can make the recipe through Step 2 one or two days ahead, refrigerating the beans and sauce separately or together. Bring back to a simmer and proceed with the recipe. The finished dish keeps well for 4 days, but for the best color you'll want to add the chard on the day you wish to serve.

LEFTOVERS: Use leftovers to make White Bean and Chard Gratin: Scrape the leftovers into a lightly oiled baking dish, sprinkle with bread crumbs and Parmesan, and drizzle on 1 or 2 tablespoons olive oil. Bake at 375°F until the top browns, 20 to 30 minutes. You can also toss the leftovers with pasta.

EASY WHITE BEANS WITH TOMATOES AND GARLIC

Italy • **Serves 4**

This is an incredibly quick and simple Italian bean dish, a perfect family meal that can practically be pulled off the pantry shelf. Serve the beans on their own, with plenty of crusty bread and a green salad, use them as a topping for Bruschetta (page 135), or toss them with pasta.

2 tablespoons extra virgin olive oil

1 or 2 garlic cloves (to taste), minced

2 to 4 fresh sage leaves (to taste), chopped

3 large ripe tomatoes, peeled, seeded, and chopped; or 1 can (14 ounces) tomatoes, drained and chopped

2 cans (15 ounces each) cannellini beans, rinsed and drained

Salt and freshly ground pepper

1 tablespoon wine vinegar or sherry vinegar (optional)

Heat the oil in a wide, heavy skillet or saucepan over medium heat and add the garlic. Cook, stirring, for 30 seconds, until fragrant. Add the sage and tomatoes and bring to a simmer. Simmer for 5 minutes, stirring often, and add the beans, salt, and pepper. Cover, reduce the heat to low, and simmer for 10 minutes. Taste and adjust seasonings. Stir in the vinegar. Serve hot or warm.

ADVANCE PREPARATION: The finished dish will keep for 3 days in the refrigerator. You might want to thin the beans out with a little water or an extra tomato when you reheat them.

Note: *You can substitute other white beans, such as navy beans, for the cannellini beans.*

LARGE WHITE BEANS WITH TOMATOES AND GARLIC (Fassoulia)

Greece and Spain • **Serves 4 as a main dish or 8 to 10 as a *meze***

I've encountered delicious, simple dishes like this one made with giant white beans in both Greece and Spain. The beans are most often served as a *meze* or tapa, but they would be equally welcome on my table as a main dish.

The large white beans can be found in Mediterranean markets and gourmet groceries. They are a bit tricky to cook, because they tend to fall apart. You can avoid this by being careful to keep the beans at a slow simmer. If they boil, they will break. You can also use smaller dried lima beans (they stay intact a bit better).

2 tablespoons extra virgin olive oil

1 onion, chopped, plus ½ small onion, minced and soaked (page 119), for garnish (optional)

4 large garlic cloves, minced

3 large tomatoes, peeled, seeded, and chopped; or 1 can (14 ounces) chopped tomatoes, with juice

1 pound dried large white beans (sometimes sold as lima beans), soaked in 8 cups water for 6 hours or overnight, drained

6 cups water

3 tablespoons tomato paste

2 teaspoons dried oregano

1 bay leaf

Salt

Juice of 1 large lemon

Freshly ground pepper

¼ cup chopped fresh flat-leaf parsley, or a mixture of parsley and dill

1. Heat 1 tablespoon of the olive oil in a large, heavy bean pot or Dutch oven over medium heat and add the chopped onion. Cook, stirring, until tender, about 5 minutes. Add half the garlic, stir together for about 30 seconds, and add the tomatoes. Cook, stirring, until the tomatoes cook down a bit, 10 to 15 minutes, and add the remaining garlic, beans, water, tomato paste, oregano, and bay leaf. Bring to a simmer, cover, and simmer over low heat for 45 minutes. Salt abundantly (2 teaspoons or more) and continue to simmer for another 15 to 30 minutes, until the beans are tender but not mushy.

2. Set a colander over a bowl and drain the beans. Return the broth to the pot and bring to a boil. Reduce until the liquid is thick and tomatoey. Return the beans to the pot and stir gently until bathed in the tomato sauce. Remove from the heat, taste, and adjust the salt.

3. Stir in the lemon juice and pepper to taste. Discard the bay leaf. Drizzle on the remaining 1 tablespoon oil. Cool, or serve hot, garnished with chopped parsley and, if you wish, minced onion.

ADVANCE PREPARATION: The finished dish will keep for 3 to 5 days in the refrigerator. Reheat gently on top of the stove, and thin out, if you wish, with water.

BLACK-EYED PEAS WITH WILD FENNEL
Greece • **Serves 6 to 8 as a starter or 4 to 6 as a main dish**

I think of black-eyed peas as a purely American food, much loved in the South and my standard dish for New Year's Day. In fact, they are native to Africa. According to food historian Clifford Wright, they arrived in the northern Mediterranean by about 300 BC and were cultivated by the Romans. Black-eyed peas traveled to South America with the slave trade, but came to North America via the Mediterranean. They are much loved in Greece, where they are often seasoned, as these are, with wild fennel. If you can't find wild fennel easily, use the feathery tops of bulb fennel.

> 4 tablespoons extra virgin olive oil
>
> 1 onion, chopped
>
> 2 garlic cloves, minced
>
> 2 cups chopped wild fennel, or the fronds from bulb fennel; plus additional for garnish (optional)
>
> 1 can (14 ounces) tomatoes, drained and puréed in a food processor

> 1 pound black-eyed peas
>
> Salt and freshly ground pepper

1. Heat 2 tablespoons of the olive oil in a large, heavy soup pot or Dutch oven over medium heat and add the onion. Cook, stirring, until tender, about 5 minutes. Add the garlic and fennel, and cook, stirring, for a minute, until the garlic is fragrant and the fennel beginning to wilt. Stir in the tomatoes and bring to a simmer. Add the black-eyed peas and enough water to cover by an inch, and stir. Bring to a boil, reduce the heat, and simmer for 30 minutes.

2. Add salt to taste (about 2 teaspoons) and pepper, and continue to simmer until the beans are tender, another 15 minutes. Stir in the remaining 2 tablespoons olive oil. Taste and adjust seasonings. Serve warm or hot, garnished with additional chopped wild fennel if desired.

ADVANCE PREPARATION: The beans will keep for up to 5 days in the refrigerator, but taste best the day after you make them.

MASHED BLACK-EYED PEAS WITH GARLIC PURÉE
Greece • **Serves 4 as a main dish or 6 as a starter**

This recipe, adapted from one in Diane Kochilas's *The Glorious Foods of Greece,* comes from the island of Límnos. The beans are cooked and mashed with a garlicky purée. I like to add a little cumin to the mix.

Serve these as a comforting supper, on toasted thick slices of country bread, or as a starter, with pita or thin toasted rounds of baguette.

FOR THE BLACK-EYED PEAS

> 1 cup dried black-eyed peas
>
> 1 onion, cut in half
>
> 2 garlic cloves, crushed
>
> 1 bay leaf
>
> Salt

FOR THE GARLIC PURÉE

4 plump or 8 smaller garlic cloves

¼ teaspoon salt (more to taste)

½ teaspoon freshly ground cumin

⅓ cup extra virgin olive oil

¼ cup fresh lemon juice (more to taste)

1. *Make the black-eyed peas:* Place the black-eyed peas in a medium saucepan or soup pot and cover by 2 inches with water. Bring to a boil and skim off any foam. Add the halved onion, crushed garlic cloves, and bay leaf. Reduce the heat, cover, and simmer gently for 30 minutes. Add salt to taste (about 1 teaspoon), cover, and continue to simmer until the beans are tender, about 15 minutes. Remove from the heat.

2. *Make the garlic purée:* While the beans are cooking, crush the whole garlic cloves, one at a time, in a mortar and pestle along with the salt, cumin, and 1 tablespoon of the olive oil. When all of the garlic has been crushed, begin drizzling in the remaining olive oil and the lemon juice, alternating the two and stirring all the while with the pestle, until you have a smooth paste. It will be very garlicky. Taste and adjust salt.

3. Drain off most of the liquid from the beans. Discard the onion halves and bay leaf. Using a potato masher, a pestle, or a wooden spoon, crush the beans while adding the garlic purée. You should have a coarse purée. Taste and adjust salt. Add a little more olive oil if desired. Serve warm.

ADVANCE PREPARATION: You can cook the beans through Step 1 up to 3 days ahead. Reheat gently, then proceed with the recipe.

ANDALUSIAN CHICK PEA AND CABBAGE STEW
Spain • Serves 6

This recipe is adapted from one in Clifford Wright's *A Mediterranean Feast*. The authentic version includes bacon. This vegetarian version is no less fragrant and soothing. It's a simple stew that's very easy to put together.

1 pound dried chick peas, picked over, rinsed, soaked overnight in 8 cups water, and drained

3 quarts water

1 large onion, chopped

4 large garlic cloves, minced or put through a press

Salt

2 tablespoons extra virgin olive oil

1 can (14 ounces) tomatoes, chopped, with juice

2 teaspoons freshly ground cumin seeds

1 medium head green cabbage (1½ to 2 pounds), cored and chopped

Freshly ground pepper

Cayenne

Crusty bread

1. Combine the chick peas and water in a large soup pot or Dutch oven. Bring to a boil. Skim off any foam, then add the onion and half the garlic. Reduce the heat, cover, and simmer for 1 hour.

2. Add salt (at least 2 teaspoons), the olive oil, tomatoes, and cumin seeds, and simmer for another hour, until the chick peas are tender.

3. Add the cabbage and remaining garlic, bring back to a simmer, and simmer, partially covered, for 30 minutes. Add pepper and cayenne, taste, and adjust salt. Serve with thick slices of crusty bread.

ADVANCE PREPARATION: You can make the dish through Step 2 ahead of time. Remove the pot from the heat and cool, then cover and refrigerate for up to 3 days. Bring back to a simmer before proceeding with the recipe.

CHICK PEA STEW
Turkey • **Serves 4**

This dish—from Edirne, an early capital of the Ottoman Empire—has all the complexity of the sophisticated palace cooking of Istanbul, with sweet, spicy, and savory overtones and a mixture of mint, dill, and parsley that define the dish as Turkish. Although there are a lot of ingredients in the stew, it's very uncomplicated to cook.

2 tablespoons extra virgin olive oil

2 onions, sliced

4 garlic cloves, chopped

1 teaspoon cumin seeds, crushed

1 teaspoon fennel seeds, crushed

1 teaspoon brown sugar or 2 teaspoons pomegranate molasses

1 tablespoon white wine vinegar, sherry vinegar, or lemon juice

4 tomatoes, peeled and chopped; or 1 can (14 ounces) tomatoes, drained and chopped

½ teaspoon Aleppo pepper

4 ounces leaf spinach

½ pound dried chick peas, cooked and drained; or 2 cans (15 ounces each) chick peas, rinsed and drained

Salt

¼ cup chopped fresh herbs, preferably a mix of flat-leaf parsley, dill, and mint

Lemon wedges

Drained yogurt (page 21)

Heat the oil in a large nonstick skillet over medium heat and add the onions. Cook, stirring, until tender, about 5 minutes, and add the garlic, cumin, and fennel seeds. Cook until the onion has colored slightly, 5 to 8 minutes. Add the sugar and stir together for a minute, then stir in the vinegar, tomatoes, and Aleppo pepper. Cook, stirring, until the tomatoes have cooked down a bit, about 10 minutes. Stir in the spinach, chick peas, and salt (about 1 teaspoon). Add enough water so that the dish can simmer. Simmer uncovered over medium heat, stirring often, for 20 to 25 minutes. The stew should be saucy but not watery. Add salt to taste

and stir in the herbs. Serve with lemon wedges and yogurt.

ADVANCE PREPARATION: This dish keeps well for a few days in the refrigerator, and benefits from being made ahead.

CHICK PEA FATTET
Middle East • **Serves 6**

Flat breads, known as *fatta,* become stale quickly, and the people of the Middle East have developed a number of wonderful ways to utilize them once they have dried out. These dishes are known collectively as *fattet.* There are many different *fattet,* often with chicken or lamb, but this lemony version is my favorite. The layered casserole, made with stale pita bread, broth, chick peas, and garlicky yogurt, is quite wonderful and comforting. Humble as this dish is, I've served it at many dinner parties with great success. It also makes an easy family dinner.

1½ cups dried chick peas, picked over, rinsed, soaked in 5 cups water for 6 hours or overnight, and drained

6 cups water

Salt

6 tablespoons fresh lemon juice

3 pita breads, white or whole wheat

4 garlic cloves, cut in half

½ to 1 teaspoon ground cumin (to taste)

2 tablespoons extra virgin olive oil

1½ cups drained yogurt (page 21)

2 tablespoons tahini

1 to 2 tablespoons chopped fresh mint (or 1 to 2 teaspoons dried mint) (to taste)

1. Combine the chick peas and water in a large pot. Bring to a boil, reduce the heat, cover, and simmer for 1 hour. Salt generously (about 2 teaspoons) and continue to simmer for another hour, until the chick peas are very tender. Drain through a colander set over a bowl. Add 2 tablespoons lemon juice to the chick pea broth, taste, and adjust salt.

2. Heat the oven to 350°F. Open the pita breads and toast in the oven until crisp, about 10 minutes. Oil a 2-quart baking dish. Break the pitas into pieces and line the dish with the bread. Leave the oven on.

3. Mash the garlic to a paste with ¼ teaspoon salt in a mortar and pestle.

4. Purée half the chick peas with the cumin and half the garlic paste in a food processor fitted with the steel blade. With the machine running, add 3 tablespoons of the lemon juice, the olive oil, and ½ cup of the chick pea broth. Add salt to taste.

5. Douse the pita bread with ¾ cup of the chick pea broth. Scrape the puréed chick peas over the pitas in an even layer. Top with the remaining chick peas. Stir the remaining garlic paste and 1 tablespoon lemon juice into the yogurt and add the tahini and salt to taste. Spread in an even layer over the chick peas.

6. Warm for 15 minutes in the hot oven, sprinkle on the mint, and serve.

ADVANCE PREPARATION: You can assemble this dish several hours before you heat and serve it. It can also be served at room temperature.

LEFTOVERS: The casserole will be good for about 3 days.

DRIED FAVA BEANS AND GREENS

Italy • **Serves 4 as a main dish or 6 as a starter**

This warm purée of skinned dried fava beans, served with cooked greens, is one of the signature dishes of Puglia. The Pugliese like chicory, but you can choose other greens, such as kale, broccoli rabe (which they also love), or a mixture of greens. I have seen and tasted different presentations of the dish. Sometimes the greens are stirred into the purée, sometimes they're served on the side. At Il Frantoio, the wonderful farm/hotel I stayed at, they deconstructed the dish and made a fantastic greens timbale, which they served with the favas. Here it is in its simplest form.

1 pound split dried peeled fava beans, picked over

Salt

5 tablespoons extra virgin olive oil

1 pound greens, such as chicory, broccoli rabe, or kale, stemmed

2 garlic cloves, minced

1. Cover the fava beans by 1 inch with water in a 4-quart pot and bring to a boil. Boil for 1 minute, cover, and turn off the heat. Let sit for 1 hour. Bring back to a boil, add salt (about 2 teaspoons), reduce the heat, and simmer, stirring occasionally, for 1 to 1½ hours, or until the beans dissolve into a mush. Have a pot of water simmering on hand and add some if the beans stick to the bottom of the pan. Remove from the heat and allow to sit for 30 minutes. Taste and adjust seasoning. Stir in 3 tablespoons of the olive oil.

2. Bring a large pot of generously salted water to a boil and add the greens. Cook until just tender, 2 to 4 minutes, depending on the green. Transfer to a bowl of ice water and drain. Squeeze out water and chop coarsely.

3. Heat the remaining 2 tablespoons olive oil in a large, heavy skillet over medium heat. Add the garlic, cook for 30 seconds, and stir in the greens. Cook for about 1 minute, stirring, until nicely coated. Season with salt and pepper. Serve with the favas.

ADVANCE PREPARATION: This dish is best served on the day it's cooked, but it makes a good leftover.

LEFTOVERS: The cooked favas will keep for 3 to 5 days in the refrigerator. The cooked greens will keep for 2 to 3 days. Reheat both before serving.

BAKED BEANS

The Balkans • Serves 6

It must be the long, slow, gentle cooking that makes these beans so tender and full of flavor. The beans never fall apart, but the broth becomes thick and heady with lots of onion and garlic, tomatoes and paprika, mint and a hint of chile.

- 1 pound dried borlotti or pinto beans, picked over, rinsed, soaked in 8 cups water for 6 hours or overnight, and drained
- 5 cups water
- 1 dried or fresh hot red chile pepper
- Salt
- 2 tablespoons extra virgin olive oil
- 2 medium onions, chopped
- 3 large garlic cloves, minced or put through a press
- 2 red bell peppers, 1 chopped, 1 sliced into strips or rounds
- 1 pound tomatoes, half chopped, half sliced into rounds
- 1 teaspoon paprika
- Freshly ground pepper
- 1 heaped tablespoon chopped fresh mint, plus additional chopped mint (or flat-leaf parsley) for garnish

1. Combine the beans, water (enough to cover by ½ inch; add more if necessary), and chile pepper in a large ovenproof casserole or Dutch oven. Bring to a boil, reduce the heat, and simmer for 45 minutes to 1 hour, until the beans are tender but intact. Stir in 1 teaspoon salt.

2. While the beans are simmering, heat the oven to 325°F. Heat the oil in a large nonstick frying pan over medium heat and add the onions. Stir, cover, and cook, stirring occasionally, for 15 minutes,

until lightly browned. Stir in the garlic and the chopped bell pepper and cook, stirring, for 5 minutes, until the pepper is just tender and the mixture is fragrant. Add the chopped tomatoes and some salt, and cook, stirring often, until the tomatoes have cooked down a little, 5 to 10 minutes. Remove from the heat and stir in the paprika, salt (1 teaspoon or more), ground pepper, and mint. Stir the vegetable mixture into the beans and blend thoroughly. Taste and adjust salt.

3. Cover the beans and bake for 1 hour, until very tender. Check from time to time to make sure the beans are covered with liquid. Add hot water if necessary. Taste and adjust salt.

4. Arrange the sliced tomatoes and sliced peppers on top of the beans. Return to the oven and bake uncovered for 1 hour more, until the vegetables on the top are tender. The beans should remain submerged in the broth; add hot water if necessary. Serve hot or warm, with additional mint sprinkled on top.

Note: *This dish looks pretty in a gratin dish. After Step 3, transfer the beans and their liquid to a 3-quart gratin dish. Arrange the sliced tomatoes and peppers over the top and proceed with the recipe.*

ADVANCE PREPARATION: The beans can be prepared through Step 2 up to a day before you bake them. You can also prepare them through Step 3, and they'll benefit from the time. Refrigerate, then bring back to a simmer on top of the stove before proceeding with Step 4.

LEFTOVERS: The baked beans will keep for 3 to 5 days in the refrigerator. If you want to transform the beans into another dish, you can toss with pasta for a delicious *pasta e fagioli*. They'd also make a wonderful, earthy dish mixed with rice. Or toss with a vinaigrette for a hearty bean salad.

BAKED BEANS WITH HONEY AND DILL

Greece • Serves 4 to 6

I first made this dish, inspired by Diane Kochilas's recipe in *The Greek Vegetarian,* with some gorgeous Christmas lima beans I'd bought at a specialty market in Los Angeles. The sweet and sour flavors of the beans are reminiscent of our American baked beans, but everything else about the dish speaks of the Mediterranean.

- 1 pound dried lima beans or Greek giant white beans, soaked if necessary for 6 hours or overnight in 8 cups water and drained (some types of limas require no soaking)
- 4 tablespoons extra virgin olive oil
- 1 large red onion, finely chopped
- 1 can (28 ounces) chopped tomatoes, with juice; or 3 cups peeled, seeded, and chopped fresh tomatoes
- 1 bay leaf
- 3 tablespoons mild honey, such as clover or acacia
- 2 cups water
- 2 tablespoons tomato paste
- ¼ cup red wine vinegar or sherry vinegar
- Salt and freshly ground black pepper
- 1 cup loosely packed chopped fresh dill
- Country bread

1. Combine the beans and water to cover by 3 inches in a large ovenproof casserole or Dutch oven and bring to a boil. Reduce the heat, cover, and simmer 30 minutes.

2. Meanwhile, heat the oven to 375°F. Heat 2 tablespoons of the olive oil in a medium, heavy skillet over medium heat and add the onion. Cook, stirring often, until tender and lightly caramelized, 10 to 15 minutes. Remove from the heat.

3. Drain the beans and return them to the pot. Add the remaining 2 tablespoons olive oil, the tomatoes, bay leaf, honey, and 2 cups water. Stir in the sautéed onion and bring the mixture to a simmer. Cover and bake for 1 hour, stirring often and adding hot water if necessary to keep the beans covered. Add the tomato paste, vinegar, salt (be generous), and pepper. Cover and bake another 30 minutes, until the beans are tender and the mixture is thick.

4. Stir in the dill and bake another 15 minutes. Taste and adjust seasonings. Discard the bay leaf. Serve hot or warm, with thick slices of country bread.

ADVANCE PREPARATION: This recipe can be made through Step 3 a day or two ahead of time and refrigerated. Add water if the mixture is too thick. Bring to a simmer on top of the stove, add the dill, and then bake in a preheated 375°F oven for 15 minutes.

LEFTOVERS: The beans will be good for 3 or 4 days.

Rice, Couscous, and Other Grains

Wheat (in the form of bread) may be the most universal staple throughout the Mediterranean, but rice is also important, particularly in the cuisines of Spain, the Veneto region of Italy, Turkey, Greece, and the Middle East. It came to the Mediterranean by way of Persia with the rise of Islam, and was well established in Spain by the 10th century. Rice was important throughout the Middle Ages, not just as a food, but as a trade commodity.

The types of rice that are grown and used in cooking differ from one part of the Mediterranean region to another, as do the methods for cooking it. The Spanish use a short- or medium-grain rice, which they don't rinse before cooking. For *arroz en paella*, which we call, simply, *paella*, they sauté the rice in abundant olive oil before adding liquid to it, then cook it uncovered in a wide pan called a *paella*. Most important, when the liquid is added, the rice is stirred once, and not touched again until all of the liquid has been absorbed. Paellas are chewy, slightly sticky (though the grains of rice are separate), and very aromatic, often with the addition of saffron. Paella is the best

313

known of the Spanish rice dishes, but rice is also the basis for other, soupier dishes that are cooked in earthenware cazuelas, such as the rice and black bean dish called *Moros y Cristianos,* and the rice and fish stew called *Caldero Murciano.*

The northern Italians developed a wonderful method for cooking their starchy short-grain rice (Arborio or Carnaroli). Their risottos are rich and creamy, bound with the starch from the rice kernels, which is coaxed out of them by slow cooking and stirring in simmering broth. The broth is an important factor in risotto: the more flavorful the broth, the better your risotto will taste. Risottos are wonderful vehicles for all sorts of vegetables, and you will find a varied selection here.

Risotto-like dishes are also made with other grains in Italy. *Orzotto* is a barley risotto, and *farrotto* is made with spelt, which is called *farro* in Italy, *épautre* in France. These grains have wonderful flavors and chewy textures. Their risottos aren't creamy like those made with rice, because the grains aren't as starchy.

Another grain that is much loved in Italy is corn (*mais*), which arrived in northern Italy in the late 15th or early 16th century. The grain was cultivated in the Veneto, its kernels ground into a meal and cooked into a porridge that came to be known as *polenta*. Polenta is popular all over Italy, particularly in the north. It's comforting in the way that mashed potatoes are comforting, very much at home with melted cheese or a savory topping. Cooled polenta can be sliced and grilled.

In Turkey, Greece, the Balkans, and the Middle East, long-grain rice is most often used (though there are exceptions, like the Balkan pilafs), and the method is completely different from the Spanish or Italian way. Here rice is cooked using the pilaf method. First it's rinsed to rid the grains of excess starch; sometimes the rice is sautéed first in butter or oil. As in the Spanish method, once liquid is added and brought to a boil, the rice isn't touched. But now it simmers slowly in a covered pot. Once the rice has absorbed all of the liquid, a towel is placed between the lid and the rice to absorb steam. This helps keep the individual grains separate. Pilafs are fluffy, the rice dry.

Pilafs are also made with bulgur, a type of cracked wheat made from wheat kernels that have been soaked in boiling water, then dried and milled into coarse, fine, or medium grinds. Bulgur, like couscous, is convenient, because it requires only a soak in hot water to reconstitute it. It's a nutty-tasting grain that is also used in vegetable fillings, *kofte* (meatballs and vegetarian patties), and salads, and it's much loved in Turkey and the Middle East.

The other grain I've included in this chapter is couscous, which is actually a pasta. A North African staple, couscous is made by rubbing together large grains of semolina with smaller, finer grains sprayed with salted water. The grains affix to each other, forming the larger grains of semolina we know as couscous. Before it can be eaten, couscous must be reconstituted and steamed (*never* boiled). Ideally, some of the broth from the stew you are serving it with will be used for reconstituting, and the grains will steam above the simmering broth, absorbing more aromas. A couscous meal can be an amazing feast, as the recipes on pages 336 to 341 attest.

HOW TO MAKE RISOTTO

Risotto is one of the world's great dishes, yet it's very difficult to get a good one in a restaurant, because it should go from the pan to your plate immediately. But this doesn't mean you can't cook risotto ahead, at least partially. You can cook the risotto halfway through, spread the rice in a thin layer in the pan while it's still hard, then finish the dish just before serving.

Creamy risotto is made with round Italian rice, Arborio or Carnaroli, which retains its chewy texture while yielding its sauce-thickening starch as it slowly cooks.

The broth is important in a risotto, because it seasons the rice as the rice cooks. Chicken broth is the most common type used; rarely would an Italian use anything else. But if you are a vegetarian, you should not be deprived of risotto! A savory vegetable broth works well, as does garlic broth. The mushroom risotto on page 318 calls for mushroom broth.

Here are the basic steps in making a risotto:

1. Prepare all your ingredients (see following recipes).

2. Bring the broth to a simmer on the stove, with a ladle nearby or in the pot. Make sure that the broth is well seasoned with salt. It will remain at a simmer the entire time you are making the risotto.

3. Heat the butter or extra virgin olive oil over medium heat in a wide, heavy nonstick skillet. The skillet should be wide so that the rice will cook evenly as it is stirred, without being submerged in liquid. I use a nonstick skillet because I use less oil than traditional risotto calls for. Add the onion if onion is called for. Cook gently until it is just tender. Do not brown.

4. Stir in the rice, and if the recipe calls for garlic, add it with the rice. Traditional risottos call for more fat than mine, and the rice absorbs it before you add the other ingredients. In my recipes you will stir the rice just until the grains become separate, which doesn't take very long.

5. Add the wine and cook, stirring, until it is absorbed. The wine is important for flavor, as it adds a delicious acidity to the dish (the alcohol boils off). The heat should be moderate; the wine should bubble as soon as you add it to the rice, but it should not boil off so quickly that the rice doesn't have time to absorb its flavor. (A dry white wine, such as pinot grigio or sauvignon blanc, is the best wine to use. Don't use chardonnay; it is too oaky and not dry enough.)

6. Once you no longer see any wine in the pan, begin adding the simmering broth about ½ cup at a time. The broth should just cover the rice, and should be bubbling, not too slowly but not too quickly. Stir often; you don't have to stir constantly, as I used to think, but you do have to stir often, to keep the grains separate and to distribute their starch throughout the mixture, and also to ascertain when it's time to add the next portion of broth. This you will do when you see that the broth has just about disappeared in the pan.

7. The rice will be cooked through but still be chewy after 20 to 25 minutes of this cooking—adding the broth in increments and stirring. When the rice is tender all the way through but still chewy, it is done. Taste now and correct seasoning.

8. Add a final ladleful of broth (about ⅓ cup) to the rice. Stir in the Parmesan if called for, and remove from the heat. The mixture should be creamy. If you put some on a plate and tilt the plate, the mound of rice should flatten out. Add freshly ground pepper, taste one last time, and adjust salt. Stir once and serve right away.

ADVANCE PREPARATION: You can begin the risotto up to several hours before serving: Proceed with the recipe and cook halfway through Step 6, that is, for about 15 minutes. The rice should still be hard when you remove it from the heat, and there should not be any liquid in the pan. Spread it in an even layer in the pan and keep it away from the heat until you resume cooking. Fifteen minutes before serving, resume cooking as instructed.

LEFTOVERS: Risotto will lose that wonderful chewy texture over time, but it will still taste good for 2 or 3 days. One marvelous way to stretch leftovers is to stir them into a frittata. Use ½ to 2 cups risotto for 4 to 10 eggs and follow the directions on page 176. Another wonderful use for leftover Risotto Milanese is to make Deep-Fried Rice and Mozzarella Balls (page 133).

RISOTTO MILANESE

Italy • **Serves 4 generously**

This is the mother of all risottos. It's utterly simple and classic—a little onion, rice, wine, broth, cheese, and a pinch of saffron. If you've never made risotto, start with this one. If you can make Risotto Milanese, you can make any risotto.

> 7 cups Garlic Broth (page 145), Simple Vegetable Broth (page 145), or chicken stock (as needed)
>
> Salt
>
> 2 tablespoons unsalted butter or extra virgin olive oil (or 1 tablespoon each)
>
> ¼ cup finely chopped onion
>
> 1½ cups Arborio or Carnaroli rice
>
> ½ cup dry white wine, such as pinot grigio or sauvignon blanc
>
> Saffron
>
> ⅔ cup freshly grated Parmesan

1. Put your broth into a saucepan and bring it to a simmer on the stove, with a ladle nearby or in the pot. Make sure that it is well seasoned with salt. It will remain at a simmer the entire time you are making the risotto, and you will add it a ladleful or two at a time to the rice.

2. Heat the butter in a wide, heavy nonstick skillet over medium heat. Add the onion and cook gently until it is just tender, about 3 minutes. Do not brown.

3. Stir in the rice and stir just until the grains become separate, which doesn't take very long. Add the wine and cook, stirring, until it is absorbed.

4. Stir in enough simmering broth to just cover the rice, and crumble in a pinch of saffron. The broth should bubble slowly. Cook, stirring often, until it is just about absorbed. Add another ladleful or two of broth and continue to cook in this fashion, not too fast and not too slowly, adding more broth when the rice is almost dry and stirring often, for 20 to 25 minutes. When the rice is tender all the way through but still chewy, it is done. Taste now and correct seasoning.

5. Add a final ⅓ cup broth to the rice. Stir in the Parmesan and remove from the heat. The mixture should be creamy. If you put some on a plate and tilt the plate, the mound of rice should flatten out. Serve right away.

ADVANCE PREPARATION and **LEFTOVERS:** See page 315.

ARTICHOKE RISOTTO

Italy • **Serves 4 generously**

Risotto can be a pantry meal, a really elegant supper that you pull out of your pantry and freezer. I try to remember to keep frozen artichoke hearts on hand for just such an occasion. Serve this risotto in wide soup bowls or on plates, spreading it in a thin layer rather than a mound.

> 7 cups Simple Vegetable Broth (page 145) or chicken stock (as needed)
>
> Salt
>
> 2 tablespoons unsalted butter or extra virgin olive oil (or 1 tablespoon each)
>
> 1 small onion, minced
>
> 1 to 2 garlic cloves (to taste), minced or put through a press
>
> 1 package (1 pound) frozen artichoke hearts, thawed and quartered
>
> 1½ cups Arborio or Carnaroli rice
>
> 1 teaspoon fresh thyme leaves (or ½ teaspoon dried)
>
> ½ cup dry white wine, such as pinot grigio or sauvignon blanc
>
> 1 tablespoon fresh lemon juice
>
> 2 tablespoon chopped fresh flat-leaf parsley
>
> ½ cup freshly grated Parmesan, or a mixture of Parmesan and Pecorino Romano
>
> Freshly ground pepper

1. Put your broth into a saucepan and bring it to a simmer on the stove, with a ladle nearby or in the pot. Make sure that it is well seasoned with salt. It will remain at a simmer the entire time you are making the risotto, and you will add it a ladleful or two at a time to the rice.

2. Heat the butter in a wide, heavy nonstick skillet over medium heat. Add the onion and cook gently until tender and just golden, about 5 minutes. Do not brown. Add the garlic and stir for about a minute, until the garlic smells fragrant. Stir in the artichoke hearts. Toss together until fragrant.

3. Stir in the rice and thyme, and stir until the grains become separate and begin to crackle. Add the wine and cook, stirring, until it has just about evaporated and been absorbed by the rice. Stir in enough of the simmering broth to just cover the rice. The broth should bubble slowly. Cook, stirring often, until it is just about absorbed. Add another ladleful or two of the broth and continue to cook in this fashion, not too fast and not too slowly, adding more broth when the rice is almost dry and stirring often, for 20 to 25 minutes. When the rice is tender all the way through but still chewy, it is done. Taste now and correct seasoning.

4. Add another ⅓ cup of broth to the rice. Stir in the lemon juice, parsley, and cheese, and remove from the heat. The mixture should be creamy. Add freshly ground pepper, taste one last time, and adjust salt. Stir once and serve right away.

ADVANCE PREPARATION and **LEFTOVERS:** See page 315.

FAVA BEAN AND GREEN GARLIC RISOTTO

Italy • **Serves 4**

This is a springtime risotto, a celebration of the young fava beans and tender bulbs of fresh garlic that hit the markets here in Los Angeles about the same time they do throughout the Mediterranean, from April through June. If you can't get green garlic, make the dish with spring onions or scallions.

> 7 cups Simple Vegetable Broth (page 145) or chicken stock (as needed)
>
> Salt
>
> 2 tablespoons extra virgin olive oil
>
> ½ cup minced green garlic, spring onions, or scallions (white and light green parts only)

> 1½ cups Arborio or Carnaroli rice
>
> ½ cup dry white wine, such as pinot grigio or sauvignon blanc
>
> ½ teaspoon saffron (optional)
>
> 3 pounds fresh fava beans, shelled and skinned (page 113)
>
> ½ cup freshly grated Parmesan
>
> ¼ cup chopped fresh flat-leaf parsley
>
> ½ teaspoon grated lemon zest
>
> Freshly ground pepper

1. Put your broth into a saucepan and bring it to a simmer on the stove, with a ladle nearby or in the pot. Make sure that it is well seasoned with salt. It will remain at a simmer the entire time you are making the risotto, and you will add it a ladleful or two at a time to the rice.

2. Heat the oil in a large nonstick skillet over medium heat and add the green garlic. Cook, stirring, for about a minute, until it begins to smell fragrant, and add the rice. Cook, stirring, until the grains of rice are separate, about 1 minute.

3. Stir in the wine and cook over medium heat, stirring constantly. The wine should bubble, but not too quickly. You want some of the flavor to cook into the rice before it evaporates. When the wine has just about evaporated, stir in a ladleful or two of the simmering broth, enough to just cover the rice. Crumble in the saffron. The broth should bubble slowly. Cook, stirring often, until it is just about absorbed. Add another ladleful of broth and continue to cook in this fashion, not too fast and not too slowly, adding more broth when the rice is almost dry, for about 15 minutes, until the rice is almost cooked through but still a bit hard in the center. Stir in the fava beans and another ladleful or two of broth. Continue adding broth and stirring the rice as you have been doing for another 10 minutes, until the rice is cooked al dente.

4. Add another ⅓ cup of broth to the rice, and stir in the Parmesan, parsley, lemon zest, and pepper. Taste and adjust salt. The rice should be creamy. Stir for a couple of seconds and serve.

ADVANCE PREPARATION: The favas can be blanched and skinned a day or two ahead and refrigerated in a covered bowl. You can begin this dish several hours ahead; see page 113.

VARIATION

ASPARAGUS AND FAVA BEAN RISOTTO: Substitute 1 pound asparagus for 1 pound of the fava beans. Trim the asparagus and cut into 1-inch lengths. Steam for 5 minutes, refresh with cold water, and set aside. Add to the rice with the final ladleful of broth.

MUSHROOM RISOTTO

Italy • **Serves 4 generously**

A rich ragout of mushrooms, both cultivated and wild, will make a risotto that you can serve time and again for a dinner party, and I guarantee that your guests will never tire of it. You find the dish on menus throughout northern Italy, and it's always worth ordering. An assortment of wild mushrooms, like chanterelles, oyster mushrooms, shiitake, and morels, will make this unforgettable.

1 ounce (about 1 heaped cup) dried
    mushrooms, preferably porcinis

3 cups boiling water

4 cups Simple Vegetable Broth (page 145)
    or chicken stock (as needed)

2 tablespoons soy sauce

Salt

2 tablespoons unsalted butter or extra virgin
    olive oil (or 1 tablespoon each)

1 small onion, minced

1 pound fresh cultivated or wild mushrooms
    (see headnote), trimmed and cut into thick
    slices

2 large garlic cloves, minced or put through
    a press

½ to 1 teaspoon chopped fresh rosemary
    (or ¼ to ½ teaspoon crumbled dried)

½ to 1 teaspoon fresh thyme (or ¼ to
    ½ teaspoon dried)

1½ cups Arborio or Carnaroli rice

½ cup dry white wine, such as pinot grigio or
    fumé blanc

¼ cup freshly grated Parmesan (more to taste)

¼ cup chopped fresh flat-leaf parsley

Freshly ground pepper

1. Place the dried mushrooms in a bowl or in a Pyrex measuring cup and pour on the boiling water. Let sit for 30 minutes. Line a strainer with cheesecloth or with a double thickness of paper towels, place it over a bowl, and drain the mushrooms. Squeeze the mushrooms over the strainer to extract all the liquid, then rinse them in several changes of water to remove sand. Chop coarsely and set aside.

2. Combine the mushroom soaking liquid with the vegetable broth; add additional broth if you need to make 7 cups. Add the soy sauce and 1 teaspoon salt (if the broth is salted, add less salt). Taste and adjust the salt. It should be well seasoned. Put your broth into a saucepan and bring to a simmer on the stove, with a ladle nearby or in the pot. It will remain at a simmer the entire time you are making the risotto, and you will add it a ladleful or two at a time to the rice.

3. Heat 1 tablespoon of the butter in a large, heavy skillet over medium heat and add the onion. Cook, stirring, until the onion begins to soften, about 3 minutes, and add the dried and fresh mushrooms. Cook, stirring, until the mushrooms begin to release liquid. Add the garlic, rosemary, and thyme. Cook, stirring, until the mushroom liquid has just about evaporated, and add the remaining butter and the rice. Cook, stirring, until the grains of rice are separate.

4. Stir in the wine and cook over medium heat, stirring constantly. The wine should bubble, but not too quickly. You want some of the flavor to cook into the rice before it evaporates. When the wine has just about evaporated, stir in a ladleful or two of the simmering broth, enough to just cover the rice. The broth should bubble slowly. Cook, stirring often, until it is just about absorbed. Add another ladleful of broth and continue to cook in this fashion, not too fast and not too slowly, adding more broth when the rice is almost dry, for 20 to 25 minutes. Taste a bit of the rice. Is it cooked through? It should taste chewy but not hard in the middle. Definitely not soft like steamed rice. If it is still hard in the middle, you need to add another ladleful of broth and cook for another 5 minutes or so. Now is the time to ascertain if there is enough salt. Add if necessary.

5. Add another ⅓ cup of broth to the rice. Stir in the Parmesan and parsley, add freshly ground pepper, taste one last time, and adjust salt. The rice should be creamy. Serve at once.

ADVANCE PREPARATION and **LEFTOVERS:** See page 315.

RED PEPPER RISOTTO WITH SAFFRON

Italy • Serves 4 generously

You can make this risotto at any time of year, because you can always find red peppers. But from the middle of summer through the fall, the local peppers will be freshly picked and sweet. Look for them at your farmers' markets. I often add a pinch of saffron, not only for its incredible rich, earthy flavor, but also for the color.

> 7 cups Simple Vegetable Broth (page 145) or chicken stock (as needed)
>
> Salt
>
> 1 tablespoon unsalted butter
>
> 1 tablespoon extra virgin olive oil
>
> 1 medium shallot, minced
>
> 2 large red bell peppers, seeded and sliced into thin 2-inch-long strips
>
> 1½ cups Arborio or Carnaroli rice
>
> ½ cup dry white wine, such as pinot grigio or sauvignon blanc
>
> ½ teaspoon saffron
>
> ½ cup freshly grated Parmesan
>
> 2 tablespoons chopped fresh flat-leaf parsley, or a mixture of parsley and thyme, oregano, or marjoram
>
> Freshly ground pepper

1. Put your broth into a saucepan and bring it to a simmer on the stove, with a ladle nearby or in the pot. Make sure that it is well seasoned with salt. It will remain at a simmer the entire time you are making the risotto, and you will add it a ladleful or two at a time to the rice.

2. Heat a large, wide, heavy skillet over medium heat and add the butter and olive oil. When the fat is hot, add the shallot and cook gently until tender and fragrant but not browned, about 3 minutes. Add the peppers and cook, stirring, until they are limp and fragrant, 8 to 10 minutes. Season to taste with salt.

3. Add the rice and cook, stirring, until all of the grains are separate and coated with oil. Add the wine and cook, stirring, until it has just about evaporated and been absorbed by the rice. Stir in a ladleful or two of the simmering broth, enough to just cover the rice. Crumble in the saffron. The broth should bubble slowly. Cook, stirring often, until it is just about absorbed. Add another ladleful of broth and continue to cook in this fashion, not too fast and not too slowly, adding more broth when the rice is almost dry and stirring often, for 20 to 25 minutes. When the rice is tender all the way through but still chewy, it is done. Taste now and correct seasoning.

4. Add another ⅓ cup of broth to the rice. Stir in the Parmesan and fresh herbs and remove from the heat. The mixture should be creamy. Add freshly ground pepper, taste one last time, and adjust salt. Stir once and serve right away.

ADVANCE PREPARATION and **LEFTOVERS:** See page 315.

RED RISOTTO WITH BEET GREENS

Italy • **Serves 4 generously**

Years ago I spent a heady week in Venice during Carnevale, in February. It was cold and gray, often rainy, but that didn't keep the hordes of costumed Italians from the streets. Every day was a party. And for me, just about every meal meant a new kind of risotto, the Veneto being risotto country. Venice was the ideal place for me to do my risotto research.

In Los Angeles, I make this dish often throughout the winter, when I buy beets with their greens attached at local farmers' markets. When I use these greens for risotto, the resulting rice is pinkish red and quite beautiful. Red chard and radicchio provide equally delicious results. I use red wine instead of white, to enhance the color. However, if white is all you have on hand, use it.

7 cups Simple Vegetable Broth (page 145)
    or chicken stock (as needed)

Salt

2 tablespoons unsalted butter or extra virgin
    olive oil (or 1 tablespoon each)

1 small onion, minced

1½ cups Arborio or Carnaroli rice

2 garlic cloves, minced or put through a press

½ cup dry, fruity red wine, such as a Côtes du
    Rhône or Syrah

¾ to 1 pound (1 bunch) beet greens or red
    chard, stemmed and cut into 1-inch strips

¼ to ½ cup freshly grated Parmesan (to taste)

Freshly ground pepper

1. Put your broth into a saucepan and bring it to a simmer on the stove, with a ladle nearby or in the pot. Make sure that it is well seasoned with salt. It will remain at a simmer the entire time you are making the risotto, and you will add it a ladleful or two at a time to the rice.

2. Heat the butter in a large nonstick skillet over medium heat and add the onion. Cook, stirring, until the onion begins to soften, about 3 minutes, and add the rice and garlic. Cook, stirring, until the grains of rice are separate.

3. Stir in the wine and cook over medium heat, stirring constantly. The wine should bubble, but not too quickly. You want some of the flavor to cook into the rice before it evaporates. When the wine has just about evaporated, stir in a ladleful or two of the simmering broth, enough to just cover the rice. The broth should bubble slowly. Cook, stirring often, until it is just about absorbed. Add another ladleful of broth and continue to cook in this fashion, not too fast and not too slowly, adding more broth when the rice is almost dry, for 10 minutes.

4. Stir in the greens and continue adding more broth, a ladleful at a time, and stirring, for another 10 to 15 minutes, until the rice is cooked al dente. Taste and adjust seasonings.

5. Add another ⅓ cup of broth to the rice. Stir the Parmesan into the rice and immediately remove from the heat. Add freshly ground pepper, taste one last time, and adjust salt. The rice should be creamy. Stir once and serve.

ADVANCE PREPARATION: See instructions on page 315. You can begin this dish several hours ahead and cook the rice for 10 minutes through Step 3. Scatter the greens over the top and remove the risotto and the broth from the heat.

LEFTOVERS: See page 315.

VARIATIONS

I often blanch greens when I get them home from the market so that they won't wilt or rot in the refrigerator if I don't get around to cooking them right away. If you do this, and want to use them for a risotto, chop the blanched greens and set aside. Add them to the risotto during the last few minutes of cooking, just to heat them through and amalgamate into the dish. The color will not be as red.

RADICCHIO RISOTTO: Substitute 2 medium heads of radicchio for the beet greens. Quarter and core the radicchio and cut into chiffonade.

RED WINE RISOTTO WITH CAULIFLOWER

Italy • **Serves 4 generously**

This dish is based on a classic, heavenly Venetian risotto that's made with Barolo wine. Cauliflower absorbs the color and flavors perfectly here.

> 2 cups robust, fruity red wine, such as an Italian Barolo or a Côtes du Rhône
>
> 5 cups Simple Vegetable Broth (page 145) or chicken stock (as needed)
>
> Salt
>
> 2 tablespoons extra virgin olive oil or unsalted butter (or 1 tablespoon each)
>
> 1 small onion, minced
>
> 2 large garlic cloves, minced or put through a press
>
> 1½ cups Arborio or Carnaroli rice
>
> 1 medium cauliflower, separated into small florets, the florets broken into smaller pieces or sliced ½ inch thick (about 4 heaped cups)
>
> ½ cup freshly grated Parmesan
>
> Freshly ground pepper

1. Combine the wine and broth and bring to a simmer with a ladle nearby or in the pot. Make sure that it is well seasoned with salt. It will remain at a simmer the entire time you are making the risotto, and you will add it a ladleful or two at a time to the rice.

2. Heat the oil in a large, heavy nonstick skillet over medium heat and add the onion. Cook, stirring, until the onion begins to soften, about 3 minutes, and add the garlic and the rice. Cook, stirring, for a couple of minutes, until the grains of rice are separate.

3. Stir in a ladleful or two of the simmering wine and broth, enough to just cover the rice. The broth should bubble slowly. Cook, stirring often, until it is just about absorbed. Add the cauliflower and another ladleful of the broth and continue to cook in this fashion, not too fast and not too slowly, adding more broth when the rice is almost dry, for 20 to 25 minutes, or until the rice is al dente. Add

salt if necessary (remembering that the Parmesan will also contribute saltiness).

4. Add another ⅓ cup of broth to the rice. Stir in the Parmesan and immediately remove from the heat. Add freshly ground pepper, taste one last time, and adjust salt. The rice should be creamy. Serve at once.

ADVANCE PREPARATION and **LEFTOVERS:** See page 315.

RISI E BISI

Italy • **Serves 4 generously**

This is the quintessential springtime risotto, made for sweet, fresh peas when they come into the market. I splurge on them during their short season. Serve it in wide soup bowls or on plates, spreading the risotto in a thin layer rather than a mound.

> 7 cups Simple Vegetable Broth (page 145) or chicken stock (as needed)
>
> Salt
>
> 2 tablespoons unsalted butter or extra virgin olive oil (or 1 tablespoon each)
>
> 1 small onion or 2 shallots, minced
>
> 1½ cups Arborio or Carnaroli rice
>
> ½ cup dry white wine, such as pinot grigio or fumé blanc
>
> 1½ pounds fresh peas, shelled
>
> ½ cup freshly grated Parmesan, or a mixture of Parmesan and Pecorino Romano
>
> 2 tablespoons chopped fresh flat-leaf parsley
>
> Freshly ground pepper

1. Put your broth into a saucepan and bring it to a simmer on the stove, with a ladle nearby or in the pot. Make sure that it is well seasoned with salt. It will remain at a simmer the entire time you are making the risotto, and you will add it a ladleful or two at a time to the rice.

2. Heat the butter in a wide, heavy nonstick skillet over medium heat. Add the onion and cook until tender and translucent, about 5 minutes. Stir in the rice and stir until the grains become separate. ▶

3. Add the wine and cook, stirring, until it has just about evaporated and been absorbed by the rice. Stir in enough of the simmering broth to just cover the rice. The broth should bubble slowly. Cook, stirring often, until it is just about absorbed. Add another ladleful or two of broth and continue to cook in this fashion, not too fast and not too slowly, adding more broth when the rice is almost dry and stirring often, for 10 minutes.

4. Add the peas and continue adding broth and stirring for another 10 to 15 minutes. The peas should be tender and the rice tender all the way through but still chewy. Taste now and correct seasoning.

5. Add another ⅓ cup broth to the rice. Stir in the cheese and parsley, and remove from the heat. The mixture should be creamy. Add freshly ground pepper, taste one last time, and adjust salt. Stir once and serve right away.

ADVANCE PREPARATION and **LEFTOVERS:** See page 315.

RISI E BISI WITH MUSHROOMS
This is a variation of Risi e Bisi (page 321).

This dish is a little more savory and hearty than *risi e bisi.* I love the contrast of the mushrooms with the sweet peas, and the bright green color that the peas add. In addition to the *risi e bisi,* you'll need:

> 1 ounce (about 1 heaped cup) dried porcini mushrooms
>
> 2 cups boiling water
>
> 1 tablespoon extra virgin olive oil
>
> 1 pound wild mushrooms, thickly sliced
>
> 2 garlic cloves, minced
>
> ½ cup red wine

1. Cover the dried mushrooms with the boiling water and let stand for 30 minutes. Line a strainer with cheesecloth or with a double thickness of paper towels, place it over a bowl, and drain the mushrooms. Squeeze the mushrooms over the strainer to extract all the liquid, then rinse in several changes of water to remove sand. Chop coarsely and set aside.

2. Heat the olive oil in a wide, heavy nonstick skillet over medium heat. When the oil is hot, add the wild mushrooms and sear for 10 minutes, stirring. Add the garlic and the reconstituted mushrooms and cook, stirring, for a minute or so, until fragrant. Add the wine and salt and pepper to taste, and cook, stirring, until the liquid in the pan has just about evaporated. Add ½ cup of the mushroom soaking liquid and continue to cook, stirring, until the liquid has just about evaporated and the mushrooms are tender, glossy, and fragrant. Taste and adjust seasonings.

3. When you serve the *risi e bisi,* make a depression in the center of each serving and fill with a spoonful of mushrooms.

SUMMER SQUASH RISOTTO
Italy • **Serves 4 generously**

An abundance of summer squash makes a particularly creamy risotto. In developing this one, I was partly inspired by an article by Marcella Hazan in *Saveur* magazine, in which she talks about *insaporire,* the essential process of bringing out the flavors of foods, which is at the heart of Italian home cooking. Each ingredient that flavors a dish is cooked until the maximum flavor is obtained before the next ingredient is added. That is what you will be doing here with the onion and summer squash. You need to cook the squash until it has given up its water and its flavors are concentrated before you add the rice. For color, I remove some of the squash from the pan before this point, to be stirred back into the risotto at the end.

Serve the risotto in wide soup bowls or on plates, spreading it in a thin layer rather than a mound.

> **7 cups Simple Vegetable Broth (page 145) or chicken stock (as needed)**

Salt

2 tablespoons unsalted butter or extra virgin
olive oil (or 1 tablespoon each)

1 small onion, minced

1 to 2 garlic cloves (to taste), minced or put
through a press

1 to 1¼ pounds mixed yellow and green summer
squash, diced

1½ cups Arborio or Carnaroli rice

1 tablespoon chopped fresh marjoram

½ cup dry white wine, such as pinot grigio
or sauvignon blanc

½ cup freshly grated Parmesan, or a mixture
of Parmesan and Pecorino Romano

Freshly ground pepper

1. Put your broth into a saucepan and bring it to a simmer on the stove, with a ladle nearby or in the pot. Make sure that it is well seasoned with salt. It will remain at a simmer the entire time you are making the risotto, and you will add it a ladleful or two at a time to the rice.

2. Heat the butter in a wide, heavy nonstick skillet over medium heat. Add the onion and cook gently until tender and just golden, about 5 minutes. Add the garlic and stir for about a minute, until the garlic smells fragrant, and stir in the squash. Cook, stirring, until the squash begins to look translucent, about 5 minutes. Add salt and continue to cook, stirring often, until the squash has released water, and the water has evaporated, 8 to 10 minutes. Remove one-third of the squash from the pan and set aside.

3. Stir the rice and marjoram into the squash in the pan and stir until the grains become separate.

4. Add the wine and cook, stirring, until it has just about evaporated and been absorbed by the rice. Stir in enough of the simmering broth to just cover the rice. The broth should bubble slowly. Cook, stirring often, until it is just about absorbed. Add another ladleful or two of broth and continue to cook in this fashion, not too fast and not too slowly, adding more broth when the rice is almost dry and stirring often, for 20 to 25 minutes. When

the rice is tender all the way through but still chewy, it is done. Taste and correct seasoning.

5. Add ⅓ cup broth to the rice. Stir in the cheese and the reserved squash, and remove from the heat. The mixture should be creamy. Add freshly ground pepper, taste one last time, and adjust salt. Stir once and serve right away.

ADVANCE PREPARATION and **LEFTOVERS:** See page 315.

TOMATO AND ZUCCHINI RISOTTO
Croatia • **Serves 4 to 6**

There is an amazing farm/restaurant (*azienda agrituristica*) called Alla Beccaccia, on the Croatian peninsula of Istria, near the village of Fazana. My friends Mira Furlan and Goran Gajic took me there for lunch on a Sunday afternoon, and we loved it so much that we went back again a few days later. The proprietor had promised to make us *beccaccia,* the wild game bird (woodcock, I think) that is the restaurant's namesake. The birds were incredible, but so was the risotto that I watched the cooks make for their own lunch. Privately, I wanted that risotto more than the special roasted birds.

Serve the risotto in wide soup bowls or on plates, spreading it in a thin layer rather than a mound.

6 cups Simple Vegetable Broth (page 145)
or chicken stock (as needed)

1 heaped tablespoon tomato paste

Salt

2 tablespoons extra virgin olive oil

½ medium or 1 small onion, minced

2 garlic cloves, minced

2 medium zucchini, sliced about ¼ inch thick

Freshly ground pepper

1½ pounds tomatoes, peeled, seeded, and diced

1½ cups Arborio or Carnaroli rice

½ cup freshly grated Parmesan, or a mixture
of Parmesan and Pecorino Romano

2 tablespoons chopped fresh flat-leaf parsley

1. Put your broth into a saucepan, add the tomato paste, and bring to a simmer on the stove, with a ladle nearby. Stir to dissolve the tomato paste. Make sure that the broth is well seasoned with salt. It will remain at a simmer the entire time you are making the risotto, and you will add it a ladleful or two at a time to the rice.

2. Heat the oil in a wide, heavy nonstick skillet over medium heat. Add the onion and cook gently until tender and just golden, about 5 minutes. Add the garlic and stir for about a minute, until the garlic smells fragrant, and stir in the zucchini. Cook, stirring, until the zucchini begins to look translucent, about 5 minutes. Season with salt and pepper. Add the tomatoes, turn the heat up slightly, and cook, stirring, until they cook down and smell fragrant, 10 to 15 minutes. Season with salt and pepper.

3. Stir in the rice and stir until the grains separate. Stir in enough of the simmering broth to just cover the rice. The broth should bubble slowly. Cook, stirring often, until it is just about absorbed. Add another ladleful or two of broth and continue to cook in this fashion, not too fast and not too slowly, adding more broth when the rice is almost dry and stirring often, for 20 to 25 minutes. When the rice is tender all the way through but still chewy, it is done. Taste now and correct seasoning.

4. Add another ⅓ cup broth to the rice. Stir in the cheese and parsley, and remove from the heat. The mixture should be creamy. Add freshly ground pepper, taste one last time, and adjust salt. Stir once and serve right away.

ADVANCE PREPARATION and **LEFTOVERS:** See page 315.

WINTER SQUASH RISOTTO
Italy • **Serves 4 generously**

Winter squash, cut into very small dice, will partially melt into the rice as this creamy, orange-hued risotto cooks. The sweet flavor of the squash makes a compelling contrast to the other, savory flavors in the risotto.

> 7 cups Simple Vegetable Broth (page 145) or chicken stock (as needed)
>
> Salt
>
> 2 tablespoons extra virgin olive oil or unsalted butter (or 1 tablespoon each)
>
> 1 small or ½ medium onion
>
> 1 pound winter squash (about half a good-size butternut, for example), such as butternut, banana, or hubbard, peeled, seeded, and finely diced
>
> 2 large garlic cloves, minced or put through a press
>
> 1½ cups Arborio or Carnaroli rice
>
> ½ cup dry white wine, such as pinot grigio or sauvignon blanc
>
> 2 teaspoons chopped fresh sage (optional)
>
> ¼ to ½ cup freshly grated Parmesan (to taste)
>
> Freshly grated nutmeg
>
> ¼ cup chopped fresh flat-leaf parsley
>
> Freshly ground pepper

1. Put your broth into a saucepan and bring it to a simmer on the stove, with a ladle nearby or in the pot. Make sure that it is well seasoned with salt. It will remain at a simmer the entire time you are making the risotto, and you will add it a ladleful or two at a time to the rice.

2. Heat the oil in a large, heavy nonstick skillet over medium heat and add the onion. Cook, stirring, until the onion begins to soften, about 3 minutes, and add the squash, garlic, and about ¼ teaspoon salt. Cook, stirring, until the squash begins to soften, about 3 minutes, and add the rice. Cook, stirring, until the grains of rice are separate.

3. Stir in the wine and cook over medium heat, stirring constantly. The wine should bubble, but not too quickly. You want some of the flavor to cook into the rice before it evaporates. When the wine has just about evaporated, stir in a ladleful or two of the simmering broth, enough to just cover the rice and squash. The broth should bubble slowly. Cook, stirring often, until it is just about absorbed. Add the sage and another ladleful of the broth, and continue to cook in this fashion, not too fast and not too slowly, adding more broth when the rice is almost dry, for 20 to 25 minutes, or until the rice is cooked al dente. Taste and adjust seasonings.

4. Add another ⅓ cup broth to the rice. Stir in the Parmesan, a pinch of nutmeg, and the parsley, and immediately remove from the heat. Add freshly ground pepper, taste one last time, and adjust salt. The rice should be creamy. Serve at once.

ADVANCE PREPARATION and **LEFTOVERS:** See page 315.

VEGETABLE PAELLA FROM EL PALMAR

Spain • **Serves 6 generously**

El Palmar is a little town filled with paella restaurants, on the rice-growing lagoon that surrounds Valencia. Here, at Restaurant Isla, I found a *paella de verduras* on the menu, and I ordered it straight-away. The waiter asked, "Thirty minutes?" A good sign, as this meant it was going to be begun right then and there. I should have also asked if I could watch the chef make it! But the chef, Maria Ange-les, whose husband owns the restaurant, and who is referred to as a "cook," not a chef, told me how she did it afterwards.

First the vegetables are fried in very hot olive oil, for about 10 minutes. The hot oil gives the squash, flat green beans, asparagus, onion, giant white beans, mushrooms, baby artichokes, and eggplant great seared flavor. The yellow rice, which was crunchy, was more colored than sea-soned with saffron; I opt for more. Paprika and pepper added some bite.

When the vegetables are nicely browned, the rice is added, stirred once, then water—not broth—is added. After 20 minutes, everything is done. This chef emphasized that, with the exception of the fish paella called *arroz abanda,* broth is not used in most paella. Maria Angeles does, however, add a vegetable bouillon cube and some tomato "for flavor." Other chefs I have talked to insist that the success of the paella is entirely dependent on the broth. In any case, this one had lots of flavor. Try making it on an outdoor grill for a wonderful smoky taste.

1 small eggplant, diced

Salt

4 cups water or Simple Vegetable Broth (page 145)

1 vegetable bouillon cube (optional)

6 tablespoons extra virgin olive oil

1 onion, chopped

4 baby artichokes, trimmed and sliced; or 4 frozen artichoke hearts, thawed and sliced (optional)

¼ pound Romano beans or green beans, cut into 2-inch lengths

1 red bell pepper or 2 lipstick peppers, thinly sliced

1 small zucchini, diced

4 medium mushrooms, sliced

¼ pound asparagus, trimmed and cut into 2-inch lengths (or omit and use ½ pound Romano or green beans)

Freshly ground pepper

4 garlic cloves, minced

2 tomatoes, peeled, seeded, and chopped

1½ teaspoons sweet Spanish paprika

2 cups short-grain rice

1 can (15 ounces) giant white beans, drained and rinsed; or 1½ cups cooked dried giant white beans

Saffron

1. Place the eggplant in a colander and salt gener-ously. Let sit in the sink for 30 minutes. Squeeze out moisture and blot dry with paper towels. ▶

2. Bring the water to a simmer in a saucepan. Add the bouillon cube and dissolve, and keep at a low simmer.

3. Heat 2 tablespoons of the olive oil in a 12-inch frying pan, paella pan, or wide casserole over medium-high heat, and add the onion. Cook, stirring, until translucent, about 5 minutes. Add another 2 tablespoons olive oil, turn the heat up to high, and heat for a couple of minutes until almost smoking. Add the artichokes, Roman beans, red pepper, zucchini, mushrooms, asparagus, and eggplant. Cook, stirring often, for 5 minutes, then reduce the heat to medium and cook, stirring often, until the vegetables are nicely browned, 10 to 15 minutes. Season to taste with salt and freshly ground pepper. Stir in the garlic and cook, stirring, for about a minute, until fragrant. Add the tomatoes and paprika, and cook, stirring, until the tomatoes begin to cook down, 5 to 10 minutes.

4. Add the remaining 2 tablespoons oil, the rice, giant white beans, 2 teaspoons salt, and a generous pinch or two of saffron. Stir together for a couple of minutes, then pour in the simmering bouillon. Bring to a simmer, stir once, and reduce the heat to low. Cook without stirring until all of the liquid has been absorbed, about 20 minutes. Turn off the heat. Cover tightly and let sit for 10 minutes without disturbing. Fold the rice from the outside of the pan into the middle, cover tightly, and let sit again for 10 minutes. Taste and adjust seasonings. Serve hot.

ADVANCE PREPARATION: Paella is a dish to make with your friends standing around. It should be served right away.

SOUR CHERRY PILAF
Turkey • Serves 6

This Turkish pilaf is traditionally made with sour cherries and rice. It can also be made with bulgur. You can find preserved sour cherries, or Morello cherries, in gourmet groceries. I've found them at my local Trader Joe's. If you can't find them, you could use dried cherries, or regular cherries, which will bleed into the rice for a beautiful pink color.

- 2 tablespoons unsalted butter
- 1 cup Morello cherries, drained and pitted; or 1 cup dried cherries, soaked for 10 minutes in hot water and drained
- 1 teaspoon sugar
- 1½ teaspoons caraway seeds or fennel seeds, ground
- 1¼ cups basmati rice, rinsed until the water runs clear
- 2¼ cups water
- 1 teaspoon salt
- ½ cup drained yogurt (page 21)

Melt the butter in a large, heavy saucepan over medium heat and add the cherries and sugar. Cook, gently shaking the pan, for 2 to 3 minutes. Stir in the caraway and rice, and cover with the water. Add the salt and bring to a boil. Reduce the heat, cover, and simmer for 15 minutes, until the water has been absorbed. Remove from the heat, remove the lid, and cover the saucepan with a clean, dry dishtowel. Return the lid to the pan and let sit for 15 minutes, undisturbed. Remove the lid. The rice should be tender, with the grains separate. Mound into a wide bowl or onto a platter, and serve with the yogurt.

ADVANCE PREPARATION: The pilaf can be made several hours ahead, transferred to a baking dish, and allowed to cool uncovered. To reheat, cover with foil and place in a 325°F oven for 20 minutes.

EGGPLANT PILAF

Turkey • **Serves 4 to 6**

The Turkish spice palate is a seductive one. Cumin seeds and coriander, along with tomato, onion, and garlic, give this pilaf its marvelous character.

Salt

1 medium eggplant, peeled in alternating strips and cut into ¾-inch dice

1 cup basmati or long-grain rice

3 tablespoons extra virgin olive oil (as needed)

1 small onion, chopped

2 garlic cloves, minced

1 teaspoon sugar

¾ teaspoon cumin seeds, whole or lightly crushed

¾ teaspoon coriander seeds, whole or lightly crushed

1 tablespoon tomato paste

2 cups water

Freshly ground pepper

1. Salt the eggplant generously and leave for 30 minutes to an hour in a colander set on a plate. Rinse briefly and pat dry.

2. If using basmati rice, rinse in several changes of water until the water runs clear.

3. Heat 1 tablespoon of the olive oil in a large, heavy saucepan or Dutch oven over medium heat and add the onion. Cook, stirring often, until tender, about 5 minutes. Add the garlic, stir until fragrant, about 30 seconds, and stir in the sugar, cumin seeds, and coriander seeds. Cook for a couple of minutes, until they begin to smell fragrant, and stir in the rice, tomato paste, water, ¾ teaspoon salt, and pepper to taste. Bring to a boil, then reduce the heat, cover, and simmer until the liquid has been absorbed, about 15 minutes. Remove the pan from the heat, cover with a clean dish towel, and replace the lid. Let sit undisturbed for 15 to 20 minutes. The rice will steam and should be fluffy.

4. Meanwhile, heat the remaining 2 tablespoons oil in a large, heavy nonstick skillet over medium-high heat and add the eggplant. Cook, stirring, until tender and lightly browned, about 15 minutes. Cover the pan, reduce the heat to medium-low, and continue to cook, stirring occasionally, for another 5 to 10 minutes, until the eggplant is nice and tender. Stir in the rice, toss together, taste, adjust seasonings, and serve.

ADVANCE PREPARATION: This pilaf can be made a day ahead and reheated. Spread in a lightly oiled baking dish and cool. Cover and chill. Reheat in a 325°F oven for 20 minutes.

TOMATO AND RICE PILAF

The Balkans • **Serves 4 as a main dish or 6 to 8 as a side dish**

According to food historian Maria Kaneva-Johnson, whose wonderful book *The Melting Pot: Balkan Food and Cookery* has been the source of many delicious recipes for me, this dish evolved from a Persian dish called *borani,* which originally contained neither rice nor tomatoes (it wouldn't have included tomatoes, as they didn't reach Europe until the 16th century). The Turks brought the dish to the Balkans and introduced rice into it. One of the most interesting aspects of the dish is that it is meant to be served at room temperature or cold.

3 tablespoons extra virgin olive oil

2 medium onions, finely chopped

1 green or yellow bell pepper, diced small

2 to 3 garlic cloves (to taste), minced

2 teaspoons paprika

1¾ pounds tomatoes, peeled, seeded, and finely chopped or put through a food mill fitted with the medium blade

Salt

1 cup short- or medium-grain rice (see **Note**)

1¾ cups water

¾ teaspoon freshly ground pepper

2 tablespoons finely chopped fresh flat-leaf parsley, plus additional for garnish

2 tablespoons finely chopped fresh dill

Imported black olives

Note: *If you want to make this dish with a long-grain rice, such as basmati, use only 1½ cups water.*

1. Heat 2 tablespoons of the olive oil in a 2- or 3-quart heavy saucepan over medium-low heat and add the onions and bell pepper. Cook gently, stirring often, until the vegetables begin to soften, 3 to 5 minutes. Cover and continue to cook, stirring often, for 5 to 10 minutes, until the vegetables are thoroughly tender but not browned. Stir in the garlic and cook, stirring, for about 1 minute, until fragrant. Add the paprika and stir for about 30 seconds, then stir in the tomatoes. Turn up the heat slightly and bring to a simmer. Cook, stirring often, for 10 minutes, until the tomatoes have cooked down somewhat and smell fragrant. Season to taste with salt.

2. Add the rice, water, and 1½ teaspoons salt, and bring to a simmer. Reduce the heat to low, cover, and simmer for 15 to 20 minutes, or until all of the liquid has been absorbed. Remove from the heat, cover the pot with a clean dishtowel, and replace the lid. Let sit for 10 minutes, while you heat the oven to 375°F.

3. Oil a 2-quart baking dish with olive oil. Uncover the rice and stir in the remaining 1 tablespoon olive oil, the black pepper, and herbs. Taste and adjust salt. Spoon into the baking dish and bake for 30 minutes, until the top is browned. Remove from the heat and cool to room temperature. Cut into diamonds or squares and serve, garnished with parsley and olives.

ADVANCE PREPARATION: You can cook the rice with the tomatoes up to a day before finishing the dish in the oven, and you could also finish the dish in the oven a day ahead. The dish will keep for 5 days in the refrigerator.

ZUCCHINI, TOMATO, AND RICE PILAF

The Balkans • Serves 4 as a main dish or 8 as a side dish

This is much like the Tomato and Rice Pilaf on page 327 that comes from the same part of the world. It can be eaten hot or cold. The Yogurt and Mint Spread makes a nice accompaniment.

   3 tablespoons extra virgin olive oil

   1 large onion, finely chopped, or 1 bunch spring onions, white and light green parts, finely chopped

   3 garlic cloves, minced; or 2 green garlic bulbs, peeled and minced

   1 pound fresh tomatoes, peeled, seeded, and chopped; or 1 can (14 ounces) tomatoes, pulsed to a coarse purée in a food processor fitted with the steel blade

   2 teaspoons paprika

   1½ pounds zucchini, sliced

   1¼ teaspoons salt

   1 cup short- or medium-grain rice

   1½ cups water

   ¼ teaspoon freshly ground pepper

   2 tablespoons chopped fresh flat-leaf parsley

   2 tablespoons chopped fresh dill, plus additional for garnish

   Imported black olives

   Turkish Yogurt and Mint Spread (page 81) or drained yogurt (page 21)

1. Heat 2 tablespoons of the olive oil in a large, heavy nonstick skillet over medium-low heat and add the onion. Cook, stirring, until tender, about 5 minutes, and add the garlic. Cook, stirring, until fragrant, about 1 minute, and add the tomatoes and paprika. Turn the heat to medium and cook, stirring, for 5 to 10 minutes, until the tomatoes cook down slightly and smell fragrant. Add the zucchini and 1 teaspoon of the salt, and cook, stirring often, for 10 minutes, until the zucchini is tender.

2. Stir in the rice, water, and remaining ¼ teaspoon salt, and bring to a simmer. Reduce the heat to low, cover, and simmer for 20 minutes, or until the rice is tender and the mixture is thick. Remove from the heat, cover the pot with a towel, and replace the lid. Let sit for 15 minutes. Stir in the pepper, parsley, dill, and remaining 1 tablespoon olive oil. Taste and adjust salt.

3. Heat the oven to 375°F. Oil a 2-quart baking dish. Scrape the rice into the dish and bake for 30 to 35 minutes, until the top is browned. Cut into diamonds or squares. Serve warm or cold, garnished with dill and olives, and with the yogurt and mint spread.

ADVANCE PREPARATION: The rice and vegetables can be cooked and transferred to the casserole a day ahead.

PERSIAN RICE (Chelo)

Iran • Serves 6 generously

This rice is the pride as well as staple of Persian cuisine. As the rice steams gently in a generous amount of butter (though an authentic recipe would call for more butter), a golden crust forms on the bottom of the pan. Called a *tah-dig*, the crust is served on the side, and is considered the measure of a cook. When I first tested this recipe, 3 cups uncooked rice seemed like too much to me, but when I served it to six people there was very little left over. Similarly, tested, 2 cups rice was not too much for four people, and my son and I polished off 1 cup with no effort.

> 3 cups basmati rice (see Note)
>
> 8 cups water
>
> 1½ teaspoons salt
>
> 4 tablespoons unsalted butter, melted
>
> 4 tablespoons hot water
>
> ¼ to ½ teaspoon ground saffron (to taste) dissolved in 2 tablespoons hot water
>
> 2 tablespoons plain yogurt

Note: *If you don't want to make such a large quantity of rice, use 2 cups rice and 6 cups water. Use the same quantities of butter, saffron, and yogurt as listed above.*

1. Place the rice in a bowl and wash in several changes of cold water, until the water runs clean.

2. Bring the water to a boil in a large, heavy pot (I recommend either enameled cast iron or nonstick). Add the salt, then the rice. Boil for 5 to 10 minutes, stirring once or twice to make sure the rice doesn't stick to the bottom of the pot, until just tender but still firm. Drain in a colander and rinse. Rinse and dry the pot.

3. Heat 3 tablespoons of the butter in the pot over medium heat. Stir in 2 tablespoons of the hot water, 1 teaspoon of the dissolved saffron mixture, and the yogurt. Now carefully mound the rice into a pyramid in the pot, a spoonful at a time, heaping it in the center. Using the handle of a long wooden spoon, poke holes in the rice in several places, down to the bottom of the pot. Mix the remaining 1 tablespoon melted butter with the remaining 2 tablespoons hot water and pour over the pyramid. Cover the pot with a clean dishtowel, and cover tightly with a lid. Fold the edges of the towel up over the lid so that they do not make contact with the flame or burner. Cook for 10 minutes over medium heat, then reduce the heat to very low and cook for 45 minutes. Remove from the heat and place the pot on a damp towel. Cool for 5 minutes without opening. Remove 4 tablespoons of the rice and mix with the remaining saffron mixture in a dish. Set aside.

4. Carefully mound the rice, a spoonful or spatula at a time, into a pyramid on a large oval or round serving platter. Do not disturb the crust on the bottom of the pot. Sprinkle the saffron rice over the top. Detach the crust on the bottom of the pan using a wooden or plastic spatula. Serve the rice with the bits of crust on the side.

ADVANCE PREPARATION: The rice can sit in the pot, with the towel and lid on, for about 1 hour before you serve it.

BARLEY RISOTTO WITH PESTO AND RICOTTA SALATA

Italy • **Serves 4 to 6**

Risotto can be made with other starchy grains, like barley or farro. Barley risotto, which is called *orzotto* in Italy, is chewier than risotto made with rice. I ate a beautiful one with arugula pesto and ricotta when I was passing through the Abruzzo region of Italy one hot summer. The risotto is equally delicious when the pesto that is stirred in at the end is made with basil.

Serve it in wide soup bowls or on plates, spreading the risotto in a thin layer rather than a mound.

FOR THE PESTO

2 large garlic cloves, peeled

1 cup tightly packed fresh basil or arugula leaves

Salt

¼ cup extra virgin olive oil

¼ cup freshly grated Parmesan

Freshly ground pepper

FOR THE ORZOTTO

7 cups Simple Vegetable Broth (page 145) or chicken stock (as needed)

Salt

2 tablespoons extra virgin olive oil

1 small onion or 2 shallots, minced

1½ cups barley

½ cup dry white wine, such as pinot grigio or sauvignon blanc

½ cup grated ricotta salata

Freshly ground pepper

1. *Make the pesto:* Turn on a processor fitted with the steel blade and drop in the garlic. Scrape down the sides of the food processor bowl, add the basil or arugula and salt (⅛ to ¼ teaspoon), and process until finely chopped. Scrape down the sides once more. Drizzle in the olive oil with the machine running. Process to a paste. Stir in the Parmesan and pepper. Taste and adjust salt.

2. *Make the orzotto:* Put your broth into a saucepan and bring it to a simmer on the stove, with a ladle nearby or in the pot. Make sure that it is well seasoned with salt. It will remain at a simmer the entire time you are making the risotto, and you will add it a ladleful or two at a time to the barley.

3. Heat the oil in a wide, heavy nonstick skillet over medium heat. Add the onion and cook gently until tender and translucent, about 5 minutes. Stir in the barley and stir until the grains become separate.

4. Add the wine and cook, stirring, until it has just about evaporated and been absorbed by the barley. Stir in enough of the simmering broth to just cover the barley. The broth should bubble slowly. Cook, stirring often, until it is just about absorbed. Add another ladleful or two of the broth and continue to cook in this fashion, not too fast and not too slowly, adding more broth when the barley is almost dry and stirring often, for 30 to 40 minutes, until the barley is just tender to the bite.

5. Add another ⅓ cup broth to the barley. Stir in the pesto and ricotta salata, and remove from the heat. The mixture should be creamy. Add freshly ground pepper, taste one last time, and adjust salt. Stir once and serve right away.

ADVANCE PREPARATION: You can begin up to several hours before serving: Proceed with the recipe and cook halfway through, that is, for about 15 minutes. The barley should still be hard in the middle when you remove it from the heat, and there should not be any liquid in the pan. Spread it in an even layer in the pan and keep it away from the heat until you resume cooking. If the pan is not wide enough for you to spread the barley in a thin layer, then transfer it to a sheet pan. Thirty minutes before serving, resume cooking as instructed.

VARIATION

BARLEY RISOTTO WITH ASPARAGUS OR GREEN BEANS AND PESTO: Add ½ pound asparagus or green beans to the risotto. Trim and parboil or steam for 5 minutes, and cut into 1-inch pieces. Stir into the risotto along with the pesto.

FARRO RISOTTO WITH DRIED MUSHROOMS, FAVAS, AND GARLIC

Italy • **Serves 4**

Spelt, called *farro* in Italy, makes a luscious, robust risotto. Its dark tawny color begs a mushroom accompaniment, and dried porcinis do the trick. And who can resist green garlic and fava beans in springtime? If you don't feel like peeling favas, or can't get them, tender green beans are also wonderful in the dish (see the variation that follows).

1½ cups farro (see Note)

1 ounce (about 1 heaped cup) dried porcini mushrooms

2 cups boiling water

4 cups Simple Vegetable Broth (page 145) or chicken stock

Salt

2 tablespoons extra virgin olive oil

1 cup minced green garlic (1 bunch, white and light green parts only) or minced spring onions

2 teaspoons chopped fresh rosemary (or 1 teaspoon crumbled dried)

½ cup dry white wine, such as pinot grigio or sauvignon blanc

2 pounds fresh fava beans, shelled and skinned (page 113)

¼ to ½ cup freshly grated Parmesan (to taste)

¼ cup chopped fresh flat-leaf parsley

Freshly ground pepper

1 large egg, beaten (optional)

Note: *For risotto, the wheat berries that we find in our whole foods stores do not make a good substitute for farro. They take too long to cook and their outer shells remain too chewy. You can find farro in some Italian and imported foods markets.*

1. Place the farro in a bowl and pour on enough hot water to cover by an inch. Let soak while you continue with Step 2.

2. Place the dried mushrooms in a large Pyrex measuring cup or bowl and pour in the boiling water. Let sit for 30 minutes. Drain the mushrooms through a cheesecloth-lined strainer set over a bowl. Squeeze the mushrooms over the strainer, then rinse in several changes of water to remove grit. Chop coarsely if the pieces are large, and set aside. Reserve the mushroom cooking liquid.

3. Drain the farro, retaining the soaking water. Add the mushroom liquid to the broth and enough soaking water from the farro to measure 7 cups. Place in a saucepan and bring to a simmer. Season generously with salt (about 2 teaspoons, more to taste).

4. Heat the oil in a large, heavy nonstick skillet over medium heat and add the green garlic. Cook, stirring, for about a minute, until it begins to smell fragrant, and add the farro, reconstituted dried mushrooms, and rosemary. Cook, stirring, until the grains of farro are separate, about 2 minutes.

5. Stir in the wine and cook over medium heat, stirring constantly. The wine should bubble, but not too quickly. You want some of the flavor to cook into the farro before it evaporates. When the wine has just about evaporated, stir in enough of the simmering broth to cover the farro by about ½ inch. The broth should bubble slowly. Cook, stirring often, until it is just about absorbed. Add another ladleful or two of broth, this time just enough to barely cover the farro, and continue to cook in this fashion, not too quickly but not too slowly, adding more broth when the farro is almost dry, for about 20 minutes, until the farro is almost cooked through but still a bit hard in the center.

6. Stir the fava beans and another ladleful or two of simmering broth into the farro. Continue adding broth and stirring the farro as you have been doing for another 15 to 20 minutes, until the farro is al dente. Add another ⅓ cup broth to the farro, and stir in the Parmesan, parsley, and pepper. Taste and adjust salt. The farro should be creamy. Stir for a couple of seconds and remove from the heat.

7. If you wish, beat the egg with a ladleful of broth and stir into the risotto, stirring for 1 or 2 minutes to cook the egg. Serve immediately.

ADVANCE PREPARATION: The favas can be blanched and skinned a day or two ahead and refrigerated. You can cook the dish through Step 5 several hours ahead and finish it just before serving. Spread the farro in an even layer in the pan. Twenty minutes before serving, reheat the farro and the broth, and resume cooking as instructed.

LEFTOVERS: Like all risottos, this keeps for a few days in the refrigerator, but the texture of the farro will soften and the mixture will become a bit mushy. It's delicious nonetheless, and I've never hesitated to eat the leftovers, but don't make this a day ahead to serve to company. Leftovers can be stirred into beaten eggs for a fabulous frittata.

VARIATION

FARRO RISOTTO WITH GREEN BEANS: Substitute ½ pound tender green beans (such as haricots verts) for the fava beans. Break the beans in half if they're long and parboil them for 4 minutes in generously salted boiling water. Transfer to a bowl of ice water, then drain. Add to the risotto with the cheese.

THE DOCTOR'S BAIANA
France • Serves 6

Here is a tradition that is dying out with the peasant way of life. A *baiana* is a traditional Provençal dish (called *bajano* in the regional dialect) in which vegetables, legumes, and sometimes grains—in particular, spelt (*épautre* in French)—are cooked together, then separated from their broth and tossed in a vinaigrette. The broth, which is served over toasted or stale bread that has been rubbed with garlic, is considered highly nutritious—high in protein and magnesium, phosphorus, and calcium. While there is little that is elegant about this dish, its flavors are comforting, and the grain and lentil salad makes a hearty and satisfying meal.

> ½ pound (1 cup plus 2 tablespoons) lentils
>
> ½ pound (1⅓ cups) farro or wheat berries
>
> 1 onion, halved
>
> 2 whole cloves

1 head garlic, cut in half crosswise

A bouquet garni made with a bay leaf and a few sprigs each fresh thyme and rosemary

Salt

4 medium carrots, quartered lengthwise and cut into 2-inch lengths

1 large leek, white and light green parts only, cut in half lengthwise and sliced

1 celery stalk, sliced

2 to 3 tablespoons chopped fresh flat-leaf parsley (to taste)

3 tablespoons red wine vinegar or sherry vinegar (more to taste)

2 small garlic cloves, 1 minced, 1 cut in half

6 to 8 tablespoons extra virgin olive oil (to taste)

Freshly ground pepper

6 thick slices country bread

1. Rinse the lentils and farro and place in a Dutch oven or large saucepan. Cover by 2 inches with water. Stick a clove into each of the onion halves and add to the pot along with the halved head of garlic and the bouquet garni. Bring to a boil. Reduce the heat, cover, and simmer for 30 minutes. Add salt to taste (about 2 teaspoons), the carrots, leek, and celery, and continue to cook for another 20 to 30 minutes, until the lentils and farro are tender.

2. Place a colander over a bowl and drain the lentil mixture. Discard the onion, garlic, and bouquet garni. Pour the broth back into the pot and transfer the lentil mixture to a salad bowl. Add the parsley. Cool.

3. Whisk together the vinegar, minced garlic, olive oil, salt, and pepper. Taste and adjust salt, then toss with the lentils.

4. Toast the bread and rub with the cut clove of garlic. Place a slice in each of 6 wide soup bowls. Taste the broth and adjust salt if it tastes bland. Bring to a simmer. Serve the salad, then serve the broth, ladling each serving over the bread.

Note: *If you don't want to serve the broth, just serve the grains and vegetables.*

BULGUR AND CHICK PEA PILAF

Greece • **Serves 4 as a main dish or 6 as a side dish**

This classic preparation from Asia Minor is one of those great Mediterranean dishes that should become a pantry staple, as it has for me (it helps to have an herb garden). Mint is the traditional herb used in Greece, but I like the pilaf equally well when seasoned with dill, parsley, or a combination of one or both of these herbs and mint. It's best if you use medium or coarse bulgur for this, but fine bulgur will do if that's what you have on hand.

> 1 cup bulgur
>
> Salt
>
> 2 cups hot water
>
> 3 to 4 tablespoons extra virgin olive oil (to taste)
>
> 1 medium onion, finely chopped
>
> 2 large garlic cloves, minced
>
> 1 cup cooked chick peas (canned or cooked dried)
>
> ¼ cup chopped fresh mint, or a combination of mint, parsley, and/or dill
>
> Juice of 1 lemon (more to taste)

1. Place the bulgur in a bowl, mix in ½ teaspoon salt, and pour on the hot water. Cover and allow to sit until all the water has been absorbed, about 1 hour. Transfer the bulgur to a strainer and press out all remaining water. (If you are in a hurry you can use boiling water and let it sit for 20 minutes. But the bulgur will be fluffier with a longer sit.) Transfer to a bowl.

2. Heat 1 tablespoon of the olive oil in a heavy skillet over medium heat and add the onion. Cook, stirring, until thoroughly tender, 5 to 7 minutes. Stir in the garlic and continue to cook until fragrant, 30 seconds to 1 minute. Stir into the bulgur.

3. Toss the bulgur with 2 tablespoons olive oil, the chick peas, herbs, and lemon juice. Taste and adjust seasonings, adding more salt, pepper, or lemon juice as desired. If you wish, drizzle 1 more tablespoon olive oil over the top. Serve hot or at room temperature.

POLENTA WITH TOMATO SAUCE AND PARMESAN

Italy • **Serves 4**

This is a great, simple polenta dish that can be easily pulled out of a pantry if you have a carton of marinara sauce or a can of tomatoes on hand.

> 1 recipe Small Batch Easy Polenta (page 334)
>
> 2 cups Basic Tomato Sauce (page 78) or commercial marinara sauce
>
> ⅓ cup freshly grated Parmesan or Gruyère

1. Heat the oven to 350°F. Prepare the polenta through Step 2.

2. Spread the tomato sauce over the polenta and top with the cheese. Turn the oven up to 375°F and return the gratin to the oven. Bake for 20 minutes, or until the sauce is bubbling and the cheese just beginning to brown. Cut into squares and serve.

POLENTA

My most vivid memory of eating polenta in Italy is at the *Festa dell'Unità,* a huge Communist fair outside of Bologna, where hundreds of people came to eat at long wooden tables. My friend Lorella's parents were active in the party, and worked behind the scenes at the fair to produce a memorable dinner that began with a polenta course. Lorella brought me back into the kitchen tent, where I witnessed two strong men pouring polenta from the biggest pots I'd ever seen into large wooden frames. As soon as it cooled enough to cut, it was portioned out and served with a porcini mushroom sauce.

The classic way to serve polenta that is cooked on top of the stove is to oil or butter a cutting board, sheet pan, or platter and pour the cooked polenta out onto it to serve right away, or to cool and slice later. Polenta can also be cooked in the oven in a baking dish, and when I make it this way, I see no reason to pour it out, as it is already in a nice serving dish. If I'm not serving it right away, I'll top it with a sauce, a ragout, and/or cheese, and heat it through in the oven until the cheese melts.

Polenta is as versatile as it is comforting. It can be spooned out like thick porridge and topped with a rich cheese like Gorgonzola or fontina, or just dotted with butter and sprinkled with Parmesan or Gruyère (or both). Or the cheese can be stirred into it while it's hot. It can also be topped with a tomato sauce or with a bean or vegetable ragout. Once cooled, it can be sliced and grilled (page 336) or browned in oil, then served as a side dish or with a sauce. It makes a terrific accompaniment to bean dishes, to grilled vegetables, and to any kind of vegetable ragout.

Two Ways to Make Polenta

The classic way to make polenta is to add the cornmeal ever so slowly to a pot of simmering water (or, for a rich polenta, milk) and to stir with a long-handled spoon until it's thick and creamy (which usually coincides with getting a blister on the inside of your thumb, if you want a handy hint for timing). Polenta made this way is undoubtedly creamier than the polenta made the easy way. That said, I invariably choose the easy way, especially when I'm planning on slicing up the polenta to use for something else, like grilled polenta (page 336). But here are both options:

Easy Polenta

Big Batch
Serves 8 generously

> 2 cups polenta (coarse stone-ground cornmeal)
>
> 8 cups water
>
> 2½ teaspoons salt
>
> 1 to 2 tablespoons unsalted butter (to taste)

Small Batch
Serves 4 generously

> 1 cup polenta (coarse stone-ground cornmeal)
>
> 4 cups water
>
> 1¼ teaspoons salt
>
> 1 tablespoon unsalted butter

1. Heat the oven to 350°F. Combine the polenta, water, salt, and butter in a 3- to 4-quart baking dish (for a big batch) or a 2-quart baking dish (for a small batch). Stir together.

2. *If you are making a big batch:* Bake for 1 hour and 20 minutes. Remove from the oven, stir with a fork, and return to the oven for 10 more minutes.

If you are making a small batch: Bake for 1 hour. Remove from the oven, stir with a fork, and return to the oven for 10 more minutes.

3. Remove from the oven, let sit for 5 minutes, and serve with the topping of your choice, or as a side dish with a vegetable gratin. Or chill for use in another recipe.

ADVANCE PREPARATION: If you are serving the polenta hot with a topping, it's best to serve it when it comes out of the oven, though it can sit for more than the required 5 minutes.

Classic Polenta

Big Batch
Serves 6 to 8

> 6 cups water
>
> 2 teaspoons salt
>
> 2 cups polenta

Small Batch
Serves 4 to 6

> 4 cups water
>
> 1¼ teaspoons salt
>
> 1⅓ cups polenta

1. Have a kettle of water at a simmer, in case you need to add more water to the polenta. Bring the water to a boil in a large (at least 3-quart) saucepan or pot. Meanwhile, prepare your platter, sheet pan, or cutting board by brushing it with butter or extra virgin olive oil. Add the salt to the water and reduce the heat to low. The water should be just boiling, with bubbles breaking through from time to time. Using a long-handled spoon, stir the water in one direction only while you add the polenta in a very slow stream. The easiest way to do this is to pick up handfuls of cornmeal and let it slip between your fingers into the water.

2. Once all of the cornmeal has been added, continue to stir in one direction for 30 minutes, or until the polenta is thick and comes away from the sides of the pot. If it becomes too thick to stir, add a little simmering water. The polenta should have a creamy consistency when done, and a spoon should stand up when stuck in the middle.

3. When the polenta is done, immediately pour it onto the platter or cutting board. Serve right away, or cool and slice, depending on your topping.

ADVANCE PREPARATION: Once cooked, polenta will keep for several days in the refrigerator, and is delicious cut into pieces to be baked in a gratin, or grilled, toasted, or broiled.

VARIATION

POLENTA MADE WITH MILK: Some very rich northern Italian polenta dishes call for milk instead of water. You can use regular, low-fat, or skim. If you'll be adding a lot of cheese or butter to the polenta, I recommend using skim.

GRILLED POLENTA

Prepare polenta using either the easy or classic method (pages 334 to 335), and cool completely.

Prepare a medium-hot fire in a grill, or heat 1 tablespoon olive oil in a nonstick skillet over medium-high heat. Cut the cooled polenta into squares or triangles. Brush each side with olive oil and grill or pan-grill until lightly browned on each side, 4 to 5 minutes per side.

POLENTA WITH MUSHROOMS
Serves 6

Polenta and mushrooms make a wonderful marriage. I think of this as a fall/winter dish. On the other hand, you could grill the polenta (above) and serve for a vegetarian barbecue.

> 1 recipe Big Batch Polenta (pages 334 to 335)
>
> 1 recipe Wild Mushroom Ragout (page 285) or Wild Mushrooms with Tomatoes and Basil (page 286)
>
> ½ cup grated Gruyère or a mixture of Gruyère and Parmesan

IF USING THE EASY METHOD

1. Heat the oven to 350°F. Make the polenta using the easy method on page 334. Top the polenta with the mushroom dish of your choice.

2. Sprinkle the cheese over the mushrooms and heat through in the oven until the cheese melts, about 10 minutes. Serve hot.

IF USING THE CLASSIC METHOD

1. Heat the mushroom dish of your choice on top of the stove while you make the polenta.

2. Pour the polenta out onto a platter or spoon directly onto plates. Make a depression in the middle and top with the mushrooms and the cheese. Serve right away.

ADVANCE PREPARATION: The ragouts will both keep for 3 to 5 days in the refrigerator, and the polenta makes a good vehicle for leftovers. You can make the polenta up to a few days ahead and grill it. Serve the grilled polenta with the ragout.

COUSCOUS WITH CHICK PEAS AND CHARD
Tunisia • Serves 6

This thick chick pea stew is typical of many Tunisian vegetable stews, fragrant with layers of flavor emanating from spices (caraway, cumin, coriander seeds) and chiles (harissa), and the beans and vegetables themselves. It makes a perfect vegetarian meal with couscous.

> 1 pound (2½ cups) dried chick peas, picked over, rinsed, soaked in 8 cups water for 6 hours or overnight, and drained
>
> 9 cups water
>
> 1 to 1½ pounds Swiss chard (2 bunches)
>
> 2 tablespoons extra virgin olive oil
>
> 1 medium onion, chopped
>
> 2 leeks, white part only, sliced
>
> 4 large garlic cloves (more to taste), minced
>
> 1 teaspoon coriander seeds, ground
>
> 1 teaspoon caraway seeds, ground
>
> 2 teaspoons cumin seeds, ground
>
> 2 tablespoons Harissa (page 86 or commercial) or ½ teaspoon ground cayenne pepper, plus additional for serving
>
> 2 tablespoons tomato paste
>
> Salt
>
> 1 large bunch fresh flat-leaf parsley, stemmed and chopped
>
> 3 cups couscous
>
> 3 cups hot water

1. Place the chick peas and 8 cups of the water in a large pot. Bring to a boil, reduce the heat, and simmer for 1 hour.

2. Tear the chard leaves off the stems. Wash the stems and slice crosswise about ¼ inch thick. Wash the leaves thoroughly and chop coarsely. Set aside.

3. Heat the oil in a heavy casserole or Dutch oven, or if you have one, in the bottom of a couscoussière over medium heat. Add the onion and leeks and cook, stirring, until tender, about 5 minutes. Add the chard stems and stir for a couple of minutes, until they begin to soften. Add the garlic and ground spices, and stir together for 30 seconds to 1 minute, until the garlic is fragrant. Add the harissa and the tomato paste, and stir together for another minute or two. Add the chick peas, their

cooking liquid, and 1 cup water. Stir and bring back to a simmer. Add salt (you will need a generous amount, 2 to 3 teaspoons), cover, and simmer for 30 minutes to 1 hour, until the chick peas are thoroughly tender and the broth fragrant. Strain off ½ cup of the liquid and set aside.

4. Stir in the chard greens, allowing each handful to cook down a bit before adding the next. Simmer for 15 to 20 minutes, until the greens are very tender and fragrant. Stir in the parsley. Remove from the heat. Taste and adjust seasonings, adding salt, garlic, or harissa as desired.

5. Place the couscous in a bowl with 1 teaspoon salt. Combine the 3 cups hot water with the ½ cup

HOW TO PREPARE PACKAGED COUSCOUS

Like pasta, couscous is a semolina product. But unlike pasta, it has been steamed. It requires reconstituting and another quick steam to make it fluffy and delicate, a very easy process that makes couscous one of today's great convenience foods.

Whenever you can, use some of the broth from the vegetable stew you serve with the couscous when you reconstitute the couscous.

Place the couscous in a bowl. Add ½ teaspoon salt per cup of couscous and mix together. Combine ½ to 1 cup of the broth from the stew you are serving with the couscous with enough hot water to cover the couscous by about ½ inch. Let sit for 20 minutes, until the water is absorbed. Stir every 5 minutes with a wooden spoon, or rub the couscous between your moistened thumbs and fingers, so that the couscous doesn't lump. The couscous will now be fairly soft; fluff it with a fork or with your hands. Taste and add salt if necessary.

You now have options for steaming the couscous.

To steam above the stew or boiling water: Place the couscous in a colander, sieve, or the top part of a couscoussière and set it over the simmering stew or boiling water, making sure that the bottom of the colander does not touch the liquid (remove some of the liquid if it does). Wrap a towel between the edge of the colander and the pot if there is a space, so that steam doesn't escape. Steam for 15 to 20 minutes.

The couscous can also steam in the oven or in the microwave. I use the oven most often when I'm entertaining, partly because it's easy to present the couscous in an attractive earthenware baking dish alongside the stew.

To steam in the oven: Place the couscous in a lightly oiled baking dish, cover tightly with foil, and place in a 350°F oven for 20 minutes.

To steam in a microwave: Transfer the couscous to a microwave-safe bowl, cover tightly with plastic wrap, and pierce the plastic a couple of times with a knife. Microwave for 2 minutes on 100 percent power. Let the couscous sit for 1 minute, then carefully remove the plastic and fluff with a fork.

Advance preparation: Couscous can be reconstituted up to a day ahead, then steamed before serving.

of the strained cooking liquid from the vegetables and pour over the couscous. The couscous should be covered by about ½ inch. Let sit for 20 minutes, until the water is absorbed. Stir every 5 minutes with a wooden spoon, or rub the couscous between your moistened thumb and fingers, so that the couscous doesn't lump. The couscous will now be fairly soft; fluff it with a fork or with your hands. Taste and add salt if necessary.

6. Follow the directions on page 337 for steaming the couscous.

7. Transfer the couscous to a wide serving bowl, such as a pasta bowl, or directly to wide soup plates. Spoon on the stew and serve, passing additional harissa at the table.

ADVANCE PREPARATION: The stew can be made through Step 4 up to 3 days ahead and refrigerated. Bring back to a simmer and proceed as directed. The couscous can be reconstituted up to a day ahead, then steamed before serving. The stew keeps well in the refrigerator for 3 or 4 days. However, the chard will lose its bright green color. If you want to get a jump on making the stew for serving the next day, I suggest you prep the chard, but don't add it or the parsley until you reheat the stew. You may also want to add a cup of water when you reheat. Adjust seasonings accordingly.

COUSCOUS WITH CHICK PEAS AND WINTER VEGETABLES

Tunisia • **Serves 6 to 8**

This is the kind of dish I love to make for a dinner party. You can get almost every bit of it done ahead, and the tagine just gets better overnight. Winter vegetables like butternut squash, turnips, carrots, and leeks make a sweet contrast to the spicy Tunisian seasonings in this incredibly warming, satisfying stew.

> ½ pound dried chick peas, picked over, rinsed, soaked in 4 cups water for 6 hours or overnight, and drained
>
> 6 to 7 cups water

Salt

1 tablespoon plus 1 teaspoon extra virgin olive oil

1 large onion, chopped

1 pound leeks, white and light green parts, sliced

2 large garlic cloves, minced or put through a press

2 teaspoons coriander seeds, ground

¾ teaspoon caraway seeds, ground

½ teaspoon cumin seeds, ground

¼ teaspoon cayenne (more to taste)

1 tablespoon Harissa (page 86 or commercial), plus additional for serving

½ pound carrots, thickly sliced

½ to ¾ pound turnips, peeled and cut into wedges

2¼ pounds winter squash, peeled, seeded, and cut into large dice

½ pound red-skinned potatoes, scrubbed and diced

1 tablespoon tomato paste

½ cup chopped fresh flat-leaf parsley

3 cups couscous

3 cups hot water

1. Place the chick peas and 4 cups of the water in a large saucepan. Bring to a boil, reduce the heat, and simmer for 1 hour. Add 1 teaspoon salt and simmer another 30 to 60 minutes, until tender. Set aside.

2. Heat the oil in a large, heavy soup pot, Dutch oven, or couscoussière over medium heat and add the onion and leeks. Cook, stirring, until tender, about 5 minutes, and stir in the garlic, ground coriander, caraway, cumin, and cayenne. Stir together for about 1 minute and add the harissa, carrots, turnips, squash, potatoes, the chick peas with their broth, and another 2 or 3 cups of the water, enough to cover everything by a good inch. Bring to a boil, then add a generous amount of salt and the tomato paste. Reduce the heat, cover, and simmer for 45 minutes, until the squash is beginning to fall apart. Taste and adjust salt, and add more harissa or cayenne to make the stew spicier if you wish. Stir in the parsley. Simmer another 15 minutes. Taste and adjust seasonings. Strain out ½ cup of the broth and set aside.

3. Place the couscous in a bowl with 1 teaspoon salt. Combine the 3 cups hot water with the ½ cup of strained cooking liquid from the stew and pour it over the couscous. The couscous should be covered by about ½ inch. Let sit for 20 minutes, until the water is absorbed. Stir every 5 minutes with a wooden spoon, or rub the couscous between your moistened thumb and fingers, so that the couscous doesn't lump. The couscous will now be fairly soft; fluff it with a fork or with your hands. Taste the couscous and add salt if necessary.

4. Follow the directions on page 337 for steaming the couscous.

5. Transfer the couscous to a wide serving bowl, such as a pasta bowl, or directly to dinner plates or wide soup plates. Spoon on the stew and serve, passing additional harissa at the table.

ADVANCE PREPARATION: The cooked chick peas will keep for 3 or 4 days in the refrigerator. The stew can be made, without the addition of the parsley, a day or two ahead and refrigerated. Bring back to a simmer and add the parsley. The couscous can be reconstituted up to a day ahead, then steamed before serving.

VARIATION

COUSCOUS WITH CHICK PEAS AND SPRING VEGETABLES: Use young, tender turnips. Omit the tomato paste. Substitute 2 pounds fava beans, shelled and skinned (page 113) and ½ pound green beans, trimmed and parboiled in boiling salted water for 4 minutes, for the winter squash. Do not add to the stew with the other vegetables in Step 3. After the other vegetables and the chick peas have simmered for 30 minutes, stir into the stew and simmer for another 5 to 10 minutes. Substitute ¼ cup chopped cilantro (or more to taste) for ¼ cup of the parsley.

CAULIFLOWER AND TOMATO COUSCOUS
Tunisia • **Serves 6 to 8**

Even if you think you don't like cauliflower, try this thick, hearty, Tunisian-inspired tagine. There's almost no fat in it at all, but it tastes as rich as can be.

- 1 pound dried chick peas, picked over, rinsed, soaked in 8 cups water for 6 hours or overnight, and drained
- 10 cups water
- 1 medium onion, chopped
- 2 leeks, white part only, sliced
- 4 large garlic cloves (to taste), minced
- 1 teaspoon coriander seeds, ground
- 1 teaspoon caraway seeds, ground
- 2 teaspoons cumin seeds, ground
- 2 tablespoons Harissa (page 86 or commercial) or ½ teaspoon ground cayenne pepper, plus additional for serving
- 2 tablespoons tomato paste
- 1 pound tomatoes, peeled, seeded, and chopped; or 1 can (14 ounces) tomatoes, with juice, chopped
- Salt
- 1 large cauliflower, broken into small florets
- ½ cup imported black olives, such as kalamatas, pitted and halved
- 3 cups couscous
- 3 cups hot water
- 1 cup chopped fresh flat-leaf parsley
- 1 cup chopped fresh cilantro

1. Place the chick peas and water in a large pot or the bottom part of a couscoussière. Bring to a boil, reduce the heat, and simmer for 1 hour.

2. Add the onion, leeks, garlic, coriander, caraway, cumin, harissa, tomato paste, tomatoes, and salt (about 1 tablespoon), and simmer another 30 minutes to 1 hour, until the chick peas are thoroughly tender and the broth fragrant. Strain out ½ cup of the broth and set aside. ▶

3. Add the cauliflower and olives to the simmering stew, and cook, partially covered, for another 15 to 20 minutes, until the cauliflower is tender. Taste and adjust seasonings, adding salt, garlic, or harissa as desired.

4. Place the couscous in a bowl with 1 teaspoon salt. Combine the 3 cups hot water with the ½ cup of strained cooking liquid from the stew and pour over the couscous. The couscous should be covered by about ½ inch. Let sit for 20 minutes, until the water is absorbed. Stir every 5 minutes with a wooden spoon, or rub the couscous between your moistened thumb and fingers, so that the couscous doesn't lump. The couscous will now be fairly soft; fluff it with a fork or with your hands. Taste and add salt if necessary.

5. Follow the directions on page 337 for steaming the couscous.

6. Bring the stew to a simmer and stir in the parsley and cilantro. Simmer for a couple of minutes, taste, and adjust seasonings. Transfer the couscous to a wide serving bowl, such as a pasta bowl, or directly to wide soup plates. Spoon on the stew and serve, passing additional harissa at the table.

ADVANCE PREPARATION: The dish can be prepared through Step 2 up to a day ahead and refrigerated. Bring back to a simmer before proceeding. The entire stew can be prepared a day ahead and refrigerated. Bring back to a simmer and proceed with the recipe.

LEFTOVERS: This couscous will be delicious for 4 or 5 days in the refrigerator. It will become quite thick, and you can thin it out with water if you wish. Leftovers can be eaten as a main dish or side dish.

COUSCOUS WITH WINTER SQUASH
Tunisia • Serves 4 generously

This comforting Tunisian winter stew should simmer until the squash and potatoes begin to fall apart, thickening the mixture.

- 1 tablespoon plus 1 teaspoon extra virgin olive oil
- 1 large onion, sliced
- 2 large garlic cloves, minced or put through a press
- 2 teaspoons coriander seeds, ground
- ¾ teaspoon caraway seeds, ground
- ¼ teaspoon cayenne
- 1 tablespoon Harissa (page 86 or commercial); more to taste
- 2¼ pounds winter squash, peeled, seeded, and cut into large dice
- ½ pound Yukon gold potatoes, scrubbed and diced
- 6 cups water
- Salt
- 1 tablespoon tomato paste
- 1 can (15 ounces) chick peas, rinsed and drained
- ½ cup chopped fresh flat-leaf parsley
- 2 cups couscous
- 2 cups hot water

1. Heat the oil in a large, heavy soup pot, Dutch oven, or couscoussière over medium heat and add the onion. Cook, stirring, until tender, about 5 minutes, and stir in the garlic, coriander, caraway, and cayenne. Stir together for about 1 minute and add the harissa, squash, potatoes, and water. Bring to a boil and add a generous amount of salt and the tomato paste. Reduce the heat, cover, and simmer for 45 minutes, until the squash is beginning to fall apart. Taste and adjust salt. Strain out ½ cup of the broth and set aside. Stir in the chick peas and parsley. Simmer another 15 minutes.

2. Place the couscous in a bowl with 1 scant teaspoon salt. Combine the 2 cups hot water with the ½ cup of strained cooking liquid from the stew and pour over the couscous. The couscous should be covered by about ½ inch. Let sit for 20 minutes, until the water is absorbed. Stir every 5 minutes with a wooden spoon, or rub the couscous between your moistened thumbs and fingers, so that the couscous doesn't lump. The couscous will now be fairly soft; fluff it with a fork or with your hands. Taste the couscous and add salt if necessary.

3. Follow the directions on page 337 for steaming the couscous.

4. Serve the couscous in wide bowls or mound onto plates and top with the stew.

ADVANCE PREPARATION: The stew can be made a day ahead and reheated.

LEFTOVERS: The couscous will keep for 3 or 4 days in the refrigerator. It can be reconstituted up to a day ahead, then steamed before serving.

Sweets and Desserts

Throughout the Mediterranean, the end of the meal is much more likely to be marked by a bowl of fresh, in-season fruit than by a piece of cake. If you happen to be in Provence in early June, you cannot do much better than a bowl of fat red cherries; or in July, a honey-ripe peach. The sweet, thirst-quenching watermelon that we were offered after every summer meal in Greece was always the perfect finale for me. But that wasn't always the case for my son, Liam, and his sweet tooth.

To Liam's delight (and, I confess, to mine), there were always sweets to be had. In Italy, for example, where there is more gelato per city block than in any place I've ever been in the world, it does seem a bit far-fetched to think that dessert is not part of the gastronomic landscape. If a coveted piece of cake or fruit tart wasn't listed on a restaurant menu, we could always find it in a pastry shop close by.

It is not always at the end of a meal that the Greek, Turk, or Italian wishes to nibble on something sweet. I am similar, and the Mediterranean rhythm suits me to a T. I am much more likely to want to eat something sweet in the afternoon, rather than after a meal.

343

In countries where lunch can linger into the early afternoon and dinner doesn't begin until after 9 o'clock, late afternoon to early evening is the time when people walk, socialize, sip a coffee or a cold drink, and eat something sweet. In Italy, this time of day has a name, the hour of the *passeggiata*. It exists all around the Mediterranean basin, when the hot afternoon sun has retreated and the streets fill up with people. Driving up to hill towns in Puglia in August, I was always amused by the bumper-to-bumper traffic jams that occurred at this time of day, everyone driving to towns so that they could get out of their cars and walk, look, talk, and nibble. At one *caffè*, they would be enjoying lemon granita; at another, *granita di caffè*. The gelaterias were always a destination for us; so many flavors, all good.

Gelaterias are packed late at night as well. On a hot, hot night in Bologna, our friends Marco de Stefani and Lorella Grossi and their two daughters, Costanza and Carlotta, walked us through the center of that beautiful city, through moonlit squares and past ornate fountains, to a popular ice cream place where at 11:30 a line stretched out the door and down the block. I waited patiently for my coffee gelato, Liam for his *stracciatella* (chocolate chip). We continued on our walk, the ice cream melting quickly in the heat, even in the dark.

Midmorning, or even breakfast, is also a time for sweets in many Mediterranean countries. Most of my favorite cookies come from Italy, and they were made fresh and served daily on the breakfast buffet at Il Frantoio, the wonderful farm/hotel in Puglia where we settled in for four blissful August days. Cookies for breakfast! Liam talked about this for months, and still chides me for not continuing the custom at home.

The fruits of the Mediterranean have inspired many of the desserts I've selected for this chapter. The fact that we can get the same fruit in our Los Angeles farmers' markets makes all of them doable here. If you live in the Northeast or the Midwest, you may not have access to fresh figs, but you can certainly make peach gelato or cherry clafouti in the summer, or poached pears in the fall. The cookies and cakes are just a smattering of what the Mediterranean has on offer.

ALMOND BISCOTTI

Italy • **Makes about 5 dozen**

Biscotti are now nothing new in the United States; you can find them at every Starbucks or Coffee Bean you walk into. But most of these biscotti don't resemble the thin, dry biscotti you get in Italy. They are twice-baked cookies, meant to be dipped into sweet wine, tea, or coffee. Mine are much less sweet than most.

- 1 cup sugar
- 4 large eggs plus 2 yolks, at room temperature
- 1 teaspoon baking powder
- ⅛ teaspoon salt
- 1 teaspoon pure vanilla extract
- 3 cups unbleached all-purpose flour
- 1⅔ cups toasted almonds, roughly chopped

1. Set a rack in the center of the oven and heat the oven to 350°F. Line a baking sheet with parchment and lightly spray the parchment with cooking spray.

2. In the bowl of a standing mixer fitted with the paddle attachment, beat together the sugar, 3 of the eggs, and the egg yolks until thick, about 4 minutes. Beat in the baking powder, salt, and vanilla extract. Add the flour and combine. Beat at medium speed while you gradually add the almonds. Beat until smooth.

3. Flour your hands and your work surface. Divide the dough into 3 pieces and roll each piece into a 2-inch-wide log. Place the logs at least 2 inches apart on the baking sheet. Beat the remaining egg and brush the logs lightly with the egg. Bake on the middle rack for 35 minutes.

4. Remove the baking sheet from the oven and reduce the oven temperature to 275°F. Slice the logs on the diagonal into ⅓-inch-thick slices and lay them cut side up on the baking sheets. Return to the oven for another 25 to 30 minutes, until brown and completely dry. Cool on racks.

ADVANCE PREPARATION: Keep the biscotti in a cookie tin and they'll keep for several weeks.

HONEY-ORANGE BISCOTTI

Italy • **Makes about 5 dozen**

Here is another biscotti that is not very sweet, perfumed with orange zest and honey, a particularly nice cookie to dip into a cup of Earl Grey tea.

- ½ cup mild honey, such as clover or acacia
- 3 large eggs plus 2 yolks, at room temperature
- 2 tablespoons finely grated orange zest
- 1 teaspoon baking powder
- ⅛ teaspoon salt
- 1 tablespoon Grand Marnier
- ½ teaspoon pure vanilla extract
- 3¼ cups unbleached all-purpose flour
- 1⅔ cups toasted almonds, roughly chopped

1. Set a rack in the middle of the oven and heat the oven to 350°F. Cover a baking sheet with parchment and lightly spray the parchment with cooking spray.

2. In the bowl of a standing mixer fitted with the paddle attachment, beat together the honey, 2 of the eggs, and the egg yolks until thick, about 4 minutes. Beat in the orange zest, baking powder, salt, Grand Marnier, and vanilla. Add the flour and combine. Beat at medium speed while you gradually add the almonds. Beat until smooth.

3. Flour your hands and your work surface. Divide the dough into 3 pieces and roll each piece into a 2-inch-wide log. Place the logs at least 2 inches apart on the baking sheet. Beat the remaining egg and brush the logs lightly with the egg. Bake on the middle rack for 35 minutes.

4. Remove the baking sheet from the oven and reduce the oven temperature to 275°F. Slice the logs on the diagonal into ⅓-inch-thick slices and lay them cut side up on the baking sheets. Return to the oven for another 25 to 30 minutes, until brown and completely dry. Cool on racks.

ADVANCE PREPARATION: Keep the biscotti in a cookie tin and they'll keep for several weeks.

FINANCIER

France • **Makes one 9-inch cake**

Financier is a rich, buttery cake that is defined by almonds. Most of the flour is almond flour, and there is often a little almond extract in the batter. It's easy to make and very adaptable; see the Cherry Financier (opposite page).

> 12 tablespoons (1½ sticks) unsalted butter
>
> 1 cup almond flour (available in gourmet markets and baking supply stores)
>
> ½ cup cake flour
>
> 1¾ cups confectioners' sugar
>
> 6 large egg whites, at room temperature
>
> 1 teaspoon almond extract

1. Melt the butter in a medium saucepan over medium heat. Cook the butter until the solids separate and you begin to see them browning. Let the butter brown to a light golden color, then remove from the heat. Cool the butter to room temperature (but make sure it remains liquid and pourable).

2. Heat the oven to 350°F. Spray a 9 × 2-inch round cake pan with cooking spray, line it with a piece of parchment paper, then spray the paper lightly with cooking spray.

3. Spread ½ cup of the almond flour in another cake pan and toast it in the oven until just golden brown and beginning to smell toasty, about 2 minutes. Watch carefully. Transfer to a bowl. Sift the cake flour, toasted and plain almond flour, and sugar together into the bowl of a standing mixer fitted with a paddle attachment. Turn the machine on low and mix the dry ingredients for 30 seconds. Add the egg whites all at once and mix at medium speed for 3 minutes.

4. Add the melted butter all at once. Be sure to scrape in all the browned bits from the bottom of the pan. Add the almond extract and mix for 3 minutes at medium speed, scraping down well (the butter tends to fall to the bottom).

5. Scrape the batter into the pan and bake for 20 minutes. Rotate the cake for even browning and

A GLASS OF DESSERT WINE

The best dessert in the world might be a glass of sweet wine, and there are a number of notable dessert wines produced in the Mediterranean. Indeed, all of the Mediterranean wines in ancient times and in the Middle Ages were sweet. Below are some of the Mediterranean dessert wines that are imported.

Serve the wine in a small glass, cold if it's a white wine, and linger. You may want to dip a biscotti into it, or just sip. The wine will definitely constitute a dessert in a glass.

Banyuls: This dark red wine is France's finest and most complex *vin doux naturel,* a sweet wine that is made by adding alcohol to grapes during the fermentation process. It is made in the Roussillon on the Mediterranean coast of France, very near the Spanish border. Banyuls age well, and go very well with chocolate.

Maury: Another complex, dark red *vin doux naturel* from the Roussillon.

Moscato, Muscat, Moscatel: These are sweet golden wines that are produced from the *muscat blanc à petits grains* grape. More than any other wine, they taste of the grape from which they're made. In Italy, the wines are called Moscato, the most famous one being the lightly fizzy, pale Moscato d'Asti. In Spain they are called Moscatel, and in France Muscat. The most esteemed French Muscat is made in Beaumes-de-Venise, in the Côtes-du-Rhône. Other highly regarded Muscats are produced in the Languedoc, southwest of the Côtes-du-Rhône, in Rivesaltes and Frontignan.

Vin Santo: This is an amber-colored dessert wine from Tuscany. A perfect dipping wine for biscotti.

bake for another 15 to 20 minutes, until a toothpick inserted in the center comes out clean and the edges are beginning to pull away from the sides of the pan. Cool the cake in the pan for 10 minutes, then invert onto a cake rack to cool completely. Wrap tightly and, if possible, leave until the next day. Transfer to a cake plate and serve.

ADVANCE PREPARATION: Wrapped airtight, the financier will keep at room temperature for 1 day, in the refrigerator for 3 days, or in the freezer for 2 weeks. Financier batter will keep in the refrigerator for up to 2 weeks. When using refrigerated batter, be sure to bring it back to room temperature, then stir the entire mixture from the bottom up to the top to reincorporate any butter that might have separated and sunk. Beat the batter by hand or in a standing mixer, to warm it up and mix it well.

CHERRY FINANCIER

France • **Makes one 9-inch cake**

If you're looking for cake as a vehicle for fruit, this is the one to choose. Like the financier, opposite, this one too is a rich, buttery/almondy cake that is incredibly easy to make. Even if you haven't made many cakes, you can feel confident about success with this one. Just make sure to give yourself time. The hot browned butter that gives the cake its distinctive taste must cool down to room temperature, which will take about 1 hour.

> 12 tablespoons (1½ sticks) unsalted butter
>
> 1 cup almond flour (available in gourmet markets and baking supply stores)
>
> ½ cup cake flour
>
> 1¾ cups confectioners' sugar
>
> 6 large egg whites, at room temperature
>
> 1 teaspoon almond extract
>
> 1 pound cherries, pitted

1. Melt the butter in a medium saucepan over medium heat. Cook the butter until the solids separate and you begin to see them browning. Let the butter brown to a light golden color, and then remove it from the heat. Cool to room temperature (but make sure it remains liquid and pourable).

2. Heat the oven to 350°F. Spray a 9 × 2-inch round cake pan with cooking spray, line it with a piece of parchment paper, then spray the paper lightly with cooking spray.

3. Spread ½ cup of the almond flour in another cake pan and toast it in the oven until just golden brown and beginning to smell toasty, about 2 minutes. Watch carefully. Transfer to a bowl to cool. Sift the cake flour, toasted and plain almond flour, and sugar together into the bowl of a standing mixer fitted with a paddle attachment. Turn the machine to low and mix the dry ingredients for 30 seconds. Add the egg whites all at once and mix at medium speed for 3 minutes.

4. Add the melted butter all at once. Be sure to scrape in all the browned bits from the bottom of the pan. Add the almond extract and mix for 3 minutes at medium speed, scraping down well (the butter tends to fall to the bottom).

5. Arrange the cherries in an even layer in the cake pan. Pour the batter over the cherries. Bake for 20 minutes. Rotate the cake for even browning, and bake for another 15 to 20 minutes, or until a toothpick inserted in the center comes out clean and the edges are beginning to pull away from the sides of the pan. After the cake has cooled in the pan for 10 minutes, invert it onto a rack to cool completely. Wrap tightly, and, if possible, leave until the next day. Transfer to a cake plate and serve.

ADVANCE PREPARATION: Wrapped airtight, the financier will keep at room temperature for 1 day, in the refrigerator for 3 days, or in the freezer for 2 weeks. Financier batter will keep in the refrigerator for up to 2 weeks. When using refrigerated batter, be sure to bring it back to room temperature, then stir the batter from the bottom up to the top to reincorporate any butter that might have separated and sunk. Beat the batter by hand or in a standing mixer, to warm it up and mix it well.

CHERRY CLAFOUTI

France • **Makes one 10-inch clafouti**

This dish actually comes from the center of France, but the most wonderful cherries come from Provence. I have spent many a month of May and June in Provence in the presence of ripe cherry trees, and if I can resist eating the fruit right off the trees, this is what I'll make. A traditional French cook would not pit the cherries, but I do.

> 1½ pounds fresh ripe cherries, pitted
>
> 3 tablespoons kirsch
>
> 7 tablespoons granulated sugar
>
> 3 large eggs
>
> 1 vanilla bean, split and scraped
>
> Salt
>
> ⅔ cup sifted unbleached all-purpose flour
>
> ¾ cup low-fat (2%) milk or buttermilk
>
> 1 tablespoon confectioners' sugar

1. Toss the cherries with the kirsch and 2 tablespoons of the granulated sugar, and let sit for 30 minutes. Drain in a colander set over a bowl. Reserve the liquid from the cherries.

2. Heat the oven to 375°F. Butter a 10- or 10½-inch ceramic tart pan or clafouti dish. Arrange the drained cherries in the dish.

3. Beat the eggs with the remaining 5 tablespoons granulated sugar and the seeds from the vanilla bean in the bowl of an electric mixer fitted with the whisk attachment, or by hand with a whisk, until the sugar is dissolved. Add a pinch of salt and the liquid from the cherries and combine well. Slowly beat in the flour and whisk until smooth. Add the milk and combine well. Pour over the cherries.

4. Bake for 30 to 40 minutes, until the top is browned and the clafouti is firm and puffed. Press gently on the top in the middle to see if it's firm. If it isn't, return to the oven for 5 minutes.

5. Cool on a rack. Serve warm or at room temperature, with the confectioners' sugar sifted over the top.

ADVANCE PREPARATION: The clafouti will hold for several hours at room temperature.

LEFTOVERS: Eat the leftovers for breakfast.

WATERMELON GRANITA

Serves 6

Watermelon was everywhere, and always so welcome, during my travels through Italy and Greece with my son, Liam, and friend/nanny, Rachel, during the summer of 2005. We arrived in Rome on a hot day in July, about a week into our trip, and lunched at a small trattoria called Da Sergio, near the Campo de' Fiori. We had good pasta with tomato sauce, and spaghetti carbonara, which is a Roman dish. I was most impressed, though, with the big wedges of watermelon we had for dessert.

Thus began a series of watermelon feasts. Over the next month we encountered big wedges of the fruit in refrigerator cases everywhere, especially in Greece. It would be delivered—cold, sweet, and juicy—to our taverna table whether we'd asked for it or not. Nothing could be better during that hot summer; we were always thirsty.

Watermelon, unembellished, is as good a dessert as anything. But if you are going to do something with it, I highly recommend this granita, which I learned from Wolfgang Puck in Los Angeles.

> ¼ cup water
>
> ½ cup sugar
>
> 2 pounds peeled watermelon (seedless if possible, or seeded if seedless is not available) cut into 1-inch chunks
>
> ¼ cup sparkling water
>
> 3 tablespoons fresh lime juice
>
> ⅛ teaspoon salt

1. Place a large, flat-bottomed pan in the freezer while you make your base. A 9 × 13-inch cake pan works well for this. Combine the water and sugar in a saucepan and bring to a simmer. Stir until the sugar dissolves and remove from the heat.

2. Working in batches, purée the watermelon in a food processor fitted with the steel blade. Put through a sieve into a bowl, and stir in the sugar syrup, the sparkling water, lime juice, and salt. Mix well.

3. Pour the watermelon mixture into the cold pan and place in the freezer.

4. Fluff the granita with a fork every 20 minutes, bringing the frozen crystals that form around the edge of the pan into the center. Set a timer for the 20-minute intervals so you don't forget to stir, or the granita will freeze into a solid block. (If this does happen, you can pulse the granita in a food processor to break it up.)

5. The granita is ready when all the liquid is frozen into small ice crystals, which should take about 2 hours. Cover tightly with plastic wrap and keep for up to a week. To serve, place wine-glasses, martini glasses, or bowls in the freezer for 30 minutes. Scrape the top of the granita with a fork, then spoon out into the glasses. Serve immediately.

ADVANCE PREPARATION: You can keep the granita for a week in the freezer. You may need to pulse it in the food processor before serving. Cut it into blocks and place in the processor. Pulse and serve.

AN UNUSUAL TREAT

On a page of one of my notebooks from my 2005 Mediterranean trip, I have one line written large:

FETA AND WATERMELON!

It's a combination I'd never considered before that summer in Greece. But of course it works. The sweet, juicy watermelon slakes any thirst created by the rich, salty feta, and the flavors complement each other beautifully.

MELON SORBET
Makes 1 quart

In Spain, I ate the sweetest, juiciest green-fleshed melons at virtually every meal. Sometimes I ate melon as a starter, with or without Serrano ham, other times for dessert, and sometimes both. In France, the cantaloupe-colored Cavaillon melons are the taste of a Provençal summer, as sweet as honeysuckle. I rarely turn them into anything else, but this melon sorbet is pretty irresistible on a hot summer evening. Either green-fleshed or orange-fleshed melon will work here, but it must be at its juiciest, sweetest, ripest best. Don't bother making this if it isn't, or its subtle perfume will be lost.

½ cup water

½ cup sugar

2½ pounds peeled ripe cantaloupe, honeydew, or similar yellow or green-fleshed melons, seeded and diced

2 tablespoons Midori liqueur (optional)

1 tablespoon fresh lime juice

Salt

1. Combine the water and sugar in a saucepan and bring to boil. Reduce the heat and simmer until the sugar has dissolved. Remove from the heat and cool. Chill a 1-quart storage container in the freezer.

2. In a food processor fitted with the steel blade, or in a blender, purée the melon until smooth. Add the sugar syrup, Midori, lime juice, and a pinch of salt. Freeze in an ice cream maker following the manufacturer's instructions. Transfer to the chilled container and freeze for 2 hours before serving. Allow to soften in the refrigerator for 15 to 30 minutes before serving.

ADVANCE PREPARATION: The sorbet will keep—if you can hang on to it—for a couple of weeks in the freezer.

VARIATION

MELON SOUP: Use only ¼ cup sugar and ¼ cup water for the syrup, or omit it altogether. Do not freeze the mixture. Serve chilled, garnished with melon balls and mint.

MELON WITH MUSCAT DE BEAUMES-DE-VENISE

France • **Serves 4 to 6**

Muscat de Beaumes-de-Venise is a sweet fortified wine from the Rhône Valley, and it tastes exactly like the green Muscat grapes from which it's made. In fact, wine writer Jancis Robinson says that this is the only wine that actually does taste like grapes. The wine makes a fine dessert on its own, with crisp biscotti for dipping. But it also goes very nicely with the wonderful sweet melons of the region. Serve additional wine in dessert wineglasses.

> 1 large ripe cantaloupe or similar yellow-fleshed melon (or 2 smaller ones), or a mixture of green-fleshed melon and yellow-fleshed melon
>
> ¾ cup chilled Muscat de Beaumes-de-Venise

Cut the melon in half and scoop out the seeds. Make melon balls with a melon baller and place in a bowl. Cover and chill. Just before serving, toss with the wine.

ADVANCE PREPARATION: The melons can be prepared a day ahead and refrigerated.

FIG AND RED WINE COMPOTE

France • **Serves 6 to 8**

This jammy compote can be served warm or chilled—with the Fig Ice Cream on the opposite page, and some Almond Biscotti (page 345) for dipping.

> 2 cups fruity red wine, such as Syrah or Côtes du Rhône
>
> ½ cup Banyuls wine or port
>
> ⅓ cup lavender, acacia, clover, or orange blossom honey
>
> 2 tablespoons sugar
>
> 1 vanilla bean, split and scraped
>
> 1 pound ripe fresh figs, stems removed

1. Combine the wines, honey, sugar, and seeds from the vanilla bean in a large saucepan and bring to a boil. Reduce the heat to medium and boil gently until reduced to 1½ cups. Reduce the heat so that the wine is at a bare simmer.

2. Meanwhile, quarter each fig from the tip to within ½ inch of the base; don't cut all the way through.

3. Place the figs in the wine syrup and simmer gently for 5 minutes, turning the figs over halfway through. Remove with a slotted spoon and place in a serving bowl or divide among individual dishes. Bring the heat up under the wine and reduce once more, to about ¾ cup. Spoon over the figs and cool. Serve warm, at room temperature, or cold.

ADVANCE PREPARATION: You can make this dessert a few hours before you wish to serve it.

HONEY-ROASTED FIGS

Serves 4

When I think of honey and figs, I think of Greek gods lying around, feasting on this delicacy. I also think of late summer in Provence, where I use lavender honey for this simple dish. Serve the figs with ice cream, or with other complementary fruit, such as raspberries or melon. They also go well with savory foods and salads.

> 12 ripe fresh figs
>
> 2 tablespoons honey, preferably lavender honey
>
> 2 teaspoons finely chopped grated orange zest (optional)
>
> Fresh mint sprigs or raspberries (or both)

1. Heat the oven to 400°F. Butter a baking dish that will accommodate all of the figs in a single layer. Cut the stems off the figs, then quarter each from the stem end down to within about ½ inch of the bottom. Open them out like flowers, arrange in the dish, and drizzle with the honey. Sprinkle on the zest.

2. Bake for 15 minutes, until the figs have softened and begun to ooze, but still hold their shape. Serve warm, garnished with mint and/or raspberries.

ADVANCE PREPARATION: You can prepare the figs hours before you bake them.

FIG ICE CREAM
Makes 1 quart

This is a luxurious summer ice cream. If you want to go even more crazy with figs, serve it with Fig and Red Wine Compote on page 350.

> 1 pound ripe fresh figs, stems removed
>
> 3 tablespoons water or red wine
>
> 1 vanilla bean, split and scraped
>
> 2 cups milk (whole or low-fat)
>
> ⅓ to ½ cup sugar (to taste)
>
> 4 large egg yolks
>
> Salt

1. Quarter the figs and place in a heavy saucepan with the water. Bring to a simmer and cook, stirring often, until the figs are very tender, 15 to 20 minutes. Remove from the heat and purée coarsely in a food processor fitted with the steel blade; be careful to maintain some texture.

2. Combine the vanilla bean (pod and seeds) with the milk and half the sugar in a heavy 3-quart saucepan. Bring to a simmer over medium heat. Remove from the heat, cover, and steep for 15 minutes.

3. While the milk is steeping, fill a large bowl with ice or ice water and nestle a smaller bowl in the ice. Place a strainer above the smaller bowl. Whisk together the egg yolks, remaining sugar, and a small pinch of salt in a medium bowl until thick and lemon colored.

4. Remove the vanilla pod from the milk and scrape any remaining seeds into the milk. Set the pod aside to dry on paper towels so that you can use it for vanilla sugar (see Tip). Bring the milk back to a simmer and remove from the heat. Ladle out ½ cup of the hot milk and drizzle it slowly into the egg yolks, whisking all the while. Then whisk the tempered egg yolks back into the milk. Scrape out the bottom of the bowl with a heatproof rubber spatula.

5. Place the pan back on the stove over low heat and cook, stirring constantly. Watch very closely. Stir in figure-eights, using a heatproof rubber spatula and scraping the bottom of the pan constantly. After 2 to 5 minutes, the sauce should begin to thicken. Do not let the mixture boil, or the eggs will curdle. If you have a digital thermometer, insert it into the mixture. Remove the sauce from the heat when it reaches 180°F, or when it coats your spatula like cream and leaves a canal when you run your finger down the middle.

6. Stir the sauce for a few seconds, then strain into the bowl set in the ice bath. Stir in the puréed figs and combine well. Stir occasionally for the next 10 to 15 minutes. As the sauce cools, it will thicken more. If there is time, cover and refrigerate for 2 hours.

7. Place a 1-quart storage container in the freezer. Freeze the fig mixture in an ice cream maker following the manufacturer's instructions. Scrape into the chilled container and freeze for 2 hours or longer. Allow to soften for 15 minutes in the refrigerator before serving.

ADVANCE PREPARATION: The ice cream will keep for several weeks in the freezer. You can make the base (which is a fig-flavored crème anglaise) a day or two before making the ice cream.

 **TIP** VANILLA SUGAR
Save the pods whenever you use the seeds from vanilla beans. Let them dry out thoroughly on paper towels (this takes a day if they've been simmered), then bury them in a jar of sugar. The sugar will begin to taste like vanilla as you keep adding vanilla pods to it. I use vanilla sugar often when recipes call for vanilla. In a pinch, if you're out of vanilla beans but you've got the sugar, you can use it and you'll still get that wonderful vanilla flavor in your dessert.

PEACH GELATO

Italy • **Makes 2 quarts**

If I could choose one fruit ice cream above all others, it would be peach, made with ripe summer fruit. This gelato is a lighter version of the ice creams I enjoyed up and down the Italian boot.

> 1½ pounds peaches
>
> ⅔ cup sugar
>
> 2 tablespoons mild honey, such as clover or acacia
>
> 3 cups milk
>
> ¼ cup powdered milk
>
> 1½ teaspoons almond extract
>
> Salt

1. Fill a medium saucepan with water and bring to a boil. Fill a bowl with ice water. Drop the peaches into the boiling water and leave for 30 seconds if the peaches are ripe and soft, 1 minute if they are hard. Transfer to the ice water and leave for a minute. Peel off the skins, cut in half, and remove the pits. If the peach clings to the pit, it's easier to cut them into quarters and pry the peach from the pit, or cut the peach away from the pit with a paring knife.

2. Measure out 1 cup of water from the saucepan and drain the rest. Return the water to the pot, add the sugar, and bring to a boil. When the sugar has dissolved, reduce the heat, add the honey and peaches, and simmer for 10 minutes. Remove from the heat and cool. Transfer the peaches with a slotted spoon to a food processor fitted with the steel blade and pulse until they are finely chopped or coarsely puréed. Reserve the purée and syrup separately.

3. Fill a large bowl with ice and water. Combine the milk and powdered milk in a medium saucepan or in a large measuring cup and whisk together. Bring to a boil (you can do this in the microwave in the measuring cup) and remove from the heat. Pour into a medium bowl and place the bowl in the ice bath. Cool to room temperature, then stir in the syrup, almond extract, and a pinch of salt.

4. Place two 1-quart storage containers in your freezer. Freeze the gelato base in an ice cream maker, following the manufacturer's directions. When the gelato has just about reached the desired constancy, add the peach purée and continue to process for another 5 to 10 minutes. Scrape into the cold containers and freeze for 2 hours or longer.

ADVANCE PREPARATION: You can poach the peaches several hours or a day before you make the gelato. The gelato will keep in the freezer for a couple of weeks.

PEACHES IN RED WINE AND BANYULS

France • **Serves 6**

My friend Christine Picasso buys peaches by the flat, and she makes this salad throughout the hot Provençal summer. We're happy to eat this for dessert every night, sometimes with a plate of cookies.

Banyuls is a fortified wine from Languedoc-Roussillon, in Catalan France. You can find it in some wine stores. If you can't get it, substitute equal parts Syrah and port.

> 6 firm, ripe peaches
>
> 2 cups fruity red wine, such as Côtes du Rhône or Syrah
>
> ½ cup Banyuls (or ¼ cup Syrah and ¼ cup Ruby port)
>
> ¼ cup mild honey, such as clover or acacia
>
> One 3-inch cinnamon stick
>
> 1 vanilla bean, split and scraped; or ½ teaspoon vanilla extract
>
> Mint sprigs

1. Bring a pot of water to a boil and drop in the peaches. Blanch for 30 seconds to 1 minute, and transfer at once to a bowl of ice water. Leave for a few minutes, then slip off the skins and slice. Place in a bowl.

2. Combine the wine, Banyuls, honey, cinnamon stick, and vanilla bean (seeds and pod) in a medium nonreactive saucepan and bring to a boil. Reduce the heat and simmer for 1 minute. Remove from the heat and pour over peaches. Refrigerate for several hours. Remove the cinnamon stick and the vanilla bean.

3. Serve cold, garnished with mint sprigs.

ADVANCE PREPARATION: This dessert will keep well for about half a day, but after time the peaches will give up too much of their flavor.

APRICOT CLAFOUTI

France • **Makes one 10-inch clafouti**

I marinate the luscious farmers' market apricots I can buy from June through August in Amaretto for this clafouti. Amaretto is an almond liqueur, and almonds and apricots have always been a classic combination.

>   1 pound apricots, halved and pitted
>
>   2 tablespoons Amaretto
>
>   7 tablespoons vanilla sugar (page 351)
>   or granulated sugar
>
>   3 large eggs
>
>   ½ teaspoon vanilla extract (if using granulated
>   sugar)
>
>   Salt
>
>   ⅔ cup sifted unbleached all-purpose flour
>
>   ¾ cup low-fat (2%) milk or buttermilk
>
>   1 tablespoon confectioners' sugar (optional)

1. Toss the apricots with the Amaretto and 2 tablespoons of the sugar, and let sit for 30 minutes. Drain through a strainer set over a bowl.

2. Heat the oven to 375°F. Butter a 10- or 10½-inch ceramic tart pan or clafouti dish. Arrange the drained apricots in the dish, rounded side up.

3. Beat the eggs with the remaining 5 tablespoons sugar (and the vanilla extract, if using) in the bowl of an electric mixer fitted with the whisk attachment, or by hand with a whisk, until the sugar is dissolved. Add a pinch of salt and the liquid from the apricots and combine well. Slowly beat in the flour and whisk until smooth. Add the milk and combine well. Pour over the apricots.

4. Bake for 30 to 40 minutes, until the top is browned and the clafouti is firm and puffed. Press gently on the top in the middle to see if it's firm. If it isn't, return to the oven for 5 minutes. Cool on a rack. When warm or cool, sift on the confectioners' sugar. Serve warm or at room temperature.

ADVANCE PREPARATION: This clafouti will hold for several hours at room temperature.

LEFTOVERS: Enjoy the leftovers for breakfast.

SUMMER STONE FRUIT STRUDEL

Croatia • **Serves 8 to 10**

One of the most interesting places to eat in the Mediterranean is the Istrian Peninsula, on the Adriatic coast of northern Croatia. Over the last several centuries, Istria has held a strategic position in a number of reigning empires, from the Roman to the Venetian, the Austro-Hungarian to the Ottoman. The cuisine here is decidedly Italian in flavor, with one exception: Many of the desserts you find have a distinctly *Mitteleuropan* character.

>   ½ pound figs, quartered (or ½ cup dried figs)
>
>   ½ pound apricots, pitted and quartered
>   (or ½ cup dried apricots)
>
>   ¾ pound ripe but firm peaches, pitted and
>   sliced (or ½ pound frozen peaches)
>
>   ¾ pound good-size red plums, such as Santa
>   Rosas, pitted and sliced
>
>   Juice of ½ lemon
>
>   ¼ cup sugar
>
>   1½ teaspoons ground cinnamon
>
>   8 sheets phyllo dough
>
>   4 tablespoons (½ stick) unsalted butter, melted
>
>   1 cup bread crumbs

1. Heat the oven to 375°F. Line a half-sheet pan with parchment. If you are using dried figs and apricots, place them in a bowl and pour on boiling water to cover. Let sit for 15 minutes, and drain. Cut the figs and the apricots in half. ▶

2. In a large bowl, toss the figs, apricots, peaches, and plums with the lemon juice, sugar, and cinnamon. Set aside.

3. Place a sheet of parchment on your work surface with a long edge facing you. Keep the phyllo sheets you aren't working with covered with a damp towel. Lay a sheet of phyllo dough on the parchment. Brush with butter and top with another sheet of phyllo. Continue to layer all eight sheets, brushing each one with butter before topping with the next one.

4. Brush the top sheet of phyllo dough with butter. Sprinkle half the bread crumbs evenly over the phyllo. With the remaining bread crumbs, create a line 4 inches from the edge of the dough nearest to you. Top this line with the fruit mixture, leaving a 1½-inch border at both ends. Fold the bottom edge of the phyllo over the filling, then tuck the ends over the filling, and roll up. Place the strudel on the baking sheet. Brush with butter and make 3 or 4 slits on the diagonal along the length of the strudel.

5. Place the strudel in the oven and bake for 20 minutes. Remove from the oven, brush again with butter, rotate the pan, and return to the oven. Continue to bake for another 20 to 25 minutes, until golden brown. Remove from the heat and serve warm or at room temperature.

ADVANCE PREPARATION: The fruit filling will keep for a couple of days in the refrigerator. The strudel can be baked a few hours before serving it. Recrisp in a low oven (250° to 300°F) for 15 minutes. Once cooled, the strudel can be wrapped airtight and frozen for 2 weeks. Thaw, and crisp in a 300°F oven for 20 minutes.

STRAWBERRY TART WITH ROSE-SCENTED PASTRY CREAM

Makes one 9- or 10-inch tart

This looks like a tart you'd buy in a French pastry shop. It tastes like one, too, except that the rosewater scented pastry cream hints of the Middle East. Make this with local sweet, ripe strawberries.

> ½ recipe Rose-Scented Pastry Cream (opposite page)
>
> One 9- or 10-inch Sweet Pie Crust, fully baked (opposite page)
>
> 1 pound 2 ounces ripe fresh strawberries, hulled
>
> Confectioners' sugar (optional)

Spread the pastry cream over the baked tart shell in an even layer. Top with the strawberries, hulled side down. Just before serving, dust with confectioners' sugar.

ADVANCE PREPARATION: Make this dessert no more than a few hours before serving. If it sits too long, the tart shell will become soggy.

VARIATION

RASPBERRY OR BLUEBERRY TART: Substitute raspberries, blueberries, or a mixture, for the strawberries.

 TIP WHAT TO DO ABOUT CURDLED PASTRY CREAM
Although the flour is supposed to prevent curdling, I have ended up with scrambled pastry cream more than once. No need to worry. Transfer it to a food processor fitted with the steel blade and process until smooth.

ROSE-SCENTED PASTRY CREAM
Makes enough pastry cream for two 9-inch fruit tarts

Sherry Yard, executive pastry chef at Spago Beverly Hills, is my pastry guru. I've had the great pleasure of working with her on both of her cookbooks, and through this experience have become a much more confident dessert maker than I'd ever dreamed I would be. This pastry cream is one example of a basic dessert building block that I had never liked before I learned to make it Sherry's way.

This version, with rose water, is wonderfully perfumed. But orange zest—which Sherry uses—also gives the pastry cream a very special flavor. See the variation that follows.

> 2 cups milk
>
> ½ cup sugar
>
> ½ vanilla bean, split and scraped; or 1 teaspoon vanilla extract
>
> 1 teaspoon rose water (available in Middle Eastern groceries)
>
> Pinch salt (less than ⅛ teaspoon)
>
> 3 tablespoons unbleached all-purpose flour or cornstarch
>
> 5 large egg yolks or 3 large eggs, cold, straight from the refrigerator
>
> 1 tablespoon unsalted butter, softened

1. If you need to cool the pastry cream quickly, line a baking sheet with plastic wrap and set aside.

2. In a medium nonreactive saucepan combine the milk, ¼ cup of the sugar, the vanilla pod and seeds (or vanilla extract), and rose water, and bring to a simmer over medium heat. While the milk is heating, sift together the remaining ¼ cup sugar, the salt, and flour onto a piece of parchment. In a large bowl, whisk the eggs yolks and add the sifted dry ingredients. Whisk until fluffy.

3. When the milk begins to simmer, remove from the heat. Let sit for a minute, then slowly whisk ½ cup into the eggs. Once the milk is incorporated into the eggs, whisk them back into the hot milk. Be sure to scrape all the egg mixture into the milk with a rubber spatula.

4. Return the pot to medium heat and immediately begin to whisk the pastry cream rapidly. In under a minute it will boil and begin to thicken. Continue to whisk for about 3 minutes, until it reaches pudding consistency. To test the cream for doneness, tilt the saucepan to one side. The cream should pull away from the pan completely.

5. Remove the pot from the heat and immediately strain the cream into a clean bowl. Add the butter and stir until it is melted and incorporated. Refrigerate until ready to use. To cool pastry cream quickly, spread it out on the lined baking sheet. To prevent a skin from forming as it cools, place another sheet of plastic wrap directly on the surface.

ADVANCE PREPARATION: The pastry cream will keep for 3 days in the refrigerator. Place a sheet of plastic directly on the surface to prevent a skin from forming.

VARIATION

ORANGE-SCENTED PASTRY CREAM: Substitute 1½ teaspoons finely chopped grated orange zest (no need to chop if you use a microplane) for the rose water.

SWEET PIE CRUST (Pâte Sucrée)
Makes two 9- or 10-inch crusts

This is one of celebrated pastry chef Sherry Yard's formulas for *pâte sucrée,* a sweet, cookie-like pastry dough.

> 2½ cups unbleached all-purpose flour
>
> ⅓ cup sugar
>
> ½ pound (2 sticks) unsalted butter, cut into ½-inch pieces, cold
>
> 2 large egg yolks, cold
>
> 2 tablespoons heavy cream, cold

1. Combine the flour and sugar in the bowl of a standing mixer fitted with the paddle attachment. Mix on low speed for 1 minute. Add the butter and mix on medium-low speed until the butter is barely visible. ▶

2. Add the egg yolks and mix on medium-low speed until the dough comes together. Turn the machine down to low and stream in the cream. Stop the machine and scrape down the bowl and beater. Continue to mix on low speed for 1 minute.

3. Remove the dough from the bowl and divide into 2 equal pieces. Place on plastic wrap and flatten to about ½ inch thick. Wrap tightly and refrigerate for 4 hours or overnight.

4. To roll out the dough, place one piece at a time in a stand mixer fitted with the hook attachment. Work the dough at medium-low speed just until pliable. Roll out on a floured surface to a ¼-inch-thick circle. Store flat between pieces of parchment in the refrigerator or freezer, or line pans, wrap tightly, and store.

PREBAKING: Set a rack in the lower third of the oven and heat the oven to 350°F. Line the dough with foil and fill with dried beans. Bake for 15 to 18 minutes. Remove the beans and foil and bake another 6 to 10 minutes, until a deep golden brown. Cool on a rack before filling.

ADVANCE PREPARATION: This rolled-out dough freezes very well, wrapped airtight. Roll it out and line the pan, then wrap and freeze. When you prebake it, you can take it directly from the freezer to the oven, and there will be no need to use beans or other pie weights.

STRAWBERRY SORBET
Makes just under 1 quart

Ice cream, gelato, sorbet, granita—these are constants when it comes to dessert throughout the Mediterranean. On a summer night, no matter what the hour, you will find the ice cream shops packed, from Malaga to Rome. Sherry Yard, of Spago Beverly Hills, makes a wonderful strawberry sauce using the ingredients that follow (and star anise). It makes me think of the vivid granitas and sorbets I ate in Italy, so I've used an approximation of her formula for my strawberry sorbet base.

1¾ pounds ripe, sweet strawberries, hulled and quartered if large, halved if small

¼ cup water

⅔ cup sugar

¾ cup fresh orange juice

1 tablespoon Grand Marnier

1 tablespoon fresh lemon juice

Salt

1. Combine the strawberries, water, sugar, orange juice, Grand Marnier, and lemon juice in a saucepan with a pinch of salt and bring to a boil. Reduce the heat and simmer, stirring often, for 10 minutes. Remove from the heat and cool.

2. Chill a 1-quart storage container in your freezer. Purée the sorbet base in a food processor fitted with the steel blade, or in a blender, and put through a fine sieve. Transfer to an ice cream maker and process following the manufacturer's instructions. Scrape into the chilled container and freeze for 2 hours.

ADVANCE PREPARATION: The sorbet will keep for several weeks in the freezer. You can make the base a day or two before you make the sorbet.

VARIATION

STRAWBERRY GRANITA: Instead of processing the mixture in an ice cream maker, freeze in a cold baking dish, following the granita instructions on page 348.

STRAWBERRY AND APRICOT SALAD
Serves 6

This is a dessert to shop for at the farmers' market, when at the height of summer you're bound to find sweet, ripe apricots and the sweetest strawberries. I would buy these by the flat in Provence in the summer, and eat this salad after meals and for breakfast, with yogurt.

2 pints strawberries, hulled and quartered

2 teaspoons sugar or, if available, lavender honey

1 pound ripe apricots, pitted and quartered

Juice of ½ lemon

Juice of ½ orange

1 tablespoon slivered fresh mint

Toss the strawberries with the sugar or honey in a bowl. Cover and refrigerate for 1 hour. Toss with the apricots, lemon and orange juice, and mint, and serve.

ADVANCE PREPARATION: You can make the salad a few hours before serving, but don't add the mint until just before you serve.

PEARS POACHED IN WINE AND HONEY
Serves 4

All of the Mediterranean countries produce wonderful honey. I use this combination of honey and wine for poaching pears and other fruits like figs and peaches. Serve this with biscotti (page 345) for dipping into the syrup.

1 bottle fruity red wine, such as a Syrah

½ cup lavender, acacia, or clover honey

½ vanilla bean, split and scraped

2 sprigs fresh thyme

4 ripe but firm pears, such as Comice or Anjou, peeled, cored, and quartered

1. Combine the wine, honey, vanilla pod and seeds, and thyme in a large saucepan and bring to a boil. Turn the heat down so that the syrup is at a simmer, and drop in the pears. Poach for 10 minutes, flipping the pears over halfway through, until they are just translucent but still firm. Remove the pears from the wine with a slotted spoon and set aside in a bowl.

2. Bring the syrup to a boil and reduce by half. Turn off the heat and cool slightly, then pour over the pears. Chill for several hours.

3. Serve in bowls or soup plates, with biscotti.

ADVANCE PREPARATION: You can keep the prepared dessert in the refrigerator for a day.

QUINCE COMPOTE
France • Serves 4

Quinces grow abundantly throughout the Mediterranean, and they're used in savory and sweet dishes alike. It's a very tart, hard fruit that needs cooking and sweetening to coax out its wonderful perfume and beautiful pink color. I was told how to make this compote years ago by a vendor in the market in Apt, in Provence's Lubéron region.

Juice of ½ lemon

2 pounds quinces (or use a combination of quinces and apples)

½ cup sugar

½ cup water

½ teaspoon ground cinnamon

1 vanilla bean, split and scraped

¼ cup raisins

1. Fill a large bowl with water and add the lemon juice. Quarter the quinces and place the pieces you aren't working with in the water while you peel, core, and slice each quarter into 1-inch-thick pieces.

2. Combine the sugar and water in a large, heavy nonreactive saucepan and bring to a boil. Reduce the heat and simmer until the sugar has dissolved. Drain the quinces and add to the pot along with the cinnamon, vanilla pod and seeds, and raisins. Bring to a simmer, cover, and reduce the heat. Simmer, stirring often, for 1 hour, by which time the quinces will be soft and pinkish.

3. Serve hot or cold. This is excellent with vanilla ice cream.

ADVANCE PREPARATION: This dessert will keep for about a week in the refrigerator.

QUINCE SPOON SWEET

Greece • **Makes about 2 cups**

When you visit a Greek family in the late morning or afternoon, you will invariably be offered coffee, a glass of ice water, and a spoon sweet. Spoon sweets are simply preserved fruits, in a syrup that is runnier than jam and thicker than syrup. They're very sweet, and one or two spoonfuls suffice, thus the name. I love them with ice cream or yogurt.

The idea for the rose geranium leaves comes from food writer Diane Kochilas. Only use them if you are sure they're free of pesticides.

> 1 pound quinces
>
> 1 cup water
>
> Juice of ½ lemon
>
> 2 cups sugar
>
> 2 rose geranium leaves or ¾ teaspoon vanilla extract

1. Peel and core the quinces, and chop very fine. Combine with the water and lemon juice in a large saucepan and bring to a boil. Reduce the heat and simmer for 10 minutes, until the quinces are slightly softened.

2. Add the sugar to the pan and continue to simmer uncovered over medium-low heat for 1 hour, until the syrup is thick. Make sure the temperature does not go over 230°F (use a candy thermometer). Remove from the heat and stir in the rose geranium leaves or the vanilla. Cool completely and remove the rose geranium leaves. Transfer to a sterilized jar and store in a cool, dark place.

3. To serve, spoon a few teaspoons onto a plate and serve with a glass of ice water. Or stir into yogurt, or spoon over vanilla ice cream.

ADVANCE PREPARATION: The spoon sweet will keep until you use it up.

ROSE GERANIUM SYRUP FOR ICED TEA

Combine 1 cup water and 1 cup sugar in a saucepan. Bring to a boil, reduce the heat, and simmer for 5 minutes, until the sugar is completely dissolved and the syrup has cooked down slightly. Add 2 or 3 sprigs of rose geranium and turn off the heat. Allow to infuse until the syrup cools. Remove the rose geranium and store the syrup in the refrigerator. I keep mine in a squeeze bottle and add it to iced tea.

ORANGE SORBET WITH BLOOD ORANGE SALAD

Makes 1½ quarts

The blood oranges that you get in Europe are dark, dark red and have a flavor that tastes of both citrus and berries. Those that we get here tend to be more sour, but they still have that beautiful color. I suggest you use regular oranges for the sorbet, or use tangerines, and it will contrast nicely with the salad.

FOR THE SORBET

½ cup sugar

½ cup water

4 cups fresh orange juice or tangerine (or clementine) juice

2 tablespoons fresh lemon juice

FOR THE SALAD

6 medium or 12 small blood oranges

2 to 3 tablespoons Grand Marnier (to taste)

2 tablespoons slivered fresh mint leaves

Fresh mint sprigs

1. *Make the sorbet:* Combine the sugar and water in a small saucepan and bring to a boil. Reduce the heat and simmer for 5 minutes, until the sugar is completely dissolved. Cool.

2. Combine the syrup with the orange juice and the lemon juice. Place a 1½-quart storage container in your freezer. Freeze the base in an ice cream maker, following the manufacturer's directions. Transfer to the cold container and freeze for at least 2 hours.

3. *Make the salad:* Using a small paring knife, peel away the skin and white pith from the oranges. Cut the sections away from the membranes, holding the oranges above a bowl so that you catch all of the juice. Toss the orange sections with their juice, the Grand Marnier, and the mint, and refrigerate until ready to serve.

4. Serve the sorbet in bowls or on plates, with the orange salad on the side. Garnish with fresh mint sprigs.

ADVANCE PREPARATION: The sorbet will keep for a few weeks in the freezer. The salad should not be prepared too far ahead, as the oranges will lose some of their sweetness.

LEMON SORBET
Makes 1 quart

The climate and landscape of Southern California is often described as Mediterranean. That certainly rings true in the spring, when the air is perfumed with heavenly aromas of jasmine and citrus blossoms. I have a dwarf Meyer lemon tree in my backyard which yields so much fruit that I can keep my freezer stocked with sorbet through the winter and spring. The regular lemons from my potted lemon trees do just fine when I don't have Meyers to work with.

This sorbet (or granita) is a welcome dessert. But there's also nothing like it at the end of a hot summer afternoon in Italy, when you've climbed up the hill of whatever village you are visiting, and sit for a while at a lively bar, like Il Tripoli in Martina Franca (Puglia), to rest and do some early evening people-watching.

> 1 cup less 2 tablespoons sugar
>
> 3 cups water

Finely grated zest of 1 lemon

1 cup fresh lemon juice (if available, use Meyer lemons)

1. Combine the sugar with 1 cup of the water in a saucepan and bring to a boil. Add the lemon zest and reduce the heat. Simmer for 5 minutes, then remove from the heat and cool.

2. Strain the syrup into a bowl. Add the remaining 2 cups water and the lemon juice. Mix together. Place a 1-quart storage container in the freezer. Freeze the sorbet base in an ice cream maker, following the manufacturer's instructions. When the sorbet reaches the right consistency, transfer to the chilled container and freeze for 2 hours.

ADVANCE PREPARATION: The sorbet will keep for several weeks in the freezer.

VARIATIONS

• Add 1 tablespoon grenadine syrup, for a beautiful pale pink sorbet.

• Make granita instead of sorbet, following the directions on page 348.

LEMON TART
Makes one 9-inch tart

This is the lemon tart that I make throughout the year with lemons that grow in my backyard. It's incredibly easy and I haven't altered the recipe, which I've published before, because it's just so good. If you have access to Meyer lemons, use them.

> ⅔ cup fresh lemon juice (if available, use Meyer lemons)
>
> ½ cup sugar
>
> 2 tablespoons drained yogurt (page 21) or crème fraîche
>
> 4 large eggs
>
> One 9-inch Sweet Pie Crust (page 355), fully baked

1. Heat the oven to 350°F.   ▶

2. Whisk together the lemon juice and sugar. When the sugar has dissolved, whisk in the yogurt. Whisk in the eggs, one at a time. Pour into the crust and bake for 25 to 30 minutes, until set and shiny. Cool on a rack.

ADVANCE PREPARATION: You can make this dessert up to a day before you wish to serve it.

COFFEE GRANITA

Italy • **Serves 8**

There is a *caffè* near the Pantheon in Rome called La Casa del Caffè-Tazza d'Oro, which I would go to every day if I lived in Rome, just for the *granita di caffè*. The barman puts a small amount of *panna,* thick whipped cream, into a plastic cup, then scrapes out about a half cup of sweet, strong granita to top the cream. Then he tops the granita with another spoonful of *panna.* When you eat the granita, you scoop down through the cream into the refreshing coffee ice, and the combination is unbelievably pleasing. On a hot summer day in Rome, nothing could be more refreshing, or addictive.

The granita formula I'm using here was given to me by Sherry Yard, the executive pastry chef at Spago Beverly Hills and Wolfgang Puck Worldwide.

> 4 cups strong brewed espresso
>
> ¾ cup sugar
>
> ¼ cup raw brown (turbinado) sugar
>
> 1 cup San Pellegrino (or other sparkling mineral water)
>
> 1 tablespoon rum (optional)
>
> 1 to 2 cups heavy cream (to taste)

1. Place a large, flat-bottomed pan in the freezer while you make your coffee. Place the hot coffee in a bowl and stir in the sugars. When the sugars have dissolved, add the Pellegrino and rum. Cool completely, then pour into the pan and place in the freezer.

2. Fluff the granita with a fork every 20 minutes. Bring the frozen crystals that form around the edge of the pan into the center. This forces the unfrozen liquid to the edge to freeze. Set a timer for the 20-minute intervals. If forgotten, the mixture will freeze into a solid block. (If this should happen, place chunks of the frozen granita in a food processor, pulse until it's liquefied, and start the freezing process over.)

3. The granita is ready when all the liquid is frozen into small ice crystals, which should take about 2 hours. Once the ice crystals are formed, the granita can be stored in the freezer, wrapped air tight, for up to a week.

4. To serve, place wineglasses or parfait glasses in the freezer for 30 minutes. Whip the cream to medium peaks. Place a spoonful of cream in the bottom of each glass. Scrape the top of the granita with a fork, then spoon out into the glasses. Top with another spoonful of whipped cream. Serve immediately—this melts fast!

ADVANCE PREPARATION: You can keep this granita on hand in the freezer for weeks and scrape it out whenever you need a sweet, caffeinated lift.

RICOTTA CHEESECAKE

Italy • **Makes one 9½- or 10-inch cheesecake**

I had just eaten one of the best meals of my life, in one of the most beautiful places, an *azienda agrituristica* called Monte Sacro, up in the mountains on the Gargano Promontory in Puglia. The meal had begun with slices of Ricotta Frittata with Zucchini (page 183) and tomato bruschetta, followed by Stewed Eggplant and Onions (page 276), Dried Fava Beans and Greens (page 309), orecchiette with ragout, and grilled meats and roasted potatoes with rosemary. How could we possibly eat more? When the ricotta cheesecake came, accompanied by ripe melon, we found a way.

I've looked at many Italian cheesecake recipes, and have found nothing quite like the one we ate in Gargano. Classic Italian ricotta cheesecake usually calls for raisins that have been soaked in rum or Marsala, and often includes pine nuts. This cheesecake was utterly simple, pure ricotta, eggs, sugar, and a sprinkling of nuts on the top. As cheesecakes go, it's the lightest I've ever tasted. You need to start draining the cheese the night before.

- 1½ pounds ricotta cheese (3½ cups)
- 3 tablespoons unsalted butter, softened
- ¼ cup fine dry bread crumbs
- 4 large eggs, separated
- ⅓ cup plus 2 tablespoons sugar
- ¼ teaspoon salt
- 1 tablespoon unbleached all-purpose flour
- ¼ cup heavy cream
- ¼ cup sour cream (or omit sour cream and use ½ cup heavy cream)
- Finely grated zest of 1 lemon or orange (or both)
- 1 teaspoon vanilla extract
- ¼ cup finely chopped walnuts
- ½ teaspoon ground cinnamon

1. The day before you wish to bake, line a strainer with cheesecloth, place over a bowl, and place the ricotta in the strainer. Refrigerate overnight. It's important to drain the ricotta so that the cake won't be too watery.

2. Set a rack in the middle of the oven and heat the oven to 350°F. Smear a 9½- or 10-inch springform pan with the softened butter and dust evenly with the bread crumbs. Tip out the excess crumbs.

3. In a food processor fitted with the steel blade, process the egg yolks, drained ricotta, ⅓ cup plus 1 tablespoon of the sugar, the salt, and flour until very smooth. Scrape down the sides of the bowl. Add the cream, sour cream, zest, and vanilla extract, and process to combine. Transfer to a bowl.

4. Beat the egg whites in a separate bowl to medium-stiff peaks. Stir one-quarter into the ricotta batter to lighten it, then carefully fold in the rest. Scrape into the pan.

5. Bake on the middle rack for 1 hour to 1 hour 15 minutes, until golden brown and set in the center. Turn off the oven.

6. Pulse together the nuts, the remaining 1 tablespoon sugar, and the cinnamon in a food processor fitted with the steel blade. Do not overprocess or you will release too much oil from the nuts. Sprinkle in an even layer over the cake. Put back in the turned-off oven, prop the door open, and cool in the oven for 30 minutes.

7. Remove from the oven and cool completely on a rack, then refrigerate for at least 2 hours. Run a knife between the edge of the pan and the cheesecake, and carefully remove the ring from the pan. Serve the cheesecake cold or at room temperature.

ADVANCE PREPARATION: You can make this cheesecake a day or two before you wish to serve it.

ANISE BUTTER COOKIES

Italy • **Makes 36 large or 72 small cookies**

Imagine being seven years old and finding a breakfast buffet laden with platters of cookies and cakes, about ten different kinds. That is what we were welcomed with every morning at Il Frantoio, the exquisite olive farm/hotel *agrituristica* in Puglia, where Liam, Rachel, and I capped off six weeks of Mediterranean travel in the summer of 2005. Needless to say, Liam couldn't wait to get to breakfast every morning. I myself went straight for the fresh fruit—huge bowls of plums and peaches, apricots and grapes, all from the farm. But I was nonetheless impressed by all of the different types of cookies that came out of this Italian kitchen.

- 12 tablespoons (1½ sticks) unsalted butter
- ⅔ cup sugar
- 1 large egg
- 1 teaspoon finely grated lemon zest
- 1 teaspoon vanilla extract
- 2 teaspoons anise seeds, crushed in a mortar and pestle
- 2¼ cups unbleached all-purpose flour
- 1 teaspoon baking powder
- ¼ teaspoon salt

1. In a standing mixer fitted with the paddle, cream the butter with the sugar until fluffy and pale, about 4 minutes. Scrape down the bowl and paddle. Add the egg, lemon zest, vanilla, and anise, and beat together.

2. Sift together the flour, baking powder, and salt. On low speed, beat the dry ingredients into the butter mixture.

3. Turn the dough onto the counter, gather it into a ball, then press down to a 1-inch thickness. Wrap tightly in plastic and refrigerate overnight or for up to 3 days, or place in the freezer for 1 to 2 hours.

If you don't want to roll out the dough: Remove spoonfuls of half of the dough and plop them down the middle of a piece of parchment paper to create a log about 2 inches in diameter. Roll the parchment up around the log and repeat with the remaining dough. Refrigerate for 2 hours or longer.

4. Set a rack in the bottom of the oven and heat the oven to 350°F. Line baking sheets with parchment.

5. Cut the dough into quarters, and roll out one piece at a time on a lightly floured work surface to about ¼ inch thick. Cut into circles or diamond shapes, dipping the cutter into flour between each cut, and place 1 inch apart on the baking sheets. Keep the remaining pieces of dough in the refrigerator or freezer.

If you have made logs, cut ⅓-inch-thick rounds and place 1 inch apart on the baking sheets.

6. Bake for 10 to 12 minutes, turning the baking sheet front to back halfway through. Remove from the oven and cool on a rack.

ADVANCE PREPARATION: These cookies will keep for 2 weeks in a tin or jar. They freeze well, for 2 months.

VARIATION

LEMON BUTTER COOKIES: Omit the anise seeds. Increase the lemon zest to 2 tablespoons. Add 1 tablespoon fresh lemon juice along with the egg. Adjust flour if dough is too sticky.

VENETIAN CORNMEAL SHORTBREAD
(Fregolata Veneziana)
Italy • **Makes 12 wedges**

These are rich shortbread pastry wedges from Venice. The ingredients are similar to ingredients used in the French cake Financier (page 346), but the dough is more like pie crust dough than a batter. This is based on a recipe in Carol Field's *The Italian Baker*.

7 tablespoons unsalted butter

1 cup almond flour (available in gourmet groceries)

½ cup sugar

2 large egg yolks

Finely grated zest of 1 lemon

2 teaspoons fresh lemon juice

¼ teaspoon almond extract

1 teaspoon vanilla extract

1 cup less 2 tablespoons fine yellow cornmeal

¾ cup unbleached all-purpose flour

⅛ teaspoon salt

1. Melt the butter in a medium saucepan over medium heat. Cook the butter until the solids separate and you begin to see them browning. Let the butter brown to a light golden color, then remove from the heat. Cool to room temperature (but make sure it remains liquid and pourable).

2. Heat the oven to 350°F. Spray a 9-inch pie pan or cake pan with cooking spray, line it with a piece of parchment paper, then spray the paper lightly.

3. Combine the almond flour and sugar in the bowl of a standing mixer fitted with the paddle. Turn to low speed and add the butter, making sure to scrape in all of the brown bits that may have settled at the bottom or on the sides of the pan. Beat until blended, and add the egg yolks, lemon zest, lemon juice, almond extract, and vanilla extract. Beat until well blended. Scrape down the bowl and the paddle.

4. Sift together the cornmeal, all-purpose flour, and salt. Sift again, into the bowl. At low speed,

Yiorgos, the Honey Man

July 12, 2005
Ikaria

This cooking day began with a morning visit to a local beekeeper's hives. Yiorgos Stenos began his career as a beekeeper when he was 17. He asked a friend in the trade to take him out to his hives so that he could see if he was allergic to bees and minded being stung. He wasn't and he didn't. So he went with his donkey over the mountains to the other side of the island and bought his first hive. Now he has many blue wooden hives, out among the pines in the hills around Christos (each beekeeper knows his hives by their color).

We all wore close-toed shoes and socks, and borrowed beekeepers' gear, the meshed helmeted aprons that keep the bees off—sort of. I noticed that Yiorgos swatted his arms a few times. (When we got back to his warehouse, I asked him how many times he'd been stung. "Twelve," he said. He'd reacted the way you or I would respond to a fly alighting on our arm, or at most a mosquito bite.)

Smoker in hand, Yiorgos checked his hives. First he pumped smoke into the hive with his bellows, which pacifies the bees. Then he pulled out the frames filled with honeycomb to check the honey. Those that were full he placed in a box to take back to his warehouse. The bees were beautiful; I felt so lucky, to be able to see them up close and in such numbers, doing their job.

We then proceeded back to Yiorgos's warehouse. Yiorgos, like all beekeepers, uses a centrifuge to extract the honey from the frames. The frames are placed inside and spun, and the honey flows from a tap into a large empty feta can. Yiorgos would later strain the honey and pack it into cans, which we would carry home from Greece.

From Yiorgos's warehouse we proceeded to Diane Kochilas's house, Villa Thalassi, for a honey and cheese tasting. Honey and salty Greek cheeses, or fresh cheeses, are extremely compatible. Whether the cheese is salty and briny, mild and fresh, or earthy, the sweet honey complements it. Honey can be complex, like cheese. Some of the honeys we tasted were dark and had bitter edges. My favorites were the pine, which must have been the type Yiorgos's bees produced, and the thyme honey for which Greece is famous.

Yogurt with honey was breakfast for me every day that I was in Greece. But it could also be dessert, as fresh ricotta drizzled with honey can be in Italy. Serve wedges of feta or spoonfuls of fresh ricotta with the honey either drizzled over or on the side. Spoon yogurt into bowls and drizzle with honey.

mix until the mixture is amalgamated. Do not overbeat.

5. Using your fingers, spread the dough in an even layer in the pan and bake for 20 minutes. Reduce the heat to 300°F and bake another 20 minutes. Cool on a rack.

6. Cut into wedges or squares and serve, with fresh fruit or tea.

ADVANCE PREPARATION: Wrapped airtight, this shortbread will keep for about 5 days. It freezes well.

BUCKWHEAT CAKE FROM THE ALTO ADIGE

Italy • **Makes one 9-inch cake**

When I lived in Paris, I used to join my friends Marco de Stefani and Lorella Grossi every winter in Alpe di Siusi, the northern Italian Tyrol, where we would go cross-country skiing. I have an indelible memory of this buckwheat cake, which I ate one afternoon at a little café I came across on the cross-country trail. I was hot—cross-country skiing is hard work—and ready for coffee. My cappuccino was fine; the cake I ate with it unforgettable. For 20 years I've been trying to find the recipe. Finally, I found one, in Carol Field's authoritative *Celebrating Italy*. This is my adaptation of her adaptation of the authentic, denser cake. Buckwheat flour has a nutty/earthy flavor, and it contrasts beautifully with the jam filling. The traditional jam filling, Carol Field tells us, is made with berries called *mirtilli rossi*, or red blueberries. I like any berry jam or preserve—raspberry or blackberry, red currant or huckleberry.

> 1 cup buckwheat flour (available in whole foods stores and specialty markets)
>
> 1 cup unbleached all-purpose flour
>
> 2 teaspoons baking powder
>
> ⅛ teaspoon salt
>
> 14 tablespoons (1¾ sticks) unsalted butter, at room temperature if using a hand mixer

> 1 cup granulated sugar
>
> 2 tablespoons grappa or brandy
>
> 1 tablespoon vanilla extract
>
> 5 large eggs, separated, plus 1 egg white, at room temperature
>
> 1 cup berry jam or preserves, such as raspberry, blackberry, huckleberry, blueberry, or red currant
>
> 1 to 2 tablespoons water (as needed)
>
> Confectioners' sugar for dusting
>
> Whipped cream (optional)

1. Set a rack in the middle of the oven and heat the oven to 350°F. Spray a 9-inch springform pan with cooking spray and line with parchment. Spray the parchment. Sift together the buckwheat and all-purpose flours, the baking powder, and salt three times. Set aside.

2. In the bowl of a standing mixer fitted with the paddle, or using electric beaters, beat the butter on medium speed for 1 minute, until soft and creamy. Continue to beat on medium speed while you gradually add the granulated sugar, 1 tablespoon at a time. This should take about 5 minutes. Beat in the grappa and vanilla. Scrape down the bowl and beaters. Add the egg yolks, one at a time, scraping down the bowl and beaters between each addition.

3. Add the dry ingredients, 1 tablespoon at a time, to the butter mixture and beat until incorporated. Scrape down the bowl and beaters.

4. In a separate, clean bowl, beat the 6 egg whites to stiff but not dry peaks. Stir one-quarter of them into the batter, then gently fold in the rest. This is most easily done with a balloon whisk. The batter will be thick and somewhat heavy, even after the egg whites have been folded in.

5. Scrape the batter into the pan. Before putting the pan into the oven, spin it on the countertop; this will help prevent the cake from forming too much of a dome in the middle. Bake for 30 minutes. Rotate the cake front to back, and continue to bake for another 30 minutes, until a toothpick comes out just about clean. Cool on a rack.

6. While the cake is cooling, heat the jam with the water and stir until smooth. Begin with 1 tablespoon of water, and if the mixture seems too thick to spread, add another tablespoon. Cool. Cut the cake in half horizontally and spread the bottom half with the jam. Top with the other layer. Dust the top with confectioners' sugar and serve, with whipped cream if you wish.

ADVANCE PREPARATION: This cake is a good keeper. Wrapped airtight, it will keep for about 5 days. It can also be frozen.

LOUKOUMADES

Greece • **Makes about 4 dozen**

Loukoumades are the Greek answer to doughnuts, and kids love them. Adults don't mind them either, drizzled as they are with fabulous Greek honey or dunked in honey syrup. The dough is a yeasted spongy batter that resembles blini batter. In Algeria, there's a similar dish with a similar name, *Loqma*.

FOR THE BATTER

2½ teaspoons (1 package) active dry yeast

3 cups lukewarm water

1 teaspoon sugar

1 cup lukewarm milk

½ teaspoon salt

2 large eggs, beaten

About 4 cups unbleached all-purpose flour

FOR THE SYRUP

1 cup honey, preferably Greek pine or thyme honey

2 cups sugar

1 cup water

Canola, peanut, or vegetable oil for frying

Ground cinnamon for sprinkling

1. *Make the batter:* In a large bowl, dissolve the yeast in 1 cup of the lukewarm water. Stir in the sugar and leave until the water clouds and begins to bubble, about 5 minutes. Add the remaining 2 cups water and the milk. Beat in the salt and eggs, and begin to stir in the flour, 1 cup at a time. Stir until you have a thick, yeasty batter. Cover and set aside in a warm place to rise for 1 hour, until very bubbly.

2. *Meanwhile, make the syrup:* Combine the honey, sugar, and water in a large saucepan and bring to a boil over medium heat. Reduce the heat and simmer for 10 to 12 minutes, until thick. Set aside to cool.

3. Heat 3 inches of vegetable oil in a large saucepan (or a deep fryer) to 350°F. Stir the batter and carefully drop spoonfuls, about 2 tablespoons each, into the hot oil. Fry until golden, flip over, and fry the other side until golden. Remove from the oil with a spider or a slotted spoon and drain briefly on a rack. Add more oil if necessary, but bring the heat back to 350°F before adding more batter.

4. Using a slotted spoon, dip the *loukoumades* into the syrup, then place on a platter and sprinkle with cinnamon. Serve hot.

ADVANCE PREPARATION: The batter can be made up to a day ahead and refrigerated.

TIP HOW TO CUT A CAKE INTO LAYERS
First, cut a small notch in the side of the cake so that you can easily line up the layers when you put it back together. Use a long serrated bread knife. Hold it horizontally against the cake where you want to cut it, resting the side of your hand on the work surface. Cut about 2 inches into the cake, then rotate the cake against the knife as you gently saw with the knife. Once you have turned the cake a full circle, slide the knife through.

BAKLAVA WITH MIXED DRIED FRUIT AND NUTS

Greece • **Makes one 15 × 17-inch pan**

Baklava is that incredibly sweet Greek dessert made with phyllo, nuts, and lots of sugar and honey. The filling is a wonderful mixture of dried fruit and nuts, spiced with cinnamon, nutmeg, allspice, and orange zest. It's sweet but not as cloying as many baklavas are, and it's fun to make. It's also pretty, and irresistible.

FOR THE BAKLAVA

½ pound phyllo dough (see Note)

2½ cups finely chopped walnuts, or a mixture of walnuts and almonds

1 cup dried fruit, such as apricots, raisins, and figs, chopped

1 teaspoon ground cinnamon

½ teaspoon freshly grated nutmeg

¼ teaspoon ground allspice

1 teaspoon finely grated orange zest

8 tablespoons (1 stick) unsalted butter, melted

30 whole cloves

FOR THE SYRUP

¾ cup sugar

¾ cup water

⅓ cup honey

1 tablespoon fresh lemon juice

Note: *Always thaw phyllo dough in the refrigerator overnight, not at room temperature. If you thaw it too quickly, it could become soggy.*

1. *Make the baklava:* Heat the oven to 350°F. Butter a 12 × 15-inch half-sheet baking pan. Unwrap the phyllo, fold it in half, and place it, like a book, on a sheet of parchment. Cover with a damp towel.

2. Combine the chopped nuts, dried fruit, cinnamon, nutmeg, allspice, and orange zest. Divide into 5 equal portions. Place the folded "book" of phyllo in front of you on the sheet of parchment, and open the first "page." Brush with melted butter, and turn the next 5 pages, brushing each page with butter. Top the sixth page with 1 portion of the filling in an even layer. Turn another 6 pages, brushing each one with butter, and top with another portion of the filling. Repeat until the phyllo is opened up to the middle of the book. Top the filled side, press down on the baklava, and continue to turn the pages, brushing each one with butter and sprinkling the filling over the top every 6 pages, until all the pages have been "turned" and all of the filling is used up. Lift up the parchment and transfer the baklava on the parchment to the baking sheet. Press down on the top sheet.

3. With a sharp knife or offset serrated knife, cut the baklava into 2-inch-wide diagonal strips. Turn the pan and cut 2-inch strips on the diagonal, to make diamonds. Make sure you cut down all the way through the bottom of the baklava. Place a clove in the middle of each diamond. Bake for 45 minutes to 1 hour, until crispy and golden brown.

4. *Meanwhile, make the syrup:* Combine the sugar, water, honey, and lemon juice in a medium saucepan and bring to a boil over medium heat. Reduce the heat and simmer for 5 minutes.

5. When the baklava is ready, remove from the oven and drizzle on the syrup, making sure to pour it all over the baklava. Cool slightly. Serve warm or at room temperature.

ADVANCE PREPARATION: The baklava will keep for 5 days, tightly covered.

SWEET DESSERT COUSCOUS WITH CITRUS AND POMEGRANATE
Tunisia and Algeria • **Serves 8 to 10**

This is called *mesfouf* in Tunisia and Algeria, where it is made with a very fine couscous that we cannot get in the United States. It sometimes contains vegetables as well as fruit, and it is served at the beginning of the evening meal, and sometimes for breakfast. It looks very nice on a buffet table, where I would serve it as a dessert.

2 cups water

⅓ cup sugar

1 tablespoon orange flower water or rose water

2 tablespoons unsalted butter

½ cup golden raisins or currants

1½ cups couscous

¾ teaspoon ground cinnamon

¼ teaspoon salt

1 tablespoon finely grated orange zest

2 navel oranges

16 dates, pitted and seeded lengthwise

Seeds from 1 pomegranate

3 tablespoons pine nuts, lightly toasted

Confectioners' sugar for dusting (optional)

1. Combine the water and sugar in a saucepan and bring to a boil. Reduce the heat and simmer gently until the sugar has dissolved and the syrup thickens slightly, about 5 minutes. Remove from the heat and add the orange flower water, butter, and raisins. Cool for 15 minutes.

2. Place the couscous in a large bowl. Stir in the cinnamon, salt, and orange zest. Pour on the syrup and stir once. Let sit for 20 minutes, until all of the liquid has been absorbed. Stir the couscous from time to time and rub between your thumbs and fingers so that it doesn't lump.

3. Steam the couscous, either in a microwave or in a colander set over a saucepan with boiling water, following the instructions on page 337. Remove from the heat and return to the bowl if you have steamed the couscous in a colander.

4. Peel the oranges, holding them above the couscous so that any juice that escapes will go into the couscous. Remove the skin and pith at the same time by holding the knife against the orange at a slight angle and turning the orange against the knife, so that the skin comes off in a spiral. Squeeze the skin over the couscous to obtain any juice from the pulp that you may have cut away with the skin. Cut one of the oranges in half crosswise, then cut the sections from between the membranes, and toss with the couscous along with half the dates. Slice the other orange into rounds.

5. Mound the couscous onto a platter, shaping it like a cone. Decorate with the remaining dates, the orange slices, pomegranate seeds, and pine nuts. Serve warm or at room temperature. If you wish, dust with confectioners' sugar just before serving.

ADVANCE PREPARATION: You can make this through Step 3 up to 3 days ahead, and keep in the refrigerator. You'll want to steam the couscous again before proceeding with the recipe. Or you can make the couscous through Step 5 several hours before serving.

ACKNOWLEDGMENTS

MANY PEOPLE HELPED ALONG THE WAY WITH THIS PROJECT. My agent, Angela Miller, helped me get it off the ground, encouraging me to write about what I felt passionate about, which was all she needed to say.

Thanks to Margot Schupf for acquiring the book for Rodale; to Marya Dalrymple for finishing the job; and especially to the hard-working, talented editor Roy Finamore. I'm so glad I finally got to work with you and profit from your skills.

I am very grateful to Dana Beier, for helping me in the early stages of this book with recipe testing. Thank you for the many hours you put in with me in my kitchen.

Diane Kochilas opened her doors and her kitchen to me in Ikaria, and I thank her for her hospitality, her generosity with recipes, and her wonderful cooking classes. I am sure that my 2005 trip to that fabulous Greek island won't be my last.

Thanks to Goran Gajic and Mira Furlan for introducing me to Istria, and for taking me to the wonderful *agrituristica* restaurant Alla Beccaccia not once but twice!

For more than 25 years, Christine Picasso, my "French mother," has been my host in Provence, and when I was working on this book she extended her hospitality beyond Provence to Màlaga. I thank her for that, and for so much more.

Thank you to Marco, Lorella, Carlotta, and Costanza for walking us through the streets of Bologna on the hottest night of the summer, and for always being such wonderful hosts and guides in Italy.

My close friend and cooking buddy Clifford Wright has been a generous and invaluable source of information about, and recipes from, the Mediterranean. He is the person I turn to whenever I have a question, and he always has an answer.

I am grateful to Rosalba and Armando Ciannamea, proprietors of Il Frantoio, in Puglia, for being such gracious and inspiring hosts. Their beautiful hotel was the most wonderful and delicious base for exploring the wonders of Puglian cuisine.

I could not have done the research required for this book had I not had Rachel Monas along with me as travel companion and "big sister" to Liam. Thank you so much for everything.

Finally, thanks to my son, Liam, for being such a good sport and curious eater on our travels and at home, for loving good food, and for being you.

Martha Rose Shulman
Los Angeles, July 2007

I like going into Italian delis, and Persian and Middle Eastern markets, for ingredients I can't find at the farmers' market or in local supermarkets. Shopping online is the next best thing.

Adriana's Caravan

www.adrianascaravan.com

A food products source that bills itself as the place for "every ingredient for every recipe you'll ever read"—and they're right.

Best Turkish Food

bestturkishfood.com

A Chicago firm offering Turkish food products.

Bubalus Bubalis Mozzarella

www.realmozzarella.com

Buffalo milk mozzarella and more.

Gastarea

www.gastarea.com

An Italian site in Italian and English offering a wide range of Italian gourmet ingredients.

Gourmet Sardinia

www.gourmetsardinia.com

A good site for all things Sardinian including food products.

Holy Land Olive Oil

www.holylandoliveoil.com

Organic Palestinian olive oil produced by small farmers in the northern West Bank; portions of proceeds will benefit children.

Kalustyan's

www.kalustyans.com

Site of a Manhattan-based spice purveyor with a wide range of spices and spice blends and Middle Eastern products.

King Arthur Flour

www.kingarthurflour.com

King Arthur Flour company website. An excellent source for a variety of flours and baking equipment.

La Tienda

www.LaTienda.com

A good source for Spanish food products.

Parthenon Foods

www.parthenonfoods.com

An excellent site for all kinds of hard-to-find Mediterranean food products.

Pasta Cheese Gourmet

www.pastacheese.com

An excellent source for hard-to-find Mediterranean products.

Penzeys Spices

www.penzeys.com

A complete catalogue of spices and herbs at very good prices.

Products from Spain

www.productsfromspain.net

A good site for Spanish products.

The Rogers Collection

www.rogersintl.com

Importers of fine Mediterranean artisanal food products.

Shamra

www.shamra.com

Mediterranean and Middle Eastern food products.

Surfas

www.surfasonline.com

An excellent source for both cookware and imported ingredients of all kinds.

Taste of Turkey

www.tasteofturkey.com

High-quality products from Turkey, the Middle East, and the Mediterranean.

Tolumba

www.tulumba.com

A great site for Turkish food products.

Yiyelim Foods

www.turkishfoodstore.com

A wide range of Turkish foods.

Zingerman's

www.zingermans.com

Web site of Zingerman's, an Ann Arbor, Michigan, purveyor offering a wide range of Mediterranean products such as olive oils, cheeses, and vinegars.

SELECT BIBLIOGRAPHY

Alford, Jeffrey, and Naomi Duguid. *Flatbreads & Flavors.* New York: William Morrow, 1995.

Basan, Ghillie. *Classic Turkish Cooking.* New York: St. Martin's Press, 1997.

Batali, Mario. *Molto Italiano.* New York: Ecco, 2005.

Boubezari, Karimène. *Ma Cuisine Algérienne.* Aix-en-Provence: Edisud, 2002.

Bsisu, May S. *The Arab Table.* New York: William Morrow, 2005.

Casas, Penelope. *The Foods and Wines of Spain.* New York: Alfred A. Knopf, 1982.

Delicioso! The Regional Cooking of Spain. New York: Alfred A. Knopf, 1996.

Certain, Christophe. *Cuisine Pied-Noir.* Aix-en-Provence: Edisud, 2001.

Chaudron, Maud. *La cuisine méditerranéenne à l'huile d'olive.* Nîmes: C. Lacour, 2001.

Downie, David. *Cooking the Roman Way.* New York: HarperCollins Publishers, 2003.

Field, Carol. *The Italian Baker.* New York: Harper & Row, 1985.

Celebrating Italy. New York: William Morrow, 1990.

Italy in Small Bites. New York: William Morrow, 1993.

Giusti-Lanham, Hedy, and Andrea Dodi. *The Cuisine of Venice and Surrounding Northern Regions.* New York: Barrons, 1978.

Helou, Anissa. *Mediterranean Street Food.* New York: HarperCollins Publishers, 2002.

Husson, René, et Philippe Galmiche. *Recettes de Provence.* Saint-Afrique, France: Éditions Fleurines, 2001.

Jenkins, Nancy Harmon. *The Mediterranean Diet Cookbook.* New York: Bantam Books, 1994.

Jenkins, Steven. *Cheese Primer.* New York: Workman Publishing, 1996

Kaneva-Johnson, Maria. *The Melting Pot: Balkan Food and Cookery.* Devon, England: Prospect Books, 1995.

Kasper, Lynne Rossetto. *The Italian Country Table.* New York: Scribner, 1999.

Kochilas, Diane. *The Food and Wine of Greece.* New York: St. Martin's Press, 1990.

The Greek Vegetarian. New York: St. Martin's Press, 1996.

The Glorious Foods of Greece. New York: William Morrow, 2001.

Maureau, Andrée. *Tians et Petits Farcis.* Aix-en-Provence: Edisud, 2003.

Desserts et Douceurs en Provence. Aix-en-Provence: Edisud, 2003.

Middione, Carlo. *The Food of Southern Italy.* New York: William Morrow, 1987.

Morse, Kitty. *The Vegetarian Table: North Africa.* San Francisco: Chronicle Books, 1996.

Plotkin, Fred. *Italy for the Gourmet Traveler.* Boston and New York: Little, Brown and Company, 1996.

Recipes from Paradise. Boston and New York: Little, Brown and Company, 1997.

Robinson, Jancis. *The Oxford Companion to Wine.* New York: Oxford University Press, 1994, 1999.

Shulman, Martha Rose. *Supper Club Chez Martha Rose.* New York: Atheneum, 1988.

Mediterranean Light. New York: Bantam Books, 1989.

Entertaining Light. New York: Bantam Books, 1991.

Provençal Light. New York: Bantam Books, 1994.

Ready When You Are. New York: Clarkson Potter/Publishers, 2003.

Wells, Patricia. *The Food Lover's Guide to France.* New York: Workman Publishing, 1987.

The Provence Cookbook. New York: HarperCollins Publishers, 2004.

Willinger, Faith. *Red, White & Greens.* New York: HarperCollins Publishers, 1996.

Wolfert, Paula. *The Cooking of the Eastern Mediterranean.* New York: HarperCollins Publishers, 1994.

Wright, Clifford A. *Cucina Paradiso.* New York: Simon & Schuster, 1992.

A Mediterranean Feast. New York: William Morrow, 1999.

Mediterranean Vegetables. Boston: The Harvard Common Press, 2001.

Little Foods of the Mediterranean. Boston: The Harvard Common Press, 2003.

Yard, Sherry. *Desserts by the Yard.* Boston: Houghton Mifflin, 2003.

ALGERIA

EGGS AND CHEESE
Chakchouka, 194
North African Fried Pepper Stew with Eggs, 194

STARTERS, SNACKS, AND MEZE
Ajlūk, 98
Eggplant Ajlūk, 98
Fava Bean Salad, 114
North African Carrot "Compote," 98
Winter Squash Ajlūk, 98
Zucchini Ajlūk, 98

SWEETS AND DESSERTS
Sweet Dessert Couscous with Citrus and
Pomegranate, 367

VEGETABLES AND BEANS
Fava Bean and Potato Stew, 280–81

THE BALKANS

RICE, COUSCOUS, AND OTHER GRAINS
Tomato and Rice Pilaf, 327–28
Zucchini, Tomato, and Rice Pilaf, 328–29

SAVORY PIES AND GRATINS
Balkan-Style Moussaka, 258–59
Cabbage Gratin, 260–61
Zucchini, Potato, and Artichoke
Moussaka, 259–60

SOUPS
Iced Cucumber Soup with Walnuts, 167
White Bean Soup, 167–68

STARTERS, SNACKS, AND MEZE
Eggplant and Red Pepper Purée, 125
Red Pepper Purée, 124–25

VEGETABLES AND BEANS
Baked Beans, 310

BOSNIA

BREADS, PIZZA, AND PANINI
Bosnian Flat Bread, 47

SAVORY PIES AND GRATINS
Coiled Summer Squash Pitta, 245–46
Potato Pitta, 244–45

BULGARIA

STARTERS, SNACKS, AND MEZE
Leeks Cooked in White Wine, 117

CROATIA

PASTA
Strozzapreti with Wild Arugula and Wild
Asparagus, 216

RICE, COUSCOUS, AND OTHER GRAINS
Tomato and Zucchini Risotto, 323–24

SOUPS
Istrian Minestrone, 151–52
Manestra, 151–52

STARTERS, SNACKS, AND MEZE
Leeks Cooked in White Wine, 117

SWEETS AND DESSERTS
Summer Stone Fruit Strudel, 353–54

EASTERN MEDITERRANEAN

BREADS, PIZZA, AND PANINI
Sesame Bread Rings, 53–54

EGYPT

STARTERS, SNACKS, AND MEZE
Lentil Salad, 119–20

FRANCE

APERITIFS
The Mauresque, 34
Sirops à l'Eau, 34
Syrup Spritzers, 34

BREADS, PIZZA, AND PANINI
Fougasse aux Olives, 44–45
Niçoise Chick Pea Flour Pancake, 53
Pissaladière, 63
Pompe à l'Huile, 52
Provençal Bread with Olives, 44–45
Provençal Green Olive and Cheese Bread, 55
Provençal Onion Pizza, 63
Provençal Orange-Scented Brioche, 52
Socca, 53

FRANCE *(cont.)*

BREADS, PIZZA, AND PANINI
Walnut Fougasse, 45
Whole Wheat Fougasse, 45

EGGS AND CHEESE
Cheese Soufflé with Truffles, 199
Large Ratatouille Omelet, 184
Piperade, 179
Provençal Flat Onion Omelet, 185
Provençal Flat Sorrel Omelet, 186
Provençal Flat Swiss Chard Omelet,
186–87
Provençal Flat Tomato Omelet, 185–86
Scrambled Eggs with Pepper, 179
Soufflé aux Truffes, 199
Truccha, 186–87
Truffle Omelet, 182–83

RICE, COUSCOUS, AND OTHER GRAINS
The Doctor's Baiana, 332–33

SAUCES, DRESSINGS, AND CONDIMENTS
Aïoli, 72–73
Béchamel, 77–78
Fresh Tomato Concassée, 79
Olive Oil Béchamel, 78
Pistou, 76
Provençal and Catalan Garlic Mayonnaise,
72–73
Rouille, 73–74
Spicy Garlic Mayonnaise, 73–74
Vinaigrette to Keep in the Refrigerator, 82
Walnut Vinaigrette, 82–83

SAVORY PIES AND GRATINS
Bohemienne Gratinée, 246
Cabbage Galette, 236–37
Eggplant and Tomato Gratin, 246
Mushroom and Greens Gratin, 234
Mushrooms and Greens Tart, 233–34
Potato and Mushroom Gratin, 252
Provençal Fennel and Tomato Gratin, 251
Provençal Greens Gratin, 253–54
Provençal Kale and Cabbage Gratin, 254
Provençal Pumpkin Torte, 237–38
Provençal Summer Potato Gratin, 252–53
Provençal Summer Squash, Red Pepper, and
Tomato Gratin, 255–56
Provençal Swiss Chard Gratin, 257–58
Provençal Zucchini and Greens Torte,
234–35
Pumpkin Galette, 238
Pumpkin Gratin, 238
Summer Squash Gratin, 256
Zucchini and Greens Gratin, 235

SOUPS
Bouillabaisse of Fresh Peas, 156–57
Garlic Soup, 161–62
Greens Bouillabaisse, 158
Lentil Soup with Goat Cheese, 160–61
Provençal Chick Pea Soup, 160
Provençal Lentil and Tomato Soup, 161
Provençal Wheat Berry Soup, 159
Provençal Winter Squash Soup, 162–63
Soupe au Pistou, 155–56
Spinach Bouillabaisse, 157–58
Tomato, Egg, and Bread Bouillabaisse, 158

STARTERS, SNACKS, AND MEZE
Beet and Beet Greens Salad, 94
Beet and Beet Greens Salad with Skordalia, 94
Cauliflower à la Grecque, 100–101
Couscous "Tabbouleh," 97
Farro Salad, 112
Green Olive and Almond Tapenade, 122
Green Olive Tapenade, 122
Mesclun Salad, 118
Provençal Chick Pea Salad, 102
Roasted Salted Almonds with Cayenne, 91
Salad with Warm Goat Cheese and Basil
Sauce, 117
Tapenade, 121–22
Warm Goat Cheese Salad, 115
Warm Tomatoes with Goat Cheese, 128
White Bean "Brandade," 91

SWEETS AND DESSERTS
Apricot Clafouti, 353
Cherry Clafouti, 348
Cherry Financier, 347
Fig and Red Wine Compote, 350
Financier, 346–47
Melon with Muscat de Beaumes-de-Venise,
350
Peaches in Red Wine and Banyuls, 352–53
Quince Compote, 357

VEGETABLES AND BEANS
Aïoli Monstre, 293–94
Artichokes à la Barigoule, 265
Artichokes à la Barigoule with Fava Beans, 265
Braised Fennel with Parmesan, 282
Garlic Green Beans, 272
Huge Aïoli Feast, 293–94
One More Ratatouille, 297
Provençal Artichoke, Mushroom, and Potato
Ragout, 268
Tian Niçoise, 298
Tomato and Bean Gratin, 304
Tomato and Bean Ragout, 303
Two Methods for One Ratatouille, 296–97

GREECE

BREADS, PIZZA, AND PANINI
Greek Country Bread, 47–48
Paximathia, 49
Rusks, 49

EGGS AND CHEESE
Baked Spicy Feta, 198
Baked Vegetable Omelet, 188–89
Greek Fried Cheese, 198
Poached Eggs with Tzatziki, 188
Saganaki, 198
Scrambled Eggs with Tomatoes and Feta, 189

PASTA
Pasta with Tomatoes, Beans, and Feta, 219

RICE, COUSCOUS, AND OTHER GRAINS
Bulgur and Chick Pea Pilaf, 333

SAUCES, DRESSINGS, AND CONDIMENTS
Garlic and Potato Purée, 80
Skordalia, 80

SAVORY PIES AND GRATINS
Cauliflower Gratin with Feta and Olives, 261
Fennel and Scallion Pie, 238–39
Greek Pie Crust, 229–30
Greens and Sweet Onion Pie, 239–40
Spanakopita, 243–44
Winter Squash and Leek Pie, 241–42
Winter Squash Pie with Bulgur and Feta,
    240–41
Zucchini, Potato, and Artichoke
    Moussaka, 259–60
Zucchini and Herb Pie, 242–43

STARTERS, SNACKS, AND MEZE
Apricot Yogurt Dip, 91
Beet and Beet Greens Salad, 94
Beet and Beet Greens Salad with Skordalia, 94
Black-Eyed Pea Salad, 122–23
Black-Eyed Pea Salad with Feta, 123
Cheese and Herb Phyllo Triangles, 137–38
Cheese and Winter Squash Phyllo
    Triangles, 138–39
Cretan Barley Rusks with Tomato Topping, 137
Diane Kochilas's Zucchini Fritters, 130
Dolmades, 114–15
Eggplant Slices with Tomato Sauce and Feta, 109
Fava, 123–24
Grape Leaves Stuffed with Rice, Onions, and
    Herbs, 114–15
Mushroom and Feta Phyllo Triangles, 139, 141
Purslane Salad, 118
Roasted Eggplant Salad with Feta and Green
    Peppers, 109

Split Pea Purée, 123–24
Summer Salad, 119
Tzatziki, 106

SWEETS AND DESSERTS
Baklava with Mixed Dried Fruit and Nuts, 366
Loukoumades, 365
Quince Spoon Sweet, 358

VEGETABLES AND BEANS
Artichoke and Fresh Fava Stew, 269–70
Artichoke and Potato Stew, 270–71
Baked Beans with Honey and Dill, 311
Black-Eyed Peas with Wild Fennel, 306
Cheese-and-Vegetable-Stuffed Eggplants, 277–78
Fassoulia, 305–6
Fried Potatoes with Tomatoes and Oregano, 291
Ikarian Summer Vegetable Stew, 300–301
Large White Beans with Tomatoes and
    Garlic, 305–6
Mashed Black-Eyed Peas with Garlic Purée, 306–7
Potato and Olive Stew, 291–92
Sautéed Peppers with Tomatoes, 288
Soufiko, 300–301
Stewed Green Beans with Tomatoes, 272

IRAN

EGGS AND CHEESE
Persian Herb Omelet, 190

RICE, COUSCOUS, AND OTHER GRAINS
Chelo, 329
Persian Rice, 329

ITALY

APERITIFS
Bellini, 33
Campari Orange Cocktail, 34
CampariSoda, 33
Il Frantoio's "Special Caffè Freddo," 35
Italian Cream Sodas, 34–35
Sirops à l'Eau, 34
Sparkling Wine and Peach Cocktail, 33
Syrup Spritzers, 34

BREADS, PIZZA, AND PANINI
Artichoke Heart and Red Pepper Panini, 66
Baby Spinach and Fontina Panini, 67
Bell Pepper Focaccia, 44
Biga, 39
Calzone with Tomato and Kale Filling, 64
Cheese Focaccia, 44
Durum Flour Bread from Altamura, 40–41
Eggplant and Red Pepper Panini, 65
Eggplant and Tomato Panini, 65
Focaccia, 43–44

ITALY *(cont.)*

BREADS, PIZZA, AND PANINI
Greens and Fontina Panini, 66
Grilled Zucchini, Goat Cheese, and Mint Panini, 65
Herb Focaccia, 44
Italian Flat Bread, 45
Mushroom and Gruyère Panini, 67
Pizza Bianca, 62
Pizza Dough, 56–57
Pizza Margherita, 58
Pizza Marinara with Tomatoes and Garlic, 57–58
Pizza with Mozzarella and Cherry Tomatoes, 59
Pizza with Mushrooms and Artichoke Hearts, 60
Pizza with Peppers, Tomato Sauce, and
    Mozzarella, 60–61
Pizza with Tomato, Eggplant, and Mozzarella, 59
Pizza with Tomato Sauce, Mozzarella, and
    Arugula, 61
Pizza with Tomato Sauce and Potatoes, 62–63
Pugliese Bread, 41–42
Semolina Bread with Sesame Seeds, 42
Semolina Bread with Tomato and Zucchini, 43
Tomato and Mozzarella Focaccia, 44
Tomato Focaccia, 44
"White" Pizza, 62
Whole Wheat Country Bread, 39–40
Whole Wheat Focaccia, 44
Whole Wheat Pizza Dough, 57

EGGS AND CHEESE
Asparagus with Egg Sauce, 181
Asparagus with Scrambled Eggs, 181
Baked Artichoke Heart Omelet, 187
Basic Strata, 196–97
Homemade Ricotta Cheese, 195
Individual Eggplant and Tomato
    Frittata, 184–85
Ricotta Frittata with Asparagus, 183
Ricotta Frittata with Fresh Herbs, 183
Ricotta Frittata with Zucchini, 183
Sformato with Ricotta and Greens, 195–96
Strata with Greens, or with Tomatoes and
    Greens, 197
Strata with Mushrooms and Sage, 197
Strata with Tomatoes and Thyme, 197
Tortino, 187
Wild Mushroom Frittata, 182

PASTA
Baked Eggplant Stuffed with Pasta, 220
Baked Semolina Gnocchi with Butter and
    Parmesan, 225
Beet Green Lasagna, 207
Garganelli with Mushroom Sauce, 210
Gnocchi, 223–24

Gnocchi with Eggplant and Peppers, 224–25
Half-Moon Ravioli with Winter Squash Filling,
    204–6
Laganari with Eggplant, Tomato Sauce, and
    Oregano, 218
Lasagna with Greens and Tomato Sauce, 222–23
Orecchiette with Broccoli Rabe, 211
Orecchiette with Raw and Cooked Tomato
    Sauce, 212
Orecchiette with Uncooked Tomatoes and
    Arugula, 211
Pansôti, 207–8
Pasta e Fagiole, 218–19
Pasta with Beans, 218–19
Pasta with Ligurian Artichoke Sauce, 213
Pasta with Uncooked Tomatoes, Basil, Capers,
    Olives, and Feta, 212–13
Penne with Asparagus and Eggs, 214
Perciatelli with Tomato Sauce and
    Ricotta, 214–15
Potato and Mint Ravioli, 208
Ravioli with Beet Greens and Ricotta, 206–7
Ravioli with Greens, Herbs, and Ricotta, 207–8
Spaghetti alla Chitarra with Arugula Pesto and
    Tomato Sauce, 215
Spaghetti with Black Pepper and Pecorino, 215
Trenette with Pesto, Green Beans, and Potatoes, 217
Whole Wheat Spaghetti with Green Beans and
    Tomato Sauce, 217

RICE, COUSCOUS, AND OTHER GRAINS
Artichoke Risotto, 316–17
Asparagus and Fava Bean Risotto, 318
Barley Risotto with Asparagus or Green Beans
    and Pesto, 330
Barley Risotto with Pesto and Ricotta Salata, 330
Farro Risotto with Dried Mushrooms, Favas, and
    Garlic, 331–32
Farro Risotto with Green Beans, 332
Fava Bean and Green Garlic Risotto, 317–18
Mushroom Risotto, 318–19
Polenta with Tomato Sauce and Parmesan, 333
Radicchio Risotto, 320
Red Pepper Risotto with Saffron, 319
Red Risotto with Beet Greens, 320
Red Wine Risotto with Cauliflower, 321
Risi e Bisi, 321–22
Risi e Bisi with Mushrooms, 322
Risotto Milanese, 316
Summer Squash Risotto, 322–23
Winter Squash Risotto, 324–25

SAUCES, DRESSINGS, AND CONDIMENTS
Almond, Basil, and Tomato Sauce, 79–80
Arugula Pesto, 75
Basic Tomato Sauce, 78

Gremolata, 85
Ligurian Walnut Sauce, 76–77
Marinara Sauce, 78
Oil and Vinegar Dressing, 82
Peperonata, 85
Pesto Genovese, 74–75
Quicker Basic Tomato Sauce, 79
Southern Tomato Sauce, 79
Stewed Peppers and Tomatoes, 85

SAVORY PIES AND GRATINS
Eggplant Parmesan, 250
Ligurian Artichoke and Greens Torta, 231–32
Purple Cauliflower Gratin, 257
Spinach and Ricotta Torta, 235

SOUPS
Cabbage and White Bean Minestrone, 152–53
Kale Minestrone, 148–49
Lemon Stracciatella, 155
Lentil Minestrone with Greens, 149, 151
Minestrone, 146–47
Pappa al Pomodoro, 148
Ribolitta, 147
Stracciatella, 154–55
Stracciatella with Asparagus, 155
Tuscan Bean and Farro Soup with Cabbage and
    Winter Squash, 153–54
Tuscan Bread and Tomato Soup, 148

STARTERS AND SNACKS
Bruschetta, 135
Cauliflower with Capers, Parsley, and Vinegar, 101
Crostini, 135
Deep-Fried Rice and Mozzarella Balls, 133–34
Frico, 132–33
Grilled Eggplant with Hot Red Pepper Flakes, 108
Grilled Mozzarella in Radicchio Bundles, 131–32
Grilled Zucchini Slices, 129
Italian Bread Salad, 129
Marinated Carrots, 99
Marinated Eggplant, 106–7
Marinated Mushrooms, 120–21
Mushroom and Celery Salad, 121
Panzanella, 129
Sautéed Eggplant with Tomatoes and Balsamic
    Vinegar, 107
Supplì al Telefono, 133–34

SWEETS AND DESSERTS
Almond Biscotti, 345
Anise Butter Cookies, 361–62
Buckwheat Cake from the Alto Adige, 364–65
Coffee Granita, 360
Fregolata Veneziana, 362, 364
Honey-Orange Biscotti, 345
Lemon Butter Cookies, 362

Peach Gelato, 352
Ricotta Cheesecake, 360–61
Venetian Cornmeal Shortbread, 362, 364

VEGETABLES AND BEANS
Asparagi alla Parmigiana, 271
Asparagus with Parmesan, 271
Asparagus with Parmesan and Eggs, 271
Braised Broccoli with White Wine, 272–73
Braised Fennel with Parmesan, 282
Broccoli alla Romana, 272–73
Caponata, 276–77
Carrots with Currants and Pine Nuts, 275
Dried Fava Beans and Greens, 309
Easy White Beans with Tomatoes and Garlic, 305
Fritteda, 268–69
Kale with Garlic and Olive Oil, 283
Ligurian Ratatouille, 298–99
Pan-Fried Zucchini with Mint and
    Pepperoncini, 292
Pugliese Stuffed Artichokes, 266
Roasted Potatoes and Root Vegetables with
    Rosemary, 290
Roasted Potatoes with Rosemary, 290
Roman-Style Braised Baby Artichokes with Parsley
    and Mint, 266
Sautéed Mushrooms with Gremolata, 284
Sicilian Spring Vegetable Stew, 268–69
Spring Peas with Sugar, 287
Stewed Eggplant and Onions, 276
Stuffed Artichokes, 265–66
Sweet and Sour Cabbage, 273
Tomato and Bean Gratin, 304
Tomato and Bean Ragout, 303
White Bean and Chard Gratin, 304
White Bean and Chard Ragout, 304
Wild Mushroom Ragout, 285
Wild Mushrooms with Tomatoes and Basil, 286

LEBANON

STARTERS, SNACKS, AND MEZE
Lebanese Beets with Yogurt, 95
Tabbouleh, 96–97

MIDDLE EAST

BREADS, PIZZA, AND PANINI
Arab Bread, 51

SAUCES, DRESSINGS, AND CONDIMENTS
Chermoula, 86
Parsley Sauce, 84
Pine Nut Tarator Sauce, 81
Tahini Garlic Sauce, 83
Turkish Tarator Sauce, 81
Za'tar, 24

MIDDLE EAST *(cont.)*

STARTERS, SNACKS, AND MEZE
Baba Gannouj, 110–11
Bread and Vegetable Salad, 128–29
Chick Pea and Bulgur Salad, 102–3
Deep-Fried Cauliflower, 101
Falafel, 104–5
Fattoush, 128–29
Grilled Eggplant Purée with Mint and Almonds, 110
Hummus, 103
Lebanese Beets with Yogurt, 95
Middle Eastern Cabbage Salad with Lemon and Dill, 98
Middle Eastern Cabbage Salad with Yogurt, Lemon, and Dill, 98
Muhammara, 126
Swiss Chard Stalk and Tahini Dip, 127–28

VEGETABLES AND BEANS
Arab Eggplant, Tomato, and Chick Pea Casserole, 280
Chick Pea Fattet, 308–9

MOROCCO

BREADS, PIZZA, AND PANINI
Moroccan Flat Bread, 54–55

SAUCES, DRESSINGS, AND CONDIMENTS
Ras al-Hanut, 24

STARTERS, SNACKS, AND MEZE
Fresh Fava Bean Purée, 113
Grilled Eggplant and Pepper Salad, 111

NORTH AFRICA

SAUCES, DRESSINGS, AND CONDIMENTS
Preserved Lemons, 87

SOUPS
Tomato Soup with Cilantro and Vermicelli, 169

STARTERS, SNACKS, AND MEZE
North African Beet Salad, 95
Orange and Olive Salad, 122

PROVENCE

VEGETABLES AND BEANS
Wild Mushroom Ragout, 285

SPAIN

APERITIFS
Sangria, 34

EGGS AND CHEESE
Bar Pilar's Tortilla Española, 177
Piperade, 179

Scrambled Eggs with Pepper, 179
Spanish Omelet with Potatoes and Onions, 176–77
Sweet Green Pepper Tortilla from Murcia, 178–79
Tortilla Española, 176–77
Tortilla Murciana, 178

RICE, COUSCOUS, AND OTHER GRAINS
Vegetable Paella from El Palmar, 325–26

SAUCES, DRESSINGS, AND CONDIMENTS
Aïoli, 72–73
Catalan Ratatouille, 72
Provençal and Catalan Garlic Mayonnaise, 72–73
Romesco Sauce, 71
Samfaina, 72

SOUPS
Castilian Garlic Soup with Paprika and Saffron, 164–65
Cold Tomato and Roasted Pepper Soup, 166
Gazpacho, 165
Majorcan Bread and Vegetable Soup, 168
Potaje de Vigilia, 163–64
Salmorejo, 166
Vegetable Soup with Chick Peas and Spinach, 163–64
White Gazpacho with Grapes, 166

STARTERS, SNACKS, AND TAPAS
Andalusian Cabbage Salad, 97–98
Catalan Bread with Tomato, 135
Giant Favas with Mint, 112
Hearts of Romaine and Tomato Salad, 116
Mushrooms al Ajillo, 120
Mushrooms in Garlic Sauce, 120
Roasted Pepper Salad with Lettuce and Tomato, 124

VEGETABLES AND BEANS
Andalusian Chick Pea and Cabbage Stew, 307
Fassoulia, 305–6
Large White Beans with Tomatoes and Garlic, 305–6
Pan-Cooked Zucchini and Tomatoes, 293
Pisto, 293
Potatoes with Green Beans and Garlic, 289
Spicy Potatoes with Aïoli, 288–89
Stuffed Lipstick Peppers, 287–88
Valencia-Style Peas, 286–87

SYRIA

VEGETABLES AND BEANS
Spinach with Spices and Yogurt, 283

TUNISIA

EGGS AND CHEESE
Baked Potato, Onion, and Parsley Omelet, 192–93
Bell Pepper, Tomato, and Potato Omelet, 193
Carrot and Parsley Omelet, 193–94
Chakchouka, 194
North African Fried Pepper Stew with Eggs, 194
Tunisian Cauliflower Omelet, 194
Tunisian Eggplant Omelet, 190, 192

RICE, COUSCOUS, AND OTHER GRAINS
Cauliflower and Tomato Couscous, 339–40
Couscous with Chick Peas and Chard, 336–38
Couscous with Chick Peas and Spring
    Vegetables, 339
Couscous with Chick Peas and Winter
    Vegetables, 338–39
Couscous with Winter Squash, 340–41

SAUCES, DRESSINGS, AND CONDIMENTS
Harissa, 86
Tabil, 24

SOUPS
Bean and Vegetable Soup with Pastina,
    169–70
Chick Pea Breakfast Soup, 170–71
Hearty Bean, Chard, and Vermicelli Soup, 171
Hlelem, 171

STARTERS, SNACKS, AND MEZE
Ajlūk, 98
Carrot Salad, 99
Eggplant Ajlūk, 98
Grilled Pepper Salad, 126–27
Mechwya, 126–27
North African Carrot "Compote," 98
Ommok Houria, 99
Spicy Beet Salad, 95
Winter Squash Ajlūk, 98
Zucchini Ajlūk, 98

SWEETS AND DESSERTS
Sweet Dessert Couscous with Citrus and
    Pomegranate, 367

VEGETABLES AND BEANS
Spicy Vegetable Stew with Swiss Chard, Black-
    Eyed Peas, and Potatoes, 302
Spicy Vegetable Stew with Swiss Chard, Favas, and
    Potatoes, 302
Vegetable Ragout with Chick Peas, Turnips, and
    Greens, 301–2

TURKEY

BREADS, PIZZA, AND PANINI
Soft Turkish Pocket Bread, 50–51
Turkish Country Bread, 49–50

EGGS AND CHEESE
Poached Eggs with Garlic Sauce, 188
Turkish Menemem, 194

RICE, COUSCOUS, AND OTHER GRAINS
Eggplant Pilaf, 327
Sour Cherry Pilaf, 326

SAUCES, DRESSINGS, AND CONDIMENTS
Tahini Dressing, 83
Yogurt and Mint Spread, 81
Za'tar, 24

STARTERS, SNACKS, AND MEZE
Apricot Yogurt Dip, 91
Baked Hummus with Pine Nuts, 104
Beet and Yogurt Salad, 94–95
Cacik, 106
Grilled Feta in Grape Leaves, 132
Grilled Pepper Salad, 125
Kisir, 95–96
Mashed Carrots with Garlicky Yogurt, 100
Shredded Romaine and Radish Salad, 116
Small Bulgur Patties, 95–96
Spinach with Yogurt and Pine Nuts, 127
Turkish Cucumber and Yogurt Salad, 106
Turkish Hummus, 104

VEGETABLES AND BEANS
Chick Pea Stew, 308
Imam Bayildi, 278
Stuffed Cabbage, 274
Stuffed Cabbage with Egg-Lemon Sauce, 274
Stuffed Cabbage with Tahini Sauce, 275
Stuffed Eggplants (or Peppers), 279
Turkish Ratatouille, 299–300
Türlü, 299–300
Türlü Topped with a Fried Egg, 300

INDEX

Underscored page references indicate sidebars.

A

Absinthe, 35
Aïoli, 72–73
    Aïoli Monstre, 293–94
    Huge Aïoli Feast, 293–94
    Spicy Potatoes with Aïoli, 288–89
Ajvar, 93
Alla Beccaccia, recollection about, 180
Almonds, 27
    Almond, Basil, and Tomato Sauce, 79–80
    Almond Biscotti, 345
    Green Olive and Almond Tapenade, 122
    Grilled Eggplant Purée with Mint and Almonds, 110
    Roasted Salted Almonds with Cayenne, 91
    Romesco Sauce, 71
    White Gazpacho with Grapes, 166
Aniseed, 23
    Anise Butter Cookies, 361–62
Anise-flavored aperitifs, 23, 35
Aperitifs, 31–32
    anise-flavored, 23, 35
    Arak, 35
    Bellini, 33
    Biz Fizz, 33
    Campari Orange Cocktail, 34
    CampariSoda, 33
    Italian Cream Sodas, 34–35
    The Mauresque, 34
    Prosecco and Midori Cocktail, 33
    Sangria, 34
    Sirops à l'Eau, 34
    Sparkling Wine and Peach Cocktail, 33
    Syrup Spritzers, 34
Apricots
    Apricot Clafouti, 353
    Apricot Yogurt Dip, 91
    Baklava with Mixed Dried Fruit and Nuts, 366
    Strawberry and Apricot Salad, 356–57
    Summer Stone Fruit Strudel, 353–54
Arak, 35
Arborio rice
    cooking, for pies, 235
    for risotto, 315 (see also Risotto)
Aroma Café, recollection about, 247–49
Artichokes, 28
    Artichoke and Fresh Fava Stew, 269–70
    Artichoke and Potato Stew, 270–71
    Artichoke Heart and Red Pepper Panini, 66
    Artichokes à la Barigoule, 265
    Artichokes à la Barigoule with Fava Beans, 265
    Baked Artichoke Heart Omelet, 187
    Fritteda, 268–69
    how to prepare, 267
    Ligurian Artichoke and Greens Torta, 231–32
    Pasta with Ligurian Artichoke Sauce, 213
    Pizza with Mushrooms and Artichoke Hearts, 60
    Provençal Artichoke, Mushroom, and Potato Ragout, 268
    Pugliese Stuffed Artichokes, 266
    Roman-Style Braised Baby Artichokes with Parsley and Mint, 166
    Sicilian Spring Vegetable Stew, 268–69
    Stuffed Artichokes, 265–66
    Tortino, 187
    Vegetable Paella from El Palmar, 325–26
    Zucchini, Potato, and Artichoke Moussaka, 259–60
Arugula
    Arugula Pesto, 75
    Barley Risotto with Pesto and Ricotta Salata, 330
    Orecchiette with Uncooked Tomatoes and Arugula, 211
    Pizza with Tomato Sauce, Mozzarella, and Arugula, 61
    Spaghetti alla Chitarra with Arugula Pesto and Tomato Sauce, 215
    Strozzapreti with Wild Arugula and Wild Asparagus, 216
Asparagus
    Asparagi alla Parmigiana, 271
    Asparagus and Fava Bean Risotto, 318
    Asparagus with Egg Sauce, 181
    Asparagus with Parmesan, 271
    Asparagus with Parmesan and Eggs, 271
    Asparagus with Scrambled Eggs, 181
    Barley Risotto with Asparagus or Green Beans and Pesto, 330
    Penne with Asparagus and Eggs, 214
    Ricotta Frittata with Asparagus, 183
    Stracciatella with Asparagus, 155
    Strozzapreti with Wild Arugula and Wild Asparagus, 216

B

Baba Gannouj, 110–11
Baking dishes, recommended, 14–15
Baking stone, for two loaves, 41
Baklava
    Baklava with Mixed Dried Fruit and Nuts, 366
The Balkans, cheeses of, 21
Banneton, 40

Barley
  Barley Risotto with Asparagus or Green Beans and
    Pesto, 330
  Barley Risotto with Pesto and Ricotta Salata, 330
  Cretan Barley Rusks with Tomato Topping, 137
Basil, 23
  Almond, Basil, and Tomato Sauce, 79–80
  Barley Risotto with Pesto and Ricotta Salata, 330
  Eggs Filled with Pesto, 131
  Pasta with Uncooked Tomatoes, Basil, Capers, Olives,
    and Feta, 212–13
  Pesto Genovese, 74–75
  Pistou, 76
  Salad with Warm Goat Cheese and Basil Sauce, 117
  Trenette with Pesto, Green Beans, and Potatoes, 217
  Wild Mushrooms with Tomatoes and Basil, 286
Beans, 28
  Baked Beans, 310
  Baked Beans with Honey and Dill, 311
  Bean and Vegetable Soup with Pastina, 169–70
  black-eyed peas (see Black-eyed peas)
  Cabbage and White Bean Minestrone, 152–53
  chick peas (see Chick peas)
  Easy White Beans with Tomatoes and Garlic, 305
  Fassoulia, 305–6
  fava (see Fava beans)
  Hearty Bean, Chard, and Vermicelli Soup, 171
  Istrian Minestrone, 151–52
  Large White Beans with Tomatoes and Garlic, 305–6
  lupini, 93
  Macaroni with Beans and Cheese, 219
  Manestra, 151–52
  Mediterranean, 263–64
  Pasta e Fagiole, 218–19
  Pasta with Beans, 218–19
  Pasta with Tomatoes, Beans, and Feta, 219
  Tomato and Bean Gratin, 304
  Tomato and Bean Ragout, 303
  Tuscan Bean and Farro Soup with Cabbage and Winter
    Squash, 153–54
  types of, 150
  uses for, 150
  Vegetable Paella from El Palmar, 325–26
  White Bean and Chard Gratin, 304
  White Bean and Chard Ragout, 304
  White Bean "Brandade," 91
  White Bean Soup, 167–68
Béchamel, 77–78
  Olive Oil Béchamel, 78
Beekeeper, recollection about, 363
Beets and beet greens
  Beet and Beet Greens Salad, 94
  Beet and Beet Greens Salad with Skordalia, 94
  Beet and Yogurt Salad, 94–95
  Beet Green Lasagna, 207
  Lebanese Beets with Yogurt, 95
  North African Beet Salad, 95
  Ravioli with Beet Greens and Ricotta, 206–7
  Red Risotto with Beet Greens, 320
  Spicy Beet Salad, 95
Biscotti
  Almond Biscotti, 345
  Honey-Orange Biscotti, 345

Black-eyed peas, 150
  Black-Eyed Pea Salad, 122–23
  Black-Eyed Pea Salad with Feta, 123
  Black-Eyed Peas with Wild Fennel, 306
  Mashed Black-Eyed Peas with Garlic Purée, 306–7
  Spicy Vegetable Stew with Swiss Chard, Black-Eyed Peas,
    and Potatoes, 302
Black pepper, 26
  Spaghetti with Black Pepper and Pecorino, 215
Blood oranges
  Orange Sorbet with Blood Orange Salad, 358–59
Blueberries
  Raspberry or Blueberry Tart, 354
Borlotti beans, 150
Bosnia, savory pies of, 228
Bouillabaisse
  Bouillabaisse of Fresh Peas, 156–57
  Greens Bouillabaisse, 158
  Spinach Bouillabaisse, 157–58
  Tomato, Egg, and Bread Bouillabaisse, 158
Brandade
  White Bean "Brandade," 91
Bread crumbs, homemade, 250
Bread puddings, savory, 196. See also Stratas
Breads, 37–38
  baking two loaves with one stone, 41
  banneton for, 40
  Biga, 39
  Bruschetta, 134, 135, 136
  Catalan Bread with Tomato, 135
  Crostini, 134, 135, 136
  Durum Flour Bread from Altamura, 40–41
  flat, 45
    Bosnian Flat Bread, 47
    Chick Pea Fattet, 308–9
    Italian Flat Bread, 45
    Moroccan Flat Bread, 54–55
  focaccia, 43–44
    Bell Pepper Focaccia, 44
    Cheese Focaccia, 44
    Herb Focaccia, 44
    Tomato and Mozzarella Focaccia, 44
    Tomato Focaccia, 44
    Whole Wheat Focaccia, 44
  fougasse
    aux Olives, 44–45
    Walnut Fougasse, 45
    Whole Wheat Fougasse, 45
  Greek Country Bread, 47–48
  Niçoise Chick Pea Flour Pancake, 53
  Pappa al Pomodoro, 148
  Paximathia, 49
  pocket
    Arab Bread, 51
    Soft Turkish Pocket Bread, 50–51
  Pompe à l'Huile, 52
  Provençal Bread with Olives, 44–45
  Provençal Orange-Scented Brioche, 52
  Pugliese Bread, 41–42
  quick
    Provençal Green Olive and Cheese Bread, 55
    Quick Olive and Cheese Bread, 56
  Rosemary and Thyme Bread, 46

Breads (cont.)
Rusks, 49
Cretan Barley Rusks with Tomato Topping, 137
made from bread on hand, 137
Rusks, 49
in salads
Bread and Vegetable Salad, 128–29
Fattoush, 128–29
Italian Bread Salad, 129
Panzanella, 129
Semolina Bread with Sesame Seeds, 42
Semolina Bread with Tomato and Zucchini, 43
Sesame Bread Rings, 53–54
Socca, 53
in soups, 144
Majorcan Bread and Vegetable Soup, 168
Tomato, Egg, and Bread Bouillabaisse, 158
Tuscan Bread and Tomato Soup, 148
stale, uses for, 147
Turkish Country Bread, 49–50
Whole Wheat Country Bread, 39–40
Brioche
Provençal Orange-Scented Brioche, 52
Broccoli
Braised Broccoli with White Wine, 272–73
Broccoli alla Romana, 272–73
Broccoli rabe
Orecchiette with Broccoli Rabe, 211
Broths
Garlic Broth, 145
for risotto, 315
Simple Vegetable Broth, 145
vegetable trimmings for, 145
Bruschetta, 134, 135
toppings for, 76, 136
Buckwheat flour
Buckwheat Cake from the Alto Adige, 364–65
Bulgur, 314
Bulgur and Chick Pea Pilaf, 333
Chick Pea and Bulgur Salad, 102–3
Kisir, 95–96
Small Bulgur Patties, 95–96
Tabbouleh, 96–97
Winter Squash Pie with Bulgur and Feta, 240–41
Butter
Anise Butter Cookies, 361–62
Baked Semolina Gnocchi with Butter and Parmesan, 225
Lemon Butter Cookies, 362

C

Cabbage
Andalusian Cabbage Salad, 97–98
Andalusian Chick Pea and Cabbage Stew, 307
Cabbage, Kale, and Potato Gratin, 255
Cabbage and White Bean Minestrone, 152–53
Cabbage Galette, 236–37
Cabbage Gratin, 260–61
leaves, preparing for stuffing, 273
Middle Eastern Cabbage Salad with Lemon and Dill, 98
Middle Eastern Cabbage Salad with Yogurt, Lemon, and Dill, 98
Provençal Kale and Cabbage Gratin, 254
Stuffed Cabbage, 274

Stuffed Cabbage with Egg-Lemon Sauce, 274
Stuffed Cabbage with Tahini Sauce, 275
Sweet and Sour Cabbage, 273
Tuscan Bean and Farro Soup with Cabbage and Winter Squash, 153–54
Cakes
Buckwheat Cake from the Alto Adige, 364–65
Cherry Financier, 347
cutting, into layers, 365
Financier, 346, 347
Ricotta Cheesecake, 360–61
Calzone
Calzone with Tomato and Kale Filling, 64
Campari
Campari Orange Cocktail, 34
CampariSoda, 33
Capers, 28
Cauliflower with Capers, Parsley, and Vinegar, 101
Pasta with Uncooked Tomatoes, Basil, Capers, Olives, and Feta, 212–13
Caponata, 93, 276–77, 295
Carbohydrates, in Mediterranean diet, 9
Carnaroli rice, for risotto, 315. See also Risotto
Carrots
Carrot and Parsley Omelet, 193–94
Carrot Salad, 99
Carrots with Chermoula, 275
Carrots with Currants and Pine Nuts, 275
Couscous with Chick Peas and Winter Vegetables, 338–39
Marinated Carrots, 99
Mashed Carrots with Garlicky Yogurt, 100
North African Carrot "Compote," 98
Ommok Houria, 99
Simple Vegetable Broth, 145
Casseroles. See also Gratins, Stratas
Arab Eggplant, Tomato, and Chick Pea Casserole, 280
cookware for, 14
Cauliflower
Cauliflower à la Grecque, 100–101
Cauliflower and Tomato Couscous, 339–40
Cauliflower Gratin with Feta and Olives, 261
Cauliflower with Capers, Parsley, and Vinegar, 101
Deep-Fried Cauliflower, 101
Fusilli with Tomato Sauce, Cauliflower, and Olives, 216
Purple Cauliflower Gratin, 257
Red Wine Risotto with Cauliflower, 321
Roasted Cauliflower with Chermoula, 275
Tunisian Cauliflower Omelet, 194
Cayenne, 23
Roasted Salted Almonds with Cayenne, 91
Celery
Mushroom and Celery Salad, 121
Simple Vegetable Broth, 145
Chakchouka, 194, 295
Cheese-making, recollection about, 191
Cheeses
Cheese and Herb Phyllo Triangles, 137–38
Cheese-and-Vegetable-Stuffed Eggplants, 277–78
Cheese and Winter Squash Phyllo Triangles, 138–39
Cheese Focaccia, 44
Cheese Soufflé with Truffles, 199

feta, 20–21
  Baked Spicy Feta, 198
  Black-Eyed Pea Salad with Feta, 123
  Cauliflower Gratin with Feta and Olives, 261
  Eggplant Slices with Tomato Sauce and Feta, 109
  feta and watermelon, 349
  Grilled Feta in Grape Leaves, 132
  Mushroom and Feta Phyllo Triangles, 139, 141
  Pasta with Tomatoes, Beans, and Feta, 219
  Pasta with Uncooked Tomatoes, Basil, Capers, Olives, and Feta, 212–13
  Roasted Eggplant Salad with Feta and Green Peppers, 109
  Scrambled Eggs with Tomatoes and Feta, 189
  Winter Squash Pie with Bulgur and Feta, 240–41
fontina, 19
  Baby Spinach and Fontina Panini, 67
  Greens and Fontina Panini, 66
Frico, 132–33
goat, 18
  Grilled Zucchini, Goat Cheese, and Mint Panini, 65
  Lentil Soup with Goat Cheese, 160–61
  Macaroni with Tomato Sauce and Goat Cheese, 220–21
  Salad with Warm Goat Cheese and Basil Sauce, 117
  Warm Goat Cheese Salad, 115
  Warm Tomatoes with Goat Cheese, 128
Greek Fried Cheese, 198
Gruyère, 18
  Basic Strata, 196–97
  Mushroom and Gruyère Panini, 67
  Provençal Green Olive and Cheese Bread, 55
  Quick Olive and Cheese Bread, 56
  Strata with Greens, or with Tomatoes and Greens, 197
  Strata with Mushrooms and Sage, 197
  Strata with Tomatoes and Thyme, 197
Macaroni with Beans and Cheese, 219
in Mediterranean cuisines, 18–21, 92, 174
mozzarella, 19
  Deep-Fried Rice and Mozzarella Balls, 133–34, 133
  Grilled Mozzarella in Radicchio Bundles, 131–32
  Pizza with Mozzarella and Cherry Tomatoes, 59
  Pizza with Peppers, Tomato Sauce, and Mozzarella, 60–61
  Pizza with Tomato, Eggplant, and Mozzarella, 59
  Pizza with Tomato Sauce, Mozzarella, and Arugula, 61
  Supplì al Telefono, 133–34, 133
  Tomato and Mozzarella Focaccia, 44
Parmesan, 19–20
  Asparagi alla Parmigiana, 271
  Asparagus with Parmesan, 271
  Asparagus with Parmesan and Eggs, 271
  Baked Semolina Gnocchi with Butter and Parmesan, 225
  Braised Fennel with Parmesan, 282
  Eggplant Parmesan, 250
  Polenta with Tomato Sauce and Parmesan, 333
  rinds for soup, 149
pecorino, 20
  Spaghetti with Black Pepper and Pecorino, 215
ricotta, 20
  Homemade Ricotta Cheese, 195
  Pansôti, 207–8

Perciatelli with Tomato Sauce and Ricotta, 214–15
Ravioli with Beet Greens and Ricotta, 206–7
Ravioli with Greens, Herbs, and Ricotta, 207–8
Ricotta Cheesecake, 360–61
Ricotta Frittata with Asparagus, 183
Ricotta Frittata with Fresh Herbs, 183
Ricotta Frittata with Zucchini, 183
Sformato with Ricotta and Greens, 195–96
Spinach and Ricotta Torta, 235
ricotta salata, 20
  Barley Risotto with Pesto and Ricotta Salata, 330
Saganaki, 198
for snacks and starters, 92
Soufflé aux Truffes, 199
Chermoula, 86
  Carrots with Chermoula, 275
  Roasted Cauliflower with Chermoula, 275
  Winter Squash with Chermoula, 275
Cherries
  Cherry Clafouti, 348
  Cherry Financier, 347
  Sour Cherry Pilaf, 326
Chick pea flour
  Niçoise Chick Pea Flour Pancake, 53
  Socca, 53, 150
  uses for, 150
Chick peas
  Andalusian Chick Pea and Cabbage Stew, 307
  Arab Eggplant, Tomato, and Chick Pea Casserole, 280
  Baked Hummus with Pine Nuts, 104
  Bulgur and Chick Pea Pilaf, 333
  Chick Pea and Bulgur Salad, 102–3
  Chick Pea Breakfast Soup, 170–71
  Chick Pea Fattet, 308–9
  Chick Pea Stew, 308
  Couscous with Chick Peas and Chard, 336–38
  Couscous with Chick Peas and Spring Vegetables, 339
  Couscous with Chick Peas and Winter Vegetables, 338–39
  Falafel, 104–5
  Hummus, 103
  Potaje de Vigilia, 163–64
  Provençal Chick Pea Salad, 102
  Provençal Chick Pea Soup, 160
  Turkish Hummus, 104
  uses for, 150
  Vegetable Ragout with Chick Peas, Turnips, and Greens, 301–2
  Vegetable Soup with Chick Peas and Spinach, 163–64
Children, Mediterranean diet for, 7–8
Chiles
  Harissa, 86
Cholesterol, Mediterranean diet reducing, 8
Cilantro, 23
  Chermoula, 86
  Tomato Soup with Cilantro and Vermicelli, 169
Clafouti
  Apricot Clafouti, 353
  Cherry Clafouti, 348
Coffee. See Espresso
Compotes
  Fig and Red Wine Compote, 350
  Quince Compote, 357

Condiments, 69–70
    Aïoli, 72–73
    Gremolata, 85
    Harissa, 86
    Peperonata, 85
    Preserved Lemons, 87
    Provençal and Catalan Garlic Mayonnaise, 72–73
    Ras al-Hanut, 24
    Roasted or Grilled Peppers, 84–85
    Rouille, 73–74
    Spicy Garlic Mayonnaise, 73–74
    Stewed Peppers and Tomatoes, 85
    Tabil, 24
    Za'tar, 24
Cookies, 344
    Anise Butter Cookies, 361–62
    Lemon Butter Cookies, 362
Cookware
    nonstick, 13–14, 13
    recommended, 13–15
Cornmeal
    Fregolata Veneziana, 362, 364
    in polenta (see Polenta)
    Venetian Cornmeal Shortbread, 362, 364
Coronary heart disease, Mediterranean diet reducing, 8, 9
Couscous, 314
    Cauliflower and Tomato Couscous, 339–40
    Couscous "Tabbouleh," 97
    Couscous with Chick Peas and Chard, 336–38
    Couscous with Chick Peas and Spring Vegetables, 339
    Couscous with Chick Peas and Winter Vegetables, 338–39
    Couscous with Winter Squash, 340–41
    packaged, how to prepare, 337
    Sweet Dessert Couscous with Citrus and Pomegranate, 367
Crostini, 134, 135
    toppings for, 76, 136
Cucumbers
    Bread and Vegetable Salad, 128–29
    Cacik, 106
    Fattoush, 128–29
    Iced Cucumber Soup with Walnuts, 167
    Summer Salad, 119
    Turkish Cucumber and Yogurt Salad, 106
    Tzatziki, 106
Currants
    Carrots with Currants and Pine Nuts, 275
    Greens with Currants and Pine Nuts, 282
Cutting boards, recommended, 12

D

Desserts. See Sweets and desserts
Dessert wines, 346
Dill, 25
    Baked Beans with Honey and Dill, 311
    Middle Eastern Cabbage Salad with Lemon and Dill, 98
    Middle Eastern Cabbage Salad with Yogurt, Lemon, and Dill, 98
Dips and spreads
    Apricot Yogurt Dip, 91
    Baba Gannouj, 110–11
    Baked Hummus with Pine Nuts, 104

Eggplant and Red Pepper Purée, 125
    Fava, 123–24
    Fresh Fava Bean Purée, 113
    Green Olive and Almond Tapenade, 122
    Green Olive Tapenade, 122
    Grilled Eggplant Purée with Mint and Almonds, 110
    Hummus, 103
    Muhammara, 126
    Red Pepper Purée, 124–25
    Split Pea Purée, 123–24
    Swiss Chard Stalk and Tahini Dip, 127–28
    Tapenade, 121–22
    Turkish Hummus, 104
    White Bean "Brandade," 91
    Yogurt and Mint Spread, 81
Dough
    Fresh Pasta Dough, 204
    phyllo (see Phyllo dough)
    Pizza Dough, 56–57
    Pizza Dough for a Thicker Crust, 57
    Whole Wheat Pizza Dough, 57
Dressings
    Oil and Vinegar Dressing, 82
    Tahini Dressing, 83
    Vinaigrette to Keep in the Refrigerator, 82
    Walnut Vinaigrette, 82–83
Drinks. See Aperitifs
Durum flour
    Durum Flour Bread from Altamura, 40–41
Dutch ovens, 14

E

Eggplant
    Arab Eggplant, Tomato, and Chick Pea Casserole, 280
    Baba Gannouj, 110–11
    Baked Eggplant Stuffed with Pasta, 220
    Balkan-Style Moussaka, 258–59
    Bohemienne Gratinée, 246
    Caponata, 276–77
    Catalan Ratatouille, 72
    Cheese-and-Vegetable-Stuffed Eggplants, 277–78
    Deep-Dish Eggplant Torta, 230–31
    Eggplant Ajlūk, 98
    Eggplant and Red Pepper Panini, 65
    Eggplant and Red Pepper Purée, 125
    Eggplant and Tomato Gratin, 246
    Eggplant and Tomato Panini, 65
    Eggplant Parmesan, 250
    Eggplant Pilaf, 327
    Eggplant Slices with Tomato Sauce and Feta, 109
    Gnocchi with Eggplant and Peppers, 224–25
    Grilled Eggplant and Pepper Salad, 111
    Grilled Eggplant Purée with Mint and Almonds, 110
    Grilled Eggplant with Hot Red Pepper Flakes, 108
    Ikarian Summer Vegetable Stew, 300–301
    Imam Bayildi, 278
    Individual Eggplant and Tomato Frittata, 184–85
    Laganari with Eggplant, Tomato Sauce, and Oregano, 218
    Large Ratatouille Omelet, 184
    Ligurian Ratatouille, 298–99
    Marinated Eggplant, 106–7
    One More Ratatouille, 297
    Pizza with Tomato, Eggplant, and Mozzarella, 59

quick roasting, <u>277</u>
in ratatouille dishes, <u>295</u>
Roasted Eggplant Salad with Feta and Green Peppers,109
salting, <u>111</u>
Samfaina, 72
Sautéed Eggplant with Tomatoes and Balsamic Vinegar, 107
smoke-flavored, <u>110</u>
Soufiko, 300–301
Stewed Eggplant and Onions, 276
Stuffed Eggplants (or Peppers), 279
Tian Niçoise, 298
Tortilla Murciana, 178
Tunisian Eggplant Omelet, 190, 192
Turkish Ratatouille, 299–300
Türlü, 299–300
Türlü Topped with a Fried Egg, 300
Two Methods for One Ratatouille, 296–97
Vegetable Paella from El Palmar, 325–26
Eggs, 173–74
at Alla Beccaccia, <u>180</u>
Asparagus with Parmesan and Eggs, 271
Chakchouka, 194
Eggs and Vegetables Stuffed with Tapenade, 130–31
frittatas
fillings for, <u>176</u>
Individual Eggplant and Tomato Frittata, 184–85
Master Frittata, 175–76
Ricotta Frittata with Asparagus, 183
Ricotta Frittata with Fresh Herbs, 183
Ricotta Frittata with Zucchini, 183
Wild Mushroom Frittata, 182
North African Fried Pepper Stew with Eggs, 194
omelets
Baked Artichoke Heart Omelet, 187
Baked Potato, Onion, and Parsley Omelet, 192–93
Baked Vegetable Omelet, 188–89
Bell Pepper, Tomato, and Potato Omelet, 193
Carrot and Parsley Omelet, 193–94
flat, 174, <u>175</u>, <u>185</u>
Large Ratatouille Omelet, 184
Persian Herb Omelet, 190
Provençal Flat Onion Omelet, 185
Provençal Flat Sorrel Omelet, 186
Provençal Flat Swiss Chard Omelet, 186–87
Provençal Flat Tomato Omelet, 185–86
Spanish Omelet with Potatoes and Onions, 176–77
Tortino, 187
Truccha, 186–87
Truffle Omelet, 182–83
Tunisian, <u>192</u>
Tunisian Cauliflower Omelet, 194
Tunisian Eggplant Omelet, 190, 192
Penne with Asparagus and Eggs, 214
poached
Poached Eggs with Garlic Sauce, 188
Poached Eggs with Tzatziki, 188
in sauces
Asparagus with Egg Sauce, 181
Stuffed Cabbage with Egg-Lemon Sauce, 274
scrambled
Asparagus with Scrambled Eggs, 181
Piperade, 179

Scrambled Eggs with Peppers, 179
Scrambled Eggs with Tomatoes and Feta, 189
soufflés
Cheese Soufflé with Truffles, 199
Soufflé aux Truffes, 199
in soups
Lemon Stracciatella, 155
Stracciatella, 154–55
Stracciatella with Asparagus, 155
Tomato, Egg, and Bread Bouillabaisse, 158
stratas
Basic Strata, 196–97
Strata with Greens, or with Tomatoes and Greens, 197
Strata with Mushrooms and Sage, 197
Strata with Tomatoes and Thyme, 197
tortillas
Bar Pilar's Tortilla Española, 177
Lower-Fat Spanish Tortilla, 177
Sweet Green Pepper Tortilla from Murcia, 178–79
Tortilla Española, 174, 176–77
Tortilla Murciana, 178
Turkish Menemem, 194
Türlü Topped with a Fried Egg, 300
Electric appliances, recommended, 15
Equipment, kitchen, recommended, 12–15
Escalivada, <u>295</u>
Espresso
Coffee Granita, 360
Il Frantoio's "Special Caffé Freddo," 35

F
Falafel, 104–5
Farro
The Doctor's Baiana, 332–33
Farro Risotto with Dried Mushrooms, Favas, and Garlic, 331–32
Farro Risotto with Green Beans, 332
Farro Salad, 112
Provençal Wheat Berry Soup, 159
Tuscan Bean and Farro Soup with Cabbage and Winter Squash, 153–54
Fattoush, 128–29
Fava beans
Artichoke and Fresh Fava Stew, 269–70
Artichokes à la Barigoule with Fava Beans, 265
Asparagus and Fava Bean Risotto, 318
Couscous with Chick Peas and Spring Vegetables, 339
Dried Fava Beans and Greens, 309
Falafel, 104–5
Farro Risotto with Dried Mushrooms, Favas, and Garlic, 331–32
Fava Bean and Green Garlic Risotto, 317–18
Fava Bean and Potato Stew, 280–81
Fava Bean Salad, 114
Fresh Fava Bean Purée, 113
Giant Favas with Mint, 112
how to prepare, <u>281</u>
Pasta with Tomatoes, Beans, and Feta, 219
Spicy Vegetable Stew with Swiss Chard, Favas, and Potatoes, 302
Fennel, 25
Black-Eyed Peas with Wild Fennel, 306
Braised Fennel with Parmesan, 282

Fennel *(cont.)*
  Fennel and Scallion Pie, 238–39
  Fritteda, 268–69
  Mushroom and Fennel Topping, 60
  Provençal Fennel and Tomato Gratin, 251
  Sicilian Spring Vegetable Stew, 268–69
  wild, 269
Figs
  Baklava with Mixed Dried Fruit and Nuts, 366
  Fig and Red Wine Compote, 350
  Fig Ice Cream, 351
  Honey-Roasted Figs, 350–51
  Summer Stone Fruit Strudel, 353–54
Financier, 346, 347
  Cherry Financier, 347
Flat breads. *See* Breads, flat
Flour, 28. *See also specific flours*
Focaccia. *See* Breads, focaccia
Food processor, for making pesto, 74
Fougasse. *See* Breads, fougasse
France. *See also* Provence
  cheeses of, 18–19, 92
  gratins of, 228
  pastis of, 35
Frico, 132–33
Frittatas. *See* Eggs, frittatas
Fritters
  Diane Kochilas's Zucchini Fritters, 130
  polenta, 150
Fruits. *See also specific fruits*
  in desserts, 344
  dried, 28
  health benefits from, 8–9

G
Gadgets, recommended, 12–13
Galettes, 231. *See also* Pies, savory
Garlic, 17–18
  Aïoli, 72–73
  Aïoli Monstre, 293–94
  Castilian Garlic Soup with Paprika and Saffron, 164–65
  Chermoula, 86
  Easy White Beans with Tomatoes and Garlic, 305
  Farro Risotto with Dried Mushrooms, Favas, and Garlic, 331–32
  Fassoulia, 305–6
  Fava Bean and Green Garlic Risotto, 317–18
  Garlic and Potato Purée, 80
  Garlic Broth, 145
  Garlic Green Beans, 272
  Garlic Soup, 161–62
  Gremolata, 85
  Huge Aïoli Feast, 293–94
  Kale with Garlic and Olive Oil, 283
  Large White Beans with Tomatoes and Garlic, 305–6
  Mashed Black-Eyed Peas with Garlic Purée, 306–7
  Mashed Carrots with Garlicky Yogurt, 100
  Mushrooms al Ajillo, 120
  Mushrooms in Garlic Sauce, 120
  Pizza Marinara with Tomatoes and Garlic, 57–58
  Poached Eggs with Garlic Sauce, 188
  Potatoes with Green Beans and Garlic, 289
  Provençal and Catalan Garlic Mayonnaise, 72–73

  puréeing, in mortar and pestle, 81
  Rouille, 73–74
  Skordalia, 80
  Spicy Garlic Mayonnaise, 73–74
  Spring Onion, Garlic, and Greens Gratin, 236
  Spring Onion, Garlic, and Greens Tart, 236
  Tahini Garlic Sauce, 83
Garlic Soup, An Ode to, 162
Gazpacho, 165
  Gazpacho, 165
  White Gazpacho with Grapes, 166
Gelato, 343, 344
  Peach Gelato, 352
Gnocchi. *See* Pasta, Gnocchi
Grains, 28, 313–14. *See also specific grains*
Granita
  Coffee Granita, 360
  Strawberry Granita, 356–57
  Watermelon Granita, 348–49
Grape leaves
  Dolmades, 114–15
  Grape Leaves Stuffed with Rice, Onions, and Herbs, 114–15
  Grilled Feta in Grape Leaves, 132
Grapes
  White Gazpacho with Grapes, 166
Grappa, 35
Gratins, 228
  Balkan-Style Moussaka, 258–59
  Bohemienne Gratinée, 246
  Cabbage, Kale, and Potato Gratin, 255
  Cabbage Gratin, 260–61
  Cauliflower Gratin with Feta and Olives, 261
  Eggplant and Tomato Gratin, 246
  Eggplant Parmesan, 250
  Mushroom and Greens Gratin, 234
  Potato and Mushroom Gratin, 252
  Provençal Fennel and Tomato Gratin, 251
  Provençal Greens Gratin, 253–54
  Provençal Kale and Cabbage Gratin, 254
  Provençal Summer Potato Gratin, 252–53
  Provençal Summer Squash, Red Pepper, and Tomato Gratin, 255–56
  Provençal Swiss Chard Gratin, 257–58
  Pumpkin Gratin, 238
  Purple Cauliflower Gratin, 257
  Spring Onion, Garlic, and Greens Gratin, 236
  Summer Squash Gratin, 256
  Tomato and Bean Gratin, 304
  White Bean and Chard Gratin, 304
  Zucchini, Potato, and Artichoke Moussaka, 259–60
  Zucchini and Greens Gratin, 235
Greece
  cheeses of, 20–21
  grappa of, 35
  meze of, 108
  ouzo of, 35
  savory pies of, 227–28
Green beans
  Barley Risotto with Asparagus or Green Beans and Pesto, 330
  Couscous with Chick Peas and Spring Vegetables, 339
  Farro Risotto with Green Beans, 332

Garlic Green Beans, 272
Potatoes with Green Beans and Garlic, 289
Stewed Green Beans with Tomatoes, 272
Trenette with Pesto, Green Beans, and Potatoes, 217
Whole Wheat Spaghetti with Green Beans and Tomato
    Sauce, 217
Greens. *See also specific greens*
Dried Fava Beans and Greens, 309
Greens and Fontina Panini, 66
Greens and Potato Torta or Galette, 232–33
Greens and Sweet Onion Pie, 239–40
Greens Bouillabaisse, 158
Greens with Currants and Pine Nuts, 282
Lasagna with Greens and Tomato Sauce, 222–23
Lentil Minestrone with Greens, 149, 151
Ligurian Artichoke and Greens Torta, 231–32
Mesclun Salad, 118
Mushroom and Greens Gratin, 234
Mushroom and Greens Tart, 233–34
Pansôti, 207–8
Provençal Greens Gratin, 253–54
Provençal Zucchini and Greens Torte, 234–35
Quicker Free-Form Lasagna with Greens, 223
Ravioli with Greens, Herbs, and Ricotta, 207–8
Sformato with Ricotta and Greens, 195–96
Spring Onion, Garlic, and Greens Gratin, 236
Spring Onion, Garlic, and Greens Tart, 236
Strata with Greens, or with Tomatoes and Greens, 197
Vegetable Ragout with Chick Peas, Turnips, and Greens,
    301–2
Zucchini and Greens Gratin, 235
Gremolata, 85
Sautéed Mushrooms with Gremolata, 284

H

Harissa, 28–29, 86
Herbs. *See also specific herbs*
Cheese and Herb Phyllo Triangles, 137–38
Dolmades, 114–15
Grape Leaves Stuffed with Rice, Onions, and Herbs,
    114–15
Herb Focaccia, 44
in Mediterranean cuisines, 22–23, 25–27
Pansôti, 207–8
Persian Herb Omelet, 190
Ravioli with Greens, Herbs, and Ricotta, 207–8
Ricotta Frittata with Fresh Herbs, 183
in tomato sauce, 78
Zucchini and Herb Pie, 242–43
Honey, 29
Baked Beans with Honey and Dill, 311
Honey-Orange Biscotti, 345
Honey-Roasted Figs, 350–51
Pears Poached in Wine and Honey, 357
production of, 363
Hummus, 103
Baked Hummus with Pine Nuts, 104
Turkish Hummus, 104

I

Ice cream
Fig Ice Cream, 351
Iced tea, rose geranium syrup for, 358

Ingredients, in Mediterranean pantry, 1–2, 15–29, 370.
    See also specific ingredients
Italian truck stop, recollection about, 209
Italy
aperitifs of, 32
cheeses of, 19–20, 92
little foods of, 90
pasta of, 201–2
pizza of, 38
polenta of, 314
risotto of, 314
savory pies of, 228
sweets of, 343, 344

K

Kale
Cabbage, Kale, and Potato Gratin, 255
Calzone with Tomato and Kale Filling, 64
Kale Minestrone, 148–49
Kale with Garlic and Olive Oil, 283
Provençal Kale and Cabbage Gratin, 254
Kitchen equipment, recommended, 12–15
Kitchen scissors, for cutting pizza, 61
Knives, recommended, 12

L

Lasagna. *See* Pasta, lasagna
Lebanon, arak in, 35
Leeks
cleaning, 244
Couscous with Chick Peas and Winter Vegetables, 338–39
Leeks Cooked in White Wine, 117
Winter Squash and Leek Pie, 241–42
Lemons
Gremolata, 85
Lemon Butter Cookies, 362
Lemon Sorbet, 359
Lemon Stracciatella, 155
Lemon Tart, 359–60
Middle Eastern Cabbage Salad with Lemon and Dill, 98
Middle Eastern Cabbage Salad with Yogurt, Lemon, and
    Dill, 98
Preserved Lemons, 87
Stuffed Cabbage with Egg-Lemon Sauce, 274
Lentils
The Doctor's Baiana, 332–33
Lentil Minestrone with Greens, 149, 151
Lentil Salad, 119–20
Lentil Soup with Goat Cheese, 160–61
Provençal Lentil and Tomato Soup, 161
uses for, 150
varieties of, 150
Lettuce. *See also* Romaine, Mesclun
Roasted Pepper Salad with Lettuce and Tomato, 124
Lima beans, 150
Longevity, Mediterranean diet improving, 8
Loukoumades, 365
Lupini beans, 93

M

Mayonnaise
Aïoli, 72–73
Provençal and Catalan Garlic Mayonnaise, 72–73

Mayonnaise (cont.)
  Rouille, 73–74
  Spicy Garlic Mayonnaise, 73–74
Meat, in Mediterranean dishes, 7
Mediterranean cuisines
  author's background in, 1–5
  for children, 7–8
  cooking
    ease of, 11
    equipment for, 12–15
  enjoyment from, 9
  ingredients in, 1–2, 15–29, 320 (see also specific
      ingredients)
  typical dishes of, 7
  variety of, 8
Mediterranean diet, health benefits from, 8–9
Melons
  Melon Sorbet, 349
  Melon Soup, 349
  Melon with Muscat de Beaumes-de-Venise, 350
  for snacks and starters, 93
Mesclun, 90
  Mesclun Salad, 118
Meze, 108. See also Starters, snacks, and meze
  aperitifs with, 35
Middle East, cheeses of, 21
Midori
  Biz Fizz, 33
  Prosecco and Midori Cocktail, 33
Milk
  Polenta Made with Milk, 335
Minestrone. See Soups, Minestrone
Mint, 25
  Giant Favas with Mint, 112
  Grilled Eggplant Purée with Mint and Almonds, 110
  Grilled Zucchini, Goat Cheese, and Mint Panini, 65
  Pan-Fried Zucchini with Mint and Pepperoncini, 292
  Potato and Mint Ravioli, 208
  Roman-Style Braised Baby Artichokes with Parsley and
      Mint, 166
  Yogurt and Mint Spread, 81
Mortar and pestle, 12
  for making pesto, 74
  puréeing garlic in, 81
Moussaka
  Balkan-Style Moussaka, 258–59
  Zucchini, Potato, and Artichoke Moussaka, 259–60
Muhammara, 126
Mushrooms
  dried, 29
  Farro Risotto with Dried Mushrooms, Favas, and Garlic,
      331–32
  Garganelli with Mushroom Sauce, 210
  Marinated Mushrooms, 120–21
  Mushroom and Celery Salad, 121
  Mushroom and Fennel Topping, 60
  Mushroom and Feta Phyllo Triangles, 139, 141
  Mushroom and Greens Gratin, 234
  Mushroom and Gruyère Panini, 67
  Mushroom Lasagna, 221–22
  Mushroom Risotto, 318–19
  Mushrooms al Ajillo, 120
  Mushroom and Greens Tart, 233–34

Mushrooms in Garlic Sauce, 120
  Pizza with Mushrooms and Artichoke Hearts, 60
  Polenta with Mushrooms, 336
  Potato and Mushroom Gratin, 252
  Provençal Artichoke, Mushroom, and Potato Ragout, 268
  Risi e Bisi with Mushrooms, 322
  Sautéed Mushrooms with Gremolata, 284
  Strata with Mushrooms and Sage, 197
  wild, types of, 285
  Wild Mushroom Frittata, 182
  Wild Mushroom Ragout, 285
  Wild Mushrooms with Tomatoes and Basil, 286

N

New World beans, 150
Nuts. See also specific nuts
  Baklava with Mixed Dried Fruit and Nuts, 366
  in Mediterranean cuisines, 27–28
  for snacks and starters, 92
  storing, 27
  toasting, 27

O

Ode to Garlic Soup, An, 162
Olive oil
  in authentic vs. author's recipes, 11
  buying, 16–17
  Kale with Garlic and Olive Oil, 283
  longevity and, 8
  Oil and Vinegar Dressing, 82
  Olive Oil Béchamel, 78
  Vinaigrette to Keep in the Refrigerator, 82
  Walnut Vinaigrette, 82–83
  Yeasted Olive Oil Pastry, 229
Olive paste, 93
Olives
  buying, 16
  Cauliflower Gratin with Feta and Olives, 261
  curing of, 15–16
  Eggs and Vegetables Stuffed with Tapenade, 130–31
  Fougasse aux Olives, 44–45
  Fusilli with Tomato Sauce, Cauliflower, and Olives, 216
  Green Olive and Almond Tapenade, 122
  Green Olive Tapenade, 122
  Orange and Olive Salad, 122
  Pasta with Uncooked Tomatoes, Basil, Capers, Olives,
      and Feta, 212–13
  pitting, 122
  Potato and Olive Stew, 291–92
  Provençal Bread with Olives, 44–45
  Provençal Green Olive and Cheese Bread, 55
  Quick Olive and Cheese Bread, 56
  for snacks and starters, 92
  Tapenade, 121–22
Omelets. See Eggs, omelets
Onions
  Baked Potato, Onion, and Parsley Omelet, 192–93
  Bar Pilar's Tortilla Española, 177
  Dolmades, 114–15
  Fritteda, 268–69
  Grape Leaves Stuffed with Rice, Onions, and Herbs,
      114–15
  Greens and Sweet Onion Pie, 239–40

Lower-Fat Spanish Tortilla, 177
Onion and Pepper Topping, 61
Pissaladière, 63
Provençal Flat Onion Omelet, 185
Provençal Onion Pizza, 63
raw, soaking, 119
Sicilian Spring Vegetable Stew, 268–69
Simple Vegetable Broth, 145
Spanish Omelet with Potatoes and Onions, 176–77
Spring Onion, Garlic, and Greens Gratin, 236
Spring Onion, Garlic, and Greens Tart, 236
Stewed Eggplant and Onions, 276
Summer Salad, 119
Tortilla Española, 174, 176–77
Orange flower water, 29
Oranges
Campari Orange Cocktail, 34
Honey-Orange Biscotti, 345
Orange and Olive Salad, 122
Orange-Scented Pastry Cream, 355
Orange Sorbet with Blood Orange Salad, 358–59
Pompe à l'Huile, 52
Provençal Orange-Scented Brioche, 52
Sweet Dessert Couscous with Citrus and Pomegranate, 367
Oregano, 25
Fried Potatoes with Tomatoes and Oregano, 291
Laganari with Eggplant, Tomato Sauce, and Oregano, 218
Ouzo, 35, 108

P

Paella, 313–14
Vegetable Paella from El Palmar, 325–26
Pancakes
Niçoise Chick Pea Flour Pancake, 53
Socca, 53, 150
Panini, 65
Artichoke Heart and Red Pepper Panini, 66
Baby Spinach and Fontina Panini, 67
Eggplant and Red Pepper Panini, 65
Eggplant and Tomato Panini, 65
Greens and Fontina Panini, 66
Grilled Zucchini, Goat Cheese, and Mint Panini, 65
Mushroom and Gruyère Panini, 67
Panini grills, 65
Panzanella, 129
Paprika, 25
Castilian Garlic Soup with Paprika and Saffron, 164–65
Parmesan rinds, for soups, 149
Parsley, 25
Baked Potato, Onion, and Parsley Omelet, 192–93
Carrot and Parsley Omelet, 193–94
Cauliflower with Capers, Parsley, and Vinegar, 101
Chermoula, 86
Couscous "Tabbouleh," 97
Gremolata, 85
Parsley Sauce, 84
preparing, 96
Roman-Style Braised Baby Artichokes with Parsley and Mint, 166
Tabbouleh, 96–97

Pasta
Baked Eggplant Stuffed with Pasta, 220
dried vs. fresh, 202
Fresh Pasta Dough, 204
Fusilli with Tomato Sauce, Cauliflower, and Olives, 216
garganelli
Garganelli with Mushroom Sauce, 210
homemade, 210
Gnocchi, 202, 223–24
Baked Semolina Gnocchi with Butter and Parmesan, 225
Gnocchi with Eggplant and Peppers, 224–25
how to cook, 205
of Italy, 201–2
Laganari with Eggplant, Tomato Sauce, and Oregano, 218
lasagna
Beet Green Lasagna, 207
Lasagna with Greens and Tomato Sauce, 222–23
Mushroom Lasagna, 221–22
Quicker Free-Form Lasagna with Greens, 223
macaroni
Macaroni with Beans and Cheese, 219
Macaroni with Tomato Sauce and Goat Cheese, 220–21
orecchiette, 201
Orecchiette with Broccoli Rabe, 211
Orecchiette with Raw and Cooked Tomato Sauce, 212
Orecchiette with Uncooked Tomatoes and Arugula, 211
Pasta e Fagiole, 218–19
Pasta with Beans, 218–19
Pasta with Ligurian Artichoke Sauce, 213
Pasta with Tomatoes, Beans, and Feta, 219
Pasta with Uncooked Tomatoes, Basil, Capers, Olives, and Feta, 212–13
Penne with Asparagus and Eggs, 214
Perciatelli with Tomato Sauce and Ricotta, 214–15
with pesto, 76
ravioli
Half-Moon Ravioli with Winter Squash Filling, 204–6
Pansôti, 207–8
Potato and Mint Ravioli, 208
Ravioli with Beet Greens and Ricotta, 206–7
Ravioli with Greens, Herbs, and Ricotta, 207–8
shaping, 206
in soups
Bean and Vegetable Soup with Pastina, 169–70
Hearty Bean, Chard, and Vermicelli Soup, 171
Tomato Soup with Cilantro and Vermicelli, 169
spaghetti, 202
Spaghetti alla Chitarra with Arugula Pesto and Tomato Sauce, 215
Spaghetti with Black Pepper and Pecorino, 215
Whole Wheat Spaghetti with Green Beans and Tomato Sauce, 217
Strozzapreti with Wild Arugula and Wild Asparagus, 216
Trenette with Pesto, Green Beans, and Potatoes, 217
types of, 203
Pastis, 35
The Mauresque, 34
Pastry. See also Pie crusts
Yeasted Olive Oil Pastry, 229

Pastry cream
 Orange-Scented Pastry Cream, 355
 Rose-Scented Pastry Cream, 355
 Strawberry Tart with Rose-Scented Pastry Cream, 354
 uncurdling, 354
Peaches. *See also* Peach purée
 Peaches in Red Wine and Banyuls, 352–53
 Peach Gelato, 352
 Summer Stone Fruit Strudel, 353–54
Peach purée
 Bellini, 33
 Sparkling Wine and Peach Cocktail, 33
Pears
 Pears Poached in Wine and Honey, 357
Peas
 Bouillabaisse of Fresh Peas, 156–57
 Fava, 123–24
 Risi e Bisi, 321–22
 Risi e Bisi with Mushrooms, 322
 Split Pea Purée, 123–24
 Spring Peas with Sugar, 287
 Valencia-Style Peas, 286–87
Pepper, black, 26
 Spaghetti with Black Pepper and Pecorino, 215
Pepper, red, 26
Pepperoncini
 Pan-Fried Zucchini with Mint and Pepperoncini, 292
Peppers
 Artichoke Heart and Red Pepper Panini, 66
 Bell Pepper, Tomato, and Potato Omelet, 193
 Bell Pepper Focaccia, 44
 Catalan Ratatouille, 72
 Chakchouka, 194
 Cold Tomato and Roasted Pepper Soup, 166
 Eggplant and Red Pepper Panini, 65
 Eggplant and Red Pepper Purée, 125
 Eggs and Vegetables Stuffed with Tapenade, 130–31
 Gnocchi with Eggplant and Peppers, 224–25
 Grilled Eggplant and Pepper Salad, 111
 Grilled Pepper Salad, 125, 126–27
 Mechwya, 126–27
 Muhammara, 126
 North African Fried Pepper Stew with Eggs, 194
 Onion and Pepper Topping, 61
 Peperonata, 85
 Piperade, 179
 Pizza with Peppers, Tomato Sauce, and Mozzarella,
  60–61
 Provençal Summer Squash, Red Pepper, and Tomato
  Gratin, 255–56
 Red Pepper Purée, 124–25
 Red Pepper Risotto with Saffron, 319
 Roasted Eggplant Salad with Feta and Green Peppers,
  109
 Roasted or Grilled Peppers, 84–85
 Roasted Pepper Salad with Lettuce and Tomato, 124
 Romesco Sauce, 71
 Salmorejo, 166
 Samfaina, 72
 Sautéed Peppers with Tomatoes, 288
 Sautéed Zucchini and Red Peppers, 292
 Scrambled Eggs with Peppers, 179
 Spanish, 71, 93

 Stewed Peppers and Tomatoes, 85
 Stuffed Eggplants (or Peppers), 279
 Stuffed Lipstick Peppers, 287–88
 Sweet Green Pepper Tortilla from Murcia, 178–79
 Turkish Menemem, 194
Pesto
 Arugula Pesto, 75
 Barley Risotto with Asparagus or Green Beans and Pesto,
  330
 Barley Risotto with Pesto and Ricotta Salata, 330
 Eggs Filled with Pesto, 131
 made with mortar and pestle vs. food processor, 74
 Pesto Genovese, 74–75
 Spaghetti alla Chitarra with Arugula Pesto and Tomato
  Sauce, 215
 Trenette with Pesto, Green Beans, and Potatoes, 217
 uses for, 76
Phyllo dough
 Cheese and Herb Phyllo Triangles, 137–38
 Cheese and Winter Squash Phyllo Triangles, 138–39
 cutting, 139
 Mushroom and Feta Phyllo Triangles, 139, 141
 substitute for, 231
 thawing, 29
 working with, 238
Pie crusts. *See also* Pastry
 Greek Pie Crust, 229–30
 Pâte Sucrée, 355–56
 Sweet Pie Crust, 355–56
Pies, savory, 227–28
 Cabbage Galette, 236–37
 Coiled Summer Squash Pitta, 245–46
 cooking Arborio rice for, 235
 Deep-Dish Eggplant Torta, 230–31
 Fennel and Scallion Pie, 238–39
 Greek Pie Crust, 229–30
 Greens and Potato Torta or Galette, 232–33
 Greens and Sweet Onion Pie, 239–40
 Ligurian Artichoke and Greens Torta, 231–32
 Mushroom and Greens Tart, 233–34
 names for, 231
 Potato Pitta, 244–45
 Provençal Pumpkin Torte, 237–38
 Provençal Zucchini and Greens Torte, 234–35
 Pumpkin Galette, 238
 Ratatouille Tart, 298
 Spanakopita, 243–44
 Spinach and Ricotta Torta, 235
 Spring Onion, Garlic, and Greens Tart, 236
 Winter Squash and Leek Pie, 241–42
 Winter Squash Pie with Bulgur and Feta, 240–41
 Yeasted Olive Oil Pastry, 229
 Zucchini and Herb Pie, 242–43
Pilaf, 314. *See also* Rice, pilaf
 Bulgur and Chick Pea Pilaf, 333
Pine nuts, 28
 Baked Hummus with Pine Nuts, 104
 Carrots with Currants and Pine Nuts, 275
 Greens with Currants and Pine Nuts, 282
 Pine Nut Tarator Sauce, 81
 Spinach with Yogurt and Pine Nuts, 127
Piquillo pimientos, 93
Pisto, 295

Pistou, 76
    Soupe au Pistou, 155–56
Pitas and pittas, 227, 228, 231. *See also* Pies, savory
Pizza-cutting wheel, 61
Pizzas, 38
    Calzone with Tomato and Kale Filling, 64
    cutting, 61
    Mushroom and Fennel Topping, 60
    Onion and Pepper Topping, 61
    Pissaladière, 63
    Pizza Bianca, 62
    Pizza Dough, 56–57
    Pizza Dough for a Thicker Crust, 57
    Pizza Margherita, 58
    Pizza Marinara with Tomatoes and Garlic, 57–58
    Pizza with Mozzarella and Cherry Tomatoes, 59
    Pizza with Mushrooms and Artichoke Hearts, 60
    Pizza with Peppers, Tomato Sauce, and Mozzarella,
        60–61
    Pizza with Tomato, Eggplant, and Mozzarella, 59
    Pizza with Tomato Sauce, Mozzarella, and Arugula, 61
    Pizza with Tomato Sauce and Potatoes, 62–63
    Provençal Onion Pizza, 63
    "White" Pizza, 62
    Whole Wheat Pizza Dough, 57
Plums
    Summer Stone Fruit Strudel, 353–54
Polenta, 314
    Classic Polenta, 335
    Easy Polenta, 334–35
    grilled, 336
    Polenta Made with Milk, 335
    Polenta with Mushrooms, 336
    Polenta with Tomato Sauce and Parmesan, 333
    preparing, 334
Polenta fritters, 150
Pomegranate
    Sweet Dessert Couscous with Citrus and Pomegranate,
        367
Pomì marinara sauce, 29
Potatoes
    Artichoke and Potato Stew, 270–71
    Baked Potato, Onion, and Parsley Omelet, 192–93
    Bar Pilar's Tortilla Española, 177
    Bell Pepper, Tomato, and Potato Omelet, 193
    Cabbage, Kale, and Potato Gratin, 255
    Fava Bean and Potato Stew, 280–81
    Fried Potatoes with Tomatoes and Oregano, 291
    Garlic and Potato Purée, 80
    Gnocchi, 223–24
    Greens and Potato Torta or Galette, 232–33
    Lower-Fat Spanish Tortilla, 177
    Pizza with Tomato Sauce and Potatoes, 62–63
    Potato and Mint Ravioli, 208
    Potato and Mushroom Gratin, 252
    Potato and Olive Stew, 291–92
    Potatoes with Green Beans and Garlic, 289
    Potato Pitta, 244–45
    Provençal Artichoke, Mushroom, and Potato Ragout,
        268
    Provençal Summer Potato Gratin, 252–53
    red-skinned, 289
    Roasted Potatoes and Root Vegetables with Rosemary, 290
    Roasted Potatoes with Rosemary, 290
    Skordalia, 80
    Spanish Omelet with Potatoes and Onions, 176–77
    Spicy Potatoes with Aïoli, 288–89
    Spicy Vegetable Stew with Swiss Chard, Black-Eyed Peas,
        and Potatoes, 302
    Spicy Vegetable Stew with Swiss Chard, Favas, and
        Potatoes, 302
    Tortilla Española, 174, 176–77
    Trenette with Pesto, Green Beans, and Potatoes, 217
    Zucchini, Potato, and Artichoke Moussaka, 259–60
Pots, recommended, 14
Prosecco
    Bellini, 33
    Biz Fizz, 33
    Prosecco and Midori Cocktail, 33
    Sparkling Wine and Peach Cocktail, 33
Provence
    egg dishes of, 174
    melons of, 93
    salads of, 90
    sauces and dressings of, 70
Pumpkin, 240
    Provençal Pumpkin Torte, 237–38
    Pumpkin Galette, 238
    Pumpkin Gratin, 238
Purslane
    Purslane Salad, 118

Q

Quinces
    Quince Compote, 357
    Quince Spoon Sweet, 358

R

Radicchio
    Grilled Mozzarella in Radicchio Bundles, 131–32
    Radicchio Risotto, 320
Radishes
    Shredded Romaine and Radish Salad, 116
    for snacks and starters, 93
Ragouts. *See also* Stews
    Provençal Artichoke, Mushroom, and Potato Ragout, 268
    Tomato and Bean Ragout, 303
    Turkish Menemem, 194
    Vegetable Ragout with Chick Peas, Turnips, and Greens,
        301–2
    White Bean and Chard Ragout, 304
    Wild Mushroom Ragout, 285
Raisins
    Baklava with Mixed Dried Fruit and Nuts, 366
Raki, 35
Ras al-Hanut, 24
Raspberries
    Raspberry or Blueberry Tart, 354
Ratatouille
    Catalan Ratatouille, 72
    Large Ratatouille Omelet, 184
    Ligurian Ratatouille, 298–99
    One More Ratatouille, 297
    Ratatouille Tart, 298
    Samfaina, 72
    stews similar to, 295

Ratatouille *(cont.)*
    Tian Niçoise, 298
    Turkish Ratatouille, 299–300
    Türlü, 299–300
    Two Methods for One Ratatouille, 296–97
Ravioli. *See* Pasta, ravioli
Red pepper flakes
    Grilled Eggplant with Hot Red Pepper Flakes, 108
Red pepper purée, 93
Ribolitta, 147
Rice, 313–14. *See also* Risotto
    Arborio, 235, 315
    Carnaroli, 315
    Chelo, 329
    Deep-Fried Rice and Mozzarella Balls, 133–34, 133
    Dolmades, 114–15
    Grape Leaves Stuffed with Rice, Onions, and Herbs,
        114–15
    Persian Rice, 329
    pilaf, 314
        Eggplant Pilaf, 327
        Sour Cherry Pilaf, 326
        Tomato and Rice Pilaf, 327–28
        Zucchini, Tomato, and Rice Pilaf, 328–29
    Supplì al Telefono, 133–34, 133
    Vegetable Paella from El Palmar, 325–26
Risotto, 314
    Artichoke Risotto, 316–17
    Asparagus and Fava Bean Risotto, 318
    Barley Risotto with Asparagus or Green Beans and Pesto,
        330
    Barley Risotto with Pesto and Ricotta Salata, 330
    Farro Risotto with Dried Mushrooms, Favas, and Garlic,
        331–32
    Farro Risotto with Green Beans, 332
    Fava Bean and Green Garlic Risotto, 317–18
    how to make, 315
    Mushroom Risotto, 318–19
    Radicchio Risotto, 320
    Red Pepper Risotto with Saffron, 319
    Red Risotto with Beet Greens, 320
    Red Wine Risotto with Cauliflower, 321
    Risi e Bisi, 321–22
    Risi e Bisi with Mushrooms, 322
    Risotto Milanese, 316
    Summer Squash Risotto, 322–23
    Tomato and Zucchini Risotto, 323–24
    Winter Squash Risotto, 324–25
Romaine
    Hearts of Romaine and Tomato Salad, 116
    Shredded Romaine and Radish Salad, 116
Root vegetables
    Roasted Potatoes and Root Vegetables with Rosemary, 290
Rose geranium, 26
    syrup, for iced tea, 358
Rosemary, 26
    Roasted Potatoes and Root Vegetables with Rosemary, 290
    Roasted Potatoes with Rosemary, 290
    Rosemary and Thyme Bread, 46
Rose water, 29
    Rose-Scented Pastry Cream, 355
    Strawberry Tart with Rose-Scented Pastry Cream, 354
Roux, 77, 77

Rusks, 49
    Cretan Barley Rusks with Tomato Topping, 137
    made from bread on hand, 137
Rusks, 49

S

Saffron, 26
    Castilian Garlic Soup with Paprika and Saffron, 164–65
    Red Pepper Risotto with Saffron, 319
Sage, 26
    Strata with Mushrooms and Sage, 197
Salads, 90. *See also* Starters, snacks, and meze
    Andalusian Cabbage Salad, 97–98
    Beet and Beet Greens Salad, 94
    Beet and Beet Greens Salad with Skordalia, 94
    Beet and Yogurt Salad, 94–95
    Black-Eyed Pea Salad, 122–23
    Black-Eyed Pea Salad with Feta, 123
    Bread and Vegetable Salad, 128–29
    Cacik, 106
    Carrot Salad, 99
    Chick Pea and Bulgur Salad, 102–3
    Couscous "Tabbouleh," 97
    Farro Salad, 112
    Fattoush, 128–29
    Fava Bean Salad, 114
    Grilled Eggplant and Pepper Salad, 111
    Grilled Pepper Salad, 125, 126–27
    Hearts of Romaine and Tomato Salad, 116
    Italian Bread Salad, 129
    Lebanese Beets with Yogurt, 95
    Lentil Salad, 119–20
    Mechwya, 126–27
    Mesclun Salad, 118
    Middle Eastern Cabbage Salad with Lemon and Dill, 98
    Middle Eastern Cabbage Salad with Yogurt, Lemon, and
        Dill, 98
    Mushroom and Celery Salad, 121
    North African Beet Salad, 95
    Ommok Houria, 99
    Orange and Olive Salad, 122
    Orange Sorbet with Blood Orange Salad, 358–59
    Panzanella, 129
    Provençal Chick Pea Salad, 102
    Purslane Salad, 118
    Roasted Eggplant Salad with Feta and Green Peppers, 109
    Roasted Pepper Salad with Lettuce and Tomato, 124
    Salad with Warm Goat Cheese and Basil Sauce, 117
    Shredded Romaine and Radish Salad, 116
    Spicy Beet Salad, 95
    Strawberry and Apricot Salad, 356–57
    Summer Salad, 119
    Tabbouleh, 96–97
    Turkish Cucumber and Yogurt Salad, 106
    Warm Goat Cheese Salad, 115
Salt, 17
Samfaina, 295
Saucepans, recommended, 14
Sauces, 69–70
    Asparagus with Egg Sauce, 181
    Béchamel, 77–78
    Catalan Ratatouille, 72
    Chermoula, 86

Garganelli with Mushroom Sauce, 210
Garlic and Potato Purée, 80
Ligurian Walnut Sauce, 76–77
Mushrooms al Ajillo, 120
Mushrooms in Garlic Sauce, 120
Olive Oil Béchamel, 78
Parsley Sauce, 84
Pasta with Ligurian Artichoke Sauce, 213
pesto (see Pesto)
Pine Nut Tarator Sauce, 81
Pistou, 76
Poached Eggs with Garlic Sauce, 188
Romesco Sauce, 71
roux-thickened, 77
Salad with Warm Goat Cheese and Basil Sauce, 117
Samfaina, 72
Skordalia, 80
Stuffed Cabbage with Egg-Lemon Sauce, 274
Stuffed Cabbage with Tahini Sauce, 275
Tahini Garlic Sauce, 83
tomato (see Tomato sauce)
Turkish Tarator Sauce, 81
Scallions
    Baked Vegetable Omelet, 188–89
    Fennel and Scallion Pie, 238–39
Semolina flour
    Baked Semolina Gnocchi with Butter and Parmesan,
        225
    Semolina Bread with Sesame Seeds, 42
    Semolina Bread with Tomato and Zucchini, 43
Sesame seeds, 28
    Semolina Bread with Sesame Seeds, 42
    Sesame Bread Rings, 53–54
Shortbread
    Fregolata Veneziana, 362, 364
    Venetian Cornmeal Shortbread, 362, 364
Skordalia, 80
    Beet and Beet Greens Salad with Skordalia, 94
Snacks. See Starters, snacks, and meze
Sofrito, 153
Sorbets
    Lemon Sorbet, 359
    Melon Sorbet, 349
    Orange Sorbet with Blood Orange Salad, 358–59
    Strawberry Sorbet, 356
Sorrel
    Provençal Flat Sorrel Omelet, 186
Soufflés
    Cheese Soufflé with Truffles, 199
    Soufflé aux Truffes, 199
Soufiko, 295, 300–301
Soups, 143–44
    Bean and Vegetable Soup with Pastina, 169–70
    bouillabaisse
        Bouillabaisse of Fresh Peas, 156–57
        Greens Bouillabaisse, 158
        Spinach Bouillabaisse, 157–58
        Tomato, Egg, and Bread Bouillabaisse, 158
    broths
        Garlic Broth, 145
        for risotto, 315
        Simple Vegetable Broth, 145
        vegetable trimmings for, 145

Castilian Garlic Soup with Paprika and Saffron, 164–65
    Chick Pea Breakfast Soup, 170–71
    Cold Tomato and Roasted Pepper Soup, 166
    Garlic Soup, 161–62
    Gazpacho, 165, 165
        White Gazpacho with Grapes, 166
    Hearty Bean, Chard, and Vermicelli Soup, 171
    Iced Cucumber Soup with Walnuts, 167
    Lentil Soup with Goat Cheese, 160–61
    Majorcan Bread and Vegetable Soup, 168
    Melon Soup, 349
    Minestrone, 144, 146–47
        Cabbage and White Bean Minestrone, 152–53
        Istrian Minestrone, 151–52
        Kale Minestrone, 148–49
        Lentil Minestrone with Greens, 149, 151
        Manestra, 151–52
    Pappa al Pomodoro, 148
    Parmesan rinds for, 149
    Potaje de Vigilia, 163–64
    Provençal Chick Pea Soup, 160
    Provençal Lentil and Tomato Soup, 161
    Provençal Wheat Berry Soup, 159
    Provençal Winter Squash Soup, 162–63
    Ribolitta, 147
    Salmorejo, 166
    sofrito in, 153
    Soupe au Pistou, 155–56
    Stracciatella, 154–55
        Lemon Stracciatella, 155
        Stracciatella with Asparagus, 155
    Tomato Soup with Cilantro and Vermicelli, 169
    Tuscan Bean and Farro Soup with Cabbage and Winter
        Squash, 153–54
    Tuscan Bread and Tomato Soup, 148
    Vegetable Soup with Chick Peas and Spinach, 163–64
    White Bean Soup, 167–68
Spaghetti. See Pasta, spaghetti
Spain
    cheeses of, 18, 92
    egg dishes of, 173–74
    melons of, 93
    paella of, 313–14
    peppers of, 71
    sauces of, 70
    tapas of, 113
Spice blends, 24
Spices. See also specific spices
    in Mediterranean cuisines, 22–23, 25–27
    Spinach with Spices and Yogurt, 283
    toasting, 23
Spinach
    Baby Spinach and Fontina Panini, 67
    Potaje de Vigilia, 163–64
    Spanakopita, 243–44
    Spinach and Ricotta Torta, 235
    Spinach Bouillabaisse, 157–58
    Spinach with Spices and Yogurt, 283
    Spinach with Yogurt and Pine Nuts, 127
    Vegetable Soup with Chick Peas and Spinach, 163–64
    wilting, 284
Spreads. See Dips and spreads
Squash. See Summer squash; Winter squash

Starters, snacks, and meze, 89–90, <u>108</u>
  Ajlūk, 98
  Andalusian Cabbage Salad, 97–98
  Apricot Yogurt Dip, 91
  Baba Gannouj, 110–11
  Baked Hummus with Pine Nuts, 104
  Beet and Beet Greens Salad, 94
  Beet and Beet Greens Salad with Skordalia, 94
  Beet and Yogurt Salad, 94–95
  Black-Eyed Pea Salad, 122–23
  Black-Eyed Pea Salad with Feta, 123
  Bread and Vegetable Salad, 128–29
  Bruschetta, <u>134</u>, 135, <u>136</u>
  Cacik, 106
  Carrot Salad, 99
  Catalan Bread with Tomato, 135
  Cauliflower à la Grecque, 100–101
  Cauliflower with Capers, Parsley, and Vinegar, 101
  Cheese and Herb Phyllo Triangles, 137–38
  Cheese and Winter Squash Phyllo Triangles, 138–39
  Chick Pea and Bulgur Salad, 102–3
  Couscous "Tabbouleh," 97
  Cretan Barley Rusks with Tomato Topping, 137
  Crostini, <u>134</u>, 135, <u>136</u>
  Deep-Fried Cauliflower, 101
  Deep-Fried Rice and Mozzarella Balls, 133–34, <u>133</u>
  Diane Kochilas's Zucchini Fritters, 130
  Dolmades, 114–15
  Eggplant Ajlūk, 98
  Eggplant and Red Pepper Purée, 125
  Eggplant Slices with Tomato Sauce and Feta, 109
  Eggs and Vegetables Stuffed with Tapenade, 130–31
  Eggs Filled with Pesto, 131
  Falafel, 104–5
  Farro Salad, 112
  Fattoush, 128–29
  Fava, 123–24
  Fava Bean Salad, 114
  Fresh Fava Bean Purée, 113
  Frico, 132–33
  Giant Favas with Mint, 112
  Grape Leaves Stuffed with Rice, Onions, and Herbs, 114–15
  Grilled Eggplant and Pepper Salad, 111
  Grilled Eggplant Purée with Mint and Almonds, 110
  Grilled Eggplant with Hot Red Pepper Flakes, 108
  Grilled Feta in Grape Leaves, 132
  Grilled Mozzarella in Radicchio Bundles, 131–32
  Grilled Pepper Salad, 125, 126–27
  Grilled Zucchini Slices, 129
  Hearts of Romaine and Tomato Salad, 116
  Hummus, 103
  Italian Bread Salad, 129
  Kisir, 95–96
  Lebanese Beets with Yogurt, 95
  Leeks Cooked in White Wine, 117
  Lentil Salad, 119–20
  Marinated Carrots, 99
  Marinated Eggplant, 106–7
  Marinated Mushrooms, 120–21
  Mashed Carrots with Garlicky Yogurt, 100
  Mechwya, 126–27
  Mesclun Salad, 118

  Middle Eastern Cabbage Salad with Lemon and Dill, 98
  Middle Eastern Cabbage Salad with Yogurt, Lemon, and Dill, 98
  Muhammara, 126
  Mushroom and Celery Salad, 121
  Mushroom and Feta Phyllo Triangles, 139, 141
  Mushrooms al Ajillo, 120
  Mushrooms in Garlic Sauce, 120
  North African Beet Salad, 95
  North African Carrot "Compote," 98
  Ommok Houria, 99
  Orange and Olive Salad, 122
  other dishes for starters, <u>140</u>
  Panzanella, 129
  Provençal Chick Pea Salad, 102
  Purslane Salad, 118
  ready-made, <u>92–93</u>
  Red Pepper Purée, 124–25
  Roasted Eggplant Salad with Feta and Green Peppers, 109
  Roasted Pepper Salad with Lettuce and Tomato, 124
  Roasted Salted Almonds with Cayenne, 91
  Salad with Warm Goat Cheese and Basil Sauce, 117
  Sautéed Eggplant with Tomatoes and Balsamic Vinegar, 107
  Shredded Romaine and Radish Salad, 116
  Small Bulgur Patties, 95–96
  Spicy Beet Salad, 95
  Spinach with Yogurt and Pine Nuts, 127
  Split Pea Purée, 123–24
  Summer Salad, 119
  Supplì al Telefono, 133–34, <u>133</u>
  Swiss Chard Stalk and Tahini Dip, 127–28
  Tabbouleh, 96–97
  tapas, <u>113</u>
  Tapenade, 121
  Turkish Cucumber and Yogurt Salad, 106
  Turkish Hummus, 104
  Tzatziki, 106
  Warm Goat Cheese Salad, 115
  Warm Tomatoes with Goat Cheese, 128
  Winter Squash Ajlūk, 98
  Zucchini Ajlūk, 98
Stews. *See also* Ragouts
  Andalusian Chick Pea and Cabbage Stew, 307
  Artichoke and Fresh Fava Stew, 269–70
  Artichoke and Potato Stew, 270–71
  Chakchouka, 194
  Chick Pea Stew, 308
  Fava Bean and Potato Stew, 280–81
  Fritteda, 268–69
  Ikarian Summer Vegetable Stew, 300–301
  North African Fried Pepper Stew with Eggs, 194
  Potato and Olive Stew, 291–92
  ratatouille-like, <u>295</u> (*see also* Ratatouille)
  Sicilian Spring Vegetable Stew, 268–69
  Soufiko, 300–301
  Spicy Vegetable Stew with Swiss Chard, Black-Eyed Peas, and Potatoes, 302
  Spicy Vegetable Stew with Swiss Chard, Favas, and Potatoes, 302
Stracciatella, 154–55
  Lemon Stracciatella, 155
  Stracciatella with Asparagus, 155

Stratas
   Basic Strata, 196–97
   Strata with Greens, or with Tomatoes and Greens, 197
   Strata with Mushrooms and Sage, 197
   Strata with Tomatoes and Thyme, 197
Strawberries
   Strawberry and Apricot Salad, 356–57
   Strawberry Granita, 356–57
   Strawberry Sorbet, 356
   Strawberry Tart with Rose-Scented Pastry Cream, 354
Strudel
   Summer Stone Fruit Strudel, 353–54
Sugar, vanilla, 351
Summer squash, 243. See also Zucchini
   Coiled Summer Squash Pitta, 245–46
   Provençal Summer Squash, Red Pepper, and Tomato
      Gratin, 255–56
   Summer Squash Gratin, 256
   Summer Squash Risotto, 322–23
Sweets and desserts, 343–44
   Almond Biscotti, 345
   Anise Butter Cookies, 361–62
   Apricot Clafouti, 353
   Baklava with Mixed Dried Fruit and Nuts, 366
   Buckwheat Cake from the Alto Adige, 364–65
   Cherry Clafouti, 348
   Cherry Financier, 347
   Coffee Granita, 360
   feta and watermelon, 349
   Fig and Red Wine Compote, 350
   Fig Ice Cream, 351
   Financier, 346, 347
   Fregolata Veneziana, 362, 364
   Honey-Orange Biscotti, 345
   Honey-Roasted Figs, 350–51
   Lemon Butter Cookies, 362
   Lemon Sorbet, 359
   Lemon Tart, 359–60
   Loukoumades, 365
   Melon Sorbet, 349
   Melon Soup, 349
   Melon with Muscat de Beaumes-de-Venise, 350
   Orange-Scented Pastry Cream, 355
   Orange Sorbet with Blood Orange Salad, 358–59
   Pâte Sucrée, 355–56
   Peaches in Red Wine and Banyuls, 352–53
   Peach Gelato, 352
   Pears Poached in Wine and Honey, 357
   Quince Compote, 357
   Quince Spoon Sweet, 358
   Raspberry or Blueberry Tart, 354
   Ricotta Cheesecake, 360–61
   Rose-Scented Pastry Cream, 355
   Strawberry and Apricot Salad, 356–57
   Strawberry Granita, 356–57
   Strawberry Sorbet, 356
   Strawberry Tart with Rose-Scented Pastry Cream, 354
   Summer Stone Fruit Strudel, 353–54
   Sweet Dessert Couscous with Citrus and Pomegranate, 367
   Sweet Pie Crust, 355–56
   vanilla sugar for, 351
   Venetian Cornmeal Shortbread, 362, 364
   Watermelon Granita, 348–49

Swiss chard
   Couscous with Chick Peas and Chard, 336–38
   Hearty Bean, Chard, and Vermicelli Soup, 171
   Provençal Flat Swiss Chard Omelet, 186–87
   Provençal Swiss Chard Gratin, 257–58
   Spicy Vegetable Stew with Swiss Chard, Black-Eyed Peas,
      and Potatoes, 302
   Spicy Vegetable Stew with Swiss Chard, Favas, and
      Potatoes, 302
   Swiss Chard Stalk and Tahini Dip, 127–28
   Truccha, 186–87
   White Bean and Chard Gratin, 304
   White Bean and Chard Ragout, 304
Syria, arak in, 35
Syrup
   Italian Cream Sodas, 34–35
   Sirops à l'Eau, 34
   Syrup Spritzers, 34

T
Tabbouleh, 96–97
   Couscous "Tabbouleh," 97
Tabil, 24
Tahini, 29, 83
   Stuffed Cabbage with Tahini Sauce, 275
   Swiss Chard Stalk and Tahini Dip, 127–28
   Tahini Dressing, 83
   Tahini Garlic Sauce, 83
Tapas, 113. See also Starters, snacks, and meze
Tapenade, 121–22
   Eggs and Vegetables Stuffed with Tapenade, 130–31
   Green Olive and Almond Tapenade, 122
   Green Olive Tapenade, 122
   store-bought, 93
Tarts, dessert
   Lemon Tart, 359–60
   Raspberry or Blueberry Tart, 354
   Strawberry Tart with Rose-Scented Pastry Cream, 354
Tarts, savory, 231. See also Pies, savory
Tea, iced, rose geranium syrup for, 358
Thyme, 27
   Rosemary and Thyme Bread, 46
   Strata with Tomatoes and Thyme, 197
Tomatoes
   Arab Eggplant, Tomato, and Chick Pea Casserole, 280
   Bell Pepper, Tomato, and Potato Omelet, 193
   Bohemienne Gratinée, 246
   Bread and Vegetable Salad, 128–29
   Calzone with Tomato and Kale Filling, 64
   canned, 29
   Catalan Bread with Tomato, 135
   Catalan Ratatouille, 72
   Cauliflower and Tomato Couscous, 339–40
   Cold Tomato and Roasted Pepper Soup, 166
   Cretan Barley Rusks with Tomato Topping, 137
   Easy White Beans with Tomatoes and Garlic, 305
   Eggplant and Tomato Gratin, 246
   Eggplant and Tomato Panini, 65
   Eggs and Vegetables Stuffed with Tapenade, 130–31
   Fassoulia, 305–6
   Fattoush, 128–29
   Fried Potatoes with Tomatoes and Oregano, 291
   Gazpacho, 165

Tomatoes *(cont.)*
    Hearts of Romaine and Tomato Salad, 116
    Individual Eggplant and Tomato Frittata, 184–85
    Italian Bread Salad, 129
    Large White Beans with Tomatoes and Garlic, 305–6
    Orecchiette with Uncooked Tomatoes and Arugula, 211
    Pan-Cooked Zucchini and Tomatoes, 293
    Panzanella, 129
    Pappa al Pomodoro, 148
    Pasta with Tomatoes, Beans, and Feta, 219
    Pasta with Uncooked Tomatoes, Basil, Capers, Olives, and Feta, 212–13
    Peperonata, 85
    Pisto, 293
    Pizza Marinara with Tomatoes and Garlic, 57–58
    Pizza with Mozzarella and Cherry Tomatoes, 59
    Pizza with Tomato, Eggplant, and Mozzarella, 59
    Provençal Fennel and Tomato Gratin, 251
    Provençal Flat Tomato Omelet, 185–86
    Provençal Lentil and Tomato Soup, 161
    Provençal Summer Squash, Red Pepper, and Tomato Gratin, 255–56
    Roasted Pepper Salad with Lettuce and Tomato, 124
    Romesco Sauce, 71
    Salmorejo, 166
    Samfaina, 72
    Sautéed Eggplant with Tomatoes and Balsamic Vinegar, 107
    Sautéed Peppers with Tomatoes, 288
    Scrambled Eggs with Tomatoes and Feta, 189
    Semolina Bread with Tomato and Zucchini, 43
    Stewed Green Beans with Tomatoes, 272
    Stewed Peppers and Tomatoes, 85
    Strata with Greens, or with Tomatoes and Greens, 197
    Strata with Tomatoes and Thyme, 197
    Summer Salad, 119
    sun-dried, as snack, 93
    Tomato, Egg, and Bread Bouillabaisse, 158
    Tomato and Bean Gratin, 304
    Tomato and Bean Ragout, 303
    Tomato and Mozzarella Focaccia, 44
    Tomato and Rice Pilaf, 327–28
    Tomato and Zucchini Risotto, 323–24
    Tomato Focaccia, 44
    in tomato sauce *(see* Tomato sauce)
    Tomato Soup with Cilantro and Vermicelli, 169
    Tuscan Bread and Tomato Soup, 148
    Warm Tomatoes with Goat Cheese, 128
    Wild Mushrooms with Tomatoes and Basil, 286
    Zucchini, Tomato, and Rice Pilaf, 328–29
Tomato paste, 29
Tomato sauce
    Almond, Basil, and Tomato Sauce, 79–80
    Basic Tomato Sauce, 78
    Eggplant Slices with Tomato Sauce and Feta, 109
    Fresh Tomato Concassée, 79
    Fusilli with Tomato Sauce, Cauliflower, and Olives, 216
    ingredients for, 78
    Laganari with Eggplant, Tomato Sauce, and Oregano, 218
    Lasagna with Greens and Tomato Sauce, 222–23
    Macaroni with Tomato Sauce and Goat Cheese, 220–21
    Marinara Sauce, 78
    Orecchiette with Raw and Cooked Tomato Sauce, 212
    Perciatelli with Tomato Sauce and Ricotta, 214–15
    Pizza with Peppers, Tomato Sauce, and Mozzarella, 60–61
    Pizza with Tomato Sauce, Mozzarella, and Arugula, 61
    Pizza with Tomato Sauce and Potatoes, 62–63
    Polenta with Tomato Sauce and Parmesan, 333
    Quicker Basic Tomato Sauce, 79
    Southern Tomato Sauce, 79
    Spaghetti alla Chitarra with Arugula Pesto and Tomato Sauce, 215
    Whole Wheat Spaghetti with Green Beans and Tomato Sauce, 217
Toppings
    for bruschetta and crostini, 76, 136
    pizza
        Mushroom and Fennel Topping, 60
        Onion and Pepper Topping, 61
Tortes and tortas. *See* Pies, savory
Tortillas. *See* Eggs, tortillas
Truck stop, Italian, recollection about, 209
Truffles
    Cheese Soufflé with Truffles, 199
    eggs and, 174
    Soufflé aux Truffes, 199
    Truffle Omelet, 182–83
Tunisia, egg dishes of, 174
Turkey
    cheeses of, 21
    raki of, 35
Türlü, 295, 299–300
    Türlü Topped with a Fried Egg, 300
Turnips
    Vegetable Ragout with Chick Peas, Turnips, and Greens, 301–2
Tzatziki, 106
    Poached Eggs with Tzatziki, 188

V

Vanilla beans, 27
Vanilla sugar, 351
Vegetables. *See also specific vegetables*
    health benefits from, 8–9
    Mediterranean, 263–64
Vegetable trimmings, for broths, 145
Vinaigrette
    Oil and Vinegar Dressing, 82
    Vinaigrette to Keep in the Refrigerator, 82
    Walnut Vinaigrette, 82–83
Vinegar
    Cauliflower with Capers, Parsley, and Vinegar, 101
    Oil and Vinegar Dressing, 82
    Sautéed Eggplant with Tomatoes and Balsamic Vinegar, 107
    Vinaigrette to Keep in the Refrigerator, 82
    Walnut Vinaigrette, 82–83

W

Walnut oil
    Walnut Vinaigrette, 82–83
Walnuts, 28
    Baklava with Mixed Dried Fruit and Nuts, 366
    Iced Cucumber Soup with Walnuts, 167
    Ligurian Walnut Sauce, 76–77

Muhammara, 126
Turkish Tarator Sauce, 81
Walnut Fougasse, 45
Watermelon
    feta and, 349
    Watermelon Granita, 348–49
Wheat berries
    The Doctor's Baiana, 332–33
    Farro Salad, 112
    Provençal Wheat Berry Soup, 159
White beans, 150. *See also* Beans
Whole wheat flour
    Whole Wheat Country Bread, 39–40
    Whole Wheat Focaccia, 44
    Whole Wheat Fougasse, 45
    Whole Wheat Pizza Dough, 57
Wines
    Braised Broccoli with White Wine, 272–73
    Broccoli alla Romana, 272–73
    dessert, 346
    Fig and Red Wine Compote, 350
    health benefits from, 9
    Leeks Cooked in White Wine, 117
    Mediterranean, 21–22
    Melon with Muscat de Beaumes-de-Venise, 350
    Peaches in Red Wine and Banyuls, 352–53
    Pears Poached in Wine and Honey, 357
    Red Wine Risotto with Cauliflower, 321
    Sangria, 34
Winter squash, 240. *See also* Pumpkin
    Cheese and Winter Squash Phyllo Triangles, 138–39
    Couscous with Chick Peas and Winter Vegetables, 338–39
    Half-Moon Ravioli with Winter Squash Filling, 204–6
    Provençal Winter Squash Soup, 162–63
    roasting, 163
    Tuscan Bean and Farro Soup with Cabbage and Winter Squash, 153–54
    Winter Squash Ajlūk, 98
    Winter Squash and Leek Pie, 241–42
    Winter Squash Pie with Bulgur and Feta, 240–41
    Winter Squash Risotto, 324–25
    Winter Squash with Chermoula, 275

Y

Yeast, active dry, 29
Yogurt
    Apricot Yogurt Dip, 91
    Beet and Yogurt Salad, 94–95
    Cacik, 106
    choosing, 21
    drained, 21
    Lebanese Beets with Yogurt, 95
    Mashed Carrots with Garlicky Yogurt, 100
    Middle Eastern Cabbage Salad with Yogurt, Lemon, and Dill, 98
    Spinach with Spices and Yogurt, 283
    Spinach with Yogurt and Pine Nuts, 127
    Turkish Cucumber and Yogurt Salad, 106
    Tzatziki, 106
    Yogurt and Mint Spread, 81

Z

Za'tar, 24
Zucchini, 243
    Baked Vegetable Omelet, 188–89
    Diane Kochilas's Zucchini Fritters, 130
    Eggs and Vegetables Stuffed with Tapenade, 130–31
    Grilled Zucchini, Goat Cheese, and Mint Panini, 65
    Grilled Zucchini Slices, 129
    Pan-Cooked Zucchini and Tomatoes, 293
    Pan-Fried Zucchini with Mint and Pepperoncini, 292
    Pisto, 293
    Provençal Zucchini and Greens Torte, 234–35
    Ricotta Frittata with Zucchini, 183
    Sautéed Zucchini and Red Peppers, 292
    Semolina Bread with Tomato and Zucchini, 43
    Tomato and Zucchini Risotto, 323–24
    Zucchini, Potato, and Artichoke Moussaka, 259–60
    Zucchini, Tomato, and Rice Pilaf, 328–29
    Zucchini Ajlūk, 98
    Zucchini and Greens Gratin, 235
    Zucchini and Herb Pie, 242–43

ABOUT THE AUTHOR

Martha Rose Shulman is the author of more than 25 books, including *Mediterranean Light* and *Provençal Light*. Her articles have appeared in *Bon Appétit*, *Food & Wine*, *Fine Cooking*, *Saveur*, the *Los Angeles Times*, and many other publications. She has taught cooking classes and has been featured on radio and television, including *Good Morning America* and the Food Network. She lives in Los Angeles.

BOOKS BY MARTHA ROSE SHULMAN

The Classic Party Fare Cookbook

Culinary Boot Camp

Entertaining Light

Every Woman's Guide to Eating During Pregnancy

Fast Vegetarian Feasts

Great Breads

Light Basics Cookbook

Martha Rose Shulman's Feasts & Fêtes

Mediterranean Light

Mexican Light

Provençal Light

Ready When You Are

Supper Club Chez Martha Rose

The Vegetarian Feast